COURTROOM EVIDENCE HANDBOOK

2024–2025

Student Edition

STEVEN GOODE

W. James Kronzer Chair in Trial and Appellate Advocacy
University Distinguished Teaching Professor
University of Texas School of Law

OLIN GUY WELLBORN III

William C. Liedtke, Sr. Professor of Law Emeritus
University of Texas School of Law

COPYRIGHT © 1995 WEST PUBLISHING CO.
© West, a Thomson business, 1997, 2000–2008
© 2009–2012 Thomson Reuters
© 2013 LEG, Inc. d/b/a West Academic Publishing
© 2014–2023 LEG, Inc. d/b/a West Academic
© 2024 LEG, Inc. d/b/a West Academic
    860 Blue Gentian Road, Suite 350
    Eagan, MN 55121
    1-877-888-1330

Published in the United States of America

ISBN: 979-8-89209-067-4

PREFACE

The law of evidence is complicated, and, in the opinion of probably every evidence student and litigator, more complicated than it needs to be. Like the tax code, however, it has proved remarkably resistant to simplification. This book is designed to make sense of evidence law, both for students taking an evidence course and students participating in trial advocacy or clinical programs. The rules of evidence are found in Chapter 1 and printed in large type for easy use.

The bulk of the book—Chapter 2—is designed to serve as a mini-treatise on the federal rules of evidence. Drawn from our Courtroom Handbook on Federal Evidence, it provides a careful, concise and up-to-date treatment of all the major points of evidence law, complete with illustrations, citations to relevant case law, and references to more extensive discussions of the rules.

But it is one thing to know the rules; it is another to know just how to introduce a letter, lay a foundation for a business record, refresh a witness's recollection, or question a character witness. The second part of this book, therefore, is designed to help you bridge the gap from knowing the law of evidence to knowing how to perform at trial.

Chapter 3, entitled "Common Objections and Responses," contains ninety-three different objections to evidence. Each objection is presented in the form of a model objection, complete with relevant supporting authority. We also provide a range of possible responses for "opposing counsel," likewise supplemented with relevant authority.

Rounding out the book is the "checklists and foundations" chapter. Here is the guide that will help you get through the daunting task of introducing documents, laying the proper foundation for hearsay exceptions, and overcoming a myriad of other evidentiary hurdles. There are checklists to consult, brief summaries of foundational elements, and "how-to-do-it" examples in question and answer format.

We hope you will find this book useful, whether you are participating in a mock trial, going to court as part of a clinical program, or just trying to understand the law of evidence.

STEVEN GOODE
O. GUY WELLBORN III

January 2024

SUMMARY OF CONTENTS

TABLE OF CONTENTS

TABLE OF CONTENTS

ARTICLE VI. WITNESSES

ARTICLE VII. OPINIONS AND EXPERT TESTIMONY

ARTICLE VIII. HEARSAY

ARTICLE IX. AUTHENTICATION AND IDENTIFICATION

ARTICLE X. CONTENTS OF WRITINGS, RECORDINGS, AND PHOTOGRAPHS

Rule

ARTICLE VIII. HEARSAY

ARTICLE IX. AUTHENTICATION AND IDENTIFICATION

ARTICLE X. CONTENTS OF WRITINGS, RECORDINGS, AND PHOTOGRAPHS

ARTICLE XI. MISCELLANEOUS RULES

COURTROOM EVIDENCE HANDBOOK

2024–2025

Student Edition

CHAPTER 1

FEDERAL RULES OF EVIDENCE

Effective July 1, 1975

Including Amendments Through December 1, 2023

ARTICLE I. GENERAL PROVISIONS

ARTICLE II. JUDICIAL NOTICE

ARTICLE III. PRESUMPTIONS IN CIVIL CASES

ARTICLE IV. RELEVANCE AND ITS LIMITS

ARTICLE V. PRIVILEGES

ARTICLE VI. WITNESSES

ARTICLE I

GENERAL PROVISIONS

Rule 101. Scope; Definitions

(a) Scope. These rules apply to proceedings in United States courts. The specific courts and proceedings to which the rules apply, along with exceptions, are set out in Rule 1101.

(b) Definitions. In these rules:

    (1) "civil case" means a civil action or proceeding;

    (2) "criminal case" includes a criminal proceeding;

    (3) "public office" includes a public agency;

    (4) "record" includes a memorandum, report, or data compilation;

    (5) a "rule prescribed by the Supreme Court" means a rule adopted by the Supreme Court under statutory authority; and

    (6) a reference to any kind of written material or any other medium includes electronically stored information.

Rule 102. Purpose

These rules should be construed so as to administer every proceeding fairly, eliminate unjustifiable expense and delay, and promote the development of evidence law, to the end of ascertaining the truth and securing a just determination.

Rule 103. Rulings on Evidence

(a) Preserving a Claim of Error. A party may claim error in a ruling to admit or exclude evidence only if the error affects a substantial right of the party and:

    (1) if the ruling admits evidence, a party, on the record:

        (A) timely objects or moves to strike; and

        (B) states the specific ground, unless it was apparent from the context; or

    (2) if the ruling excludes evidence, a party informs the court of its substance by an offer of proof, unless the substance was apparent from the context.

(b) Not Needing to Renew an Objection or Offer of Proof. Once the court rules definitively on the record—either before or at trial—a party need not renew an objection or offer of proof to preserve a claim of error for appeal.

(c) Court's Statement About the Ruling; Directing an Offer of Proof. The court may make any statement about the character or form of the evidence, the objection made, and the ruling. The court may direct that an offer of proof be made in question-and-answer form.

(d) Preventing the Jury from Hearing Inadmissible Evidence. To the extent practicable, the court must conduct a jury trial so that inadmissible evidence is not suggested to the jury by any means.

(e) Taking Notice of Plain Error. A court may take notice of a plain error affecting a substantial right, even if the claim of error was not properly preserved.

Rule 104. Preliminary Questions

(a) **In General.** The court must decide any preliminary question about whether a witness is qualified, a privilege exists, or evidence is admissible. In so deciding, the court is not bound by evidence rules, except those on privilege.

(b) **Relevance That Depends on a Fact.** When the relevance of evidence depends on whether a fact exists, proof must be introduced sufficient to support a finding that the fact does exist. The court may admit the proposed evidence on the condition that the proof be introduced later.

(c) **Conducting a Hearing So That the Jury Cannot Hear It.** The court must conduct any hearing on a preliminary question so that the jury cannot hear it if:

　　(1) the hearing involves the admissibility of a confession;

　　(2) a defendant in a criminal case is a witness and so requests; or

　　(3) justice so requires.

(d) **Cross-Examining a Defendant in a Criminal Case.** By testifying on a preliminary question, a defendant in a criminal case does not become subject to cross-examination on other issues in the case.

(e) **Evidence Relevant to Weight and Credibility.** This rule does not limit a party's right to introduce before the jury evidence that is relevant to the weight or credibility of other evidence.

Rule 105. Limiting Evidence That Is Not Admissible Against Other Parties or for Other Purposes

If the court admits evidence that is admissible against a party or for a purpose—but not against another party or for another purpose—the court, on timely request, must restrict the evidence to its proper scope and instruct the jury accordingly.

Rule 106. Remainder of or Related Statements

If a party introduces all or part of a statement, an adverse party may require the introduction, at that time, of any other part—or any other statement—that in fairness ought to be considered at the same time. The adverse party may do so over a hearsay objection.

ARTICLE II

JUDICIAL NOTICE

Rule 201. Judicial Notice of Adjudicative Facts

(a) **Scope.** This rule governs judicial notice of an adjudicative fact only, not a legislative fact.

(b) **Kinds of Facts That May Be Judicially Noticed.** The court may judicially notice a fact that is not subject to reasonable dispute because it:

　　(1) is generally known within the trial court's territorial jurisdiction; or

　　(2) can be accurately and readily determined from sources whose accuracy cannot reasonably be questioned.

(c) **Taking Notice.** The court:

　　(1) may take judicial notice on its own; or

    (2) must take judicial notice if a party requests it and the court is supplied with the necessary information.

(d) **Timing.** The court may take judicial notice at any stage of the proceeding.

(e) **Opportunity to Be Heard.** On timely request, a party is entitled to be heard on the propriety of taking judicial notice and the nature of the fact to be noticed. If the court takes judicial notice before notifying a party, the party, on request, is still entitled to be heard.

(f) **Instructing the Jury.** In a civil case, the court must instruct the jury to accept the noticed fact as conclusive. In a criminal case, the court must instruct the jury that it may or may not accept the noticed fact as conclusive.

ARTICLE III

PRESUMPTIONS IN CIVIL CASES

Rule 301. Presumptions in Civil Cases Generally

In a civil case, unless a federal statute or these rules provide otherwise, the party against whom a presumption is directed has the burden of producing evidence to rebut the presumption. But this rule does not shift the burden of persuasion, which remains on the party who had it originally.

Rule 302. Applying State Law to Presumptions in Civil Cases

In a civil case, state law governs the effect of a presumption regarding a claim or defense for which state law supplies the rule of decision.

ARTICLE IV

RELEVANCE AND ITS LIMITS

Rule 401. Test for Relevant Evidence

Evidence is relevant if:

(a) it has any tendency to make a fact more or less probable than it would be without the evidence; and

(b) the fact is of consequence in determining the action.

Rule 402. General Admissibility of Relevant Evidence

Relevant evidence is admissible unless any of the following provides otherwise:

- the United States Constitution;
- a federal statute;
- these rules; or
- other rules prescribed by the Supreme Court.

Irrelevant evidence is not admissible.

Rule 403. Excluding Relevant Evidence for Prejudice, Confusion, Waste of Time, or Other Reasons

The court may exclude relevant evidence if its probative value is substantially outweighed by a danger of one or more of the following: unfair prejudice, confusing the issues, misleading the jury, undue delay, wasting time, or needlessly presenting cumulative evidence.

Rule 404. Character Evidence; Other Crimes, Wrongs, or Acts

(a) **Character Evidence.**

    (1) *Prohibited Uses.* Evidence of a person's character or character trait is not admissible to prove that on a particular occasion the person acted in accordance with the character or trait.

    (2) *Exceptions for a Defendant or Victim in a Criminal Case.* The following exceptions apply in a criminal case:

        (A) a defendant may offer evidence of the defendant's pertinent trait, and if the evidence is admitted, the prosecutor may offer evidence to rebut it;

        (B) subject to the limitations in Rule 412, a defendant may offer evidence of an alleged victim's pertinent trait, and if the evidence is admitted, the prosecutor may:

            (i) offer evidence to rebut it; and

            (ii) offer evidence of the defendant's same trait; and

        (C) in a homicide case, the prosecutor may offer evidence of the alleged victim's trait of peacefulness to rebut evidence that the victim was the first aggressor.

    (3) *Exceptions for a Witness.* Evidence of a witness's character may be admitted under Rules 607, 608, and 609.

(b) **Other Crimes, Wrongs, or Acts.**

    (1) *Prohibited Uses.* Evidence of any other crime, wrong, or act is not admissible to prove a person's character in order to show that on a particular occasion the person acted in accordance with the character.

    (2) *Permitted Uses.* This evidence may be admissible for another purpose, such as proving motive, opportunity, intent, preparation, plan, knowledge, identity, absence of mistake, or lack of accident.

    (3) *Notice in a Criminal Case.* In a criminal case, the prosecutor must:

        (A) provide reasonable notice of any such evidence that the prosecutor intends to offer at trial, so that the defendant has a fair opportunity to meet it;

        (B) articulate in the notice the permitted purpose for which the prosecutor intends to offer the evidence and the reasoning that supports the purpose; and

        (C) do so in writing before trial—or in any form during trial if the court, for good cause, excuses lack of pretrial notice.

Rule 405. Methods of Proving Character

(a) **By Reputation or Opinion.** When evidence of a person's character or character trait is admissible, it may be proved by testimony about the person's reputation or by testimony in the form of an opinion. On cross-examination of the character witness, the court may allow an inquiry into relevant specific instances of the person's conduct.

(b) By Specific Instances of Conduct. When a person's character or character trait is an essential element of a charge, claim, or defense, the character or trait may also be proved by relevant specific instances of the person's conduct.

Rule 406. Habit; Routine Practice

Evidence of a person's habit or an organization's routine practice may be admitted to prove that on a particular occasion the person or organization acted in accordance with the habit or routine practice. The court may admit this evidence regardless of whether it is corroborated or whether there was an eyewitness.

Rule 407. Subsequent Remedial Measures

When measures are taken that would have made an earlier injury or harm less likely to occur, evidence of the subsequent measures is not admissible to prove:

- negligence;
- culpable conduct;
- a defect in a product or its design; or
- a need for a warning or instruction.

But the court may admit this evidence for another purpose, such as impeachment or—if disputed—proving ownership, control, or the feasibility of precautionary measures.

Rule 408. Compromise Offers and Negotiations

(a) Prohibited Uses. Evidence of the following is not admissible—on behalf of any party—either to prove or disprove the validity or amount of a disputed claim or to impeach by a prior inconsistent statement or a contradiction:

(1) furnishing, promising, or offering—or accepting, promising to accept, or offering to accept— a valuable consideration in compromising or attempting to compromise the claim; and

(2) conduct or a statement made during compromise negotiations about the claim—except when offered in a criminal case and when the negotiations related to a claim by a public office in the exercise of its regulatory, investigative, or enforcement authority.

(b) Exceptions. The court may admit this evidence for another purpose, such as proving a witness's bias or prejudice, negating a contention of undue delay, or proving an effort to obstruct a criminal investigation or prosecution.

Rule 409. Offers to Pay Medical and Similar Expenses

Evidence of furnishing, promising to pay, or offering to pay medical, hospital, or similar expenses resulting from an injury is not admissible to prove liability for the injury.

Rule 410. Pleas, Plea Discussions, and Related Statements

(a) Prohibited Uses. In a civil or criminal case, evidence of the following is not admissible against the defendant who made the plea or participated in the plea discussions:

(1) a guilty plea that was later withdrawn;

(2) a nolo contendere plea;

(3) a statement made during a proceeding on either of those pleas under Federal Rule of Criminal Procedure 11 or a comparable state procedure; or

    (4) a statement made during plea discussions with an attorney for the prosecuting authority if the discussions did not result in a guilty plea or they resulted in a later-withdrawn guilty plea.

(b) Exceptions. The court may admit a statement described in Rule 410(a)(3) or (4):

    (1) in any proceeding in which another statement made during the same plea or plea discussions has been introduced, if in fairness the statements ought to be considered together; or

    (2) in a criminal proceeding for perjury or false statement, if the defendant made the statement under oath, on the record, and with counsel present.

Rule 411. Liability Insurance

Evidence that a person was or was not insured against liability is not admissible to prove whether the person acted negligently or otherwise wrongfully. But the court may admit this evidence for another purpose, such as proving a witness's bias or prejudice or proving agency, ownership, or control.

Rule 412. Sex-Offense Cases: The Victim's Sexual Behavior or Predisposition

(a) Prohibited Uses. The following evidence is not admissible in a civil or criminal proceeding involving alleged sexual misconduct:

    (1) evidence offered to prove that a victim engaged in other sexual behavior; or

    (2) evidence offered to prove a victim's sexual predisposition.

(b) Exceptions.

    (1) *Criminal Cases.* The court may admit the following evidence in a criminal case:

        (A) evidence of specific instances of a victim's sexual behavior, if offered to prove that someone other than the defendant was the source of semen, injury, or other physical evidence;

        (B) evidence of specific instances of a victim's sexual behavior with respect to the person accused of the sexual misconduct, if offered by the defendant to prove consent or if offered by the prosecutor; and

        (C) evidence whose exclusion would violate the defendant's constitutional rights.

    (2) *Civil Cases.* In a civil case, the court may admit evidence offered to prove a victim's sexual behavior or sexual predisposition if its probative value substantially outweighs the danger of harm to any victim and of unfair prejudice to any party. The court may admit evidence of a victim's reputation only if the victim has placed it in controversy.

(c) Procedure to Determine Admissibility.

    (1) *Motion.* If a party intends to offer evidence under Rule 412(b), the party must:

        (A) file a motion that specifically describes the evidence and states the purpose for which it is to be offered;

        (B) do so at least 14 days before trial unless the court, for good cause, sets a different time;

        (C) serve the motion on all parties; and

        (D) notify the victim or, when appropriate, the victim's guardian or representative.

    (2) *Hearing.* Before admitting evidence under this rule, the court must conduct an in camera hearing and give the victim and parties a right to attend and be heard. Unless the court orders otherwise, the motion, related materials, and the record of the hearing must be and remain sealed.

(d) **Definition of "Victim."** In this rule, "victim" includes an alleged victim.

Rule 413. Similar Crimes in Sexual-Assault Cases

(a) **Permitted Uses.** In a criminal case in which a defendant is accused of a sexual assault, the court may admit evidence that the defendant committed any other sexual assault. The evidence may be considered on any matter to which it is relevant.

(b) **Disclosure to the Defendant.** If the prosecutor intends to offer this evidence, the prosecutor must disclose it to the defendant, including witnesses' statements or a summary of the expected testimony. The prosecutor must do so at least 15 days before trial or at a later time that the court allows for good cause.

(c) **Effect on Other Rules.** This rule does not limit the admission or consideration of evidence under any other rule.

(d) **Definition of "Sexual Assault."** In this rule and Rule 415, "sexual assault" means a crime under federal law or under state law (as "state" is defined in 18 U.S.C. § 513) involving:

(1) any conduct prohibited by 18 U.S.C. chapter 109A;

(2) contact, without consent, between any part of the defendant's body—or an object—and another person's genitals or anus;

(3) contact, without consent, between the defendant's genitals or anus and any part of another person's body;

(4) deriving sexual pleasure or gratification from inflicting death, bodily injury, or physical pain on another person; or

(5) an attempt or conspiracy to engage in conduct described in subparagraphs (1)–(4).

Rule 414. Similar Crimes in Child-Molestation Cases

(a) **Permitted Uses.** In a criminal case in which a defendant is accused of child molestation, the court may admit evidence that the defendant committed any other child molestation. The evidence may be considered on any matter to which it is relevant.

(b) **Disclosure to the Defendant.** If the prosecutor intends to offer this evidence, the prosecutor must disclose it to the defendant, including witnesses' statements or a summary of the expected testimony. The prosecutor must do so at least 15 days before trial or at a later time that the court allows for good cause.

(c) **Effect on Other Rules.** This rule does not limit the admission or consideration of evidence under any other rule.

(d) **Definition of "Child" and "Child Molestation."** In this rule and Rule 415:

(1) "child" means a person below the age of 14; and

(2) "child molestation" means a crime under federal law or under state law (as "state" is defined in 18 U.S.C. § 513) involving:

(A) any conduct prohibited by 18 U.S.C. chapter 109A and committed with a child;

(B) any conduct prohibited by 18 U.S.C. chapter 110;

(C) contact between any part of the defendant's body—or an object—and a child's genitals or anus;

(D) contact between the defendant's genitals or anus and any part of a child's body;

(E) deriving sexual pleasure or gratification from inflicting death, bodily injury, or physical pain on a child; or

    (F) an attempt or conspiracy to engage in conduct described in subparagraphs (A)–(E).

Rule 415. Similar Acts in Civil Cases Involving Sexual Assault or Child Molestation

(a) Permitted Uses. In a civil case involving a claim for relief based on a party's alleged sexual assault or child molestation, the court may admit evidence that the party committed any other sexual assault or child molestation. The evidence may be considered as provided in Rules 413 and 414.

(b) Disclosure to the Opponent. If a party intends to offer this evidence, the party must disclose it to the party against whom it will be offered, including witnesses' statements or a summary of the expected testimony. The party must do so at least 15 days before trial or at a later time that the court allows for good cause.

(c) Effect on Other Rules. This rule does not limit the admission or consideration of evidence under any other rule.

ARTICLE V

PRIVILEGES

Rule 501. Privilege in General

The common law—as interpreted by United States courts in the light of reason and experience—governs a claim of privilege unless any of the following provides otherwise:

- the United States Constitution;
- a federal statute; or
- rules prescribed by the Supreme Court.

But in a civil case, state law governs privilege regarding a claim or defense for which state law supplies the rule of decision

Rule 502. Attorney-Client Privilege and Work Product; Limitations on Waiver

The following provisions apply, in the circumstances set out, to disclosure of a communication or information covered by the attorney-client privilege or work-product protection.

(a) Disclosure Made in a Federal Proceeding or to a Federal Office or Agency; Scope of a Waiver. When the disclosure is made in a Federal proceeding or to a Federal office or agency and waives the attorney-client privilege or work-product protection, the waiver extends to an undisclosed communication or information in a Federal or State proceeding only if:

    (1) the waiver is intentional;

    (2) the disclosed and undisclosed communications or information concern the same subject matter; and

    (3) they ought in fairness to be considered together.

(b) Inadvertent Disclosure. When made in a Federal proceeding or to a Federal office or agency, the disclosure does not operate as a waiver in a Federal or State proceeding if:

    (1) the disclosure is inadvertent;

    (2) the holder of the privilege or protection took reasonable steps to prevent disclosure; and

(3) the holder promptly took reasonable steps to rectify the error, including (if applicable) following Federal Rule of Civil Procedure 26(b)(5)(B).

(c) **Disclosure Made in a State Proceeding.** When the disclosure is made in a State proceeding and is not the subject of a State-court order concerning waiver, the disclosure does not operate as a waiver in a Federal proceeding if the disclosure:

(1) would not be a waiver under this rule if it had been made in a Federal proceeding; or

(2) is not a waiver under the law of the State where the disclosure occurred.

(d) **Controlling Effect of a Court Order.** A Federal court may order that the privilege or protection is not waived by disclosure connected with the litigation pending before the court—in which event the disclosure is also not a waiver in any other Federal or State proceeding.

(e) **Controlling Effect of a Party Agreement.** An agreement on the effect of disclosure in a Federal proceeding is binding only on the parties to the agreement, unless it is incorporated into a court order.

(f) **Controlling Effect of this Rule.** Notwithstanding Rules 101 and 1101, this rule applies to State proceedings and to Federal court-annexed and Federal court-mandated arbitration proceedings, in the circumstances set out in the rule. And notwithstanding Rule 501, this rule applies even if State law provides the rule of decision.

(g) **Definitions.** In this rule:

(1) "attorney-client privilege" means the protection that applicable law provides for confidential attorney-client communications; and

(2) "work-product protection" means the protection that applicable law provides for tangible material (or its intangible equivalent) prepared in anticipation of litigation or for trial.

ARTICLE VI

WITNESSES

Rule 601. Competency to Testify in General

Every person is competent to be a witness unless these rules provide otherwise. But in a civil case, state law governs the witness's competency regarding a claim or defense for which state law supplies the rule of decision.

Rule 602. Need for Personal Knowledge

A witness may testify to a matter only if evidence is introduced sufficient to support a finding that the witness has personal knowledge of the matter. Evidence to prove personal knowledge may consist of the witness's own testimony. This rule does not apply to a witness's expert testimony under Rule 703.

Rule 603. Oath or Affirmation to Testify Truthfully

Before testifying, a witness must give an oath or affirmation to testify truthfully. It must be in a form designed to impress that duty on the witness's conscience.

Rule 604. Interpreter

An interpreter must be qualified and must give an oath or affirmation to make a true translation.

Rule 605. Judge's Competency as a Witness

The presiding judge may not testify as a witness at the trial. A party need not object to preserve the issue.

Rule 606. Juror's Competency as a Witness

(a) At the Trial. A juror may not testify as a witness before the other jurors at the trial. If a juror is called to testify, the court must give a party an opportunity to object outside the jury's presence.

(b) During an Inquiry into the Validity of a Verdict or Indictment.

    (1) *Prohibited Testimony or Other Evidence.* During an inquiry into the validity of a verdict or indictment, a juror may not testify about any statement made or incident that occurred during the jury's deliberations; the effect of anything on that juror's or another juror's vote; or any juror's mental processes concerning the verdict or indictment. The court may not receive a juror's affidavit or evidence of a juror's statement on these matters.

    (2) *Exceptions.* A juror may testify about whether:

        (A) extraneous prejudicial information was improperly brought to the jury's attention;

        (B) an outside influence was improperly brought to bear on any juror; or

        (C) a mistake was made in entering the verdict on the verdict form.

Rule 607. Who May Impeach a Witness

Any party, including the party that called the witness, may attack the witness's credibility.

Rule 608. A Witness's Character for Truthfulness or Untruthfulness

(a) Reputation or Opinion Evidence. A witness's credibility may be attacked or supported by testimony about the witness's reputation for having a character for truthfulness or untruthfulness, or by testimony in the form of an opinion about that character. But evidence of truthful character is admissible only after the witness's character for truthfulness has been attacked.

(b) Specific Instances of Conduct. Except for a criminal conviction under Rule 609, extrinsic evidence is not admissible to prove specific instances of a witness's conduct in order to attack or support the witness's character for truthfulness. But the court may, on cross-examination, allow them to be inquired into if they are probative of the character for truthfulness or untruthfulness of:

    (1) the witness; or

    (2) another witness whose character the witness being cross-examined has testified about.

By testifying on another matter, a witness does not waive any privilege against self-incrimination for testimony that relates only to the witness's character for truthfulness.

Rule 609. Impeachment by Evidence of a Criminal Conviction

(a) In General. The following rules apply to attacking a witness's character for truthfulness by evidence of a criminal conviction:

    (1) for a crime that, in the convicting jurisdiction, was punishable by death or by imprisonment for more than one year, the evidence:

        (A) must be admitted, subject to Rule 403, in a civil case or in a criminal case in which the witness is not a defendant; and

    (B) must be admitted in a criminal case in which the witness is a defendant, if the probative value of the evidence outweighs its prejudicial effect to that defendant; and

  (2) for any crime regardless of the punishment, the evidence must be admitted if the court can readily determine that establishing the elements of the crime required proving—or the witness's admitting—a dishonest act or false statement.

(b) Limit on Using the Evidence After 10 Years. This subdivision (b) applies if more than 10 years have passed since the witness's conviction or release from confinement for it, whichever is later. Evidence of the conviction is admissible only if:

  (1) its probative value, supported by specific facts and circumstances, substantially outweighs its prejudicial effect; and

  (2) the proponent gives an adverse party reasonable written notice of the intent to use it so that the party has a fair opportunity to contest its use.

(c) Effect of a Pardon, Annulment, or Certificate of Rehabilitation. Evidence of a conviction is not admissible if:

  (1) the conviction has been the subject of a pardon, annulment, certificate of rehabilitation, or other equivalent procedure based on a finding that the person has been rehabilitated, and the person has not been convicted of a later crime punishable by death or by imprisonment for more than one year; or

  (2) the conviction has been the subject of a pardon, annulment, or other equivalent procedure based on a finding of innocence.

(d) Juvenile Adjudications. Evidence of a juvenile adjudication is admissible under this rule only if:

  (1) it is offered in a criminal case;

  (2) the adjudication was of a witness other than the defendant;

  (3) an adult's conviction for that offense would be admissible to attack the adult's credibility; and

  (4) admitting the evidence is necessary to fairly determine guilt or innocence.

(e) Pendency of an Appeal. A conviction that satisfies this rule is admissible even if an appeal is pending. Evidence of the pendency is also admissible.

Rule 610. Religious Beliefs or Opinions

Evidence of a witness's religious beliefs or opinions is not admissible to attack or support the witness's credibility.

Rule 611. Mode and Order of Examining Witnesses and Presenting Evidence

(a) Control by the Court; Purposes. The court should exercise reasonable control over the mode and order of examining witnesses and presenting evidence so as to:

  (1) make those procedures effective for determining the truth;

  (2) avoid wasting time; and

  (3) protect witnesses from harassment or undue embarrassment.

(b) Scope of Cross-Examination. Cross-examination should not go beyond the subject matter of the direct examination and matters affecting the witness's credibility. The court may allow inquiry into additional matters as if on direct examination.

(c) Leading Questions. Leading questions should not be used on direct examination except as necessary to develop the witness's testimony. Ordinarily, the court should allow leading questions:

(1) on cross-examination; and

(2) when a party calls a hostile witness, an adverse party, or a witness identified with an adverse party.

Rule 612. Writing Used to Refresh a Witness's Memory

(a) Scope. This rule gives an adverse party certain options when a witness uses a writing to refresh memory:

(1) while testifying; or

(2) before testifying, if the court decides that justice requires the party to have those options.

(b) Adverse Party's Options; Deleting Unrelated Matter. Unless 18 U.S.C. § 3500 provides otherwise in a criminal case, an adverse party is entitled to have the writing produced at the hearing, to inspect it, to cross-examine the witness about it, and to introduce in evidence any portion that relates to the witness's testimony. If the producing party claims that the writing includes unrelated matter, the court must examine the writing in camera, delete any unrelated portion, and order that the rest be delivered to the adverse party. Any portion deleted over objection must be preserved for the record.

(c) Failure to Produce or Deliver the Writing. If a writing is not produced or is not delivered as ordered, the court may issue any appropriate order. But if the prosecution does not comply in a criminal case, the court must strike the witness's testimony or—if justice so requires—declare a mistrial.

Rule 613. Witness's Prior Statement

(a) Showing or Disclosing the Statement During Examination. When examining a witness about the witness's prior statement, a party need not show it or disclose its contents to the witness. But the party must, on request, show it or disclose its contents to an adverse party's attorney.

(b) Extrinsic Evidence of a Prior Inconsistent Statement. Extrinsic evidence of a witness's prior inconsistent statement is admissible only if the witness is given an opportunity to explain or deny the statement and an adverse party is given an opportunity to examine the witness about it, or if justice so requires. This subdivision (b) does not apply to an opposing party's statement under Rule 801(d)(2).

Rule 614. Court's Calling or Examining a Witness

(a) Calling. The court may call a witness on its own or at a party's request. Each party is entitled to cross-examine the witness.

(b) Examining. The court may examine a witness regardless of who calls the witness.

(c) Objections. A party may object to the court's calling or examining a witness either at that time or at the next opportunity when the jury is not present.

Rule 615. Excluding Witnesses from the Courtroom; Preventing an Excluded Witness's Access to Trial Testimony

(a) **Excluding Witnesses.** At a party's request, the court must order witnesses excluded from the courtroom so that they cannot hear other witnesses' testimony. Or the court may do so on its own. But this rule does not authorize excluding:

    (1) a party who is a natural person;

    (2) one officer or employee of a party that is not a natural person if that officer or employee has been designated as the party's representative by its attorney;

    (3) any person whose presence a party shows to be essential to presenting the party's claim or defense; or

    (4) a person authorized by statute to be present.

(b) **Additional Orders to Prevent Disclosing and Accessing Testimony.** An order under (a) operates only to exclude witnesses from the courtroom. But the court may also, by order:

    (1) prohibit disclosure of trial testimony to witnesses who are excluded from the courtroom; and

    (2) prohibit excluded witnesses from accessing trial testimony.

ARTICLE VII

OPINIONS AND EXPERT TESTIMONY

Rule 701. Opinion Testimony by Lay Witnesses

If a witness is not testifying as an expert, testimony in the form of an opinion is limited to one that is:

(a) rationally based on the witness's perception;

(b) helpful to clearly understanding the witness's testimony or to determining a fact in issue; and

(c) not based on scientific, technical, or other specialized knowledge within the scope of Rule 702.

Rule 702. Testimony by Expert Witnesses

A witness who is qualified as an expert by knowledge, skill, experience, training, or education may testify in the form of an opinion or otherwise if the proponent demonstrates to the court that it is more likely than not that:

(a) the expert's scientific, technical, or other specialized knowledge will help the trier of fact to understand the evidence or to determine a fact in issue;

(b) the testimony is based on sufficient facts or data;

(c) the testimony is the product of reliable principles and methods; and

(d) the expert's opinion reflects a reliable application of the principles and methods to the facts of the case.

Rule 703. Bases of an Expert's Opinion Testimony

An expert may base an opinion on facts or data in the case that the expert has been made aware of or personally observed. If experts in the particular field would reasonably rely on those kinds of facts or data in forming an opinion on the subject, they need not be admissible for the opinion to be admitted. But if the facts or data would otherwise be inadmissible, the proponent of the opinion may disclose them to the jury only if their probative value in helping the jury evaluate the opinion substantially outweighs their prejudicial effect.

Rule 704. Opinion on an Ultimate Issue

(a) **In General—Not Automatically Objectionable.** An opinion is not objectionable just because it embraces an ultimate issue.

(b) **Exception.** In a criminal case, an expert witness must not state an opinion about whether the defendant did or did not have a mental state or condition that constitutes an element of the crime charged or of a defense. Those matters are for the trier of fact alone.

Rule 705. Disclosing the Facts or Data Underlying an Expert's Opinion

Unless the court orders otherwise, an expert may state an opinion—and give the reasons for it—without first testifying to the underlying facts or data. But the expert may be required to disclose those facts or data on cross-examination.

Rule 706. Court-Appointed Expert Witnesses

(a) **Appointment Process.** On a party's motion or on its own, the court may order the parties to show cause why expert witnesses should not be appointed and may ask the parties to submit nominations. The court may appoint any expert that the parties agree on and any of its own choosing. But the court may only appoint someone who consents to act.

(b) **Expert's Role.** The court must inform the expert of the expert's duties. The court may do so in writing and have a copy filed with the clerk or may do so orally at a conference in which the parties have an opportunity to participate. The expert:

(1) must advise the parties of any findings the expert makes;

(2) may be deposed by any party;

(3) may be called to testify by the court or any party; and

(4) may be cross-examined by any party, including the party that called the expert.

(c) **Compensation.** The expert is entitled to a reasonable compensation, as set by the court. The compensation is payable as follows:

(1) in a criminal case or in a civil case involving just compensation under the Fifth Amendment, from any funds that are provided by law; and

(2) in any other civil case, by the parties in the proportion and at the time that the court directs—and the compensation is then charged like other costs.

(d) **Disclosing the Appointment to the Jury.** The court may authorize disclosure to the jury that the court appointed the expert.

(e) **Parties' Choice of Their Own Experts.** This rule does not limit a party in calling its own experts.

ARTICLE VIII

HEARSAY

Rule 801. Definitions That Apply to This Article; Exclusions from Hearsay

(a) **Statement.** "Statement" means a person's oral assertion, written assertion, or nonverbal conduct, if the person intended it as an assertion.

(b) **Declarant.** "Declarant" means the person who made the statement.

(c) **Hearsay.** "Hearsay" means a statement that:

    (1) the declarant does not make while testifying at the current trial or hearing; and

    (2) a party offers in evidence to prove the truth of the matter asserted in the statement.

(d) **Statements That Are Not Hearsay.** A statement that meets the following conditions is not hearsay:

    (1) *A Declarant-Witness's Prior Statement.* The declarant testifies and is subject to cross-examination about a prior statement, and the statement:

        (A) is inconsistent with the declarant's testimony and was given under penalty of perjury at a trial, hearing, or other proceeding or in a deposition;

        (B) is consistent with the declarant's testimony and is offered:

            (i) to rebut an express or implied charge that the declarant recently fabricated it or acted from a recent improper influence or motive in so testifying; or

            (ii) to rehabilitate the declarant's credibility as a witness when attacked on another ground; or

        (C) identifies a person as someone the declarant perceived earlier.

    (2) *An Opposing Party's Statement.* The statement is offered against an opposing party and:

        (A) was made by the party in an individual or representative capacity;

        (B) is one the party manifested that it adopted or believed to be true;

        (C) was made by a person whom the party authorized to make a statement on the subject;

        (D) was made by the party's agent or employee on a matter within the scope of that relationship and while it existed; or

        (E) was made by the party's coconspirator during and in furtherance of the conspiracy.

    The statement must be considered but does not by itself establish the declarant's authority under (C); the existence or scope of the relationship under (D); or the existence of the conspiracy or participation in it under (E).

Rule 802. The Rule Against Hearsay

Hearsay is not admissible unless any of the following provides otherwise:

- a federal statute;
- these rules; or
- other rules prescribed by the Supreme Court.

Rule 803. Exceptions to the Rule Against Hearsay—Regardless of Whether the Declarant Is Available as a Witness

The following are not excluded by the rule against hearsay, regardless of whether the declarant is available as a witness:

(1) ***Present Sense Impression.*** A statement describing or explaining an event or condition, made while or immediately after the declarant perceived it.

(2) ***Excited Utterance.*** A statement relating to a startling event or condition, made while the declarant was under the stress of excitement that it caused.

(3) ***Then-Existing Mental, Emotional, or Physical Condition.*** A statement of the declarant's then-existing state of mind (such as motive, intent, or plan) or emotional, sensory, or physical condition (such as mental feeling, pain, or bodily health), but not including a statement of memory or belief to prove the fact remembered or believed unless it relates to the validity or terms of the declarant's will.

(4) ***Statement Made for Medical Diagnosis or Treatment.*** A statement that:

(A) is made for—and is reasonably pertinent to—medical diagnosis or treatment; and

(B) describes medical history; past or present symptoms or sensations; their inception; or their general cause.

(5) ***Recorded Recollection.*** A record that:

(A) is on a matter the witness once knew about but now cannot recall well enough to testify fully and accurately;

(B) was made or adopted by the witness when the matter was fresh in the witness's memory; and

(C) accurately reflects the witness's knowledge.

If admitted, the record may be read into evidence but may be received as an exhibit only if offered by an adverse party.

(6) ***Records of a Regularly Conducted Activity.*** A record of an act, event, condition, opinion, or diagnosis if:

(A) the record was made at or near the time by—or from information transmitted by—someone with knowledge;

(B) the record was kept in the course of a regularly conducted activity of a business, organization, occupation, or calling, whether or not for profit;

(C) making the record was a regular practice of that activity;

(D) all these conditions are shown by the testimony of the custodian or another qualified witness, or by a certification that complies with Rule 902(11) or (12) or with a statute permitting certification; and

(E) the opponent does not show that the source of information or the method or circumstances of preparation indicate a lack of trustworthiness.

(7) ***Absence of a Record of a Regularly Conducted Activity.*** Evidence that a matter is not included in a record described in paragraph (6) if:

(A) the evidence is admitted to prove that the matter did not occur or exist;

(B) a record was regularly kept for a matter of that kind; and

(C) the opponent does not show that the possible source of the information or other circumstances indicate a lack of trustworthiness.

(8) ***Public Records.*** A record or statement of a public office if:

    (A) it sets out:

        (i) the office's activities;

        (ii) a matter observed while under a legal duty to report, but not including, in a criminal case, a matter observed by law-enforcement personnel; or

        (iii) in a civil case or against the government in a criminal case, factual findings from a legally authorized investigation; and

    (B) the opponent does not show that the source of information or other circumstances indicate a lack of trustworthiness.

(9) ***Public Records of Vital Statistics.*** A record of a birth, death, or marriage, if reported to a public office in accordance with a legal duty.

(10) ***Absence of a Public Record.*** Testimony—or a certification under Rule 902—that a diligent search failed to disclose a public record or statement if:

    (A) the testimony or certification is admitted to prove that

        (i) the record or statement does not exist; or

        (ii) a matter did not occur or exist, if a public office regularly kept a record or statement for a matter of that kind; and

    (B) in a criminal case, a prosecutor who intends to offer a certification provides written notice of that intent at least 14 days before trial, and the defendant does not object in writing within 7 days of receiving the notice—unless the court sets a different time for the notice or the objection.

(11) ***Records of Religious Organizations Concerning Personal or Family History.*** A statement of birth, legitimacy, ancestry, marriage, divorce, death, relationship by blood or marriage, or similar facts of personal or family history, contained in a regularly kept record of a religious organization.

(12) ***Certificates of Marriage, Baptism, and Similar Ceremonies.*** A statement of fact contained in a certificate:

    (A) made by a person who is authorized by a religious organization or by law to perform the act certified;

    (B) attesting that the person performed a marriage or similar ceremony or administered a sacrament; and

    (C) purporting to have been issued at the time of the act or within a reasonable time after it.

(13) ***Family Records.*** A statement of fact about personal or family history contained in a family record, such as a Bible, genealogy, chart, engraving on a ring, inscription on a portrait, or engraving on an urn or burial marker.

(14) ***Records of Documents That Affect an Interest in Property.*** The record of a document that purports to establish or affect an interest in property if:

    (A) the record is admitted to prove the content of the original recorded document, along with its signing and its delivery by each person who purports to have signed it;

    (B) the record is kept in a public office; and

    (C) a statute authorizes recording documents of that kind in that office.

(15) ***Statements in Documents That Affect an Interest in Property.*** A statement contained in a document that purports to establish or affect an interest in property if the matter stated was relevant to the document's purpose—unless later dealings with the property are inconsistent with the truth of the statement or the purport of the document.

(16) ***Statements in Ancient Documents.*** A statement in a document that was prepared before January 1, 1998, and whose authenticity is established.

(17) ***Market Reports and Similar Commercial Publications.*** Market quotations, lists, directories, or other compilations that are generally relied on by the public or by persons in particular occupations.

(18) ***Statements in Learned Treatises, Periodicals, or Pamphlets.*** A statement contained in a treatise, periodical, or pamphlet if:

> **(A)** the statement is called to the attention of an expert witness on cross-examination or relied on by the expert on direct examination; and

> **(B)** the publication is established as a reliable authority by the expert's admission or testimony, by another expert's testimony, or by judicial notice.

If admitted, the statement may be read into evidence but not received as an exhibit.

(19) ***Reputation Concerning Personal or Family History.*** A reputation among a person's family by blood, adoption, or marriage—or among a person's associates or in the community—concerning the person's birth, adoption, legitimacy, ancestry, marriage, divorce, death, relationship by blood, adoption, or marriage, or similar facts of personal or family history.

(20) ***Reputation Concerning Boundaries or General History.*** A reputation in a community—arising before the controversy—concerning boundaries of land in the community or customs that affect the land, or concerning general historical events important to that community, state, or nation.

(21) ***Reputation Concerning Character.*** A reputation among a person's associates or in the community concerning the person's character.

(22) ***Judgment of a Previous Conviction.*** Evidence of a final judgment of conviction if:

> **(A)** the judgment was entered after a trial or guilty plea, but not a nolo contendere plea;

> **(B)** the conviction was for a crime punishable by death or by imprisonment for more than a year;

> **(C)** the evidence is admitted to prove any fact essential to the judgment; and

> **(D)** when offered by the prosecutor in a criminal case for a purpose other than impeachment, the judgment was against the defendant.

The pendency of an appeal may be shown but does not affect admissibility.

(23) ***Judgments Involving Personal, Family, or General History or a Boundary.*** A judgment that is admitted to prove a matter of personal, family, or general history, or boundaries, if the matter:

> **(A)** was essential to the judgment; and

> **(B)** could be proved by evidence of reputation.

(24) **[Other exceptions.]** [Transferred to Rule 807.]

Rule 804. Exceptions to the Rule Against Hearsay—When the Declarant Is Unavailable as a Witness

(a) **Criteria for Being Unavailable.** A declarant is considered to be unavailable as a witness if the declarant:

     (1) is exempted from testifying about the subject matter of the declarant's statement because the court rules that a privilege applies;

     (2) refuses to testify about the subject matter despite a court order to do so;

     (3) testifies to not remembering the subject matter;

     (4) cannot be present or testify at the trial or hearing because of death or a then-existing infirmity, physical illness, or mental illness; or

     (5) is absent from the trial or hearing and the statement's proponent has not been able, by process or other reasonable means, to procure:

         (A) the declarant's attendance, in the case of a hearsay exception under Rule 804(b)(1) or (5); or

         (B) the declarant's attendance or testimony, in the case of a hearsay exception under Rule 804(b)(2), (3), or (4).

But this subdivision (a) does not apply if the statement's proponent procured or wrongfully caused the declarant's unavailability as a witness in order to prevent the declarant from attending or testifying.

(b) **The Exceptions.** The following are not excluded by the rule against hearsay if the declarant is unavailable as a witness:

     (1) *Former Testimony.* Testimony that:

         (A) was given as a witness at a trial, hearing, or lawful deposition, whether given during the current proceeding or a different one; and

         (B) is now offered against a party who had—or, in a civil case, whose predecessor in interest had—an opportunity and similar motive to develop it by direct, cross-, or redirect examination.

     (2) *Statement Under the Belief of Imminent Death.* In a prosecution for homicide or in a civil case, a statement that the declarant, while believing the declarant's death to be imminent, made about its cause or circumstances.

     (3) *Statement Against Interest.* A statement that:

         (A) a reasonable person in the declarant's position would have made only if the person believed it to be true because, when made, it was so contrary to the declarant's proprietary or pecuniary interest or had so great a tendency to invalidate the declarant's claim against someone else or to expose the declarant to civil or criminal liability; and

         (B) is supported by corroborating circumstances that clearly indicate its trustworthiness, if it is offered in a criminal case as one that tends to expose the declarant to criminal liability.

     (4) *Statement of Personal or Family History.* A statement about:

         (A) the declarant's own birth, adoption, legitimacy, ancestry, marriage, divorce, relationship by blood, adoption, or marriage, or similar facts of personal or family history, even though the declarant had no way of acquiring personal knowledge about that fact; or

(B) another person concerning any of these facts, as well as death, if the declarant was related to the person by blood, adoption, or marriage or was so intimately associated with the person's family that the declarant's information is likely to be accurate.

(5) **[Other exceptions.]** [Transferred to Rule 807.]

(6) ***Statement Offered Against a Party That Wrongfully Caused the Declarant's Unavailability.*** A statement offered against a party that wrongfully caused—or acquiesced in wrongfully causing—the declarant's unavailability as a witness, and did so intending that result.

Rule 805. Hearsay Within Hearsay

Hearsay within hearsay is not excluded by the rule against hearsay if each part of the combined statements conforms with an exception to the rule.

Rule 806. Attacking and Supporting the Declarant's Credibility

When a hearsay statement—or a statement described in Rule 801(d)(2)(C), (D), or (E)—has been admitted in evidence, the declarant's credibility may be attacked, and then supported, by any evidence that would be admissible for those purposes if the declarant had testified as a witness. The court may admit evidence of the declarant's inconsistent statement or conduct, regardless of when it occurred or whether the declarant had an opportunity to explain or deny it. If the party against whom the statement was admitted calls the declarant as a witness, the party may examine the declarant on the statement as if on cross-examination.

Rule 807. Residual Exception

(a) **In General.** Under the following conditions, a hearsay statement is not excluded by the rule against hearsay even if the statement is not admissible under a hearsay exception in Rule 803 or 804:

    (1) the statement is supported by sufficient guarantees of trustworthiness—after considering the totality of circumstances under which it was made and evidence, if any, corroborating the statement; and

    (2) it is more probative on the point for which it is offered than any other evidence that the proponent can obtain through reasonable efforts.

(b) **Notice.** The statement is admissible only if the proponent gives an adverse party reasonable notice of the intent to offer the statement—including its substance and the declarant's name—so that the party has a fair opportunity to meet it. The notice must be provided in writing before the trial or hearing—or in any form during the trial or hearing if the court, for good cause, excuses a lack of earlier notice.

ARTICLE IX

AUTHENTICATION AND IDENTIFICATION

Rule 901. Authenticating or Identifying Evidence

(a) **In General.** To satisfy the requirement of authenticating or identifying an item of evidence, the proponent must produce evidence sufficient to support a finding that the item is what the proponent claims it is.

(b) **Examples.** The following are examples only—not a complete list—of evidence that satisfies the requirement:

(1) ***Testimony of a Witness with Knowledge.*** Testimony that an item is what it is claimed to be.

(2) ***Nonexpert Opinion About Handwriting.*** A nonexpert's opinion that handwriting is genuine, based on a familiarity with it that was not acquired for the current litigation.

(3) ***Comparison by an Expert Witness or the Trier of Fact.*** A comparison with an authenticated specimen by an expert witness or the trier of fact.

(4) ***Distinctive Characteristics and the Like.*** The appearance, contents, substance, internal patterns, or other distinctive characteristics of the item, taken together with all the circumstances.

(5) ***Opinion About a Voice.*** An opinion identifying a person's voice—whether heard firsthand or through mechanical or electronic transmission or recording—based on hearing the voice at any time under circumstances that connect it with the alleged speaker.

(6) ***Evidence About a Telephone Conversation.*** For a telephone conversation, evidence that a call was made to the number assigned at the time to:

    (A) a particular person, if circumstances, including self-identification, show that the person answering was the one called; or

    (B) a particular business, if the call was made to a business and the call related to business reasonably transacted over the telephone.

(7) ***Evidence About Public Records.*** Evidence that:

    (A) a document was recorded or filed in a public office as authorized by law; or

    (B) a purported public record or statement is from the office where items of this kind are kept.

(8) ***Evidence About Ancient Documents or Data Compilations.*** For a document or data compilation, evidence that it:

    (A) is in a condition that creates no suspicion about its authenticity;

    (B) was in a place where, if authentic, it would likely be; and

    (C) is at least 20 years old when offered.

(9) ***Evidence About a Process or System.*** Evidence describing a process or system and showing that it produces an accurate result.

(10) ***Methods Provided by a Statute or Rule.*** Any method of authentication or identification allowed by a federal statute or a rule prescribed by the Supreme Court.

Rule 902. Evidence That Is Self-Authenticating

The following items of evidence are self-authenticating; they require no extrinsic evidence of authenticity in order to be admitted:

(1) ***Domestic Public Documents That Are Sealed and Signed.*** A document that bears:

    (A) a seal purporting to be that of the United States; any state, district, commonwealth, territory, or insular possession of the United States; the former Panama Canal Zone; the Trust Territory of the Pacific Islands; a political subdivision of any of these entities; or a department, agency, or officer of any entity named above; and

    (B) a signature purporting to be an execution or attestation.

(2) ***Domestic Public Documents That Are Not Sealed but Are Signed and Certified.*** A document that bears no seal if:

(A) it bears the signature of an officer or employee of an entity named in Rule 902(1)(A); and

(B) another public officer who has a seal and official duties within that same entity certifies under seal—or its equivalent—that the signer has the official capacity and that the signature is genuine.

(3) *Foreign Public Documents.* A document that purports to be signed or attested by a person who is authorized by a foreign country's law to do so. The document must be accompanied by a final certification that certifies the genuineness of the signature and official position of the signer or attester—or of any foreign official whose certificate of genuineness relates to the signature or attestation or is in a chain of certificates of genuineness relating to the signature or attestation. The certification may be made by a secretary of a United States embassy or legation; by a consul general, vice consul, or consular agent of the United States; or by a diplomatic or consular official of the foreign country assigned or accredited to the United States. If all parties have been given a reasonable opportunity to investigate the document's authenticity and accuracy, the court may, for good cause, either:

(A) order that it be treated as presumptively authentic without final certification; or

(B) allow it to be evidenced by an attested summary with or without final certification.

(4) *Certified Copies of Public Records.* A copy of an official record—or a copy of a document that was recorded or filed in a public office as authorized by law—if the copy is certified as correct by:

(A) the custodian or another person authorized to make the certification; or

(B) a certificate that complies with Rule 902(1), (2), or (3), a federal statute, or a rule prescribed by the Supreme Court.

(5) *Official Publications.* A book, pamphlet, or other publication purporting to be issued by a public authority.

(6) *Newspapers and Periodicals.* Printed material purporting to be a newspaper or periodical.

(7) *Trade Inscriptions and the Like.* An inscription, sign, tag, or label purporting to have been affixed in the course of business and indicating origin, ownership, or control.

(8) *Acknowledged Documents.* A document accompanied by a certificate of acknowledgment that is lawfully executed by a notary public or another officer who is authorized to take acknowledgments.

(9) *Commercial Paper and Related Documents.* Commercial paper, a signature on it, and related documents, to the extent allowed by general commercial law.

(10) *Presumptions Under a Federal Statute.* A signature, document, or anything else that a federal statute declares to be presumptively or prima facie genuine or authentic.

(11) *Certified Domestic Records of a Regularly Conducted Activity.* The original or a copy of a domestic record that meets the requirements of Rule 803(6)(A)–(C), as shown by a certification of the custodian or another qualified person that complies with a federal statute or a rule prescribed by the Supreme Court. Before the trial or hearing, the proponent must give an adverse party reasonable written notice of the intent to offer the record—and must make the record and certification available for inspection—so that the party has a fair opportunity to challenge them.

(12) *Certified Foreign Records of a Regularly Conducted Activity.* In a civil case, the original or a copy of a foreign record that meets the requirements of Rule 902(11), modified as follows: the certification, rather than complying with a federal statute or Supreme Court rule, must be signed in a manner that, if falsely made, would subject the maker to a criminal penalty in the country where the certification is signed. The proponent must also meet the notice requirements of Rule 902(11).

(13) ***Certified Records Generated by an Electronic Process or System.*** A record generated by an electronic process or system that produces an accurate result, as shown by a certification of a qualified person that complies with the certification requirements of Rule 902(11) or (12). The proponent must also meet the notice requirements of Rule 902(11).

(14) ***Certified Data Copied from an Electronic Device, Storage Medium, or File.*** Data copied from an electronic device, storage medium, or file, if authenticated by a process of digital identification, as shown by a certification of a qualified person that complies with the certification requirements of Rule 902(11) or (12). The proponent also must meet the notice requirements of Rule 902(11).

Rule 903. Subscribing Witness's Testimony

A subscribing witness's testimony is necessary to authenticate a writing only if required by the law of the jurisdiction that governs its validity.

ARTICLE X

CONTENTS OF WRITINGS, RECORDINGS, AND PHOTOGRAPHS

Rule 1001. Definitions That Apply to This Article

In this article:

(a) A "writing" consists of letters, words, numbers, or their equivalent set down in any form.

(b) A "recording" consists of letters, words, numbers, or their equivalent recorded in any manner.

(c) A "photograph" means a photographic image or its equivalent stored in any form.

(d) An "original" of a writing or recording means the writing or recording itself or any counterpart intended to have the same effect by the person who executed or issued it. For electronically stored information, "original" means any printout—or other output readable by sight—if it accurately reflects the information. An "original" of a photograph includes the negative or a print from it.

(e) A "duplicate" means a counterpart produced by a mechanical, photographic, chemical, electronic, or other equivalent process or technique that accurately reproduces the original.

Rule 1002. Requirement of the Original

An original writing, recording, or photograph is required in order to prove its content unless these rules or a federal statute provides otherwise.

Rule 1003. Admissibility of Duplicates

A duplicate is admissible to the same extent as the original unless a genuine question is raised about the original's authenticity or the circumstances make it unfair to admit the duplicate.

Rule 1004. Admissibility of Other Evidence of Content

An original is not required and other evidence of the content of a writing, recording, or photograph is admissible if:

(a) all the originals are lost or destroyed, and not by the proponent acting in bad faith;

(b) an original cannot be obtained by any available judicial process;

(c) the party against whom the original would be offered had control of the original; was at that time put on notice, by pleadings or otherwise, that the original would be a subject of proof at the trial or hearing; and fails to produce it at the trial or hearing; or

(d) the writing, recording, or photograph is not closely related to a controlling issue.

Rule 1005. Copies of Public Records to Prove Content

The proponent may use a copy to prove the content of an official record—or of a document that was recorded or filed in a public office as authorized by law—if these conditions are met: the record or document is otherwise admissible; and the copy is certified as correct in accordance with Rule 902(4) or is testified to be correct by a witness who has compared it with the original. If no such copy can be obtained by reasonable diligence, then the proponent may use other evidence to prove the content.

Rule 1006. Summaries to Prove Content

The proponent may use a summary, chart, or calculation to prove the content of voluminous writings, recordings, or photographs that cannot be conveniently examined in court. The proponent must make the originals or duplicates available for examination or copying, or both, by other parties at a reasonable time and place. And the court may order the proponent to produce them in court.

Rule 1007. Testimony or Statement of a Party to Prove Content

The proponent may prove the content of a writing, recording, or photograph by the testimony, deposition, or written statement of the party against whom the evidence is offered. The proponent need not account for the original.

Rule 1008. Functions of the Court and Jury

Ordinarily, the court determines whether the proponent has fulfilled the factual conditions for admitting other evidence of the content of a writing, recording, or photograph under Rule 1004 or 1005. But in a jury trial, the jury determines—in accordance with Rule 104(b)—any issue about whether:

(a) an asserted writing, recording, or photograph ever existed;

(b) another one produced at the trial or hearing is the original; or

(c) other evidence of content accurately reflects the content.

ARTICLE XI

MISCELLANEOUS RULES

Rule 1101. Applicability of the Rules

(a) To Courts and Judges. These rules apply to proceedings before:

- United States district courts;
- United States bankruptcy and magistrate judges;
- United States courts of appeals;
- the United States Court of Federal Claims; and
- the district courts of Guam, the Virgin Islands, and the Northern Mariana Islands.

(b) To Cases and Proceedings. These rules apply in:

- civil cases and proceedings, including bankruptcy, admiralty, and maritime cases;
- criminal cases and proceedings; and
- contempt proceedings, except those in which the court may act summarily.

(c) Rules on Privilege. The rules on privilege apply to all stages of a case or proceeding.

(d) Exceptions. These rules—except for those on privilege—do not apply to the following:

(1) the court's determination, under Rule 104(a), on a preliminary question of fact governing admissibility;

(2) grand-jury proceedings; and

(3) miscellaneous proceedings such as:

- extradition or rendition;
- issuing an arrest warrant, criminal summons, or search warrant;
- a preliminary examination in a criminal case;
- sentencing;
- granting or revoking probation or supervised release; and
- considering whether to release on bail or otherwise.

(e) Other Statutes and Rules. A federal statute or a rule prescribed by the Supreme Court may provide for admitting or excluding evidence independently from these rules.

Rule 1102. Amendments

These rules may be amended as provided in 28 U.S.C. § 2072.

Rule 1103. Title

These rules may be cited as the Federal Rules of Evidence.

CHAPTER 2

EVIDENCE RULES WITH AUTHORS' COMMENTARY

ARTICLE I. GENERAL PROVISIONS

ARTICLE II. JUDICIAL NOTICE

ARTICLE III. PRESUMPTIONS IN CIVIL CASES

ARTICLE IV. RELEVANCE AND ITS LIMITS

ARTICLE V. PRIVILEGES

ARTICLE VI. WITNESSES

ARTICLE VII. OPINIONS AND EXPERT TESTIMONY

ARTICLE VIII. HEARSAY

ARTICLE IX. AUTHENTICATION AND IDENTIFICATION

ARTICLE X. CONTENTS OF WRITINGS, RECORDINGS, AND PHOTOGRAPHS

ARTICLE XI. MISCELLANEOUS RULES

ARTICLE I

GENERAL PROVISIONS

Rule 101. Scope; Definitions

(a) **Scope.** These rules apply to proceedings in United States courts. The specific courts and proceedings to which the rules apply, along with exceptions, are set out in Rule 1101.

(b) **Definitions.** In these rules:

    (1) "civil case" means a civil action or proceeding;

    (2) "criminal case" includes a criminal proceeding;

    (3) "public office" includes a public agency;

    (4) "record" includes a memorandum, report, or data compilation;

    (5) a "rule prescribed by the Supreme Court" means a rule adopted by the Supreme Court under statutory authority; and

    (6) a reference to any kind of written material or any other medium includes electronically stored information.

AUTHORS' COMMENTS

(1) **Scope and purpose of Rule 101.** Rule 101(a) describes in general terms the proceedings in which the rules apply. Rule 1101 prescribes more specifically the courts, proceedings, and issues to which the rules apply. Rule 101(b), which was added as part of the restyling effective in 2011, contains a few simple and straightforward definitions.

CROSS-REFERENCES

Treatises

2 Graham, Handbook of Federal Evidence § 101:1 (9th ed. 2020)

21 Wright & Graham, Federal Practice and Procedure §§ 5011–5014 (2005)

Rule 102. Purpose

These rules should be construed so as to administer every proceeding fairly, eliminate unjustifiable expense and delay, and promote the development of evidence law, to the end of ascertaining the truth and securing a just determination.

AUTHORS' COMMENTS

(1) **Scope and purpose of Rule 102.** Rule 102 is a rule of liberal construction applicable to all the rules of evidence.

Example. Court of Appeals cited Rule 102 in declining to construe Rule 608(b) to require exclusion of prior specific act evidence that it regarded as highly probative in the circumstances of the case. "We believe that the ultimate purpose of the rules of evidence should not be lost by a rigid, blind application of a single rule of evidence. Individual rules of evidence, in this instance Rule 608(b), should not be read in isolation, when to do so destroys the purpose of ascertaining the truth." United States v. Batts, 558 F.2d 513, 517 (9th Cir.1977), opinion withdrawn on other grounds, 573 F.2d 599 (9th Cir.1978).

CROSS-REFERENCES

Treatises

2 Graham, Handbook of Federal Evidence § 102:1 (9th ed. 2020)

21 Wright & Graham, Federal Practice and Procedure §§ 5021–5027 (2005)

Rule 103. Rulings on Evidence

(a) **Preserving a Claim of Error.** A party may claim error in a ruling to admit or exclude evidence only if the error affects a substantial right of the party and:

    (1) if the ruling admits evidence, a party, on the record:

        (A) timely objects or moves to strike; and

(B) states the specific ground, unless it was apparent from the context; or

(2) if the ruling excludes evidence, a party informs the court of its substance by an offer of proof, unless the substance was apparent from the context.

(b) **Not Needing to Renew an Objection or Offer of Proof.** Once the court rules definitively on the record—either before or at trial—a party need not renew an objection or offer of proof to preserve a claim of error for appeal.

(c) **Court's Statement About the Ruling; Directing an Offer of Proof.** The court may make any statement about the character or form of the evidence, the objection made, and the ruling. The court may direct that an offer of proof be made in question-and-answer form.

(d) **Preventing the Jury from Hearing Inadmissible Evidence.** To the extent practicable, the court must conduct a jury trial so that inadmissible evidence is not suggested to the jury by any means.

(e) **Taking Notice of Plain Error.** A court may take notice of a plain error affecting a substantial right, even if the claim of error was not properly preserved.

AUTHORS' COMMENTS

(1) **Scope and purpose of Rule 103.** Rule 103 addresses objections, motions to strike, and offers of proof. To preserve error for appeal, a party complaining of the admission of evidence must make a timely and specific objection or motion to strike. To preserve error as to the exclusion of evidence, the proponent must make an offer of proof.

(2) **Effect of erroneous ruling—Harmless error.** The opening clause of Rule 103(a) incorporates the common-law doctrine of harmless error, by stating as a prerequisite to any claim of error in the admission or exclusion of evidence that a substantial right of the party must have been affected by the ruling. See also 28 U.S.C.A. § 2111; Fed. R. Civ. P. 61; Fed. R. Crim. P. 52(a). "A number of factors have guided the courts in their determinations of whether error is harmless, including (1) whether erroneously admitted evidence was the primary evidence relied upon, (2) whether the aggrieved party was nonetheless able to present the substance of its claim, (3) the existence and usefulness of curative jury instructions, (4) the extent of jury argument based on tainted evidence, (5) whether erroneously admitted evidence was merely cumulative, and (6) whether other evidence was overwhelming." ATD Corp. v. Lydall, Inc., 159 F.3d 534, 549–50 (Fed.Cir.1998). See also Griffin v. Finkbeiner, 689 F.3d 584, 599 (6th Cir.2012) (finding exclusion of "other acts" evidence was not harmless where employment-discrimination plaintiff relied largely on circumstantial evidence in presenting case of retaliation to jury).

(3) **Objections—Timeliness.** To be timely, an objection or motion to strike must be made as soon as the ground of it is known, or reasonably should be known, to the objector. United States v. Check, 582 F.2d 668, 676 (2d Cir.1978).

In the case of an offer of real or documentary evidence, the proper time for objection is when the item is formally offered; after it has been admitted is too late. United States v. Benavente Gomez, 921 F.2d 378, 385 (1st Cir.1990); Vallejos v. C. E. Glass Co., 583 F.2d 507, 511 (10th Cir.1978).

In the case of oral testimony, normally the objection must precede the witness's answer. Hutchinson v. Groskin, 927 F.2d 722, 725 (2d Cir.1991); Reagan v. Brock, 628 F.2d 721, 723 (1st Cir.1980).

In some circumstances, an objection after the answer, accompanied by a motion to strike and a request for an instruction to the jury to disregard the answer, will be timely; for example, where a witness gives an objectionable answer to a question that was unobjectionable; where the witness answers an objectionable question too quickly for the objection to be interposed; where the witness volunteers an objectionable statement; or where the defect does not appear on the face of the testimony but is revealed later, such as where improper basis of expert opinion does not appear until cross-examination, Benjamin v. Peter's Farm Condominium Owners Ass'n, 820 F.2d 640, 642 n.5 (3d Cir.1987). See also Jones v. Lincoln Electric Co., 188 F.3d 709, 727 (7th Cir.1999) ("[W]e do not believe it to always be the case that an objection has to be perfectly contemporaneous with the challenged testimony in order to satisfy Rule 103(a) and be considered 'timely.' Instead, an objection can still be deemed 'timely' if it is raised within a sufficient time after the proffer of testimony so as to allow the district court an adequate opportunity to correct any error"). The motion to strike is itself subject to a requirement of timeliness. Terrell v. Poland, 744 F.2d 637, 639 (8th Cir.1984); United States v. Gibbs, 739 F.2d 838, 849 (3d Cir.1984) (en banc). An overruled objection is sufficient to preserve error; "the law imposes no obligation on a party opposing the admission of evidence *both* to object *and* to move to strike." United States v. Meserve, 271 F.3d 314, 325 (1st Cir.2001).

An objection to a closing argument may be timely even if made after the jury verdict in some circumstances. If the party repeatedly objected to the introduction of evidence at trial that was mentioned in the closing statement, the objection may be timely even if the party failed to object during the closing statement. United States v. Carpenter, 494 F.3d 13, 20–21 (1st Cir.2007).

(4) Objections—Timeliness—Connecting up. Where an objection is conditionally overruled upon the proponent's representation that required connecting or foundation evidence will be presented later, and the proponent fails to present the required connecting or foundation proof, a waiver occurs unless the objector renews his earlier objection by a motion to strike at an appropriate time, usually the close of the proponent's case. United States v. Dougherty, 895 F.2d 399, 403 (7th Cir.1990).

(5) Continuing objections. A continuing objection, if requested and granted, will preserve error with regard to a series of similar or connected questions or offers of evidence, to the extent that the continuing objection is adequately specific and unambiguous. United States v. Gomez-Norena, 908 F.2d 497, 500 n. 2 (9th Cir.1990).

(6) Depositions. Time requirements for objections in depositions are governed by Fed. R. Civ. P. 32, which is made applicable to depositions in criminal cases by Fed. R. Crim. P. 15. In general, objections that might be obviated or cured at the deposition, such as to the form of a question, are waived unless made at the deposition. All other objections, such as to the competency of the witness or to the competency or relevancy of the evidence, are reserved until the deposition is offered at trial.

(7) Motions in limine. "[U]nder the Federal Rules of Evidence, it is no longer necessary for a party to renew an objection to evidence when the district court has definitively ruled on the party's motion in limine. In relevant part, Rule 103 provides, 'Once the court rules definitively on the record—either before or at trial—a party need not renew an objection or offer of proof to preserve a claim of error for appeal.' Fed. R. Evid. 103(b). As the commentary explains, 'The amendment applies to all rulings on evidence whether they occur at or before trial, including so-called "in limine" rulings.' Fed. R. Evid. 103 advisory committee's note. Thus, we review claims of error raised and decided in an in limine motion as long as the district court's ruling was definitive." Tampa Bay Water v. HDR Engineering, Inc., 731 F.3d 1171, 1178 (11th Cir.2013). Compare United States v. Wilson, 788 F.3d 1298, 1313 (11th Cir.2015) ("Here, the district court did not definitively rule on the admissibility of Brown's testimony. Addressing Wilson's pretrial objection to Brown's testimony, the district court merely issued a provisional ruling. Throughout its discussion, the court used equivocal language stating, '[k]eeping in mind that none of this evidence has been actually offered yet,' and 'should Sherman Brown testify,' and 'I think Mr. Brown's testimony can be either intrinsic or extrinsic.' The court neither 'denied' or 'overruled' the objection nor used decisive language such as 'rule,' 'decide,' or 'conclude.' "); United States v. Big Eagle, 702 F.3d 1125, 1130 (8th Cir.2013) ("We must decide in this case whether Big Eagle's pretrial objections, in light of the district court's rulings, sufficiently preserved his evidentiary challenges on appeal. The district court's tentative ruling on the admissibility of uncharged crimes evidence was not final, and not sufficient to preserve Big Eagle's objections on appeal. The district court explicitly stated the ruling was 'preliminary,' noted the court had not heard the evidence the government intended to present, and emphasized the court would 'make further rulings on objections as the case progresses.' Taken in context, it is clear the district court did not intend this ruling to be definitive, but intended to address Big Eagle's concerns in light of the evidence the government offered at trial, subject to Big Eagle's specific objections to such evidence. Big Eagle's failure to object at trial limits our review of these challenges to plain error."). "Rule 103 requires the objecting party (here, Takesian) 'to clarify whether an in limine or other evidentiary ruling is definitive when there is doubt on that point.' See Crowe v. Bolduc, 334 F.3d 124, 133 (1st Cir.2003) (quoting Fed. R. Evid. 103 advisory committee's note to 2000 amendment)." United States v. Takesian, 945 F.3d 553, 562 (1st Cir.2019).

(8) Objections—Specificity—In general. There are four aspects as to which an objection may be wanting in specificity and may therefore be inadequate to protect the rights of the objector: grounds, parts, parties, and purposes. A failure of specificity in any of the four respects may have the result that the objector cannot successfully complain on appeal if the objection is overruled, even though the evidence was in fact not properly admissible or not admissible as offered. The problems of specificity of objections as to parties and purposes are addressed in Rule 105. Rule 103(a)(1) refers to stating "the specific ground." This language is interpreted to refer to specificity as to parts as well as to legal grounds. Collins v. Seaboard Coast Line R.R., 675 F.2d 1185, 1194 (11th Cir.1982); Dente v. Riddell, Inc., 664 F.2d 1, 2 n. 1 (1st Cir.1981); 2 Graham, Handbook of Federal Evidence § 103:2 (9th ed. 2020).

(9) Objections—Specificity—Grounds. An objection only preserves the specific ground or grounds named. United States v. Gomez-Norena, 908 F.2d 497, 500 (9th Cir.1990). A so-called "general" objection, such as the notorious "irrelevant, incompetent, and immaterial," preserves no ground for appeal, except perhaps the ground of total irrelevancy to any issue in the case. Owen v. Patton, 925 F.2d 1111, 1114 (8th Cir.1991); United States v. O'Brien, 601 F.2d 1067, 1071 (9th Cir.1979). If the proper ground of objection is a relevancy problem under Rules 401 and 402, however, an objection on that ground may suffice, if its meaning is clear. 2 Graham, Handbook of Federal Evidence § 103:2 (9th ed. 2020).

> **Example—Not Specific.** "We have not located cases with facts as egregious as this case: where an appellant affirmatively misleads the court regarding the legal standard that controls the objection. Until Seale filed his reply brief in this court, Seale never strayed from his erroneous argument that the pre-Miranda standard of general voluntariness applied. * * * He never put the district court on notice that the admissibility of his statement should be analyzed under Miranda. Fed. R. Evid. 103(a)(1) and the cases interpreting that rule establish that when the objection is not specific as to the legal basis for the objection, the error is not preserved and can only be reviewed for plain error." United States v. Seale, 600 F.3d 473, 484–488 (5th Cir.2010).

Rule 103(a)(1)(B) contemplates that an objection general by itself may acquire specific meaning in the context, which will be recognized on appeal. United States v. Musacchia, 900 F.2d 493, 497 (2d Cir.1990), vac'd in part on other grounds, 955 F.2d 3 (2d Cir.1991).

Since an objection only preserves the specific grounds named, if an objection naming an untenable ground is overruled, the ruling will be affirmed on appeal even though a good but unnamed ground existed for exclusion of the evidence. United States v. Gomez-Norena, 908 F.2d 497, 500 (9th Cir.1990). If an objection naming an untenable ground is sustained, the ruling will not be upheld on appeal on the basis of an unnamed valid ground if the valid ground might have been obviated by the proponent had it been raised at the trial.

(10) Objections—Specificity—Parts. An objection must be specific as to parts as well as grounds. If part of an offer is admissible and part inadmissible, an objection to the whole, even if it names a valid specific ground, may be properly overruled, and the entire offer admitted, if the objector fails to specify properly which part or parts of the offer are inadmissible. Collins v. Seaboard Coast Line R.R., 675 F.2d 1185, 1194 (11th Cir.1982); Dente v. Riddell, Inc., 664 F.2d 1, 2 n. 1 (1st Cir.1981).

(11) Offers—Overbroad. If a party offers evidence that is partly admissible and partly inadmissible, without limiting the offer to the admissible part, the party may not complain on appeal if the court excludes the entire offer. United States v. West, 670 F.2d 675, 684 (7th Cir.1982); United States v. Stout, 667 F.2d 1347, 1354 (11th Cir.1982).

(12) Offer of proof—In general. To preserve error in the exclusion of evidence, Rule 103(a)(2) requires that the substance of the evidence be shown by offer of proof. The primary purpose of the offer of proof is to enable an appellate court to determine whether the exclusion was erroneous and harmful. A secondary purpose is to permit the trial judge to reconsider the ruling in light of the actual evidence.

> **Example.** "The requirement that an offer of proof be made is essential in two ways. First, it gives the trial judge the information he or she needs to make an informed ruling. Judges are not mind readers, and even the most prepared judge cannot possibly know as much about a party's case (and strategy) as the lawyer who is trying it. When the relevance of a particular line of questioning is not self-evident, an explanation of what the anticipated answers will be and how those answers advance the party's theory of the case is critical. Second, without that explanation there is no way for a reviewing court to determine whether excluding the evidence was prejudicial." Wilson v. City of Chicago, 758 F.3d 875, 885 (7th Cir.2014).

Where there are multiple parties, an offer of proof by a co-party suffices. United States v. Davis, 261 F.3d 1, 40–41 (1st Cir.2001).

(13) Offer of proof—"Apparent from the context"; cross-examination. An offer of proof is unnecessary where "the substance was apparent from the context."

> **Example.** "In this case, the substance of Leiva's proffered testimony was obvious from its context. Ibacache had already been questioned about his alleged conversation with Leiva, and the question Appellants' counsel posed to Leiva was obviously directed at that same conversation. No doubt the district court denied Appellants' request for a sidebar conference because it already knew the substance of the proffered testimony. Therefore, as soon as the district court made a definitive ruling by sustaining the hearsay objection, the issue was preserved for appeal." Lamonica v. Safe Hurricane Shutters, Inc., 711 F.3d 1299, 1316 (11th Cir.2013).

This exception may frequently apply during cross-examination. Otherwise, the requirement of offer of proof to preserve error in exclusion of evidence applies to cross-examination. Saltzman v. Fullerton Metals Co., 661 F.2d 647, 653 n. 8 (7th Cir.1981); United States v. Vitale, 596 F.2d 688, 689–90 (5th Cir.1979).

(14) Offer of proof—Motions in limine. "A 2000 amendment to Rule 103 states '[o]nce the court rules definitively on the record—either before or at trial—a party need not renew an objection or offer of proof to preserve a claim of error on appeal.' * * * Because the order limiting the testimony of Lawrey's experts was the subject of a definitive motion in limine, Lawrey's counsel was not required to make an offer of proof at trial to preserve a claim of error on appeal." Lawrey v. Good Samaritan Hosp., 751 F.3d 947, 952 (8th Cir.2014). Compare United States v. Grullon, 996 F.3d 21, 30–31 (1st Cir.2021) ("Where a judge issues an unconditional ruling on a motion in limine, the defendant need not renew the objection or take 'additional steps to preserve the issue for appeal.' On the other hand, when a judge issues a preliminary, conditional, or 'tentative' ruling that 'clearly invites the party to offer the evidence at trial,' then the party has an obligation to raise it again to preserve the claim. As the judge announced and as Grullon's attorney understood, the ruling on the motion in limine was 'preliminary,' not final, and Grullon made no attempt to raise the Clarke evidence during trial. Accordingly, Federal Rule of Evidence 103(b) gives him no shield and he has not preserved the claim. When Grullon's counsel responded to the judge's question during trial about whether he would be going further into Clarke's bad behavior with 'No. No. No. No.,' he intentionally relinquished, and thus waived, his right to appeal the denial of his motion in limine.") (citations omitted).

(15) Offer of proof—Form. Rule 103(c) accords the trial judge discretion as to the form of an offer of proof. Fidelity Savings & Loan Ass'n v. Aetna Life & Cas. Co., 647 F.2d 933, 937 (9th Cir.1981). An avowal by counsel may be sufficient if it includes with particularity the substance of the excluded evidence. United States v. Peak, 856 F.2d 825, 832–33 (7th Cir.1988). A formal offer, in question-and-answer form, is a more reliable method. A question-and-answer offer eliminates doubt as to the harm caused by the exclusion, and may encourage the trial judge to reconsider the ruling. An opponent may request that the court direct the question-and-answer form in order to "call the bluff" of a proponent whose avowal may be optimistic.

> **Example.** "To answer the standard of review, we must first determine whether Silver Mountain made the requisite offer of proof. An offer of proof is necessary to permit the trial judge to make an informed evidentiary ruling as well as 'to create a clear record that an appellate court can review to "determine whether there was reversible error in excluding the [testimony]."' But '"merely telling the court of the content of * * * proposed testimony" is not an offer of proof.' Instead, the proponent must 'describe the evidence and what it tends to show and * * * identify the grounds for admitting the evidence.' Where both proper and improper purposes for proffered evidence exist, the offer of proof must rule out the improper purposes because the trial judge is not required to 'imagine some admissible purpose.' Finally, Rule 103 does not require any specific form for offers of proof. Instead the trial judge has discretion to shape the manner and form of the offer of proof. We agree the district court did not err in excluding the evidence. While given ample opportunity, Silver Mountain failed to make an adequate offer of proof concerning the content and admissibility of the August 2005 cell phone payment, so plain error review governs." Perkins v. Silver Mt. Sports Club & Spa, LLC, 557 F.3d 1141, 1147–49 (10th Cir.2009) (citations omitted).

(16) Plain error. "Plain error means an error that not only is clear in retrospect but also causes a miscarriage of justice." Wilson v. Williams, 182 F.3d 562, 568 (7th Cir.1999). "There are four prerequisites to a finding that the district court committed plain error in admitting specified evidence: (1) an error; (2) that is clear and obvious under current law; (3) that affects the defendant's substantial rights; and (4) that would seriously affect the fairness, integrity or public reputation of judicial proceedings if left uncorrected." Tompkins v. Cyr, 202 F.3d 770, 779 (5th Cir.2000). "Plain error review of a forfeited evidentiary issue in a civil case is available only under extraordinary circumstances when the party seeking review can demonstrate that: (1) exceptional circumstances exist; (2) substantial rights are affected; and (3) a miscarriage of justice will occur if plain error review is not applied." Jimenez v. City of Chicago, 732 F.3d 710, 720 (7th Cir.2013) (quoting Estate of Moreland v. Dieter, 395 F.3d 747, 756 (7th Cir.2005)).

CROSS-REFERENCES

Treatises

2 Graham, Handbook of Federal Evidence §§ 103:1–103:10 (9th ed. 2020)

1 McCormick, Evidence §§ 51, 52, 55, 58 (8th ed. 2020)

21 Wright & Graham, Federal Practice and Procedure §§ 5031–5043 (2005)

Rule 104. Preliminary Questions

(a) **In General.** The court must decide any preliminary question about whether a witness is qualified, a privilege exists, or evidence is admissible. In so deciding, the court is not bound by evidence rules, except those on privilege.

(b) **Relevance That Depends on a Fact.** When the relevance of evidence depends on whether a fact exists, proof must be introduced sufficient to support a finding that the fact does exist. The court may admit the proposed evidence on the condition that the proof be introduced later.

(c) **Conducting a Hearing So That the Jury Cannot Hear It.** The court must conduct any hearing on a preliminary question so that the jury cannot hear it if:

    (1) the hearing involves the admissibility of a confession;

    (2) a defendant in a criminal case is a witness and so requests; or

    (3) justice so requires.

(d) **Cross-Examining a Defendant in a Criminal Case.** By testifying on a preliminary question, a defendant in a criminal case does not become subject to cross-examination on other issues in the case.

(e) **Evidence Relevant to Weight and Credibility.** This rule does not limit a party's right to introduce before the jury evidence that is relevant to the weight or credibility of other evidence.

AUTHORS' COMMENTS

    (1) **Scope and purpose of Rule 104.** The admissibility of evidence often turns upon an issue of fact. For example, if a hearsay statement is offered as a dying declaration, the admissibility of the statement depends upon whether it was made while the declarant believed his death was imminent. Or, if a claim of attorney-client privilege is made with respect to a communication, the claim may depend upon whether the communication was made confidentially and for the purpose of obtaining legal services from an attorney. Questions of this sort are termed preliminary questions. Rule 104 sets forth the respective roles of the judge and the jury in deciding preliminary questions and also addresses some procedural matters concerning the disposition of preliminary questions.

    (2) **Questions of admissibility generally.** Rule 104(a) embodies the orthodox common-law doctrine that the judge, not the jury, decides preliminary questions of fact that determine the admissibility of evidence under the rules of evidence.

    Example. "Faced with a proffer of expert scientific testimony, then, the trial judge must determine at the outset, pursuant to Rule 104(a), whether the expert is proposing to testify to (1) scientific knowledge that (2) will assist the trier of fact to understand or determine a fact in issue."

Daubert v. Merrell Dow Pharmaceuticals, Inc., 509 U.S. 579, 591, 113 S.Ct. 2786, 2796 (1993) (footnotes omitted).

Example. When an out-of-court statement is offered as a coconspirator statement under Rule 801(d)(2)(E), the issues of the existence of a conspiracy, its pendency, whether the party against whom the statement is offered was a member, and whether the statement was made in furtherance of it, are for the court. Bourjaily v. United States, 483 U.S. 171, 175–76, 107 S.Ct. 2775, 2778 (1987).

Example. The determination whether a particular witness is qualified to testify as an expert is for the court under Rule 104(a) and the trial judge's determination will not be disturbed on appeal unless a clear abuse of discretion is shown. United States v. Diallo, 40 F.3d 32, 34 (2d Cir.1994).

Example. Whether facts or data relied upon by an expert witness are of a type reasonably relied upon by experts in the field is a matter for preliminary determination by the trial court. United States v. Lawson, 653 F.2d 299, 302 n. 7 (7th Cir.1981).

Example. "The trial court could readily have accepted that the victim, the declarant of the statements, did, in fact, believe that death was imminent. Tex.R.Crim.Evid., Rule 104(a)." Green v. State, 840 S.W.2d 394, 411 (Tex.Crim.App.1992).

Rule 104(a) does not confer any additional discretion to the trial court to exclude evidence that is established to be admissible. United States v. Evans, 728 F.3d 953, 961 (9th Cir.2013) ("Rule 104(a) provides the trial court with the authority to decide questions that might make evidence inadmissible under some other rule of evidence (or under the Constitution, a federal statute, or other Supreme Court rules), but it does not itself provide a substantive basis for excluding the evidence."); Blake v. Pellegrino, 329 F.3d 43, 48 (1st Cir.2003) ("Rule 104(a) is inapposite here, for no foundational facts were in issue. * * * In this instance, those facts (e.g., the authenticity of the death certificate and the authority of the medical examiner to sign it) were never in dispute. The district court's problem did not go to any foundational fact, but, rather, to the very core of the evidence: its persuasiveness. Where, as here, a piece of evidence rests upon a proper foundation, Rule 104(a) does not permit a trial judge to usurp the jury's function and exclude the evidence based on the judge's determination that it lacks persuasive force.").

(3) Rules of evidence, except privileges, inapplicable on preliminary questions. The second sentence of Rule 104(a) liberates the judge from the rules of evidence, except privileges, in determining preliminary questions relating to admissibility. United States v. Matlock, 415 U.S. 164, 173–74, 94 S.Ct. 988, 994 (1974).

Example—Admissible. "Campbell additionally argues that the district court erred in admitting, over his objection, the government's Exhibit 90, which was a letter from Cage to Rogers in which Cage acknowledged waiving the attorney-client privilege on behalf of the Partnership. * * * The government responds that, when Campbell objected to Rogers's testimony on the basis of attorney-client privilege, it offered Exhibit 90 to demonstrate that any such privilege had been waived. * * * [Under Rule 104(a)], the court could have considered Exhibit 90 to determine whether the attorney-client privilege had been waived even if the letter was hearsay not within any exception." United States v. Campbell, 73 F.3d 44, 48 (5th Cir.1996).

Example. "The district judge should not have allowed the jury to see Rimland's affidavit, which in addition to being hearsay was not relevant to any issue in the prosecution. Its only function was to get the receipt into evidence. The prosecutor, the defense attorney, and the judge all appear to have assumed that the jury needed the affidavit in order to decide whether the receipt is a business record. Yet judges, not juries, decide whether evidence is admissible, and for the purpose of that decision the hearsay rule does not apply. See Fed. R. Evid. 104(a). The judge should have decided for himself whether the receipt is a business record (which it is) and, having made that decision, allowed only the receipt into the trial record. Although the affidavit should not have been admitted, the error was harmless precisely because it served only to pin down the status of the receipt." United States v. Brown, 744 F.3d 474, 478 (7th Cir.2014).

(4) Relevancy conditioned on fact. Paragraph (b) of Rule 104 in effect gives to the jury issues that go only to the relevancy, as opposed to the competency, of evidence. As to these issues, the judge exercises only the usual judicial control over jury fact issues, i.e., the judge permits the issue to proceed to the jury only if there is evidence "sufficient to support a finding" of the fact. "Even if a trial court is satisfied that the proffered past act evidence satisfies Rule 104(b), however, it may still exclude it under Federal Rule of Evidence 403 * * *." Johnson v. Elk Lake School Dist., 283 F.3d 138, 155 (3d Cir.2002).

> **Example—Admissible.** The Seventh Circuit held that evidence introduced under the "cat's paw theory" (proving discrimination when the decisionmaker is unbiased) is to be governed by Rule 104(b). "That rule instructs courts to admit conditionally relevant evidence—here, animosity by a nondecisionmaker—'upon * * * the introduction of evidence sufficient to support a finding of the fulfillment of the condition.' In other words, the jury could only properly consider evidence of animosity by Mulally (or any other nondecisionmaker) if the court determined that there was sufficient evidence to support a finding of singular influence by Mulally (or another) over Buck." Staub v. Proctor Hosp., 560 F.3d 647, 657–58 (7th Cir.2009), rev'd on other grounds, 562 U.S. 411, 131 S.Ct. 1186 (2011).

The most common example of a situation of "conditional relevancy" is authentication or identification. The authentication of a document or an item of real evidence requires evidence sufficient to support a jury finding that the offered item is what its proponent claims. The function of the judge is merely to determine whether a prima facie case has been presented, not to decide the actual issue of genuineness. This traditional doctrine is codified not only in Rule 104(b), but also in Rule 901(a). Ricketts v. City of Hartford, 74 F.3d 1397, 1409–11 (2d Cir.1996); United States v. Espinoza, 641 F.2d 153, 169–70 (4th Cir.1981).

> **Example—Admissible.** "The district court's determination that it 'was not satisfied that the voice on the tape was that of Davis' * * * is inconsistent with these principles. So long as a jury is entitled to reach a contrary conclusion, it must be given the opportunity to do so. * * * [T]he district court erred in excluding the tape on authentication grounds without making a finding that no rational juror could have concluded that Davis made the statement at issue." Ricketts v. City of Hartford, supra, 74 F.3d at 1411.

(5) **"Connecting up."** Rule 104(b) also embraces the traditional practice referred to as "connecting up." Where evidence is presented that is subject to exclusion on an objection that its relevancy has not been shown or that it lacks adequate foundation, the judge may admit the evidence conditionally upon counsel's promise to "connect it up later." If sufficient "connecting" evidence fails to appear by the close of the proponent's evidence, the judge, upon the opponent's motion, will strike the conditionally admitted evidence and instruct the jury to disregard it. A waiver may occur, however, if the opponent fails to renew his original objection by a motion to strike at an appropriate time, usually the close of the proponent's case. United States v. Dougherty, 895 F.2d 399, 403 (7th Cir.1990).

(6) **Other crimes, wrongs, or acts.** Rule 104(b) also applies to evidence of other crimes, wrongs, or acts offered under Rule 404(b) as proof of motive, opportunity, intent, preparation, plan, knowledge, identity, absence of mistake, or lack of accident, or for another proper purpose. Huddleston v. United States, 485 U.S. 681, 108 S.Ct. 1496 (1988); United States v. Bergrin, 682 F.3d 261, 278–79 (3d Cir.2012) (finding that the district court had "usurped the jury's role" where it excluded witness's "other acts" testimony based on a lack of corroboration and questions about credibility).

(7) **Hearing of jury.** Rule 104(c) addresses whether hearings on preliminary questions must be out of the hearing of the jury. Sometimes a hearing on a preliminary matter does not threaten to expose the jury to prejudicial inadmissible matters; if not, then the interests of justice do not require the inconvenience of withdrawing the jury. Determining this issue is a matter of the trial judge's discretion, in general. United States v. Odom, 736 F.2d 104, 110–11 (4th Cir.1984). In two situations Rule 104(c) eliminates discretion and makes withdrawal of the jury a matter of right: (1) when the hearing is to determine the admissibility of a confession, and (2) when an accused is a witness on the issue and requests withdrawal of the jury.

(8) **Weight and credibility.** The purpose of Rule 104(e) is to clarify that the procedures provided in Rule 104 for the disposition of preliminary questions determining admissibility do not limit the introduction of other evidence before the jury for purposes of weight and credibility.

> **Example.** The judge decides, under Rule 104(a), whether a person is competent to testify as a witness. Yet a favorable determination by the judge on the preliminary issue does not preclude the opponent from introducing before the jury evidence as to the witness's lack of credibility. United States v. Strahl, 590 F.2d 10, 12 (1st Cir.1978).

Example. "Once the trial judge renders a 'clear-cut determination that the confession * * * was in fact voluntary,' the defendant generally retains the freedom to 'familiarize a jury with circumstances that attend the taking of his confession, including facts bearing upon its weight and voluntariness.' Lego [v. Twomey,] 404 U.S. [477,] 483, 486, 92 S.Ct. 619 [(1972)]. That is so because the jury is empowered to 'assess the truthfulness of confessions,' id. at 485, 92 S.Ct. 619—their credibility—as part of their decision on 'the ultimate factual issue of the defendant's guilt or innocence.' Crane [v. Kentucky], 476 U.S. [683,] 689, 106 S.Ct. 2142 [(1986)]; see 18 U.S.C. § 3501(a); Fed. R. Evid. 104(e)." United States v. Feliz, 794 F.3d 123, 130 (1st Cir.2015).

(9) Testimony by accused out of the hearing of the jury. Rule 104(d) does not address questions of subsequent use of testimony given by the accused on a preliminary matter out of the hearing of the jury. In general, the prosecution may not use such testimony against the accused as evidence in chief, but under some conditions it may be used for impeachment. See Simmons v. United States, 390 U.S. 377, 392, 88 S.Ct. 967, 976 (1968); Harris v. New York, 401 U.S. 222, 224, 91 S.Ct. 643, 645 (1971); Walder v. United States, 347 U.S. 62, 66, 74 S.Ct. 354, 356 (1954).

CROSS-REFERENCES

Treatises

2 Graham, Handbook of Federal Evidence §§ 104:1–104:4 (9th ed. 2020)

1 McCormick, Evidence §§ 53, 58, 162; 2 id. § 227 (8th ed. 2020)

21A Wright & Graham, Federal Practice and Procedure §§ 5051–5058 (2005)

Rule 105. Limiting Evidence That Is Not Admissible Against Other Parties or for Other Purposes

If the court admits evidence that is admissible against a party or for a purpose—but not against another party or for another purpose—the court, on timely request, must restrict the evidence to its proper scope and instruct the jury accordingly.

AUTHORS' COMMENTS

(1) Scope and purpose of Rule 105. Rule 105 addresses situations of limited admissibility, i.e., when evidence is offered that is admissible as to one party or for one purpose but not admissible as to another party or for another purpose. It prescribes the use of limiting instructions upon request of a party.

(2) Limiting instruction a matter of right. If evidence is admissible only for a limited purpose and an appropriate limiting instruction is requested, it is error to refuse it. Frederick v. Kirby Tankships, Inc., 205 F.3d 1277, 1285 (11th Cir.2000); United States v. Eckmann, 656 F.2d 308, 314 (8th Cir.1981).

"A limiting instruction must be given upon request. See Fed. R. Evid. 105. But a defendant may choose to go without one to avoid highlighting the evidence. * * * We caution against judicial freelancing in this area; sua sponte limiting instructions in the middle of trial, when the evidence is admitted, may preempt a defense preference to let the evidence come in without the added emphasis of a limiting instruction. The court should consult counsel about whether and when to give a limiting instruction." United States v. Gomez, 763 F.3d 845, 860 (7th Cir.2014).

(3) Responsibilities of party. If evidence is offered that is admissible against party-opponent A but not against party-opponent B—for example, A's admission—Rule 105 codifies the common-law practice of admission with a limiting instruction. If party B fails to request the instruction, however, he may not complain on appeal if the judge admits the evidence without limitation. United States v. Christian, 786 F.2d 203, 213 (6th Cir.1986). Similarly, if evidence is admissible only for a limited purpose, Rule 105 authorizes admitting it with a limiting instruction; but if the opponent fails to request the instruction, he may not complain on appeal if the evidence is admitted without limitation, United States v. Bridwell, 583 F.2d 1135, 1140 (10th Cir.1978), absent a determination of "plain error," United States v. Brawner, 32 F.3d 602, 605–06 (D.C.Cir.1994). An overbroad objection, demanding total exclusion of the evidence instead of a limiting instruction, likewise operates as a waiver. Gray v. Busch Entertainment Corp., 886 F.2d 14, 16 (2d Cir.1989); United States v. Espinoza, 641 F.2d 153, 167 (4th Cir.1981).

(4)　Time of limiting instruction. Rule 105 does not specify the time at which a limiting instruction should be given. Ordinarily, the court instructs the jury concerning limited admissibility at the time the evidence is admitted. The timing of the instruction is a matter of the trial court's discretion, however, and the instruction may be deferred until the giving of the general charge. United States v. Beasley, 495 F.3d 142, 150–51 (4th Cir.2007) ("In this case, the district court met its obligation under Rule 105 when it instructed the jury at the conclusion of the trial that it 'is your duty to give separate, personal consideration to the case of each individual defendant. When you do so, you should analyze what the evidence in the case shows with respect to that individual, leaving out of consideration entirely any evidence admitted solely against some other defendant or defendants.' "); United States v. Garcia, 848 F.2d 1324, 1334–35 (2d Cir.1988), rev'd on other grounds, 490 U.S. 858, 109 S.Ct. 2237 (1989).

While the judge may postpone a limiting instruction, counsel who delays requesting an instruction risks a finding of waiver. United States v. Thirion, 813 F.2d 146, 155–57 (8th Cir.1987).

(5)　Exclusion under Rule 403. In some circumstances a limiting instruction may be insufficient to protect a party from unfair prejudice. If the danger of unfair prejudice substantially outweighs the probative value of the evidence for its admissible purpose, taking into consideration the probable effectiveness of a limiting instruction, the evidence should be excluded under Rule 403.

Example. Confession of nontestifying codefendant implicating accused inadmissible even with limiting instruction. Bruton v. United States, 391 U.S. 123, 88 S.Ct. 1620 (1968).

Example. Defendant's offer of hearsay confession of another man to possession of the firearm in question was properly excluded rather than admitted with limiting instruction to show effect on the state of mind of the investigator who heard it. "Here, the danger of unfair prejudice carried by Deen's confession was enormous. The consequence of even one jury member taking Deen's confession for the truth asserted rather than for its effect on the listener would be Elysee's acquittal. Thus, Deen's confession belongs to the category of statements that presents the greatest danger of unfair prejudice—those statements that go directly to the issue of guilt and innocence. Furthermore, any limiting instruction the Court would give would likely be difficult to understand and apply. The reasoning the jury would have to follow to use the evidence for its instructed purpose would be attenuated, especially compared to the obviousness of the impermissible use." United States v. Elysee, 993 F.3d 1309, 1343 (11th Cir.2021) (citation omitted).

CROSS-REFERENCES

Treatises

2 Graham, Handbook of Federal Evidence § 105:1 (9th ed. 2020)

1 McCormick, Evidence § 59 (8th ed. 2020)

21A Wright & Graham, Federal Practice and Procedure §§ 5061–5067 (2005)

Rule 106.　Remainder of or Related Statements

If a party introduces all or part of a statement, an adverse party may require the introduction, at that time, of any other part—or any other statement—that in fairness ought to be considered at the same time. The adverse party may do so over a hearsay objection.

AUTHORS' COMMENTS

(1)　Scope and purpose of Rule 106. Rule 106 codifies the common-law "rule of completeness" as applied to writings and recorded statements. It is based on two considerations: the danger that material may be made misleading by being taken out of context, and the inadequacy of a delayed repair.

(2)　Oral conversations. Rule 106 applies only to writings or recorded statements. United States v. Verdugo, 617 F.3d 565, 579 (1st Cir.2010) ("The short answer to this claim is that Rule 106 does not apply to testimony about unrecorded oral statements such as the one that Verdugo gave to Naylor and Cardello when he was arrested."). If a witness testifies to only part of an unrecorded conversation, transaction, or event, the opposing party may not invoke Rule 106 to insist upon presentation of the remainder of the conversation, transaction, or event at that time. United States v. Garcia, 530 F.3d 348, 353–54 (5th

Cir.2008) (Rule 106 not applicable where witness testified about interrogation that was recorded but where proponent offered neither transcript nor tape recording of the interrogation). The opposing party may, however, develop the remainder on cross-examination or as part of his own case. Beech Aircraft Corp. v. Rainey, 488 U.S. 153, 171–72, 109 S.Ct. 439, 450–51 (1988); United States v. Williams, 930 F.3d 44, 59 (2d Cir.2019) ("[I]n this Circuit, the completeness principle applies to oral statements through Rule 611(a), * * * so as to require completion, whether contemporaneous or on cross-examination, in instances in which testimony regarding oral statements is elicited in fragments that fail to present 'the tenor of the utterance as a whole.' "); United States v. Li, 55 F.3d 325, 329 (7th Cir.1995); United States v. Castro, 813 F.2d 571, 576 (2d Cir.1987).

(3) Writing need not be formally introduced to trigger rule. Rule 106 applies when the contents of a writing are effectively presented even if the writing itself is not introduced into evidence. Rainey v. Beech Aircraft Corp., 784 F.2d 1523, 1529–30 (11th Cir.1986), reinstated en banc, 827 F.2d 1498 (11th Cir.1987), rev'd on other grounds, 488 U.S. 153, 109 S.Ct. 439 (1988).

(4) Remainder must be relevant and must qualify or explain admitted portion. Admissibility under Rule 106 is limited to other parts or writings "that in fairness to be considered at the same time." To meet this standard, the other writing or recording must be relevant to the issues and must be "necessary to (1) explain the admitted portion, (2) place the admitted portion in context, (3) avoid misleading the trier of fact, or (4) insure a fair and impartial understanding." United States v. Soures, 736 F.2d 87, 91 (3d Cir.1984). Accord, United States v. Reese, 666 F.3d 1007, 1019 (7th Cir.2012); United States v. Glover, 101 F.3d 1183, 1190 (7th Cir.1996); United States v. Branch, 91 F.3d 699, 727–29 (5th Cir.1996).

> **Example—Inadmissible.** "The defense took what inconsistencies it could find in Officer Hanson's prior testimony and police report and made the most of them, but revealing these inconsistencies did not warrant a submission of the officer's entire prior grand jury testimony, the entirety of his suppression hearing testimony, and his police report. The government made no attempt to specify which portions of these documents were relevant to the issues raised on cross-examination. * * * [T]he district court abused its discretion in admitting the transcripts and the police report in their entirety." United States v. Ramos-Caraballo, 375 F.3d 797, 803 (8th Cir.2004).

> **Example—Inadmissible.** " 'The completeness doctrine does not, however, require introduction of portions of a statement that are neither explanatory of nor relevant to the admitted passages.' * * * We don't believe Bayless' testimony was confusing or misleading, nor do we believe the testimony Billingsley wished to pursue was explanatory of or relevant to the admitted testimony. Rather, what Billingsley wished to have admitted was merely explanatory of his theory of the case. Therefore, we disagree that the doctrine of completeness should have been invoked here, and believe that the district judge was well within her discretion in finding that Billingsley's proposed cross-examination of Bayless was an attempt to bring impermissible hearsay before the jury." United States v. Lewis, 641 F.3d 773, 785 (7th Cir.2011).

> **Example—Inadmissible.** "The district court properly concluded that the Rule of Completeness is not so broad as to require the admission of all redacted portions of a statement, without regard to content. * * * The district court explained that '[j]ust because somebody is putting in part of a transcript * * * does not mean for the sake of completeness, everything comes in,' and it properly rejected Vallejos's argument that the redacted portions should be admitted to show the jury the 'flavor of the interview,' to 'humanize' Vallejos, to prove his 'character,' and to convey to the jury the voluntariness of the statement. The district court did not abuse its discretion when it determined that—while this evidence might be relevant to 'sympathy' and sentencing—the redacted statement was not misleading and therefore that the Rule of Completeness did not require admission of the full statement into evidence." United States v. Vallejos, 742 F.3d 902, 905 (9th Cir.2014).

> **Example—Inadmissible.** "Williams argues that the district court erred in preventing him from eliciting testimony at trial from Detectives Latorre and Fichter that he first denied knowledge or ownership of the firearm found in the center console of the Nissan before admitting, as both Detectives Latorre and Fichter testified, that the gun was his. * * * To require completion under the doctrine of completeness, Williams had to demonstrate that admission of his initial

statements denying ownership of the gun was 'necessary to explain' his later statements that the gun was his, 'to place [these statements] in context, to avoid misleading the jury, or to ensure fair and impartial understanding' of these later statements. Williams did not make such a showing. It is not uncommon for a suspect, upon interrogation by police, to first claim in a self-serving manner that he did not commit a crime, only thereafter to confess that he did. * * * [T]he mere fact that a suspect denies guilt before admitting it, does not—without more—mandate the admission of his self-serving denial." United States v. Williams, 930 F.3d 44, 60–61 (2d Cir.2019).

(5) Foundation. "To lay a sufficient foundation at trial for a rule of completeness claim, the offeror need only specify the portion of the [evidence] that is relevant to the issue at trial and that qualifies or explains portions already admitted." United States v. Sweiss, 814 F.2d 1208, 1212 (7th Cir.1987). Accord, United States v. King, 351 F.3d 859, 866 (8th Cir.2003).

(6) Otherwise inadmissible matters. Courts have disagreed as to whether Rule 106 permits otherwise inadmissible evidence. United States v. Garcia, 530 F.3d 348, 354 (5th Cir.2008) ("it remains unsettled whether Rule 106 trumps other evidentiary rules and makes the inadmissible admissible"); compare, e.g., United States v. Adams, 722 F.3d 788, 826 (6th Cir.2013) (no), United States v. Lentz, 524 F.3d 501, 526 (4th Cir.2008) (no) and United States v. Collicott, 92 F.3d 973, 983 (9th Cir.1996) (no) with United States v. Bucci, 525 F.3d 116, 133 (1st Cir.2008), and United States v. Sutton, 801 F.2d 1346, 1368 (D.C.Cir.1986) (yes). In light of the principle of waiver known as "opening the door" or "curative admissibility," otherwise inadmissible matters will often become admissible in Rule 106 situations. 2 Graham, Handbook of Federal Evidence §§ 106:1, 106:2 (8th ed. 2016). Admissibility under these principles and Rule 106 is limited, however, by Rule 403. Id.; Merrick v. Mercantile-Safe Deposit & Trust Co., 855 F.2d 1095, 1104 n. 10 (4th Cir.1988). See also United States v. Williams, 930 F.3d 44, 60 (2d Cir.2019) ("With respect to the government's suggestion that evidence proffered under the rule of completeness may be excluded whenever not independently admissible due to the hearsay rule, this is simply not correct. True, a party cannot circumvent the hearsay rule simply by invoking the doctrine of completeness so as to render otherwise inadmissible evidence admissible for its truth. * * * But when the omitted portion of a statement is properly introduced to correct a misleading impression or place in context that portion already admitted, it is for this very reason admissible for a valid, *nonhearsay* purpose: to explain and ensure the fair understanding of the evidence that has already been introduced.); United States v. Verdugo, 617 F.3d 565, 579 (1st Cir.2010) ("[Rule 106] does not ordinarily allow otherwise inadmissible evidence to be used to create doubt as to whether the admitted statement was ever made.").

CROSS-REFERENCES

Treatises

2 Graham, Handbook of Federal Evidence §§ 106:1–106:2 (9th ed. 2020)

1 McCormick, Evidence §§ 56, 57 (8th ed. 2020)

21A Wright & Graham, Federal Practice and Procedure §§ 5071–5079 (2005)

ARTICLE II

JUDICIAL NOTICE

Rule 201. Judicial Notice of Adjudicative Facts

(a) Scope. This rule governs judicial notice of an adjudicative fact only, not a legislative fact.

(b) Kinds of Facts That May Be Judicially Noticed. The court may judicially notice a fact that is not subject to reasonable dispute because it:

    (1) is generally known within the trial court's territorial jurisdiction; or

    (2) can be accurately and readily determined from sources whose accuracy cannot reasonably be questioned.

(c) Taking Notice. The court:

(1) may take judicial notice on its own; or

(2) must take judicial notice if a party requests it and the court is supplied with the necessary information.

(d) Timing. The court may take judicial notice at any stage of the proceeding.

(e) Opportunity to Be Heard. On timely request, a party is entitled to be heard on the propriety of taking judicial notice and the nature of the fact to be noticed. If the court takes judicial notice before notifying a party, the party, on request, is still entitled to be heard.

(f) Instructing the Jury. In a civil case, the court must instruct the jury to accept the noticed fact as conclusive. In a criminal case, the court must instruct the jury that it may or may not accept the noticed fact as conclusive.

AUTHORS' COMMENTS

(1) Scope and purpose of Rule 201. Rule 201 governs judicial notice of "adjudicative facts"—the facts of the particular case. Rule 201 does not regulate judicial notice of so-called "legislative facts"—general facts, not peculiar to the case at bar, to which a court may refer in framing or interpreting a rule of law. Judicial notice of legislative facts is not subject to the requirements of Rule 201. For example, if a fact is adjudicative, it cannot be judicially noticed unless it is "not subject to reasonable dispute" (Rule 201(b)). By contrast, if a fact is legislative, it may be judicially noticed without evidentiary basis even though it is disputable.

Example—Legislative facts. In determining constitutionality of statute restricting sale of contraceptives to persons under sixteen, court judicially noticed, as legislative fact, that persons under sixteen do engage in sexual intercourse and that the result is "often venereal disease, unwanted pregnancy, or both." Population Services, Int'l v. Wilson, 398 F.Supp. 321, 332–33 (S.D.N.Y.1975), aff'd sub nom., Carey v. Population Services, Int'l, 431 U.S. 678, 97 S.Ct. 2010 (1977).

Example—Legislative facts. That the United States Medical Center for Federal Prisoners in Springfield, Missouri is a place that falls within the special maritime and territorial jurisdiction of the United States. The legal question of special maritime and territorial jurisdiction requires the determination of legislative facts, rather than adjudicative facts. Because Federal Rule of Evidence 201 applies only to adjudicative facts, a district court need not submit judicially noticed legislative facts to the jury. United States v. Love, 20 F.4th 407, 410–12 (8th Cir.2021).

Similarly, Rule 201 does not apply to "background" or "reasoning" facts.

Example—"Background" facts. "Whether Hilton's computer contained a modem would be an adjudicative fact; what a modem generally does is less easily categorized because (among other problems) it is a fact but not really peculiar to the case. In some contexts (but not all) a modem's functioning might be a subject of reasonable dispute. Yet as a practical matter, a large number of 'background' facts are taken for granted in the courtroom unless and until someone wants to challenge them." United States v. Hilton, 257 F.3d 50, 55 & n. 2 (1st Cir.2001).

Example—"Background" facts. "[R]ule [201] is irrelevant here because the practice of customs searches for foreign but not domestic arrivals is not an adjudicative fact, and Rule 201(b)'s limits do not apply to the vast array of 'background' facts commonly considered by judges and juries in deciding cases." United States v. Amado-Nunez, 357 F.3d 119, 121 (1st Cir.2004).

Example—Not an adjudicative fact. "The fourth document is a lawyer's motion filed in the same state case. That document is not subject to judicial notice because it is not evidence of an adjudicative fact. A lawyer's appellate brief in the Seventh Circuit is not evidence; neither is a lawyer's motion in state court. If the document were being offered just to show that it had been filed, that fact might be subject to judicial notice, but the 'Request' does not suggest that appellant wants this court to take notice that a particular document was filed * * *." In the Matter of Lisse, 905 F.3d 495, 497 (7th Cir.2018).

(2) Kinds of facts that may be judicially noticed—Two-stage test. Rule 201(b) sets forth a two-stage test for judicial notice of adjudicative facts. The first stage, which must always be satisfied, is indisputability ("not subject to reasonable dispute"). It requires that the judge find that reasonable persons would not doubt the fact. The second stage requires the judge to find that the fact is either generally known ("generally known within the trial courts' territorial jurisdiction") or verifiable ("can be accurately and readily determined from sources whose accuracy cannot reasonably be questioned").

(3) Indisputability. A fact cannot be judicially noticed unless it is "not subject to reasonable dispute."

Example. In light of scientific disagreement, court could not take judicial notice that asbestos causes mesothelioma. Hardy v. Johns-Manville Sales Corp., 681 F.2d 334, 347–48 (5th Cir.1982).

Example. "[T]aking judicial notice of findings of fact from another case exceeds the limits of Rule 201." Wyatt v. Terhune, 280 F.3d 1238, 1242 (9th Cir.2002).

Example. "The nature of the Ku Klux Klan, and its historic commitment to violence against blacks in particular, is generally known throughout this country and is not subject to reasonable dispute." Marshall v. Bramer, 828 F.2d 355, 358 (6th Cir.1987).

Example. "That banks send customers monthly statements which inform customers to whom their money was paid and in what amounts is not reasonably subject to dispute * * *." Kaggen v. I.R.S., 71 F.3d 1018, 1020 (2d Cir.1995).

Example. "[W]e cannot simply take judicial notice of the transformation of American society since 1943 to conclude, as the City urges, that the safety of Englewood's residents depends upon prohibiting door-to-door canvassing after 6 P.M. To do so would 'turn [judicial notice] into a pretext for dispensing with a trial.'" Ohio Citizen Action v. City of Englewood, 671 F.3d 564, 579–80 (6th Cir.2012) (quoting Garner v. Louisiana, 368 U.S. 157, 173, 82 S.Ct. 248 (1961)).

Example. Court declined to take judicial notice of a New York certificate of disposition where New York courts had found that the certificates' references to New York Penal Law subsections were unreliable. United States v. Castillo-Marin, 684 F.3d 914, 926–27 (9th Cir.2012).

Example. "[A] power of attorney filed in state court. The fact that a document is in a state court's record does not make it an appropriate subject of notice, however, because its provenance may be disputed. Is it authentic? See Rules 901 to 903. Are the four signatures real or forged? (The signature lines say that all four signers are officers of Bank of America; none is a party to this proceeding.) Is it the original, or perhaps a duplicate admissible under Rule 1003? Is the document even relevant? See Rule 402. If the power of attorney had been submitted in this proceeding it would not be subject to judicial notice. It does not get a privileged status because it was filed in a state suit." In the Matter of Lisse, 905 F.3d 495, 496–97 (7th Cir.2018).

(4) Facts generally known. A matter does not qualify as "generally known" merely because the individual judge knows it. Switzer v. Coan, 261 F.3d 985, 989 (10th Cir.2001) ("Plaintiff asserts that judges in this circuit have issued decisions which they have not read. While the district judge may personally know this allegation is false, such knowledge is not a proper basis for judicial notice."); Housing Works, Inc. v. City of New York, 203 F.3d 176, 179 (2d Cir.2000) (Jacobs, C.J., concurring); United States v. Sorrells, 714 F.2d 1522, 1527 n. 6 (11th Cir.1983). Knowledge of a matter within a trade or special class of persons is not sufficient notoriety for this category of judicial notice. United States v. Bramble, 641 F.2d 681, 683 (9th Cir.1981) (that 21 marijuana plants constituted a commercial crop so as to support inference of intent to sell); Fielder v. Bosshard, 590 F.2d 105, 110–11 (5th Cir.1979) (that impairment of function of portion of liver would reduce life expectancy). Facts within the knowledge of a trade or specialty may be judicially noticed if found within a source that meets the tests of Rule 201(b)(2).

If a fact is generally known, a request that it be judicially noticed need not be accompanied by any supporting materials or information. Apostolic Church v. American Honda Motor Co., 833 S.W.2d 553, 556 (Tex.App.1992) ("Whether Highway 96 North links Center and the neighboring Shelby County community of Tenaha is a fact of such notoriety that there is no necessity of accompanying the request for judicial notice with additional background information, in order for it to be mandatorily judicially noticed.").

Example—Facts generally known. "In this case, the district court took judicial notice of the fact that color is indicative of flavor in ice cream. This fact is adjudicative in nature and is generally known among consumers. * * * In order to judicially notice that color is indicative of flavor, it is not necessary that consumers generally know that, for example, pink coloring denotes strawberry ice cream. Rather, it is necessary that consumers generally know that pink coloring denotes some flavor of ice cream, for example, strawberry, bubble gum, or cherry." Dippin' Dots, Inc. v. Frosty Bites Distribution, LLC, 369 F.3d 1197, 1205 & n.8 (11th Cir.2004).

(5) Verifiable facts. Rule 201(b)(2) requires two conditions: (i) that the adjudicative fact in question is "capable of accurately and ready determination," and (ii) that the source used to determine it is accurate beyond reasonable question. These two conditions are in addition to Rule 201(b)'s general requirement of indisputability. Examples of facts judicially noticed:

• "[I]t is a well-settled principle that the decision of another court or agency, including the decision of an administrative law judge, is a proper subject of judicial notice." Opoka v. I.N.S., 94 F.3d 392, 394 (7th Cir.1996). Accord, Najjar v. Ashcroft, 257 F.3d 1262, 1283 (11th Cir.2001) ("[W]e may, and do, take judicial notice of the fact that Mazen's custody proceeding occurred and the subject matter thereof."). Judicial notice is limited, however, to the existence and terms of the judicial record; it does not extend to the truth of statements quoted in the record, or to factual findings. Wyatt v. Terhune, 315 F.3d 1108, 1114 n.5 (9th Cir.2003). Accord, Khoja v. Orexigen Therapeutics, Inc., 899 F.3d 988, 999 (9th Cir.2018) (investor call transcript submitted to the SEC; "Just because the document itself is susceptible to judicial notice does not mean that every assertion of fact within that document is judicially noticeable for its truth.").

• Public disclosure documents filed with the SEC. In re NAHC, Inc., Securities Litigation, 306 F.3d 1314, 1331 (3d Cir.2002); Oran v. Stafford, 226 F.3d 275, 289 (3d Cir.2000). But see Kushner v. Beverly Enterprises, Inc., 317 F.3d 820, 832 (8th Cir.2003) ("We have noted previously that courts have considered SEC filings on a motion to dismiss where the filings were required by law and were not offered to prove the truth of the documents' contents. * * * The documents the investors seek to have judicially noticed, for the most part, are not SEC filings, they are offered for the truth of the matters asserted in them, and Beverly disputes the facts and inferences that the investors attempt to establish through these documents. Accordingly, the district court did not abuse its discretion by declining to take judicial notice of these extra-record matters.").

• Judicial acts of state court, as reflected in its records. In the Matter of Lisse, 905 F.3d 495, 496 (7th Cir.2018) (orders entered by a state court in Wisconsin); Colonial Leasing v. Logistics Control Group Intern., 762 F.2d 454, 459 (5th Cir.1985).

• Stock price data compiled by the Dow Jones news service. In re NAHC, Inc., Securities Litigation, 306 F.3d 1314, 1331 (3d Cir.2002).

• Prevailing interest rates. Havens Steel Co. v. Randolph Engineering Co., 813 F.2d 186, 189 (8th Cir.1987).

• Fishing license records of Merchant Document Division of Coast Guard. Massachusetts v. Westcott, 431 U.S. 322, 323 n. 2, 97 S.Ct. 1755, 1756 n. 2 (1977).

• History and beliefs of Mennonites. Bethel Conservative Mennonite Church v. C.I.R., 746 F.2d 388, 392 (7th Cir.1984).

• Published budget of municipality. Association Against Discrimination in Employment, Inc. v. City of Bridgeport, 647 F.2d 256, 277 (2d Cir.1981).

• "[T]hat Graves' disease is a condition that is capable of substantially limiting major life activities if left untreated by medication." Harris v. H & W Contracting Co., 102 F.3d 516, 522 (11th Cir.1996).

• That certain matters have been posted on a website. Denius v. Dunlap, 330 F.3d 919, 926 (7th Cir.2003).

• "[T]he fact that various newspapers, magazines, and books have published information * * *. Courts may take judicial notice of publications introduced to 'indicate what was in the public realm at the time, not whether the contents of those articles were in fact true.'" Von Saher v. Norton Simon Museum of Art at Pasadena, 578 F.3d 1016, 1022 (9th Cir.2009) (citations omitted).

- The existence of trademarks, "as we determine that the registration documents by the PTO are capable of accurate and ready determination by resort to sources whose accuracy cannot reasonably be questioned." In re Chippendales USA, Inc., 622 F.3d 1346, 1356 (Fed.Cir.2010).

- The median and mean sentences imposed for a particular crime on a local and national level. United States v. White, 620 F.3d 401, 416 (4th Cir.2010).

- FDA grant of pre-market approval. Funk v. Stryker Corp., 631 F.3d 777, 783 (5th Cir.2011).

- The Consumer Price Index. Pickett v. Sheridan Health Care Center, 664 F.3d 632, 648 (7th Cir.2011).

- A Google map. "It is a 'source[ ]' whose accuracy cannot reasonably be questioned,' at least for the purpose of identifying the area where Burroughs was arrested and the general layout of the block." United States v. Burroughs, 810 F.3d 833, 835 n.1 (D.C.Cir.2016).

- "This court and numerous others routinely take judicial notice of information contained on state and federal government websites." United States v. Garcia, 855 F.3d 615, 621 (4th Cir.2017).

It has been held improper for a court to take judicial notice of the contents of an archived webpage found on a private archive service (Wayback Machine), absent testimony from "someone with personal knowledge of the reliability of the archive service." Weinhoffer v. Davie Shoring, Incorporated, 23 F.4th 579, 583–84 (5th Cir.2022).

(6) Sua sponte. If an adjudicative fact is appropriate for judicial notice under the standards of Rule 201, a court, trial or appellate, may take judicial notice of the fact sua sponte. Rule 201(c)(1); Zimomra v. Alamo Rent-a-Car, Inc., 111 F.3d 1495, 1503–04 (10th Cir.1997). In exercising this power, the court must comply with Rule 201(e), which entitles all parties, upon request, to an opportunity to be heard concerning judicial notice of any adjudicative fact. Cooperativa de Ahorro y Credito Aguada v. Kidder, Peabody & Co., 993 F.2d 269, 273 (1st Cir.1993); United States v. Garcia, 672 F.2d 1349, 1356 n. 9 (11th Cir.1982).

(7) Mandatory notice. Rule 201(c)(2) requires the court to take judicial notice if a party requests it and supplies the necessary information.

Example. Trial court abused its discretion in withdrawing judicial notice of information on the official website of the National Personnel Records Center, Military Personnel Records. Denius v. Dunlap, 330 F.3d 919, 927 (7th Cir.2003).

Example. It was error, but harmless, for a trial court to refuse to take judicial notice, based upon proffered calculations, of distances a car would travel in specific time periods at specific speeds. Drake v. Holstead, 757 S.W.2d 909, 910–11 (Tex.App.1988).

(8) Request must be timely. Although not specified in the rule, in order for a party to be entitled to mandatory judicial notice as provided in Rule 201(c)(1), the party must request it and supply the necessary information in a timely fashion. 21B Wright & Graham, Federal Practice and Procedure § 5107 (2005); Duderstadt Surveyors Supply, Inc. v. Alamo Express, Inc., 686 S.W.2d 351, 354 (Tex.App.1985).

(9) Rules of evidence inapplicable to supporting information. The rules of evidence do not apply to the process of judicial notice. Therefore, information supplied to the court in support of (or against) a request for judicial notice need not be in a form that would be admissible as evidence. Garner v. First Nat'l City Bank, 465 F.Supp. 372, 382 n. 12 (S.D.N.Y.1979); 21B Wright & Graham, Federal Practice and Procedure § 5108 (2005).

(10) Opportunity to be heard. Rule 201(e) does not require the court to notify the parties and give them an opportunity to be heard before judicially noticing a fact. Instead, Rule 201(e) makes prior notification optional, and provides for an after-the-fact right to be heard in cases where judicial notice is taken without prior notification. Center for Biological Diversity, Inc. v. BP America Production Co., 704 F.3d 413, 423 (5th Cir.2013). If no advance notification is afforded, the rule provides that a party may request to be heard after the judicial notice has been taken. Once requested, the opportunity to be heard is a matter of right. If no party "timely" requests to be heard, the matter is foreclosed. Edwards v. Hurtel, 724 F.2d 689 (8th Cir.1984).

The "opportunity to be heard" does not mean, in all circumstances, a formal hearing. Center for Biological Diversity, Inc. v. BP America Production Co., supra, at 423; American Stores Co. v. C.I.R., 170 F.3d 1267, 1271 (10th Cir.1999). Although Rule 201(e) is not limited to a party opposing judicial notice, it may be satisfied as to a proponent of judicial notice by consideration of briefs. Id.

> **Example—Opportunity to be heard not required.** "We also reject the Robinsons' argument that the district court could not take 'judicial notice' of dictionary definitions without first affording them a hearing. * * * But Rule 201 'governs judicial notice of an adjudicative fact only, not a legislative fact.' Fed. R. Evid. 201(a). '[A]djudicative facts are those developed in a particular case,' while '[l]egislative facts are established truths, facts or pronouncements that do not change from case to case but apply universally.' W. Ala. Women's Ctr. v. Williamson, 900 F.3d 1310, 1316 (11th Cir.2018) (internal quotation marks omitted); see also Fed. R. Evid. 201(a) advisory committee's note to 1972 proposed rule ('Adjudicative facts are simply the facts of the particular case.'). Dictionary definitions establish legislative facts when used to answer a question of law, such as how to interpret contractual terms. See Fed. R. Evid. 201(a) advisory committee's note to 1972 proposed rule ('Legislative facts * * * are those which have relevance to legal reasoning and the lawmaking process * * * in the formulation of a legal principle or ruling by a judge or court * * *.')." Robinson v. Liberty Mut. Ins. Co., 958 F.3d 1137, 1142 (11th Cir.2020).

It is implicit in Rule 201(e) that if a court takes judicial notice of an adjudicative fact sua sponte, it must at some point notify the parties that it has done so, so that they in fact receive the opportunity to be heard granted by the rule. Pickett v. Sheridan Health Care Center, 664 F.3d 632, 648 (7th Cir.2011); Cooperativa de Ahorro y Credito Aguada v. Kidder, Peabody & Co., 993 F.2d 269, 273 (1st Cir.1993); United States v. Garcia, 672 F.2d 1349, 1356 n. 9 (11th Cir.1982). This is probably required by the Constitution as well as by the rule. Garner v. Louisiana, 368 U.S. 157, 173–74, 82 S.Ct. 248, 256–57 (1961); Ohio Bell Tel. Co. v. Public Utilities Comm., 301 U.S. 292, 302–03, 57 S.Ct. 724, 729–30 (1937).

(11) Time of taking notice; judicial notice on appeal. The reference in Rule 201(d) to "any stage of the proceedings" clearly embraces appeal. Opoka v. I.N.S., 94 F.3d 392, 394–95 (7th Cir.1996); United States v. Esquivel, 88 F.3d 722, 726–27 (9th Cir.1996).

> **Example.** "The right place to propose judicial notice, once a case is in a court of appeals, is in a brief. When evidence is 'not subject to reasonable dispute,' there's no need to multiply the paperwork by filing motions or 'Requests.' Just refer to the evidence in the brief and explain there why it is relevant and subject to judicial notice. If the assertion is questionable, the opposing litigant can protest. 'On timely request, a party is entitled to be heard on the propriety of taking judicial notice and the nature of the fact to be noticed.' Rule 201(e). That 'timely request' and the 'opportunity to be heard' both belong in the next brief. So if an appellant proposes judicial notice, the appellee's objection can be presented in its own brief. If it is an appellee who proposes judicial notice, the appellant's reply brief provides the opportunity to be heard in opposition. There's no need to engage in motions practice, require the attention of additional appellate judges, and defer briefing." In the Matter of Lisse, 905 F.3d 495, 497 (7th Cir.2018).

An appellate court is not required to take judicial notice, however, if it was not requested below or if necessary supporting materials were not first presented to the trial court. Johnson v. Chater, 108 F.3d 942, 946 (8th Cir.1997); Conway v. Chemical Leaman Tank Lines, Inc., 610 F.2d 360, 365 n. 5 (5th Cir.1980).

(12) Instructing jury—Civil cases. Rule 201(f) prescribes a peremptory instruction to the jury on any judicially noticed adjudicative fact in a civil case. As a corollary, once the judge has judicially noticed a fact in a civil case, no evidence is admissible to rebut it. Hardy v. Johns-Manville Sales Corp., 681 F.2d 334, 348 (5th Cir.1982).

Rule 201(f) is mandatory. That is, it requires a peremptory instruction in every instance in which a court takes judicial notice of an adjudicative fact in a civil case. Nevertheless, a party may not complain on appeal of the failure of the trial court to give the instruction unless the party made a timely request for it.

(13) Instructing jury—Criminal cases. In criminal cases, Rule 201(f) prescribes a permissive, rather than peremptory, jury instruction concerning any judicially noticed adjudicative fact. United States v. Bello, 194 F.3d 18, 22–26 (1st Cir.1999) (permissive instruction complied with Rule 201(f)). The decision to forbear the peremptory instruction in criminal cases arose from concerns about its constitutionality. Rule

201 only applies to adjudicative facts, and the prohibition against peremptory instructions in criminal cases is accordingly applicable only to adjudicative facts. When the court instructs the jury on the law to be applied to the case, it may be necessary or appropriate for the court to make general factual statements that are legislative, not adjudicative facts. Since Rule 201 is inapplicable to legislative facts, it is not improper for the court to refer to them in peremptory rather than permissive terms.

Example. Trial court properly instructed jury that Raybrook Federal Correctional Institution "is a place that falls within the territorial jurisdiction of the United States"; "any factual issues whose resolution is necessary to a determination of such a geographical/jurisdictional issue would invoke judicial notice of legislative facts to which Rule 201 is inapplicable." United States v. Hernandez-Fundora, 58 F.3d 802, 809–12 (2d Cir.1995). Accord, United States v. Love, 20 F.4th 407, 411–12 (8th Cir.2021). But see United States v. Bello, 194 F.3d 18, 22–23 & n. 4 (1st Cir.1999) (whether facility where assault occurred was "within the special maritime and territorial jurisdiction of the United States" was an adjudicative fact governed by Rule 201; permissive instruction complied with Rule 201).

Example. Trial court took judicial notice that cocaine hydrochloride is a derivative of coca leaves and thereby is a schedule II controlled substance under 21 U.S.C.A. § 812; court proceeded to instruct jury to that effect, without instructing them that they were not required to accept the fact. Court of Appeals affirmed; Rule 201(g) was inapplicable because fact was legislative, not adjudicative. United States v. Gould, 536 F.2d 216 (8th Cir.1976).

CROSS-REFERENCES

Treatises

2 Graham, Handbook of Federal Evidence §§ 201:1–201:9 (9th ed. 2020)

2 McCormick, Evidence §§ 328–335 (8th ed. 2020)

21B Wright & Graham, Federal Practice and Procedure §§ 5101–5111.1 (2005)

ARTICLE III

PRESUMPTIONS IN CIVIL CASES

Rule 301. Presumptions in Civil Cases Generally

In a civil case, unless a federal statute or these rules provide otherwise, the party against whom a presumption is directed has the burden of producing evidence to rebut the presumption. But this rule does not shift the burden of persuasion, which remains on the party who had it originally.

AUTHORS' COMMENTS

    (1) Scope and purpose of Rule 301. Rule 301 stipulates that in civil cases, presumptions have the limited effect of shifting to the party opposing the presumption the burden of producing evidence to rebut the presumption; they do not shift the burden of persuasion. Rule 301 thus adopts the Thayer, or "bursting bubble," approach to presumptions. See Nunley v. City of Los Angeles, 52 F.3d 792, 796 (9th Cir.1995). A presumption may be given a different effect where an Act of Congress so provides. In addition, some courts have held that long-standing principles of substantive law regarding presumptions take precedence over the command of Rule 301. See, e.g., Kelly v. Armstrong, 141 F.3d 799, 802–03 (8th Cir.1998).

    (2) Presumption defined; conclusive vs. rebuttable presumptions. Presumptions are not evidence; they are merely procedural devices. If a presumption exists, proof of a fact or set of facts (the "basic fact") establishes the existence of another fact (the "presumed fact"). Presumptions may be conclusive or rebuttable. Conclusive presumptions are irrebuttable; if the basic fact is established, the existence of the presumed fact may not be controverted. Conclusive presumptions are really substantive rules of law. E.g., 12 U.S.C.A. § 1849(a) (certain merger transactions conclusively presumed not to violate antitrust laws). Rebuttable presumptions allow the party against whom the presumption is directed to overcome the presumption. Rule 301 addresses how much evidence is necessary to overcome a presumption.

(3) Presumption shifts burden of production. Rule 301 gives presumptions only minimal effect. It provides that a presumption shifts to its opponent merely the burden of producing evidence to rebut the presumed fact—what is sometimes referred to as the burden of production or the burden of going forward with the evidence. Under Rule 301, a presumption does not shift the burden of persuasion. Texas Dept. of Community Affairs v. Burdine, 450 U.S. 248, 256, 101 S.Ct. 1089, 1095 (1981). In other words, the opponent of a presumption may negate the procedural effect of a presumption by introducing enough evidence so that a reasonable juror could find the non-existence of the presumed fact. ITC Ltd. v. Punchgini, Inc., 482 F.3d 135, 149 (2d Cir.2007). If the opponent meets this burden, the presumption disappears from the case. Nichino America, Inc. v. Valent U.S.A. LLC, 44 F.4th 180, 186 (3d Cir.2022) ("disappears like a bursting bubble"). If the opponent fails to meet this burden, the fact finder must find that the presumed fact exists. St. Mary's Honor Center v. Hicks, 509 U.S. 502, 503–11, 113 S.Ct. 2742, 2746–50 (1993).

(4) Statutory presumptions. Rule 301 applies only in civil cases, and, even then, may be supplanted if "a federal statute or these rules provide otherwise." Thus, a statutory presumption may provide explicitly that it is to be given an effect other than that provided for in Rule 301. See, e.g., 29 U.S.C.A. § 1401(a)(3)(A), (B) (shifting burden of persuasion). Even when the statute creating the presumption is not explicit as to its procedural effect, the court may construe it as shifting the burden of persuasion. E.g., Microsoft Corp. v. i4i Ltd. Partnership, 564 U.S. 91, 131 S.Ct. 2238 (2011) (presumption of patent validity in § 282 of Patent Act of 1952 places burden of persuasion on party seeking to establish invalidity of patent and requires proof by clear and convincing evidence).

(5) Basic facts must be established. A presumption comes into play only if the basic facts—the facts giving rise to the presumption—are established. E.g., Godfrey v. United States, 997 F.2d 335, 338–39 (7th Cir.1993) (government not entitled to presumption of delivery of check absent evidence about check mailing process).

(6) Inference permitted if presumption eliminated. If the opponent of a presumption meets the burden of production, the presumption is eliminated from the case. Cappuccio v. Prime Capital Funding L.L.C., 649 F.3d 180, 191–92 (3d Cir.2011). Nevertheless, as a matter of logic, the basic facts may tend to prove the presumed fact, and the court may instruct the jury accordingly.

Example. In Lupyan v. Corinthian Colleges Inc., 761 F.3d 314, 319 (3d Cir.2014), the court explained that once the presumption that a mailed letter has been received by the addressee is rebutted, the jury may still logically infer receipt from the likelihood that a mailed letter will be delivered. The court observed that sending a letter by certified mail creates a stronger "presumption" (meaning, inference) of receipt, while sending a letter by regular mail creates a weaker "presumption."

CROSS-REFERENCES

Treatises

2 Graham, Handbook of Federal Evidence §§ 301:1–301:14 (9th ed. 2020)

2 McCormick, Evidence §§ 342–345 (8th ed. 2020)

21B Wright and Graham, Federal Practice and Procedure §§ 5121–5129 (2005)

Rule 302. Applying State Law to Presumptions in Civil Cases

In a civil case, state law governs the effect of a presumption regarding a claim or defense for which state law supplies the rule of decision.

AUTHORS' COMMENTS

(1) Scope and purpose of Rule 302. Rule 302, like Rules 501 and 601, conforms the evidence rules to the dictates of Erie Railroad Co. v. Tompkins, 304 U.S. 64, 58 S.Ct. 817 (1938). Several Supreme Court decisions make clear that *Erie* applies to questions of burden of proof and presumptions. E.g., Dick v. New York Life Ins. Co., 359 U.S. 437, 79 S.Ct. 921 (1959). Rule 302 thus provides that when state law supplies the rule of decision as to a civil claim or defense, state presumption law applies as well. See, e.g., Rudisill v. Ford Motor Co., 709 F.3d 595, 609 (6th Cir.2013); Kokins v. Teleflex, Inc., 621 F.3d 1290, 1299–1306 (10th Cir.2010).

(2) Limit on application of state law. Note that Rule 302 limits the application of state presumption law to those instances in which the state presumption operates on an element of a claim or defense. State law does not apply when the presumption is merely a tactical one, that is, one that affects a lesser aspect of the case. Advisory Committee's Note.

CROSS-REFERENCES

Treatises

2 Graham, Handbook of Federal Evidence § 302:1 (9th ed. 2020)

2 McCormick, Evidence § 349 (8th ed. 2020)

21B Wright and Graham, Federal Practice and Procedure §§ 5131–5137 (2005)

Proposed Rule 303.   Presumptions in Criminal Cases

[NOT ENACTED]

(a) Scope. Except as otherwise provided by Act of Congress, in criminal cases, presumptions against an accused, recognized at common law or created by statute, including statutory provisions that certain facts are prima facie evidence of other facts or of guilt, are governed by this rule.

(b) Submission to Jury. The judge is not authorized to direct the jury to find a presumed fact against the accused. When the presumed fact establishes guilt or is an element of the offense or negatives a defense, the judge may submit the question of guilt or of the existence of the presumed fact to the jury, if, but only if, a reasonable juror on the evidence as a whole, including the evidence of the basic facts, could find guilt or the presumed fact beyond a reasonable doubt. When the presumed fact has a lesser effect, its existence may be submitted to the jury if the basic facts are supported by substantial evidence, or are otherwise established, unless the evidence as a whole negatives the existence of the presumed fact.

(c) Instructing the Jury. Whenever the existence of presumed fact against the accused is submitted to the jury, the judge shall give an instruction that the law declares that the jury may regard the basic facts as sufficient evidence of the presumed fact but does not require it to do so. In addition, if the presumed fact establishes guilt or is an element of the offense or negatives a defense, the judge shall instruct the jury that its existence must, on all the evidence, be proved beyond reasonable doubt.

AUTHORS' COMMENTS

(1) Scope and purpose of Proposed Rule 303. Proposed Rule 303 was designed to govern the use of presumptions in criminal cases. The proposed rule was deleted by the House of Representatives, however, because the House intended to deal with the subject in other legislation. Congress failed to act, however, and the Supreme Court has since issued a number of opinions dealing with presumptions. A list of federal statutory criminal presumptions can be found in 1 McLaughlin, Weinstein's Federal Evidence (2d ed. 1998) § 303 App.100[2].

(2) Permissive and mandatory inferences distinguished. In County Court of Ulster County v. Allen, 442 U.S. 140, 99 S.Ct. 2213 (1979), and subsequent decisions the Supreme Court has distinguished between permissive presumptions (or inferences) and mandatory presumptions (or inferences).

(a) *Permissive inferences.* A permissive inference arises when the jury is instructed that it may, but need not, infer a presumed fact (often, an element of the crime) from proof of other facts. Id., 442 U.S. at 157, 99 S.Ct. at 2224. A permissive inference is constitutional if, considering the facts of the case, the presumed fact is more likely than not to flow from the basic facts. 442 U.S. at 165, 99 S.Ct. at 2228.

(b) *Mandatory inferences.* A mandatory inference arises when the jury is instructed that it must find the presumed fact upon proof of the basic fact unless the defendant rebuts the presumed fact. A mandatory inference thus shifts to the defendant either the burden of production or the burden of persuasion. In *Ulster County*, the Court stated that such a presumption is constitutional if, looking at the presumption on its face, the presumed fact flows from the basic facts beyond a reasonable doubt. 442 U.S. at 157–58, 99 S.Ct. at

2224–26. Since *Ulster County*, however, the Supreme Court has yet to uphold the constitutionality of a mandatory presumption. See Carella v. California, 491 U.S. 263, 109 S.Ct. 2419 (1989) (instruction that person "shall be presumed to have embezzled" a vehicle if not returned within 5 days of expiration of rental agreement); Francis v. Franklin, 471 U.S. 307, 105 S.Ct. 1965 (1985) (instruction that person intends the natural and probable consequences of his acts); Sandstrom v. Montana, 442 U.S. 510, 99 S.Ct. 2450 (1979) (instruction that person presumes the ordinary consequences of his voluntary acts).

(3) **Instructing the jury.** A presumption's status as permissive or mandatory is determined by looking at the instruction given the jury. "The question * * * is * * * what a reasonable juror could have understood the charge as meaning." Francis v. Franklin, 471 U.S. 307, 315–16, 105 S.Ct. 1965, 1972 (1985). See also Estelle v. McGuire, 502 U.S. 62, 112 S.Ct. 475 (1991). The form of instruction mandated by Proposed Rule 303(c) establishes a permissive inference.

CROSS-REFERENCES

Treatises

2 Graham, Handbook of Federal Evidence §§ 303:1–303:5 (9th ed. 2020)

2 McCormick, Evidence §§ 346–348 (8th ed. 2020)

21B Wright and Graham, Federal Practice and Procedure §§ 5141–5148 (2005)

ARTICLE IV

RELEVANCE AND ITS LIMITS

Rule 401. Test for Relevant Evidence

Evidence is relevant if:

(a) it has any tendency to make a fact more or less probable than it would be without the evidence; and

(b) the fact is of consequence in determining the action.

AUTHORS' COMMENTS

(1) **Scope and purpose of Rule 401.** Rule 401 defines "relevant evidence." To be relevant, evidence must possess logical probative value toward some fact that is legally of consequence to the case. Relevance (as well as prejudice under Rule 403) must be "determined in the context of the facts and arguments in a particular case." Sprint/United Management Co. v. Mendelsohn, 552 U.S. 379, 128 S.Ct. 1140, 1147 (2008).

(2) **Relationship to Rules 402 and 403.** Rule 402 makes all relevant evidence admissible unless it is excluded by another rule or law. Rule 403 permits exclusion of relevant evidence on grounds of prejudice, confusion, or waste of time. In practice, determinations of basic relevancy under Rule 401 often merge with the balancing test of Rule 403; evidence that is of doubtful relevancy under Rule 401 is apt to be excluded under Rule 403.

(3) **Two requirements: probative value, fact of consequence.** "Implicit in that definition are two distinct requirements: (1) the evidence must be probative of the proposition it is offered to prove, and (2) the proposition to be proved must be one that is of consequence to the determination of the action." United States v. Hall, 653 F.2d 1002, 1005 (5th Cir.1981).

(4) **Fact of consequence is determined by substantive law.** "Whether a proposition is of consequence to the determination of the action is a question that is governed by the substantive law." United States v. Hall, 653 F.2d 1002, 1005 (5th Cir.1981).

> **Example—Inadmissible.** "Long's out-of-court statements are probative of why Deputy Needham went to the mobile home. However, his reasons for going there are not of consequence to the determination of the action, i.e., they do not bear on any issue involving the elements of the charged offense." United States v. Dean, 980 F.2d 1286, 1288 (9th Cir.1992).

Example—Inadmissible. In a prosecution for throwing blood and ashes on the walls of the Pentagon, evidence that United States nuclear weapons policies violate international law was properly excluded. United States v. Cassidy, 616 F.2d 101 (4th Cir.1979).

Example—Inadmissible. "Fifer argues that the district court wrongly excluded evidence regarding his knowledge (or lack of knowledge) of C.T.'s age. As this court held * * *, a defendant's knowledge of the victim's age is not an element of the offense of producing child pornography * * *. Evidence that Fifer misjudged C.T.'s age therefore has no bearing on his guilt or innocence under the statute, and the district court properly excluded that evidence as irrelevant. See Fed. R. Evid. 401." United States v. Fifer, 863 F.3d 759, 767 (7th Cir.2017).

Example—Inadmissible. "Did the District Court err in excluding expert testimony suggesting that Heinrich photographed the girls to create art, not sexually explicit pictures? No, it did not. That testimony is irrelevant and risks confusing and misleading the jury. * * * The report here does not disprove Heinrich's intent. It casts no doubt on his intent to strip the girls, pose them, and take their pictures. Rather, it addresses Heinrich's purpose for taking the photos. But that purpose is irrelevant to the statute." United States v. Heinrich, 57 F.4th 154, 166 (3rd Cir.2023).

Example—Inadmissible. In a prosecution for making false statements on a tax return, evidence offered by taxpayer that he actually overpaid his taxes by failure to take permissible deductions was properly excluded. United States v. Johnson, 558 F.2d 744 (5th Cir.1977).

Example—Inadmissible. Since the issue in an insurance bad faith case is whether the company had a reasonable basis for denying the claim, the company's subsequent litigation tactics and strategy are seldom relevant. Timberlake Construction Co. v. United States Fidelity & Guaranty Co., 71 F.3d 335, 340–41 (10th Cir.1995).

Example—Inadmissible. "The fact of consequence in this case was whether Hawkins possessed the gun, and the ammunition found in the upper unit has nothing to do with possession. While the ammunition may be relevant to proving ownership of the gun, ownership is not relevant to the offense in question." United States v. Hawkins, 215 F.3d 858 (8th Cir.2000).

Example—Inadmissible. "Here, the redacted statement introduced by the government sought to establish that Dotson sexually exploited a minor and unlawfully possessed child pornography. * * * The district court concluded that the redacted portions of Dotson's statement were not relevant to any issues in the case, that is, they did not have 'any tendency to make a fact [of consequence in determining the action] more or less probable than it would be without the evidence.' Fed. R. Evid. 401(a)–(b). We agree. The omitted portions—which illustrated that Dotson had a rough upbringing and had been sexually abused as a child; that he considered his girlfriend to be a 'blessing' and had intended to marry her prior to encountering financial difficulties; and his concern that the victim knew he was exploiting her—did not make any fact of consequence related to these statutory offenses more or less probable than it would have been without them." United States v. Dotson, 715 F.3d 576, 582–83 (6th Cir.2013).

Example—Inadmissible. "The evidence excluded was irrelevant. The defendants' fiduciary duty * * * to hold and spend union funds for the benefit of the organization itself remains regardless of whether SEIU is a model international union. Any evidence showing SEIU had questionable leadership and ethics would not lessen the defendants' obligation to refrain from using union resources to weaken their own union and engage in dual unionism. This evidence could only prove facts that were not 'of consequence in determining the action.' Fed. R. Evid. 401(b). The district court did not abuse its discretion by excluding irrelevant evidence." Services Employees Intern. Union v. National Union of Healthcare Workers, 718 F.3d 1036, 1050 (9th Cir.2013).

Example—Inadmissible. "[B]ecause the intent to permanently deprive is neither a required element of, nor a defense to, the 'conver[sion]' or 'steal[ing]' that 18 U.S.C. § 664 criminalizes, the district court did not abuse its discretion when it excluded evidence of Van Elsen's eventual repayment of his employees' funds in a bankruptcy proceeding as irrelevant." United States v. Van Elsen, 652 F.3d 955, 962 (8th Cir.2011).

Example—Inadmissible. "The jury convicted Buendia of federal-programs bribery, which requires her to have "corruptly solicit[ed]" the kickbacks. She argues that she lacked the requisite corruptness because, as this evidence allegedly would have shown, she spent the kickbacks to benefit the school. But regardless of how Buendia might have eventually spent the kickback money, she "corruptly solicit[ed]" it because, by awarding contracts to Shy in exchange for kickbacks, she subverted the normal bidding process in a manner inconsistent with her duty to obtain goods and services for her school at the best value." United States v. Buendia, 907 F.3d 399, 402 (6th Cir.2018).

Example—Inadmissible. "The Government argues that 'evidence of what the store employees felt is probative of whether a reasonable person would have been afraid under the same circumstances.' In so arguing, the Government seemingly contends that the victim store employees' testimony bears on whether they feared injury. But as Appellant points out, the robberies were committed using firearms. Moreover, the Government elicited testimony about what the store employees were thinking and feeling during the robbery, such that testimony about how the robbery impacted them afterward was—at best—unnecessary. Specifically, Bene testified that when Brown was handcuffing her during the Elizabeth City robbery, she thought she was 'going to die,' and Soler-Garcia testified that when Brown asked her to lay down on her stomach during the Garner robbery, she refused because she 'didn't want him to put a bullet in the back of [her] head.' Perhaps the testimony about how Bene lost her marriage and her children, Swain was afraid to leave her home, and Soler-Garcia tried to go back to work but had to quit her job because she had panic attacks helps to demonstrate that the robberies were traumatizing for the store employee—more akin to a victim impact statement at sentencing. But it is only minimally relevant to proof of an element of the crime charged—the store employees' fear of injury during the robbery." United States v. Walker, 32 F.4th 377, 388–89 (4th Cir.2022), cert. denied, 143 S.Ct.450 (2022).

(5) Probative value. "Evidence is relevant if 'it has *any* tendency to make a fact [of consequence] more or less probable than it would be without the evidence.' Fed. R. Evid. 401 (emphasis added). The word 'any' signals that evidence is relevant even if it only slightly or marginally alters the likelihood of a consequential fact." United States v. Leonard-Allen, 739 F.3d 948, 956 (7th Cir.2013). "[T]he test of relevance is very liberal and does not entail a determination of the sufficiency of the evidence." Douglass v. Eaton Corp., 956 F.2d 1339, 1345 (6th Cir.1992). A trial judge's determination as to relevance is reviewed under an abuse of discretion standard. Transgo, Inc. v. Ajac Transmission Parts Corp., 768 F.2d 1001, 1020 (9th Cir.1985).

Example—Irrelevant. In mail and wire fraud prosecution, defendant's recorded racist and misogynist statements were not relevant. "The recordings of Hazelwood's highly offensive comments fail to meet even the lenient 'step on one evidentiary route' standard. As the district court instructed the jury, the recordings 'do[ ] not go to any of the elements of the offenses with which Mr. Hazelwood is charged in the indictment.' In other words, there is simply no 'route' on which the recordings make it more likely that Hazelwood committed fraud. Moreover, the recordings do not rebut Hazelwood's argument that he was a 'good businessman.' Having a bad set of personal beliefs did not make it more likely that Hazelwood made bad business decisions." United States v. Hazelwood, 979 F.3d 398, 409 (6th Cir.2020).

Example—Irrelevant. "Mr. Palms's first argument is not persuasive because the sexual behavior evidence is not probative of a central issue in this case. Evidence that a sex trafficking victim previously engaged in prostitution is irrelevant to whether that victim was forced or coerced into working as a prostitute at a later date. * * * Even if M.W. participated in commercial sex work in 2017 and knew how to post ads for commercial sex, that does not tend to prove Mr. Palms did not force her to engage in prostitution during the period charged. Indeed, this lack of probative value is exactly why Rule 412 exists. It 'preclude[s] defendants from arguing that because the victim previously consented to have sex—for love or money—her claims of coercion should not be believed.' " United States v. Palms, 21 F.4th 689, 703 (10th Cir.2021).

(6) Fact need not be disputed; "background evidence." The fact of consequence to which the evidence is directed need not be disputed. United States v. Douglas, 482 F.3d 591, 597 (D.C.Cir.2007) (evidentiary relevance under Rule 401 is not affected by the availability of alternative proofs of the element, such as a defendant's concession or offer to stipulate) (citing, inter alia, Old Chief v. United States, 519 U.S. 172, 179, 117 S.Ct. 644 (1997)). Evidence offered to prove a conceded point may be excluded, but on the basis of Rule 403 considerations, not Rule 401. Advisory Committee's Note to Rule 401. "Background evidence," such as photographs, views of real estate, murder weapons, and basic biographical information concerning a witness, is relevant according to the standard of Rule 401. Id.; United States v. Boros, 668 F.3d 901, 908 (7th Cir.2012); Faigin v. Kelly, 184 F.3d 67, 81 (1st Cir.1999); United States v. Blackwell, 853 F.2d 86, 88 (2d Cir.1988); Government of Virgin Islands v. Grant, 775 F.2d 508, 513 (3d Cir.1985); Conway v. Chemical Leaman Tank Lines, Inc., 525 F.2d 927, 930 (5th Cir.1976).

(7) Flight, escape, and other "admissions by conduct." The probative value of flight "as circumstantial evidence of guilt depends upon the degree of confidence with which four inferences can be drawn: (1) from the defendant's behavior to flight; (2) from flight to consciousness of guilt; (3) from consciousness of guilt to consciousness of guilt concerning the crime charged; (4) from consciousness of guilt concerning the crime charged to actual guilt of the crime charged." United States v. Myers, 550 F.2d 1036, 1049 (5th Cir.1977). Accord, United States v. Murphy, 996 F.2d 94, 96 (5th Cir.1993). "Evidence of an accused's flight may be admitted at trial as indicative of a guilty mind, so long as there is an adequate factual predicate for the inference that the defendant's movement was indicative of a guilty conscience, and not normal travel." United States v. Zanghi, 189 F.3d 71, 83 (1st Cir.1999). The relevancy of evidence of escape depends upon a similar analysis. United States v. Hankins, 931 F.2d 1256, 1261–62 (8th Cir.1991).

Other conduct that may have relevance similar to that of flight or escape:

- Threats to witnesses. United States v. Guerrero-Cortez, 110 F.3d 647, 652 (8th Cir.1997); United States v. Monahan, 633 F.2d 984, 985 (1st Cir.1980).

- Attempts to bribe witnesses. United States v. Mendez-Ortiz, 810 F.2d 76, 79 (6th Cir.1986).

- Refusal to provide handwriting exemplars. United States v. Jackson, 886 F.2d 838, 845–48 (7th Cir.1989).

- Bad faith destruction of documentary evidence. Brown & Williamson Tobacco Corp. v. Jacobson, 827 F.2d 1119, 1134 (7th Cir.1987).

- Use of false name. United States v. Valencia-Lucena, 925 F.2d 506, 513 (1st Cir.1991).

- Flight from the country in disguise using false name. United States v. Otero-Mendez, 273 F.3d 46, 53 (1st Cir.2001).

- Running into the woods and throwing something into the tree line immediately following automobile accident. Learmonth v. Sears, Roebuck and Co., 631 F.3d 724, 733 (5th Cir.2011).

See also Rule 804(b)(6).

(8) Occurrence or absence of similar accidents. In a negligence or product liability case, the occurrence of other accidents may be relevant to show the existence of a dangerous condition or defect, causation, or notice to the defendant of danger. Kinser v. Gehl Co., 184 F.3d 1259, 1273 (10th Cir.1999); Nachtsheim v. Beech Aircraft Corp., 847 F.2d 1261, 1268–69 (7th Cir.1988) (citing many other cases). In order for such evidence to be admissible, the proponent must show that the other accidents occurred under substantially similar circumstances and conditions. Kinser v. Gehl Co., supra, at 1273.

Example—Inadmissible. "Lovett next contends that the district court erred by excluding evidence of four similar incidents involving Jeep Cherokees. The district court excluded the evidence because the incidents were not 'substantially similar' to Lovett's accident, noting that none: (1) involved a 1985 Cherokee, (2) involved a collision with a locomotive, (3) occurred at a railroad crossing, (4) resulted in the Cherokee rolling over, (5) occurred in a similar topographical area, and (6) involved similar speeds. * * * [W]e are satisfied that the incidents were not 'substantially similar' to Lovett's accident and that the district court correctly excluded them." Lovett ex rel. Lovett v. Union Pacific R. Co., 201 F.3d 1074, 1080–81 (8th Cir.2000).

Example—Inadmissible. Evidence of other rifle failures was properly excluded where the other incidents were not "substantially similar" to the plaintiff's accident. The other rifle muzzleloaders involved different breech plugs and threads, were of a different model and design, and had been in use for longer periods of time than the plaintiff's. Katzenmeier v. Blackpowder Products, Inc., 628 F.3d 948, 951 (8th Cir.2010).

Similarity of conditions is especially important when the other accidents are offered to show the existence of a dangerous condition or causation. Mihailovich v. Laatsch, 359 F.3d 892, 907–08 (7th Cir.2004); Kinser v. Gehl Co., supra, at 1273; Nachtsheim v. Beech Aircraft Corp., supra, at 1268–69. Even when substantial similarity of circumstances is shown, the evidence is subject to exclusion in the trial court's discretion on account of dangers of unfair prejudice, confusion of issues, and undue expenditure of time in the trial of collateral issues. Nachtsheim v. Beech Aircraft Corp., supra, at 1268–69.

If the other accident is relevant to show notice, the requirement of similarity is less strict. Kinser v. Gehl Co., supra, at 1273; (citing many other cases); Benedi v. McNeil-P.P.C., Inc., 66 F.3d 1378, 1386 (4th Cir.1995). A prior accident may be used to establish notice only if it occurred sufficiently prior to the date of the subject incident that the defendant could have taken steps to remedy the situation. Kinser v. Gehl Co., supra, at 1274.

Similarly, the lack of other accidents may be relevant to show the absence of dangerous condition or defect, lack of causal relation, and lack of notice. Pandit v. American Honda Motor Co., 82 F.3d 376, 380–81 (10th Cir.1996); Espeaignnette v. Gene Tierney Co., 43 F.3d 1, 9–10 (1st Cir.1994). The admissibility of evidence of absence of accidents is also subject to a foundation showing similarity of conditions and the trial court's exercise of discretion under Rule 403. Pandit v. American Honda Motor Co., 82 F.3d 376, 381 (10th Cir.1996); Espeaignnette v. Gene Tierney Co., 43 F.3d 1, 10 (1st Cir.1994); Klonowski v. International Armament Corp., 17 F.3d 992, 996 (7th Cir.1994).

Accidents that would otherwise be inadmissible on account of dissimilarity may become admissible to impeach a witness's broad assertions concerning safety. Cooper v. Firestone Tire & Rubber Co., 945 F.2d 1103, 1105 (9th Cir.1991). But see Drabik v. Stanley-Bostitch, Inc., 997 F.2d 496 (8th Cir.1993).

(9) Experiments and demonstrations. Experiments or demonstrations designed to show how a particular event occurred are subject to the same general test of admissibility as other accidents, i.e., substantial similarity of conditions. United States v. Gaskell, 985 F.2d 1056, 1060 (11th Cir.1993); Four Corners Helicopters, Inc. v. Turbomeca, S.A., 979 F.2d 1434, 1442 (10th Cir.1992).

Experiments or demonstrations that are intended to demonstrate general principles rather than to recreate a particular event are exempt from the similarity of conditions requirement. Gilbert v. Cosco, Inc., 989 F.2d 399, 402 (10th Cir.1993); Champeau v. Fruehauf Corp., 814 F.2d 1271, 1278 (8th Cir.1987).

(10) Similar contracts or transactions. A party's business transactions with third parties in similar circumstances may be relevant to prove the probable terms or meaning of terms of a disputed agreement. Cibro Petroleum Products, Inc. v. Sohio Alaska Petroleum Co., 602 F.Supp. 1520, 1551 (N.D.N.Y.1985), aff'd, 798 F.2d 1421 (Em.App.1986).

(11) Similar claims by plaintiff. Evidence that a plaintiff has brought similar claims that were fraudulent may be relevant to the merits of the present claim. On the other hand, evidence merely indicating that the plaintiff is "claim-minded" is generally excluded. Bunion v. Allstate Ins. Co., 502 F.Supp. 340 (E.D.Pa.1980).

(12) Real and demonstrative evidence. Real evidence is physical evidence having, or alleged to have, an actual connection to the events that are the subject of the trial, such as a murder weapon, a substance seized from possession of the accused, or a product alleged to have broken and caused the plaintiff's injury. Demonstrative or illustrative evidence includes all tangible items presented at trial that did not have any real connection to the events, but that are employed to aid the trier to comprehend testimony or other evidence. Examples of demonstrative or illustrative evidence are charts, models, maps, drawings, and most photographs, films, and videotapes.

Both real and demonstrative or illustrative evidence, like testimonial evidence, are subject to the general relevancy requirements of Rules 401, 402, and 403. In addition, real and documentary evidence are subject to the requirement of authentication or identification. See Rules 901 and 902 and the Authors' Comments to those provisions. In general, with respect to an item of real evidence, a foundation must be presented establishing that the item is relevant, its identity, and that its condition has not materially changed. United States v. Dickerson, 873 F.2d 1181, 1185 (9th Cir.1988).

With respect to an item used demonstratively or illustratively, the foundation must establish that the item depicts relevant information that is or will be proven by other, substantive evidence; that it is accurate; and that it will probably aid the trier of fact in understanding the evidence. Perfect accuracy is not required, so long as, on balance, the item is helpful. Roland v. Langlois, 945 F.2d 956, 963 (7th Cir.1991).

If an item such as a chart is presented solely as illustrative and not as substantive (real) evidence, it should not go to the jury room absent consent of all parties. United States v. Wood, 943 F.2d 1048, 1053 (9th Cir.1991); Pierce v. Ramsey Winch Co., 753 F.2d 416, 431 (5th Cir.1985).

Other items received as illustrative or demonstrative evidence, subject to Rule 403 and the trial court's discretion:

• Computer reenactment of accident accompanying expert testimony. Robinson v. Missouri Pacific Railroad Co., 16 F.3d 1083, 1086–88 (10th Cir.1994).

• Posed photographic reconstruction of accident accompanying expert testimony. Johnson v. Matlock, 771 F.2d 1432, 1434 (10th Cir.1985).

• "Day in the life" film or video depicting activities of injured plaintiff. Bannister v. Town of Noble, Okl., 812 F.2d 1265, 1269–70 (10th Cir.1987); Grimes v. Employers Mutual Liability Ins. Co. of Wisconsin, 73 F.R.D. 607, 610 (D.Alaska 1977).

(13) Exhibiting personal injuries; bodily demonstrations. Exhibition of a personal injury, and demonstrating its effects, is permissible, subject to Rule 403. Allen v. Seacoast Products, Inc., 623 F.2d 355, 365 n. 23 (5th Cir.1980) (plaintiff's demonstration of removal and replacement of artificial eye).

(14) View of property or scene by trier. Whether a view of property or a scene should be taken by the trier of fact is a matter within the trial court's discretion, subject to review only for abuse. The discretion is usually exercised in the negative, and affirmed on appeal. United States v. Culpepper, 834 F.2d 879, 883 (10th Cir.1987); Stokes v. Delcambre, 710 F.2d 1120, 1129 (5th Cir.1983); Auto Owners Ins. Co. v. Bass, 684 F.2d 764, 769 (11th Cir.1982). "With respect to taking a jury for a view, the disruption and confusion likely to result closely resembles that associated with taking a third grade class to a firehouse." 1 Graham, Handbook of Federal Evidence § 401:11 (6th ed. 2006).

CROSS-REFERENCES

Common Objections (Chapter 3)

51. Irrelevant (immaterial, not probative)
61. Other accidents
62. Other claims by plaintiff
63. Other contracts or transactions involving a party

Checklists (Chapter 4)

10. Steps in Offering an Exhibit (Documentary, Real, or Illustrative Evidence)

Treatises

2 Graham, Handbook of Federal Evidence §§ 401:1–401:11 (9th ed. 2020)

1 McCormick, Evidence §§ 185, 196–200, 202; 2 id. §§ 212–217 (8th ed. 2020)

22 Wright & Graham, Federal Practice and Procedure §§ 5161–5190 (2d ed. 2012)

Rule 402. General Admissibility of Relevant Evidence

Relevant evidence is admissible unless any of the following provides otherwise:

• the United States Constitution;

• a federal statute;

• these rules; or

• other rules prescribed by the Supreme Court.

Irrelevant evidence is not admissible.

AUTHORS' COMMENTS

(1) Scope and purpose of Rule 402. Rule 402 establishes the general principles that (1) all relevant evidence is admissible unless it is made inadmissible by some particular rule or law, and (2) irrelevant evidence is not admissible.

(2) Excluded relevant evidence—"[T]he United States Constitution." The most important constitutional provisions that are applied to exclude relevant evidence in some circumstances are the Fourth, Fifth, and Sixth Amendments. See the Authors' Comments to Rules 501, 608, 611, 703, and 802.

(3) Excluded relevant evidence—"[A] Federal statute." Many federal statutes contain provisions that exclude, restrict, or place conditions upon the admissibility of relevant evidence.

(4) Excluded relevant evidence—"[T]hese rules." Many of the Federal Rules of Evidence exclude, restrict, or place conditions upon the admissibility of relevant evidence. Examples are Rules 404 and 405, which restrict the admissibility of character evidence, and Rule 802, which generally excludes hearsay.

(5) Excluded relevant evidence—"[O]ther rules prescribed by the Supreme Court." A number of provisions in the Federal Rules of Civil Procedure and the Federal Rules of Criminal Procedure operate in some circumstances to exclude, restrict, or place conditions upon the admissibility of evidence.

CROSS-REFERENCES

Common Objections (Chapter 3)

51.   Irrelevant (immaterial, not probative)

61.   Other accidents

62.   Other claims by plaintiff

63.   Other contracts or transactions involving a party

Checklists (Chapter 4)

10.   Steps in Offering an Exhibit (Documentary, Real, or Illustrative Evidence)

Treatises

2 Graham, Handbook of Federal Evidence § 402:1 (9th ed. 2020)

1 McCormick, Evidence § 184 (8th ed. 2020)

22A Wright & Graham, Federal Practice and Procedure §§ 5191–5203 (2d ed. 2014)

Rule 403. Excluding Relevant Evidence for Prejudice, Confusion, Waste of Time, or Other Reasons

The court may exclude relevant evidence if its probative value is substantially outweighed by a danger of one or more of the following: unfair prejudice, confusing the issues, misleading the jury, undue delay, wasting time, or needlessly presenting cumulative evidence.

AUTHORS' COMMENTS

(1) Scope and Purpose of Rule 403. Rule 403 authorizes the exclusion of relevant evidence if the legitimate probative value of the evidence is substantially outweighed by the potential damage that the evidence might do to the orderly, efficient, and fair process of the trial. Since Rule 403 calls for a weighing or balancing judgment, its application necessarily involves the exercise of the trial court's discretion. Rule 403 applies to all forms of evidence (real, demonstrative, documentary, and testimonial) and to both direct and cross-examination. The failure of the trial court to enter express findings into the record as to the balancing of probative value and unfair prejudice is not reversible error; it suffices that the balancing decision is supported by evidence of the record. Smith v. Tenet Healthsystem SL, Inc., 436 F.3d 879, 885 (8th Cir.2006).

(2) Rule favors admission. "In weighing the probative value of evidence against the dangers and considerations enumerated in Rule 403, the general rule is that the balance should be struck in favor of admission." United States v. Dennis, 625 F.2d 782, 797 (8th Cir.1980). "Courts have characterized Rule 403 as an extraordinary remedy to be used sparingly because it permits the trial court to exclude otherwise relevant evidence." United States v. Meester, 762 F.2d 867, 875 (11th Cir.1985) (citing many other cases).

Example—Admissible. In murder prosecution, trial court properly overruled Rule 403 objections to photographs of deceased and death scene. "Relevant evidence is inherently prejudicial; but it is only unfair prejudice, substantially outweighing probative value, which permits exclusion of relevant matter under Rule 403. Unless trials are to be conducted on scenarios, on unreal facts tailored and sanitized for the occasion, the application of Rule 403 must be cautious and sparing. Its major function is limited to excluding matter of scant or cumulative probative force, dragged in by the heels for the sake of its prejudicial effect. As to such, Rule 403 is meant to relax the iron rule of relevance, to permit the trial judge to preserve the fairness of the proceedings by exclusion despite its relevance. It is not designed to permit the court to 'even out' the weight of the evidence, to mitigate a crime, or to make a contest where there is little or none." United States v. McRae, 593 F.2d 700, 707 (5th Cir.1979).

Example—Admissible. In fraud and money laundering prosecution, trial court properly admitted evidence that when female confederate sought to withdraw from scheme, defendant threatened her by inserting gun in her vagina. "Rule 403 does not provide a shield for defendants who engage in outrageous acts, permitting only the crimes of Caspar Milquetoasts to be described fully to a jury. It does not generally require the government to sanitize its case, to deflate its witnesses' testimony, or to tell its story in a monotone." United States v. Gartmon, 146 F.3d 1015, 1021 (D.C.Cir.1998).

(3) Trial court discretion. "Particular deference is appropriate" to trial court determinations of the Rule 403 balance; "[i]ndeed, a trial judge's decision to admit or exclude evidence under Fed. R. Evid. 403 may not be reversed unless it is 'arbitrary and irrational.' " Bhaya v. Westinghouse Electric Corp., 922 F.2d 184, 187 (3d Cir.1990). Accord, Foley v. City of Lowell, Mass., 948 F.2d 10, 15 (1st Cir.1991).

"Rule 403 controversies by their very nature present competing considerations, and compromise is often the best solution for a particularly knotty Rule 403 problem." Faigin v. Kelly, 184 F.3d 67, 80 (1st Cir.1999).

Example. In § 1983 action alleging political discrimination, plaintiffs sought to admit documents from related litigation. Trial court identified risk of jury confusion as to the import of the documents but summarized the relevant parts of the documents to provide background information. Held, affirmed. " * * * [T]his compromise solution struck a fair balance between the policy favoring the admission of relevant evidence and the risk that the evidence might taint the proceedings. When a district judge carefully reconciles conflicting considerations and reaches a sensible solution as to the handling of volatile evidence, an appellate court should hesitate to intervene." Torres-Arroyo v. Rullan, 436 F.3d 1, 8 (1st Cir.2006).

(4) "Probative value"—In general. "[W]hat counts as the Rule 403 'probative value' of an item of evidence, as distinct from its Rule 401 'relevance,' may be calculated by comparing evidentiary alternatives." Old Chief v. United States, 519 U.S. 172, 184, 117 S.Ct. 644, 652 (1997). "Probity in this context is not an absolute; its value must be determined with regard to the extent to which the [fact] is established by other evidence, stipulation, or inference. It is the incremental probity of the evidence that is to be balanced against its potential for undue prejudice." United States v. Beechum, 582 F.2d 898, 914 (5th Cir.1978). "[W]hile prosecutorial need alone does not mean probative value outweighs prejudice, * * * the more essential the evidence, the greater its probative value, and the less likely that a trial court should order the evidence excluded." United States v. King, 713 F.2d 627, 631 (11th Cir.1983).

(5) "Probative value"—Judge not to determine credibility. "Weighing probative value against unfair prejudice under F.R.Evid. 403 means probative value with respect to a material fact if the evidence is believed, not the degree the court finds it believable." Bowden v. McKenna, 600 F.2d 282, 284–85 (1st Cir.1979). Accord, United States v. Evans, 728 F.3d 953, 963 (9th Cir.2013); United States v. Bergrin, 682 F.3d 261, 280 (3d Cir.2012); Ballou v. Henri Studios, Inc., 656 F.2d 1147, 1154 (5th Cir.1981).

(6) "Unfair prejudice." Rule 403 "does not offer protection against evidence that is merely prejudicial, in the sense of being detrimental to a party's case. Rather, the rule only protects against evidence that is *unfairly* prejudicial. Evidence is unfairly prejudicial only if it has 'an undue tendency to suggest decision on an improper basis,' commonly, though not necessarily, an emotional one. Advisory Committee's Note, F.R.Evid. 403. It is unfairly prejudicial if it 'appeals to the jury's sympathies, arouses its sense of horror, provokes its instinct to punish,' or otherwise 'may cause a jury to base its decision on something other than the established propositions in the case.' " Carter v. Hewitt, 617 F.2d 961, 972 (3d Cir.1980). Accord, Old Chief v. United States, 519 U.S. 172, 180, 117 S.Ct. 644, 650 (1997); United States v. Skillman, 922 F.2d 1370, 1374 (9th Cir.1990).

> **Example—Admissible.** In § 1983 action against city and police officers, evidence of deceased arrestee's criminal record, time in prison, and drug addiction was improperly excluded. Since Illinois makes surviving relatives' emotional loss and familial ties relevant to damages, evidence was probative of appropriate amount of damages and not unfairly prejudicial. Cobige v. City of Chicago, Ill., 651 F.3d 780, 784–84 (7th Cir.2011).

> **Example—Inadmissible.** Videos of prepubescent children being bound, raped, and violently assaulted were unfairly prejudicial where other available evidence was sufficient to prove the defendant knowingly possessed, received, and distributed child pornography. United States v. Cunningham, 694 F.3d 372, 391 (3d Cir.2012).

> **Example—Inadmissible.** In prosecution for conspiracy to import controlled substances, conspiracy to possess controlled substances with intent to distribute, and conspiracy to launder money, danger of unfair prejudice substantially outweighed probative value of expert testimony about potential side effects and birth defects resulting from drugs sold through defendant's internet pharmacy. United States v. Boros, 668 F.3d 901, 910 (7th Cir.2012).

Evidence presenting dangers of unfair prejudice can often be dealt with by compromise on the part of the trial court.

> **Example.** In sexual harassment case, victim wanted to testify that she had heard that alleged harasser had severely beaten and injured his wife, to show why she so feared him. Trial court forbade account of the specifics but allowed her to testify that she had heard "something" that increased her fear. Held, affirmed. "The compromise reached by the district court was a perfect example of a reasonable call that is not an abuse of discretion." Gray v. Genlyte Group, Inc., 289 F.3d 128, 139 (1st Cir.2002).

(7) **"Confusing the issues."** Evidence may be excluded as confusing the issues if it would tend to distract the jury from the proper issues.

> **Example—Inadmissible.** Criminal conviction of coworker for state misdemeanor of "accosting" was properly excluded in sexual harassment case because of danger of confusion. The statute was applicable to conduct that would fall short of sexual harassment. Gray v. Genlyte Group, Inc., 289 F.3d 128, 140 (1st Cir.2002).

> **Example—Inadmissible.** "Military specifications [for forklifts] would appear to carry the imprimatur of government sanction, and might therefore resemble in the jury's mind something akin to actual regulation. In addition, both the legal effect and the genesis of these specifications might have been put at issue by introducing the specifications themselves, resulting in confusion of the issues for the jury as well as in an unnecessary waste of the court's time." McEuin v. Crown Equipment Corp., 328 F.3d 1028, 1034 (9th Cir.2003).

> **Example—Inadmissible.** "The videotape improperly focused attention on what took place in International Falls on September 9, 1989 instead of what was actually said at the October 24, 1991 meeting in McGehee, Arkansas." BE & K Construction Co. v. United Brotherhood of Carpenters & Joiners, 90 F.3d 1318, 1331 (8th Cir.1996).

> **Example—Inadmissible.** Evidence that bank recovered its investment confused issue of intent to defraud. United States v. Tidwell, 559 F.2d 262, 266 (5th Cir.1977).

> **Example—Inadmissible.** "The introduction of evidence about subsequent changes in the product or its design threatens to confuse the jury by diverting its attention from whether the product was defective at the relevant time to what was done later." Grenada Steel Indus. v. Alabama Oxygen Co., 695 F.2d 883, 888 (5th Cir.1983).

Example—Inadmissible. Plaintiff claimed defendant was negligent because it did not retrofit its Chrysler Ram with a device that might have prevented the accident. Chrysler had previously retrofitted its Dodge Cherokee with the same device after reports of unintended acceleration. "[E]vidence of the Jeep-retrofit program raised substantial issues of confusion and prejudice with regard to the Dodge Ram. Given that the Jeep-retrofit evidence involved an entirely different vehicle, its probative value for the negligence and strict-liability claims was minimal." Ahlberg v. Chrysler Corp., 481 F.3d 630, 632–634 (8th Cir.2007).

Example—Inadmissible. In prosecution for possession of child pornography, district court properly excluded psychologist's expert testimony that defendant was not a pedophile. The evidence "might well 'shift attention away from [a] key question—whether the defendant had knowledge of the contents of the videos—to a wholly irrelevant one—whether or not he is a pedophile.' " United States v. Pires, 642 F.3d 1, 11 (1st Cir.2011).

Example—Inadmissible. "Endeavor argues that the district court erred when it excluded evidence related to the title defects. When Endeavor delivered its termination letter to Broad Street, it included a box of documentation. The district court excluded the documentation, citing the possibility of 'unnecessary confusion for the jury.' A court may exclude evidence on this basis if the 'probative value is substantially outweighed by a danger of * * * confusing the issues.' Fed. R. Evid. 403. The probative value of this evidence was low because it was cumulative. * * * Plus, the possibility the evidence might confuse was not insignificant. The documentation was dense and highly technical, and included legal opinions, lease assignments, land records, and spreadsheets." Broad Street Energy Co. v. Endeavor Ohio, LLC, 806 F.3d 402, 409 (6th Cir.2015).

(8) "Misleading the jury." Cases invoking the danger of misleading the jury often refer to the possibility that the jury might attach undue weight to the evidence.

Example—Inadmissible. Government report on safety of tire excluded under Rule 403 because the "jury may have been influenced by the official character of the report to afford it greater weight than it was worth." Bright v. Firestone Tire & Rubber Co., 756 F.2d 19, 23 (6th Cir.1984).

Example—Inadmissible. Doctors' testimony regarding defendant's impaired judgment was relevant to his state of mind in fraud prosecution but relevancy was outweighed by danger jury would be misled into thinking that the condition amounted to temporary insanity or ameliorated the offense. United States v. Schneider, 111 F.3d 197, 203 (1st Cir.1997).

Example—Inadmissible. Probable cause determination by EEOC. "A strong argument can be made that a jury would attach undue weight to this type of agency determination, viewing it as a finding of discrimination—as the plaintiff himself suggests it should be viewed—rather than as a mere finding of probable cause." Williams v. Nashville Network, 132 F.3d 1123, 1129 (6th Cir.1997).

Example—Inadmissible. "There is also the danger that the jury may overvalue polygraph results as an indicator of truthfulness because of the polygraph's scientific nature." United States v. Call, 129 F.3d 1402, 1406 (10th Cir.1997).

Example—Inadmissible. Findings in a sanctions order from a previous trial. "A lay jury is quite likely to give special weight to judicial findings merely because they are judicial findings." Faigin v. Kelly, 184 F.3d 67, 80 (1st Cir.1999).

Demonstrative evidence may be excluded as misleading if it distorts or misrepresents underlying evidence.

Example—Inadmissible. In copyright infringement action against singer-composer Michael Jackson, trial court properly excluded plaintiff's demonstrative tapes designed to compare plaintiff's song "Dangerous" with defendant's song of the same title; the tapes altered the tempo, changed the key, repeated musical phrases not repeated in the originals, and spliced together portions not adjacent in the originals; "the changes made to the songs in these recordings were so significant that the tapes no longer represented the songs in question." Cartier v. Jackson, 59 F.3d 1046, 1049 (10th Cir.1995).

(9) "Undue delay, wasting time, or needlessly presenting cumulative evidence." "As a general rule, evidence may not be excluded solely to avoid delay. * * * Under Rule 403, the court should consider the probative value of the proffered evidence and balance it against the harm of delay." General Signal Corp. v. MCI Telecommunications Corp., 66 F.3d 1500, 1509–10 (9th Cir.1995).

Evidence may be excluded on account of waste of time because it has scant probative value. Stathos v. Bowden, 728 F.2d 15, 19 (1st Cir.1984).

"In the normal evidentiary sense cumulative evidence is excluded because it is repetitious." Brown v. Wainwright, 785 F.2d 1457, 1466 (11th Cir.1986). Accord, International Minerals and Resources, S.A. v. Pappas, 96 F.3d 586, 596 (2d Cir.1996).

Example—Inadmissible. "[E]vidence of the prior judgment was cumulative, because the Government had earlier introduced seven documents from Bejar's earlier deportation that would strongly tend to prove that he was an alien." United States v. Bejar-Matrecios, 618 F.2d 81, 84 (9th Cir.1980).

Example—Inadmissible. "The ruling in question involved the court telling the City to 'move on' after counsel had asked McDonough several repetitive questions about his relationship with Captain Falco. * * * The court provided the City with ample opportunity to highlight McDonough's sour relationship with the City. It was within the court's discretion to draw the line where it did." McDonough v. City of Quincy, 452 F.3d 8, 20 (1st Cir.2006).

The concept of "cumulative" evidence should not, however, be employed to interfere with a party's right to present a persuasive case. For example, evidence that is corroborative of a defendant's testimony should not be excluded as "cumulative." Towner v. State, 685 P.2d 45, 49–50 (Wyo.1984).

(10) Surprise. "The rule does not enumerate surprise as a ground for exclusion * * *. * * * [T]he granting of a continuance is a more appropriate remedy than exclusion of the evidence." Advisory Committee's Note to Rule 403. "Although [Rule 403] does not list 'surprise' as a specific ground for excluding evidence, testimony which results in surprise may be excluded if the surprise would require a continuance causing undue delay or if surprise is coupled with the danger of prejudice and confusion of issues." Lease America Corp. v. Insurance Co. of North America, 88 Wis.2d 395, 276 N.W.2d 767, 769 (1979).

CROSS-REFERENCES

Common Objections (Chapter 3)

27. Confusion of the issues

29. Cumulative

59. Misleading the jury

61. Other accidents

62. Other claims by plaintiff

63. Other contracts or transactions involving a party

69. Photograph inflammatory and unfairly prejudicial

70. Prejudicial effect outweighs probative value

Treatises

2 Graham, Handbook of Federal Evidence §§ 403:1–403:2 (9th ed. 2020)

1 McCormick, Evidence § 185 (8th ed. 2020)

22A Wright & Graham, Federal Practice and Procedure §§ 5211–5224 (2d ed. 2014)

Rule 404(a). Character Evidence

(a) Character Evidence.

 (1) *Prohibited Uses.* Evidence of a person's character or character trait is not admissible to prove that on a particular occasion the person acted in accordance with the character or trait.

(2) ***Exceptions for a Defendant or Victim in a Criminal Case.*** The following exceptions apply in a criminal case:

    (A) a defendant may offer evidence of the defendant's pertinent trait, and if the evidence is admitted, the prosecutor may offer evidence to rebut it;

    (B) subject to the limitations in Rule 412, a defendant may offer evidence of an alleged victim's pertinent trait, and if the evidence is admitted, the prosecutor may:

        (i) offer evidence to rebut it; and

        (ii) offer evidence of the defendant's same trait; and

    (C) in a homicide case, the prosecutor may offer evidence of the alleged victim's trait of peacefulness to rebut evidence that the victim was the first aggressor.

(3) ***Exceptions for a Witness.*** Evidence of a witness's character may be admitted under Rules 607, 608, and 609.

AUTHORS' COMMENTS

(1) Scope and purpose of Rule 404(a)(1). Rule 404(a)(1) iterates the general principle that character evidence is not admissible to prove that a person acted in conformity with his or her character on a particular occasion. The rule is based on the view that the probative value of such evidence is outweighed by the danger of unfair prejudice and confusion of issues. Michelson v. United States, 335 U.S. 469, 475–76, 69 S.Ct. 213, 218–19 (1948). There are, however, three exceptions to this general principle listed in Rule 404(a).

    (1) An accused may offer evidence of his good character and the prosecution may then offer character evidence in rebuttal. Rule 404(a)(2)(A).

    (2) An accused may offer evidence of his alleged victim's bad character. Rule 404(a)(2)(B). In response, the prosecution may offer evidence of the alleged victim's good character and the accused's bad character. Rule 404(a)(2)(B). In homicide cases, the prosecution may offer evidence of the alleged victim's peaceable character to rebut any evidence that the alleged victim started the altercation. Rule 404(a)(2)(C).

    (3) In both civil and criminal cases, evidence of a witness's character for truthfulness or untruthfulness may be offered. Rule 404(a)(3).

As Rule 404(a) is concerned only with the use of character evidence to show conformity, it does not govern other uses of such evidence. Thus, Rules 401–403 govern the admissibility of character evidence when it is offered because character is itself in issue or is being offered to prove something other than conformity. Rule 404(b) governs the use of evidence of other acts when offered for other purposes, such as to prove motive or intent.

When character evidence is admissible, Rule 405 dictates how it may be proved.

(2) Circumstantial use of character to prove conforming conduct generally inadmissible. Rule 404(a) expresses the general rule that a person's conduct or state of mind on a particular occasion may not be proved circumstantially by offering evidence of the person's character from which the fact finder is to infer that the person acted in accordance with that character on the particular occasion. Character has been defined as "a generalized description of a person's disposition, or of the disposition in respect to a general trait, such as honesty, temperance or peacefulness." McCormick, Evidence § 195 (5th ed. 1999). See also United States v. Doe, 149 F.3d 634, 638 (7th Cir.1998). Although most often invoked in criminal cases, the prohibition on character evidence to prove conformity applies in civil cases as well.

Example—Civil case—Inadmissible. In Kebede v. Hilton, 580 F.3d 714 (8th Cir.2009), the plaintiff brought an alienation of affections action against one of her former husband's co-workers. The court ruled that evidence that the defendant had previously had affairs with two other co-workers was inadmissible to prove that she had a propensity for having such affairs.

Example—Civil case—Inadmissible. In Kanida v. Gulf Coast Medical Personnel LP, 363 F.3d 568, 581–82 (5th Cir.2004), the plaintiff claimed that her supervisor retaliated against her for claiming unpaid overtime compensation. She sought to introduce evidence that the supervisor became angry with another employee who claimed unpaid overtime compensation. The court ruled that this was inadmissible character evidence.

Rules 413 and 414 permit the introduction of character evidence against the defendant in sexual assault and child molestation cases. Similarly, Rule 415 authorizes admission of such evidence against a party in a civil action predicated on alleged acts of sexual assault or child molestation. See Authors' Commentary to Rules 413–415.

(3) Circumstantial use of character to prove something other than conformity. Rule 404(a) does not govern the admissibility of character evidence when it is offered as circumstantial proof of something other than conforming conduct. The admissibility of such evidence is controlled by Rules 401–403.

Example. In Cobige v. City of Chicago, 651 F.3d 780 (7th Cir.2011), the plaintiff brought a § 1983 action against the defendants after his mother died in police lockup. He sought damages for his loss of companionship and for his mother's loss of enjoyment of life. The court of appeals held that the trial court erred in excluding evidence that the mother was a frequently-imprisoned drug addict. The evidence was not offered "to establish propensity .* * *. [I]t is relevant to how much loss [her] estate and son suffered by her death."

(4) Character an element of claim or defense. Rule 404(a) does not apply if a person's character is directly in issue—that is, if it is "a material fact that under the substantive law determines rights and liabilities of the parties." Perrin v. Anderson, 784 F.2d 1040, 1045 (10th Cir.1986). In such an instance, the character evidence is not being used to prove conformity. Character, however, is rarely present as an element of a charge or defense in a criminal case. One instance in which it may be an element is entrapment. Some courts view the issue of an accused's predisposition to commit the crime as implicating the accused's character. E.g., United States v. Gomez, 6 F.4th 992, 1004–06 (9th Cir.2021) (prior acts admissible to prove predisposition; United States v. Abumayyaleh, 530 F.3d 641, 650 (8th Cir.2008) (accord); United States v. Franco, 484 F.3d 347, 352 (6th Cir.2007) (accord); United States v. Thomas, 134 F.3d 975 (9th Cir.1998) (allowing defendant to introduce evidence of good character to prove lack of criminal predisposition). Other courts, however, consider predisposition a matter of the accused's state of mind, and not his character. E.g., United States v. McLaurin, 764 F.3d 372, 380–81 (4th Cir.2014); United States v. Cervantes, 706 F.3d 603, 616 (5th Cir.2013); United States v. Richardson, 764 F.2d 1514, 1522 n. 2 (11th Cir.1985). These courts address the admissibility of specific act evidence under Rule 404(b).

In civil cases, character is ordinarily an element of a claim in a negligent entrustment, hiring, or supervision case or where the defendant is claimed to have been grossly negligent in hiring the person who caused the plaintiff's injury. It is an element of a defense when a defamation defendant raises a defense of truth. Schafer v. Time, Inc., 142 F.3d 1361, 1370–73 (11th Cir.1998). If character is in issue, Rule 405 provides that it may be proved by evidence of opinion, reputation or specific conduct.

Example—Admissible. In Parrish v. Luckie, 963 F.2d 201, 205 (8th Cir.1992), a civil rights action against a police officer and his police chief, the plaintiff offered evidence of previous acts of violence by defendant police officer. The evidence was admissible to prove the police chief's knowledge of the officer's violent tendencies.

It is important to distinguish between "character directly in issue" (i.e., character is itself *an* issue in the case) and "putting character in issue" (i.e., when an accused offers evidence of his good character to prove he acted in conformity with that good character).

(5) Circumstantial use of character evidence—Exception for criminal defendant. Rule 404(a)(2)(A) expresses the first exception to the general rule that bars character evidence to prove conformity. A criminal defendant may offer evidence of his good character to support an inference that he acted in conformity with that good character and thus did not commit the crime with which he is charged. United States v. Yarbrough, 527 F.3d 1092, 1100–02 (10th Cir.2008). This is referred to as "putting character in issue." The evidence must relate to a character trait pertinent to the charge. In re Sealed Case, 352 F.3d 409, 411–13 (D.C. Cir.2003).

Example—Inadmissible. In United States v. Harris, 491 F.3d 440, 445–48 (D.C. Cir.2007), the defendant was charged with possession of cocaine with intent to distribute. Evidence of his character as a good family man was held inadmissible as it was not pertinent to the crime charged.

Example—Inadmissible. In United States v. Nazzaro, 889 F.2d 1158, 1168 (1st Cir.1989), evidence of the defendant's character for bravery and attention to duty was held inadmissible, as it was not pertinent to the charges against him of mail fraud and perjury.

Evidence that an accused is "law abiding" is admissible under Rule 404(a)(2)(A). Cf. United States v. Diaz, 961 F.2d 1417, 1419–20 (9th Cir.1992) (holding admissible character trait for "being prone to criminal activity or conduct" as within notion of "law abidingness," but excluding character trait for "being prone to large-scale drug dealing").

The accused may offer evidence of his good character through witnesses competent either to testify to his reputation in the relevant community for a pertinent trait or to offer their personal opinions concerning such a trait. He may not offer evidence of specific acts suggesting good character. United States v. Hill, 40 F.3d 164, 169 (7th Cir.1994); see Rule 405.

Example—Inadmissible. "Ahmed argues that the district court should have allowed his former attorney, Justin Claud, to testify about Ahmed's response to a deceptive advertising allegation and Ahmed's efforts to ensure zoning compliance. The district court rejected that argument, and so do we. * * * Claud's testimony would have covered specific acts of Ahmed's conduct to establish traits unrelated to the fraud charges. Ahmed would have used this evidence of supposed good conduct 'to negate [his] criminal intent,' which makes it precisely the kind of evidence that Rules 404(a) and 405(b) prohibit." United States v. Ahmed, 73 F.4th 1363, 1384 (11th Cir.2023).

(6) Exception for criminal defendant—Rebuttal by prosecution. After an accused has offered evidence of his good character, the prosecution may rebut the evidence. First, the prosecution may cross-examine the accused's reputation or opinion witnesses. Ordinarily, a reputation witness may be asked whether she "has heard" about specific acts committed by the accused that would be inconsistent with the reputation, while an opinion witness may be asked whether she knows about such acts. Courts should, however, permit either form of question to be put to both reputation and opinion witnesses. United States v. Scholl, 166 F.3d 964, 974 (9th Cir.1999). Of course, the cross-examiner must have a good faith belief that the defendant committed the specific acts. See United States v. Bruguier, 161 F.3d 1145, 1149 (8th Cir.1998). Second, the prosecution may call its own reputation or opinion witnesses to testify to the accused's bad character. Id.

(7) Reasonable doubt instruction. The overwhelming majority of courts of appeals hold that the trial court need not instruct the jury that evidence of the defendant's good character, standing alone, may be sufficient evidence to create a reasonable doubt. See United States v. Pujana-Mena, 949 F.2d 24, 28 n. 2 (2d Cir.1991). A few circuits hold that an accused is entitled to such an instruction either in certain circumstances, see United States v. Foley, 598 F.2d 1323, 1336–37 (4th Cir.1979); Oertle v. United States, 370 F.2d 719, 726–27 (10th Cir.1966), or whenever the defendant offers character evidence, see United States v. Lewis, 482 F.2d 632, 637 (D.C.Cir.1973).

(8) Circumstantial evidence of character—Accused may prove character of alleged victim. Rule 404(a)(2)(B) presents the second exception to the general rule by providing for the admissibility of evidence of an alleged victim's character and rebuttal evidence. Under Rule 404(a)(2)(B), the accused may offer evidence of the alleged victim's character (in the form of reputation or opinion testimony) to show that the alleged victim acted in conformity with his character. See United States v. Gulley, 526 F.3d 809, 817–19 (5th Cir.2008) (allowing reputation evidence, but excluding specific acts evidence); United States v. Gregg, 451 F.3d 930, 933–35 (8th Cir.2006)(same); United States v. Smith, 230 F.3d 300, 307–08 (7th Cir.2000) (same). Typically, this exception is invoked when the defendant claims he acted in self-defense and offers evidence of the alleged victim's violent character to prove the alleged victim was the first aggressor. E.g., United States v. Emeron Taken Alive, 262 F.3d 711 (8th Cir.2001); United States v. Keiser, 57 F.3d 847, 852–57 (9th Cir.1995).

In cases involving alleged sexual misconduct, Rule 412 governs the admissibility of evidence concerning the alleged victim's other sexual behavior or sexual predisposition.

(9) Circumstantial evidence of alleged victim's character—Prosecution response. Once the accused has offered evidence of the victim's bad character to support a claim of self-defense or provocation, Rule 404(a)(2)(B) allows the prosecution to offer rebuttal evidence in two different ways. First, the prosecution may offer evidence of the alleged victim's peaceable character (in the form of reputation or opinion testimony). Rule 404(a)(2)(B)(i). Second, the prosecution may offer evidence regarding the same trait of the defendant's character (also by reputation or opinion testimony). Rule 404(a)(2)(B)(ii). Thus, if an accused offers evidence of the alleged victim's violent character, the prosecution may offer evidence of the accused's violent character. Rule 404(a)(2)(C) contains a special provision for homicide cases. In such cases, the prosecution may offer evidence of the alleged victim's peaceable character in response to any kind of evidence that the alleged victim was the aggressor.

(10) Character of alleged victim—Communicated character. Under one theory of self-defense, an accused may claim that his knowledge of the alleged victim's violent character and acts contributed to his reasonable belief that the immediate use of force was necessary to protect himself. This self-defense theory does not implicate Rule 404(a)(2)(B) because the evidence concerning the alleged victim is not being offered to prove he acted in conformity with his character on that occasion. Rather, it is being used to prove the accused's state of mind. United States v. Gregg, 451 F.3d 930, 935 (8th Cir.2006). Note that unless the accused was aware of the alleged victim's violent character or acts, they would not be relevant to his claimed fear. United States v. Drapeau, 644 F.3d 646, 655 (8th Cir.2011) (requiring "pre-incident knowledge of the evidence"). Communicated character evidence may also be relevant to the defense of other claims, such as a civil action charging the use of excessive force.

> **Example.** In United States v. Saenz, 179 F.3d 686, 688–89 (9th Cir.1999), defendant sought to introduce evidence that he knew that his victim had recently been carrying brass knuckles and a length of pipe and that the victim had attempted to seriously injure a relative because the relative slighted him. The court of appeals held such evidence admissible, stating, "a defendant claiming self-defense may show his own state of mind by testifying that he knew of the victim's prior acts of violence."

(11) Application of exceptions to civil cases. Some courts interpreted the original version of Rule 404(a)—despite its use of the terms "accused" and "prosecution"—as allowing civil litigants to invoke, in limited instances, the first two exceptions to the character evidence rule. See, e.g., Perrin v. Anderson, 784 F.2d 1040, 1044 (10th Cir.1986); Bolton v. Tesoro Petroleum Corp., 871 F.2d 1266, 1277 (5th Cir.1989). Rule 404(a) was amended in 2006 to reject these rulings, and Rule 404(a)(2) states explicitly that these exceptions apply only in criminal cases.

(12) Exception for character of witness. Rule 404(a)(3) provides a third exception to the general prohibition against character evidence to show conformity. Evidence of a witness's character may be offered for impeachment and rehabilitation purposes in accordance with the dictates of Rules 607 through 609.

CROSS-REFERENCES

Common Objections (Chapter 3)

18. Character evidence inadmissible

Checklists and Foundations (Chapter 4)

2. Character Evidence

Treatises

3 Graham, Handbook of Federal Evidence §§ 404:1–404:4 (9th ed. 2020)

1 McCormick, Evidence §§ 186–189, 191–194 (8th ed. 2020)

22B Wright and Graham, Federal Practice and Procedure §§ 5231–5241 (2d ed. 2017)

Rule 404(b). Other Crimes, Wrongs, or Acts

(b) Other Crimes, Wrongs, or Acts.

> **(1)** *Prohibited Uses.* Evidence of any other crime, wrong, or act is not admissible to prove a person's character in order to show that on a particular occasion the person acted in accordance with the character.

(2) ***Permitted Uses.*** This evidence may be admissible for another purpose, such as proving motive, opportunity, intent, preparation, plan, knowledge, identity, absence of mistake, or lack of accident.

(3) ***Notice in a Criminal Case.*** In a criminal case, the prosecutor must:

    (A) provide reasonable notice of any such evidence that the prosecutor intends to offer at trial, so that the defendant has a fair opportunity to meet it;

    (B) articulate in the notice the permitted purpose for which the prosecutor intends to offer the evidence and the reasoning that supports the purpose; and

    (C) do so in writing before trial—or in any form during trial if the court, for good cause, excuses lack of pretrial notice.

AUTHORS' COMMENTS

(1) Scope and purpose of Rule 404(b). Rule 404(b)(1) echoes Rule 404(a)'s prohibition of the use of character evidence to prove conforming character, specifying that evidence of "a crime, wrong, or other act" is not admissible for this purpose. But Rule 404(b)(2) then provides that evidence of a crime, wrong, or other act may be admissible when it is offered to prove something other than character, and offers a smorgasbord of possible alternative uses for such evidence. Rule 404(b) is thus a rule of inclusion, not exclusion. United States v. Benjamin, 711 F.3d 371, 380 (3d Cir.2013).

Rule 404(b)(1) "reflects the revered and longstanding policy that . . . an accused is tried for *what* he did, not *who* he is." United States v. Caldwell, 760 F.3d 267, 276 (3d Cir.2014) (emphasis in original). Permitting the introduction of "other crimes" evidence (particularly in a criminal case) poses the danger that the jury will view it as reflecting on the party's character and reach a verdict because it has concluded that the party is a bad person deserving of punishment. United States v. Linares, 367 F.3d 941, 945–46 (D.C. Cir.2004). Protection against such a danger comes from four sources: (1) from adherence to the command of Rule 404(b) that such evidence may be admitted only for a non-character purpose; (2) from the relevancy requirement embraced in Rule 402; (3) from Rule 403; and (4) from the use of limiting instructions. Huddleston v. United States, 485 U.S. 681, 691–92, 108 S.Ct. 1496, 1502 (1988). See United States v. Gomez, 763 F.3d 845, 860–61 (7th Cir.2014) (discussing proper instruction). The requirement that other crimes evidence may be admitted only for a non-character purpose means that proponents of such evidence "must do more than conjure up a proper purpose—they must also establish a chain of inferences no link of which is based on a propensity inference." United States v. Smith, 725 F.3d 340, 345 (3d Cir.2013); United States v. Gomez, 763 F.3d 845, 856, 860 (7th Cir.2014).

Because the ban on character evidence is based largely on concerns about prejudice to a defendant whose character is being impugned, some circuits have held that Rule 404(b) should apply differently to other-act evidence offered to prove a non-party's character. See Ermini v. Scott, 937 F.3d 1329, 1342 (11th Cir.2019) (noting circuit precedent that Rule 404(b) does not apply to evidence of non-party's character but stating it seems to "flatly contradict" text of rule); United States v. Espinoza, 880 F.3d 506 (9th Cir.2018) (standard of admissibility not as restrictive when defendant offers evidence of third-party's character).

Since December 1, 2020, Rule 404(b)'s notice requirement has been located in Rule 404(b)(3) and has been mandatory. See Authors' Comments 404(b)(4) and 404(b)(11).

(2) Other crimes, wrongs, or acts—Generally; Admissibility standard by circuit. Although often referred to as "other crimes" evidence, Rule 404(b) makes clear that the other crime, wrong, or act need not have been criminal, much less have resulted in an arrest or conviction. United States v. Scott, 677 F.3d 72, 78 (2d Cir.2012) ("Rule 404(b) extends to non-criminal acts") (citing cases). Nor is it necessary that the other act have occurred prior to the one for which the accused is being tried. United States v. Briley, 770 F.3d 267, 275 (4th Cir.2014) ("Rule 404(b) permits the admission of evidence of not only prior but also subsequent acts."); United States v. Curley, 639 F.3d 50, 51 (2d Cir.2011) (citing cases).

Example—Subsequent other crime. In a prosecution of an insurance broker for defrauding insureds and insurers, evidence of the defendant's false answers on applications he subsequently filed for his license renewal were held admissible as evidence of his consciousness of guilt. United States v. Shenker, 933 F.2d 61, 63 (1st Cir.1991).

Any other crimes evidence offered under Rule 404(b) must be probative of the non-character purpose for which it is offered.

> **Example—Inadmissible.** In United States v. Forcelle, 86 F.3d 838 (8th Cir.1996), defendant was charged with mail fraud in relation to his use of company monies to pay for a portion of a drag-racing chassis and a portion of a beach-front house. The court of appeals held that the trial court improperly admitted evidence that defendant had stolen platinum scrap from the company. As this was entirely distinct from the charged crimes, it was probative only as evidence of the defendant's character.

With one exception, each circuit has announced a test for admitting other bad acts evidence under Rule 404(b). Many of these tests incorporate factors that merely restate relevancy requirements or the Rule 403 balancing standard. The Seventh Circuit recently abandoned its four-part test "in favor of a more straightforward rules-based approach." United States v. Gomez, 763 F.3d 845, 853 (7th Cir.2014).

CA1:

(1) other bad act must have "special relevance" to an issue in the case such as intent or knowledge, and must not include "bad character or propensity as a necessary link in the inferential chain;" and

(2) evidence may still be excluded if its probative value is substantially outweighed by the danger of unfair prejudice. United States v. Lopez-Cotto, 884 F.3d 1, 13 (1st Cir.2018).

CA2:

(1) other bad act must be offered for a proper purpose;

(2) evidence must be relevant to a disputed issue;

(3) probative value of the evidence must substantially outweigh the danger of unfair prejudice; and

(4) the court must administer an appropriate limiting instruction. United States v. Cadet, 664 F.3d 27, 32 (2d Cir.2011).

CA3:

(1) other-acts evidence must be proffered for a non-propensity purpose;

(2) the evidence must be relevant to the identified non-propensity purpose;

(3) its probative value must not be substantially outweighed by the danger of unfair prejudice; and

(4) it must be accompanied by a limiting instruction, if requested. United States v. Repak, 852 F.3d 230, 241 (3d Cir.2017).

CA4:

(1) other bad act must be relevant to an issue, such as an element of an offense, and must not be offered to establish the general character of the defendant;

(2) evidence must be necessary in the sense that it is probative of an essential claim or element of the offense;

(3) evidence must be reliable; and

(4) probative value of the evidence must not be substantially outweighed by confusion or unfair prejudice. United States v. Cole, 631 F.3d 146, 154 (4th Cir.2011).

CA5:

(1) other bad act evidence must be offered for a purpose other than proving the defendant's propensity to commit crimes;

(2) unfair prejudice associated with the evidence must not substantially outweigh its probative value. United States v. Gutierrez-Mendez, 752 F.3d 418, 423 (5th Cir.2014).

CA6:

(1) sufficient evidence must exist that crime, wrong, or other act occurred;

(2)   crime, wrong, or other act must be offered for a proper purpose, that is, must be probative of a material issue other than character;

(3)   evidence must pass Rule 403 balancing test. United States v. Barnes, 822 F.3d 914, 920 (6th Cir.2016).

CA7:

Rejects special test. See United States v. Gomez, 763 F.3d 845, 853 (7th Cir.2014).

CA8:

(1)   prior bad act must be relevant to a material issue;

(2)   prior bad act must be proved by a preponderance of the evidence;

(3)   evidence must be higher in probative value than in prejudicial effect; and

(4)   prior bad act must be similar in kind and close in time to the crime charged. United States v. Wright, 866 F.3d 899, 904 (8th Cir.2017).

CA9:

(1)   other bad act must tend to prove material point in issue;

(2)   other bad act must not be too remote in time;

(3)   other bad act must be proven with evidence sufficient to show the act was committed: and

(4)   if admitted to prove intent, other bad act must be similar to the offense charged. United States v. Charley, 1 F.4th 637, 647 (9th Cir.2021).

CA10:

(1)   other bad act must be introduced for a proper purpose;

(2)   evidence must be relevant;

(3)   the court must make a Rule 403 determination whether the probative value of the similar act is substantially outweighed by its potential for unfair prejudice; and

(4)   upon request, the court must give a proper limiting instruction. United States v. Benford, 875 F.3d 1007, 1012 (10th Cir.2017).

CA11:

(1)   the evidence must be relevant to an issue other than the defendant's character;

(2)   sufficient proof must be presented to allow a jury to find by a preponderance of the evidence that the defendant committed the extrinsic act; and

(3)   the probative value of the evidence must not be substantially outweighed by the risk of unfair prejudice. United States v. Green, 873 F.3d 846, 858 (11th Cir.2017).

CADC:

(1)   other bad act must be probative of a material issue other than character; and

(2)   probative value of the evidence must not be substantially outweighed by its potential prejudice. United States v. Miller, 895 F.2d 1431, 1434 (D.C. Cir.1990).

    (3) Procedure—Burden of proof; limiting instructions. The admissibility of other crimes evidence is a question of conditional relevancy under Rule 104(b). Thus, the judge need only find that the jury could reasonably conclude by a preponderance of the evidence that the defendant committed or is responsible for the other crime, wrong, or act. Huddleston v. United States, 485 U.S. 681, 689–90, 108 S.Ct. 1496, 1501 (1988); United States v. Riddle, 103 F.3d 423, 433 (5th Cir.1997). If the accused was convicted of the extraneous offense, the standard will obviously be met. The conditional relevancy standard may, however, be met with a far lesser showing of proof. Indeed, the fact that the defendant was previously tried for and acquitted of the other crime does not bar its use under Rule 404(b). Dowling v. United States, 493 U.S. 342, 350, 110 S.Ct. 668, 673 (1990).

When the judge concludes that the evidence is admissible, the defendant is entitled, upon timely request, to an instruction limiting the jury's consideration of the extraneous offense evidence to the purpose or purposes for which it was admitted. See Huddleston v. United States, 485 U.S. 681, 691–92, 108 S.Ct. 1496, 1502 (1988); United States v. McGill, 815 F.3d 846, 889 (D.C. Cir.2016) ("a proper Rule 404(b) jury instruction should identify the evidence at issue and the particular purpose for which a jury could permissibly use it, rather than providing an incomplete description of the evidence are issue and an undifferentiated laundry list of evidentiary uses"), cert. denied, 138 S.Ct. 58 (2017). For an example of what one court of appeals termed an "admirable instruction," see United States v. Gilbert, 181 F.3d 152, 159–60 (1st Cir.1999).

(4) Procedure—Articulation of purpose; stipulations. Determining the admissibility of other crimes evidence requires the proponent and court to focus on the purpose for which the evidence is offered. Effective December 1, 2020, prosecutors are required to provide defendants with reasonable notice if they intend to offer other crimes evidence at trial. See Authors' Comment 404(b)(11). In this notice, prosecutors must articulate "the permitted purpose for which the prosecutor intends to offer the evidence and the reasoning that supports the purpose." This latter requirement codifies a practice many appellate courts have for some time strongly advised or even required. See, e.g., United States v. Moore, 641 F.3d 812, 823 (7th Cir.2011) (court must explain rationale for admitting evidence and identify applicable Rule 404(b) exception); United States v. Caldwell, 760 F.3d 267, 276–77 (3d Cir.2014) (proponent must identify non-propensity purpose for evidence and explain how evidence is relevant to that purpose); United States v. Murphy, 241 F.3d 447, 452–53 (6th Cir.2001) (both proponent and court should identify specific purpose for which evidence is offered); United States v. Youts, 229 F.3d 1312, 1318 (10th Cir.2000) (prior to deciding whether to admit evidence, court must articulate specific purpose for which evidence is offered and inferences to be drawn from evidence); United States v. Morley, 199 F.3d 129, 133 (3d Cir.1999) (proponent must articulate chain of inferences). This requirement should discourage prosecutors (and trial courts) from the often-criticized practice of reciting as grounds for admission the "laundry list" of permissible uses contained in Rule 404(b)(2). E.g., United States v. Brown, 765 F.3d 278, 294 (3d Cir.2014); United States v. Patterson, 20 F.3d 809, 813 n.3 (10th Cir.1994); United States v. Kern, 12 F.3d 122, 125 n.3 (8th Cir.1993).

The Supreme Court has held that a defendant may not render other crimes evidence inadmissible by stipulating to the element of the crime to which the other crimes proof is directed. This is the message of Old Chief v. United States, 519 U.S. 172, 117 S.Ct. 644 (1997), even though the unusual circumstances in *Old Chief* impelled the Court to create an exception to this general rule. Old Chief was prosecuted for being a felon in possession of a firearm. He offered to stipulate to the fact of his prior conviction. Since the prosecution could fully establish the defendant's status as a convicted felon through the stipulation and had no need to establish the exact nature of Old Chief's prior conviction, the Court held that the prosecution should not have been permitted to adduce the name and nature of his prior conviction.

The Court, however, distinguished this situation from the typical case in which the prosecution seeks to prove evidence of other crimes "on some issue other than status (i.e., to prove 'motive, opportunity, intent, preparation, plan, knowledge, identity, or absence of mistake or accident,' Rule 404(b))." Id. at 190, 117 S.Ct. at 654. In such instances, the Court affirmed the prosecution's ability to "prove its case free from any defendant's option to stipulate the evidence away." Id. See, e.g., United States v. Tan, 254 F.3d 1204, 1213 (10th Cir.2001) (citing and quoting other cases); United States v. Hill, 249 F.3d 707, 712 (8th Cir.2001) ("several other circuits have recognized that *Old Chief* eliminates the possibility that a defendant can escape the introduction of past crimes under Rule 404(b) by stipulating to the element of the crime at issue").

Nevertheless, at least some courts emphasize that the admissibility of other crimes evidence depends on whether it bears on an issue actually in dispute. See, e.g., United States v. Siddiqui, 699 F.3d 690, 702 (2d Cir.2012) ("A defendant may, however, forestall the admission of Rule 404(b) evidence by advancing a theory that makes clear that the object the 404(b) evidence seeks to establish, while technically at issue, is not really in dispute. * * * For example, a defense theory that the defendant did not commit the charged act effectively removes issues of intent and knowledge from the case."); United States v. Caldwell, 760 F.3d 267, 276–77 (3d Cir.2014) (proponent must identify non-propensity purpose for evidence and explain how evidence is relevant to that purpose); United States v. Bell, 516 F.3d 432, 441–42 (6th Cir.2008) (prior crime evidence not admissible to prove absence of mistake where defendant contended he never possessed the substances seized by police, not that he was mistaken as to their illegality). But see United States v. Smith, 741 F.3d 1211, 1225 (11th Cir.2013) ("There is '[a]mple precedent . . . in this circuit finding that a not guilty plea in a drug conspiracy case . . . makes intent a material issue and opens the door to admission of prior drug-related offenses as highly probative, and not overly prejudicial, evidence of a defendant's intent.' ") (quoting United States v. Calderon, 127 F.3d 1314, 1332 (11th Cir.1997)).

(5) Other purposes—Intent. The reasoning and holdings in cases concerning intent also apply to proof of other states of mind such as knowledge, and overlap with the use of such evidence to rebut claims of mistake or accident. Arguably, such use often violates the prohibition on the use of character evidence to prove conforming conduct. Assume the charge is theft by deception and that, to prove that the accused did not intend to pay when he ordered the goods, the prosecution offers witnesses to testify about other transactions where the defendant failed to pay for goods or services. This evidence normally tends to prove the defendant's fraudulent intent only because the jury may infer (a) the defendant's dishonest character and (b) that the defendant acted in conformity with that dishonest character on the occasion in question. Yet the courts routinely admit such evidence, seldom acknowledging—and often denying—that it often involves a prohibited use of character evidence.

> **Example.** In United States v. Henthorn, 864 F.3d 1241 (10th Cir.2017), the defendant was tried for the first-degree murder of his second wife. She died after falling from a cliff while hiking with the defendant in a remote site. The trial court admitted evidence that the defendant's first wife died when she was crushed under a car while she and the defendant were changing a tire on the side of a remote road. The appellate affirmed, holding the evidence tended to prove the defendant's intent, motive, and plan without requiring an inference about defendant's character. The court agreed with the district court's observation that "a string of improbable incidents is unlikely to be the result of chance."

> **Example.** In United States v. Gellene, 182 F.3d 578, 594–96 (7th Cir.1999), the defendant, an attorney, was charged with fraudulently make false statements in a bankruptcy case. He admitted the falsity of the statements, but denied that he made them with the requisite fraudulent intent. Therefore, the court of appeals held that the trial court properly allowed the prosecution to offer evidence that (1) the defendant had misrepresented his status as a member of the bar of one district court when he applied to become a member of the bar of another district court, and (2) that he falsely represented himself to be a member of the New York bar for almost nine years. Defendant's intent to deceive concerning his bar status was similar enough in nature to the charged offenses to be probative.

> **Example.** In United States v. York, 933 F.2d 1343, 1350 (7th Cir.1991), the defendant was tried for using the mails in an attempt to defraud an insurer. His scheme allegedly involved killing his partner and torching their tavern in an effort to collect on her life insurance policy. The trial court admitted evidence that the defendant had previously murdered his wife and collected on her life insurance policy. The court of appeals affirmed, stating that the inference that two such episodes could not be the vagaries of chance had nothing to do with a subjective assessment of the defendant's character. In reality, the conclusion that the episodes could not be the vagaries of chance meant that they were the product of a malevolent character.

Other crimes evidence is often most probative when the primary issue in dispute is the party's state of mind. This is particularly true when little or no dispute exists as to the party's actions.

> **Example—Admissible.** In United States v. Boone, 828 F.3d 705 (8th Cir.2016), the defendant was charged with willfully depriving an arrestee of his right to be free from the use of unreasonable force by an officer. Because the defendant contended that he did not intend to injure the victim, the court held the prosecution was properly allowed to offer evidence of the defendant's unreasonable use of force on another arrestee five years earlier.

> **Example—Admissible.** In United States v. Valenzuela, 57 F.4th 518 (5th Cir.2023), defendant was stopped while crossing into the United States from Mexico. Border officials found methamphetamine and fentanyl hidden in her car. To disprove defendant's claim that she did not know drugs were in her car, the prosecution proved that, seventeen years before, defendant was convicted for smuggling drugs into the country. In that instance, the drugs were hidden in her car and defendant professed ignorance of the drugs' presence. The court of appeals affirmed the admission of the prior incident.

Many courts of appeals routinely hold that extrinsic offense evidence is admissible to prove intent in drug cases. E.g., United States v. Dunnican, 961 F.3d 859, 874 (6th Cir.2020) ("We have 'repeatedly recognized that prior drug-distribution evidence is admissible [under Rule 404(b)] to show intent to distribute.'" (quoting United States v. Ayoub, 498 F.3d 532, 548 (6th Cir.2007)); United States v. Watson, 766 F.3d 1219, 1237 (10th Cir.2014) ("Our court has time and again held that past drug-related activity is admissible other-acts evidence under Rule 404(b) to prove * * * knowledge or intent"); United States v. Misher, 99 F.3d 664, 670 (5th Cir.1996) ("it is settled in this Circuit that Rule 404(b) permits the admission of other crime evidence when a defendant places his intent at issue in a drug conspiracy case by pleading not guilty"). But see United States v. Gomez, 763 F.3d 845, 858–59 (7th Cir.2014) (distinguishing between admissibility in cases requiring prosecution to prove intent to distribute—e.g., conspiracy or possession with intent to distribute—and those requiring only proof of general intent—e.g., drug distribution); United States v. McBride, 676 F.3d 385, 395–99 (4th Cir.2012) (evidence of prior involvement in sale of crack cocaine not admissible to prove charged crime of possessing cocaine with intent to distribute); United States v. Miller, 673 F.3d 688, 696 (7th Cir.2012) ("admission of prior drug crimes to prove intent to commit present drug crimes has become too routine").

While the relevance of the other crimes evidence to the defendant's intent often requires some degree of similarity between the two crimes, the degree of similarity required is ordinarily not as great as that required when the other crime is offered to prove identity. United States v. Luna, 21 F.3d 874, 878 n. 1 (9th Cir.1994). See United States v. Davis, 154 F.3d 772, 779 (8th Cir.1998) ("the degree of similarity required necessarily depends on the purpose for which the past acts evidence is admitted").

(6) Other purposes—Motive. Although motive itself is rarely an element of a crime, evidence of motive is often probative of the accused's guilt. Because it does not involve the use of character to prove conformity, other crimes evidence may be used to prove motive under Rule 404(b).

The other crimes may themselves provide the motive for committing the charged crime. Proof of the other crimes may help establish why this particular person is likely to have committed the crime. Where identity is not an issue, other crimes evidence may tend to prove the defendant's state of mind.

Example—Admissible. In United States v. Earls, 704 F.3d 466, 470–72 (7th Cir.2012), defendant was charged with obtaining a passport in another's name and fleeing to Panama. Evidence that the defendant faced three state felony charges with a potential penalty of sixty years in prison was admissible to show his motive for obtaining the fraudulent passport and fleeing.

Example—Admissible. In United States v. Moon, 802 F.3d 135, 144 (1st Cir.2015), defendant was charged with being a felon in possession of a firearm. The court held that evidence of the defendant's drug dealing was admissible to prove his motive to possess (and therefore his possession of) the gun found in defendant's bedroom.

Example—Admissible. In United States v. Lafond, 783 F.3d 1216 (11th Cir.2015), defendants, who were prison inmates, were charged with murdering another inmate. The prosecution was permitted to present evidence that the defendants belonged to a white supremacist gang whose members believed white inmates should not share a cell with a black inmate. This provided the motive for their attack on their victim, a white inmate who had refused to take any action to have his black cellmate replaced.

Other crimes may also be admissible where they are reflective and therefore probative of the defendant's motive.

Example—Admissible. In United States v. Berckmann, 971 F.3d 999 (9th Cir.2020), the court properly admitted evidence of other assaults by defendant against his wife. These were probative of his feelings toward his wife and therefore were admissible to prove that he intended to assault and strangle her.

(7) Other purposes—Identity. A common basis for admitting other crimes evidence is to show, via a *modus operandi* theory, that the accused was the person who committed the charged crime. This requires a showing that the crime or its perpetrator and the other crime share distinctive characteristics that evince "a 'unique pattern or signature' linking the other conduct to the alleged offense." United States v. Edwards, 26 F.4th 449, 454 (7th Cir.2022). If the accused is shown to have committed the other crime, it is more likely that he committed this one. Of course, this use of other crimes evidence applies only if identity is an issue in the case.

The *modus operandi* theory works only if the two crimes share distinctive characteristics. United States v. Simpson, 479 F.3d 492, 498 (7th Cir.2007). A showing that they share features that are generic to the type of crime committed is insufficient.

Example—Inadmissible. In United States v. Luna, 21 F.3d 874, 881 (9th Cir.1994), a bank robbery prosecution, the government was erroneously permitted to introduce evidence of two other bank robberies in which the defendant was allegedly involved. The court of appeals held that the features common to the crimes were largely generic to "takeover" bank robberies and were insufficiently distinctive in nature.

Example—Admissible. In United States v. Robinson, 161 F.3d 463, 466–68 (7th Cir.1998), the court pointed to numerous similarities between two bank robberies that made them "clearly distinctive from the thousands of other bank robberies committed each year." In both robberies, the robber donned an orange ski mask before entering, carried a distinctive duffel bag in one hand and a handgun in the other, vaulted over the teller counter and demanded money, emptied the teller drawers by himself after putting down the handgun, and used a blue Chevrolet Cavalier as a getaway car.

The degree of similarity in the characteristics must be substantial, but cannot be reduced to any formula. United States v. Shumway, 112 F.3d 1413, 1420 (10th Cir.1997) (listing elements relevant to "signature quality"). Courts should focus primarily on the similarities between the charged offense and the other crimes rather than the dissimilarities, as no two crimes are ever committed in precisely the same way. United States v. Powers, 978 F.2d 354, 361 (7th Cir.1992). Proximity in time and location between the charged and extrinsic offenses may also be important. United States v. Carroll, 207 F.3d 465, 469 (8th Cir.2000).

Example—Admissible. In United States v. Sanchez, 988 F.2d 1384, 1393–94 (5th Cir.1993), evidence of the defendant's participation in another transaction was admissible where both transactions involved the sale in front of the same house of heroin in pink balloons and where, in both instances, the defendant used a primer gray Volkswagen bug and was accompanied by the apparent owner of the car.

(8) Other purposes—List not exclusive. The purposes listed in Rule 404(b)(2) for which other crimes evidence may be offered is not exhaustive. United States v. Sanchez, 118 F.3d 192, 195 (4th Cir.1997). The following are among the other purposes, listed and unlisted, for which other crimes evidence may be offered:

- To prove absence of mistake. E.g., King v. Ahrens, 16 F.3d 265, 269 (8th Cir.1994) (defendant's license suspension for over-prescribing Percodan offered to prove his omission of prescription from medical chart was deliberate; but evidence excluded under Rule 403).

- To demonstrate a common plan or scheme. E.g., United States v. DeCicco, 370 F.3d 206 (1st Cir.2004) (previous attempt by defendant to burn down same building that defendant now charged with burning down); Lewis v. United States, 771 F.2d 454, 456 (10th Cir.1985) (burglary of garage to obtain equipment used to commit charged burglary of post office). See Becker v. ARCO Chemical Co., 207 F.3d 176, 195–97 (3d Cir.2000) (stressing that charged and extrinsic offenses must both constitute steps toward same final goal).

- Where the charged offense and the other crimes are inextricably intertwined See Authors' Comment 404(a)(9).

- To show knowledge. E.g., United States v. Cassell, 292 F.3d 788, 793 (D.C. Cir.2002) (to prove unlawful possession, evidence that defendant possessed "the same or similar things at other times is often quite relevant to his knowledge and intent with regard to the crime charged"). But there must be "a logical connection between the knowledge gained as a result of the commission of the prior act and the knowledge at issue in the charged act." United States v. Martin, 796 F.3d 1101, 1106 (9th Cir.2015).

• To show opportunity or capacity. E.g., United States v. Cruz-Garcia, 344 F.3d 951 (9th Cir.2003) (cohort's six prior drug convictions admissible to rebut prosecution's theory that cohort was too dumb to plan drug deal without defendant's help).

• To show consciousness of guilt. E.g., United States v. Castleman, 795 F.3d 904, 914–16 (8th Cir.2015) (killing witness); United States v. Rocha, 916 F.2d 219, 241 (5th Cir.1990) (threat against witness).

• To support or rebut a claim of entrapment. E.g., United States v. Thomas, 134 F.3d 975 (9th Cir.1998) (allowing defendant to introduce evidence of good character to prove lack of criminal predisposition); United States v. Knox, 112 F.3d 802, 810–12 (5th Cir.1997), aff'd in relevant part en banc, 120 F.3d 42 (5th Cir.1997); United States v. Emerson, 501 F.3d 804, 812–13 (7th Cir.2007) (allowing prosecution to introduce evidence of defendant's bad character to prove criminal predisposition).

• To rebut a duress defense. E.g., United States v. Verduzco, 373 F.3d 1022, 1029 (9th Cir.2004) (citing cases).

(9) Intrinsic offenses. Evidence of another offense is admissible when it is inextricably intertwined with the charged offense. United States v. Kupfer, 797 F.3d 1233, 1238 (10th Cir.2015). This occurs primarily in two situations: (1) where the other offense constitutes a part of the transaction that serves as the basis for the criminal charge and (2) when a coherent and comprehensible story of the charged crime cannot be told without mentioning the other offense. See United States v. Sumlin, 956 F.3d 879, 889–90 (6th Cir.2020) (intrinsic acts are those that are part of single criminal episode); United States v. Brizuela, 962 F.3d 784, 795 (4th Cir.2020) ("for evidence of uncharged conduct to be admissible to 'complete the story' of a charged offense, the evidence must be probative of an integral component of the crime on trial or provide information without which the factfinder would have an incomplete or inaccurate view of other evidence or of the story of the crime itself"); United States v. Loftis, 843 F.3d 1173, 177–78 (9th Cir.2016). See, e.g., Elliot v. Turner Construction Co., 381 F.3d 995, 1003–04 (10th Cir.2004) (worker injured in construction of bridge permitted to prove series of negligent acts by defendant in construction of bridge to prove defendant's overall lack of planning for the project). But see United States v. Green, 617 F.3d 233, 248–49 (3d Cir.2010) (criticizing inextricably intertwined test as "vague, overbroad, and prone to abuse," and recognizing two categories of intrinsic offenses); United States v. Gorman, 613 F.3d 711, 719 (7th Cir.2010) (declaring that "inextricable intertwinement doctrine has outlived its usefulness"); United States v. Bowie, 232 F.3d 923, 927–29 (D.C. Cir.2000) (surveying case law and criticizing broad interpretation of "intrinsic offense").

(10) Rule 403. Rule 403 balancing "is an integral step toward a determination of admissibility" under Rule 404(b). King v. Ahrens, 16 F.3d 265, 269 (8th Cir.1994). Among the factors courts should consider are the following:

• The strength of the evidence of the other crime. E.g., United States v. Bradley, 5 F.3d 1317, 1320–21 (9th Cir.1993).

• The need for the evidence. United States v. Varoudakis, 233 F.3d 113, 122 (1st Cir.2000).

• The proximity in time of the other crime. E.g., United States v. Fields, 871 F.2d 188, 198 (1st Cir.1989).

• The degree of similarity of the other crime. E.g., United States v. Aguilar-Aranceta, 58 F.3d 796, 801–02 (1st Cir.1995).

• The efficacy of a limiting instruction. Huddleston v. United States, 485 U.S. 681, 691–92, 108 S.Ct. 1496, 1502 (1988).

(11) Notice. Before December 1, 2020, in a criminal case, the prosecution had to provide reasonable notice of any other crimes evidence it intended to introduce at trial only if the accused requested such notice. Now, an accused no longer needs to make such a request. Rule 404(b)(3)(A) requires a prosecutor to provide reasonable notice of any other-crime evidence the prosecutor intends to introduce. See United States v. Crow Ghost, 79 F.4th 927, 934 (8th Cir.2023); United States v. Perez-Tosta, 36 F.3d 1552, 1560–62 (11th Cir.1994) (discussing factors for determining reasonableness of notice). Rule 404(b)(3)(C) requires the prosecutor ordinarily to provide this notice in writing before trial. But the court may, for good cause, allow the prosecutor to provide the notice during trial and in any form. See, e.g., United States v. Lopez-Gutierrez, 83 F.3d 1235, 1240–41 (10th Cir.1996) (finding good cause where government first learned of evidence one day before trial and trial court took steps to ensure defendant would be able to effectively cross-examine witness). Finally, Rule 404(b)(3)(B) requires more than just notice of intent. The prosecutor must articulate both (1) the "permissible purpose" for which the evidence will be offered and (2) how the evidence tends to prove that permissible purpose without relying on an inference about the accused's character. E.g., United States v. Abarca, 61 F.4th 578, 580–81 (8th Cir.2023) (providing defendant with copy of witness's pretrial interview did not comply with (3)(B) requirement because it provided notice only of general nature of testimony). The notice requirement does not apply to offenses that are inextricably intertwined with the charged offense ("intrinsic" offenses). E.g., United States v. Mahdi, 598 F.3d 883, 891 (D.C. Cir.2010).

CROSS-REFERENCES

Common Objections (Chapter 3)

64.   Other crimes evidence; insufficient notice of intent to offer
65.   Other crimes evidence not adequately proven
66.   Other crimes evidence not admissible to prove character
67.   Other crimes evidence offered for an undisputed point

Treatises

3 Graham, Handbook of Federal Evidence § 404:5 (9th ed. 2020)

1 McCormick, Evidence §§ 190–190.11 (8th ed. 2020)

22B Wright and Graham, Federal Practice and Procedure §§ 5242–5259 (2d ed. 2017)

Rule 405. Methods of Proving Character

(a)   **By Reputation or Opinion.** When evidence of a person's character or character trait is admissible, it may be proved by testimony about the person's reputation or by testimony in the form of an opinion. On cross-examination of the character witness, the court may allow an inquiry into relevant specific instances of the person's conduct.

(b)   **By Specific Instances of Conduct.** When a person's character or character trait is an essential element of a charge, claim, or defense, the character or trait may also be proved by relevant specific instances of the person's conduct.

AUTHORS' COMMENTS

(1)   **Scope and purpose of Rule 405.** Rule 405 prescribes the permissible methods of proving the character or trait of character of a person. It must be viewed in relation to Rule 404, which severely restricts the use of character evidence in any form for the purpose of proving a person's conduct on a particular occasion.

(2)   **Character in issue versus character used circumstantially.** A person's character may be relevant in either of two ways:

(a)   *Character in issue.* A trait of the person's character may be, in itself, an ultimate issue in the case under the governing substantive law ("an essential element of a charge, claim, or defense"). This relatively rare situation is known as "character in issue." The most important example of character in issue in practice arises in the so-called "negligent entrustment" case. If plaintiff contends that defendant was negligent in entrusting a dangerous instrumentality to a particular servant, the trait of incompetence of the servant to handle the instrumentality safely is an element of the claim. In re Aircrash In Bali, Indonesia, 684 F.2d 1301, 1314–15 (9th Cir.1982); Crawford v. Yellow Cab Co., 572 F.Supp. 1205, 1210 (N.D.Ill.1983).

(b)   *Character used circumstantially (character to prove conduct).* A trait of the person's character, though not an element of a charge, claim, or defense, may be logically relevant for the circumstantial inference that the person acted in a particular way on a particular occasion. For example, it is not an element of a charge of murder that the defendant is a violent person. United States v. Gulley, 526 F.3d 809, 819 (5th Cir.2008). But his violent or peaceable disposition would be logically relevant to whether he committed the murder, because a violent man is at least somewhat more likely to commit a murder than a peaceable man.

Rule 404(a) generally forbids the circumstantial use of character evidence, with three listed exceptions. Rule 404 does not restrict proof of character when it is in issue. Advisory Committee's Note to Rule 404.

(3) Three methods of proof: reputation, opinion, specific instances of conduct. Rule 405 prescribes three methods of proving character: reputation, opinion, and specific instances of conduct. When character is in issue, any or all three methods may be used.

Example. In entrapment defense, defendant's lack of predisposition to commit the offense is an element and a trait of his character; therefore, trial court erred in excluding defendant's evidence of his lack of criminal or arrest record. United States v. Thomas, 134 F.3d 975, 978–80 (9th Cir.1998).

When character is permitted to be shown circumstantially under one of the exceptions in Rule 404(a), only reputation and/or opinion evidence may be used; specific instances of conduct may not be proved for the purpose of establishing the pertinent trait.

Example. "[E]vidence of the victim's aggressive character may be admissible * * * to establish that the victim was the aggressor. * * * However, Fed. R. Evid. 405 limits the type of character evidence to reputation or opinion evidence unless the character or trait of character is an essential element of the charge, claim or defense. * * * [T]he use of evidence of a victim's violent character to prove that the victim was the aggressor is circumstantial use of character evidence. * * * Therefore, Bautista could have introduced evidence of Carillo's reputation for aggressiveness, but he could not introduce specific instances of aggressive conduct." United States v. Bautista, 145 F.3d 1140, 1152 (10th Cir.1998).

Relevant specific instances of conduct may, however, be addressed on cross-examination of a reputation or opinion witness, in order to test the witness's credibility.

(4) Reputation. A reputation witness must be qualified by showing that the witness has a sufficient acquaintance with the person, the community in which he has lived or worked, and the circles in which he has moved to speak with authority of the terms in which he is generally regarded. United States v. Watson, 669 F.2d 1374, 1381 (11th Cir.1982). If the reputation testimony is offered on the issue of the accused's character with regard to the charged offense, negative reputation after the charge is not likely to be relevant because it may be tainted by gossip accompanying the charge. United States v. Curtis, 644 F.2d 263, 268 (3d Cir.1981).

(5) Opinion; experts. As with reputation, a witness must have sufficient familiarity to be qualified to express an opinion as to a person's character. United States v. Koessel, 706 F.2d 271, 275 (8th Cir.1983) (witness who had met person only once not qualified). Rule 405(a) embraces expert as well as lay opinion as to a person's traits. United States v. Roberts, 887 F.2d 534, 536 (5th Cir.1989); United States v. Hill, 655 F.2d 512, 516–17 (3d Cir.1981); United States v. Staggs, 553 F.2d 1073, 1075 (7th Cir.1977).

(6) Cross-examination of reputation or opinion witness concerning specific instances of conduct. A witness who has testified in reputation or opinion form as to the character of a person may be asked on cross-examination about relevant specific instances of the person's conduct. The form of the question may be either "have you heard?" or "do you know?," regardless of whether the form of the direct testimony was opinion or reputation. United States v. Scholl, 166 F.3d 964, 974 (9th Cir.1999); S.E.C. v. Peters, 978 F.2d 1162, 1170 (10th Cir.1992); Advisory Committee's Note to Rule 405.

(7) Cross-examination of reputation or opinion witness concerning specific instances of conduct—Purpose. The purpose of the "have you heard" inquiries is twofold. If the witness has not heard of the matter, the extent of the witness's knowledge is called into question. If the witness admits having heard of the damaging matter, then the witness's standard for characterizing a character or reputation as "good" is challenged. United States v. Hewitt, 663 F.2d 1381, 1390–91 (11th Cir.1981).

(8) Cross-examination of reputation or opinion witness concerning specific instances of conduct—Good-faith basis, relevancy to particular trait. There are "two important limitations upon judicial discretion in admitting inquiries concerning such prior misconduct: first, a requirement that the prosecution have some good-faith factual basis for the incidents inquired about, and second, a requirement that the incidents inquired about are relevant to the character traits involved at trial." United States v. Wells, 525 F.2d 974, 977 (5th Cir.1976). It is not sufficient as to the first requirement that the prosecutor have a good faith belief that the incidents occurred; there must also be a good faith belief that the events are of a type that are likely to become a matter of general knowledge or reputation in the community. United States v. Monteleone, 77 F.3d 1086, 1090 (8th Cir.1996).

> **Example—Admissible.** Prosecution made required showing of good faith by offer of letter of reprimand. United States v. Bright, 588 F.2d 504, 512 (5th Cir.1979).

> **Example—Admissible.** Affidavit from F.B.I. agent that defendant told agent she committed act was adequate basis for questions. United States v. Alvarez, 860 F.2d 801, 828 (7th Cir.1988).

> **Example—Admissible.** In prosecution for conspiracy to evade federal gasoline taxes, witnesses who testified to defendant's good character for veracity and honesty could be asked whether they had heard about pending state court indictment of defendant for evasion of state gasoline taxes. United States v. West, 58 F.3d 133, 141 (5th Cir.1995).

> **Example—Admissible.** Witness who testified defendant had good reputation for truth and honesty was properly cross-examined concerning defendant's prior convictions for filing false unemployment claim and making false statement to the police. United States v. Grady, 665 F.2d 831, 834 n. 3 (8th Cir.1981).

> **Example—Inadmissible.** Testimony to good character for peaceableness does not justify cross-examination about arrests for drunkenness and traffic violations. United States v. George, 778 F.2d 556, 565 (10th Cir.1985).

> **Example—Inadmissible.** Testimony to good reputation for peaceableness does not justify cross-examination about instances of lying. United States v. Curtis, 644 F.2d 263, 268 (3d Cir.1981).

> **Example—Inadmissible.** Although Government may have had good faith basis to believe that defendant had lied before a grand jury, it did not have a good faith belief that the alleged perjury was likely to have become a topic of discussion in the community, because of the secrecy of grand jury proceedings; therefore, it was reversible error to permit questions on the subject during cross-examination of defendant's good character witness. United States v. Monteleone, 77 F.3d 1086, 1090 (8th Cir.1996).

> **Example—Inadmissible.** Improper for prosecutor to cross-examine witness, who had testified to defendant's law abiding reputation, concerning defendant's sales of manuals on how to convert semiautomatic weapons into fully automatic and a book on how to make explosives; sale of the materials was not unlawful. United States v. Holt, 170 F.3d 698, 701–02 (7th Cir.1999).

(9) Cross-examination of reputation or opinion witness concerning specific instances of conduct—Extrinsic proof not permitted. If the witness answers in the negative concerning a specific instance of conduct, neither the act nor the witness's knowledge of it may be shown by extrinsic evidence; the cross-examiner must abide the witness's answer. United States v. Ling, 581 F.2d 1118, 1120–21 (4th Cir.1978); United States v. Benedetto, 571 F.2d 1246, 1250 (2d Cir.1978).

(10) Cross-examination of reputation or opinion witness concerning specific instances of conduct—Hypothetical question assuming guilt of charged offense improper. It is improper to ask the character witness if his or her opinion would change if the witness assumed the act or acts for which the accused is on trial. United States v. Guzman, 167 F.3d 1350, 1352 (11th Cir.1999); United States v. Mason, 993 F.2d 406, 409 (4th Cir.1993) (citing many other cases). "Asking a character witness whether he has heard of some of the defendant's alleged misbehavior is arguably appropriate," however, "because if the witness has not heard of the behavior, then he may be perceived by the jury as not attuned to the community and the defendant's reputation, and his effectiveness as a character witness is undermined." United States v. Smith-Bowman, 76 F.3d 634, 636 (5th Cir.1996). Some circuits have held that a guilt-assuming hypothetical may be used to cross-examine an opinion witness but not a reputation witness. United States v. Guerrero, 665 F.3d 1305, 1312 (D.C.Cir.2012); United States v. Kellogg, 510 F.3d 188, 192–97 (3d Cir.2007). Defense counsel may open the door to guilt-assuming hypotheticals on cross by asking the character witness on direct whether his or her opinion would change in light of the allegations under trial. United States v. Hough, 803 F.3d 1181, 1192 (11th Cir.2015).

(11) Cross-examination of reputation or opinion witness concerning specific instances of conduct—Limiting instruction. The jury should be instructed that they are to consider any incidents brought out in cross-examination only as bearing on the credibility and weight of the witness's testimony. United States v. Apfelbaum, 621 F.2d 62, 65 (3d Cir.1980).

(12) Rebuttal. Where character is not an essential element of a charge, claim, or defense, Rule 405(a) restricts proof to reputation or opinion evidence. Accordingly, if an accused offers reputation or opinion testimony as to his good character under Rule 404(a)(1), prosecutorial rebuttal evidence is likewise limited to reputation or opinion form, and may not include proof of particular instances of conduct such as prior convictions. United States v. Hazelwood, 979 F.3d 398, 410 (6th Cir.2020); United States v. Herman, 589 F.2d 1191, 1197 (3d Cir.1978); United States v. Reese, 568 F.2d 1246, 1251 (6th Cir.1977).

CROSS-REFERENCES

Common Objections (Chapter 3)

17. Character evidence in form of opinion testimony
19. Character evidence, specific acts inadmissible
20. Character witness, improper cross-examination as to specific acts
21. Character witness not qualified to testify in the form of reputation or opinion

Treatises

3 Graham, Handbook of Federal Evidence §§ 405:1–405:2 (9th ed. 2020)

1 McCormick, Evidence §§ 186–187, 189, 191 (8th ed. 2020)

22B Wright & Graham, Federal Practice and Procedure §§ 5261–5269 (2d ed. 2017)

Rule 406. Habit; Routine Practice

Evidence of a person's habit or an organization's routine practice may be admitted to prove that on a particular occasion the person or organization acted in accordance with the habit or routine practice. The court may admit this evidence regardless of whether it is corroborated or whether there was an eyewitness.

AUTHORS' COMMENTS

(1) Scope and purpose of Rule 406. Rule 406 provides that evidence of a person's habit or an organization's routine practice is admissible to prove that the person or organization acted in conformity with that habit or routine practice on a particular occasion. The rule thus places habit and routine practice on a different footing than character evidence. Habit and routine practice evidence is admissible to prove conforming conduct; character evidence ordinarily is not. Therefore, admissibility often hinges on whether the particular conduct is classified as habit (or routine practice) or character.

(2) Habit vs. character. Habit is much narrower than character. Character refers to "a generalized description of a person's disposition, or of the disposition in respect to a general trait, such as honesty, temperance, or peacefulness." McCormick, Evidence § 195 (5th ed. 1999). In contrast, habit has been described as "one's regular response to a repeated specific situation," a "regular practice of meeting a particular kind of situation with a specific type of conduct," or "uniformity" of or "semi-automatic" behavior. McCormick, Evidence § 195 (5th ed. 1999); Camfield v. City of Oklahoma City, 248 F.3d 1214, 1232 (10th Cir.2001); Simplex, Inc. v. Diversified Energy Sys., 847 F.2d 1290, 1293 (7th Cir.1988). Some courts seem to restrict habit evidence to "nonvolitional activity that occurs with invariable regularity." Weil v. Seltzer, 873 F.2d 1453, 1460 (D.C.Cir.1989). One prominent treatise summarizes the salient difference between habit and character by noting that "one could reasonably testify to having observed habitual behavior, but character is almost always a matter of opinion." 22 Wright and Graham, Federal Practice and Procedure § 5233, at 354 (1978).

In deciding whether the conduct in question qualifies as a habit, two distinct issues must be resolved. First, even if the conduct is shown to have occurred with frequency and regularity, is it the type of conduct that could constitute a habit? Second, even if it is the type of conduct that could constitute a habit, has sufficient evidence been produced to establish that the particular person possessed the habit?

(3) Habit vs. non-habit. Two factors influence whether a type of conduct can qualify as habit. The first is the specificity of the conduct; the more particularized the conduct, the more likely it will qualify as habit. Second, the more a person seems to engage in the conduct without thinking about it, the more likely it will be deemed to qualify as habit. United States v. Angwin, 271 F.3d 786, 799 (9th Cir.2001). Thus, courts have little difficulty concluding that repetitive, particularized conduct that does not require conscious thought (e.g., braking with one's left foot, latching a particular fence) qualifies as habit. Conduct that is less particularized and seems to involve a greater degree of conscious thought presents more difficulty for courts.

The following are examples of the types of conduct that have been held to constitute a habit:

- A judge's practice of not giving instructions to court clerk before a matter is filed and judge looked at the law. Doe by next friend Rothert v. Chapman, 30 F.4th 766, 769–71 (8th Cir.2022).

- A prosecutor's regular practice of sharing court orders with relevant agencies. Howard v. City of Durham, 68 F.4th 934, 950–51 (4th Cir.2023). See also United States v. Arredondo, 349 F.3d 310, 315 (6th Cir.2003) (lawyer's regular practice of passing settlement offers to clients).

- The deceased driver's habit of wearing a seat belt. Babcock v. General Motors Corp., 299 F.3d 60, 66 (1st Cir.2002).

- A mechanic's habit of drinking on the job. Loughan v. Firestone Tire & Rubber Co., 749 F.2d 1519, 1522–23 (11th Cir.1985).

- The deceased's habit of invariably reacting with extreme violence to any contact with police officers. Perrin v. Anderson, 784 F.2d 1040, 1045–46 (10th Cir.1986).

The following are examples of the types of conduct that have been held not to constitute a habit:

- That a state investment officer had never before conditioned an award of state business upon the making of a political contribution did not constitute a habit of refraining from extortion. United States v. Troutman, 814 F.2d 1428, 1455 (10th Cir.1987).

- That truck drivers accept jobs without checking the fuel tanks of the trucks. United States v. Rangel-Arreola, 991 F.2d 1519, 1523 (10th Cir.1993).

- In a malpractice suit, evidence that the defendant doctor prescribed steroids to five patients other than the plaintiff and led them to believe that the steroids were antihistamines. Weil v. Seltzer, 873 F.2d 1453 (D.C.Cir.1989).

(4) Proof of habit—Method. Rule 406 does not specify how habit may be proved. It is well accepted, however, that both opinion testimony and evidence of specific instances of conduct are acceptable methods of proof. Maynard v. Sayles, 817 F.2d 50, 52 (8th Cir.1987) ("The foundation for Rule 406 evidence can be established by a lay opinion."), opinion vac'd and judgment aff'd by equally divided court, 831 F.2d 173 (8th Cir.1987); Weil v. Seltzer, 873 F.2d 1453, 1461 (D.C.Cir.1989) (specific instances). The court may limit the number of witnesses and amount of testimony offered to establish the habit. Perrin v. Anderson, 784 F.2d 1040, 1046 (10th Cir.1986) (court permitted only four of eight proffered witnesses so as to prevent unfair prejudice).

(5) Proof of habit—Sufficiency. The proponent of habit evidence must prove the existence of a pattern of repeated behavior. This involves consideration both of (1) the frequency of the given behavior and (2) the regularity of the behavior. Evidence of the number of times that a person engaged in the conduct is only part of the equation; the other part is the number of occasions on which the person might have engaged in the conduct. United States v. Angwin, 271 F.3d 786, 799 (9th Cir.2001); Weil v. Seltzer, 873 F.2d 1453, 1461 (D.C.Cir.1989).

    Example—Habit established. In Crawford v. Tribeca Lending Corp., 815 F.3d 121, 124–25 (2d Cir.2016), an attorney testified that he had conducted more than a thousand loan signings and always showed the borrower the documents to be signed one-by-one and briefly explained the significance of each. The court held that this qualified as habit evidence and was admissible to prove how he performed on the occasion in question.

    Example—Habit not established. In Leonard v. Nationwide Mutual Ins. Co., 499 F.3d 419, 442 (5th Cir.2007), evidence that, over the course of a decade, an insurance agent told five customers that they should not purchase flood insurance unless they lived in a flood-prone area did "not remotely qualify or quantify as a habit within the meaning of Rule 406."

Example—Routine practice established. In Mobil Exploration and Producing U.S., Inc. v. Cajun Const. Serv., Inc., 45 F.3d 96, 100 (5th Cir.1995), evidence regarding the manner in which the defendant loaded its trucks in over 3400 instances was held sufficient to establish that routine practice of the defendant.

Example—Routine practice not established. In United States v. West, 22 F.3d 586, 591–92 (5th Cir.1994), the defendant attempted to prove that it was the routine practice of the FDIC to allow parties to purchase their own discounted notes, held by a failed institution, through third party straw purchasers. The trial court properly excluded the evidence because the defendant failed to make a comparison of the number of transactions in which the FDIC allowed straw purchasers with the number in which it did not.

(6) Routine practice of an organization. Evidence of the customary practice of a business is admissible to prove that the business acted in accordance with that practice on a particular occasion. Hancock v. American Tel. and Tel. Co., 701 F.3d 1248, 1262–64 (10th Cir.2012) (evidence of standard practice followed by installation technicians in obtaining customer acceptance of terms of service admissible to prove that plaintiffs accepted terms of service). Such evidence is often considered even more probative than individual habit evidence. Mobil Exploration and Producing U.S., Inc. v. Cajun Const. Serv., Inc., 45 F.3d 96, 99 (5th Cir.1995). Rule 406 substitutes the term "routine practice" for the more traditional "custom." The common law allowed evidence of routine practice only if it corroborated other evidence that the conduct in question had occurred or if other evidence corroborated that the routine practice was followed on the occasion in question. Rule 406 requires no such corroboration as a prerequisite to the admission of routine practice evidence.

(7) Routine practice—Admissible. The following are examples of conduct that has been held to constitute "routine practice":

• A military base's practice of using base facilities to make authorized retirement gifts. United States v. Sheffield, 992 F.2d 1164, 1169–70 (11th Cir.1993).

• That an insurance company's agents routinely waived written policy conditions. Rosenburg v. Lincoln Am. Life Ins. Co., 883 F.2d 1328, 1336 (7th Cir.1989).

• The City of Cleveland's routine practice of posting notices on condemned properties. First Floor Living LLC v. City of Cleveland, 83 F.4th 445, 456–57 (6th Cir.2023).

(8) Routine practice—Inadmissible. The following are examples of conduct that has been held not to constitute "routine practice":

• Evidence that Johnson & Johnson and some of its subsidiaries paid kickbacks in four countries over ten years where Johnson & Johnson had hundreds of subsidiaries operating in sixty countries. In re DePuy Orthopaedics, Inc., Pinnacle Hip Implant Prod. Liab. Litig., 888 F.3d 753, 785 n.69 (5th Cir.2018).

• Three instances of an Indian tribe approving emergency assistance applications for personal transportation expenses. United States v. Oldbear, 568 F.3d 814, 822 (10th Cir.2009).

(9) Trade custom and industry standards. Evidence of general business customs or industry standards is admissible as bearing on the standard of care to which a particular business enterprise is held and on whether a product is "unreasonably dangerous" in a strict liability case. Anderson v. Malloy, 700 F.2d 1208, 1212 (8th Cir.1983); Griggs v. Firestone Tire & Rubber Co., 513 F.2d 851, 862 (8th Cir.1975). While relevant, however, the general custom or industry standard is not determinative on the issue of negligence or unreasonable dangerousness. Sorrels v. NCL (Bahamas) Ltd., 796 F.3d 1275, 1282 (11th Cir.2015).

CROSS-REFERENCES

Common Objections (Chapter 3)

38. Habit evidence not admissible

Treatises

3 Graham, Handbook of Federal Evidence §§ 406:1–406:4 (9th ed. 2020)

1 McCormick, Evidence § 195 (8th ed. 2020)

23 Wright and Gold, Federal Practice and Procedure §§ 5271–5277 (2d ed. 2018)

Rule 407. Subsequent Remedial Measures

When measures are taken that would have made an earlier injury or harm less likely to occur, evidence of the subsequent measures is not admissible to prove:

- negligence;
- culpable conduct;
- a defect in a product or its design; or
- a need for a warning or instruction.

But the court may admit this evidence for another purpose, such as impeachment or—if disputed—proving ownership, control, or the feasibility of precautionary measures.

AUTHORS' COMMENTS

(1) Scope and purpose of Rule 407. Rule 407 carries on the common-law tradition of excluding evidence of a party's subsequent remedial measures as proof of the party's negligence or culpable conduct. Rule 407 also makes subsequent remedial measure evidence inadmissible to prove a product or design defect or the need for a warning or instruction. The rule is based both on public policy and relevance concerns. The policy is one of encouraging parties to take safety measures. Frye v. CSX Transportation, Inc., 933 F.3d 591, 603–04 (6th Cir.2019). The relevancy concern questions whether evidence of a subsequent remedial measure is a good indicator of a party's liability. Kelly v. Crown Equipment Co., 970 F.2d 1273, 1276 (3d Cir.1992).

(2) Remedial measure defined. A remedial measure is one that—had it been taken before the event that caused an injury or harm—would have made the injury or harm less likely to occur. The following are examples of remedial measures:

- A repair. Stanley v. Amoco Oil Co., 965 F.2d 203 (7th Cir.1992).
- A design change. Flaminio v. Honda Motor Co., Ltd., 733 F.2d 463 (7th Cir.1984).
- Installation of safety features. Baker v. Canadian National/Ill. Central R.R., 536 F.3d 357, 366–67 (5th Cir.2008).
- The firing of or disciplinary action against an employee. Nolan v. Memphis City Schools, 589 F.3d 257, 274 (6th Cir.2009).
- A change in rules or policies. Estate of Hamilton v. City of New York, 627 F.3d 50, 53 (2d Cir.2010); First Security Bank v. Union Pacific Railroad Co., 152 F.3d 877, 881 (8th Cir.1998).
- A new or modified warning. Chlopek v. Federal Ins. Co., 499 F.3d 692, 700 (7th Cir.2007).

Post-accident analyses or studies are generally not considered subsequent remedial measures. Novick v. Shipcom Wireless, Inc., 946 F.3d 735, 739–40 (5th Cir.2020); Brazos River Auth. v. GE Ionics, Inc., 469 F.3d 416, 430–31 (5th Cir.2006); Prentiss & Carlisle Co., Inc. v. Koehring-Waterous Div., 972 F.2d 6, 10 (1st Cir.1992). But see Complaint of Consolidation Coal Co., 123 F.3d 126, 136–37 (3d Cir.1997).

(3) Timing of remedial measure. The remedial measure must be taken after the occurrence of the accident or event that allegedly caused the injury or harm. Thus, a remedial measure taken after a product was purchased, but before the accident or event that caused the alleged injury does not qualify as a subsequent remedial measure. Bogosian v. Mercedes-Benz of North America, Inc., 104 F.3d 472, 481 (1st Cir.1997); Traylor v. Husqvarna Motor, 988 F.2d 729, 733 (7th Cir.1993).

(4) Third party remedial measures. Rule 407 does not bar the admission of remedial measures taken by third parties. A third party will not be deterred from taking a remedial step by the fear that its action will later be used as proof in a case to which it is not a party. Millennium Partners, L.P. v. Colmar Storage, LLC, 494 F.3d 1293, 1302–03 (11th Cir.2007); Diehl v. Blaw-Knox, 360 F.3d 426, 430 (3d Cir.2004) (citing cases). Such evidence may, however, be excluded under Rule 403. See Authors' Comment (10) infra.

(5) Compelled remedial measures. Some courts have held that evidence of a party's own subsequent remedial measure should be admissible when the party was compelled by the government to take the precautionary act. The compulsory nature of the action negates the danger that the party would be deterred from taking it by the fear that it would be used as evidence against it. O'Dell v. Hercules, Inc., 904 F.2d 1194, 1204 (8th Cir.1990) ("An exception to Rule 407 is recognized for evidence of remedial action mandated by superior governmental authority . . . because the policy goal of encouraging remediation would not necessarily be furthered by exclusion of such evidence."); Pineda v. Ford Motor Co., 520 F.3d 237, 246 n.13 (3d Cir.2008) (noting "possible exception"). See, e.g., In re Aircrash in Bali, Indonesia, 871 F.2d 812, 817 (9th Cir.1989) (FAA investigation).

(6) Strict liability cases. A 1997 amendment to Rule 407 resolved the question whether subsequent remedial measure evidence should be treated differently in a products liability case based on a strict liability theory. The rule now expressly provides that such evidence is inadmissible to prove either a product or design defect or the need for a warning or instruction. This codifies the majority position that had evolved when the rule barred the admissibility of subsequent remedial evidence only when offered to prove "negligence or culpable conduct." See Wood v. Morbark Indus., Inc., 70 F.3d 1201, 1206–07 (11th Cir.1995), and cases cited therein.

(7) Admissibility for other purposes—Generally. Rule 407 explicitly provides that subsequent remedial measure evidence may be admissible when offered for some purpose other than to prove negligence or culpable conduct. The rule then supplies a non-exclusive listing of such alternative uses for subsequent remedial measure evidence. The two most widely-used "other purposes"—feasibility and impeachment—are discussed infra. The following are illustrative of less-commonly invoked "other purposes":

- To prove ownership or control. Clausen v. Sea-3, Inc., 21 F.3d 1181, 1189–92 (1st Cir.1994).

- To rebut a defensive theory based upon the condition of the accident scene. Pitasi v. Stratton Corp., 968 F.2d 1558, 1561 (2d Cir.1992).

- Where the defendant has destroyed the relevant object, allegedly as a remedial measure. Albrecht v. Baltimore & Ohio R. Co., 808 F.2d 329, 332 (4th Cir.1987).

Note that the "other purpose" for which the subsequent remedial measure evidence is offered must be controverted. Hull v. Chevron U.S.A., Inc., 812 F.2d 584, 587 (10th Cir.1987) (evidence offered to show control inadmissible where control was not disputed). Although the text of the rule seemingly exempts impeachment from this requirement, a witness's credibility is always subject to dispute and so impeachment automatically meets this requirement.

(8) Admissibility for other purposes—Feasibility. Evidence of a subsequent remedial measure may be offered to prove that such a measure was physically, technologically or economically feasible. E.g., Abernathy v. Eastern Illinois R. Co., 940 F.3d 982, 992–94 (7th Cir.2019) (evidence that railroad bought new tie crane after plaintiff's injury admissible to rebut its contention that cost of repairing or replacing present tie crane was prohibitively high); Donahue v. Phillips Petroleum Co., 866 F.2d 1008, 1013 (8th Cir.1989) (evidence of subsequent warning admissible to rebut contention that it was not feasible to provide warnings).

Feasibility must, however, be in dispute before such evidence is admitted. This effectively allows the party that took the subsequent remedial measure to preclude its admission by choosing not to controvert feasibility. Some courts take the position that a defendant can remove the issue of feasibility from a case only by expressly admitting that a precautionary measure would have been feasible. E.g., Ross v. Black & Decker, Inc., 977 F.2d 1178, 1185 (7th Cir.1992) (feasibility was controverted because defendant failed to stipulate to feasibility, or admit to it in pretrial memorandum or motion). Other courts hold that the defendant must affirmatively contest the feasibility issue before it is deemed to be in dispute. E.g., Gauthier v. AMF, Inc., 788 F.2d 634, 637–38 (9th Cir.1986), amended, 805 F.2d 337 (9th Cir.1986). Under this view, a defendant's silence as to whether a precautionary measure would have been feasible precludes the use of subsequent remedial measure evidence to prove feasibility.

(9) Admissibility for other purposes—Impeachment. Rule 407 lists impeachment as one of the other purposes for which subsequent remedial measure evidence is admissible. Courts have warned, however, that interpreting this "other purpose" too liberally would result in the exception swallowing the rule. E.g., Wilkinson v. Carnival Cruise Lines, Inc., 920 F.2d 1560, 1567 (11th Cir.1991). Such impeachment should be permitted only where the witness either makes factual assertions that are contradicted by the subsequent remedial measure or claims that the product or condition was the "best" or "safest" that it could be. Harrison v. Sears, Roebuck and Co., 981 F.2d 25, 31–32 (1st Cir.1992); McCormick, Evidence § 267 (5th ed. 1999).

Example—Impeachment allowed. In Wood v. Morbark Indus., Inc., 70 F.3d 1201, 1205–08 (11th Cir.1995), plaintiff claimed that a wood chipper manufactured by defendant was defective because its infeed chute was too short. The trial court excluded evidence that after the accident in question (plaintiff's husband had been pulled into the machine and died), defendant had lengthened the infeed chute. But the court of appeals held that once the president of the defendant company testified about the original length chute, "I've said it once and a thousand times, it's the safest length chute you could possibly put on the machine," evidence of the subsequent change should have been admitted for impeachment purposes.

Example—Impeachment allowed. In Petree v. Victor Fluid Power, Inc., 887 F.2d 34, 38–41 (3d Cir.1989), the defendant's expert testified that a particular hazard had been designed out of the product. The court of appeals held that the trial court should have allowed the plaintiff to impeach the expert by questioning him about the defendant's post-accident placement of a decal warning about this danger.

Example—Impeachment not allowed. In Minter v. Prime Equipment Co., 451 F.3d 1196, 1212 (10th Cir.2006), the plaintiff offered evidence that, after plaintiff fell from a scissor lift, the defendant replaced the chainlink entry to the lift with a solid guardrail. The evidence was not admissible for impeachment purposes because the defense contended that the plaintiff fell because he failed to properly latch the chainlink entry and defendant's expert testified only that, when properly latched, a chainlink entry is basically equivalent to a solid guardrail.

Example—Impeachment not allowed. In Kelly v. Crown Equipment Co., 970 F.2d 1273, 1279 (3d Cir.1992), the defendant's expert testified that a forklift's design was excellent and proper. The court disallowed an attempt to impeach the expert with evidence of a subsequent design change, finding that the witness had not testified that the forklift's design was the best or only one possible.

(10) Use of Rule 403. Even when Rule 407 does not bar the introduction of subsequent remedial measure evidence, it may still be ruled inadmissible under Rule 403. The court must weigh the probative value of its permissible use against the danger that it will be impermissibly used as evidence of negligence, culpable conduct, the existence of a defect, or the need for a warning or instruction. E.g., Trull v. Volkswagen of America, Inc., 187 F.3d 88, 96–97 (1st Cir.1999) (excluding evidence of pre-accident design change); Harrison v. Sears, Roebuck and Co., 981 F.2d 25, 31–32 (1st Cir.1992) (impeachment not allowed).

(11) Application of state law in diversity case. In a diversity case, the *Erie* doctrine, see Erie R. Co. v. Tompkins, 304 U.S. 64, 58 S.Ct. 817 (1938), arguably requires the court to resolve the admissibility of subsequent remedial measure evidence by reference to the governing state law rather than Federal Rule 407. See 23 Wright & Graham, Federal Practice and Procedure § 5291, at 157 (1980). The Tenth Circuit has so held. Wheeler v. John Deere Co., 862 F.2d 1404, 1410 (10th Cir.1988); Moe v. Avions Marcel Dassault-Breguet Aviation, 727 F.2d 917, 931–33 (10th Cir.1984). The Third, Fifth and Seventh Circuits have rejected this argument and apply Rule 407. Kelly v. Crown Equipment Co., 970 F.2d 1273, 1277–78 (3d Cir.1992); Flaminio v. Honda Motor Co., Ltd., 733 F.2d 463, 470–72 (7th Cir.1984); Grenada Steel Ind., Inc. v. Alabama Oxygen Co., Inc., 695 F.2d 883, 885 (5th Cir.1983). See also Rosa v. Taser International, Inc., 684 F.3d 941, 948–49 (9th Cir.2012) (dicta). But see Sims v. Great American Life Ins. Co., 469 F.3d 870 (10th Cir.2006) (holding *Erie* inapplicable because Federal Rules are congressional enactment).

CROSS-REFERENCES

Common Objections (Chapter 3)

90.   Subsequent remedial measure

Treatises

3 Graham, Handbook of Federal Evidence § 407:1 (9th ed. 2020)

2 McCormick, Evidence § 267 (8th ed. 2020)

23 Wright and Gold, Federal Practice and Procedure §§ 5281–5291 (2d ed. 2018)

Rule 408. Compromise Offers and Negotiations

(a) Prohibited Uses. Evidence of the following is not admissible—on behalf of any party—either to prove or disprove the validity or amount of a disputed claim or to impeach by a prior inconsistent statement or a contradiction:

(1) furnishing, promising, or offering—or accepting, promising to accept, or offering to accept—a valuable consideration in compromising or attempting to compromise the claim; and

(2) conduct or a statement made during compromise negotiations about the claim—except when offered in a criminal case and when the negotiations related to a claim by a public office in the exercise of its regulatory, investigative, or enforcement authority.

(b) Exceptions. The court may admit this evidence for another purpose, such as proving a witness's bias or prejudice, negating a contention of undue delay, or proving an effort to obstruct a criminal investigation or prosecution.

AUTHORS' COMMENTS

(1) Scope and purpose of Rule 408. Rule 408 excludes evidence that a party (a) offered to compromise a claim or (b) actually compromised a claim, when offered to prove the validity of the claim, the invalidity of the claim, or the amount of damages. The rule is premised primarily on the notion that without this protection parties would be deterred from entering into settlement discussions with their opponents Klauber v. VMware, Inc., 80 F.4th 1, 8 (1st Cir.2023).

Rule 408 may apply even when the claim presently being litigated is not identical to the claim that was the subject of the compromise negotiations. See Lyondell Chemical Co. v. Occidental Chemical Corp., 608 F.3d 284, 295–300 (5th Cir.2010) (surveying case law regarding scope of Rule 408).

(2) Requirement of a dispute. Rule 408 protects only offers to compromise and compromises of claims that are disputed as to either validity or amount. Thus the rule does not protect an offer to pay a claim that is admittedly owed. See Molinos Valle del Cibao, C. por A. v. Lama, 633 F.3d 1330, 1352–54 (11th Cir.2011).

Although the formal commencement of legal proceedings is sufficient to establish the existence of a dispute, neither it nor the threat of legal action is necessary for a dispute to be found. Weems v. Tyson Foods, Inc., 665 F.3d 958, 965 (8th Cir.2011). When the facts fall short of the filing of a lawsuit or the threat of litigation, courts will have to determine on a case-by-case basis whether the offer was made in the context of an existing dispute.

Example—No existing dispute. In MCI Communications Services, Inc. v. Hagan, 641 F.3d 112, 116–17 (5th Cir.2011), the defendant allegedly severed the plaintiff's underground cable. After an employee fixing the cable the next day told the defendant that cable down-time was costing $20,000 per minute, the defendant called his attorney, who then called the plaintiff. The court of appeals said that the trial court's decision to exclude under Rule 408 evidence of what the defendant's attorney said to the plaintiff was erroneous. When the call was made, "there was not yet an actual dispute or a difference of opinion about who caused the damage to MCI's cable and how much the damage was costing MCI."

Example—Existing dispute. In Macsherry v. Sparrows Point, LLC, 973 F.3d 212, 221–24 (4th Cir.2020), the court of appeals held that the trial court improperly admitted a compromise statement made about two months before the plaintiff filed suit. The parties clearly differed over whether the plaintiff was entitled to the commission he sought, and the defendant had already terminated the plaintiff without paying him the commission he claimed he was due.

Ordinary business negotiations are generally not protected. E.g., Deere & Co. v. International Harvester Co., 710 F.2d 1551, 1557 (Fed.Cir.1983) (offer to license uncontested patent not protected).

(3) Must be an offer to compromise. Rule 408 protects statements only if they constitute or are made in pursuit of a compromise. Rodriguez-Garcia v. Municipality of Caguas, 495 F.3d 1, 12 (1st Cir.2007) (letter that would have granted plaintiff reinstatement without condition not protected); Wall Data Inc. v. Los Angeles County Sheriff's Dept., 447 F.3d 769, 783–84 (9th Cir.2006) (memo prepared before settlement discussions began not protected); Lightfoot v. Union Carbide Corp., 110 F.3d 898, 909 (2d Cir.1997). The context and character of the statement or offer must evince some element of concession. Pierce v. F.R. Tripler & Co., 955 F.2d 820, 827 (2d Cir.1992) (factors considered include timing of offer, existence of disputed claim, conditional nature of offer, and presence of counsel).

(4) What is protected. The rule protects the following:

(a) *Offers to settle.* The fact that a party offered to settle a claim cannot be offered against the party as evidence of the validity of its opponent's claim, the invalidity of the party's claim, or the amount of damages.

(b) *Settlements.* The fact that a party settled a claim cannot be offered against that party as evidence of the validity of its opponent's claim, the invalidity of the party's claim, or the amount of damages.

> **Example—Inadmissible.** In McInnis v. A.M.F., Inc., 765 F.2d 240 (1st Cir.1985), plaintiff motorcyclist, injured in a collision with a car, sued the motorcycle manufacturer. To prove the invalidity of plaintiff's claim, the manufacturer introduced evidence that the plaintiff had reached a settlement with the driver of the car before suing the manufacturer. The court of appeals held that the evidence should have been excluded under Rule 408.

The first sentence of Rule 408(a) states that compromise evidence is not admissible "on behalf of any party." The rule thus makes clear that Rule 408 excludes compromise evidence even when a party seeks to admit either its own settlement offer or statements made in settlement negotiations or evidence of a third party's settlement offer or settlement statements, or settlement. See Sheng v. M&TBank Corp., 848 F.3d 78, 84–86 (2d Cir.2017).

(c) *Conduct or statements made in the course of settlement negotiations.* Factual admissions made during settlement negotiations are generally protected by Rule 408 even if they were neither inseparable from the actual offer nor made "hypothetically" or "without prejudice." Ramada Dev. Co. v. Rauch, 644 F.2d 1097, 1106–07 (5th Cir.1981). Under the 2006 amendment, however, some conduct and statements are not protected from subsequent use in criminal cases. See Authors' Comment 408(9).

Rule 408 also may cover materials a party creates specifically for the compromise process, even if not communicated to the other party, Lyondell Chemical Co. v. Occidental Chemical Corp., 608 F.3d 284, 295 (5th Cir.2010) (rule covers "legal conclusions, factual statements, internal memoranda, and the work of non-lawyers and lawyers alike" if intended as part of compromise negotiations); E.E.O.C. v. UMB Bank Financial Corp., 558 F.3d 784, 791 (8th Cir.2009), as well as statements made by non-parties if the parties intended them to be part of the compromise process. Blu-J, Inc. v. Kemper C.P.A. Group, 916 F.2d 637, 641–42 (11th Cir.1990) (independent evaluation prepared by mutual agreement of parties as part of settlement negotiations held inadmissible).

(5) Evidence otherwise discoverable. Before 2006, Rule 408 expressly provided that the rule did "not require the exclusion of any evidence otherwise discoverable merely because it is presented in the course of compromise negotiations." This simply made clear that a party could not immunize evidence from discovery by offering it in compromise negotiations. While statements made during compromise negotiations are protected by Rule 408, the information revealed may still be discovered, and proved through other evidence. See Ramada Dev. Co. v. Rauch, 644 F.2d 1097, 1107 (5th Cir.1981). The 2006 amendment deleted the quoted language from Rule 408, but solely on the ground that it was unnecessary. See Advisory Committee's Note to 2006 Amendment ("The sentence of the Rule referring to evidence 'otherwise discoverable' has been deleted as superfluous.").

(6) Admissible for other purposes. Rule 408 excludes compromise evidence only when it is offered to prove the validity of the claim, the invalidity of the claim, or the amount of damages. Such evidence may be admissible when it is offered for some other purpose, a non-exclusive listing of which is provided in Rule 408. The other purpose for which the evidence is offered must, however, be at issue in the case. The following are illustrative:

- To show the bias, prejudice or interest of a witness. Croskey v. BMW of North America, Inc., 532 F.3d 511, 519 (6th Cir.2008).

- To rebut a claim of undue delay. Freidus v. First Nat'l Bank, 928 F.2d 793, 795 (8th Cir.1991).

- To prove the motive or intent of a party. Bankcard America, Inc. v. Universal Bancard Systems, Inc., 203 F.3d 477, 483–84 (7th Cir.2000); Johnson v. Hugo's Skateway, 949 F.2d 1338, 1345–46 (4th Cir.1991).

- In a suit to enforce the terms of the settlement agreement. Catullo v. Metzner, 834 F.2d 1075, 1079 (1st Cir.1987).

- To prove knowledge. United States v. Austin, 54 F.3d 394, 399–400 (7th Cir.1995).

- To prove an effort to obstruct justice. United States v. Technic Services, Inc., 314 F.3d 1031, 1045 (9th Cir.2002).

- As an indicator of the measure of a litigant's success for purposes of determining the appropriate amount of attorney's fees. Lohman v. Duryea Borough, 574 F.3d 163, 167–68 (3d Cir.2009).

- Where the statement made in the settlement negotiation constitutes the wrongful conduct that is the basis of the claim. Starter Corp. v. Converse, Inc., 170 F.3d 286, 292–94 (2d Cir.1999); Uforma/Shelby Business Forms, Inc. v. N.L.R.B., 111 F.3d 1284, 1293–94 (6th Cir.1997). Cf. PRL USA Holdings, Inc. v. United States Polo Ass'n, Inc., 520 F.3d 109, 112–16 (2d Cir.2008) (holding admissible that plaintiff consented, during settlement discussions regarding various marks, to defendant's use of double horsemen mark where offered to prove estoppel-by-acquiescence defense to trademark infringement claim).

- To prove bad faith. Clerveaux v. East Ramapo Central School District, 984 F.3d 213, 243–44 (2d Cir.2021).

(7) Use as prior inconsistent statement to impeach. Before 2006, courts differed over whether a statement made in compromise negotiations could be offered for impeachment purposes, either as a prior inconsistent statement or to prove a contradiction. Compare, e.g., Cochenour v. Cameron Savings and Loan, F.A., 160 F.3d 1187, 1190 (8th Cir.1998) (statement in letter written by plaintiff, which included settlement demand, that she planned to retire at fifty held admissible to rebut her testimony that she had no plans to retire); with EEOC v. Gear Petroleum, Inc., 948 F.2d 1542, 1545–46 (10th Cir.1991) (excluding settlement letter written by defense counsel that stated age was factor in employee's discharge, offered to impeach deposition testimony of defendant's executives that age was not a factor). A 2006 amendment to the first sentence of Rule 408(a) made clear that compromise evidence could not be used "to impeach through a prior inconsistent statement or contradiction."

(8) Use of Rule 403. Even when Rule 408 does not bar the introduction of compromise evidence, it may still be inadmissible under Rule 403. "[W]hen the issue is doubtful, the better practice is to exclude evidence of compromises or compromise offers." Bradbury v. Phillips Petroleum Co., 815 F.2d 1356, 1364 (10th Cir.1987); e.g., Myers v. Pennzoil Co., 889 F.2d 1457, 1461 (5th Cir.1989) (although admissible for impeachment purposes, evidence excluded under Rule 403).

(9) Applicability in criminal cases. Prior to the 2006 amendment to Rule 408, courts disagreed . . . as to whether Rule 408 precludes the admission in a criminal case of evidence that an accused settled or attempted to settle a related civil claim. Compare, e.g., United States v. Logan, 250 F.3d 350, 366–67 (6th Cir.2001) (inapplicable), with United States v. Arias, 431 F.3d 1327, 1336 (11th Cir.2005) (applicable). The amendment struck a compromise. Rule 408 does not bar the introduction in a criminal case of statements or conduct during compromise negotiations regarding a civil claim made by a government regulatory, investigative, or enforcement agency. The amendment thus draws two distinctions. First, it distinguishes between settlement discussions between private parties and those involving a government regulatory, investigative, or enforcement agency. Conduct and statements made in settlement discussions between private parties are ordinarily protected from later use in criminal cases. United States v. Davis, 596 F.3d 852, 860 (D.C. Cir.2010). Second, when addressing compromise negotiations involving a government regulatory, investigative, or enforcement agency, the rule distinguishes between statements and conduct (such as a direct admission of fault) and an offer or acceptance of a compromise offer. Only the conduct or statements may ordinarily be used in a criminal case. E.g., United States v. Paulus, 894 F.3d

267, 280 (6th Cir.2018) (admitting statement made by defendant in stipulated agreement with state medical board that medical board could conclude he engaged in illegal activity).

The 2006 amendment states only that Rule 408 does not protect a party's conduct or statements. The Advisory Committee's Note to the amendment provides, however, that such evidence may still be excluded under Rule 403.

CROSS-REFERENCES

Common Objections (Chapter 3)

22.   Compromise of or offer to compromise a civil claim

Treatises

3 Graham, Handbook of Federal Evidence § 408:1 (9th ed. 2020)

2 McCormick, Evidence § 266 (8th ed. 2020)

23 Wright and Gold, Federal Practice and Procedure §§ 5301–5315 (2d ed. 2018)

Rule 409. Offers to Pay Medical and Similar Expenses

Evidence of furnishing, promising to pay, or offering to pay medical, hospital, or similar expenses resulting from an injury is not admissible to prove liability for the injury.

AUTHORS' COMMENTS

(1) Scope and purpose of Rule 409. Rule 409 bars the admission of evidence of offers to pay or payments of medical, hospital, or similar expenses when offered as proof of the payor's (or offeror's) liability for the injury. The rule is based on the notion that the law should not discourage or penalize humanitarian gestures or contractual arrangements, such as insurance, that help an injured party before a court has determined legal liability.

(2) What is protected. Rule 409 covers both the fact of payment and offers to pay medical and hospital expenses occasioned by an injury. The rule also refers to "similar" expenses. Presumably this refers to expenses incidental to the medical care and treatment, such as ambulance services, but does not embrace other expenses, such as lost wages or property damage or destruction. 23 Wright and Graham, Federal Practice and Procedure § 5326 (1980).

(3) What is not protected. Evidence of incidental statements or conduct accompanying payment, or such behavior accompanying offers or promises to pay are not protected by Rule 409. Thus, a statement of liability made in conjunction with such an offer is not rendered inadmissible by Rule 409. See Advisory Committee's Note.

(4) Admissibility for other purposes. Unlike Rule 407, dealing with subsequent remedial measures, and Rule 408, dealing with offers of compromise, Rule 409 contains no provision stating that although such evidence is inadmissible when offered to prove liability, it is nevertheless admissible to prove other issues, such as agency, ownership, or control, or for impeachment. Commentators disagree on the significance of this omission. Compare 23 Wright & Graham, Federal Practice and Procedure § 5329 (1980) (arguing that use of term "liability" in Rule 409 logically precludes the use of such evidence to prove the identity of a tortfeasor, or ownership or control) with 1 Graham, Handbook of Federal Evidence § 409.1 (5th ed. 2001) (arguing that such evidence may be admitted if otherwise relevant to a consequential fact). The caselaw is sparse. See Savoie v. Otto Candies, Inc., 692 F.2d 363, 370 n. 7 (5th Cir.1982) (payment of maintenance payments admissible to prove recipient's status as seaman).

CROSS-REFERENCES

Common Objections (Chapter 3)

57.   Medical, hospital, or similar expenses, payment of

Treatises

3 Graham, Handbook of Federal Evidence § 409:1 (9th ed. 2020)

2 McCormick, Evidence § 267 (8th ed. 2020)

23 Wright and Gold, Federal Practice and Procedure §§ 5321–5330 (2d ed. 2018)

Rule 410. Pleas, Plea Discussions, and Related Statements

(a) Prohibited Uses. In a civil or criminal case, evidence of the following is not admissible against the defendant who made the plea or participated in the plea discussions:

(1) a guilty plea that was later withdrawn;

(2) a nolo contendere plea;

(3) a statement made during a proceeding on either of those pleas under Federal Rule of Criminal Procedure 11 or a comparable state procedure; or

(4) a statement made during plea discussions with an attorney for the prosecuting authority if the discussions did not result in a guilty plea or they resulted in a later-withdrawn guilty plea.

(b) Exceptions. The court may admit a statement described in Rule 410(a)(3) or (4):

(1) in any proceeding in which another statement made during the same plea or plea discussions has been introduced, if in fairness the statements ought to be considered together; or

(2) in a criminal proceeding for perjury or false statement, if the defendant made the statement under oath, on the record, and with counsel present.

AUTHORS' COMMENTS

(1) Scope and purpose of Rule 410. Rule 410 protects a defendant who has participated in the plea bargaining process from having his statements and certain pleas later used against him. The rule recognizes the essential role played by plea bargaining. See Blackledge v. Allison, 431 U.S. 63, 71, 97 S.Ct. 1621, 1627 (1977) ("the guilty plea and the often concomitant plea bargain are important components of this country's criminal justice system"). By assuring defendants that their statements and actions will not redound to their detriment, Rule 410 thus facilitates the plea bargaining process.

(2) Protected and unprotected pleas. Rule 410 protects both pleas and statements. The following pleas are protected:

(a) *Guilty plea later withdrawn*. Rule 410(a)(1). If a defendant is permitted to withdraw a plea pursuant to Federal Rule of Criminal Procedure 32(d), the withdrawn plea may not be offered in evidence against him. A guilty plea set aside by an appellate court should be treated as a withdrawn plea. 23 Wright and Graham, Federal Practice and Procedure § 5343 (1980). A guilty plea that is not accepted by the court is merely an offer to plead guilty and should be treated as a statement, not a plea. See Authors' Comment (3) infra.

(b) *Nolo contendere plea later withdrawn*. Rule 410(a)(2).

(c) *Nolo contendere plea not withdrawn*. Rule 410(a)(2). The defining characteristic of the nolo contendere plea is that it may not be used as an admission against the pleading party in subsequent litigation.

A guilty plea that is not withdrawn is left unprotected by Rule 410 and may be used against the defendant in the case at bar or in other litigation.

(3) Protected and unprotected statements. In the interest of fostering free and open plea negotiations, United States v. Davis, 617 F.2d 677, 683 (D.C.Cir.1979), Rule 410 also protects statements made during the course of plea proceedings conducted pursuant either to Federal Rule of Criminal Procedure 11 or any comparable state plea procedure. Rule 410(a)(3). This includes statements made by an accused for the purpose of establishing for the court that a factual basis exists for the plea.

Rule 410(a)(4) also renders inadmissible statements made in the course of plea discussions that fail to result in a guilty plea or that result in a subsequently withdrawn guilty plea. Note, however, that the statements must be made during the course of plea discussions with an attorney for the prosecution. Rule 410, therefore, does not protect the following:

• Statements made to law enforcement officers. E.g., United States v. Mangine, 302 F.3d 819, 822 (8th Cir.2002) (statements to sheriff's lieutenant); United States v. Lewis, 117 F.3d 980, 983–84 (7th Cir.1997) (statements made to state trooper and IRS agent). Statements may be protected, however, if a law enforcement agent has express authority to negotiate a plea on behalf of the prosecutor. United States v. McCauley, 715 F.3d 1119, 1125 (8th Cir.2013).

• Statements made without the intent to negotiate a plea. E.g., United States v. Edelman, 458 F.3d 791, 804–06 (8th Cir.2006) (statements made in hope of avoiding indictment altogether not protected). The accused must believe he is engaged in plea negotiations and this belief must be reasonable. United States v. Merrill, 685 F.3d 1002, 1013 (11th Cir.2012).

Example. In United States v. Hare, 49 F.3d 447, 449–51 (8th Cir.1995), the court held that Rule 410 did not protect statements made by the defendant, an attorney, to IRS agents and the Assistant United States Attorney over a two month period. The statements had been made unconditionally in an effort to cooperate. However, the court also found that Rule 410 did protect statements made after the defendant and his attorney entered into plea discussions with the government.

• Statements made after a plea agreement has been finalized. United States v. Davis, 617 F.2d 677, 684–86 (D.C.Cir.1979) (post-agreement testimony before grand jury not protected where defendant subsequently withdrew plea).

• Statements made during negotiations that result in a final plea of guilty. United States v. Paden, 908 F.2d 1229, 1235 (5th Cir.1990).

(4) Who is protected. Rule 410 renders pleas and statements made in plea discussions and proceedings inadmissible only when offered "against the defendant who made the plea or was a participant in the plea discussions." Thus, a defendant's plea and statements may not later be used against him, either as substantive evidence or for impeachment purposes. United States v. Acosta-Ballardo, 8 F.3d 1532, 1535–36 (10th Cir.1993).

A defendant's plea and statements may, however, be offered against someone other than the defendant. Thus, if otherwise admissible, one person's plea statements may be offered against someone else.

Example. In United States v. Dortch, 5 F.3d 1056, 1067 (7th Cir.1993), one of the defendants called Taylor as a witness. Taylor testified that he had never purchased cocaine from the defendant. The prosecution was permitted to impeach Taylor with inconsistent statements he had made during plea discussions.

(5) Admissibility against government. As Rule 410 prohibits the use of pleas and related statements only when offered against a defendant, it does not bar a defendant from offering evidence that he rejected the prosecution's offer of a plea bargain (to show consciousness of innocence) or of statements made by the prosecution during plea negotiations. Arnold v. Wilder, 657 F.3d 353, 366–67 (6th Cir.2011). But the Eighth Circuit has held such evidence inadmissible under Rule 408. United States v. Alexander, 679 F.3d 721, 732 (8th Cir.2012). But cf. United States v. Biaggi, 909 F.2d 662, 690–91 (2d Cir.1990) (defendant should have been permitted to prove he rejected offer of immunity).

(6) Use of judgments. Rule 410 does not govern the admissibility or procedural effects of convictions based upon pleas of nolo contendere. See, e.g., United States v. Adedoyin, 369 F.3d 337, 343–44 (3d Cir.2004) (admissible to prove defendant had prior felony conviction); Olsen v. Correiro, 189 F.3d 52, 58–62 (1st Cir.1999) (admissible to prove plaintiff had been validly incarcerated); Sharif v. Picone, 740 F.3d 263, 271–72 (3d Cir.2014) (admissible to impeach under Rule 609); Walker v. Schaeffer, 854 F.2d 138, 142–43 (6th Cir.1988) (collateral estoppel). See also Rule 803(22) (hearsay exception for judgments of conviction).

(7) Exceptions. Rule 410(b) creates two exceptions to the general rule of inadmissibility. The first is essentially a rule of optional completeness. A statement made in the course of plea discussions or proceedings is admissible if another such statement has been introduced and fairness dictates that the statement ought to be considered contemporaneously with the already introduced statement. Rule 410(b)(1).

The second exception provides for admissibility in a criminal proceeding for perjury or false statement if the statement was made by the defendant under oath, on the record and in the presence of counsel. Rule 410(b)(2). A defendant may thus be punished for perjurious statements made during a plea proceeding.

(8) Waiver. A defendant may waive the protections of Rule 410, but must do so knowingly and voluntarily. United States v. Mezzanatto, 513 U.S. 196, 115 S.Ct. 797 (1995). The extent of the waiver depends on the language of the proffer or plea agreement. See, e.g., United States v. Elbeblawy, 899 F.3d 925, 934 (11th Cir.2018); United States v. Shannon, 803 F.3d 778, 783 (6th Cir.2015). Some agreements allow the prosecution to freely use a defendant's plea statements during its case-in-chief. E.g., United States v. Elbeblawy, 899 F.3d 925, 934 (11th Cir.2018); United States v. Hall, 877 F.3d 800, 804 (8th Cir.2017). Others limit prosecutors to using such statements to rebut either factual assertions the defendant has made or evidence the defendant has offered. E.g., United States v. Rosemond, 841 F.3d 95, 103, 109–10 (2d Cir.2016) (discussing when factual assertions are or are not sufficient to trigger Rule 410 waiver); United States v. Jimenez-Bencevi, 788 F.3d 7, 16 (1st Cir.2015) (agreement authorized prosecutor to use plea statements only for impeachment).

CROSS-REFERENCES

Common Objections (Chapter 3)

71.   Pleas and plea bargaining

Treatises

3 Graham, Handbook of Federal Evidence § 410:1 (9th ed. 2020)

1 McCormick, Evidence §§ 160; 2 id. § 266 (8th ed. 2020)

23 Wright and Gold, Federal Practice and Procedure §§ 5341–5348 (2d ed. 2018)

Rule 411. Liability Insurance

Evidence that a person was or was not insured against liability is not admissible to prove whether the person acted negligently or otherwise wrongfully. But the court may admit this evidence for another purpose, such as proving a witness's bias or prejudice or proving agency, ownership, or control.

AUTHORS' COMMENTS

(1) Scope and purpose of rule. Rule 411 follows the common-law rule that evidence that a person was or was not insured is inadmissible to prove that the person acted in a negligent or wrongful manner. The rule is based on the notion that whether a person is insured has very little, if any, bearing on the degree of care exercised by the person on a given occasion. On the other hand, the admission of such evidence could be highly prejudicial.

(2) Prohibited use of liability insurance. The rule excludes evidence of liability insurance when offered as proof that the insured (or uninsured) behaved carelessly. Thus, it is inadmissible to prove the insured's (or uninsured's) negligence or comparative negligence. See Advisory Committee's Note.

Evidence that a party lacks insurance is also inadmissible if it constitutes an improper "plea of poverty." Van Bumble v. Wal-Mart Stores, Inc., 407 F.3d 823, 826 (7th Cir.2005).

(3) Admissibility for other purposes. The second sentence of Rule 411 expressly sanctions the use of evidence of liability insurance on issues other than fault. It provides a non-exclusive listing of such alternative uses for liability insurance evidence. The following are illustrative:

• To prove the bias of a witness. Conde v. Starlight I, Inc., 103 F.3d 210, 213–14 (1st Cir.1997). Cf. Ventura v. Kyle, 825 F.3d 876, 882–86 (8th Cir.2016) (holding impermissible questions about insurance to show bias where any connection between witnesses and insurance company were too remote to create risk of bias).

• To establish a trade custom of limiting liability. Posttape Associates v. Eastman Kodak Co., 537 F.2d 751 (3d Cir.1976).

• To establish why a safety inspection was made. Morrissey v. Welsh Co., 821 F.2d 1294, 1305 (8th Cir.1987).

- To prove the existence of an effective contract exculpating the defendants from all risks of loss or damage. B.H. Morton v. Zidell Explorations, Inc., 695 F.2d 347 (9th Cir.1982).

- To contradict a factual assertion made by the policy owner. Wheeling Pittsburgh Steel Corp. v. Beelman River Terminals, Inc., 254 F.3d 706, 717–18 (8th Cir.2001).

Note that Rule 411 bars liability insurance evidence only when it is offered to prove the negligence or wrongful conduct of the insured. Such evidence may be used to prove the liability of a third party.

Example. The plaintiff in a negligent entrustment case may introduce evidence that the defendant hired a driver who was able to obtain personal liability insurance through an assigned risk pool.

(4) Use of Rule 403. Even when Rule 411 does not bar the introduction of liability insurance evidence, it may still be inadmissible, or its admissibility may be limited, under Rule 403. See Charter v. Chleborad, 551 F.2d 246 (8th Cir.1977).

(5) Non-evidentiary use of insurance evidence. Although Rule 411 does not govern the propriety of asking jurors about insurance on voir dire or making reference to insurance during closing argument, courts may certainly consider the extent to which the evidence rule will be undermined if insurance is freely mentioned during other phases of the trial. Courts sometimes exercise their discretion in favor of allowing jurors to be questioned about connections with or interests in an insurance company affected by the litigation. See Socony Mobil Oil Co. v. Taylor, 388 F.2d 586, 589 (5th Cir.1967).

CROSS-REFERENCES

Common Objections (Chapter 3)

50. Insurance

Treatises

3 Graham, Handbook of Federal Evidence § 411:1 (9th ed. 2020)

1 McCormick, Evidence § 201 (8th ed. 2020)

23 Wright and Gold, Federal Practice and Procedure §§ 5361–5369 (2d ed. 2018)

Rule 412. Sex-Offense Cases: The Victim's Sexual Behavior or Predisposition

(a) Prohibited Uses. The following evidence is not admissible in a civil or criminal proceeding involving alleged sexual misconduct:

(1) evidence offered to prove that a victim engaged in other sexual behavior; or

(2) evidence offered to prove a victim's sexual predisposition.

(b) Exceptions.

(1) *Criminal Cases.* The court may admit the following evidence in a criminal case:

    (A) evidence of specific instances of a victim's sexual behavior, if offered to prove that someone other than the defendant was the source of semen, injury, or other physical evidence;

    (B) evidence of specific instances of a victim's sexual behavior with respect to the person accused of the sexual misconduct, if offered by the defendant to prove consent or if offered by the prosecutor; and

    (C) evidence whose exclusion would violate the defendant's constitutional rights.

(2) *Civil Cases.* In a civil case, the court may admit evidence offered to prove a victim's sexual behavior or sexual predisposition if its probative value substantially outweighs the danger of harm to any victim and of unfair prejudice to any party. The court may admit evidence of a victim's reputation only if the victim has placed it in controversy.

(c) Procedure to Determine Admissibility.

(1) *Motion.* If a party intends to offer evidence under Rule 412(b), the party must:

    (A) file a motion that specifically describes the evidence and states the purpose for which it is to be offered;

    (B) do so at least 14 days before trial unless the court, for good cause, sets a different time;

    (C) serve the motion on all parties; and

    (D) notify the victim or, when appropriate, the victim's guardian or representative.

(2) *Hearing.* Before admitting evidence under this rule, the court must conduct an in camera hearing and give the victim and parties a right to attend and be heard. Unless the court orders otherwise, the motion, related materials, and the record of the hearing must be and remain sealed.

(d) Definition of "Victim." In this rule, "victim" includes an alleged victim.

AUTHORS' COMMENTS

(1) **Scope and purpose of Rule 412.** Rule 412, commonly known as the rape shield provision, contains both substantive and procedural terms. Substantively, it limits the admissibility in both civil and criminal cases of evidence of the sexual behavior or predisposition of an alleged victim of sexual misconduct. In criminal cases, such evidence may be offered only in the narrowly circumscribed situations detailed in Rule 412(b)(1). For civil cases, Rule 412(b)(2) provides a new balancing test.

Procedurally, Rule 412(c) includes both a notice requirement and a provision for an in camera hearing on the admissibility of sexual behavior and predisposition evidence.

The rule is based both on relevancy and public policy concerns. The probative value of such evidence is often quite low; in comparison, the danger of unfair prejudice is often quite high. Moreover, the rule is designed to protect the alleged victim against "the invasion of privacy [and] potential embarrassment and sexual stereotyping that is associated with public disclosure of intimate sexual details." United States v. Pablo, 696 F.3d 1280, 1297 (10th Cir.2012). The rule thus seeks to protect the privacy of those victims who pursue legal actions and to encourage others who might otherwise be deterred from pressing their claims to pursue them. See Advisory Committee's Note to 1994 Amendments to Rule 412.

(2) **Relationship to character evidence—Criminal cases.** Rule 404(a)(2)(B) authorizes a defendant to offer evidence of his alleged victim's character in order to prove the alleged victim acted in conformity with that character on the occasion in question. Rule 412 effectively forecloses this option in criminal cases. Neither enumerated exception found in Rule 412(b)(1) involves the use of character evidence, and rarely, if ever, will the constitution compel the admission of evidence of an alleged victim's character.

(3) **Relationship to character evidence—Civil cases.** The exception in Rule 404(a)(2)(B) that permits a defendant to offer evidence of an alleged victim's character to prove the alleged victim acted in accordance with that character applies only in criminal cases. Although the exception in Rule 404(a)(2)(C)—allowing use of a witness's untruthful character to impeach the witness—applies in civil as well as criminal cases, evidence of a witness's sexual behavior is not a legitimate means of proving the witness's untruthful character.

(4) **Types of cases.** Rule 412 applies in all cases that involve alleged sexual misconduct. On the criminal side, this will typically embrace cases in which the defendant faces charges of criminal sexual misconduct (e.g., sexual assault). It also reaches cases in which the defendant is charged with an offense that does not contain sexual misconduct as an element but where the defendant's sexual misconduct is relevant to prove motive or as background evidence.

Example. If a defendant is charged with kidnapping, evidence that he sexually assaulted the victim might be admissible to establish his motive for the kidnapping. Cf. United States v. Galloway, 937 F.2d 542 (10th Cir.1991) (holding earlier version of Rule 412 inapplicable to such facts).

On the civil side, Rule 412 applies in an case in which a person claims to be the victim of sexual misconduct. This includes actions for sexual battery and sexual harassment. Wilson v. City of Des Moines, 442 F.3d 637, 643 (8th Cir.2006); Wolak v. Spucci, 217 F.3d 157, 160 (2d Cir.2000).

In both civil and criminal cases, Rule 412 applies even if the alleged victim or the person accused of the sexual misconduct is neither the complainant nor the defendant. For example, Rule 412 protects witnesses called to testify to other acts of sexual misconduct by a defendant from being interrogated about their past sexual behavior.

(5) Types of evidence generally inadmissible. Rule 412(a) generally bars the admissibility of two categories of evidence, whether offered as substantive evidence or for impeachment purposes. See United States v. Azure, 845 F.2d 1503, 1506 (8th Cir.1988).

Other sexual behavior. Rule 412(a)(1) proscribes the use of any evidence offered to prove that an alleged victim engaged in other sexual behavior. This includes:

- All activities that involve actual physical contact such as sexual intercourse and sexual contact.

- All activities that imply sexual intercourse or contact. See, e.g., United States v. Galloway, 937 F.2d 542, 548 (10th Cir.1991) (victim's use of contraceptives); United States v. Duran, 886 F.2d 167 (8th Cir.1989) (victim had illegitimate child).

- Statements that indicate a desire to engage in sexual activity. United States v. Papakee, 573 F.3d 569, 573 (8th Cir.2009).

- Fantasies or dreams that imply sexual activity. See Advisory Committee's Note.

- Reputation or opinion evidence about the alleged victim.

The rule only reaches evidence of "other" sexual behavior. The Advisory Committee's Note indicates that evidence of sexual behavior intrinsic to the alleged sexual misconduct is not "other" sexual behavior and may thus be admissible.

Sexual predisposition. Rule 412(a)(2) renders inadmissible evidence offered to prove the sexual predisposition of an alleged victim. This includes evidence relating to the alleged victim's mode of dress, speech and life-style if offered for its sexual connotation.

Prior false claims are not considered sexual behavior. United States v. Kettles, 970 F.3d 637, 642 (6th Cir.2020); Redmond v. Kingston, 240 F.3d 590, 592 (7th Cir.2001). Although not rendered inadmissible by Rule 412, their admissibility must still be tested under Rules 404, 405 and 608; See Boggs v. Collins, 226 F.3d 728, 736–43 (6th Cir.2000).

(6) Exceptions—Criminal cases. Rule 412(b)(1) creates for criminal cases a number of exceptions to the general rule prohibiting evidence of an alleged victim's sexual behavior or predisposition. Whether an accused has presented sufficient evidence to establish the applicability of any of the exceptions is a question of conditional relevancy governed by Rule 104(b). United States v. Platero, 72 F.3d 806 (10th Cir.1995).

(a)   The accused may offer evidence of specific instances of an alleged victim's sexual behavior to prove that someone other than the accused was the source of semen, injury, or other physical evidence. Rule 412(b)(1)(A). The other sexual behavior must, of course, have occurred at such a time that it actually tends to rebut or explain the prosecution's physical evidence.

Example—Admissible. In United States v. Begay, 937 F.2d 515, 519–23 (10th Cir.1991), the prosecution offered evidence that a physical examination of the eight-year old alleged victim revealed an unusually large hymenal opening and a vaginal abrasion. The trial court erroneously refused to allow the defendant to prove that the alleged victim had been sexually assaulted three times a few months preceding the charged sexual assault, even though the prosecution's expert conceded (outside the jury's presence) that the injuries could have been caused by such earlier assaults.

Example—Inadmissible. In United States v. Torres, 937 F.2d 1469, 1473–74 (9th Cir.1991), the defense offered evidence that the alleged victim had engaged in sexual intercourse six months after the alleged assault in an effort to prove that someone else was the source of the semen found on her panties. The trial court properly excluded this evidence because the panties were in police custody at the time the other sexual act occurred.

(b) The accused may offer evidence of specific instances of sexual behavior by the alleged victim with respect to the accused to prove consent. Rule 412(b)(1)(B). E.g., United States v. Mack, 808 F.3d 1074, 1084 (6th Cir.2015) (exception applies only to victim's conduct with defendant, and not to victim's conduct with others).

(c) The prosecution may offer evidence of specific instances of sexual behavior between the alleged victim and the accused. Rule 412(b)(1)(B). This is designed to allow the prosecution to offer evidence of uncharged sexual activity to the extent permitted under Rule 404(b).

(d) Evidence of other sexual behavior or predisposition is admissible when exclusion would violate the accused's constitutional right to confrontation or due process. Rule 412(b)(1)(C). This generally requires that the evidence be highly probative, typically to rebut an aspect of the prosecution's case or to impeach a witness. See generally United States v. Brandon, 64 F.4th 1009, 1015–19 (8th Cir.2023).

> **Example—Admissible.** In Olden v. Kentucky, 488 U.S. 227, 109 S.Ct. 480 (1988), the Supreme Court held that the defendant had a constitutional right to introduce evidence of the complainant's relationship with another man in order to show that she had a motive to falsely accuse the defendant of rape.

> **Example—Admissible.** In United States v. Zephier, 989 F.3d 629 (8th Cir.2021), the court held that the trial court erred in excluding evidence that the sexual assault complainant had previously been sexually assaulted. The prosecution had presented expert testimony that sexual assault victims often experience difficulties like drug use and cutting behaviors and evidence that the complainant had started using drugs again and cutting herself. In light of that evidence, the defendant was constitutionally entitled to present evidence of an alternative explanation for the complainant's drug use and cutting behavior.

> **Example—Admissible.** In Redmond v. Kingston, 240 F.3d 590 (7th Cir.2001), the trial court refused to allow the defendant in a sexual assault case to prove that his 15-year-old accuser had made a prior false charge of being sexually assaulted in order to get her mother's attention. The court of appeals held that the exclusion of this evidence violated the defendant's Confrontation Clause rights.

> **Example—Inadmissible.** In United States v. Palms, 21 F.4th 689, 703–04 (10th Cir.2021), a sex-trafficking prosecution, the trial court did not err in excluding evidence that the victim had previously engaged in prostitution. The appellate stated that "evidence that a sex trafficking victim previously engaged in prostitution is irrelevant to whether that victim was forced or coerced into working as a prostitute at a later date."

(7) **Exceptions—Civil cases.** Rule 412(b)(2) provides that evidence of an alleged victim's sexual behavior or predisposition may be admitted in civil cases only if a stringent balancing test is met. The probative value of the evidence must substantially outweigh the danger of harm to any victim and of unfair prejudice to any party. This reverses the balancing test ordinarily applied under Rule 403. Rodriguez-Hernandez v. Miranda-Velez, 132 F.3d 848, 856 (1st Cir.1998).

Before the rules were restyled in 2011, Rule 412(b)(2) stipulated that the evidence of an alleged victim's sexual behavior or predisposition must also be "otherwise admissible." That requirement was deleted from the text of restyled Rule 412(b)(2) because the drafters believed it unnecessary. The general principle of the rules is that evidence deemed admissible by one rule may nevertheless be rendered inadmissible by another rule. See Minutes of May 1–2, 2008 Meeting of the Advisory Committee on Evidence Rules. Thus, Rule 404(a) may still be invoked to exclude evidence of an alleged victim's sexual behavior if offered to prove the alleged victim acted in accordance with his or her character. What Rule 412(b)(2) sanctions is the use of sexual behavior or predisposition evidence when it is offered for some other purpose.

> **Example.** In Meritor Savings Bank, FSB v. Vinson, 477 U.S. 57, 69, 106 S.Ct. 2399, 2406–07 (1986), the Supreme Court held that evidence of an alleged victim's "sexually provocative speech or dress" may be admissible in a workplace harassment case as bearing on whether the victim found particular sexual advances unwelcome.

Example. In Stampf v. Long Island R. Co., 761 F.3d 192, 203 (2d Cir.2014), plaintiff sued defendant for malicious prosecution, alleging that defendant had falsely filed criminal charges that plaintiff had sexually touched defendant. The trial court properly allowed plaintiff to offer evidence of defendant's sexual conduct on the job, including her participation in sexually provocative touching. The court held that this evidence was highly probative as to whether the defendant was motivated to accuse the plaintiff by actual malice or genuine fear for her own safety.

Evidence of an alleged victim's reputation is admissible only if the alleged victim places the reputation in controversy.

(8) Procedural requirements. Rule 412 conditions the admissibility of sexual behavior and predisposition evidence on compliance with certain procedural requirements. A party that wishes to offer such evidence must file a written motion at least fourteen days prior to trial, unless the court for good cause relaxes the time limit. See, e.g., United States v. Ramone, 218 F.3d 1229, 1234–37 (10th Cir.2000) (exclusion of evidence due to failure to comply with notice requirement did not violate defendant's constitutional rights); United States v. Rouse, 111 F.3d 561, 569 (8th Cir.1997) (defendant failed to give adequate notice of intent to offer sexual behavior evidence). But see LaJoie v. Thompson, 217 F.3d 663 (9th Cir.2000) (exclusion of evidence due to defendant's failure to comply with state rape shield notice requirement violated defendant's constitutional rights). The motion must be served on all parties and must specifically describe the proffered evidence and the purpose for which it is being offered. In addition, the alleged victim (or her guardian or representative) must be notified. Rule 412(c)(1).

The court may not admit such evidence without first conducting an in camera hearing. It must afford the parties and alleged victim a right to attend and be heard. The motion, related papers, and the record of the hearing must be sealed and remain under seal unless the court orders otherwise. Rule 412(c)(2).

CROSS-REFERENCES

Common Objections (Chapter 3)

87.   Sexual conduct or predisposition of alleged victim of sexual misconduct; civil case

88.   Sexual conduct or predisposition of alleged victim of sexual misconduct; criminal case

Treatises

3 Graham, Handbook of Federal Evidence § 412:1 (9th ed. 2020)

1 McCormick, Evidence § 193 (8th ed. 2020)

23 Wright and Gold, Federal Practice and Procedure §§ 5371–5378 (2d ed. 2018)

Rule 413. Similar Crimes in Sexual-Assault Cases

(a)   **Permitted Uses.** In a criminal case in which a defendant is accused of a sexual assault, the court may admit evidence that the defendant committed any other sexual assault. The evidence may be considered on any matter to which it is relevant.

(b)   **Disclosure to the Defendant.** If the prosecutor intends to offer this evidence, the prosecutor must disclose it to the defendant, including witnesses; statements or a summary of the expected testimony. The prosecutor must do so at least 15 days before trial or at a later time that the court allows for good cause.

(c)   **Effect on Other Rules.** This rule does not limit the admission or consideration of evidence under any other rule.

(d)   **Definition of "Sexual Assault."** In this rule and Rule 415, "sexual assault" means a crime under federal law or under state law (as "state" is defined in 18 U.S.C. § 513) involving:

    (1)   any conduct prohibited by 18 U.S.C. chapter 109A;

    (2)   contact, without consent, between any part of the defendant's body—or an object—and another person's genitals or anus;

(3) contact, without consent, between the defendant's genitals or anus and any part of another person's body;

(4) deriving sexual pleasure or gratification from inflicting death, bodily injury, or physical pain on another person; or

(5) an attempt or conspiracy to engage in conduct described in subparagraphs (1)–(4).

AUTHORS' COMMENTS

(1) Scope and purpose of Rule 413. Rule 413 is designed to supersede in sexual assault cases the general rule, expressed in Rule 404, that excludes character evidence when offered to prove conforming conduct. United States v. Luger, 837 F.3d 870, 873–74 (8th Cir.2016). Rule 413 is based on the notion that informing the jury of a defendant's commission of other sexual assaults is often crucial to the accurate determination of sexual assault cases because such cases often turn on a dispute as to whether the complainant consented.

(2) Types of cases. Rule 413 applies only in criminal cases where the defendant is accused of sexual assault. United States v. Courtright, 632 F.3d 363, 368–69 (7th Cir.2011) (to be "accused of an offense of sexual assault" means to be charged in indictment with sexual-assault offense). Rule 413 defines "sexual assault" in part through cross-reference to 18 U.S.C.A. chapter 109A (§§ 2241 et seq.). United States v. Blazek, 431 F.3d 1104, 1108–09 (8th Cir.2005) (accused need not be charged with a chapter 109A offense; charged offense need only involve conduct proscribed by chapter 109A).

(3) Type of evidence admissible. Contrary to the general rule barring evidence of a person's character to prove that the person acted in conformity with that character, Rule 413(a) expressly states that evidence of other sexual assaults committed by the defendant "may be considered on any matter to which it is relevant." See United States v. Rogers, 587 F.3d 816, 821 (7th Cir.2009). The other instances need not have resulted in conviction and may have been either prior or subsequent to the charged offense. United States v. Sioux, 362 F.3d 1241 (9th Cir.2004). Although the Rule makes no mention of the quantum of proof required to prove the defendant committed the other sexual assault or assaults, this will in all likelihood be viewed as a question of conditional relevancy. See Huddleston v. United States, 485 U.S. 681, 108 S.Ct. 1496 (1988). Therefore, the proponent of the evidence will be required to offer only enough evidence so that a reasonable juror could find that the defendant committed the other sexual assault. Any other act offered under this rule must constitute an act of sexual assault or attempted sexual assault. United States v. Blue Bird, 372 F.3d 989, 992 (8th Cir.2004) (trial court erred in admitting evidence of other acts by defendant that were not sexual acts, sexual contact or attempts thereof).

(4) Notice requirement. The prosecution must provide the defendant with notice of its intent to introduce evidence under Rule 413. It must disclose the statements of witnesses or a summary of the substance of their expected testimony at least fifteen days prior to trial. The court may, for good cause, allow the prosecution to disclose the evidence at a later time. E.g., United States v. Guidry, 456 F.3d 493, 504–05 (5th Cir.2006).

(5) Rule 403. Rule 413 clearly favors admissibility of other sexual assault evidence. United States v. Hawpetoss, 478 F.3d 820, 823–826 (7th Cir.2007) (discussing factors to be considered). See, e.g., United States v. Julian, 427 F.3d 471, 485–88 (7th Cir.2005) (upholding admission of twelve-year-old offense). But courts should still exclude such evidence when its probative value is substantially outweighed by the danger of unfair prejudice; United States v. Mound, 149 F.3d 799, 800 (8th Cir.1998). United States v. Guardia, 135 F.3d 1326, 1329–30 (10th Cir.1998).

CROSS-REFERENCES

Common Objections (Chapter 3)

67.   Other crimes evidence offered for an undisputed point

Treatises

3 Graham, Handbook of Federal Evidence § 413:1 (9th ed. 2020)

1 McCormick, Evidence § 190.10 (8th ed. 2020)

23 Wright and Gold, Federal Practice and Procedure §§ 5381–5387 (2d ed. 2018)

Rule 414. Similar Crimes in Child-Molestation Cases

(a) **Permitted Uses.** In a criminal case in which a defendant is accused of child molestation, the court may admit evidence that the defendant committed any other child molestation. The evidence may be considered on any matter to which it is relevant.

(b) **Disclosure to the Defendant.** If the prosecutor intends to offer this evidence, the prosecutor must disclose it to the defendant, including witnesses' statements or a summary of the expected testimony. The prosecutor must do so at least 15 days before trial or at a later time that the court allows for good cause.

(c) **Effect on Other Rules.** This rule does not limit the admission or consideration of evidence under any other rule.

(d) **Definition of "Child" and "Child Molestation."** In this rule and Rule 415:

(1) "child" means a person below the age of 14; and

(2) "child molestation" means a crime under federal law or under state law (as "state" is defined in 18 U.S.C. § 513) involving:

(A) any conduct prohibited by 18 U.S.C. chapter 109A and committed with a child;

(B) any conduct prohibited by 18 U.S.C. chapter 110;

(C) contact between any part of the defendant's body—or an object—and a child's genitals or anus;

(D) contact between the defendant's genitals or anus and any part of a child's body;

(E) deriving sexual pleasure or gratification from inflicting death, bodily injury, or physical pain on a child; or

(F) an attempt or conspiracy to engage in conduct described in subparagraphs (A)–(E).

AUTHORS' COMMENTS

(1) **Scope and purpose of Rule 414.** Rule 414 is designed to supersede in child molestation cases the general rule, expressed in Rule 404, that excludes character evidence when offered to prove conforming conduct. United States v. Hanson, 936 F.3d 876, 881 (9th Cir.2019). Rule 414 is based on the notion that evidence that a defendant has engaged in other acts of child molestation is highly probative in that it reveals the defendant's unusual sexual or sadosexual interest in children. Even before enactment of Rule 414, courts were quite willing to admit evidence of prior sexual acts in prosecutions for child sexual abuse. E.g., United States v. Yellow, 18 F.3d 1438, 1440–41 (8th Cir.1994).

(2) **Types of cases.** Rule 414 applies only in criminal cases in which the defendant is accused of child molestation. Rule 414(d) defines "child" as a person below the age of fourteen. It defines the term "child molestation" in part through cross-reference to 18 U.S.C.A. chapters 109A (§ 2241 et seq.) and 110 (§ 2251 et seq.).

(3) **Type of evidence admissible.** Contrary to the general rule barring evidence of a person's character to prove that the person acted in conformity with that character, Rule 414(a) expressly states that evidence of other acts of child molestation committed by the defendant "may be considered on any matter to which it is relevant." See United States v. Hruby, 19 F.4th 963, 965 (6th Cir.2021) ("Under Federal Rule of Evidence 414(a), a court may admit evidence that a defendant previously molested a child to show that he is inclined to molest children."); United States v. Weber, 987 F.3d 789, 793 (8th Cir.2021) (evidence of prior acts probative because they "established [defendant's] propensity to molest young boys"). The defendant need not have been convicted for the other acts of child molestation. E.g., United States v. Larson, 112 F.3d 600, 604–05 (2d Cir.1997). Although the Rule makes no mention of the quantum of proof required to prove the defendant committed the other sexual assault or assaults, this is a conditional relevancy matter governed by Rule 104(b). United States v. Hruby, 19 F.4th 963, 966–67 (6th Cir.2021). Therefore, the proponent of the evidence will be required to offer only enough evidence so that a reasonable juror could find that the defendant committed the other acts of child molestation.

(4) Notice requirement. The prosecution must provide the defendant with notice of its intent to introduce evidence under Rule 414. It must disclose the statements of witnesses or a summary of the substance of their expected testimony at least fifteen days prior to trial. The court may, for good cause, allow the prosecution to disclose the evidence at a later time.

(5) Rule 403. Rule 414 clearly favors admissibility of evidence of other acts of child molestation. United States v. Schave, 55 F.4th 671, 677 (8th Cir.2022) ("Rule 414 reveals a 'strong legislative judgment that evidence of prior sexual offenses should ordinarily be admissible.'") (quoting United States v. LeCompte, 131 F.3d 767, 769 (8th Cir.1997)); see, e.g., United States v. Kelly, 510 F.3d 433, 437 (4th Cir.2007) (upholding admission of twenty-two-year-old conviction); United States v. Meacham, 115 F.3d 1488, 1491–95 (10th Cir.1997) (upholding admission of twenty-five year old incident). But courts should still exclude such evidence when its probative value is substantially outweighed by the danger of unfair prejudice. United States v. Perrault, 995 F.3d 748, 765–71 (10th Cir.2021) (reviewing factors to be considered); United States v. Joubert, 778 F.3d 247, 254 (1st Cir.2015) (in applying Rule 403 to Rule 414 evidence, court should recognize congressional judgment to allow propensity evidence in such cases). E.g., United States v. Davis, 624 F.3d 508, 511–12 (2d Cir.2010) (excluding three-year-old conviction as unduly inflammatory, while admitting 19-year-old conviction with details of offense redacted).

CROSS-REFERENCES

Common Objections (Chapter 3)

18. Character evidence inadmissible
19. Character evidence, specific acts inadmissible
64. Other crimes evidence; insufficient notice of intent to offer
65. Other crimes evidence not adequately proven
66. Other crimes evidence not admissible to prove character
67. Other crimes evidence offered for an undisputed point

Treatises

3 Graham, Handbook of Federal Evidence § 414:1 (9th ed. 2020)

1 McCormick, Evidence § 190.10 (8th ed. 2020)

23 Wright and Gold, Federal Practice and Procedure §§ 5391–5395 (2d ed. 2018)

Rule 415. Similar Acts in Civil Cases Involving Sexual Assault or Child Molestation

(a) Permitted Uses. In a civil case involving a claim for relief based on a party's alleged sexual assault or child molestation, the court may admit evidence that the party committed any other sexual assault or child molestation. The evidence may be considered as provided in Rules 413 and 414.

(b) Disclosure to the Opponent. If a party intends to offer this evidence, the party must disclose it to the party against whom it will be offered, including witnesses' statements or a summary of the expected testimony. The party must do so at least 15 days before trial or at a later time that the court allows for good cause.

(c) Effect on Other Rules. This rule does not limit the admission or consideration of evidence under any other rule.

AUTHORS' COMMENTS

(1) Scope and purpose of Rule 415. Rule 415 provides that a party in a civil case who is seeking relief based on the other party's alleged act of sexual assault or child molestation may offer the same types of evidence authorized for admission under Rules 413 and 414 in analogous criminal cases. Thus, a plaintiff may offer evidence that the defendant committed other sexual assaults or acts of child molestation to prove that he committed the sexual assault or act of child molestation on which the plaintiff's claim for relief is based.

(2) Types of cases. Rule 415 applies in civil cases in which a party seeks damages or other relief that is predicated on the other party's commission of a sexual assault or act of child molestation.

(3) Type of evidence admissible. Contrary to the general rule prohibiting evidence of a person's character to prove that the person acted in conformity with that character, Rule 415 specifically approves of such evidence by reference to Rules 413 and 414. See Authors' Comments 413(3) and 414(3). The quantum of proof required to establish the person committed the other acts of sexual assault or child molestation is governed by Rule 104(b). Johnson v. Elk Lake School Dist., 283 F.3d 138, 151–55 (3d Cir.2002). Therefore, the proponent of such evidence is required to offer only enough evidence so that a reasonable juror could find that the person committed the other acts.

(4) Notice requirement. A party that intends to introduce evidence under Rule 415 must provide to the opposing party the statements of its witnesses or a summary of the substance of their expected testimony at least fifteen days prior to trial. The court may, for good cause, allow a party to disclose the evidence at a later time.

(5) Rule 403. Although Rule 415 clearly favors admissibility of evidence of other acts of sexual assault and child molestation, courts should still exclude such evidence when its probative value is substantially outweighed by the danger of unfair prejudice. Compare Seeley v. Chase, 443 F.3d 1290, 1295 (10th Cir.2006) (court must make "reasoned, recorded statement of its 403 decision"); with Martinez v. Cui, 608 F.3d 54, 60 (1st Cir.2010) (surveying courts' approach to use of Rule 403 in considering evidence under Rule 415 and rejecting any "special rules constraining . . . usual exercise of discretion under Rule 403).

CROSS-REFERENCES

Common Objections (Chapter 3)

18.   Character evidence inadmissible
19.   Character evidence, specific acts inadmissible
64.   Other crimes evidence; insufficient notice of intent to offer
65.   Other crimes evidence not adequately proven
66.   Other crimes evidence not admissible to prove character
67.   Other crimes evidence offered for an undisputed point

Treatises

3 Graham, Handbook of Federal Evidence § 415:1 (9th ed. 2020)

1 McCormick, Evidence § 190.10 (8th ed. 2020)

23 Wright and Gold, Federal Practice and Procedure §§ 5401–5404 (2d ed. 2018)

ARTICLE V

PRIVILEGES

Rule 501. Privilege in General

The common law—as interpreted by United States courts in the light of reason and experience—governs a claim of privilege unless any of the following provides otherwise:

- the United States Constitution;

- a federal statute; or

-     rules prescribed by the Supreme Court.

But in a civil case, state law governs privilege regarding a claim or defense for which state law supplies the rule of decision.

AUTHORS' COMMENTS

(1) **Scope and purpose of Rule 501.** Rule 501 provides that privileges are ordinarily to be found in four sources: the Constitution, federal statutes, other rules promulgated by the Supreme Court, and the principles of the common law as interpreted by the federal courts in light of reason and experience. In addition, in civil cases, state privilege law applies with respect to an element of a claim or defense as to which state substantive law governs.

Although Congress did not enact the privilege rules contained in the version of the rules of evidence transmitted to it by the Supreme Court, courts often refer to the proposed rules for guidance. United States v. Moscony, 927 F.2d 742, 751 (3d Cir.1991). The proposed rules are reproduced and discussed in the pages immediately following the discussion of Rule 502.

Testimonial privileges "contravene the fundamental principle that 'the public * * * has a right to every man's evidence.'" Trammel v. United States, 445 U.S. 40, 50, 100 S.Ct. 906, 912 (1980). Therefore, testimonial privileges must "be strictly construed." University of Pennsylvania v. Equal Employment Opportunity Commission, 493 U.S. 182, 189, 110 S.Ct. 577, 582 (1990).

(2) **Flexible approach to privileges.** Rule 501 allows the courts to address privilege claims flexibly. For example, in Trammel v. United States, 445 U.S. 40, 100 S.Ct. 906 (1980), the Supreme Court rejected the traditional rule of spousal incompetency in criminal cases, a rule that had been embraced in Proposed Rule 505. See Authors' Comments to Proposed Rule 505 infra. The Court based its decision both on its view that the contemporary justification offered for the incompetency rule was illegitimate and on the movement in the states away from the traditional rule. Nevertheless, courts remain reluctant to create new privileges. See University of Pennsylvania v. Equal Employment Opportunity Commission, 493 U.S. 182, 189, 110 S.Ct. 577, 582 (1990) ("we are disinclined to exercise this authority expansively").

(3) **Privileges recognized and rejected.** In addition to the privileges based on the proposed privilege rules discussed in the following pages, numerous statutory privileges, typically of limited applicability, also exist. Courts are also frequently asked to create privileges where neither a statute nor a proposed privilege rule recognizes one. Courts generally decline the invitation. The privilege claims made to the courts include:

-     A journalist's privilege. Branzburg v. Hayes, 408 U.S. 665, 92 S.Ct. 2646 (1972) (rejecting privilege in criminal case); United States v. Sterling, 724 F.3d 482, 492–510 (4th Cir.2013) (rejecting constitutional and common-law privilege in criminal case). Some courts recognize a qualified privilege in criminal cases, see, e.g., United States v. Burke, 700 F.2d 70, 76–77 (2d Cir.1983), and civil cases, see, e.g., Shoen v. Shoen, 5 F.3d 1289, 1292 (9th Cir.1993) (citing cases).

-     An academic peer-review privilege. University of Pennsylvania v. Equal Employment Opportunity Commission, 493 U.S. 182, 110 S.Ct. 577 (1990) (rejecting privilege).

-     A parent-child privilege. Under Seal v. United States, 755 F.3d 213 (4th Cir.2014) (citing cases); In re Grand Jury, 103 F.3d 1140 (3d Cir.1997) (rejecting both testimonial and communication privileges).

-     A privilege for critical self-analysis. See Dowling v. American Hawaii Cruises, Inc., 971 F.2d 423, 425–27 (9th Cir.1992) (noting some courts have recognized qualified privilege, but holding any such privilege is inapplicable to voluntary routine safety reviews).

-     A privilege for statements between a parolee and probation officer. United States v. Simmons, 964 F.2d 763, 768–69 (8th Cir.1992) (rejecting privilege).

-     An accountant-client privilege. United States v. Arthur Young & Co., 465 U.S. 805, 104 S.Ct. 1495 (1984) (rejecting work product protection for accountants); Cavallaro v. United States, 284 F.3d 236, 246 (1st Cir.2002); In re Grand Jury Proceedings, 220 F.3d 568 (7th Cir.2000) (rejecting privilege). But see 26 U.S.C.A. § 7525 (limited privilege for communications between taxpayer and federally authorized tax practitioner).

- A law enforcement investigatory privilege. In re United States Dept. of Homeland Security, 459 F.3d 565 (5th Cir.2006) (citing cases); Tuite v. Henry, 98 F.3d 1411 (D.C.Cir.1996) (discussing qualified nature of privilege).

- A medical peer review privilege. Hamdan v. Indiana Univ. Health North Hosp., Inc., 880 F.3d 416, 421 (7th Cir.2018); Adkins v. Christie, 488 F.3d 1324 (11th Cir.2007).

- An ombudsman privilege. Carman v. McDonnell Douglas Corp., 114 F.3d 790 (8th Cir.1997) (rejecting privilege).

- A legislative privilege. In re Hubbard, 803 F.3d 1298 (11th Cir.2015) (recognizing privilege).

- A non-attorney patent-agent privilege. In re Queen's University at Kingston, 820 F.3d 1287 (Fed.Cir.2016) (recognizing privilege).

(4) Use of state privilege law. Federal privilege law always governs in federal criminal proceedings. In civil actions, however, Rule 501 provides that state privilege law applies when (1) the privilege concerns an element of a claim or defense and (2) the claim or defense is one as to which state law supplies the substantive law. When evidence covered by a privilege is relevant to both a federal and state claim or defense, the courts generally apply the federal law of privilege. See Wilcox v. Arpaio, 753 F.3d 872, 876–77 (9th Cir.2014); Pearson v. Miller, 211 F.3d 57, 66 (3d Cir.2000).

CROSS-REFERENCES

Common Objections (Chapter 3)

77.   Privileged

Treatises

4 Graham, Handbook of Federal Evidence § 501:1 (9th ed. 2020)

1 McCormick, Evidence §§ 72–77, 112–143 (8th ed. 2020)

23A Wright and Graham, Federal Practice and Procedure §§ 5421–5438 (Supp. 2018)

Rule 502. Attorney-Client Privilege and Work Product; Limitations on Waiver

The following provisions apply, in the circumstances set out, to disclosure of a communication or information covered by the attorney-client privilege or work-product protection.

(a) Disclosure Made in a Federal Proceeding or to a Federal Office or Agency; Scope of a Waiver. When the disclosure is made in a Federal proceeding or to a Federal office or agency and waives the attorney-client privilege or work-product protection, the waiver extends to an undisclosed communication or information in a Federal or State proceeding only if:

    (1) the waiver is intentional;

    (2) the disclosed and undisclosed communications or information concern the same subject matter; and

    (3) they ought in fairness to be considered together.

(b) Inadvertent Disclosure. When made in a Federal proceeding or to a Federal office or agency, the disclosure does not operate as a waiver in a Federal or State proceeding if:

    (1) the disclosure is inadvertent;

    (2) the holder of the privilege or protection took reasonable steps to prevent disclosure; and

    (3) the holder promptly took reasonable steps to rectify the error, including (if applicable) following Federal Rule of Civil Procedure 26(b)(5)(B).

(c) Disclosure Made in a State Proceeding. When the disclosure is made in a State proceeding and is not the subject of a State-court order concerning waiver, the disclosure does not operate as a waiver in a Federal proceeding if the disclosure:

(1) would not be a waiver under this rule if it had been made in a Federal proceeding; or

(2) is not a waiver under the law of the State where the disclosure occurred.

(d) Controlling Effect of a Court Order. A Federal court may order that the privilege or protection is not waived by disclosure connected with the litigation pending before the court—in which event the disclosure is also not a waiver in any other Federal or State proceeding.

(e) Controlling Effect of a Party Agreement. An agreement on the effect of disclosure in a Federal proceeding is binding only on the parties to the agreement, unless it is incorporated into a court order.

(f) Controlling Effect of this Rule. Notwithstanding Rules 101 and 1101, this rule applies to State proceedings and to Federal court-annexed and Federal court-mandated arbitration proceedings, in the circumstances set out in the rule. And notwithstanding Rule 501, this rule applies even if State law provides the rule of decision.

(g) Definitions. In this rule:

(1) "attorney-client privilege" means the protection that applicable law provides for confidential attorney-client communications; and

(2) "work-product protection" means the protection that applicable law provides for tangible material (or its intangible equivalent) prepared in anticipation of litigation or for trial.

AUTHORS' COMMENTS

(1) Scope and purpose of Rule 502. The primary purpose of New Rule 502, which was signed into law on September 19, 2008, is the reduction of costs associated with the production of documents in discovery. It aims to reduce the time and effort lawyers spend screening documents before producing them by limiting the risk that disclosure of documents or information protected by the attorney-client privilege or work-product doctrine will result in a broad waiver of that protection.

Rule 502 accomplishes this in several ways. First, it limits the circumstances in which the inadvertent disclosure of protected material constitutes waiver as to the documents actually disclosed. Second, even when the disclosure of protected materials does constitute a waiver, Rule 502 severely limits the circumstances under which the waiver will extend beyond the communications or information actually disclosed. Third, Rule 502 provides that when parties disclose privileged documents pursuant to a federal court order stipulating that such disclosure does not constitute a waiver, other courts must honor that order. Fourth, Rule 502 makes these protections applicable in subsequent state as well as federal proceedings.

Rule 502 does not attempt to change the substantive contours of the attorney-client privilege or work-product doctrine. Nor does it supplant existing waiver law either as to other privileges or, as to the attorney-client privilege or work-product doctrine, where the disclosure is made in circumstances other than those expressly covered in Rule 502. Note that, for purposes of determining waiver by voluntary disclosure, courts have applied different standards for attorney-client privilege and work-product protection. United States v. Sanmina Corp., 968 F.3d 1107, 1120–21 (9th Cir.2020).

(2) Inadvertent disclosure. Rule 502 resolves a conflict in federal law regarding when a waiver results from a party's inadvertent disclosure—to a federal office or agency or during a federal proceeding—of attorney-client privileged or work-product protected material. Under Rule 502(b), a disclosure is considered inadvertent if it was unintended. Coburn Group, LLC v. Whitecap Advisors LLC, 640 F.Supp.2d 1032 (N.D.Ill. 2009). Rule 502(b) provides that such an inadvertent disclosure does not amount to a waiver if the party took reasonable steps to prevent the disclosure and then took prompt and reasonable steps to rectify the inadvertent disclosure. Carmody v. Board of Trustees of Univ. of Illinois, 893 F.3d 397, 406 n.2 (7th Cir.2018). In determining whether a party took reasonable steps to prevent the disclosure, a court may consider factors such as the volume and complexity of discovery and time constraints for production. In determining whether a party took reasonable steps to rectify, a court should consider the alacrity with which the party followed up on obvious indications that it might have inadvertently produced protected material. See Advisory Committee's Note to Rule 502.

If a party fails to meet these requirements and its inadvertent disclosure is held to constitute a waiver, the waiver extends only to the material actually disclosed. See Rule 502(a).

(3) Subject matter waiver. A party waives the attorney-client privilege and work-product protection when it deliberately discloses material or when its inadvertent disclosure is found to constitute waiver under Rule 502(b). Rule 502(a) is designed to limit the scope of that waiver. When a party discloses communications to a federal office or agency or during a federal proceeding, the waiver ordinarily will extend only to the material actually disclosed. Subject matter waiver—that is, waiver as to undisclosed protected communications and information—will be found only when (1) the party intended to waive the privilege by disclosure; (2) the disclosed material and the undisclosed material concern the same subject matter; and (3) the disclosed material and the undisclosed material ought in fairness to be considered together. See, e.g., Baxter International, Inc. v. AXA Versicherung, 224 F.Supp. 3d 648, 655–58 (N.D. Ill. 2016); In re King's Daughters Health System, Inc., 31 F.4th 520, 527–29 (6th Cir.2022) (hospital's disclosure of some information regarding its experts' review of cardiologist's performance waived privilege as to related, undisclosed information); Bear Republic Brewing Co. v. Central City Brewing Co., 275 F.R.D. 43, 46–49 (D.Mass. 2011). Note that the first of these three requirements means that inadvertent disclosures will never qualify for subject matter waiver. E.g., Salmon v. Lang, 57 F.4th 296, 326–27 (1st Cir.2022).

(4) Waiver determination binding on other courts. The purpose of Rule 502 can be accomplished only if lawyers are assured that the risks of waiver associated with the disclosure of privileged material in the instant proceeding are limited in future litigation—federal or state—as well. Therefore, the waiver standards of Rule 502(a) and (b) extend beyond the arena in which the disclosure occurs. They apply to subsequent proceedings in both federal and state court. Thus, if a party makes a disclosure to a federal office or agency or in a federal proceeding, a state court must follow Rule 502(a) in determining whether that disclosure constituted a subject matter waiver. Similarly, if a party makes an inadvertent disclosure to a federal office or agency or in a federal proceeding, a state court must follow Rule 502(b) in determining whether that inadvertent disclosure constituted a waiver.

(5) Disclosure made pursuant to court order. To expedite discovery, a federal court may enter an order providing that parties may disclose to one another privileged material without waiving the privilege. See Fed. R. Civ. P. 26(f)(3)(C) (whether to ask court for Rule 502 order included in discovery plan requirements). Rule 502(d) ensures that such orders must be honored in other federal and state proceedings. See e.g., In re General Motors LLC Ignition Switch Litigation, 80 F. Supp. 3d 521, 526 (S.D. N.Y. 2015).

Despite the language of Rule 502(d) (and 502(e)), some courts have held that Rule 502(b)'s waiver-by-inadvertent-disclosure test governs unless the court's order (or the parties' own agreement) specifically includes a standard for determining waiver. See IRTH Solutions, LLC v. Windstream Communications, LLC, 2018 WL 575911 (S.D. Ohio 2018) (discussing different approaches); In re Testosterone Replacement Therapy Products Liability Litigation, 301 F. Supp. 3d 917, 924–925 (N.D. Il. 2018) (protective order, not Rule 502(b) standard, applies); Maxtena, Inc. v. Marks, 289 F.R.D. 427, 444 n. 16 (D. Md. 2012) (Rule 502(b) standard applies absent specific directives in order).

Moreover, court orders entered under Rule 502(d) typically protect only against waiver by disclosure. A party's failure to object in a timely manner to its opponent's use of the disclosed document may still constitute a waiver. Certain Underwriters at Lloyd's London v. National Railroad Passenger Corp., 218 F.Supp.3d 197, 201–02 (E.D.N.Y. 2016); United States v. Wells Fargo Bank, N.A., 2015 WL 5051679, at *4 (S.D.N.Y. 2015).

(6) Party agreements. Parties may enter into their own agreement about the waiver effect of disclosure. Rule 502(e) makes clear, however, that unless such an agreement is incorporated into a court order, it will bind only the parties to the agreement.

(7) Disclosure made in state proceedings. Rule 502(c) governs the waiver effect in federal proceedings of a disclosure—made in a state proceeding and not subject to a state court order concerning waiver—of attorney-client privileged or work-product protected material. If the state and federal rules regarding waiver are the same, no problem exists. But if waiver would be found under one rule but not the other, Rule 502(c) requires the federal court to apply the rule that is more protective of privilege and work product.

The rule does not specify what happens when a disclosure is made in a state proceeding pursuant to a state court confidentiality order. The Advisory Committee's Note to Rule 502 takes the position that 28 U.S.C. § 1738 and principles of federalism and comity mandate the enforceability in a subsequent federal proceeding of a state court order protecting the privileged status of disclosed material.

(8) Applicability of Rule 502. Rule 502(f) provides that this rule applies in federal court-annexed and federal court-mandated arbitration proceedings as well as state court proceedings in the circumstances set forth in the other paragraphs of the rule.

CROSS-REFERENCES

Common Objections (Chapter 3)

77. Privileged

78. Privileged attorney-client communication

Treatises

4 Graham, Handbook of Federal Evidence § 502:1 (9th ed. 2020)

1 McCormick, Evidence §§ 93, 96 (8th ed. 2020)

23 Wright & Graham, Federal Practice and Procedure §§ 5438–5448 (2d ed. 2018)

23A Wright and Graham, Federal Practice and Procedure §§ 5441–5448 (Supp. 2018)

Proposed Rule 502. Required Reports Privileged by Statute

[NOT ENACTED]

A person, corporation, association, or other organization or entity, either public or private, making a return or report required by law to be made has a privilege to refuse to disclose and to prevent any other person from disclosing the return or report, if the law requiring it to be made so provides. A public officer or agency to whom a return or report is required by law to be made has a privilege to refuse to disclose the return or report if the law requiring it to be made so provides. No privilege exists under this rule in actions involving perjury, false statements, fraud in the return or report, or other failure to comply with the law in question.

AUTHORS' COMMENTS

(1) Scope and purpose of required report privilege. Proposed Rule 502 provides that one who makes a required report may prevent its disclosure if the law requiring the report to be made so provides. Moreover, the public officer or agency to whom the report must be made may refuse to disclose it if the law requiring the report to be made so provides. A person's or agency's ability to assert this privilege, therefore, must be determined by reference to the particular statutory provision. See, e.g., In re Domestic Air Transportation Antitrust Litigation, 141 F.R.D. 556, 560 (N.D.Ga.1992) (party making required report has no privilege unless statute so provides). Such confidentiality provisions are often included in required report laws to enhance the government's ability to gather data cheaply and efficiently.

(2) Exception. Since the confidentiality provisions are designed to encourage accurate self-reporting, the privilege may not be invoked in actions involving perjury, false statements, fraud in the return or report, or any other failure to comply with the law in question.

CROSS-REFERENCES

Common Objections (Chapter 3)

84. Privileged required report

Treatises

4 Graham, Handbook of Federal Evidence § 502:1.1 (9th ed. 2020)

1 McCormick, Evidence § 112 (8th ed. 2020)

24 Wright and Graham, Federal Practice and Procedure §§ 5451–5461 (1986)

Proposed Rule 503. Lawyer-Client Privilege

[NOT ENACTED]

(a) Definitions. As used in this rule:

(1) A "client" is a person, public officer, or corporation, association, or other organization or entity, either public or private, who is rendered professional legal services by a lawyer, or who consults a lawyer with a view to obtaining professional legal services from him.

(2) A "lawyer" is a person authorized, or reasonably believed by the client to be authorized, to practice law in any state or nation.

(3) A "representative of the lawyer" is one employed to assist the lawyer in the rendition of professional legal services.

(4) A communication is "confidential" if not intended to be disclosed to third persons other than those to whom disclosure is in furtherance of the rendition of professional legal services to the client or those reasonably necessary for the transmission of the communication.

(b) General Rule of Privilege. A client has a privilege to refuse to disclose and to prevent any other person from disclosing confidential communications made for the purpose of facilitating the rendition of professional legal services to the client, (1) between himself or his representative and his lawyer or his lawyer's representative, or (2) between his lawyer and the lawyer's representative, or (3) by him or his lawyer to a lawyer representing another in a matter of common interest, or (4) between representatives of the client or between the client and a representative of the client, or (5) between lawyers representing the client.

(c) Who May Claim the Privilege. The privilege may be claimed by the client, his guardian or conservator, the personal representative of a deceased client, or the successor, trustee, or similar representative of a corporation, association, or other organization, whether or not in existence. The person who was the lawyer at the time of the communication may claim the privilege but only on behalf of the client. His authority to do so is presumed in the absence of evidence to the contrary.

(d) Exceptions. There is no privilege under this rule:

(1) *Furtherance of crime or fraud.* If the services of the lawyer were sought or obtained to enable or aid anyone to commit or plan to commit what the client knew or reasonably should have known to be a crime or fraud; or

(2) *Claimants through same deceased client.* As to a communication relevant to an issue between parties who claim through the same deceased client, regardless of whether the claims are by testate or intestate succession or by *inter vivos* transaction; or

(3) *Breach of duty by lawyer or client.* As to a communication relevant to an issue of breach of duty by the lawyer to his client or by the client to his lawyer; or

(4) *Document attested by lawyer.* As to a communication relevant to an issue concerning an attested document to which the lawyer is an attesting witness; or

(5) *Joint clients.* As to a communication relevant to a matter of common interest between two or more clients if the communication was made by any of them to a lawyer retained or consulted in common, when offered in an action between any of the clients.

AUTHORS' COMMENTS

(1) Scope and purpose of attorney-client privilege. For the most part, Proposed Rule 503 codifies the traditional attorney-client privilege. Although Congress did not adopt the proposed rule, it accurately embodies the current state of the law. The rationale behind the attorney-client privilege is well-established. "The purpose of the privilege is to encourage clients to make full disclosure to their attorneys." Fisher v. United States, 425 U.S. 391, 403, 96 S.Ct. 1569, 1577 (1976). By doing so, the privilege "promote[s] broader public interests in the observance of law and administration of justice. The privilege recognizes that sound legal advice or advocacy . . . depends upon the lawyer being fully informed by the client." Upjohn Co. v. United States, 449 U.S. 383, 389, 101 S.Ct. 677, 682 (1981).

The basic elements of the attorney-client privilege are set forth in Proposed Rule 503(b), which enumerates the various combinations of lawyer, client, representative of the lawyer and representative of the client among whom communications are privileged. Many courts employ the standard articulated in United States v. United Shoe Machinery Corp., 89 F.Supp. 357, 358–59 (D.Mass.1950). See, e.g., Hawkins v. Stables, 148 F.3d 379, 383 (4th Cir.1998).

Proposed Rule 503(a) provides definitions for certain key terms, including client, lawyer, representative of the lawyer, and confidential. Proposed Rule 503(c) addresses who may claim the privilege and Proposed Rule 503(d) sets forth five exceptions to the privilege.

The burden of establishing the existence of the privilege falls on the party asserting it. E.E.O.C. v. BDO USA, L.L.P., 876 F.3d 690, 695 (5th Cir.2017); United States v. Adlman, 68 F.3d 1495, 1500 (2d Cir.1995).

(2) Client is holder. The attorney-client privilege is held by the client, and it is the client's privilege to assert or waive. National Security Counselors v. Central Intelligence Agency, 969 F.3d 406, 411 (D.C. Cir.2020). The attorney, however, may invoke or waive the privilege on the client's behalf. Fisher v. United States, 425 U.S. 391, 402 n. 8, 96 S.Ct. 1569, 1577 n. 8 (1976) ("universally accepted" that attorney may invoke attorney-client privilege). The rule also acknowledges that a representative of the client may invoke or waive the privilege for the client. E.g., Commodity Futures Trading Comm'n v. Weintraub, 471 U.S. 343, 105 S.Ct. 1986 (1985) (trustee in bankruptcy has power to waive privilege); United States v. Yielding, 657 F.3d 688, 706–08 (8th Cir.2011) (personal representative of deceased client may waive privilege only when waiver is in best interest of client's estate and would not damage client's reputation).

(3) Communications between lawyer, client, and representatives. The attorney-client privilege protects communications only between or among the lawyer and client, and their representatives. It does not cover communications that either the lawyer or client has with a third party. Matter of Fischel, 557 F.2d 209, 211 (9th Cir.1977). Under Proposed Rule 503(b), only communications between or among the following are privileged:

- A client (or the client's representative) and the lawyer (or the lawyer's representative). Proposed Rule 503(b)(1).

- A lawyer and the lawyer's representative. Proposed Rule 503(b)(2).

- A client and the client's representative. Proposed Rule 503(b)(4).

- Representatives of the client. Proposed Rule 503(b)(4).

- A lawyer representing the client and another lawyer representing the client. Proposed Rule 503(b)(5).

- A client or the client's lawyer and a lawyer representing another client in a matter of common interest. This is sometimes referred to as the common interest, "pooled information" or (less appropriately) "joint defense" privilege. In re Teleglobe Communications Corp., 493 F.3d 345, 363–66 (3d Cir.2007) ("common interest" privilege arising in civil case); In re Grand Jury Subpoena Duces Tecum, 112 F.3d 910, 922–23 (8th Cir.1997) ("common interest" privilege arising in criminal case). But see Lionbridge Technologies, LLC v. Valley Forge Ins. Co., 53 F.4th 711, 724–25 (1st Cir.2022) (erroneously referring to situation where attorney represented both insured and insurer as invoking "common-interest doctrine"; insured and insurer were joint clients of attorney).

> **Example—Privileged.** In In re Blue Cross Blue Shield Antitrust Litigation MDL 2406, 85 F.4th 1070, 1096 (11th Cir.2023), sub-groups of health insurance plan subscribers—fully-insured claimants and self-funded claimants—settled their antitrust suit. A self-funded claimant objected to the allocation of settlement funds between the two groups and sought discovery of communications between counsel for the fully-insured claimants and the self-funded claimants' economic expert witness. The court held that the communications were privileged, noting that

the two groups of claimants "had a substantially similar interest in the litigation against Blue Cross and in the settlement negotiations."

Example—Written agreement not required. In United States v. Gonzalez, 669 F.3d 974 (9th Cir.2012), co-defendants husband and wife were represented by separate counsel, but were tried separately. The court held that statements between their lawyers could be protected by the attorney-client privilege even in the absence of a written joint defense agreement. But the court remanded the case for the trial court to determine whether the joint defense agreement had implicitly terminated and, if so, whether the communication in question was made before or after the agreement's termination.

Example—Not privileged. In United States v. Gotti, 771 F.Supp. 535, 545 (E.D.N.Y.1991), the court held that the attorney-client privilege did not apply to communications between defendants in the absence of any lawyer. The privilege protects communications to a lawyer representing another client in a matter of common interest, but not client-to-client communications.

One party to a common interest or joint defense agreement may not unilaterally waive the privilege for the other parties to the agreement. United States v. BDO Seidman, L.L.P., 492 F.3d 806, 817 (7th Cir.2007); Restatement (Third) of the Law Governing Lawyers § 76, cmt. g. But courts disagree about whether a party to a joint defense agreement may still assert the privilege if he later testifies against a fellow party to the agreement. Compare United States v. Almeida, 341 F.3d 1318, 1323–26 (11th Cir.2003) (by testifying for state against former co-defendant, witness waived privilege created by joint defense agreement) with United States v. Henke, 222 F.3d 633, 636–38 (9th Cir.2000) (defense counsel had conflict of interest when former co-defendant testified for state because he could not fully cross-examine former co-defendant without breaching confidentiality imposed by joint defense agreement).

(4) Communications, not underlying facts, protected. The attorney-client privilege allows a client both to refuse to disclose and prevent others from disclosing confidential attorney-client communications. It does not, however, create a privilege for the underlying facts contained in an attorney-client communication. Upjohn Co. v. United States, 449 U.S. 383, 395–96, 101 S.Ct. 677, 685–86 (1981).

Example. In In re Six Grand Jury Witnesses, 979 F.2d 939, 944–45 (2d Cir.1992), employees of the target corporation were called before the grand jury and asked to reveal factual information they had uncovered while performing cost analyses of contracts at the behest of counsel. The court of appeals held the factual information was not privileged. It did, however, uphold the privilege claim with respect to a few questions that risked revealing what the witnesses had conveyed to the lawyer.

(5) Communications for the purpose of facilitating professional legal services. The privilege protects only communications made for the purpose of facilitating the rendition of professional legal services. E.g., United States v. Ivers, 967 F.3d 709, 715–17 (8th Cir.2020) (holding unprivileged threats potential client made to judge's life after attorneys told him that case lacked merit and they would not represent him); United States v. Leonard-Allen, 739 F.3d 948, 952–53 (7th Cir.2013) (privilege does not protect name of person who referred client to bankruptcy attorney); United States v. Williams, 698 F.3d 374, 379–80 (7th Cir.2012) (lawyer may testify that imprisoned client asked lawyer to forward sealed letter to client's cousin asking cousin to fabricate alibi); Antoine v. Atlas Turner, Inc., 66 F.3d 105, 109–10 (6th Cir.1995) (whether attorney forwarded default judgments to client is not privileged); United States v. Gray, 876 F.2d 1411, 1415–16 (9th Cir.1989) (whether lawyer informed client of date of sentencing hearing is not privileged). If a lawyer is acting in a non-legal capacity, the attorney-client privilege does not apply. See, e.g., United States v. Sanmina Corp., 968 F.3d 1107, 1117–19 (9th Cir.2020) (communications made to law firm so that it could conduct fair market analysis for purposes of tax compliance not privileged); In re Grand Jury Subpoena (Mr. S.), 662 F.3d 65, 72 (1st Cir.2011) (documents created by attorney to facilitate consummation of real estate transaction not privileged); In re Lindsey, 158 F.3d 1263, 1270 (D.C.Cir.1998) (advice on political, strategic or policy issues not privileged). A circuit conflict exists regarding the proper standard for determining whether the attorney-client privilege applies when a client has dual motives for communicating with counsel. Compare, e.g., In re Grand Jury, 23 F.4th 1088 (9th Cir.2021), and In re County of Erie, 473 F.3d 413, 420 (2d Cir.2007) ("predominant purpose") with In re Kellogg Brown & Root, Inc., 756 F.3d 754, 758–60 (D.C. Cir.2014) ("significant purpose").

(6) Client defined. A client may be an individual or any kind of entity, including a governmental unit, corporation, or unincorporated association. United States v. Jicarilla Apache Nation, 564 U.S. 162, 170, 131 S.Ct. 2313, 2321 (2011); e.g., In re County of Erie, 473 F.3d 413 (2d Cir.2007) (protecting communications between county attorney and county officials). Town of Norfolk v. United States Army Corps of Engineers, 968 F.2d 1438, 1457–58 (1st Cir.1992) (protecting communications between U.S. Attorney and Corps of Engineers). Cf. In re Grand Jury Subpoena, 909 F.3d 26 (1st Cir.2018) (discussing when state may assert attorney-client privilege in response to federal grand jury subpoena). Even if the person or entity does not actually become a client of the attorney, the privilege attaches to communications made while the potential client was consulting the lawyer with a view toward obtaining legal services. In re Auclair, 961 F.2d 65, 70 (5th Cir.1992). Communications made after the attorney has declined employment, however, remain unprivileged. United States v. Dennis, 843 F.2d 652, 656–57 (2d Cir.1988).

(7) Representative of client. (a) *Client is natural person.* Someone who has the authority to obtain professional legal services, or to act on advice rendered by counsel, on behalf of the client qualifies as the client's representative. Thus, the privilege covers communications between a lawyer representing a child and the child's parent or guardian.

(b) *Client is entity.* The Supreme Court has declared that a corporate client's representatives are not restricted to those persons high enough up in the corporate hierarchy to have the authority to obtain legal services for the corporation or to act on counsel's advice. Upjohn Co. v. United States, 449 U.S. 383, 392–93, 101 S.Ct. 677, 684 (1981). Although the Court declined in *Upjohn* to articulate a test to govern all future situations, it pointed to the following factors in holding that the employees of the corporate client who communicated with counsel qualified as "representatives of the client." 449 U.S. at 394–95, 101 S.Ct. at 685.

- The employees communicated to counsel in his capacity as counsel for the corporation.

- They were acting at the behest of their corporate superiors.

- The communications were made to enable the corporation to secure legal advice from its counsel and the employees were aware of this.

- The communications concerned matters within the scope of the employees' duties.

- The communications were considered highly confidential when made.

Communications between counsel and former employees of the client also may be privileged. In re Allen, 106 F.3d 582, 605–06 (4th Cir.1997). But see Infosystems, Inc. v. Ceridian Corp., 197 F.R.D. 303, 306 (E.D.Mich.2000).

(c) *Privilege is client's, not employee's.* The privilege belongs to the client, not to an employee who qualifies as a representative of the client. See Commodity Futures Trading Comm'n v. Weintraub, 471 U.S. 343, 349, 105 S.Ct. 1986, 1991 (1985) ("Displaced managers may not assert the privilege over the wishes of current managers, even as to statements that the former might have made to counsel concerning matters within the scope of their corporate duties."); United States v. International Brotherhood of Teamsters, Chauffeurs, Warehousemen and Helpers of Amer., AFL-CIO, 119 F.3d 210 (2d Cir.1997) (reasonable belief by employee that attorney represented him in individual capacity not sufficient to allow employee to claim attorney-client privilege). Cf. In re Grand Jury Subpoenas, 144 F.3d 653, 658–59 (10th Cir.1998) (recognizing that attorney-client relationship existed with both corporate client and its CEO, but holding that CEO may invoke privilege only as to those communications in which he sought personal legal advice).

(8) Lawyer defined. A lawyer need not be a member of the bar of the jurisdiction in which his counsel is sought. Confidential communications by a client to a person she reasonably believes to be a lawyer fall within the privilege's ambit. See, e.g., United States v. Tyler, 745 F.Supp. 423 (W.D.Mich.1990).

(9) Representative of lawyer defined. Under Proposed Rule 503(a)(3), a representative of a lawyer includes anyone employed to assist the lawyer in the rendition of professional legal services. The following may qualify as a lawyer's representative:

- Law clerks, secretaries and paralegals. von Bulow by Auersperg v. von Bulow, 811 F.2d 136, 146 (2d Cir.1987).

- An investigator acting at the direction of counsel. In re Kellogg Brown & Root, Inc., 796 F.3d 137, 149 (D.C. Cir.2015).

- A consulting expert employed to help the lawyer in the performance of his legal representation. E.g., In re Grand Jury Proceedings, 220 F.3d 568 (7th Cir.2000) (accountant); United States v. Schwimmer, 892 F.2d 237 (2d Cir.1989) (accountant); Brown v. Trigg, 791 F.2d 598, 601 (7th Cir.1986) (polygrapher).

Note that a consulting expert qualifies as a representative of a lawyer only when the consultation is effected for the purpose of helping the lawyer provide legal advice. Cavallaro v. United States, 284 F.3d 236, 247 (1st Cir.2002); United States v. Bornstein, 977 F.2d 112, 116–17 (4th Cir.1992).

(10) Communications must be confidential. The attorney-client privilege extends only to communications made confidentially. United States v. Robinson, 121 F.3d 971 (5th Cir.1997). Whether or not a communication is confidential turns on the intent of the parties to the communication. See United States v. Moscony, 927 F.2d 742, 752 (3d Cir.1991) (confidentiality of communication not destroyed when unsophisticated clients signed "affidavit" without intending its disclosure). Thus, the presence of an eavesdropper does not destroy the confidentiality of a communication. See United States v. Noriega, 917 F.2d 1543, 1550–51 (11th Cir.1990) (recording of attorney-client telephone conversations privileged if client had reasonable expectation of confidentiality).

If a client communicates information to a lawyer for the purpose of having the lawyer disclose it to third persons, the attorney-client privilege does not apply. United States v. Rockwell International, 897 F.2d 1255, 1265 (3d Cir.1990).

Example—Not privileged. In United States v. Oloyede, 982 F.2d 133, 141 (4th Cir.1992), a prosecution of an attorney for falsifying documents for citizenship applications, the court held that the attorney-client privilege did not protect communications made to the attorney by clients seeking citizenship. Since the clients intended that the communicated information was to be used to file their citizenship applications, their communications to the attorney were not confidential.

A limited amount of disclosure outside the circle of lawyer, client, and their representatives may be made without necessarily destroying confidentiality:

- Disclosure to third persons for the purpose of furthering the rendition of legal services is permissible. This may include disclosures to a client's spouse, parent, or business partner, or a joint client. Advisory Committee's Note. See Jenkins v. Bartlett, 487 F.3d 482, 490–91 (7th Cir.2007) (police liaison officer present to assist attorney appointed by union to represent police officer); In re Auclair, 961 F.2d 65, 69–70 (5th Cir.1992) (joint client).

- Disclosure to someone who is reasonably necessary for the transmission of the communication, such as an interpreter, is permissible. See, e.g., United States v. Evans, 113 F.3d 1457, 1464 (7th Cir.1997) (privilege inapplicable absent showing that third party's presence was necessary to accomplish object of consultation).

(11) Documents. Documents prepared to facilitate the rendition of legal services qualify as communications. However, documents that antedate the lawyer-client relationship are not within the privilege and cannot be immunized from disclosure by being placed in the attorney's hands. Fisher v. United States, 425 U.S. 391, 403–04, 96 S.Ct. 1569, 1577 (1976).

Example—Privileged. In Mason C. Day Excavating, Inc. v. Lumbermens Mut. Cas. Co., 143 F.R.D. 601 (M.D.N.C.1992), at the behest of counsel, the president of the plaintiff corporation tape recorded his observations of certain events for the sole purpose of obtaining legal advice. He turned the recordings over to counsel, who had them transcribed. The court held that the recordings and transcriptions were protected by the attorney-client privilege.

Example—Not privileged. Telephone company records of a grand jury target's wholly owned corporation were held unprotected by the attorney-client privilege. The fact that they had been turned over to an attorney did not convert them into privileged attorney-client communications. Matter of Grand Jury Subpoenas Dated October 22, 1991 and November 1, 1991, 959 F.2d 1158, 1165–66 (2d Cir.1992).

While a client's documents held by an attorney may be unprotected by the attorney-client privilege, the act of producing the documents may implicate the client's privilege against self-incrimination. Fisher v. United States, 425 U.S. 391, 410–11, 96 S.Ct. 1569, 1581 (1976).

(12) Client identity, fee arrangements. The identity of a client, fee arrangements, and the general purpose of the work performed are ordinarily considered outside the protection of the attorney-client privilege. United States v. Legal Services for New York City, 249 F.3d 1077, 1081–82 (D.C.Cir.2001) ("the general subject matters of clients' representations are not privileged"); In re Grand Jury Subpoena, 204 F.3d 516, 520 (4th Cir.2000) (client identity held not privileged); Montgomery County v. Microvote Corp., 175 F.3d 296, 304 (3d Cir.1999) (fee arrangement letter not privileged); Clarke v. American Commerce National Bank, 974 F.2d 127, 129–30 (9th Cir.1992) (attorney billing statements not privileged). In special circumstances, however, this information may be privileged. Although in the past courts used several different tests in identifying these special circumstances, most courts now agree that such information is protected only if its disclosure would be tantamount to revealing the substance of privileged communications. Vingelli v. United States, Drug Enforcement Agency, 992 F.2d 449, 452 (2d Cir.1993).

> **Example—Fee record information not privileged.** In Avgoustis v. Shinseki, 639 F.3d 1340, 1343–46 (Fed.Cir.2011), the court held that a provision requiring an attorney seeking attorney's fees to provide the general subject matter of his billing entries did not violate the attorney-client privilege. Descriptions such as "seeking the client's input," or "seeking approval for actions that require the consent of the client" do not require the attorney to reveal the nature of the advice sought or given.

> **Example—Client identity privileged.** In United States v. Liebman, 742 F.2d 807 (3d Cir.1984), the IRS served a summons on a law firm seeking the names of clients who had received specified advice from the law firm. The court held that the names of the firm's clients were privileged. Disclosing the names of the clients would effectively reveal the legal advice which they had received.

> **Example—Client identity not privileged.** In Taylor Lohmeyer Law Firm P.L.L.C. v. United States, 957 F.3d 510 (5th Cir.2020), the court upheld against an attorney-client privilege objection an IRS John Doe summons served on a law firm. The subpoena sought the names of U.S. taxpayers who, between 1995 and 2017, used the firm's services "to acquire, establish, maintain, operate, or control (1) any foreign financial account or other asset; (2) any foreign corporation, company, trust, foundation or other legal entity; or (3) any foreign or domestic financial account or other asset in the name of such foreign entity." The court held that the client identities were not "connected inextricably with a privileged communication." Their disclosure, therefore, would not effectively reveal privileged communications.

Despite agreement over the relevant legal standard, courts have reached markedly different conclusions in their application of the standard. Compare In re Subpoenaed Grand Jury Witness, 171 F.3d 511 (7th Cir.1999); Ralls v. United States, 52 F.3d 223 (9th Cir.1995) (fee payor's identity held privileged) with In re Grand Jury Subpoenas (Anderson), 906 F.2d 1485, 1488–89 (10th Cir.1990)(fee payor's identity held not privileged).

(13) Duration of privilege. The attorney-client privilege continues even after the attorney-client relationship has terminated. In fact, the attorney-client privilege may be asserted even after the death of the client. Swidler & Berlin v. United States, 524 U.S. 399, 118 S.Ct. 2081 (1998).

(14) Crime-fraud exception. The attorney-client privilege is inapplicable if the lawyer's services were knowingly sought or obtained to further a criminal or fraudulent endeavor.

(a)   This exception is directed only to communications concerning future acts. It does not apply where a client is seeking advice relating to crimes or frauds already committed. Advisory Committee's Note. The exception focuses on whether the client knew or should have known of the fraudulent or illegal nature of the conduct. But cf. In re Grand Jury 2021 Subpoenas, 87 F.4th 229, 255 (4th Cir.2023) (holding crime-fraud exception applicable to work-product privilege despite client's innocence of attorney's criminal conduct). The exception may apply even if the lawyer was unaware of the client's intentions. United States v. Doe, 429 F.3d 450, 454 (3d Cir.2005); In re Grand Jury Proceedings, John Doe No. N–92–86, Grand Jury No. 95–1, 102 F.3d 748, 751 (4th Cir.1996).

(b)   The party seeking to take advantage of the exception has the burden of establishing its applicability. Most courts state that the party seeking to pierce the privilege must establish that the client was engaged in an ongoing crime or fraud or was seeking to commit a crime or fraud at the time the communication was made. *United States v. Davis*, 1 F.3d 606, 609–10 (7th Cir.1993); *Haines v. Liggett Group Inc.*, 975 F.2d 81, 95–96 (3d Cir.1992). Some courts state that the communication must relate to the intended or ongoing crime or fraud. *In re Grand Jury Subpoena*, 2 F.4th 1339, 1349–51 (11th Cir.2021); *In re Chevron Corp.*, 633 F.3d 153, 166–67 (3d Cir.2011); *In re Grand Jury Proceedings*, 87 F.3d 377, 382–83 (9th Cir.1996). Other courts, however, require proof that the advice was used in furtherance of the crime or fraud. *In re Grand Jury Subpoena*, 745 F.3d 681, 692–93 (3d Cir.2014); *United States v. White*, 887 F.2d 267, 271 (D.C. Cir.1989).

Courts generally state that the party seeking to invoke the crime-fraud exception bears the burden of establishing a prima facie case, but have devised an array of standards in their struggle to define the meaning of "prima facie." See, e.g., *In re Grand Jury Subpoena*, 2 F.4th 1339, 1345 (11th Cir.2021) ("some foundation in fact"); *United States v. Gorski*, 807 F.3d 451, 460 (1st Cir.2015) ("reasonable basis . . . something less than a mathematical (more likely than not) probability"); *In re John Doe, Inc.*, 13 F.3d 633, 637 (2d Cir.1994) ("probable cause to believe"); *United States v. BDO Seidman, L.L.P.*, 492 F.3d 806, 818–19 (7th Cir.2007) (prima facie evidence must "give[ ] colour [sic] to the charge"); *In re Green Grand Jury Proceedings*, 492 F.3d 976, 983 (8th Cir.2007) (citing cases); *In re Grand Jury Proceedings #5 Empanelled Jan. 28, 2004*, 401 F.3d 247, 251 (4th Cir.2005) ("proof must be such as to subject the opposing party to the risk of non-persuasion if the evidence as to the disputed fact is left unrebutted"). In civil cases, the Ninth Circuit requires a preponderance of the evidence. *In re Napster, Inc. Copyright Litigation*, 479 F.3d 1078, 1094–95 (9th Cir.2007).

(c) The court may conduct an in camera review of allegedly privileged communications to determine whether the crime-fraud exception applies. The party seeking the in camera review must show that there exists "a factual basis adequate to support a good faith belief by a reasonable person" that an in camera review "may reveal evidence to establish the claim that the crime-fraud exception applies." *United States v. Zolin*, 491 U.S. 554, 572, 109 S.Ct. 2619, 2631 (1989). This showing must be made through the use of non-privileged materials. 491 U.S. at 573, 109 S.Ct. at 2631. See *United States v. Christensen*, 828 F.3d 763, 797–802 (9th Cir.2015) (applying *Zolin*), amended (7/8/2016).

(15) Other exceptions. There are four other exceptions to the attorney-client privilege listed in Proposed Rule 503. They apply to:

• Communications relevant to a dispute in which both parties claim through the same deceased client. See *United States v. Osborn*, 561 F.2d 1334, 1340 (9th Cir.1977).

• Communications relevant to an issue of breach of duty either by the lawyer to the client or by the client to the lawyer, such as a malpractice action or a suit to collect a fee. See *United States v. Pinson*, 584 F.3d 972, 977–78 (10th Cir.2009) (allegation of ineffective assistance of counsel waives privilege with respect to communications relating to attorney's strategic decisions); *Willy v. Administrative Review Board*, 423 F.3d 483 (5th Cir.2005) (breach of duty exception applies in suit by former in-house counsel against employer for retaliatory discharge).

• Communications relevant to an issue concerning an attested document to which the lawyer was an attesting witness.

• Communications relevant to a dispute between two or more clients who jointly consulted an attorney on a matter of common interest if the communications were made by any of the clients to the lawyer retained or consulted in common. *F.D.I.C. v. Ogden Corp.*, 202 F.3d 454, 461–64 (1st Cir.2000).

Courts have also recognized a "fiduciary exception," which precludes a trustee who obtains legal advice relating to his fiduciary obligations from asserting the attorney-client privilege against the trust's beneficiaries. See *United States v. Jicarilla Apache Nation*, 564 U.S. 162, 131 S.Ct. 2313 (2011). E.g., *Solis v. Food Employers Labor Relations Ass'n*, 644 F.3d 221 (4th Cir.2011) (applying fiduciary exception to communications between ERISA trustee and plan attorney; citing cases).

CROSS-REFERENCES

Common Objections (Chapter 3)

78. Privileged attorney-client communication

Treatises

4 Graham, Handbook of Federal Evidence §§ 503:1–503:7 (9th ed. 2020)

1 McCormick, Evidence §§ 87–97 (8th ed. 2020)

24 Wright and Graham, Federal Practice and Procedure §§ 5471–5507.2 (1986)

Proposed Rule 504. Psychotherapist-Patient Privilege

[NOT ENACTED]

(a) Definitions.

(1) A "patient" is a person who consults or is examined or interviewed by a psychotherapist.

(2) A "psychotherapist" is (A) a person authorized to practice medicine in any state or nation, or reasonably believed by the patient so to be, while engaged in the diagnosis or treatment of a mental or emotional condition, including drug addiction, or (B) a person licensed or certified as a psychologist under the laws of any state or nation, while similarly engaged.

(3) A communication is "confidential" if not intended to be disclosed to third persons other than those present to further the interest of the patient in the consultation, examination, or interview, or persons reasonably necessary for the transmission of the communication, or persons who are participating in the diagnosis and treatment under the direction of the psychotherapist, including members of the patient's family.

(b) General Rule of Privilege. A patient has a privilege to refuse to disclose and to prevent any other person from disclosing confidential communications, made for the purposes of diagnosis or treatment of his mental or emotional condition, including drug addiction, among himself, his psychotherapist, or persons who are participating in the diagnosis or treatment under the direction of the psychotherapist, including members of the patient's family.

(c) Who May Claim the Privilege. The privilege may be claimed by the patient, by his guardian or conservator, or by the personal representative of a deceased patient. The person who was the psychotherapist may claim the privilege but only on behalf of the patient. His authority so to do is presumed in the absence of evidence to the contrary.

(d) Exceptions.

(1) *Proceedings for hospitalization.* There is no privilege under this rule for communications relevant to an issue in proceedings to hospitalize the patient for mental illness, if the psychotherapist in the course of diagnosis or treatment has determined that the patient is in need of hospitalization.

(2) *Examination by order of judge.* If the judge orders an examination of the mental or emotional condition of the patient, communications made in the course thereof are not privileged under this rule with respect to the particular purpose for which the examination is ordered unless the judge orders otherwise.

(3) *Condition an element of claim or defense.* There is no privilege under this rule as to communications relevant to an issue of the mental or emotional condition of the patient in any proceeding in which he relies upon the condition as an element of his claim or defense, or, after the patient's death, in any proceeding in which any party relies upon the condition as an element of his claim or defense.

Authors' Note: Proposed Rule 504 was not enacted. In many ways it does not reflect the current state of the law.

AUTHORS' COMMENTS

(1) Scope and purpose of psychotherapist-patient and physician-patient privileges. Proposed Rule 504 embraced a privilege for psychotherapist-patient communications but rejected a privilege for physician-patient communications. The Advisory Committee believed that the special nature of the psychotherapist-patient relationship justified a privilege.

Various federal statutes, cited below, provide for confidentiality of certain treatment records. In addition, regulations promulgated to implement the federal Health Insurance Portability and Accountability Act of 1996 (HIPAA), see 45 C.F.R. Parts 160 and 164, protect the privacy of medical information.

(2) Psychotherapist-patient privilege recognized. In Jaffee v. Redmond, 518 U.S. 1, 116 S.Ct. 1923 (1996), the Supreme Court recognized the existence of a federal psychotherapist-patient privilege. The Court observed that a privilege would serve "the public interest by facilitating the provision of appropriate treatment for individuals suffering the effects of a mental or emotional problem." 518 U.S. at 11, 116 S.Ct. at 1929. The Court held that the privilege protects communications made to licensed social workers providing psychotherapy as well as to psychiatrists and psychologists. The Ninth Circuit has extended the privilege to unlicensed counselors. Oleszko v. State Compensation Ins. Fund, 243 F.3d 1154 (9th Cir.2001) (counselor in Employee Assistance Program). But see United States v. Wynn, 827 F.3d 778, 787 (8th Cir.2016) (privilege not applicable to statements made to nurses during calls to VA Crisis Line because nurses were not licensed psychotherapists). The privilege protects communications only when the patient is seeking or receiving diagnosis or treatment. See United States v. Bolander, 722 F.3d 199, 223 (4th Cir.2013) (privilege does not protect communications to psychotherapist for purpose of obtaining evaluation of mental condition rather than diagnosis or treatment); United States v. Ghane, 673 F.3d 771, 781–84 (8th Cir.2012) (statements to physician's assistant during emergency room intake not privileged).

(3) Psychotherapist-patient privilege—Exceptions. The Supreme Court provided little guidance as to what exceptions exist to the psychotherapist-patient privilege. It rejected the view of the lower court that the privilege may be breached whenever a court determines that the need for the evidence outweighs the patient's privacy interest. 518 U.S. at 17, 116 S.Ct. at 1932. Although the Court stated that it had no doubt that some exceptions do exist, id. at n.19, it declined to articulate what these are. The only example it gave—if a serious threat of harm to the patient or another could be averted only by disclosure—ordinarily would apply outside the context of an adjudicatory proceeding and thus would not even implicate the evidentiary privilege. See United States v. Glass, 133 F.3d 1356 (10th Cir.1998) (indicating further confusion about distinction between evidentiary privilege and non-judicial disclosure).

The First Circuit has held that the crime-fraud exception applies to the psychotherapist-patient privilege. In re Grand Jury Proceedings (Gregory P. Violette), 183 F.3d 71 (1st Cir.1999). Presumably, some sort of patient-litigant exception will be recognized as well. See Koch v. Cox, 489 F.3d 384 (D.C. Cir.2007) (plaintiff who was not seeking damages for emotional distress did not waive privilege); Doe v. Oberweis Dairy, 456 F.3d 704, 718 (7th Cir.2006) (plaintiff who was seeking damages for emotional distress waived privilege).

Courts are split as to whether a "dangerous-patient" exception should be recognized. Compare United States v. Ghane, 673 F.3d 771, 784–86 (8th Cir.2012); United States v. Chase, 340 F.3d 978 (9th Cir.2003) (en banc); United States v. Hayes, 227 F.3d 578, 583–86 (6th Cir.2000) (rejecting exception) with United States v. Glass, 133 F.3d 1356, 1359 (10th Cir.1998) (adopting exception). The Fifth Circuit has held the privilege does not apply when a patient conveys a threat to his therapist after being warned that the therapist will convey the threat to the authorities or his victims. In such instances, the requisite confidentiality is absent. United States v. Auster, 517 F.3d 312 (5th Cir.2008).

The Fifth Circuit has questioned whether the psychotherapist-patient privilege applies in the sentencing phase of a capital murder trial. United States v. Fackrell, 991 F.3d 589, 605–06 (5th Cir.2021).

(4) Physician-patient privilege. The federal courts have been unanimous in rejecting a physician-patient privilege. E.g., Gilbreath v. Guadalupe Hospital Foundation, 5 F.3d 785, 791 (5th Cir.1993); Hancock v. Dodson, 958 F.2d 1367, 1373 (6th Cir.1992) ("the federal courts do not recognize a federal physician-patient privilege"). But these cases all preceded Jaffee v. Redmond, 518 U.S. 1, 116 S.Ct. 1923 (1996). Although the Court there both distinguished ordinary medical care from psychotherapy and relied on the Advisory Committee's decision to promulgate a psychotherapist-patient privilege in Proposed Rule 504, 518 U.S. at 10, 116 S.Ct. at 1928, its decision may nonetheless prompt a reevaluation of the status of a physician-patient privilege. One important factor in the *Jaffee* decision was the widespread acceptance of a psychotherapist-patient privilege among the states. Since most states also recognize at least a limited physician-patient privilege, the case can be made for acceptance of such a privilege in federal court. But see United States v. Bek, 493 F.3d 790, 802 (7th Cir.2007) ("we can find no circuit authority in support of a physician-patient privilege, even after *Jaffee*").

CROSS-REFERENCES

Common Objections (Chapter 3)

82.   Privileged physician-patient communication

83.   Privileged psychotherapist-patient communication

Treatises

4 Graham, Handbook of Federal Evidence § 504:1 (9th ed. 2020)

1 McCormick, Evidence §§ 98–105 (8th ed. 2020)

25 Wright and Graham, Federal Practice and Procedure §§ 5521–5553 (1989)

Proposed Rule 505.   Husband-Wife Privilege

[NOT ENACTED]

(a)   General Rule of Privilege. An accused in a criminal proceeding has a privilege to prevent his spouse from testifying against him.

(b)   Who May Claim the Privilege. The privilege may be claimed by the accused or by the spouse on his behalf. The authority of the spouse to do so is presumed in the absence of evidence to the contrary.

(c)   Exceptions. There is no privilege under this rule (1) in proceedings in which one spouse is charged with a crime against the person or property of the other or of a child of either, or with a crime against the person or property of a third person committed in the course of committing a crime against the other, or (2) as to matters occurring prior to the marriage, or (3) in proceedings in which a spouse is charged with importing an alien for prostitution or other immoral purpose in violation of 8 U.S.C.A. § 1328, with transporting a female in interstate commerce for immoral purposes or other offense in violation of 18 U.S.C.A. §§ 2421–2424, or with violation of other similar statutes.

Authors' Note: Proposed Rule 505 was not enacted. It does not reflect the current state of the law.

AUTHORS' COMMENTS

(1)   Scope and purpose of spousal privileges. Proposed Rule 505, which embodied the common-law tradition that an accused could prevent his spouse from testifying against him, was squarely rejected in Trammel v. United States, 445 U.S. 40, 100 S.Ct. 906 (1980). Federal courts now recognize two distinct spousal privileges: (1) a testimonial (or anti-marital facts) privilege, which allows the spouse of a criminal defendant to refuse to testify against him; and (2) a communications privilege, which permits a spouse to protect confidential communications made to his spouse in confidence.

The marital privileges "must be narrowly construed because they are in derogation of the search for truth." United States v. Short, 4 F.3d 475, 478 (7th Cir.1993).

(2)   Testimonial privilege—Generally. The testimonial privilege, which is available only in criminal cases, provides that the spouse of an accused may not be compelled to testify against the accused spouse. See United States v. Premises Known as 281 Syosset Woodbury Rd., Woodbury, New York, 71 F.3d 1067, 1070–71 (2d Cir.1995) (testimonial privilege inapplicable in civil forfeiture proceeding brought against property owned by testifying spouse); cf. United States v. Yerardi, 192 F.3d 14 (1st Cir.1999) (privilege applies in criminal forfeiture proceeding ancillary to criminal case where answers might lead to criminal prosecution of spouse on related matters). Unlike the traditional rule of spousal incompetency, however, the testimonial privilege is vested in the witness spouse. She may choose to testify against her spouse. See United States v. Bad Wound, 203 F.3d 1072, 1075 (8th Cir.2000) (spouse voluntarily waived privilege not to testify by entering into plea agreement that required her to testify at "other proceedings as required").

114

Vesting the privilege in the witness spouse is consistent with the rationale for the privilege: the preservation of marital harmony. Presumably, the witness spouse will choose to testify only when she feels the marriage is not worth preserving. Trammel v. United States, 445 U.S. 40, 53, 100 S.Ct. 906, 913 (1980). The testimonial privilege is not based on notions of confidentiality and, consequently, is not waived simply because the witness-spouse chose to testify at an earlier proceeding. United States v. Lilley, 581 F.2d 182, 189 (8th Cir.1978).

The testimonial privilege only applies when the witness-spouse's testimony would be adverse to the defendant spouse. A witness-spouse may be compelled to give testimony that is favorable to the defendant-spouse or neutral in effect. In re Grand Jury Proceedings, 664 F.2d 423, 430 (5th Cir.1981).

(3) Testimonial privilege—Exceptions. The testimonial privilege applies only when the witness-spouse and defendant-spouse are still validly married. In accordance with the underlying justification for the privilege, courts have interpreted the marriage requirement quite stringently. See Authors' Comment (8) infra. Otherwise, the law regarding possible exceptions to the testimonial privilege is relatively undeveloped. At least one court has accepted each of the following exceptions and compelled the witness-spouse to testify:

- As to matters that occurred before the marriage. United States v. Clark, 712 F.2d 299, 302 (7th Cir.1983). But cf. United States v. Blunt, 930 F.3d 119 (3d Cir.2019) (finding privilege applicable without discussing that marriage took place after events in question).

- When the spousal testimony relates to the abuse of a minor child within the household. United States v. Allery, 526 F.2d 1362, 1365–67 (8th Cir.1975) (exception to former rule of spousal incompetency when crime is against person or property of witness-spouse or minor child of either spouse). But compare United States v. Castillo, 140 F.3d 874, 884–85 (10th Cir.1998) (seeming to recognize exception) with United States v. Jarvison, 409 F.3d 1221, 1231–32 (10th Cir.2005) (declining to recognize exception).

- When the testifying spouse is the victim of the defendant's violent acts. United States v. Seminole, 865 F.3d 1150 (9th Cir.2017). Cf. Wyatt v. United States, 362 U.S. 525, 80 S.Ct. 901 (1960) (exception to former rule of spousal incompetency when defendant-spouse is accused of Mann Act violation).

- When the spouses were joint participants in the crime. The Seventh Circuit has recognized a joint-participant exception to the testimonial privilege. United States v. Clark, 712 F.2d 299, 301 (7th Cir.1983). But the First, Second, Third, and Ninth Circuits have refused to create such an exception. United States v. Pineda-Mateo, 905 F.2d 13 (1st Cir.2018); In re Grand Jury Subpoena United States, 755 F.2d 1022 (2d Cir.1985), judgment vac'd on other grounds, 475 U.S. 133, 106 S.Ct. 1253 (1986); Appeal of Malfitano, 633 F.2d 276, 278–80 (3d Cir.1980); United States v. Ramos-Osequera, 120 F.3d 1028, 1042 (9th Cir.1997).

(4) Communication privilege—Generally. The marital communication privilege protects confidential communications made during marriage. It is premised on the notion that the existence of a privilege encourages spouses to confide in one another. United States v. Brock, 724 F.3d 817, 820–21 (7th Cir.2013). Although Proposed Rule 505 contained no such privilege, it is universally accepted, and applies both in civil and criminal cases.

(5) Communication privilege—Elements. The marital communication privilege applies only to confidential communications between spouses.

(a) *Communication.* Conduct that does not attempt to convey a message does not qualify as a communication and thus is left unprotected by this privilege.

Example. In United States v. Pugh, 945 F.3d 9, 19 (2d Cir.2019), the court held that defendant-husband failed to show that he intended to convey to his wife a draft of a letter that was found on his laptop. Defendant wrote the letter in English, and it had not been translated into Arabic, the only language his wife spoke.

Example. In United States v. Estes, 793 F.2d 465, 466–67 (2d Cir.1986), the defendant's wife testified that he told her that he stole some money. She also described her husband's actions in counting, hiding and laundering the money. The court of appeals held that the husband's statement that he stole the money qualified as a privileged communication, and should not have been admitted. The wife's testimony about her husband's subsequent conduct, however, was admissible as it did not involve communicative activity.

(b) *Confidential.* Statements between spouses that are made in the presence of third persons or that are not intended to be confidential are not privileged. United States v. Strobehn, 421 F.3d 1017, 1021 (9th Cir.2005).

Example—Not confidential. In United States v. Hamilton, 701 F.3d 404, 407–09 (4th Cir.2012), the court held that emails a husband sent to his spouse on his workplace computer were not privileged. His employer's computer policy stated that users have "no expectation of privacy in their use of the Computer System" and that all information on the system "is subject to inspection and monitoring at any time." Therefore, the husband did not have a reasonable expectation that the emails were confidential.

Example—Not confidential. In United States v. Taylor, 92 F.3d 1313, 1331–32 (2d Cir.1996), the court affirmed the trial judge's decision to admit into evidence a recording of a telephone conversation between defendant and his wife. Because the tape included an aside made by defendant to someone who appeared to be within normal speaking range, the judge held that defendant had failed to meet his burden of proving that the communication was made outside the presence of third parties.

Example—Not confidential. In United States v. Madoch, 149 F.3d 596, 602 (7th Cir.1998), tape-recorded conversations between defendant and her husband, who was in jail, were held not privileged. The court held that neither spouse could reasonably expect that their conversations would be confidential in this setting.

(c) *During marriage.* The communication must be made during a viable marriage. See Authors' Comment (8) infra. A confidential marital communication retains its privileged status after the marriage has ended. Pereira v. United States, 347 U.S. 1, 6, 74 S.Ct. 358, 361 (1954).

(6) Communication privilege—Exceptions. Although courts have interpreted the marriage requirement stringently for the marital testimonial privilege, see Authors' Comment 505(3), courts have not created an analogous exception to the marital communication privilege for sham marriages. See United States v. Fomichev, 899 F.3d 766 (9th Cir.2018), amended, 909 F.3d 1078 (9th Cir.2018). Courts have, however, recognized exceptions to the marital communications privilege:

• As to communications concerning present or future crimes in which both spouses are participants. E.g., United States v. Miller, 588 F.3d 897, 904–05 (5th Cir.2009); United States v. Vo, 413 F.3d 1010, 1017 (9th Cir.2005); United States v. Westmoreland, 312 F.3d 302, 308–09 (7th Cir.2002) (statement made to wife before she became joint participant is privileged; statements made after wife became participant are not); United States v. Bey, 188 F.3d 1, 4–6 (1st Cir.1999). But see United States v. Premises Known as 281 Syosset Woodbury Rd., Woodbury, New York, 71 F.3d 1067, 1073 (2d Cir.1995) (exception applies only where spouse would testify willingly about joint criminal activities).

• When the communication relates to a crime against the spouse or the child of a spouse. United States v. Underwood, 859 F.3d 386, 390–92 (6th Cir.2017) (sexual abuse of testifying spouse's granddaughter) (citing cases); United States v. Breton, 740 F.3d 1, 10–12 (1st Cir.2014) (offense against child of either spouse); United States v. Rakes, 136 F.3d 1, 4 n.5 (1st Cir.1998) (abuse of spouse or some other family member); United States v. Bahe, 128 F.3d 1440, 1445–46 (10th Cir.1997) (abuse of any minor child within the household). The Eighth Circuit extended this exception to a case in which the crimes with which the defendant was charged were against third parties but were committed in the course of the defendant's attempt to kill his spouse. United States v. White Owl, 39 F.4th 527 (8th Cir.2022).

Example—Not privileged. In United States v. White, 974 F.2d 1135, 1137–38 (9th Cir.1992), defendant was charged with causing his stepdaughter's death. His wife was permitted to testify that a week before her daughter died, the defendant told her that if she left the girl with him again he would kill the daughter and then kill the wife.

(7) Testimonial and communication privileges distinguished. The testimonial and communication privileges may be distinguished in the following ways:

(a) *Types of cases.* The testimonial privilege applies only in criminal cases; the communication privilege applies both in civil and criminal cases.

(b) *What it applies to.* The testimonial privilege applies only to the current spouse of a criminal defendant. The spouse may refuse to testify about anything that would be adverse to the defendant-spouse. The communication privilege applies only to confidential communications made during marriage and does not apply to facts observed by the spouse or pre-marital communications.

(c) *Holder of privilege.* The witness-spouse holds the testimonial privilege; it is hers to assert or waive. The communicating spouse certainly holds and may assert the communication privilege. The trend is to vest the privilege in the non-communicating spouse as well. This enables the non-communicating spouse to prevent the communicating spouse from waiving the privilege. United States v. Brock, 724 F.3d 817, 820 (7th Cir.2013); United States v. Montgomery, 384 F.3d 1050, 1058–59 (9th Cir.2004) ("either spouse may assert the privilege to prevent testimony regarding communications between the spouses"); United States v. Porter, 986 F.2d 1014, 1019 (6th Cir.1993).

(d) *Duration of privilege.* The testimonial privilege applies only during the marriage. It terminates with the marriage. The communication privilege applies both during and after the marriage.

(8)   Determination of marital status. The person asserting either of the marital privileges has the burden of establishing the existence of a valid marriage. United States v. Acker, 52 F.3d 509, 514–15 (4th Cir.1995) (defendant who lived together with alleged witness-spouse as man and wife for twenty-five years in states that did not recognize common-law marriage failed to establish existence of valid marriage). A good faith belief that a marriage is valid is not sufficient. United States v. Hamilton, 19 F.3d 350, 354 (7th Cir.1994) (communication privilege inapplicable where defendant's "wife" had not been legally divorced from first husband).

Even when a legally valid marriage exists, courts are increasingly unwilling to apply the marital privileges where the marriage has ceased being viable. United States v. Singleton, 260 F.3d 1295, 1300 (11th Cir.2001) ("the privilege is not available when the parties are permanently separated").

Example—Not privileged. In United States v. Porter, 986 F.2d 1014, 1019 (6th Cir.1993), the defendant communicated with his wife 10 or 12 days after she moved out. A week earlier, she had been hospitalized and the defendant had not visited her. The court of appeals held that the trial court did not abuse its discretion in concluding that the communication was made when the spouses were permanently separated and thus was not privileged.

CROSS-REFERENCES

Common Objections (Chapter 3)

80.   Privileged marital communication

81.   Privileged; marital testimonial privilege

Treatises

4 Graham, Handbook of Federal Evidence §§ 505:1–505:2 (9th ed. 2020)

1 McCormick, Evidence §§ 78–86 (8th ed. 2020)

25 Wright and Graham, Federal Practice and Procedure §§ 5571–5602 (1989)

Proposed Rule 506.   Communications to Clergymen

[NOT ENACTED]

(a)   Definitions. As used in this rule:

(1)   A "clergyman" is a minister, priest, rabbi, or other similar functionary of a religious organization, or an individual reasonably believed so to be by the person consulting him.

(2)   A communication is "confidential" if made privately and not intended for further disclosure except to other persons present in furtherance of the purpose of the communication.

(b) General Rule of Privilege. A person has a privilege to refuse to disclose and to prevent another from disclosing a confidential communication by the person to a clergyman in his professional character as spiritual adviser.

(c) Who May Claim the Privilege. The privilege may be claimed by the person, by his guardian or conservator, or by his personal representative if he is deceased. The clergyman may claim the privilege on behalf of the person. His authority so to do is presumed in the absence of evidence to the contrary.

AUTHORS' COMMENTS

(1) Scope and purpose of clergy privilege. Proposed Rule 506 provides a privilege for confidential communications made to a clergyman in his capacity as a spiritual adviser. Although the issue arises infrequently, this privilege has been recognized by the federal courts. See In re Grand Jury Investigation, 918 F.2d 374 (3d Cir.1990). It has been justified on a number of grounds, including the demands of religious liberty, the need for individuals to be able to disclose "flawed acts or thoughts" to a spiritual counselor, and the desire to avoid confrontations with members of the clergy who would refuse to divulge communications they feel ethically obligated to keep confidential. See Mullen v. United States, 263 F.2d 275, 280 (D.C.Cir.1958) (Fahy, J., concurring).

(2) Clergy broadly defined. Proposed Rule 506 defines a member of the clergy as including a minister, priest, rabbi, accredited Christian Science Practitioner, or other similar functionary of a religious organization or an individual reasonably believed so to be by the communicant. See In re Grand Jury Investigation, 918 F.2d 374, 384 n. 13 (3d Cir.1990) (approving this definition).

(3) Communication must be made for spiritual advice. Communications made to members of the clergy in their professional capacity as spiritual advisers are protected. A communication need not, however, be penitential in nature.

> **Example—Not privileged.** In Cox v. Miller, 296 F.3d 89, 111 (2d Cir.2002), the court rejected defendant's claim that his confessions of murder, made to fellow members of Alcoholics Anonymous, were privileged. The defendant confessed "primarily to unburden himself, to seek empathy and emotional support, and perhaps in some instances to seek practical guidance . . . [but not] 'for the purpose of obtaining spiritual guidance.'"

> **Example—Not privileged.** In United States v. Dube, 820 F.2d 886, 889–90 (7th Cir.1987), the court rejected the defendant's assertion of the clergy-communicant privilege. The communications at issue involved defendant's efforts to obtain assistance in avoiding tax obligations, rather than spiritual advice.

(4) Communications must be confidential. Communications made to a member of a clergy in a group setting, such as a joint consultation by a husband and wife, may be privileged. The test is whether the communications were made with a reasonable expectation of confidentiality. In re Grand Jury Investigation, 918 F.2d 374, 385–88 (3d Cir.1990) (remanding for determination as to whether confidentiality was destroyed by presence of person not related by blood to family members who together sought counseling).

CROSS-REFERENCES

Common Objections (Chapter 3)

79. Privileged; clergy-communicant privilege

Treatises

4 Graham, Handbook of Federal Evidence § 506:1 (9th ed. 2020)

1 McCormick, Evidence § 76.2 (8th ed. 2020)

26 Wright and Graham, Federal Practice and Procedure §§ 5611–5626 (1992)

Proposed Rule 507. Political Vote

[NOT ENACTED]

Every person has a privilege to refuse to disclose the tenor of his vote at a political election conducted by secret ballot unless the vote was cast illegally.

AUTHORS' COMMENTS

(1) Scope and purpose of voter's privilege. Proposed Rule 507 recognizes that "[s]ecrecy after the ballot has been cast is as essential as secrecy in the act of voting." Advisory Committee's Note. It thus provides that voters are privileged from disclosing how they voted. While federal caselaw supporting (or rejecting) the voter's privilege is non-existent, many states recognize it. 26 Wright and Graham, Federal Practice and Procedure § 5632 (1992).

(2) Exception for illegal vote. Proposed Rule 507 withdraws the privilege for an individual whose vote was cast illegally. See Oliphint v. Christy, 157 Tex. 1, 9, 299 S.W.2d 933, 939 (1957) ("the privilege of nondisclosure belongs only to the legal voter").

CROSS-REFERENCES

Treatises

4 Graham, Handbook of Federal Evidence § 507:1 (9th ed. 2020)

26 Wright and Graham, Federal Practice and Procedure §§ 5631–5638 (1992)

Proposed Rule 508. Trade Secrets

[NOT ENACTED]

A person has a privilege, which may be claimed by him or his agent or employee, to refuse to disclose and to prevent other persons from disclosing a trade secret owned by him, if the allowance of the privilege will not tend to conceal fraud or otherwise work injustice. When disclosure is directed, the judge shall take such protective measure as the interests of the holder of the privilege and of the parties and the furtherance of justice may require.

AUTHORS' COMMENTS

(1) Scope and purpose of trade secrets privilege. The federal courts have long recognized a qualified privilege for trade secrets. Federal Open Market Committee of the Federal Reserve System v. Merrill, 443 U.S. 340, 356, 99 S.Ct. 2800, 2810 (1979). The qualified nature of the privilege reflects the courts' desire to accommodate the needs of litigants while fostering technological innovation and advances in business practices. Therefore, the privilege protects trade secrets from disclosure, but only if allowing the privilege will not tend to conceal a fraud or otherwise work an injustice. Federal Rule of Civil Procedure 26(c)(7) protects trade secrets during discovery.

(2) Trade secrets defined. Proposed Rule 508 offers no definition of "trade secret." For guidance, courts most frequently refer to the six-factor test that first appeared in the Restatement of Torts § 757 comment b (1939)—now referenced in the Restatement (Third) of Unfair Competition § 39 Reporter's note to comment d (1995)—as well as the Uniform Trade Secrets Act § 1(4).

(3) Protective measures. When disclosure is necessary, the court must take whatever measures the interests of the trade secret's owner, the parties, and the furtherance of justice may require. Such measures may include:

- Taking testimony in camera. E.g., In re Iowa Freedom of Information Council, 724 F.2d 658 (8th Cir.1983).

- Allowing inspection, but not copying, of trade secret materials. See Struthers Scientific and Int'l Corp. v. General Foods Corp., 51 F.R.D. 149 (D.Del.1970).

•   Requiring counsel to whom disclosure is made not to reveal the information to their clients. E.I. Du Pont De Nemours Powder Co. v. Masland, 244 U.S. 100, 37 S.Ct. 575 (1917); R.C. Olmstead, Inc. v. CU Interface, LLC, 606 F.3d 262, 267–69 (6th Cir.2010).

CROSS-REFERENCES

Treatises

4 Graham, Handbook of Federal Evidence § 508:1 (9th ed. 2020)

26 Wright and Graham, Federal Practice and Procedure §§ 5641–5652 (1992)

Proposed Rule 509.   Secrets of State and Other Official Information

[NOT ENACTED]

(a) Definitions.

(1)   *Secret of state.* A "secret of state" is a governmental secret relating to the national defense or the international relations of the United States.

(2)   *Official information.* "Official information" is information within the custody or control of a department or agency of the government the disclosure of which is shown to be contrary to the public interest and which consists of: (A) intragovernmental opinions or recommendations submitted for consideration in the performance of decisional or policy making functions, or (B) subject to the provisions of 18 U.S.C. § 3500, investigatory files compiled for law enforcement purposes and not otherwise available, or (C) information within the custody or control of a governmental department or agency whether initiated within the department or agency or acquired by it in its exercise of its official responsibilities and not otherwise available to the public pursuant to 5 U.S.C. § 552.

(b) General Rule of Privilege. The government has a privilege to refuse to give evidence and to prevent any person from giving evidence upon a showing of reasonable likelihood of danger that the evidence will disclose a secret of state or official information, as defined in this rule.

(c) Procedures. The privilege for secrets of state may be claimed only by the chief officer of the government agency or department administering the subject matter which the secret information sought concerns, but the privilege for official information may be asserted by any attorney representing the government. The required showing may be made in whole or in part in the form of a written statement. The judge may hear the matter in chambers, but all counsel are entitled to inspect the claim and showing and to be heard thereon, except that, in the case of secrets of state, the judge upon motion of the government, may permit the government to make the required showing in the above form *in camera*. If the judge sustains the privilege upon a showing *in camera*, the entire text of the government's statements shall be sealed and preserved in the court's records in the event of appeal. In the case of privilege claimed for official information the court may require examination *in camera* of the information itself. The judge may take any protective measure which the interests of the government and the furtherance of justice may require.

(d) Notice to Government. If the circumstances of the case indicate a substantial possibility that a claim of privilege would be appropriate but has not been made because of oversight or lack of knowledge, the judge shall give or cause notice to be given to the officer entitled to claim the privilege and shall stay further proceedings a reasonable time to afford opportunity to assert a claim of privilege.

(e) Effect of Sustaining Claim. If a claim of privilege is sustained in a proceeding to which the government is a party and it appears that another party is thereby deprived of material evidence, the judge shall make any further orders which the interests of justice require, including striking the testimony of a witness, declaring a mistrial, finding against the government upon an issue as to which the evidence is relevant, or dismissing the action.

AUTHORS' COMMENTS

(1)　Scope and purpose of state secrets and official information privilege. In an effort to protect the national security and to foster informed decision-making, various types of governmental information and communications have traditionally been held privileged. Proposed Rule 509 sought to bring together under one heading several distinct common law privileges, not all of which have been accorded the same degree of protection.

Several statutes bear on privilege questions in this area. See, e.g., 5 U.S.C.A. § 552 (Freedom of Information Act); 18 U.S.C.A. App. 3 § 1 et seq. (Classified Information Procedures Act). See Federal Bureau of Investigation v. Fazaga 595 U.S. 344, 142 S.Ct. 1051 (2022) (50 U.S.C. § 1806(f) does not modify or displace state secrets privilege).

(2)　Types of privileged information. The courts have never defined precisely what qualifies as a state secret. Among the governmental information and communications held privileged are:

• 　Military, intelligence, and diplomatic information, disclosure of which would be inimical to the national security. United States v. Reynolds, 345 U.S. 1, 73 S.Ct. 528 (1953). E.g., General Dynamics Corp. v. United States, 563 U.S. 478, 131 S.Ct. 1900 (2011) (stealth aircraft technology); Abilt v. C.I.A., 848 F.3d 305, 314–15 (4th Cir.2017) (various information relating to CIA programs and officers); United States v. Stewart, 590 F.3d 93, 131–32 (2d Cir.2009) (details of National Security Agency surveillance operations); Tenet v. Doe, 544 U.S. 1, 125 S.Ct. 1230, 1236–37 (2005).

• 　Advisory opinions and recommendations contained in communications between government personnel, or between government personnel and outside consultants, that were part of the deliberative or policy-making process. NLRB v. Sears, Roebuck & Co., 421 U.S. 132, 150–52, 95 S.Ct. 1504, 1516–17 (1975); see also In re Sealed Case, 121 F.3d 729 (D.C.Cir.1997) (privilege for communication made by presidential advisers). This privilege applies only to "predecisional" communications and does not protect communications made subsequent to an agency decision. See Loving v. Department of Defense, 550 F.3d 32, 38 (D.C. Cir.2008). Nor does it protect purely factual information. Natural Resources Defense Council v. United States Environmental Protection Agency, 954 F.3d 150, 156–57 (2d Cir.2020); Assembly of State of California v. United States Department of Commerce, 968 F.2d 916, 921–22 (9th Cir.1992). The privilege is only a qualified one; communications must be disclosed upon a showing that the need for them outweighs the government's interest in non-disclosure. Hinckley v. United States, 140 F.3d 277, 285–86 (D.C.Cir.1998); Texaco Puerto Rico, Inc. v. Department of Consumer Affairs, 60 F.3d 867, 885 (1st Cir.1995).

• 　The investigative reports and files of a government agency charged with enforcement of civil or criminal law that are compiled for law enforcement purposes. This privilege is "inextricably intertwined" with the law enforcement records exemption in the FOIA, 5 U.S.C.A. § 552(b)(7). McCormick, Evidence § 108 (5th ed. 1999). This privilege is also a qualified one. See, e.g., Mapother v. Department of Justice, 3 F.3d 1533, 1540 (D.C.Cir.1993).

(3)　Government is privilege holder. The government is the holder of these privileges. The state secrets privilege must be asserted by the chief officer of the department or agency that has control over the material in question. United States v. Reynolds, 345 U.S. 1, 8, 73 S.Ct. 528, 531 (1953).

CROSS-REFERENCES

Treatises

4 Graham, Handbook of Federal Evidence § 509:1 (9th ed. 2020)

1 McCormick, Evidence §§ 106–110 (8th ed. 2020)

26 Wright and Graham, Federal Practice and Procedure §§ 5661–5672 (1992)

26A Wright and Graham, Federal Practice and Procedure §§ 5673–5693 (1992)

Proposed Rule 510.　Identity of Informer

[NOT ENACTED]

(a)　Rule of Privilege. The government or a state or subdivision thereof has a privilege to refuse to disclose the identity of a person who has furnished information relating to or assisting in an investigation of a possible violation of law to a law enforcement officer or member of a legislative committee or its staff conducting an investigation.

(b) Who May Claim. The privilege may be claimed by an appropriate representative of the government, regardless of whether the information was furnished to an officer of the government or of a state or subdivision thereof. The privilege may be claimed by an appropriate representative of a state or subdivision if the information was furnished to an officer thereof, except that in criminal cases the privilege shall not be allowed if the government objects.

(c) Exceptions.

(1) *Voluntary disclosure; informer a witness.* No privilege exists under this rule if the identity of the informer or his interest in the subject matter of his communication has been disclosed to those who would have cause to resent the communication by a holder of the privilege or by the informer's own action, or if the informer appears as a witness for the government.

(2) *Testimony on merits.* If it appears from the evidence in the case or from other showing by a party that an informer may be able to give testimony necessary to a fair determination of the issue of guilt or innocence in a criminal case or of a material issue on the merits in a civil case to which the government is a party, and the government invokes the privilege, the judge shall give the government an opportunity to show *in camera* facts relevant to determining whether the informer can, in fact, supply that testimony. The showing will ordinarily be in the form of affidavits, but the judge may direct that testimony be taken if he finds that the matter cannot be resolved satisfactorily upon affidavit. If the judge finds that there is a reasonable probability that the informer can give the testimony, and the government elects not to disclose his identity, the judge on motion of the defendant in a criminal case shall dismiss the charges to which the testimony would relate, and the judge may do so on his own motion. In civil cases, he may make any order that justice requires. Evidence submitted to the judge shall be sealed and preserved to be made available to the appellate court in the event of an appeal, and the contents shall not otherwise be revealed without consent of the government. All counsel and parties shall be permitted to be present at every stage of proceedings under this subdivision except a showing *in camera*, at which no counsel or party shall be permitted to be present.

(3) *Legality of obtaining evidence.* If information from an informer is relied upon to establish the legality of the means by which evidence was obtained and the judge is not satisfied that the information was received from an informer reasonably believed to be reliable or credible, he may require the identity of the informer to be disclosed. The judge shall, on request of the government, direct that the disclosure be made *in camera.* All counsel and parties concerned with the issue of legality shall be permitted to be present at every stage of proceedings under this subdivision except a disclosure *in camera*, at which no counsel or party shall be permitted to be present. If disclosure of the identity of the informer is made *in camera*, the record thereof shall be sealed and preserved to be made available to the appellate court in the event of an appeal, and the contents shall not otherwise be revealed without consent of the government.

AUTHORS' COMMENTS

(1) Scope and purpose of privilege for informer's identity. The existence of a qualified privilege for an informer's identity allows law enforcement officials to promise anonymity to potential informers who would otherwise be deterred from providing information by the fear of physical or economic retaliation. Roviaro v. United States, 353 U.S. 53, 59, 77 S.Ct. 623, 627 (1957). The privilege extends only to the informer's identity. The contents of an informer's communications to law enforcement officials are protected only if their disclosure would tend to reveal the informer's identity. Id.; United States v. Sanchez, 988 F.2d 1384, 1391 (5th Cir.1993).

(2) Who may claim. The privilege may be claimed by a representative of the federal government, even if the United States is a not party to the action or was not the recipient of the information. The privilege may also be asserted by a representative of a state or a subdivision of the state if the information was furnished to one of its officers. In criminal cases, the federal government may veto a state's claim of the privilege.

(3)　Civil cases. Although invoked infrequently, the privilege is applicable in civil cases. See, e.g., Wade v. Ramos, 26 F.4th 440, 445–47 (7th Cir.2022); In re Walsh, 15 F.4th 1005, 1008–11 (9th Cir.2021); In re Perez, 749 F.3d 849 (9th Cir.2014). To overcome the government's privilege claim in a civil case, the party seeking disclosure must establish that its need for the information outweighs the government's interest in nondisclosure. In re Walsh, 15 F.4th 1005, 1009 (9th Cir.2021).

(4)　Criminal cases—Testimony on merits—Procedure. Once the privilege is invoked, the defendant has the burden of making a threshold showing that the informer may be able to give testimony necessary to a fair determination of guilt or innocence. United States v. Amador-Galvan, 9 F.3d 1414, 1417 (9th Cir.1993). If the defendant satisfies this burden, the following procedures should be followed.

(a)　The court should conduct an in camera hearing to allow the government to demonstrate facts pertinent to whether the informer can indeed provide such testimony. United States v. Spires, 3 F.3d 1234, 1238 (9th Cir.1993). This may often be done via affidavit, but the court may direct the taking of testimony.

(b)　Although Proposed Rule 510(c)(2) states that no counsel shall be present at the in camera hearing, some courts have suggested that counsel should be permitted to participate. United States v. Henderson, 241 F.3d 638, 645 (9th Cir.2000) (suggesting presence of counsel in conjunction with gag order); United States v. Mendoza-Burciaga, 981 F.2d 192, 195–96 (5th Cir.1992) (same). See United States v. Spires, 3 F.3d 1234, 1238 n. 1 (9th Cir.1993).

(c)　If the court determines that a reasonable probability exists that the informer can give testimony necessary to a fair determination of guilt or innocence, the government must choose whether to disclose the identity. If the government elects not to disclose, the court must, upon the defendant's request, dismiss the charges to which the testimony would relate. Even if the defendant fails to move to dismiss, the court may dismiss the charges sua sponte.

(5)　Criminal case—Relevant factors. In deciding whether to order disclosure, the court must balance "the public interest in protecting the flow of information against the individual's right to prepare his defense." Roviaro v. United States, 353 U.S. 53, 62, 77 S.Ct. 623, 629 (1957). This requires consideration of (1) the informant's degree of involvement in the crime, (2) the extent to which disclosure would be helpful to the defense, and (3) the government's interest in non-disclosure. United States v. Jones, 930 F.3d 367, 381 (5th Cir.2019). Courts are most likely to require disclosure when:

•　The informer was an active participant in the crime. United States v. Mendoza-Salgado, 964 F.2d 993, 1001 (10th Cir.1992).

•　The informer is the "only witness in a position to amplify or contradict the testimony of government witnesses." United States v. Martinez, 922 F.2d 914, 920–21 (1st Cir.1991).

When, however, the informant is a "mere tipster," disclosure typically is unnecessary. United States v. Leonard, 884 F.3d 730, 735 (7th Cir.2018).

(6)　Criminal case—Legality of obtained evidence. If an issue is raised concerning the adequacy of information obtained from an informer that was relied upon to supply probable cause for an arrest, search or seizure, the court has discretion to conduct an in camera hearing and order the government to disclose the informer's identity. United States v. Harris, 531 F.3d 507, 515–16 (7th Cir.2008).

(7)　Waiver. The privilege is waived if either:

•　The government or the informer divulges the informer's identity to one who would have cause "to resent the communication." Roviaro v. United States, 353 U.S. 53, 60, 77 S.Ct. 623, 627 (1957).

•　The government calls the informer as a witness.

CROSS-REFERENCES

Treatises

4 Graham, Handbook of Federal Evidence §§ 510:1–510:2 (9th ed. 2020)

1 McCormick, Evidence § 111 (8th ed. 2020)

26A Wright and Graham, Federal Practice and Procedure §§ 5701–5717 (1992)

Proposed Rule 511. Waiver of Privilege by Voluntary Disclosure

[NOT ENACTED]

A person upon whom these rules confer a privilege against disclosure of the confidential matter or communication waives the privilege if he or his predecessor while holder of the privilege voluntarily discloses or consents to disclosure of any significant part of the matter or communication. This rule does not apply if the disclosure is itself a privileged communication.

Authors' Note: Rule 502, which was enacted in 2008, addresses some waiver issues concerning the attorney-client privilege and work-product protection.

AUTHORS' COMMENTS

(1) Scope and purpose of Proposed Rule 511. Privileges are neither self-executing nor unwaivable. Proposed Rule 511 expresses the well-established principle that a privilege should terminate after its holder destroys confidentiality, either by disclosing the privileged matter or failing to protect against its disclosure. Some of the traditional rules governing waiver of attorney-client privileged communications have been modified by Rule 502, which governs the waiver effect of disclosures of attorney-client privileged and work-product protected materials to a federal office or agency or in litigation.

(2) Waiver—Generally. A holder's voluntary disclosure of privileged material ordinarily constitutes waiver, even if the holder was unaware of the legal effect of disclosure or the existence of the privilege. 26A Wright and Graham, Federal Practice and Procedure § 5726 (1992). Under Rule 502(d), however, a federal court may enter an order providing that parties may disclose privileged material to one another without waiving the privilege. See Authors' Comments to Rule 502.

(3) Who may waive. The holder of the privilege possesses the power to waive it. Waiver may arise when either the holder or his agent voluntarily discloses privileged material, or when the holder consents to disclosure by a third person.

> **Example—Waiver.** In In re von Bulow, 828 F.2d 94, 100–101 (2d Cir.1987), a client allowed (and encouraged) the attorney who successfully represented him in a criminal matter to publish a book about the case which revealed some attorney-client communications. The court of appeals held that the client thereby consented to the disclosure of those communications and waived the attorney-client privilege as to those communications.

(4) Voluntary disclosure. The most obvious means of waiving a privilege is by deliberately and voluntarily disclosing privileged material. See Westinghouse Electric Corp. v. Republic of the Philippines, 951 F.2d 1414, 1423–27 (3d Cir.1991) (rejecting selective waiver theory); United States v. Lara, 850 F.3d 686, 690–92 (4th Cir.2017) (probationer's agreement to consent to disclosure of communications with therapist to state corrections department waived psychotherapist-patient privilege); United States v. Brock, 724 F.3d 817, 821–22 (7th Cir.2013) (marital communication privilege waived when, without objection, wife disclosed at husband's detention hearing what husband told her). Once the privilege is waived, it can no longer be asserted. United States v. Suarez, 820 F.2d 1158, 1160 (11th Cir.1987). Note that Rule 502 provides that a disclosure made pursuant to a federal court's confidentiality order does not constitute a waiver. See Authors' Comments to Rule 502.

(5) Implied waiver—Failure to timely object. A failure by the holder (or the holder's attorney) to assert the privilege in a timely fashion amounts to a waiver. United States v. Bolander, 722 F.3d 199, 223 (4th Cir.2013) (privilege waived where patient asserted privilege only after willingly providing psychotherapy records to expert); United States v. Sanders, 979 F.2d 87, 92 (7th Cir.1992) (waiver found where only objection raised to disclosure of privileged communication was hearsay).

(6) Implied waiver—Partial disclosure. Rule 502 modifies the traditional principle codified in Proposed Rule 511 that the disclosure of "any significant portion" of a confidential matter or communication waives the privilege as to the entire matter or communication. Traditionally, courts have construed the scope of such a waiver in light of fairness concerns. A party's disclosure during the course of a judicial proceeding of only part of a privileged communication often led to a finding that that the party waived the privilege as to the rest of the communication; the disclosure of part of a series of privileged communications often resulted in waiver as to other, if not all, the other communications concerning the same subject matter. In re Keeper of Records (Grand Jury Subpoena Addressed to XYZ Corp.), 348 F.3d 16, 23–25 (1st Cir.2003). E.g., Fort James Corp. v. Solo Cup Co., 412 F.3d 1340, 1349 (Fed.Cir.2005); Hawkins v. Stables, 148 F.3d 379, 384 n.4 (4th Cir.1998) (disclosure waives privilege as to "subject matter" of disclosure). But see In re Sealed Case, 877 F.2d 976, 980–81 (D.C.Cir.1989).

Rule 502—which applies only to attorney-client privileged and work-product protected material— strongly emphasizes fairness concerns, with the aim of significantly limiting the circumstances under which a subject matter waiver will be found. When a party discloses communications to a federal office or agency or during a federal proceeding, "subject matter waiver is limited to situations in which a party intentionally puts protected information into the litigation in a selective, misleading and unfair manner." Advisory Committee's Note to Rule 502. See Authors' Comments to Rule 502.

Rule 502 applies only to disclosures made in litigation or to federal offices or agencies. Therefore, it does not affect existing case law governing extrajudicial disclosures. But courts traditionally have been inclined to limit such waivers to the material actually disclosed, a position consistent with the Rule 502 standard. E.g., Wi-LAN, Inc. v. Kilpatrick Townsend & Stockton LLP, 684 F.3d 1364, 1368–74 (Fed.Cir.2012); John Doe Co. v. United States, 350 F.3d 299 (2d Cir.2003); In re von Bulow, 828 F.2d 94, 101–04 (2d Cir.1987).

Another area where "disclosure" may be seen as a waiver is where a witness uses a privileged document to refresh her recollection. If done before the jury, fairness requires that opposing counsel be permitted to examine the document for possible use in cross-examination. See Rule 612. When a witness reviews privileged writings prior to testifying, the court's discretionary authority to order disclosure may trump a claim of privilege. E.g., Barrer v. Women's Nat. Bank, 96 F.R.D. 202, 205 (D.D.C.1982).

(7) Implied waiver—Placing matter in issue. Waiver is frequently found when a party raises a claim or defense that places privileged matters in issue. Knox v. Roper Pump Co., 957 F.3d 1237, 1248–49 (11th Cir.2020). This is consistent with notions of fair play. Courts often invoke the maxim that a privilege may not be used as a sword instead of a shield. See Frontier Refining, Inc. v. Gorman-Rupp Co., 136 F.3d 695, 699–702 (10th Cir.1998) (discussing different tests employed by courts).

Example—Privilege waived. In Chevron Corp. v. Pennzoil Co., 974 F.2d 1156, 1162–63 (9th Cir.1992), defendant responded to plaintiff's allegation that defendant's Schedule 13D was materially misleading by contending that its tax position was "reasonable" according to advice given by its tax counsel. The court of appeals held that defendant thereby waived its attorney-client privilege with respect to all documents touching on the tax issue in question.

Example—Privilege waived. In United States v. Workman, 138 F.3d 1261 (8th Cir.1998), the defendant claimed that he had relied on his attorney's advice in cashing railroad retirement benefits checks issued in his father's name. The court of appeals held that the defendant thus waived the attorney-client privilege and that the prosecution was entitled to question the attorney about the advice he gave defendant.

Example—Privilege waived. In United States v. Fackrell, 991 F.3d 589, 606 (5th Cir.2021), the court held that a capital murder defendant waived the psychotherapist-patient privilege in the sentencing phase by offering evidence about his mental health history as mitigating evidence.

The Advisory Committee's Note to Rule 502 indicates that the rule was not intended to modify case law in these kinds of situations.

(8) Implied waiver—Inadvertent disclosure. Whether a voluntary, but inadvertent, disclosure of privileged communications results in the waiver of the privilege has been a matter of some dispute. See Gray v. Bicknell, 86 F.3d 1472, 1483–84 (8th Cir.1996) (comparing "lenient," "strict," and "middle of the road" approaches). Rule 502 now governs the waiver effect of an inadvertent disclosure of attorney-client privileged or work-product protected material to a federal office or agency or in litigation. Under Rule 502(b), such an inadvertent disclosure does not amount to a waiver if the party took reasonable steps to prevent the disclosure and then took prompt and reasonable steps to rectify the inadvertent disclosure. Although Rule 502 does not govern the waiver effect of inadvertent disclosure for other privileges and in other situations, courts are likely to look to the rule for guidance. In determining whether a party took reasonable steps to prevent the inadvertent disclosure and prompt and reasonable steps to rectify the disclosure, courts will almost certainly continue to look at factors such as the volume and complexity of the discovery, the time constraints for production, the amount to time taken to rectify the error, the amount of material inadvertently disclosed, and considerations of fairness. See Alldread v. City of Grenada, 988 F.2d 1425, 1433–34 (5th Cir.1993).

(9) Privileged disclosure. Voluntary disclosure of privileged materials does not constitute a waiver if the disclosure is itself privileged. For example, a client may confidentially reveal to her husband privileged communications she had with her attorney. The "pooled information" or "joint defense" attorney-client privilege is another example of this principle.

Attempts to selectively disclose privileged information, i.e., to disclose privileged information for a limited purpose to someone to whom disclosure is not ordinarily privileged, have generally been rejected. See In re Pacific Pictures Corp., 679 F.3d 1121 (9th Cir.2012) (citing cases); In re Qwest Communications Int'l, Inc., 450 F.3d 1179, 1186–1201 (10th Cir.2006) (surveying case law). But see Diversified Industries, Inc. v. Meredith, 572 F.2d 596 (8th Cir.1977).

CROSS-REFERENCES

Common Objections (Chapter 3)

77.   Privileged

Treatises

4 Graham, Handbook of Federal Evidence § 511:1 (9th ed. 2020)

1 McCormick, Evidence §§ 83, 93, 103 (8th ed. 2020)

26A Wright and Graham, Federal Practice and Procedure §§ 5721–5734 (1992)

Proposed Rule 512. Privileged Matter Disclosed Under Compulsion or Without Opportunity to Claim Privilege

[NOT ENACTED]

Evidence of a statement or other disclosure of privileged matter is not admissible against the holder of the privilege if the disclosure was (a) compelled erroneously or (b) made without opportunity to claim the privilege.

AUTHORS' COMMENTS

(1) Scope and purpose of Proposed Rule 512. Proposed Rule 512 provides that the disclosure of privileged matters by means other than the voluntary act of the holder or her agent does not constitute a waiver of the privilege. By prohibiting the use of the evidence despite its loss of confidentiality, the rule was designed to afford "some measure of repair" to the injured privilege holder. Advisory Committee's Note.

(2) Erroneously compelled disclosure. If a privilege claim is overruled, the holder of the privilege ought not be required to defy the order to disclose, risk a judgment of contempt, and pursue all avenues of relief in order to sustain the privilege. Thus, if a trial court erroneously compels the disclosure of privileged materials, the holder does not forever waive the privilege by complying with the court's ruling. The issue may be raised in the ordinary course of appeal and if the lower court's decision is reversed, the party may prevent the once-disclosed materials from being offered again into evidence. See In re Vargas, 723 F.2d 1461, 1466 (10th Cir.1983).

(3) Disclosure without opportunity to claim the privilege. Proposed Rule 512 expresses the view that a privilege should not be lost if the disclosure occurred in circumstances in which the holder lacked an opportunity to assert the privilege. The following are common examples of such situations:

- Where an eavesdropper discloses what he heard. Cf. 18 U.S.C.A. § 2517.

- Where a spouse makes an extrajudicial disclosure of a confidential marital communication.

- Where one participant in joint therapy discloses communications made by another participant.

CROSS-REFERENCES

Treatises

4 Graham, Handbook of Federal Evidence § 512:1 (9th ed. 2020)

1 McCormick, Evidence §§ 73–74.2, 83, 93, 103 (8th ed. 2020)

26A Wright and Graham, Federal Practice and Procedure §§ 5741–5749 (1992)

Proposed Rule 513. Comment Upon or Inference From Claim of Privilege; Instruction

[NOT ENACTED]

(a) Comment or Inference Not Permitted. The claim of a privilege, whether in the present proceeding or upon a prior occasion, is not a proper subject of comment by judge or counsel. No inference may be drawn therefrom.

(b) Claiming Privilege Without Knowledge of Jury. In jury cases, proceedings shall be conducted, to the extent practicable, so as to facilitate the making of claims of privilege without the knowledge of the jury.

(c) Jury Instruction. Upon request, any party against whom the jury might draw an adverse inference from a claim of privilege is entitled to an instruction that no inference may be drawn therefrom.

AUTHORS' COMMENTS

(1) Scope and purpose of Proposed Rule 513. The directives set forth in Proposed Rule 513 are aimed at enhancing the value of privileges by minimizing the cost to privilege holders of their exercise of a privilege. Proposed Rule 513(a) does not, however, accurately express the current state of the law, particularly with regard to the privilege against self-incrimination.

(2) Claim of privilege against self-incrimination—Present criminal proceeding. An accused's decision not to testify in the present proceeding is not the proper subject of comment by counsel or the court. Nor may an adverse inference be drawn from the defendant's silence. Griffin v. California, 380 U.S. 609, 85 S.Ct. 1229 (1965). A non-party witness who validly invokes the privilege against self-incrimination may, however, be impeached by allowing the jury to draw adverse inferences from his silence.

> **Example—Impeachment through adverse inference.** In United States v. Kaplan, 832 F.2d 676, 682–84 (1st Cir.1987) the defense attempted to impeach a prosecution witness by inquiring about his cocaine use around the time of the events to which he was testifying. The trial court allowed the witness to invoke his privilege against self-incrimination outside the presence of the jury. The court of appeals held that the district court erred in not forcing the witness to assert the privilege before the jury so that the jury might infer that the witness had used cocaine.

A party, however, may not call witnesses it knows will invoke a privilege in a conscious effort to build its case out of the adverse inferences arising from the claim of privilege. Namet v. United States, 373 U.S. 179, 186, 83 S.Ct. 1151, 1154–55 (1963); United States v. Deutsch, 987 F.2d 878, 883–84 (2d Cir.1993).

(3) Claim of privilege against self-incrimination—Present civil proceeding. In a civil suit, the invocation of the privilege against self-incrimination is the proper subject of comment and an adverse inference may be drawn therefrom. Baxter v. Palmigiano, 425 U.S. 308, 318, 96 S.Ct. 1551, 1558 (1976) (party's invocation); Mirlis v. Greer, 952 F.3d 36, 44–48 (2d Cir.2020) (party's invocation); United States v. Mallory, 988 F.3d 730, 739–40 (4th Cir.2021) (non-party's invocation). E.g., Coquina Investments v. TD Bank, N.A., 760 F.3d 1300, 1310–12 (11th Cir.2014); Pagel, Inc. v. Securities and Exchange Comm'n, 803 F.2d 942, 946 (8th Cir.1986). In deciding whether to allow any comment or adverse inference, a court should balance the competing interests of the person invoking the privilege and the party against whom the privilege is invoked, S.E.C. v. Jasper, 678 F.3d 1116, 1125 (9th Cir.2012), as well as the probative value of the invocation of privilege against the danger of unfair prejudice. In re 650 Fifth Avenue and Related

Properties, 934 F.3d 147, 171–72 (2d Cir.2019); Woods v. START Treatment & Recovery Centers, Inc., 864 F.3d 158, 170–71 (2d Cir.2017).

    (4)   **Previous invocation of privilege.** Proposed Rule 513(a) stipulates that a claim of privilege on a previous occasion is not a proper basis for comment or adverse inference. The courts tend to agree.

    (a) *Prior claim by accused.* Although the Supreme Court has held that the constitution does not bar the prosecution from cross-examining an accused about his claim of privilege at an earlier proceeding, Raffel v. United States, 271 U.S. 494, 46 S.Ct. 566 (1926), more recent decisions emphasize the importance of insuring that the prior privilege claim is sufficiently inconsistent with the accused's present testimony to warrant its use for impeachment purposes. E.g., Grunewald v. United States, 353 U.S. 391, 418–24, 77 S.Ct. 963, 981–84 (1957).

    (b) *Non-party witnesses.* Courts have consistently refused to allow a prosecutor to question a defense witness about that witness's earlier invocation of a privilege before a grand jury. United States v. Morris, 988 F.2d 1335, 1339 (4th Cir.1993) (witness had invoked marital testimonial privilege); Nezowy v. United States, 723 F.2d 1120, 1124 (3d Cir.1983) (witness had invoked privilege against self-incrimination).

    (5)   **Claiming privilege without knowledge of jury.** When a witness's invocation of a privilege would not be the proper subject of an adverse inference, the witness should be allowed, to the extent practicable, to invoke the privilege outside the presence of the jury. The party wishing to insure that the jury does not learn of the invocation may accomplish this through a motion in limine. Moreover, if the prosecution has good reason to believe that one of its witnesses plans to invoke a privilege, it should so inform the court, which may then conduct a voir dire hearing outside the jury's presence. United States v. Victor, 973 F.2d 975, 978 (1st Cir.1992) (witness's invocation of privilege against self-incrimination); United States v. Chapman, 866 F.2d 1326, 1333 (11th Cir.1989) (witness's invocation of marital testimonial privilege).

    The prosecution may elicit from a witness who is testifying pursuant to a grant of immunity the circumstances of the testimony, including the fact that the witness has been immunized. Such questioning must be conducted in good faith and in a non-inflammatory fashion. United States v. Lizza Industries, Inc., 775 F.2d 492, 495–97 (2d Cir.1985).

    (6)   **Jury instruction.** Upon request by a party against whom an adverse inference might improperly be drawn from a claim of privilege, the trial court must instruct the jury not to draw any such inference. Carter v. Kentucky, 450 U.S. 288, 101 S.Ct. 1112 (1981). The court may constitutionally give such an instruction over the objection of the accused. Lakeside v. Oregon, 435 U.S. 333, 98 S.Ct. 1091 (1978).

CROSS-REFERENCES

Common Objections (Chapter 3)
74.   Privilege, comment on or adverse inference from invocation
Treatises
4 Graham, Handbook of Federal Evidence § 513:1 (9th ed. 2020)
1 McCormick, Evidence §§ 74.1, 126–128, 136 (8th ed. 2020)
26A Wright and Graham, Federal Practice and Procedure §§ 5751–5757 (1992)

ARTICLE VI

WITNESSES

Rule 601. Competency to Testify in General

Every person is competent to be a witness unless these rules provide otherwise. But in a civil case, state law governs the witness's competency regarding a claim or defense for which state law supplies the rule of decision.

AUTHORS' COMMENTS

(1) Scope and purpose of Rule 601. Rule 601 abolishes all objections to a witness's competency except those specifically mentioned in the rules of evidence. It thereby eliminates such grounds for incompetency as age, religion, conviction of a crime, interest, and mental capacity, treating these (with the exception of religion) as bearing on a witness's credibility. By its second sentence, however, Rule 601 defers in civil actions to state rules regarding competency with respect to any claim or defense as to which state law governs.

The other federal rules addressing witness competency are Rules 602 (personal knowledge requirement), 603 (oath or affirmation requirement), 605 (competency of judge) and 606 (competency of juror). Several statutes also include competency provisions.

(2) Discretion to exclude witness. Despite the seemingly unambiguous command of Rule 601 ("every person is competent to be a witness"), many courts hold that a trial judge may rule that a witness lacks sufficient capacity to testify. United States v. Barnes, 803 F.3d 209, 219 (5th Cir.2015) (despite Rule 601, trial court must determine whether witness is capable of communicating relevant evidence and understands obligation to do so). Although a person may be competent, the court may nevertheless decide, under Rule 403, that the probative value of the person's testimony would be substantially outweighed by the countervailing considerations listed in that rule. E.g., United States v. Ramirez, 871 F.2d 582, 584 (6th Cir.1989). Thus, the courts have simply transformed the traditional concerns of competency—the witness's appreciation of the duty to testify truthfully and her capacity to observe, recall and communicate events— into an inquiry about relevance. See United States v. Phibbs, 999 F.2d 1053, 1070 (6th Cir.1993). Even under this analysis, however, the courts should, and ordinarily do, allow a witness to testify if a minimal threshold level of relevancy is met.

> **Example—Competent.** In United States v. Callahan, 801 F.3d 606, 622–23 (6th Cir.2015), the trial court properly denied defendant's motion to have a witness undergo a psychological exam to determine her competency to testify. The court reasoned the witness could testify as long as she took an oath and understood her obligation to tell the truth.

> **Example—Competent.** In United States v. Villalta, 662 F.2d 1205 (5th Cir.1981), the district court excluded the testimony of a witness concerning conversations conducted in Spanish on the ground that the witness lacked sufficient comprehension of Spanish. The court of appeals reversed, holding that any deficiencies in the witness's comprehension of Spanish should go to the weight accorded his testimony, not its admissibility.

The courts commonly state that the question of a witness's competency is a preliminary question for the court's determination under Rule 104(a). E.g., United States v. Hyson, 721 F.2d 856, 864 (1st Cir.1983). Any objection to a witness's competency must be raised in a timely fashion. United States v. Odom, 736 F.2d 104, 109–12 (4th Cir.1984).

(3) Procedure—Hearings and examinations—Generally. The trial court is granted substantial discretion in deciding whether to conduct a hearing as to a witness's competency. See, e.g., United States v. Roach, 590 F.2d 181, 185 (5th Cir.1979) (court conducted hearing); United States v. Odom, 736 F.2d 104, 109–11 (4th Cir.1984) (court refused to conduct hearing). Psychiatric examinations of witnesses for purposes of assessing their competency should be granted only upon a showing of substantial need. United States v. Skorniak, 59 F.3d 750, 755 (8th Cir.1995).

(4) Procedure—Hearings and examinations—Children. 18 U.S.C.A. § 3509(c) sets forth procedures for determining the competency of a child witness who is alleged to be either the victim of child abuse or exploitation or a witness to a crime committed against another person. The statute provides that a competency examination by the court may be conducted only upon a written motion and an offer of proof of incompetency. Id. § 3509(c)(3). If the court then determines that compelling reasons exist, it may conduct a hearing outside the jury's presence. Id. § 3509(c)(4), (6). The court may not order a psychological assessment of the child without a showing of compelling need. Id. § 3509(c)(9). See generally United States v. Snyder, 189 F.3d 640, 645–46 (7th Cir.1999).

(5) Drug or alcohol use. That a witness was under the influence of drugs or alcohol when she perceived the matter in question does not automatically establish her incompetency. E.g., United States v. Ramirez, 871 F.2d 582, 584 (6th Cir.1989) (witness addicted to cocaine at time of event held competent).

Neither is incompetency established by the fact that a witness is under the influence of drugs or alcohol while testifying or is a habitual user of drugs or alcohol. E.g., United States v. Van Meerbeke, 548 F.2d 415 (2d Cir.1976) (witness in drug case who ingested some of heroin offered into evidence held competent).

(6) Adjudication of insanity or incompetency. An adjudication that a person is insane or incompetent to stand trial does not, by itself, render her incompetent to testify. Andrews v. Neer, 253 F.3d 1052, 1062–63 (8th Cir.2001).

> **Example—Competent.** In United States v. Lightly, 677 F.2d 1027 (4th Cir.1982), the trial judge ruled a witness incompetent because he had earlier been found criminally insane and incompetent to stand trial. The court of appeals reversed, noting that the witness's physician testified that the witness had a sufficient memory, could understand the oath, and could communicate what he saw.

(7) Competency of hearsay declarant. A witness's lack of competency (or inability to meet the minimal threshold relevancy test) does not necessarily render that person's hearsay statements inadmissible. See, e.g., Morgan v. Foretich, 846 F.2d 941, 945–46 (4th Cir.1988).

(8) Use of state law. In civil actions in which state law supplies the rule of decision with respect to an element of a claim or defense, a witness's competency must be determined in accordance with state law. Thus, in a diversity case, a state Dead Man's Act may be applicable. E.g., Lovejoy Electronics, Inc. v. O'Berto, 873 F.2d 1001, 1005 (7th Cir.1989).

CROSS-REFERENCES

Common Objections (Chapter 3)
49.   Incompetent; witness is incompetent

Treatises
4 Graham, Handbook of Federal Evidence §§ 601:1–601:5 (9th ed. 2020)
1 McCormick, Evidence §§ 61–71 (8th ed. 2020)
27 Wright and Gold, Federal Practice and Procedure §§ 6001–6012 (2d ed. 2007)

Rule 602. Need for Personal Knowledge

A witness may testify to a matter only if evidence is introduced sufficient to support a finding that the witness has personal knowledge of the matter. Evidence to prove personal knowledge may consist of the witness's own testimony. This rule does not apply to a witness's expert testimony under Rule 703.

AUTHORS' COMMENTS

(1) Scope and purpose of Rule 602. Rule 602 provides that a witness may not testify unless sufficient evidence is introduced to demonstrate that she has personal knowledge of the matter. This rule is designed to improve the reliability of evidence admitted at trial by insisting that witnesses testify only as to their own observations and perceptions.

Experts are exempt from the personal knowledge requirement. See infra and Rule 703.

(2) Establishing personal knowledge. A witness's personal knowledge may be established through the witness's testimony that she has personal knowledge or it may be inferred from the circumstances. The personal knowledge requirement "is not difficult to meet." United States v. Walker, 85 F.4th 973, 980 (10th Cir.2023) (quoting United States v. Gutierrez de Lopez, 761 F.3d 1123, 1132 (10th Cir.2014)).

> **Example—Personal knowledge inferred.** In United States v. Doe, 960 F.2d 221, 223 (1st Cir.1992), the district court properly admitted a sport shop owner's testimony that he knew a certain type of pistol was manufactured in Brazil. The court of appeals noted that a witness's personal knowledge includes inferences and opinions that are grounded in personal observation and experience. As a reasonable fact finder could find that this witness had firsthand knowledge from which he could infer that the pistol was manufactured in Brazil, his testimony was admissible.

130

(3) Standard of proof. Whether a witness possesses the requisite personal knowledge is a conditional relevancy question to be determined under Rule 104(b). All that is required, therefore, is enough evidence for a reasonable juror to find that it is more likely than not that the witness's testimony is based on firsthand knowledge. United States v. Gutierrez de Lopez, 761 F.3d 1123, 1132 (10th Cir.2014). The burden of proof is on the offering party. United States v. Hickey, 917 F.2d 901, 904 (6th Cir.1990).

Example—Admissible. In a bid rigging and mail fraud case, the trial court allowed a witness to testify about the agreement between the bid riggers, even though another person had negotiated the agreement and the witness testified he was unsure how he had come to know about it. The court of appeals held that the trial court did not abuse its discretion. The witness's significant contact with the president of one of the bidders and attendance at both meetings between the bidders provided sufficient evidence of his personal knowledge. United States v. MMR Corp. (LA), 907 F.2d 489, 495–96 (5th Cir.1990).

Example—Inadmissible. In McCrary-El v. Shaw, 992 F.2d 809, 810–11 (8th Cir.1993), a civil rights case in which the plaintiff inmate alleged that prison guards used excessive force against him, the trial court properly excluded the testimony of an inmate who occupied the adjacent cell. The trial court found that the inch and one-half crack at the corner of the witness's cell did not afford him the opportunity to observe what happened in plaintiff's cell.

(4) Lack of certainty—"I believe," "I think," etc. A witness need not claim to be absolutely certain about the accuracy of her observations. Testimony phrased in terms of "I believe" or "I think" or which in some other manner concedes a modicum of doubt does not necessarily fail for lack of personal knowledge. E.g., M.B.A.F.B. Fed. Credit Union v. Cumis Ins. Soc., 681 F.2d 930, 932 (4th Cir.1982).

(5) Relationship to opinion testimony. The personal knowledge rule precludes a witness from speculating as to how an event occurred or from offering an opinion based on conjecture rather than facts. Even though a lay witness is permitted to testify in the form of an opinion, she must base her opinion on personal knowledge. See Hart v. O'Brien, 127 F.3d 424, 428 (5th Cir.1997).

Example—Admissible. In United States v. Flores-Rivera, 787 F.3d 1, 28 (1st Cir.2015), a witness was properly permitted to testify that a notation written by a co-conspirator in a drug ledger could have referred to either the defendant or another co-conspirator. Given the witness's role in the conspiracy, this inference was adequately grounded in her personal knowledge.

Example—Inadmissible. In United States v. Lanci, 669 F.2d 391, 394–95 (6th Cir.1982), the defendant offered prior state court testimony of a witness that he "imagine[d]" that the defendant's fingerprints appeared on some FBI documents because of the defendant's curiosity about the documents. The trial court did not abuse its discretion in excluding this evidence because the witness was merely speculating. He did not know whether the defendant had ever read or glanced through the documents.

Expert witnesses are exempt from the personal knowledge requirement. Rule 703 provides that expert testimony may be based entirely on hearsay as long as it is of a type reasonably relied upon by other experts in the same field. This exception is noted in the last sentence of Rule 602. See Rule 703.

(6) Relationship to hearsay rule. "The personal knowledge requirement and the hearsay rule 'are cut at least in part from the same cloth.' " United States v. El-Mezain, 664 F.3d 467, 495 (5th Cir.2011) (quoting United States v. Quezada, 754 F.2d 1190, 1195 (5th Cir.1985)). Thus, the personal knowledge rule prevents a witness who did not observe an incident from adopting another's report of the incident and relating it as the witness's own. United States v. Davis, 596 F.3d 852, 856 (D.C. Cir.2010).

Example—Inadmissible. In Kemp v. Balboa, 23 F.3d 211, 212–13 (8th Cir.1994), a nurse testified that the plaintiff, a prisoner, had failed to pick up his medication from the prison infirmary on seven occasions. On cross-examination, it became clear that the witness had not been on duty at the relevant times and that the sole basis for her testimony was what she had read in the medical records (which had not themselves been introduced in evidence). The court of appeals held that the trial judge should have struck the testimony because the witness lacked personal knowledge.

Even when a witness relates admissible hearsay, the witness must have personal knowledge that the hearsay statement was made. See Advisory Committee's Note.

CROSS-REFERENCES

Common Objections (Chapter 3)

68. Personal knowledge lacking

89. Speculation, question calls for

Treatises

4 Graham, Handbook of Federal Evidence §§ 602:1–602:2 (9th ed. 2020)

1 McCormick, Evidence § 10 (8th ed. 2020)

27 Wright and Gold, Federal Practice and Procedure §§ 6021–6028 (2d ed. 2007)

Rule 603. Oath or Affirmation to Testify Truthfully

Before testifying, a witness must give an oath or affirmation to testify truthfully. It must be in a form designed to impress that duty on the witness's conscience.

AUTHORS' COMMENTS

(1) Scope and purpose of Rule 603. Rule 603 reflects the broadly-held belief that administering an oath or affirmation impresses upon a witness his obligation to tell the truth. This is accomplished either by appealing to the witness's conscience or religious beliefs or by imposing the threat of criminal sanctions for false testimony. Testimony given by a witness who has taken neither an oath nor affirmation is inadmissible. United States v. Hawkins, 76 F.3d 545, 551 (4th Cir.1996).

(2) Oath vs. affirmation. An oath invokes a deity; an affirmation is simply a solemn pledge. Rule 603 provides that either is acceptable, requiring only that the oath or affirmation must be in a form designed to impress upon the witness's conscience the duty to testify truthfully.

(3) Conflict with religious beliefs—Alternative forms. When a witness objects on religious grounds to taking either an oath or affirmation, the court should attempt to devise, in consultation with the witness if necessary, some alternative form of "serious public commitment to answer truthfully that does not transgress the prospect's sincerely held beliefs." Society of Separationists, Inc. v. Herman, 939 F.2d 1207, 1219 (5th Cir.1991), aff'd, 959 F.2d 1283 (5th Cir.1992).

Example—Acceptable alternative. In United States v. Ward, 989 F.2d 1015 (9th Cir.1992), the court of appeals held that the trial judge erred in refusing to allow the defendant to take the affirmation he proposed: "Do you affirm to speak with fully integrated Honesty, only with fully integrated Honesty and nothing but fully integrated Honesty?"

A court need not accept a proposed oath that would allow the witness to lie with impunity. If the court wishes to preserve the threat of perjury, the court may compel the witness to acknowledge that he is subject to penalties for perjury. Ferguson v. Commissioner of Internal Revenue, 921 F.2d 588, 590 (5th Cir.1991).

Example—Unacceptable alternative. In United States v. Fowler, 605 F.2d 181, 185 (5th Cir.1979), the trial court acted properly in excluding the testimony of a witness who refused to affirm, "I state that I will tell the truth in my testimony," and was willing only to state, "I am a truthful man" or "I would not tell a lie to stay out of jail."

(4) Waiver. Failure to make a timely objection when a witness testifies without first having affirmed or sworn that he will testify truthfully waives any such error. E.g., United States v. Odom, 736 F.2d 104, 114 (4th Cir.1984).

CROSS-REFERENCES

Treatises

4 Graham, Handbook of Federal Evidence § 603:1 (9th ed. 2020)

1 McCormick, Evidence §§ 62–63 (8th ed. 2020)

27 Wright and Gold, Federal Practice and Procedure §§ 6041–6045 (2d ed. 2007)

Rule 604. Interpreter

An interpreter must be qualified and must give an oath or affirmation to make a true translation.

AUTHORS' COMMENTS

(1)   Scope and purpose of Rule 604. Rule 604 makes clear that an interpreter (a) must be qualified to translate and (b) must swear or affirm that he will translate accurately. Various statutory provisions and rules of procedure also address the use of interpreters. Both Federal Rule of Civil Procedure 43 and Federal Rule of Criminal Procedure 28 authorize the court to appoint an interpreter and fix the interpreter's compensation. In addition, the Court Interpreters Act, 18 U.S.C.A. §§ 1827–1828 provides further guidance on matters such as the certification and compensation of interpreters and when interpreters should be appointed in proceedings instituted by the United States. See United States v. Jayavarman, 871 F.3d 1050, 1064–65 (9th Cir.2017) (trial court did not err in concluding defendant did not need interpreter).

The failure to afford a criminal defendant adequate interpretation services raises constitutional questions. See United States v. Johnson, 248 F.3d 655, 663–64 (7th Cir.2001) (citing cases).

(2)   Use of interpreters. Interpreters may be used to (a) translate the testimony of a witness who is unable to communicate sufficiently well in spoken English; and (b) translate the testimony of witnesses for a party who is unable to understand or communicate in spoken English.

(3)   Qualifications of interpreters. Ordinarily, Rule 702 governs whether an interpreter is qualified. United States v. Gutierrez, 757 F.3d 785, 788 (8th Cir.2014). Therefore, the court must ask whether the interpreter is qualified by means of his "knowledge, skill, experience, training, or education" to interpret accurately. See United States v. Bell, 367 F.3d 452, 463–64 (5th Cir.2004) (permitting interpretation by sister of deaf and mute witness who communicated in manner understood only by family and friends); United States v. Ball, 988 F.2d 7, 9–10 (5th Cir.1993) (wife of deaf witness whose speech was unintelligible appointed as interpreter). See also 18 U.S.C.A. § 1827(d) (court "shall utilize the services of the most available certified interpreter").

(4)   Oath. Rule 604 makes clear that interpreters are subject to an oath or affirmative requirement. But one court of appeals has held that interpreters need not take an oath or affirmation every time they testify. Thus, courts that employ staff interpreters may administer the oath to an interpreter once and keep it on file. United States v. Solorio, 669 F.3d 943, 950 (9th Cir.2012).

(5)   Method of interpretation. An interpreter "should * * * strive to translate exactly what is said." United States v. Gomez, 908 F.2d 809, 811 (11th Cir.1990). Perfection in translation, however, is not required. Valladares v. United States, 871 F.2d 1564, 1566 (11th Cir.1989). Minor deviations from word-for-word translations do not necessarily constitute fatal error; in some instances, summary translations may even be permissible. United States v. Bell, 367 F.3d 452, 464 (5th Cir.2004). But translators may not comment on the testimony. Id.; see United States v. Gomez, 908 F.2d 809, 811 (11th Cir.1990) (interpreter improperly embellished witness's testimony).

(6)   Transcription of recordings. Transcriptions of recorded English-language conversations are often used to help the jury better understand what was said. United States v. Anderson, 452 F.3d 66, 70–72 (1st Cir.2006). When, however, the recorded conversation is in a foreign language, it must be translated for the jury. See United States v. Rivera-Rosario, 300 F.3d 1, 5–6 (1st Cir.2002). In such cases, translated transcriptions of audio recordings may be admitted into evidence. See United States v. Morales-Madera, 352 F.3d 1, 9 (1st Cir.2003) (translated transcripts "should be marked and admitted in evidence in addition to the wiretaps themselves"); United States v. Cruz-Rea, 626 F.3d 929, 936 (7th Cir.2010) (discussing appropriate jury instruction if transcript is used); United States v. Rrapi, 175 F.3d 742, 746–48 (9th Cir.1999). Some courts both play the recorded foreign-language conversation and admit the translated transcript. See, e.g., United States v. Chavez, 976 F.3d 1178, 1193–1203 (10th Cir.2020) (failure to introduce audio recording violated best evidence rule); United States v. Vazquez Guadalupe, 407 F.3d 492, 497 (1st Cir.2005). Other courts admit the transcript without having the jury listen to the recording, reasoning that the jury will not profit from hearing a foreign-language conversation. See, e.g., United States v. Estrada, 256 F.3d 466, 472–73 (7th Cir.2001); United States v. Valencia, 957 F.2d 1189, 1193–96 (5th Cir.1992). For an extensive discussion of the use of transcripts of recordings where no translation is involved, see United

States v. Holton, 116 F.3d 1536, 1540–46 (D.C.Cir.1997), and where a translation is involved, see United States v. Morales-Madera, 352 F.3d 1, 7–9 (1st Cir.2003).

CROSS-REFERENCES

Treatises

4 Graham, Handbook of Federal Evidence § 604:1 (9th ed. 2020)

1 McCormick, Evidence § 62 (8th ed. 2020)

27 Wright and Gold, Federal Practice and Procedure §§ 6051–6056 (2d ed. 2007)

Rule 605. Judge's Competency as a Witness

The presiding judge may not testify as a witness at the trial. A party need not object to preserve the issue.

AUTHORS' COMMENTS

(1)   Scope and purpose of Rule 605. Rule 605 bars a judge from testifying in a trial over which the judge presides. Several rationales support the rule: (1) the inconsistency of placing the judge in the role of both neutral arbiter and witness; (2) the practical procedural difficulties that would ensue; (3) the fear that the jury would give undue credence to the judge's testimony because of the aura of impartiality surrounding the judge; and (4) the chilling effect such action by the judge might have on opposing counsel's advocacy. See Advisory Committee's Note.

Rule 605 does not address questions of judicial disqualification or recusal, which are governed by constitutional, statutory and procedural rules. See, e.g., 28 U.S.C.A. § 455 (judge must disqualify self in case in which judge is or has been material witness).

(2)   Judge must testify "as a witness." Rule 605 prohibits a presiding judge from testifying "as a witness." Obviously, this prevents a presiding judge from taking the stand during the course of the trial. But Rule 605 may be invoked even where the judge does not formally take the stand. Courts have found Rule 605 to be applicable:

•   Where the judge in a bench trial viewed the accident scene without notice to counsel. Lillie v. United States, 953 F.2d 1188, 1191 (10th Cir.1992).

•   Where a party sought to take the judge's deposition in connection with its recusal motion. Cheeves v. Southern Clays, Inc., 797 F.Supp. 1570, 1582 (M.D.Ga.1992).

•   Where the judge injects a factual comment from the bench. E.g., United States v. Nickl, 427 F.3d 1286, 1292–95 (10th Cir.2005) (judge answered question posed to witness about whether she intended to defraud bank by stating that witness had intended to defraud).

•   Where the judge, in a suppression hearing, relied on his personal knowledge about the location of stop signs and speed limits. United States v. Berber-Tinoco, 510 F.3d 1083, 1089–91 (9th Cir.2007).

•   Where the judge's comments about a witness's credibility, made during a suppression hearing, are read into evidence at trial. United States v. Blanchard, 542 F.3d 1133, 1144–49 (7th Cir.2008).

The following are examples of judicial actions that do not constitute impermissible judicial testimony:

•   Informing the jury that they may draw an inference from facts in evidence. United States v. Sanchez, 790 F.2d 245, 252 (2d Cir.1986).

•   Commenting on facts that are subject to judicial notice. Fox v. City of West Palm Beach, 383 F.2d 189, 194–95 (5th Cir.1967).

(3)   Must be presiding judge in that trial. Judges are barred from testifying only in trials over which they preside. A judge, therefore, may testify as a witness in a trial or proceeding over which some other judge presides. E.g., United States v. Frankenthal, 582 F.2d 1102, 1107–08 (7th Cir.1978) (non-presiding judge testified about statements made to him by defense witness). Cf. 28 U.S.C.A. § 2245 (in habeas corpus proceeding trial judge may file written explanation of what happened at trial).

(4) Other court personnel. Rule 605 has been held applicable to a judge's law clerk. See Kennedy v. Great Atlantic & Pacific Tea Co., Inc., 551 F.2d 593 (5th Cir.1977). Cf. Gary W. v. State of Louisiana, 861 F.2d 1366 (5th Cir.1988) (special master could not be deposed about quasi-judicial functions).

(5) Other grounds for barring judges from testifying. Rule 3.3 of the A.B.A.'s 2007 Model Code of Judicial Conduct provides that a judge should not testify as a character witness "except when duly summoned." Comment [1] to this Rule adds that, except "where the demands of justice" require such testimony, a judge should discourage a party from requiring the judge to so testify. This is consistent with Canon 2 of the A.B.A.'s 1990 Code of Judicial Conduct, which declares that a judge "should not lend the prestige of his office to advance the private interests of others" and specifically enjoins a judge from testifying voluntarily as a character witness.

(6) No objection required. Rule 605 waives the normal requirement that a timely objection be made in order to preserve error. No such objection is required when a judge testifies in contravention of Rule 605.

CROSS-REFERENCES

Common Objections (Chapter 3)
52. Judge as witness
Treatises
4 Graham, Handbook of Federal Evidence § 605:1 (9th ed. 2020)
1 McCormick, Evidence § 68 (8th ed. 2020)
27 Wright and Gold, Federal Practice and Procedure §§ 6061–6065 (2d ed. 2007)

Rule 606. Juror's Competency as a Witness

(a) At the Trial. A juror may not testify as a witness before the other jurors at the trial. If a juror is called to testify, the court must give a party an opportunity to object outside the jury's presence.

(b) During an Inquiry into the Validity of a Verdict or Indictment.

(1) *Prohibited Testimony or Other Evidence.* During an inquiry into the validity of a verdict or indictment, a juror may not testify about any statement made or incident that occurred during the jury's deliberations; the effect of anything on that juror's or another juror's vote; or any juror's mental processes concerning the verdict or indictment. The court may not receive a juror's affidavit or evidence of a juror's statement on these matters.

(2) *Exceptions.* A juror may testify about whether:

(A) extraneous prejudicial information was improperly brought to the jury's attention;

(B) an outside influence was improperly brought to bear on any juror; or

(C) a mistake was made in entering the verdict on the verdict form.

AUTHORS' COMMENTS

(1) Scope and purpose of Rule 606. Rule 606 addresses two different aspects of juror testimony. Rule 606(a) bars a juror from testifying as a witness in a trial in which the juror is sitting.

Rule 606(b) restricts the role of jurors in attacking (or supporting) the validity of a verdict or indictment. By limiting the ability of jurors to testify in an inquiry into the validity of a verdict, the rule reflects a desire to protect jurors and promote the finality of judgments. Tanner v. United States, 483 U.S. 107, 119, 107 S.Ct. 2739, 2747–48 (1987).

A 2006 amendment created a new exception to Rule 606(b). See Authors' Comment 606(6).

(2) Juror testimony during trial. Rule 606(a) disqualifies a juror only from testifying as a witness before the jury during the trial. Cf. United States v. Kills Enemy, 3 F.3d 1201, 1204 (8th Cir.1993) (questioning wisdom of permitting former venireman to testify). It does not prevent a juror from being questioned on voir dire or by the court during trial concerning attempted tampering or other such matters.

If a juror is called to testify as a witness, counsel must be given an opportunity to object outside the jury's presence.

(3) Inquiry into validity of verdict or indictment—Scope of prohibited inquiry. In an inquiry into the validity of a verdict or indictment, Rule 606(b)(1) expressly prohibits a juror from testifying as to:

- Any incident or statement that occurred during the course of the jury's deliberations.

- The mental processes by which the jurors arrived at their decision.

- The effect that anything had on the juror's or other jurors' minds or emotions.

Rule 606(b)(1) also disallows:

- An affidavit by the juror as to any such matter.

- Evidence of any hearsay statements made by a juror as to any such matter.

Note that Rule 606(b)(1) bars testimony about statements and incidents that occur "during the jury's deliberations." By its terms, therefore, it does not bar testimony about matters that occur before the jury begins deliberations. United States v. Farmer, 717 F.3d 559, 565 (7th Cir.2013). But in Tanner v. United States, 483 U.S. 107, 107 S.Ct. 2739 (1987), without addressing this issue the Supreme Court applied Rule 606(b) to bar post-verdict testimony about jurors' alcohol and drug use before deliberations began.

Rule 606(b) clearly does not preclude the testimony of a non-juror who possesses personal knowledge of juror misconduct. E.g., United States v. Taliaferro, 558 F.2d 724, 725–26 (4th Cir.1977) (records of club at which jurors dined held admissible).

(4) Inquiry into validity of verdict or indictment—Illustrative cases. Examples of the type of juror testimony and affidavits rendered inadmissible by Rule 606(b)(1) include:

- Evidence regarding a juror's mental competency or fitness. E.g., Tanner v. United States, 483 U.S. 107, 107 S.Ct. 2739 (1987) (jurors consumed alcohol, marijuana and cocaine during the trial).

- That the jury reached a decision on an inappropriate basis. E.g., Multiflex, Inc. v. Samuel Moore & Co., 709 F.2d 980 (5th Cir.1983) (quotient verdict).

- That the jury misunderstood the jury instructions. E.g., United States v. Wickersham, 29 F.3d 191, 1945th Cir.1994).

- That jurors bullied another juror. United States v. Foster, 878 F.3d 1297, 1309–10 (11th Cir.2018).

- That the jury considered defendant's failure to testify United States v. Kelley, 461 F.3d 817, 831–32 (6th Cir.2006) (citing cases); United States v. Rutherford, 371 F.3d 634, 640 (9th Cir.2004).

(5) Exception—Extraneous prejudicial information and outside influence. Rule 606(b)(2) creates exceptions that allow jurors to testify (or submit affidavits) that they were exposed to "extraneous prejudicial information," Rule 606(b)(2)(A), or that an "outside influence" was improperly brought to bear upon them. Rule 606(b)(2)(B). "Extraneous prejudicial information" typically refers to information that relates specifically to the case, was not admitted into evidence, and emanates from a source external to the jury. Warger v. Shauers, 547 U.S. 40, 51, 135 S.Ct. 521, 529–30 (2014). An "outside influence" denotes improper exposure to a third party. United States v. Jones, 132 F.3d 232, 245 (5th Cir.1998), aff'd, 527 U.S. 373, 119 S.Ct. 2090 (1999). Courts, however, have not always distinguished carefully between the two categories. Citing one or the other exception, courts have received evidence that a juror:

- Consulted books or newspapers. E.g., Oliver v. Quarterman, 541 F.3d 329, 336–40 (5th Cir.2008) (Bible); United States v. Siegelman, 561 F.3d 1215, 1237–42 (11th Cir.2009) (information on the Internet, superseded indictment), judgmt. vacated on other grounds, 561 U.S. 1040, 130 S.Ct. 3542 (2010); United States v. Bagnariol, 665 F.2d 877, 883–85 (9th Cir.1981) (business publications).

- Looked up defendant's Facebook profile and did a Google search for information relating to the case. Ewing v. Horton, 914 F.3d 1027, 1029–30 (6th Cir.2019).

- Conducted an experiment or investigation. E.g., In re Beverly Hills Fire Litigation, 695 F.2d 207 (6th Cir.1982).

- Reviewed unadmitted court documents inadvertently left in the jury room. E.g., Government of Virgin Islands v. Joseph, 685 F.2d 857, 862–64 (3d Cir.1982).

- Was subjected to bribes or threats by third parties. E.g., Remmer v. United States, 347 U.S. 227, 74 S.Ct. 450 (1954) (bribes); Krause v. Rhodes, 570 F.2d 563, 566–70 (6th Cir.1977) (threats).

- Had an ex parte communication with the trial judge. E.g., United States v. Scisum, 32 F.3d 1479, 1481–83 (10th Cir.1994).

- Discussed a prior conviction of defendant that had not been admitted into evidence. United States v. Swinton, 75 F.3d 374, 380–82 (8th Cir.1996).

- Considered a related party's guilty plea and payment of a fine, neither of which was admitted in evidence. United States v. Brown, 108 F.3d 863, 866–67 (8th Cir.1997).

The general body of experience that jurors bring to their deliberations is considered "internal" to the deliberative process and falls outside both the "extraneous prejudicial information" and "outside influence" exceptions. Warger v. Shauers, 574 U.S. 40, 135 S.Ct. 521, 529–30 (2014). But a juror's personal knowledge of specific information about a party or the events of the litigation constitutes extraneous prejudicial information. Mancuso v. Olivarez, 292 F.3d 939, 951 (9th Cir.2002).

(6) Exceptions—Correction of clerical error. Rule 606(b)(2)(C) allows jurors to testify that the reported verdict resulted from a mistake in entering the verdict on the verdict form. This exception was added to Rule 606(b) in 2006 to codify court decisions creating such an exception. E.g., Munafo v. Metropolitan Transportation Auth., 381 F.3d 99, 107 (2d Cir.2004); United States v. DiDomenico, 78 F.3d 294, 302 (7th Cir.1996). This amendment specifically rejects a broader exception, adopted by some courts, that authorized jurors to testify that the jury had misapprehended the consequences of the result that they agreed upon. E.g., Attridge v. Cencorp Div. of Dover Techs. Int'l, Inc., 836 F.2d 113, 116 (2d Cir.1987).

(7) Exceptions—Effect on jurors. The exceptions in Rule 606(b)(2) allow testimony only as to whether the jury was exposed to extraneous prejudicial information or outside influence or whether a clerical mistake was made in entering the verdict Jurors may not testify about the manner in which such exposure affected the deliberative process. Kirk v. Exxon Mobil Corp., 870 F.3d 669, 680 (7th Cir.2017); United States v. Honken, 541 F.3d 1146, 1168–69 (8th Cir.2008) (citing cases). But see Tarango v. McDaniel, 837 F.3d 936, 950–52 (9th Cir.2016); United States v. Herndon, 156 F.3d 629, 637 (6th Cir.1998). The court must make an objective assessment of the impact the exposure would have on the average juror. United States v. Lloyd, 269 F.3d 228, 238–43 (3d Cir.2001); Wilson v. Vermont Castings, Inc., 170 F.3d 391, 394 (3d Cir.1999).

> **Example.** In Pyles v. Johnson, 136 F.3d 986, 992 (5th Cir.1998), the court considered those portions of a juror's affidavit that indicated that she visited the crime scene, but declined to consider those portions of the affidavit in which the juror described her perceptions of the crime scene. The juror's statements concerning her perceptions constituted impermissible testimony about her mental processes.

(8) Exceptions—Racial bias. In Peña-Rodriguez v. Colorado, 580 U.S. 206, 137 S.Ct. 855 (2017), the Supreme Court held that the Sixth Amendment trumps Rule 606(b) when a juror seeks to testify about overt racial bias in the deliberation of a criminal case. "[W]here a juror makes a clear statement that indicates he or she relied on racial stereotypes or animus to convict a criminal defendant," 580 U.S. at 225, 137 S.Ct. at 869, Rule 606(b)'s prohibition on juror testimony must give way. See, e.g., United States v. Nucera, 67 F.4th 146, 168 (3d Cir.2023) (*Pena-Rodriguez* exception inapplicable because defendant failed to show that juror voted to convict defendant because of his race); United States v. Birchette, 908 F.3d 50, 54–60 (4th Cir.2018) (defendant failed to make sufficient showing to warrant court order permitting counsel to interview jurors to establish racial bias). Invoking the Equal Protection Clause, the Sixth Circuit held that a juror's testimony about racial bias in the deliberation of civil cases is also admissible despite Rule 606(b). Harden v. Hillman, 993 F.2d 465, 478–85 (6th Cir.2021).

CROSS-REFERENCES

Common Objections (Chapter 3)

53.   Juror as witness at trial

54.   Juror as witness to impeach verdict

Treatises

4 Graham, Handbook of Federal Evidence §§ 606:1–606:3 (9th ed. 2020)

1 McCormick, Evidence § 68 (8th ed. 2020)

27 Wright and Gold, Federal Practice and Procedure §§ 6071–6077 (2d ed. 2007)

Rule 607. Who May Impeach a Witness

Any party, including the party that called the witness, may attack the witness's credibility.

AUTHORS' COMMENTS

(1)   Scope and purpose of Rule 607. Rule 607 eliminates the common-law voucher rule. It explicitly permits a party to impeach its own witness.

The three impeachment techniques not specifically addressed by other rules of evidence (bias, capacity, and contradiction) are discussed in this section.

(2)   Methods of impeachment. The point of impeachment is to impugn a witness's credibility by attacking his ability to perceive the event, recall accurately that which he perceived, or communicate his story accurately, or his desire to testify truthfully.

Five methods of impeachment are permitted.

(a)   *Untruthful character.* A witness's character for truthfulness may be attacked.

(b)   *Bias.* A witness may be shown to be biased or interested, i.e., to have some reason to slant or fabricate his testimony.

(c)   *Prior inconsistent statements.* A witness may be shown to have made statements inconsistent with his testimony at trial.

(d)   *Defects of capacity.* A witness's capacity to perceive, recall or relate may be shown to be impaired.

(e)   *Contradiction.* The substance of a witness's testimony may be contradicted. United States v. Chaparro, 956 F.3d 462, 478 (7th Cir.2020).

Rules 608 and 609 govern impeachment through a showing of untruthful character. Rule 613 governs impeachment by showing that the witness has made prior inconsistent statements. The other three techniques are not specifically addressed by the rules.

(3)   Bias—Generally. Bias describes "the relationship between a party and a witness which might lead the witness to slant, unconsciously or otherwise, his testimony in favor of or against a party." United States v. Abel, 469 U.S. 45, 52, 105 S.Ct. 465, 469 (1984). Bias also embraces "interest," which results from the relationship between the witness and the issues at bar, as well as "corruption," which refers to a witness's decision to testify falsely due to bribery. 3A Wigmore, Evidence § 945 (Chadbourn rev. 1970). Although the federal rules do not specifically address impeachment by bias, the Supreme Court has unequivocally declared that it is a proper impeachment technique. United States v. Abel, 469 U.S. 45, 52, 105 S.Ct. 465, 469 (1984).

The opportunity to reveal a witness's motivation to lie is sufficiently important as to enjoy constitutional protection in criminal cases. Olden v. Kentucky, 488 U.S. 227, 109 S.Ct. 480 (1988); Davis v. Alaska, 415 U.S. 308, 316–17, 94 S.Ct. 1105, 1110 (1974). E.g., United States v. Salem, 578 F.3d 682 (7th Cir.2009) (defendant should have been given opportunity to impeach government's star witness about his involvement in a murder for which he may have been given immunity). The trial court may, however, place reasonable limits on inquiries into bias. Delaware v. Van Arsdall, 475 U.S. 673, 679, 106 S.Ct. 1431, 1435 (1986) (reasonable limits permissible based on concerns about "harassment, prejudice, confusion of the issues, the witness's safety, or interrogation that is repetitive or only marginally relevant"). E.g., Bui v.

DiPaolo, 170 F.3d 232, 245 (1st Cir.1999) (trial court did not err in precluding impeachment based on theory that witness was being coerced where defendant failed to present satisfactory foundation that coercive relationship existed); United States v. Lin, 101 F.3d 760, 767–68 (D.C.Cir.1996) (cross-examination limited where counsel lacked reasonable basis for asking question designed to establish bias).

(4) Bias—Examples. Bias may arise in innumerable ways, including:

- The witness has a personal relationship with a party or someone related to the litigation. E.g., Justice v. Hoke, 90 F.3d 43 (2d Cir.1996) (witness motivated to fabricate story because of dispute with defendant); United States v. Buchanan, 891 F.2d 1436, 1442 (10th Cir.1989) (witness's romantic involvement with government agent).

- The witness has a financial stake. E.g., United States v. Sedaghaty, 728 F.3d 885, 898–903 (9th Cir.2013) (government's failure to disclose FBI payments to witness prevented defendant from impeaching witness's credibility and constituted *Brady* violation); Collins v. Wayne Corp., 621 F.2d 777, 783 (5th Cir.1980) (fees earned by expert in previous cases).

- The witness has a penal interest. Davis v. Alaska, 415 U.S. 308, 316–17, 94 S.Ct. 1105, 1110 (1974) (witness's probationary status provides motive to accuse defendant); United States v. Larson, 495 F.3d 1094, 1096–1107 (9th Cir.2007) (en banc) (discussing limits of questioning witness about expectation that sentence will be reduced because of cooperation with prosecution); United States v. Schoneberg, 396 F.3d 1036 (9th Cir.2005) (terms of witness's plea agreement required government to file motion to reduce his sentence if it determined he provided "substantial assistance").

- The witness fears a party. United States v. Thompson, 359 F.3d 470 (7th Cir.2004) (evidence of threats by defendant); United States v. Hankey, 203 F.3d 1160, 1171–73 (9th Cir.2000) (fear of gang retaliation).

(5) Bias—Procedure and extrinsic evidence. Extrinsic evidence ordinarily is admissible to prove a witness's bias. Thus, an impeaching party is not bound by the witness's answer. United States v. Abel, 469 U.S. 45, 52, 105 S.Ct. 465, 469 (1984); ML Healthcare Serv., LLC v. Publix Super Markets, Inc., 881 F.3d 1293, 1302 (11th Cir.2018). An offer of extrinsic evidence may, however, be limited by the trial court pursuant to Rule 403 because of its tendency to prejudice the jury, embarrass the witness or waste time. United States v. Weiss, 930 F.2d 185, 197–98 (2d Cir.1991).

No foundation requirement for bias impeachment is contained in the federal rules. United States v. Manske, 186 F.3d 770, 778–79 (7th Cir.1999). Nonetheless, several courts of appeals have indicated that the impeaching party must afford the impeached witness the opportunity to admit or deny facts or statements manifesting the bias. See, e.g., United States v. Betts, 16 F.3d 748, 764 (7th Cir.1994); United States v. Weiss, 930 F.2d 185, 197–98 (2d Cir.1991).

(6) Defects of capacity. A witness may be attacked by showing that he suffered from an infirmity that affected his ability to perceive the event in question, now suffers from an infirmity that affects his ability to testify accurately, or suffered an intervening disability that affected his memory. A witness may also be impeached by establishing that he lacked the opportunity to observe the event.

The rules of evidence do not explicitly address this method of impeachment. It is, therefore, governed by reference to Rules 401–403 and Rule 611. A witness's capacity to observe, recall or relate may certainly be probed on cross-examination. Extrinsic evidence is also generally admissible, subject to the court's discretion to place reasonable limits on such evidence.

Among the many potential sources of defects in capacity are the following:

(a) *A mental illness or infirmity afflicting the witness,* if it evinces "an 'impairment' of the witness's 'ability to comprehend, know, and correctly relate the truth.' " United States v. Jimenez, 256 F.3d 330, 343 (5th Cir.2001) (quoting United States v. Partin, 493 F.2d 750, 763 (5th Cir.1974)). Courts should consider the nature of the illness, its recency, and whether the witness suffered from it at the time of the event witnessed. United States v. Crowley, 318 F.3d 401, 419 (2d Cir.2003).

> **Example—Admissible.** In United States v. Gonzalez-Maldonado, 115 F.3d 9, 15–17 (1st Cir.1997), the trial court erroneously excluded expert testimony concerning the mental illness of a declarant whose taped out-of-court statements formed a major element of the prosecution's case.

Example—Inadmissible. In United States v. Fattah, 914 F.3d 112, 180–82 (3d Cir.2019), the court of appeals held that the trial court properly refused to allow the defendant to cross-examine a witness about his bipolar disorder and the medications he used. The trial court otherwise allowed the defendant to cross-examine the witness about memory and perception problems, but concluded that the defendant failed to show specifically how inquiry into the bipolar disorder and medication would throw doubt on the witness's credibility or competence.

(b) *Alcohol or drug use by the witness.* Evidence that the witness was under the influence of drugs or alcohol near the time of the event or is under the influence while testifying is admissible. Grimes v. Mazda North American Operations, 355 F.3d 566, 573 (6th Cir.2004). Courts are more likely to exclude or limit evidence of drug or alcohol use not contemporaneous with the event or testimony. E.g., Kunz v. DeFelice, 538 F.3d 667, 676–77 (7th Cir.2008); United States v. Gallardo, 497 F.3d 727, 732–33 (7th Cir.2007) (holding evidence inadmissible absent showing that drug use impaired witness's ability to recall or relate events). But see United States v. Smith, 156 F.3d 1046, 1054–55 (10th Cir.1998) (permitting questions about witness's use of LSD 20 years earlier). While it may be probative (for example, as to its effects on memory), such evidence carries the possibility of unfair prejudice. See, e.g., United States v. Neely, 980 F.2d 1074, 1081 (7th Cir.1992).

(c) *A witness's bad eyesight, memory, hearing, etc.* E.g., United States v. Love, 329 F.3d 981, 984–85 (8th Cir.2003) (mental defect of impaired memory); United States v. Ciocca, 106 F.3d 1079, 1082–83 (1st Cir.1997) (memory loss due to accident); Battle v. United States, 345 F.2d 438, 440 (D.C.Cir.1965) (eyesight). Federal courts have been quite cautious in admitting expert testimony about the reliability of eyewitness testimony. See United States v. Moore, 786 F.2d 1308, 1312–13 (5th Cir.1986).

(7) Contradiction—Generally. Obviously, the impeaching party may attempt to elicit from a witness testimony that contradicts part or all of the witness's own testimony. The issue that arises with regard to this method of impeachment is under what circumstances a party is permitted to introduce *extrinsic evidence* to establish a contradiction. Two situations must be distinguished.

First, a party might try to offer evidence that contradicts a witness's testimony as to a material fact. Suppose in a bank robbery case that Bank Teller X testifies for the prosecution and identifies Defendant as the bank robber. The defense might call Bank Teller Y to testify that Defendant was not the bank robber. In such a case, Bank Teller Y's testimony is substantive evidence as to a material fact (the identity of the robber); it has probative value independent of any incidental impact it may have on Bank Teller X's credibility. It is not being offered as impeachment evidence and is unquestionably admissible.

Second, a party might try to offer evidence that contradicts a witness's testimony as to a tangential fact, solely for the purpose of impeaching the witness. Proof that the witness is mistaken or lying about the tangential fact may tend to prove that the witness is mistaken or lying about some other, more germane aspect of his testimony. Suppose Bank Teller X is asked on cross-examination what color dress she was wearing the day of the robbery; she answers, "Red." The defense might try to call Bank Teller Y to testify that Bank Teller X was wearing a blue dress on that day. Since the color of Bank Teller X's dress is inconsequential to the merits of the case, Bank Teller Y's testimony has no probative value independent of the impact it may have on Bank Teller X's credibility. Courts traditionally would label this a "collateral matter" and exclude Bank Teller Y's testimony.

(8) Contradiction as to collateral matters. The classic standard for whether a matter is collateral, and thus not susceptible to proof by extrinsic evidence is, "Could the fact, * * * have been shown in evidence for any purpose independently of the contradiction?" 3A Wigmore, Evidence § 1003, at 961 (Chadbourn rev. 1970). See also United States v. Scott, 243 F.3d 1103, 1107 (8th Cir.2001) ("contradiction offered through the testimony of another witness is customarily excluded unless it is independently relevant or admissible"); United States v. Mulinelli-Navas, 111 F.3d 983, 988 (1st Cir.1997); Simmons, Inc. v. Pinkerton's, Inc., 762 F.2d 591, 604–05 (7th Cir.1985).

Courts, however, sometimes permit extrinsic proof of a contradiction even though the contradiction relates only to a "tangential" matter. This ordinarily happens in cases in which a witness is unlikely to have been mistaken about the "tangential" fact were his story true. United States v. Lopez, 979 F.2d 1024, 1034 (5th Cir.1992) ("Extrinsic evidence is material, not collateral, if it contradicts 'any part of the witness's account of the background and circumstances of a material transaction, which as a matter of human experience he would not have been mistaken about if his story were true' ....") (quoting McCormick, Evidence § 47, at 112 (3d ed. 1984)).

Example—Admissible. In United States v. Opager, 589 F.2d 799, 801–03 (5th Cir.1979), to show defendant's predisposition to sell cocaine, a prosecution witness testified that he had observed defendant engage in previous cocaine transactions. On cross-examination, he stated that he had observed the transactions during 1974 and 1976, when he worked with defendant at a beauty salon. The defendant sought to introduce the business records of the salon to prove that the witness and defendant had not worked there together in 1974. The court of appeals held that the district court's decision to exclude the evidence was erroneous.

Ultimately, the admissibility of extrinsic evidence that is offered to contradict a witness's testimony must be judged under Rules 401–403. Morgan v. Covington Township, 648 F.3d 172, 179–80 (3d Cir.2011); United States v. DeCologero, 530 F.3d 36, 60 (1st Cir.2008). Among the factors the court should consider are the significance of the contradicted fact to the witness's story, the ease with which the contradiction can be proved, and whether the contradicted fact was elicited on direct or cross-examination. United States v. Kincaid-Chauncey, 556 F.3d 923, 932–33 (9th Cir.2009).

(9) Impeaching one's own witness. Rule 607 abandons the common-law voucher rule which barred a party from impeaching its own witnesses. A party seeking to impeach its own witness no longer has to show that it has been surprised and injured by the witness's testimony.

Complications arise, however, when an attempt is made to impeach a witness with evidence that would otherwise be inadmissible. The most common example is an attempt to impeach a witness with his prior inconsistent statement. Unless the prior inconsistent statement is defined in Rule 801(d) as non-hearsay or fits within a hearsay exception, the statement is inadmissible if offered for its truth. Thus, the prior inconsistent statement may be used by the jury only for impeachment purposes and not as substantive evidence. But since Rule 607 allows a party to impeach its own witness, the danger exists that a party might call a witness who once made statements favorable to its cause, even though the party knows that the witness has had a change of heart and will not testify favorably, solely so that it can impeach the witness with his prior inconsistent statements. Thus, in the guise of impeachment, a party might get the prior statements before the jury in the hope that the jury will impermissibly use them as substantive evidence.

This is objectionable under Rule 403. The opponent can argue persuasively in such instances that the probative value of the evidence (as impeachment) is substantially outweighed by the danger of unfair prejudice (that the jury will use the prior statement as substantive evidence). United States v. Logan, 121 F.3d 1172, 1174–77 (8th Cir.1997); United States v. Ince, 21 F.3d 576, 579–82 (4th Cir.1994). Courts generally sustain such objections, sometimes stating that impeachment may not be used as a "mere subterfuge," United States v. Johnson, 802 F.2d 1459, 1466 (D.C.Cir.1986), or for the "primary purpose" of placing otherwise inadmissible evidence before the jury. United States v. Buffalo, 358 F.3d 519, 522–23 (8th Cir.2004) (citing cases, but maintaining proper inquiry is Rule 403 balancing test regardless of party's motivation). But see United States v. Davis, 845 F.3d 282, 289–91 (7th Cir.2016) (party may impeach own witness unless party calls witness in bad faith); United States v. Burt, 495 F.3d 733, 736–38 (7th Cir.2007) (witness presented enough favorable evidence to calling party that calling party was properly allowed to impeach him with prior inconsistent statement regarding testimony he gave that was not favorable to calling party).

If, however, the prior inconsistent statement is defined as non-hearsay under Rule 801(d)(1)(A) or falls within a hearsay exception, the jury may properly use it as substantive evidence. The danger of unfair prejudice thus is eliminated and the impeachment should be allowed.

(10) Bolstering—Generally. Bolstering ordinarily refers to a proponent's attempt to offer otherwise inadmissible evidence solely for the purpose of enhancing his witness's credibility where there has not yet been an attack on the witness's credibility. The traditional rule is that such evidence is inadmissible. United States v. Rosario-Diaz, 202 F.3d 54, 65 (1st Cir.2000); United States v. LeFevour, 798 F.2d 977, 983 (7th Cir.1986). Rules 608(a) and 801(d)(1)(B), which limit the admissibility of truthful character evidence and prior consistent statements respectively, are particular applications of this rule. But the rules contain no other provision about "bolstering." Thus, the admissibility of other types of evidence offered solely to enhance the credibility of a witness who has not been impeached must be measured against the standards of Rules 401–403. See United States v. Scott, 267 F.3d 729, 735 (7th Cir.2001).

Another form of bolstering occurs when the prosecution implies that a witness's testimony is corroborated by other evidence known by the government, but does not offer that evidence. This is improper. United States v. Valdivia, 680 F.3d 33, 48–49 (1st Cir.2012).

(11) Bolstering—Cooperation agreements. Courts disagree as to whether the prosecution may elicit details of a cooperation agreement entered into with a witness, especially details regarding the consequences of perjurious testimony by the witness. The majority of courts hold such evidence admissible even in the absence of an attack on the witness's credibility, but the Second, Ninth and Eleventh Circuits exclude it. Compare, e.g., United States v. Certified Environmental Services, Inc., 753 F.3d 72, 86 (2d Cir.2014) (evidence inadmissible until witness's credibility attacked) with United States v. McClellon, 578 F.3d 846, 858–59 (8th Cir.2009) (upholding admission of plea agreement on direct exam, but noting that trial court has discretion whether to admit full written plea agreement); United States v. Thornton, 197 F.3d 241, 252–53 (7th Cir.1999) (holding plea agreements admissible if they do not contain repetitive references to truthfulness, but expressing doubt about admissibility of proffer letters); United States v. Romer, 148 F.3d 359, 369 (4th Cir.1998) (admissible if: prosecutor's questions do not imply that government has special knowledge of witness's veracity; judge instructs jury on caution required in evaluating witness's testimony; and prosecutor's closing argument contains no improper use of witness's promise of truthful cooperation). See United States v. Spriggs, 996 F.2d 320, 323–24 (D.C.Cir.1993) (admitting evidence and surveying case law).

(12) Removing the sting. The proponent of a witness will often elicit impeaching information from the witness on direct examination to deprive his adversary "of the psychological advantage of revealing it to the jury for the first time during cross-examination." United States v. Cosentino, 844 F.2d 30, 32 (2d Cir.1988). This is neither bolstering nor impeaching; it is simply a permissible means of trying to "take the sting out" of the cross-examination. See also United States v. Universal Rehabilitation Services (PA), Inc., 205 F.3d 657 (3d Cir.2000) (evidence of witness's guilty plea admissible even when defendants offered to stipulate that they would not challenge witness's credibility); United States v. Montani, 204 F.3d 761, 765–67 (7th Cir.2000) (accord).

(13) Rehabilitation. Rehabilitation refers to a proponent's attempt to offer otherwise inadmissible evidence for the purpose of enhancing a witness's credibility after the witness's credibility has been attacked. Rules 608 and 801(d)(1)(B) respectively govern the use of character evidence and prior consistent statements to rehabilitate. Otherwise, Rules 401–403 govern rehabilitation, consistent with the general principle that the method of rehabilitation must be responsive to the method of attack. See McCormick, Evidence § 47 (5th ed. 1999).

CROSS-REFERENCES

Common Objections (Chapter 3)

15.   Bolstering

43.   Impeachment; bias

45.   Impeachment of own witness

46.   Impeachment of own witness with prior inconsistent statement

47.   Impeachment on collateral matter

Checklists and Foundations (Chapter 4)

3A.   The five methods of impeachment

3B.   Bias

3D.   Contradiction

3E.   Capacity

Treatises

4 Graham, Handbook of Federal Evidence §§ 607:1–607:8 (9th ed. 2020)

1 McCormick, Evidence §§ 33, 38, 39, 44, 45, 47, 49 (8th ed. 2020)

27 Wright and Gold, Federal Practice and Procedure §§ 6091–6098 (2d ed. 2007)

Rule 608. A Witness's Character for Truthfulness or Untruthfulness

(a) Reputation or Opinion Evidence. A witness's credibility may be attacked or supported by testimony about the witness's reputation for having a character for truthfulness or untruthfulness, or by testimony in the form of an opinion about that character. But evidence of truthful character is admissible only after the witness's character for truthfulness has been attacked.

(b) Specific Instances of Conduct. Except for a criminal conviction under Rule 609, extrinsic evidence is not admissible to prove specific instances of a witness's conduct in order to attack or support the witness's character for truthfulness. But the court may, on cross-examination, allow them to be inquired into if they are probative of the character for truthfulness or untruthfulness of:

(1) the witness; or

(2) another witness whose character the witness being cross-examined has testified about.

By testifying on another matter, a witness does not waive any privilege against self-incrimination for testimony that relates only to the witness's character for truthfulness.

AUTHORS' COMMENTS

(1) Scope and purpose of Rule 608. Rule 608, along with Rule 609, governs proof of a witness's truthful or untruthful character if offered to attack or rehabilitate the witness's credibility. Rule 608(a) sanctions the use of reputation and opinion testimony to establish the truthful or untruthful character of a witness. Rule 608(b) provides that a witness may be cross-examined about specific instances of his conduct that did not result in a conviction but that bear on his truthful or untruthful nature. The rule, however, proscribes extrinsic proof of such acts.

It is important to note that Rule 608 addresses the use of reputation, opinion and specific act evidence only when it is offered to prove a witness's truthful or untruthful character so that the fact finder may infer that the witness is acting in conformity with that character and is thus more likely to be testifying truthfully or untruthfully. United States v. Cudlitz, 72 F.3d 992, 996 (1st Cir.1996). Attempts to impeach a witness through other techniques, such as bias and capacity, are not addressed by Rule 608. See United States v. Burnette, 65 F.4th 591, 606–07 (11th Cir.2023); United States v. Delgado-Marrero, 744 F.3d 167, 179 (1st Cir.2014).

An accused who testifies is subject to impeachment in the same manner as any other witness. United States v. McMurray, 20 F.3d 831, 834 (8th Cir.1994).

(2) Untruthful character—Reputation witness. One way of establishing a witness's (the "fact witness") untruthful character is by calling another witness (the "character witness") to testify as to the fact witness's reputation—in the community or among his associates—for untruthfulness. See Wilson v. City of Chicago, 6 F.3d 1233, 1239 (7th Cir.1993) (family members and people who worked with witness constitute "community"). As was true at common law, the testimony must concern the pertinent character trait—untruthfulness—and may not advert to other characteristics of the fact witness. The testimony must be limited to the fact witness's reputation; the character witness cannot give examples or explain why the reputation exists.

A witness testifying to the reputation of a fact witness must have personal knowledge of that reputation. United States v. Whitmore, 359 F.3d 609, 616 (D.C. Cir.2004).

(3) Untruthful character—Opinion witness. A second way of establishing the fact witness's untruthful nature is by calling a witness to give her opinion of the fact witness's untruthfulness. Such a witness must, of course, be personally acquainted with the fact witness. United States v. Turning Bear, 357 F.3d 730, 734 (8th Cir.2004). As is true for reputation witnesses, the testimony must be limited to the pertinent character trait—untruthfulness.

The testimony must also be confined to a statement of opinion; the character witness cannot relate specific incidents that support her opinion. While it is proper to ask a character witness whether she would believe the fact witness under oath, United States v. McMurray, 20 F.3d 831, 834 (8th Cir.1994), it is impermissible to ask her whether she believes the fact witness's story. United States v. Harris, 471 F.3d 507, 511 (3d Cir.2006).

Courts are extremely reluctant to allow psychiatrists to testify as experts concerning a witness's truthful character, see United States v. Cecil, 836 F.2d 1431, 1441–42 (4th Cir.1988) (citing cases), or otherwise allow experts to vouch for a witness's credibility under either Rule 608 or 702. See, e.g., United States v. Pereira, 848 F.3d 17, 21–22 (1st Cir.2017); United States v. Charley, 189 F.3d 1251, 1267 (10th Cir.1999). Cf. United States v. Parson, 84 F.4th 930, 937–40 (10th Cir.2023) (expert testimony about characteristics of sexually abused children does not necessarily constitute vouching for alleged victim's credibility).

(4) Untruthful character—Specific instances. A third way of establishing a fact witness's untruthful nature is to show that the witness has committed specific acts of conduct that are probative of untruthfulness. E.g., United States v. Ramirez-Rivera, 800 F.3d 1, 41–43 (1st Cir.2015) (defendant may ask witness whether, in violation of cooperation agreement, he failed to disclose murder he had committed, but may not ask witness whether he committed the murder). Rule 608(b) governs only the use of specific acts that did not result in convictions; convictions are governed by Rule 609. United States v. Osazuwa, 564 F.3d 1169, 1170–75 (9th Cir.2009).

Under Rule 608(b), the court may allow a party to cross-examine a witness about specific acts that are probative of the witness's character for truthfulness or untruthfulness. Several limitations, however, apply to such inquiries:

(a) Although counsel may ask the witness about the specific act, he may not ask whether the witness was arrested or charged for the act. Nelson v. City of Chicago, 810 F.3d 1061, 1068 (7th Cir.2016) ("an *arrest* is not, in itself, probative of the arrested person's character for truthfulness") (emphasis in original). Cf. United States v. Dvorkin, 799 F.3d 867, 883 (7th Cir.2015) (question whether witness had been barred by state from issuing stock not precluded by Rule 608(b), but may be objectionable on other grounds).

(b) Counsel must have a good faith basis for making the inquiry. United States v. Abair, 746 F.3d 260, 264 (7th Cir.2014) (cross-examiner must "have reason to believe the witness actually engaged in conduct that is relevant to her character for truthfulness"); United States v. Zaccaria, 240 F.3d 75, 81–82 (1st Cir.2001) ("a party who seeks to cross-examine a witness for the purpose of impeaching his credibility cannot base his queries solely on hunch or innuendo"); Hynes v. Coughlin, 79 F.3d 285, 294 (2d Cir.1996).

(c) Counsel is bound by the witness's answer. Extrinsic evidence to prove the specific act is inadmissible. United States v. McGee, 408 F.3d 966, 979–82 (7th Cir.2005).

> **Example—Extrinsic evidence inadmissible.** In United States v. Sabean, 885 F.3d 27, 39 (1st Cir.2018), the trial court permitted defendant to ask a witness on cross-examination about having provided her probation officer with false documents and having lied under oath. But the court refused to allow the defendant to introduce an audiotape that would have confirmed that the witness engaged in these dishonest acts. The court of appeals affirmed.

(d) The court may use Rule 403 to refuse to allow such inquiries to be made. United States v. Morales-Quinones, 812 F.2d 604, 613 (10th Cir.1987).

(5) Specific instances—Illustrations. Inquiry into a witness's specific acts is permissible only if the acts are probative of truthfulness or untruthfulness. The following are illustrative of the types of acts that courts find probative:

- Prior use of a false name. United States v. Ojeda, 23 F.3d 1473, 1476–77 (8th Cir.1994).

- Filing false tax returns. United States v. Chevalier, 1 F.3d 581 (7th Cir.1993).

- Running a business that sold false diplomas. Paldo Sign & Display Co. v. Wagener Equities, Inc., 825 F.3d 793, 799–800 (7th Cir.2016).

- Forgery. United States v. Waldrip, 981 F.2d 799, 802–03 (5th Cir.1993).

- Omitting a material fact from an official report. United States v. Seymour, 472 F.3d 969 (7th Cir.2007).

- Attempts to threaten potential witnesses to keep them from testifying truthfully. United States v. Manske, 186 F.3d 770, 774–76 (7th Cir.1999).

- Lying in other court proceedings. United States v. White, 692 F.3d 235, 248 (2d Cir.2012).

The following are illustrative of the types of acts that courts exclude as insufficiently probative of untruthfulness:

- Attempted murder. United States v. Young, 567 F.2d 799, 803 (8th Cir.1977).

- Threats against judicial officers in a prior prosecution. United States v. Van Dorn, 925 F.2d 1331, 1335 (11th Cir.1991).

- Drug use. United States v. Clemons, 32 F.3d 1504, 1511 (11th Cir.1994).

- Speeding. United States v. Nazarenus, 983 F.2d 1480, 1486 (8th Cir.1993).

- Filing for bankruptcy. Ad-Vantage Telephone Directory Consultants, Inc. v. GTE Directories Corp., 37 F.3d 1460, 1464 (11th Cir.1994).

Other types of conduct are more controversial. Compare United States v. Wilson, 985 F.2d 348, 352 (7th Cir.1993) (inquiry about bribery permissible) with United States v. Rosa, 891 F.2d 1063 (3d Cir.1989) (inquiry about bribery impermissible).

(6) Truthful character—Witness not yet attacked. Rule 608(a) stipulates that evidence of a witness's truthful character may not be offered unless an attack has first been made on the witness's veracity. Opposing counsel often object to such evidence as impermissible "bolstering." The more precise, and thus more prudent ground for objection, however, is that such evidence violates Rule 608(a).

(7) Truthful character—Rehabilitation. Once an attack has been made on a witness's truthful character, evidence of the witness's good character for truthfulness is admissible. Attacks on truthful character typically take the form of reputation or opinion testimony, inquiry into specific acts, or proof of convictions pursuant to Rule 609. Ordinarily, impeaching a witness through evidence of bias, contradiction or prior inconsistent statements does not constitute an assault on character. United States v. Martinez, 923 F.3d 806, 816–17 (10th Cir.2019). Occasionally, however, such forms of attack are viewed as sufficiently aimed at a witness's truthful character as to permit good character evidence in response. Renda v. King, 347 F.3d 550, 554–55 (3d Cir.2003). E.g., United States v. Dring, 930 F.2d 687, 691 (9th Cir.1991) (vigorous cross-examination or presentation of contradiction evidence); Beard v. Mitchell, 604 F.2d 485, 503 (7th Cir.1979) (prior inconsistent statement). But an attack that consists only of opposing counsel's "pointing out inconsistencies in testimony and arguing that the accused's testimony is not credible does not constitute an attack on the accused's reputation for truthfulness." United States v. Drury, 396 F.3d 1303, 1315 (11th Cir.2005).

Rehabilitation may be accomplished by presenting evidence of the witness's good character for truthfulness. Rule 608(a) sanctions the use of reputation and opinion testimony for this purpose. Rule 608(b) proscribes the use of extrinsic evidence of specific acts when offered to prove the witness's good character for truthfulness. United States v. Murray, 103 F.3d 310, 321–22 (3d Cir.1997).

(8) Cross-examination of character witness. Character witnesses who testify to a fact witness's character for truthfulness are subject to the same type of cross-examination as character witnesses who testify to other character traits pursuant to Rule 404(a). United States v. Skelton, 514 F.3d 433, 443–445 (5th Cir.2008).

(a) Reputation witnesses may be asked "have you heard" questions about specific acts of the fact witness that are inconsistent with a truthful nature. Similarly, opinion witnesses may be asked "did you know" questions. Rule 608(b)(2). In both instances, it is the credibility of the character witness that is being probed by testing just how familiar the character witness is with the fact witness or his reputation. United States v. Whiting, 28 F.3d 1296, 1301 (1st Cir.1994). In theory at least, the purpose of such questioning is to discredit the character witness, not the fact witness.

(b) Although "have you heard" questions are technically proper for reputation witnesses and "did you know" questions are correct for opinion witnesses, rigid adherence to one form or the other is not essential and Rule 405 does not mandate the use of one form rather than the other. Securities & Exch. Comm'n v.

Peters, 978 F.2d 1162, 1169–70 (10th Cir.1992). But see United States v. Curtis, 644 F.2d 263, 269 (3d Cir.1981) (dictum).

(c) Counsel must have a good faith basis before asking a "have you heard" or "did you know" question. United States v. Monteleone, 77 F.3d 1086, 1090–91 (8th Cir.1996).

(d) A character witness who has testified to a defendant-witness's truthful character may not be asked on cross-examination whether her opinion would change if the defendant were guilty of the pending charge. United States v. Oshatz, 912 F.2d 534, 537–41 (2d Cir.1990).

(9) Occupation and background information. Although evidence of a witness's good character for truthfulness is not permitted until the witness's character has been attacked, the calling party may nevertheless elicit some general information regarding the witness's occupation, residence and background. This gives the jury some information by which to gauge his standing and thus assess his credibility.

(10) Specific instances—Offered for other purpose. Rule 608 applies only when evidence is being offered to prove a witness's character for truthfulness so that the jury may infer that the witness is more or less likely to be testifying truthfully. It does not apply when evidence of specific acts is offered for some other purpose. United States v. Montelongo, 420 F.3d 1169, 1175 (10th Cir.2005). Thus, extrinsic evidence may be admissible:

• When the evidence is relevant to a material issue in the case. Foster v. General Motors Corp., 20 F.3d 838, 839 (8th Cir.1994).

• To prove the witness's bias toward one of the litigants. E.g., United States v. Abel, 469 U.S. 45, 105 S.Ct. 465 (1984).

• To rebut factual assertions made by the witness on direct examination. E.g., United States v. Crockett, 435 F.3d 1305, 1312–13 (10th Cir.2006) (referring to "specific contradiction"); United States v. Antonakeas, 255 F.3d 714, 724–25 (9th Cir.2001).

• To cure a witness's misleading statements as to the extent of his troubles with the law. E.g., United States v. Callaway, 938 F.2d 907, 910–12 (8th Cir.1991).

However, a party may not bootstrap proof of a witness's misconduct into evidence by trying to elicit the misleading statements or factual assertions on cross-examination and then adducing the evidence to contradict the witness's statements. Bonilla v. Yamaha Motors Corp., 955 F.2d 150, 154–55 (1st Cir.1992).

(11) No waiver of self-incrimination privilege. The last paragraph of Rule 608 ensures that a witness may still invoke the privilege against self-incrimination in response to inquiries about specific acts directed solely at establishing the witness's untruthful character. Air et Chaleur, S.A. v. Janeway, 757 F.2d 489, 496 (2d Cir.1985).

CROSS-REFERENCES

Rule 609. Impeachment by Evidence of a Criminal Conviction

(a) In General. The following rules apply to attacking a witness's character for truthfulness by evidence of a criminal conviction:

(1) for a crime that, in the convicting jurisdiction, was punishable by death or by imprisonment for more than one year, the evidence:

    (A) must be admitted, subject to Rule 403, in a civil case or in a criminal case in which the witness is not a defendant; and

    (B) must be admitted in a criminal case in which the witness is a defendant, if the probative value of the evidence outweighs its prejudicial effect to that defendant; and

(2) for any crime regardless of the punishment, the evidence must be admitted if the court can readily determine that establishing the elements of the crime required proving—or the witness's admitting—a dishonest act or false statement.

(b) **Limit on Using the Evidence After 10 Years.** This subdivision (b) applies if more than 10 years have passed since the witness's conviction or release from confinement for it, whichever is later. Evidence of the conviction is admissible only if:

    (1) its probative value, supported by specific facts and circumstances, substantially outweighs its prejudicial effect; and

    (2) the proponent gives an adverse party reasonable written notice of the intent to use it so that the party has a fair opportunity to contest its use.

(c) **Effect of a Pardon, Annulment, or Certificate of Rehabilitation.** Evidence of a conviction is not admissible if:

    (1) the conviction has been the subject of a pardon, annulment, certificate of rehabilitation, or other equivalent procedure based on a finding that the person has been rehabilitated, and the person has not been convicted of a later crime punishable by death or by imprisonment for more than one year; or

    (2) the conviction has been the subject of a pardon, annulment, or other equivalent procedure based on a finding of innocence.

(d) **Juvenile Adjudications.** Evidence of a juvenile adjudication is admissible under this rule only if:

    (1) it is offered in a criminal case;

    (2) the adjudication was of a witness other than the defendant;

    (3) an adult's conviction for that offense would be admissible to attack the adult's credibility; and

    (4) admitting the evidence is necessary to fairly determine guilt or innocence.

(e) **Pendency of an Appeal.** A conviction that satisfies this rule is admissible even if an appeal is pending. Evidence of the pendency is also admissible.

AUTHORS' COMMENTS

(1) **Scope and purpose of Rule 609.** Rule 609 governs impeachment by proof of a witness's criminal convictions. The rule is premised on the belief that a witness's criminal past is indicative of a dishonest character or a willingness to flaunt the law. Therefore, jurors may infer that a witness with a criminal past is less deserving of credit than one with an unblemished past. Walden v. Georgia-Pacific Corp., 126 F.3d 506, 523 (3d Cir.1997).

Rule 609(a)(2) provides that a conviction for any crime involving dishonesty or false statement may be used for impeachment. Conviction for a crime not involving dishonesty or false statement may be used only if it (a) was punishable by death or imprisonment in excess of one year and (b) meets the appropriate balancing test prescribed in Rule 609(a)(1).

Rule 609 is concerned primarily with only one form of impeachment—attacking a witness's character for truthfulness. The first sentence of Rule 609(a) makes this clear. Thus, (except for the use of juvenile adjudications under Rule 609(d)), Rule 609 does not govern when a conviction may be used to attack a witness's credibility on some basis other than the witness's character. Nor does it allow a witness's conviction to be offered for the purpose of showing that the facts that formed the basis of the witness's conviction are inconsistent with his testimony. The admissibility of a conviction as substantive evidence of the facts underlying the conviction is governed by Rule 803(22).

(2) Crimes involving dishonesty or false statement. Under Rule 609(a)(2), a witness may be impeached by showing that he has been convicted of a crime involving dishonesty or false statement, regardless of the punishment. This applies to all witnesses, and (except for remote convictions) the court may not invoke a balancing test to foreclose such impeachment. Burke v. Regalado, 935 F.3d 960, 1018 (10th Cir.2019).

Crimes such as perjury, fraud, embezzlement, or false pretense clearly qualify as crimes involving dishonesty or false statement. Crimes of violence do not. Under Rule 609(a)(2), a conviction qualifies under this subdivision only if establishing the elements of the crime required either proof or admission of an act of dishonesty or false statement by the witness. It is not enough that the witness exhibited dishonesty or made a false statement in committing the crime for which he was convicted. That a witness acted deceitfully in the course of committing a murder does not convert murder, a crime of violence, into a crime involving dishonesty or false statement. Crimes involving dishonesty or false statement are limited to those for which the fact finder was required to find (or the defendant to admit) an act of dishonesty or false statement. Among the crimes that courts have held to involve dishonesty or false statement are the following:

- Counterfeiting. United States v. Morrow, 977 F.2d 222, 228 (6th Cir.1992).

- Tampering with an electric meter. Altobello v. Borden Confectionary Prod., Inc., 872 F.2d 215 (7th Cir.1989).

- Theft by check. United States v. Harper, 527 F.3d 396, 408 (5th Cir.2008). But see United States v. Barb, 20 F.3d 694, 695 (6th Cir.1994) (worthless check conviction not per se a crime involving dishonesty or false statement).

- Failure to file income tax return. Dean v. Trans World Airlines, Inc., 924 F.2d 805, 811 (9th Cir.1991). But see Cree v. Hatcher, 969 F.2d 34, 36–38 (3d Cir.1992) (not a crime involving dishonesty or false statement).

- Receiving stolen property. United States v. Foster, 227 F.3d 1096, 1099–1100 (9th Cir.2000).

Among the crimes courts have held not to involve dishonesty or false statement are the following:

- Theft. United States v. Smart, 60 F.4th 1084, 1092 (8th Cir.2023); Clarett v. Roberts, 657 F.3d 664, 669 (7th Cir.2011) (retail theft); United States v. Johnson, 388 F.3d 96, 100 (3d Cir.2004) (purse snatching).

- Unauthorized acquisition and possession of food stamps. United States v. Mejia-Alarcon, 995 F.2d 982, 989–90 (10th Cir.1993).

- Robbery. Walker v. Horn, 385 F.3d 321, 334 (3d Cir.2004); United States v. Brackeen, 969 F.2d 827, 829–31 (9th Cir.1992).

- Burglary. United States v. Sellers, 906 F.2d 597, 603 (11th Cir.1990).

- Drug use. Medrano v. City of Los Angeles, 973 F.2d 1499, 1507 (9th Cir.1992).

Typically, the statutory elements of the crime will reveal whether it is one of dishonesty or false statement. But where the statutory elements do not indicate this, the trial judge may still determine that, in the particular case, proof or admission of an act of dishonesty or false statement by the witness was required to obtain a conviction. Under Rule 609(a)(2), this determination must be made only through readily available proof, such as the indictment, a statement of admitted facts, or the jury instructions.

Example. In United States v. Jefferson, 623 F.3d 227, 234–35 (5th Cir.2010), the witness had previously been convicted of obstruction of justice. Because the statutory elements of the crime authorize conviction for acts of violence as well as dishonesty, the trial court reviewed the indictment under which the witness had been convicted and found that the acts of obstruction with which he had been charged involved acts of dishonesty—knowingly and corruptly persuading another to lie to federal law enforcement authorities. Therefore, it found that the witness's prior conviction required proof of an act of dishonesty or false statement, and allowed him to be impeached with the conviction.

(3) Crimes not involving dishonesty or false statement. Rule 609(a)(1) authorizes impeachment by convictions for crimes that do not involve dishonesty or false statement if two conditions are met. First, the witness must have been convicted of a crime that is punishable by death or imprisonment in excess of one year. Second, a balancing test must be met. The balancing test depends on the status of the witness; one test is employed for criminal defendant-witnesses, another for all other witnesses. See United States v. Tse, 375 F.3d 148, 159–64 (1st Cir.2004) (discussing different balancing tests).

(a) *Criminal defendant as witness.* If the witness is the accused, he may be impeached under Rule 609(a)(1)(B) only if the court finds that the probative value of the conviction as credibility evidence outweighs its prejudicial effect to the accused. The burden of proof falls on the impeaching party.

(b) *All other witnesses.* Under Rule 609(a)(1)(A), if the witness is anyone other than the accused, he may be impeached unless the court determines that the probative value of the conviction as credibility evidence is substantially outweighed by the danger of unfair prejudice, confusion of issues, or misleading the jury, or the other countervailing considerations listed in Rule 403. United States v. Cavender, 228 F.3d 792, 799 (7th Cir.2000). The burden of proof falls on the party opposing impeachment.

Note that the crime only need be punishable by more than one year's imprisonment; the punishment actually imposed is irrelevant.

(4) Balancing factors. Courts consider a number of factors in balancing the probative value of an impeaching conviction against the danger of unfair prejudice. Some of the factors are particular to the situation where the accused is the witness, as that is where the danger of unfair prejudice is most acute. Several courts of appeals have endorsed the following five-factor test. E.g., United States v. Smalls, 752 F.3d 1227, 1240 (10th Cir.2014); United States v. Martinez-Martinez, 369 F.3d 1076, 1086 (9th Cir.2004).

(a) *The impeachment value of the prior crime.* The more the crime seems related to veracity, the greater its probative value. E.g., United States v. Hayes, 553 F.2d 824, 827–28 (2d Cir.1977) (drug smuggling more probative of credibility than is drug possession).

(b) *The point in time of the conviction and the witness's subsequent history.* Crimes committed during youth or long ago may have less bearing on the witness's present character. United States v. Pritchard, 973 F.2d 905, 909 (11th Cir.1992). Subsequent convictions, however, indicate that the earlier conviction was probably not a youthful aberration.

(c) *The similarity between the past crime and the charged crime.* The similarity of the previous offense poses a greater risk of prejudicial effect without concomitantly enhancing its probative value as evidence of untruthful character. United States v. Sanders, 964 F.2d 295, 297–98 (4th Cir.1992).

(d) *The importance of the defendant's testimony.* The court should consider both the risk that the defendant will be deterred from taking the stand by the fear that the jury will learn of his past convictions and the need for his testimony.

(e) *The centrality of the credibility issue.* The need for full exploration of credibility is greatest when the case boils down to a swearing match between witnesses. American Modern Home Ins. Co. v. Thomas, 993 F.3d 1068, 1071 (8th Cir.2021). But see American Home Assurance Co. v. American President Lines, Ltd., 44 F.3d 774, 779 (9th Cir.1994) (rejecting centrality of credibility as a factor).

While some appellate courts have noted that an explicit on-the-record finding regarding the probative value/prejudicial effect balance would be helpful, as would some indication of the trial court's reasoning, United States v. Walker, 817 F.2d 461, 464 (8th Cir.1987), neither is required by Rule 609(a)(1). United States v. Morrow, 977 F.2d 222, 228 (6th Cir.1992).

(5) Remote convictions. Rule 609(b) mandates a more stringent balancing test for convictions that are at least ten years old. A remote conviction is admissible only if the court makes a finding, supported by specific facts and circumstances, that the probative value of the conviction substantially outweighs its prejudicial effect. The balancing factors are the same ones used in making Rule 609(a)(1) determinations, see United States v. Collins, 799 F.3d 554, 571 (6th Cir.2015), but the stringent balancing test effectively creates a presumption against admissibility. United States v. Redditt, 381 F.3d 597, 601 (7th Cir.2004) (remote convictions should be admitted "very rarely and only in exceptional circumstances"). The time frame for measuring the ten-year time limit begins with the date of conviction or the date of the witness's release from any confinement imposed for that conviction, whichever is later. It ends on the date on which the witness testifies. United States v. Watler, 461 F.3d 1005, 1008–09 (8th Cir.2006). Time spent on probation or parole is not considered confinement. United States v. Moore, 76 F.4th 1355, 1367–68 (11th Cir.2023); United States v. Stoltz, 683 F.3d 934, 939 (8th Cir.2012). A party planning to use a remote conviction must provide his opponent reasonable written notice to afford him a fair opportunity to contest the evidence. United States v. Vgeri, 51 F.3d 876, 880 (9th Cir.1995) (trial court did not abuse discretion in barring defendant from cross-examining witness about remote conviction where defendant failed to comply with notice provision). But see United States v. Sloman, 909 F.2d 176, 180 (6th Cir.1990) (no prejudicial error in allowing impeachment of defendant despite lack of advance notice where defense counsel was aware of conviction). Cf. Fed. R. Crim. P., Rule 16(a)(1)(B) (upon request, government must furnish defendant copy of prior criminal record).

(6) Method of proof. Rule 609 does not stipulate how a witness's conviction is to be proved. Typically, it is either elicited from the witness on cross-examination or established through the introduction of a public record. No special foundation questions must be propounded before either asking the witness whether he has been convicted of the impeaching offense or introducing the public record.

Occasionally a party will attempt to impeach his own witness by questioning the witness on direct examination about (or introducing the public record of) past convictions. This is permissible, subject to Rule 403. See United States v. Gomez-Gallardo, 915 F.2d 553 (9th Cir.1990). More common, and less problematic, is the tactic of eliciting convictions on direct examination for the purpose of "removing the sting" from anticipated cross-examination. See, e.g., United States v. Bad Cob, 560 F.2d 877, 883 (8th Cir.1977). By attempting in this way to "remove the sting," however, a party waives the right to appeal an in limine ruling that the conviction was inadmissible. Ohler v. United States, 529 U.S. 753, 120 S.Ct. 1851 (2000).

(7) Details surrounding conviction. The impeaching party should ordinarily be permitted to establish the nature, time and place of, and the punishment for each conviction that qualifies for impeachment purposes. United States v. Estrada, 430 F.3d 606, 615–16 (2d Cir.2005) (citing cases). Details of the crime, however, may not be explored. United States v. Shelledy, 961 F.3d 1014, 1023 (8th Cir.2020); United States v. Commanche, 577 F.3d 1261, 1270–71 (10th Cir.2009). Courts sometimes allow the witness to offer brief explanations or denials, but such explanations or denials may open the door to rebuttal evidence, including further cross-examination concerning the details of the crime. United States v. Moon, 802 F.3d 135, 146 (1st Cir.2015); United States v. Collier, 527 F.3d 695, 700 (8th Cir.2008).

(8) Pardons, annulments, and certificates of rehabilitation. A witness may not be impeached with a conviction if it has been the subject of:

(a) a pardon, annulment, certificate of rehabilitation, or some equivalent procedure based on a finding that the witness has been rehabilitated, unless the witness has since committed a crime punishable by death or more than one year's imprisonment, Rule 609(c)(1); or

(b) a pardon, annulment, or some equivalent procedure based on a finding of innocence, regardless of the witness's subsequent history, Rule 609(c)(2).

In both instances, the witness's proponent shoulders the burden of establishing that the pardon, annulment, etc. was based on a finding of innocence or rehabilitation. United States v. Swanson, 9 F.3d 1354, 1357 (8th Cir.1993). Automatic pardons that restore the civil rights of the offender do not imply a finding of innocence or rehabilitation. Smith v. Tidewater Marine Towing, Inc., 927 F.2d 838, 840–41 (5th Cir.1991).

(9) Juvenile adjudications. Rule 609(d) ordinarily proscribes the use of juvenile adjudications. It sanctions their use in criminal cases, however, if (a) the witness being impeached with the adjudication is not the defendant, (b) an adult's conviction for such an offense would be admissible to attack the adult's credibility, and (c) use of the adjudication is necessary for a fair determination of guilt or innocence. The use of a juvenile adjudication under Rule 609(d) is not limited to showing the witness's character for truthfulness. It may, for example, be used to show a witness's bias. Compare Davis v. Alaska, 415 U.S. 308, 94 S.Ct. 1105 (1974) (admission of juvenile adjudication constitutionally required to show bias) with United

States v. Mangual-Corchado, 139 F.3d 34, 43 n.23 (1st Cir.1998) (court properly excluded evidence of juvenile adjudications).

(10) Procedure—Motions in limine. Parties often seek a pre-trial ruling as to whether the court will permit a particular witness (often the criminal defendant) to be impeached with a conviction. If the court rules that the impeachment will be allowed and the defendant decides not to testify, the defendant may not raise on appeal the validity of the *in limine* ruling. Luce v. United States, 469 U.S. 38, 105 S.Ct. 460 (1984).

(11) Conviction pending appeal. A witness may be impeached with a conviction that is still on appeal. E.g., Wilson v. City of Chicago, 6 F.3d 1233, 1237 (7th Cir.1993). Rule 609(e) permits the witness's proponent to establish that the conviction is not yet final.

(12) Conviction offered for other purpose. Like Rule 608, Rule 609 ordinarily applies only when the conviction is being offered to demonstrate the witness's untruthful character. Except for juvenile adjudications under Rule 609(d), Rule 609 does not apply when the conviction is offered for some other purpose, such as:

- To prove a material issue in the case. E.g., United States v. Rogers, 918 F.2d 207, 210–11 (D.C.Cir.1990) (previous conviction admissible under Rule 404(b) to prove intent).

- To rebut factual assertions made by the witness. E.g., United States v. Portillo, 969 F.3d 144, 183–84 (5th Cir.2020) (witness's convictions admissible to contradict his testimony that Hell's Angels was simply a "fun-loving motorcycle club"); United States v. Gilmore, 553 F.3d 266, 270–73 (3d Cir.2009) (permitting defendant to be impeached with two prior drug distribution convictions after he testified, on direct examination, that he never dealt drugs).

CROSS-REFERENCES

Common Objections (Chapter 3)

48.   Impeachment, prior conviction inadmissible

Checklists and Foundations (Chapter 4)

3F.   Character

3G.   Impeachment By Conviction—Factors for Balancing Probative Value Against Prejudice

Treatises

5 Graham, Handbook of Federal Evidence §§ 609:1–609:9 (9th ed. 2020)

1 McCormick, Evidence § 42 (8th ed. 2020)

28 Wright and Gold, Federal Practice and Procedure §§ 6131–6141 (2d ed. 2012)

Rule 610. Religious Beliefs or Opinions

Evidence of a witness's religious beliefs or opinions is not admissible to attack or support the witness's credibility.

AUTHORS' COMMENTS

(1) Scope and purpose of Rule 610. Rule 610 provides that evidence of the religious beliefs or opinions of a witness is inadmissible to attack the witness's credibility. Such evidence is also inadmissible to bolster or rehabilitate a witness's credibility. See United States v. Acosta, 924 F.3d 288, 204–06 (6th Cir.2019); Tisdale v. Federal Express Corp., 415 F.3d 516, 536 (6th Cir.2005). As the Advisory Committee's Note makes clear, Rule 610 precludes the use of a witness's religious beliefs or opinions only for the purpose of showing that the witness is a truthful or untruthful person.

(2) Use of religious beliefs for other purpose. Rule 610 does not prohibit all inquiries into religious beliefs or affiliations for impeachment purposes. An inquiry directed at showing bias or interest does not implicate the rule. United States v. Teicher, 987 F.2d 112, 118 (2d Cir.1993).

Example. In Firemen's Fund Ins. Co. v. Thien, 63 F.3d 754, 760–61 (8th Cir.1995), the trial court properly admitted testimony that two witnesses were members of the church to which one of the defendants belonged. The evidence tended to show possible bias on the part of the two witnesses.

Likewise, the rule does not govern the admissibility of evidence of religious beliefs that bears directly on the merits of the case. E.g., United States v. Beasley, 72 F.3d 1518, 1527 (11th Cir.1996) (holding admissible in RICO trial evidence of religious teachings that were used to justify and promote racketeering acts of murder and arson); Mauldin v. Upjohn Co., 697 F.2d 644, 649 (5th Cir.1983) (plaintiff's testimony that injuries caused by defendant prevented him from attending church held admissible because relevant to damages).

CROSS-REFERENCES

Common Objections (Chapter 3)

85.   Religious belief or opinion

Treatises

5 Graham, Handbook of Federal Evidence § 610:1 (9th ed. 2020)

1 McCormick, Evidence § 46 (8th ed. 2020)

28 Wright and Gold, Federal Practice and Procedure §§ 6151–6153 (2d ed. 2012)

Rule 611. Mode and Order of Examining Witnesses and Presenting Evidence

(a)   **Control by the Court; Purposes.** The court should exercise reasonable control over the mode and order of examining witnesses and presenting evidence so as to:

    (1)   make those procedures effective for determining the truth;

    (2)   avoid wasting time; and

    (3)   protect witnesses from harassment or undue embarrassment.

(b)   **Scope of Cross-Examination.** Cross-examination should not go beyond the subject matter of the direct examination and matters affecting the witness's credibility. The court may allow inquiry into additional matters as if on direct examination.

(c)   **Leading Questions.** Leading questions should not be used on direct examination except as necessary to develop the witness's testimony. Ordinarily, the court should allow leading questions:

    (1)   on cross-examination; and

    (2)   when a party calls a hostile witness, an adverse party, or a witness identified with an adverse party.

AUTHORS' COMMENTS

    (1)   **Scope and purpose of Rule 611.** Rule 611 addresses the order of interrogating witnesses and presenting evidence as well as the method by which these are done.

    First, the rule directs trial courts to exercise reasonable control over the order of interrogation of witnesses and presentation of evidence with three goals in mind: (1) making the interrogation and presentation effective for the ascertainment of the truth; (2) avoiding unnecessary consumption of time; and (3) protecting witnesses from harassment or undue embarrassment. Rule 611(a).

    Second, Rule 611(b) adopts a flexible approach to the traditional American rule that limits the scope of cross-examination to the subject matter of direct examination and matters affecting the witness's credibility.

    Third, Rule 611(c) addresses the use of leading questions both on direct and cross-examination.

    (2)   **Order of interrogation and presentation of evidence.** The trial court's discretion regarding the taking of evidence is relatively unfettered by other rules or statutory directives. See Fed. R. Crim. P. 26 (testimony must be taken orally in open court except as elsewhere provided); 18 U.S.C.A. § 3509 (testimony of child victim by closed-circuit television or videotaped deposition; use of adult attendant). Control over non-evidentiary aspects of the trial such as voir dire and opening and closing arguments is also vested in the trial court, as supplemented by various court rules. See Fed. R. Civ. P. 47(a) (examination of jurors); Fed. R. Crim. P. 24(a) (examination of jurors); Fed. R. Crim. P. 29.1 (closing argument).

The trial court's discretion over the manner in which witnesses are examined includes placing reasonable limits on the way in which a pro se litigant testifies.

Example. In United States v. Beckton, 740 F.3d 303 (4th Cir.2014), the trial did not abuse its discretion in requiring a pro se defendant to propound questions to himself rather than testifying in narrative form, particularly in light of the defendant's repeated attempts to present inadmissible evidence to the jury.

Similarly, the trial court is granted wide discretion to allow witnesses to testify out-of-turn. For example, the court is free to accommodate the schedule of an expert witness, e.g., Berroyer v. Hertz, 672 F.2d 334, 342 (3d Cir.1982), or to allow witnesses to be recalled so that evidence may be presented in chronological order, e.g., United States v. Puckett, 147 F.3d 765, 770 (8th Cir.1998), or so that relevant evidence may be presented. United States v. Fields, 763 F.3d 443, 464–65 (6th Cir.2014). See also United States v. Bailey, 973 F.3d 548, 563–64 (6th Cir.2020) (trial court did not abuse discretion in allowing witness to testify three times during trial); United States v. Hoover, 246 F.3d 1054, 1060–61 (7th Cir.2001) (trial court did not abuse discretion in allowing one of defendants to testify after prosecution began its rebuttal case). Nevertheless, it must exercise its discretion reasonably.

Example—Abuse of discretion. In Loinaz v. EG & G, Inc., 910 F.2d 1 (1st Cir.1990), the trial judge refused to allow a key defense witness to testify early in the plaintiff's case; the witness was unable to testify later due to his wife's surgery. The court of appeals held that, given the critical nature of the witness's testimony, the trial court abused its discretion.

Trial judges may place reasonable time limits on a party's presentation of its case. United States v. Morrison, 833 F.3d 491, 503–06 (5th Cir.2016). But see United States v. Colomb, 419 F.3d 292, 297–98 (5th Cir.2005) (power to set reasonable time limits does not authorize trial court to specifically exclude particular witnesses or categories of witnesses); United States v. Vest, 116 F.3d 1179, 1187–88 (7th Cir.1997) (expressing concern about "rigid hour limits").

The rebuttal and surrebuttal stages of the trial are ordinarily confined to a party's attempts to refute evidence presented by his opponent in the preceding stage. United States v. Pon, 963 F.3d 1207, 1224–25 (11th Cir.2020). The trial judge, however, has discretion to admit or exclude evidence that the party should have offered at an earlier stage of the trial or to exclude evidence because it is cumulative. United States v. O'Brien, 119 F.3d 523, 531 (7th Cir.1997); United States v. Koon, 34 F.3d 1416, 1429 (9th Cir.1994), aff'd in part, rev'd in part, 518 U.S. 81, 116 S.Ct. 2035 (1996). E.g., United States v. Gaertner, 705 F.2d 210, 217 (7th Cir.1983) (upholding both admission of prosecution rebuttal evidence and exclusion of defense surrebuttal evidence). The trial judge also has wide discretion as to whether to reopen testimony after the close of evidence. United States v. Rodriguez, 43 F.3d 117, 125 (5th Cir.1995) (listing factors to consider).

(3) Alternative means of presenting testimony. Technological advances such as closed-circuit television and two-way video conferencing have created the means by which testimony can be taken without a witness having to physically appear in a party's presence. But the right to confrontation, guaranteed by the Sixth Amendment, limits the prosecution's ability to take advantage of such alternate means of presenting testimony.

(a) *Child victims.* Maryland v. Craig, 497 U.S. 836, 110 S.Ct. 3157 (1990), held that the Confrontation Clause allows a child witness in a child abuse case to testify via closed-circuit television only when the state makes an adequate showing of necessity. In *Craig*, the state successfully demonstrated that resort to closed-circuit television testimony was necessary to protect child witness from the trauma of having to testify in the presence of the defendant. 18 U.S.C.A. § 3509(b) now provides a statutory basis for the use of testimony via closed-circuit television or videotaped depositions in proceedings involving an alleged offense of physical abuse, sexual abuse, or exploitation against a child.

(i) *Closed-circuit television.* This procedure may be used if the court finds that the child is unable to testify in open court in the accused's presence due to (a) fear; (b) the substantial likelihood that she would suffer emotional trauma; (c) a mental or other infirmity; or (d) conduct by the accused or his counsel. 18 U.S.C.A. § 3509(b)(1)(B). The court must make its finding on the record following a hearing. 18 U.S.C.A. § 3509(b)(1)(C). See, e.g., United States v. Protho, 41 F.4th 812, 825–26 (7th Cir.2022) (finding, after evidentiary hearing, that child was in fear and would suffer substantial emotional trauma); United States v. Cox, 871 F.3d 479, 484–85 (6th Cir.2017) (upholding case-specific finding made by trial court that child witnesses would suffer substantial fear and be unable to testify in defendant's presence). See generally United States v. Weekley, 130 F.3d 747, 753 (6th Cir.1997) (suggested instruction to jury regarding use of closed-circuit testimony).

(ii) *Videotaped deposition.* Pursuant to 18 U.S.C.A. § 3509(b)(2)(B), upon a preliminary finding that the child is likely to be unable to testify in open court, the court may order the child's videotaped deposition be taken. The videotaped deposition may be admitted into evidence if the court later finds, on the record, that the child is unable to testify in open court because of fear. 18 U.S.C.A. § 3509(b)(2)(C). See generally United States v. Boyles, 57 F.3d 535, 545–46 (7th Cir.1995).

If the record supports the court's finding, these procedures appear to conform to the demands of Maryland v. Craig.

18 U.S.C.A. § 3509(i) also provides that the child has the right to be accompanied by an adult attendant and authorizes the court to allow the attendant to remain in close physical proximity to or in contact with the child while the child testifies.

(b) *Two-way video.* Unlike the one-way closed-circuit television used in Maryland v. Craig, 497 U.S. 836, 110 S.Ct. 3157 (1990), two-way closed-circuit television (or video conferencing) enables the witness and the accused to see one another. Nevertheless, most courts have found that testimony presented through a two-way video monitor falls short of face-to-face confrontation. See, e.g., United States v. Yates, 438 F.3d 1307, 1313 (11th Cir.2006) (citing cases). These courts hold that Maryland v. Craig supplies the proper standard for the use of two-way video. For such testimony to be admissible, therefore, the court must first find that denial of physical, face-to-face confrontation is necessary to further an important public policy. *Yates*, at 1315. But see United States v. Khan, 794 F.3d 1288, 1307–11 (11th Cir.2015) (describing attempt to use videoconferencing to obtain testimony from defense witnesses in Pakistan); United States v. Gigante, 166 F.3d 75 (2d Cir.1999).

(4) Leading question defined. "A leading question is a question phrased in such a way as to hint at the answer the witness should give." United States v. Cephus, 684 F.3d 703, 707 (7th Cir.2012). Questions that begin, "Isn't it true that" or "Don't you agree that" typically suggest the answer and are leading. Other types of questions, such as questions that call merely for a yes or no answer or that ask the witness to choose between alternatives posed by the questioner, may or may not be leading, depending on the context in which the question is asked, the tone of voice employed, and the body language or conduct of counsel. See, e.g., United States v. Warf, 529 F.2d 1170 (5th Cir.1976) (prosecutor improperly led witness to make identification by pointing at accused).

(5) Direct examination—Use of leading questions. Ordinarily, non-leading questions must be used on direct examination. Rule 611(c). But the rule is phrased in suggestive, not mandatory, language. There are three instances in which leading questions are clearly sanctioned. They are:

• When a witness is unable to convey information meaningfully in response to non-leading questions, e.g., a witness who is a child, infirm, has language difficulties, or memory problems. E.g., United States v. Torres, 894 F.3d 305, 316–18 (D.C. Cir.2018) (reluctant minor); United States v. Johnson, 519 F.3d 816, 822 (8th Cir.2008) (child); United States v. Ajmal, 67 F.3d 12, 16 (2d Cir.1995) (language); United States v. Callahan, 801 F.3d 606, 623 (6th Cir.2015) (cognitive impairment); Litherland v. Petrolane Offshore Construction Serv., 546 F.2d 129, 134 (5th Cir.1977) (mental deficiency); United States v. Templeman, 965 F.2d 617, 619 (8th Cir.1992) (memory); United States v. Grassrope, 342 F.3d 866, 867–69 (8th Cir.2003) (sexual assault victim); United States v. Greaux-Gomez, 52 F.4th 426, 437–38 (1st Cir.2022) (teen-aged sexual assault victim "shaking uncontrollably and extremely nervous").

• When the questions relate to preliminary or other undisputed matters. United States v. Londondio, 420 F.3d 777, 789 (8th Cir.2005). E.g., United States v. Indorato, 628 F.2d 711, 718 (1st Cir.1980).

• When the witness is an adverse party, is identified with an adverse party, or is hostile to the calling party. Rule 611(c)(2). E.g., Rosa-Rivera v. Dorado Health, Inc., 787 F.3d 614, 616–17 (1st Cir.2015) (nurse who assisted physician in alleged medical malpractice); Chonich v. Wayne County Community College, 874 F.2d 359, 368 (6th Cir.1989) (employee of party); United States v. Hicks, 748 F.2d 854, 859 (4th

Cir.1984) (girlfriend of party); United States v. Tsui, 646 F.2d 365, 368 (9th Cir.1981) (investigating agent); National Railroad Pass. Corp. v. Certain Temporary Easements Above R.R. Right of Way, 357 F.3d 36, 42 (1st Cir.2004) (hostile witness).

(6) Cross-examination—Generally. Although frequently associated with leading questions, cross-examination refers simply to a stage in the interrogation of a witness. It is considered a right, denial of which often constitutes reversible error. Davis v. Alaska, 415 U.S. 308, 94 S.Ct. 1105 (1974); Rhodes v. Dittmann, 903 F.3d 646 (7th Cir.2018). Nevertheless, the trial court may place reasonable limitations on a party's cross-examination. Delaware v. Van Arsdall, 475 U.S. 673, 679, 106 S.Ct. 1431, 1435 (1986) ("trial judges retain wide latitude * * * to impose reasonable limits on such cross-examination based on concerns about, among other things, harassment, prejudice, confusion of the issues, the witness's safety, or interrogation that is repetitive or only marginally relevant").

(7) Cross-examination—Leading questions. Rule 611(c)(1) codifies the familiar rule that leading questions are ordinarily permitted on cross-examination. The qualifying language—that such questions should be permitted "ordinarily"—authorizes the trial court to limit the use of leading questions when, for example, the cross-examiner is interrogating a friendly witness. Shultz v. Rice, 809 F.2d 643, 654 (10th Cir.1986) (cross-examination of client called by opponent as adverse witness).

(8) Cross-examination—Scope. Rule 611(b) provides that cross-examination should be limited to subjects raised on direct examination and credibility issues. Courts generally allow the cross-examiner wide latitude, interpreting the subject matter of direct examination to include all "inferences and implications" arising from the direct testimony. United States v. Tomblin, 46 F.3d 1369, 1386 (5th Cir.1995). See also United States v. Bozovich, 782 F.3d 814, 816 (7th Cir.2015) (standard is whether cross-examination is "reasonably related" to subject matter of direct exam and should be "liberally interpreted"). The rule explicitly authorizes courts to permit cross-examination on matters beyond the scope of direct examination, with the questioning proceeding "as if on direct examination." E.g., United States v. Carter, 910 F.2d 1524, 1530 (7th Cir.1990).

(9) Redirect and recross-examination. Rule 611 makes no mention of redirect and recross-examination. Much is left, therefore, to the discretion of the trial court pursuant to its power to control the order and mode of interrogating witnesses and presenting evidence. Although the traditional rule of thumb is that redirect examination should be limited to the subject matter brought out during cross-examination, United States v. Walker, 613 F.2d 1349, 1353 (5th Cir.1980), courts may allow new matters to be raised on redirect. United States v. O'Neal, 844 F.3d 271, 275 (D.C. Cir.2016). Similar discretion is afforded the court with respect to recross. "Recross is to redirect as cross-examination is to direct." United States v. Riggi, 951 F.2d 1368, 1375 (3d Cir.1991). See, e.g., United States v. Whitten, 610 F.3d 168, 181–83 (2d Cir.2010). If new subject matter is developed on redirect examination, recross-examination must be permitted.

> **Example.** In United States v. Vasquez, 82 F.3d 574, 575–77 (2d Cir.1996), the prosecution was trying to establish that defendant possessed a shotgun while he was fleeing from the police. On redirect examination, one of the arresting officers testified for the first time that he was unable to see defendant's hands during the chase. The trial court did not allow defendant to recross-examine the officer about this statement. The court of appeals, however, held that this was error since the officer had not made this point specifically during direct examination and the prosecution considered it an important piece of circumstantial evidence.

(10) Objections as to form of question—Generally. Many grounds exist for objecting to the form in which a question is posed. The rules of evidence do not address most of the common objections. Much, therefore, is left to the trial judge's discretion.

(11) Objections as to form—Specific objections. The following are commonly-lodged objections:

- *Ambiguous, confusing, unintelligible.* The question may be interpreted in different ways, or is so vague or unclear that it is likely to confuse either the jury or the witness. E.g., United States v. Clark, 613 F.2d 391, 406–07 (2d Cir.1979).

- *Argumentative.* Counsel may not, in the guise of asking a question, make a jury argument or attempt to summarize, draw inferences from, or comment on the evidence. E.g., Smith v. Estelle, 602 F.2d 694, 700 n. 7 (5th Cir.1979) ("Dr. Grigson, you're kind of the hatchet man down here for the District

Attorney's Office, aren't you?"), aff'd, 451 U.S. 454, 101 S.Ct. 1866 (1981). In addition, questions that ask a witness to testify as to his own credibility are improper.

• *Asked and answered.* Counsel has already posed, and the witness has already answered, the particular question. E.g., United States v. Collins, 996 F.2d 950, 952 (8th Cir.1993).

• *Assuming facts not in evidence.* E.g., United States v. Medel, 592 F.2d 1305, 1314 (5th Cir.1979).

• *Compound.* The witness is asked to respond to two or more questions posed jointly. E.g., United States v. Smith, 354 F.3d 390, 396 (5th Cir.2003).

• *Harassing, embarrassing the witness.* Rule 611(a) directs the court to "protect witnesses from harassment or undue embarrassment." E.g., United States v. Singh, 628 F.2d 758, 763–64 (2d Cir.1980) (unnecessarily delving into witnesses' personal lives).

• *Lack of foundation.* This is typically a shorthand way of protesting that the requisites of some other rule of evidence have not been met. For example, the "lack of foundation" may derive from a failure (a) to show that the witness has personal knowledge of the event to which she is about to testify, see Rule 602; (b) to authenticate the proffered exhibit, see Rule 901; (c) to establish that the requirements for a particular hearsay exception (e.g., the business record exception) have been met, see Rule 803; (d) to qualify the proffered witness as an expert, see Rule 702; or (e) to show that the facts underlying an expert's opinion constitute a permissible basis, see Rule 703.

• *Misstating testimony, misleading.* A question that misstates the witness's or another witness's testimony is misleading and improper. E.g., United States v. Pantone, 609 F.2d 675, 681 (3d Cir.1979).

• *Narrative.* Although the narrative form is not per se objectionable, it is well within the court's discretion to require counsel to employ more pointed questions. When a narrative question is likely to provoke a response containing hearsay or other inadmissible evidence, the court ought to exercise its discretion and require more specific questions. See United States v. Pless, 982 F.2d 1118, 1123 (7th Cir.1992).

• *Nonresponsive.* This objection goes to the form of the answer, rather than the question. Many courts allow only questioning counsel to object and move to strike the answer on this ground. E.g., United States v. Shillingstad, 632 F.3d 1031, 1036 (8th Cir.2011). Opposing counsel may object only if the answer is objectionable on some other ground. Although counsel must object in as timely a manner as possible, the nonresponsiveness of the answer may excuse counsel's failure to object more quickly.

• *Repetitious.* Unduly repetitious questions are not likely to elicit additional evidence of probative value and tend to waste time. E.g., United States v. Dowdy, 960 F.2d 78, 80 (8th Cir.1992).

• *Speculation, conjecture.* This objection goes to the substance of the anticipated response. Questions inviting the witness to speculate or guess as to what occurred or caused an event may either run afoul of the personal knowledge requirement (Rules 602 and 701) or constitute an impermissible attempt to elicit an opinion beyond the scope of the witness's expertise (Rule 702). E.g., United States v. Stewart, 104 F.3d 1377, 1383–84 (D.C.Cir.1997); Beissel v. Pittsburgh and Lake Erie R. Co., 801 F.2d 143, 151 (3d Cir.1986).

(12) Summary charts; Overview and summary witnesses. Appellate courts have recognized the trial court's authority to permit the use of summary charts and testimony under certain circumstances. Courts must distinguish between two basic types of summary charts: (1) charts that summarize data contained in other writings that are not themselves offered in evidence (Rule 1006 summary charts); and (2) charts that summarize testimony and other evidence already offered at trial (pedagogical summary charts). See United States v. White, 737 F.3d 1121, 1135 (7th Cir.2013); 572 U.S. 1157, 134 S.Ct. 2717 (2014); United States v. Irvin, 682 F.3d 1254, 1262–63 (10th Cir.2012).

(a) *Rule 1006 summary charts.* The admissibility of the first type of summary chart hinges on compliance with the Best Evidence Rule. The underlying data must itself be admissible and voluminous and must have been made available to opposing parties for examination or copying. See Authors' Comments to Rule 1006.

(b) *Pedagogical summary charts.* The admissibility of pedagogical summary charts is more complicated. Some courts give trial judges the discretion to allow the use such charts to clarify or as an aid in the presentation of evidence, but not to admit the charts into evidence or allow them to be taken to the jury room. In such instances, the trial judge should instruct the jury that the summary chart itself is not evidence. See, e.g., United States v. Janati, 374 F.3d 263, 273 (4th Cir.2004); United States v. Buck, 324 F.3d 786, 790–91 (5th Cir.2003). Other courts allow such charts to be admitted into evidence and taken to the jury room, but only in rare instances. See, e.g., United States v. Bray, 139 F.3d 1104, 1112 (6th Cir.1998) (referring to pedagogical summary charts that accurately and reliably summarize complex or difficult evidence and that have been admitted into evidence as "secondary-evidence summaries"). Other courts seem to give somewhat more discretion to trial judges as to whether to admit pedagogical summary charts into evidence. See, e.g., United States v. White, 737 F.3d 1121, 1135–36 (7th Cir.2013); United States v. Milkiewicz, 470 F.3d 390, 395–99 (1st Cir.2006). In determining whether pedagogical summary charts should be used, trial courts should consider the length of the trial, the complexity of the case, and the number of exhibits and witnesses in determining whether such testimony would be helpful to the jury. See, e.g., United States v. Johnson, 54 F.3d 1150, 1156–62 (4th Cir.1995). A court should not allow pedagogical evidence that is not admitted into evidence to be taken to the jury room. See Baugh v. Cuprum S.A. de C.V., 730 F.3d 701 (7th Cir.2013). But see United States v. Robinson, 872 F.3d 760, 779–80 (6th Cir.2017) (stating that law is unclear whether court may provide jury with demonstrative aid that was not admitted into evidence).

(c) *Overview and summary witnesses.* The use of an overview witness (early in a party's case presentation) or a summary witness (near the end) is more problematic. See, e.g., United States v. Lacerda, 958 F.3d 196, 208 (3d Cir.2020) (allowing limited overview testimony, but holding inadmissible overview testimony that "opines on ultimate issues of guilt, makes assertions of fact outside of the officer's personal knowledge, or delves into aspects of the investigation in which he did not participate"); United States v. Armstrong, 619 F.3d 380, 385 (5th Cir.2016) (holding that summary witnesses permitted only in "limited circumstances" in complex cases and noting potential dangers); United States v. Brooks, 736 F.3d 921, 930–34 (10th Cir.2013) (detailing possible abuses of overview testimony and recommending that such testimony be limited to high level of generality).

(13) Questioning by jurors. Courts of appeals have unanimously concluded that a court may allow jurors to ask questions of the witnesses in some circumstances. See, e.g., United States v. Richardson, 233 F.3d 1285, 1288–89 (11th Cir.2000) (surveying cases); S.E.C. v. Koenig, 557 F.3d 736, 741–43 (7th Cir.2009). While acknowledging that this is a matter that falls within the sound discretion of the trial court, some courts have urged that it be used sparingly. E.g., United States v. Collins, 226 F.3d 457, 464 (6th Cir.2000) (juror questions should be allowed "only rarely"); United States v. Ajmal, 67 F.3d 12, 14–15 (2d Cir.1995) (requiring extraordinary or compelling circumstances). Others emphasize the importance of procedural protections. United States v. Feinberg, 89 F.3d 333, 336–37 (7th Cir.1996) (criticizing judge for allowing jurors to ask questions orally). See United States v. Bush, 47 F.3d 511, 516 (2d Cir.1995) (outlining proper procedures).

CROSS-REFERENCES

Common Objections (Chapter 3)

1–12. Objections to form of question

25.   Confrontation Clause: Face-to-Face Confrontation

28.   Cross-examination, beyond scope of direct

60.   Nonresponsive answer

89.   Speculation, question calls for

Treatises

5 Graham, Handbook of Federal Evidence §§ 611:1–611:23 (9th ed. 2020)

1 McCormick, Evidence §§ 4–7, 19–32 (8th ed. 2020)

28 Wright and Gold, Federal Practice and Procedure §§ 6161–6168 (2d ed. 2012)

Rule 612. Writing Used to Refresh a Witness's Memory

(a)   **Scope.** This rule gives an adverse party certain options when a witness uses a writing to refresh memory:

(1) while testifying; or

(2) before testifying, if the court decides that justice requires the party to have those options.

(b) Adverse Party's Options; Deleting Unrelated Matter. Unless 18 U.S.C. § 3500 provides otherwise in a criminal case, an adverse party is entitled to have the writing produced at the hearing, to inspect it, to cross-examine the witness about it, and to introduce in evidence any portion that relates to the witness's testimony. If the producing party claims that the writing includes unrelated matter, the court must examine the writing in camera, delete any unrelated portion, and order that the rest be delivered to the adverse party. Any portion deleted over objection must be preserved for the record.

(c) Failure to Produce or Deliver the Writing. If a writing is not produced or is not delivered as ordered, the court may issue any appropriate order. But if the prosecution does not comply in a criminal case, the court must strike the witness's testimony or—if justice so requires—declare a mistrial.

AUTHORS' COMMENTS

(1) Scope and purpose of Rule 612. Rule 612 provides procedural protections to the opponent of a party that attempts to refresh a witness's recollection through the use of a writing. The rule applies both when a writing is shown to a witness in an effort to refresh recollection *while* the witness testifies and *before* the witness testifies.

(2) Present recollection refreshed distinguished from past recollection recorded. The practice of refreshing a witness's present recollection is often confused with the hearsay exception for past recollection recorded. See, e.g., United States v. Cash, 394 F.3d 560 (7th Cir.2005).

(a) Refreshing recollection refers simply to the procedure by which counsel uses some item in an effort to trigger a witness's faulty memory. If the effort is successful, the witness testifies from his now-revived memory. As a consequence, the refreshing object is not evidence and may not be introduced as such by the refreshing party. Therefore, a document may be used to refresh recollection even if it is not itself admissible. United States v. Vasquez, 635 F.3d 889, 895 (7th Cir.2011).

(b) Past recollection recorded is used when a witness's memory cannot be refreshed. If the witness testifies that he made a writing near the time of the event and that it accurately reflected the event, the writing may be substituted for the witness's memory under the past recollection recorded exception to the hearsay rule. Rule 803(5).

(3) Refreshing recollection with leading questions. When a witness's memory proves faulty, the court may allow counsel to attempt to jog his memory via leading questions. United States v. Templeman, 965 F.2d 617, 619 (8th Cir.1992). Courts should exercise caution, however, in permitting counsel to pose leading questions to a friendly witness in the guise of refreshing recollection. When a key witness suffers a memory lapse, the court may require that any oral statement that might jog his memory be reduced to writing and shown to him or that any attempt to refresh recollection by leading questions be undertaken outside the presence of the jury. See Rush v. Illinois Central R. Co., 399 F.3d 705, 717 (6th Cir.2005).

(4) Refreshing recollection with writings—Procedure. Once counsel establishes that a witness's memory is exhausted, counsel may use a writing to refresh the witness's recollection. The following steps should be observed.

(a) Counsel should show the writing to the witness and allow him to read it silently. Counsel should not read the writing to the witness in the presence of the jury. United States v. Shoupe, 548 F.2d 636, 641 (6th Cir.1977).

(b) If the witness testifies that he now recalls the matter independently of the writing, he may testify to that independent recollection. The witness should not, however, be permitted to testify to the contents of the writing under the guise of refreshed recollection. United States v. Carey, 589 F.3d 187, 191 (5th Cir.2009). If the court believes the witness's memory has not truly been refreshed, it may refuse to allow the witness to testify. United States v. Riccardi, 174 F.2d 883, 889 (3d Cir.1949). The court may also require the witness to relinquish possession of the writing after reading it and testify without referring to it. One factor the court may consider is the witness's ability to recall details beyond those comprising the writing. United States v. Rinke, 778 F.2d 581, 588 (10th Cir.1985).

(c)   If the witness cannot recall the matter after having reviewed the writing, his testimony is forestalled unless counsel can lay the predicate for admitting the contents of the writing under the past recollection recorded exception to the hearsay rule, Rule 803(5), or some other hearsay exception.

(d)   Courts commonly permit witnesses such as experts and police officers to consult writings as they testify, particularly where the subject matter of the testimony is lengthy and detailed. See Rush v. Illinois Central R. Co., 399 F.3d 705, 718 n.16 (6th Cir.2005).

(5)   Refreshing recollection with writings—Types of writings. Any writing, made at any time, may be used to jog a witness's memory. The writing need not be one made by the witness. In fact, the refreshing object need not even be a writing.

Example—Writing prepared by another. In United States v. Marrero, 651 F.3d 453, 471–72 (6th Cir.2011), a police officer was permitted to refresh her recollection with a report made by another officer.

Example—Writing not contemporaneous. In United States v. Horton, 526 F.2d 884, 889 (5th Cir.1976), witnesses were permitted to refresh their recollection with statements they had made non-contemporaneously with the events in question.

The trial court retains discretion to refuse to allow a writing to be used to refresh recollection when good cause exists to believe the writing will generate a false memory.

Example—Use of document disallowed. In United States v. Weller, 238 F.3d 1215, 1221–22 (10th Cir.2001), the court upheld the trial court's refusal to allow a witness to consult a document. The witness had been able to testify about the property that was the subject of the document, and the document itself was inadmissible hearsay. "[T]he court has the discretion to withhold any writing from a witness where the judge believes that the document will be a source of direct testimony rather than the key to refreshing the witness' independent recollection."

Example—Use of document disallowed. In Parliament Ins. Co. v. Hanson, 676 F.2d 1069, 1073 (5th Cir.1982), the court refused to permit counsel to refresh a witness's recollection with notes made in anticipation of litigation where the documents from which the notes were created were missing.

(6)   Refreshing recollection with writings—Adversary's rights. Rule 612(b) provides that when a writing is used during testimony to refresh recollection, the adverse party has the right to inspect it, cross-examine the witness about it, and introduce into evidence any portions of the writing related to the witness's testimony. If a dispute arises as to whether certain matters in the writing are related to the testimony, the court must examine the writing in camera, redact any irrelevant portions, and order delivery of the remainder. See Pollard v. C.I.R., 786 F.2d 1063, 1067 (11th Cir.1986) (limiting amount of material ordered disclosed).

(7)   Refreshing recollection before witness testifies. Sometimes, before testifying, a witness may review a writing to refresh his recollection. In such instances, if the court determines that justice so requires, Rule 612(a)(2) authorizes the court to order disclosure of the writing to the adversary. Note that the rule applies only when the purpose of the review was to refresh the witness's recollection for the purpose of testifying. United States v. Sheffield, 55 F.3d 341, 343 (8th Cir.1995). Documents that would otherwise be protected from disclosure by the attorney-client privilege or work-product doctrine may be the subject of a production order. See Thomas v. Euro RSCG Life, 264 F.R.D. 120 (S.D.N.Y. 2010) (ordering disclosure of attorney-client privileged notes reviewed by witness before deposition testimony, but protecting notes covered by work-product). But see In re Kellogg Brown & Root, Inc., 796 F.3d 137, 143–45 (D.C. Cir.2015) (trial court erred in ordering disclosure of privileged documents reviewed before deposition by witness designated by organization under Fed. R. Civ. P. 30(b)(6)).

(8)   Application to depositions. Citing Fed. R. Civ. P. 30(c), courts have near-unanimously held that Rule 612 applies when a witness testifies at a deposition. E.g., Thomas v. Euro RSCG Life, 264 F.R.D. 120 (S.D.N.Y. 2010).

(9) **Effect of Jencks Act.** Rule 612(b) begins by subordinating its provisions to those of the Jencks Act, 18 U.S.C.A. § 3500. The effect of this language is a matter of controversy, however, especially in light of amendments to Fed. R. Crim. P. 26.2 and 17(h), which effectively supplant the Jencks Act. See 28 Wright and Gold, Federal Practice and Procedure § 6186 (1993).

CROSS-REFERENCES

Checklists and Foundations (Chapter 4)

4.   Present Recollection Refreshed

Treatises

5 Graham, Handbook of Federal Evidence §§ 612:1–612:2 (9th ed. 2020)

1 McCormick, Evidence § 9 (8th ed. 2020)

28 Wright and Gold, Federal Practice and Procedure §§ 6181–6189 (2d ed. 2012)

Rule 613. Witness's Prior Statement

(a) **Showing or Disclosing the Statement During Examination.** When examining a witness about the witness's prior statement, a party need not show it or disclose its contents to the witness. But the party must, on request, show it or disclose its contents to an adverse party's attorney.

(b) **Extrinsic Evidence of a Prior Inconsistent Statement.** Extrinsic evidence of a witness's prior inconsistent statement is admissible only if the witness is given an opportunity to explain or deny the statement and an adverse party is given an opportunity to examine the witness about it, or if justice so requires. This subdivision (b) does not apply to an opposing party's statement under Rule 801(d)(2).

AUTHORS' COMMENTS

(1) **Scope and purpose of Rule 613.** Rule 613 governs the impeachment of a witness by proof of her prior inconsistent statements. A statement used for this type of impeachment must be the witness's own statement. Carnell Const. Corp. v. Danville Redevelopment & Housing Authority, 745 F.3d 704, 718 (4th Cir.2013) ("For a statement to qualify as a witness' prior inconsistent statement under Rule 613(b), the statement must be one that the witness has made or adopted, or to which the witness otherwise has subscribed."). Rule 613 does not apply to impeachment by conduct of the witness inconsistent with her testimony at trial. See Advisory Committee's Note.

(2) **Hearsay and prior inconsistent statements.** A witness's own out-of-court statement is hearsay if offered for its truth. When a witness's prior inconsistent statement is offered for impeachment, however, it is being offered merely to show that the witness told a different story at a different time. Thus, the statement is not being offered for its truth and is not hearsay when offered for this purpose. United States v. Yarrington, 634 F.3d 440, 448 (11th Cir.2011). However, a witness's prior inconsistent statement may be admitted for its truth as well as for impeachment purposes in certain situations:

•   When the statement meets the requirements of Rule 801(d)(1)(A), which defines certain prior inconsistent statements as non-hearsay.

•   When the statement qualifies as a prior statement of identification, Rule 801(d)(1)(C).

•   When the statement qualifies as an opposing party's statement under Rule 801(d)(2).

•   When the statement qualifies under an exception to the hearsay rule. For example, the prior inconsistent statement may have been an excited utterance. Rule 803(2).

(3) **Kinds of statements.** A witness may be impeached with any kind of prior statement—oral or written, sworn or unsworn. See Jankins v. TDC Management Corp., Inc., 21 F.3d 436, 442 (D.C.Cir.1994). A witness may also sometimes be impeached with her prior silence. See Authors' Comment (4) infra. Statements by an accused that were taken in violation of *Miranda*, and thus rendered inadmissible as substantive evidence, may nevertheless be used to impeach the accused's testimony at trial. Harris v. New York, 401 U.S. 222, 91 S.Ct. 643 (1971). Similarly, an accused's statements to an informer that were taken

160

in violation of the accused's Sixth Amendment right to counsel may be used to impeach contradictory testimony given by the accused at trial. Kansas v. Ventris, 556 U.S. 586, 129 S.Ct. 1841 (2009). Evidence that an accused gave and then withdrew a notice of intent either to offer an alibi defense, to rely on an insanity defense or introduce expert testimony concerning her mental condition, or to claim a defense of public authority may not be used against the accused. See Fed. R. Crim. P., Rules 12.1(f), 12.2(e), 12.3(e).

(4) Prior statement must be inconsistent with testimony. Although the witness's prior statement must be inconsistent with her trial testimony, direct contradiction is not required. United States v. Stewart, 907 F.3d 677, 686–88 (2d Cir.2018); United States v. Richardson, 515 F.3d 74, 84 (1st Cir.2008). One frequently-invoked test is "could the jury reasonably find that a witness who believed the truth of the facts testified to would have been unlikely to make a prior statement of this tenor?" McCormick, Evidence § 34 (5th ed. 1999). See also United States v. Barile, 286 F.3d 749, 755 (4th Cir.2002) ("A prior statement is inconsistent if it, 'taken as a whole, either by what it says or by what it omits to say affords some indication that the fact was different from the testimony of the witness whom it sought to contradict.' ").

(a) *Direct inconsistency.* Testimony that varies from a witness's previous statement regarding a material fact certainly meets any standard of inconsistency.

(b) *Prior silence or less detailed prior statement.* A witness may sometimes be impeached by her prior silence or with prior statements that she made that were less detailed than her testimony. The circumstances surrounding the prior silence or statements must have been such that the witness would have been expected to speak out or to provide greater detail. United States v. Catalan-Roman, 585 F.3d 453, 466–68 (1st Cir.2009).

Example—Prior silence admissible. In United States v. Strother, 49 F.3d 869, 874–75 (2d Cir.1995), a witness testified that the defendant had specifically asked her to make payment on a particular check. However, in a memorandum she had prepared shortly after the incident, she failed to mention such a request. The court of appeals held that the trial court improperly refused to allow the defendant to impeach her with this inconsistency because it would have been "natural" for the witness to have mentioned defendant's request to make payment in her memorandum.

Example—Pre-arrest silence admissible. In Jenkins v. Anderson, 447 U.S. 231, 100 S.Ct. 2124 (1980), the murder defendant testified that he acted in self-defense. The prosecution was then permitted to impeach him with his failure to mention for two weeks following the killing that he acted in self-defense.

The Supreme Court has held that the Fifth Amendment ordinarily prohibits the use of a defendant's post-*Miranda* warning silence to impeach her testimony at trial, Doyle v. Ohio, 426 U.S. 610, 96 S.Ct. 2240 (1976). But see United States v. Rodriguez, 260 F.3d 416, 420–22 (5th Cir.2001) (prosecutor may introduce post-arrest silence to impeach defendant's testimony that he told exculpatory story at time of arrest). A defendant's post-arrest, but pre-*Miranda* warning silence may be used against her. Fletcher v. Weir, 455 U.S. 603, 102 S.Ct. 1309 (1982).

Example—Post-arrest, pre-Miranda warning silence admissible. In United States v. Musquiz, 45 F.3d 927, 930–31 (5th Cir.1995), the defendant testified on direct examination that he was not dealing drugs, but was merely trying to earn a reward for turning in drug traffickers. The prosecution was permitted to question him about his failure to offer such an explanation in the interval between his arrest and Miranda warning.

Statements made after a *Miranda* warning is given may also be used. Anderson v. Charles, 447 U.S. 404, 100 S.Ct. 2180 (1980).

(c) *Prior claim of lack of memory.* A witness may be impeached when she testifies concerning an event about which she previously claimed to have no memory. United States v. Shoupe, 548 F.2d 636, 638–39 (6th Cir.1977).

(d) *Current claim of lack of memory.* A witness's claim that she is now unable to recall an event about which she has previously made a statement is problematic. Experience, however, shows that in many instances such testimony is untruthful; the witness is claiming lack of memory to avoid having to repeat her story. When the trial judge concludes that the witness is feigning lack of memory, courts typically allow the witness to be impeached with the prior statement. E.g., United States v. Mayberry, 540 F.3d 506, 516 (6th Cir.2008) ("limited and vague recall of events, equivocation, and claims of memory loss" can constitute prior inconsistent statements); United States v. Cisneros-Gutierrez, 517 F.3d 751, 757–59 (5th Cir.2008). But in some instances, a witness's claim of lack of memory may be truthful. If so, her testimony is logically not inconsistent with the prior statement. Nevertheless, some courts deem a witness's asserted lack of memory sufficient to allow impeachment by prior statements even in the absence of a finding that the witness is feigning forgetfulness. United States v. McGirt, 71 F.4th 755, 759–60 (10th Cir.2023) ("the great weight of authority treats a prior assertion of a fact as inconsistent with a present assertion of a lack of memory for purposes of Federal Rule of Evidence 801(d)(1)(A)"). Courts also may find an inconsistency exists when a witness simply refuses to answer questions the witness had previously answered. United States v. Truman, 688 F.3d 129, 142 (2d Cir.2012).

(e) *Omission of details previously related.* Witnesses sometimes omit from their testimony material details that they have previously related and which they would be expected to include in their testimony. This may be the unfortunate product of a faulty memory or the corrupt product of a selective memory. If the former, impeachment is generally inappropriate. United States v. Grubbs, 776 F.2d 1281, 1287 (5th Cir.1985). If the latter, impeachment should be permitted. United States v. Gajo, 290 F.3d 922, 930–32 (7th Cir.2002) (citing cases).

(f) *Witness has not yet testified.* If a witness has not yet testified, there can be no inconsistency; impeachment via prior statements is impermissible. United States v. Colombo, 869 F.2d 149, 153 (2d Cir.1989).

(5) Foundation requirement—While questioning witness. Rule 613(a) jettisons the Rule in the Queen's Case, 129 Eng.Rep. 976 (1820), which required the cross-examiner to show the witness her written inconsistent statement before examining her about it. Rule 613(a) still provides, however, that the impeaching party must show the statement or disclose its contents to opposing counsel. See United States v. Lawson, 683 F.2d 688, 694 (2d Cir.1982) (disclosure is mandatory, not discretionary).

(6) Foundation requirement—Extrinsic evidence of prior inconsistent statement. Rule 613(b) substantially modifies the traditional foundation requirement for establishing a witness's prior inconsistent statement through extrinsic evidence. The impeaching party may now offer the extrinsic proof without first questioning the witness about the prior statement. United States v. Della Rose, 403 F.3d 891, 903 (7th Cir.2005). Rule 613(b) imposes only two requirements. At some point, (a) the witness must be afforded the opportunity to explain or deny the statement and (b) opposing counsel must be afforded the opportunity to question the witness about it. As long as the witness is available to be recalled, therefore, Rule 613(b) sanctions an offer of extrinsic evidence. United States v. Feliciano, 761 F.3d 1202, 1210 (11th Cir.2014) (Rule 613(b) does not specify time sequence for introduction of extrinsic evidence of prior inconsistent statement). But see United States v. John-Baptiste, 747 F.3d 186, 213 (3d Cir.2014) (stating that Rule 613 requires impeached witness be given opportunity to explain or deny prior inconsistent statement before extrinsic evidence of statement may be introduced). Even if the witness is unavailable, the court may, in the interests of justice, admit the extrinsic proof. See Wammock v. Celotex Corp., 793 F.2d 1518, 1523–23 (11th Cir.1986) (court may admit extrinsic evidence if inconsistent statement is discovered after witness has become unavailable).

Note, however, that some appellate courts, citing the trial court's power to control the presentation of evidence pursuant to Rule 611, have upheld the trial court's decision to exclude extrinsic evidence unless the witness is first given the opportunity to explain or deny the prior inconsistent statement. E.g., United States v. Schnapp, 322 F.3d 564, 570–72 (8th Cir.2003); United States v. Bonnett, 877 F.2d 1450, 1462 (10th Cir.1989).

Courts differ as to whether extrinsic proof of a prior inconsistent statement is admissible if the witness has admitted making the statement. Compare United States v. Lopez, 870 F.3d 573, 582 (7th Cir.2017) (admissible) with United States v. Hale, 685 F.3d 522, 539 (5th Cir.2012) (inadmissible).

(7) Extrinsic evidence—Collateral matters. If the inconsistency relates to a collateral matter, extrinsic evidence may not be offered to prove that the prior statement was made. United States v. Torres-Correa, 23 F.4th 129, 135–36 (1st Cir.2022).

Example. If the victim of an assault testifies that she was wearing a kelly green sweater on the day in question, the fact that she had previously stated that she was wearing a chartreuse sweater may not be proved through extrinsic evidence.

(8) Statements by party opponent. The provisions of Rule 613(b) do not apply when the prior inconsistent statement qualifies as a statement by party opponent under Rule 801(d)(2).

(9) Rehabilitation—Prior consistent statements. A witness who has been impeached with a prior inconsistent statement may rehabilitate herself by effectively explaining away the inconsistency or denying that the statement was made. E.g., United States v. Marshall, 75 F.3d 1097, 1113 (7th Cir.1996) (witness explained inconsistent statement was motivated by promise of a job). Rule 801(d)(1)(B) now provides that prior consistent statements that are used to rehabilitate a witness may also be used as substantive evidence. Before 2014, only prior consistent statements that were admitted "to rebut an express or implied charge" that the witness "recently fabricated" his testimony or "acted from a recent improper influence or motive in so testifying" were admissible both to rehabilitate and for their truth. See Tome v. United States, 513 U.S. 150, 115 S.Ct. 696 (1995). Rule 801(d)(1)(B) was amended in 2014, however, and now prior consistent statements that tend to rehabilitate a witness whose credibility is attacked on other grounds are also admissible as substantive evidence. See Authors' Comments 801(d)(4)–(6).

CROSS-REFERENCES

Common Objections (Chapter 3)

73.   Prior consistent statement not admissible to rehabilitate
74.   Prior inconsistent statement; extrinsic evidence inadmissible
75.   Prior inconsistent statement; must disclose contents of writing

Checklists and Foundations (Chapter 4)

3C.   Prior Inconsistent Statements

Treatises

5 Graham, Handbook of Federal Evidence §§ 613:1–613:6 (9th ed. 2020)

1 McCormick, Evidence §§ 34–38, 47 (8th ed. 2020)

28 Wright and Gold, Federal Practice and Procedure §§ 6201–6206 (2d ed. 2012)

Rule 614. Court's Calling or Examining a Witness

(a) Calling. The court may call a witness on its own or at a party's request. Each party is entitled to cross-examine the witness.

(b) Examining. The court may examine a witness regardless of who calls the witness.

(c) Objections. A party may object to the court's calling or examining a witness either at that time or at the next opportunity when the jury is not present.

AUTHORS' COMMENTS

(1) Scope and purpose of Rule 614. Rule 614 codifies what has traditionally been thought to be the judge's inherent power to call and interrogate witnesses. Although the decision to abandon the voucher rule, see Rule 607, reduces the necessity of having the court call a witness, occasions still arise in which courts choose to exercise this authority.

The appointment and calling of expert witnesses is governed by Rule 706.

(2) Calling witnesses. Rule 614(a) permits the court to call witnesses *sua sponte* or at the request of a party. One reason a party might make such a request is to avoid having the jury associate it with a witness whom the party expects to have an aura of untrustworthiness.

Example. In United States v. Leslie, 542 F.2d 285, 288–89 (5th Cir.1976), the trial court called three accomplices of the defendant, all of whom had informed the prosecution that their testimony would differ from the statements they had given the FBI.

All parties are entitled to cross-examine witnesses called by the court.

The decision to call or not call a witness rests firmly in the court's discretion. United States v. Cochran, 955 F.2d 1116, 1122 (7th Cir.1992). If the court calls a witness, it may instruct the jury that witnesses called by the court are not inherently more credible than other witnesses. See United States v. Karnes, 531 F.2d 214, 216–17 (4th Cir.1976).

(3) Interrogating witnesses. The trial judge may interrogate any witness. Rule 614(b). Most often, judicial questioning is aimed at clarifying a witness's testimony. See United States v. Slone, 833 F.2d 595, 597 (6th Cir.1987) (discussing situations requiring clarification); Harris v. Steelweld Equip. Co., Inc., 869 F.2d 396, 402–03 (8th Cir.1989) (attempt to clarify technical and confusing expert testimony). The judge, however, may also seek to elicit facts in an effort to ascertain the truth. United States v. Perez-Melis, 882 F.3d 161, 165 (5th Cir.2018); e.g., Moore v. United States, 598 F.2d 439, 442–43 (5th Cir.1979) (no abuse of discretion where judge asked witness 105 questions, compared to total of 107 asked by prosecutor and defense counsel). While the judge is thus not confined to the role of moderator or umpire, United States v. Ottaviano, 738 F.3d 586, 595–97 (3d Cir.2013), the judge must maintain the appearance of impartiality. The court may not signal to the jury its sympathy or antipathy toward a party either by the frequency or the content of its questions. United States v. Lefsih, 867 F.3d 459, 467–69 (4th Cir.2017); United States v. Barnhart, 599 F.3d 737, 742–45 (7th Cir.2010). See, e.g., United States v. Rivera-Rodriguez, 761 F.3d 105, 110–18 (1st Cir.2014) (court improperly engaged in extended inquiry into witnesses' truth-telling obligation under plea agreements); United States v. Melendez-Rivas, 566 F.3d 41, 48–51 (1st Cir.2009) (reversing conviction because trial court's inquiries elicited inadmissible and harmful hearsay and appeared to enhance prosecution's effort to impeach defense witness).

(4) Objections. To avoid placing counsel in the embarrassing position of having to object in the presence of the jury to judicial interrogation of a witness or the judge's decision to call a witness, Rule 614(c) provides an exception to the general requirement of contemporaneous objection. Counsel must still object at the first available opportunity when the jury is not present. E.g., United States v. Smith, 452 F.3d 323, 330 (4th Cir.2006) (post-trial motion not timely).

CROSS-REFERENCES

Treatises

5 Graham, Handbook of Federal Evidence §§ 614:1–614:3 (9th ed. 2020)

1 McCormick, Evidence § 8 (8th ed. 2020)

29 Wright and Gold, Federal Practice and Procedure §§ 6231–6236 (2d ed. 2016)

Rule 615. Excluding Witnesses from the Courtroom; Preventing an Excluded Witness's Access to Trial Testimony

(a) Excluding Witnesses. At a party's request, the court must order witnesses excluded from the courtroom so that they cannot hear other witnesses' testimony. Or the court may do so on its own. But this rule does not authorize excluding:

(1) a party who is a natural person;

(2) one officer or employee of a party that is not a natural person if that officer or employee has been designated as the party's representative by its attorney;

(3) any person whose presence a party shows to be essential to presenting the party's claim or defense; or

(4) a person authorized by statute to be present.

(b) Additional Orders to Prevent Disclosing and Accessing Testimony. An order under (a) operates only to exclude witnesses from the courtroom. But the court may also, by order:

(1) prohibit disclosure of trial testimony to witnesses who are excluded from the courtroom; and

(2) prohibit excluded witnesses from accessing trial testimony.

AUTHORS' COMMENTS

(1) Scope and purpose of Rule 615. Rule 615, often referred to as "The Rule," provides for the exclusion of witnesses from the courtroom so that they will be unable to hear the testimony of other witnesses. It thereby hinders witnesses from tailoring their testimony to fit or rebut that of other witnesses and assists counsel in detecting and exposing false testimony. Geders v. United States, 425 U.S. 80, 87, 96 S.Ct. 1330, 1335 (1976).

Except for witnesses exempted from the Rule, the court must exclude all witnesses from the courtroom at the request of a party. The court may also invoke the Rule on its own motion.

Rule 615 was amended in 2023 by adding a new Rule 615(b). It authorizes courts to make orders to prevent excluded witnesses from learning about, obtaining, or being provided with trial testimony. See Authors' Comments 615(4). In addition, an amendment to Rule 615(a)(2) clarifies that the exclusion for entity representatives, see Authors' Comment 615(2), is limited to one representative per entity.

(2) Who is exempted. Rule 615 lists four categories of witnesses who may not be excluded:

(a) A party who is a natural person. See Perry v. Leeke, 488 U.S. 272, 281, 109 S.Ct. 594, 600 (1989) (criminal defendant has constitutional right to remain in courtroom).

(b) One officer or employee of a party that is not a natural person and who is designated by counsel as the party's representative. E.g., Varlack v. SWC Caribbean, Inc., 550 F.2d 171, 175 (3d Cir.1977) (stressing need to clearly designate person as representative); see Opus 3 Ltd. v. Heritage Park, Inc., 91 F.3d 625, 630 (4th Cir.1996) (witness who is not officer or employee of party cannot be designated representative). This exemption embraces case agents United States v. Edwards, 34 F.4th 570, 585 (7th Cir.2022) (referring to "Rule 615(b) case agent exemption"), cert. denied, 143 S.Ct. 307 (2022). A court may, in its discretion, allow an entity party to change one representative for another as the trial progresses. Advisory Committee's Note to 2023 amendment.

The limitation on the number of entity-party representatives does not apply to the exemption for persons whose presence is essential to the presentation of a party's case. See Authors' Comment 615(2)(c).

(c) A person whose presence is essential to the presentation of a party's case. An expert whose opinion is to be based upon the testimony of other witnesses ordinarily qualifies under this exemption, e.g., United States v. Seschillie, 310 F.3d 1208, 1214 (9th Cir.2002). But cf. United States v. Olofson, 563 F.3d 652, 660 (7th Cir.2009) (noting that "Rule 703 is not an automatic exemption for expert witnesses from Rule 615 sequestration"). So too does one whose knowledge or advice is needed by counsel during the testimony of other witnesses.

Example—Nonexpert. In United States ex rel. Bahrani v. ConAgra, Inc., 624 F.3d 1275, 1295–97 (10th Cir.2010), the court properly exempted from the rule a former employee of the defendant. Because he was the person most knowledgeable about the "history and complex factual details of the matter at issue," he qualified as a person whose presence was essential to the presentation of the defendant's case.

Example—Expert. In Malek v. Federal Ins. Co., 994 F.2d 49, 53–54 (2d Cir.1993), the court of appeals held that the trial court erred in refusing to allow the plaintiff's expert to remain in the courtroom during the testimony of the defendant's expert. Because the defense expert's testimony differed from his reports in important respects, plaintiff's counsel needed the advice of his expert. A ten-minute recess granted by the court so that counsel could confer with the expert prior to cross-examination was an inadequate substitute for the expert's presence.

The party relying on this exemption has the burden of establishing that the witness's presence is essential. Opus 3 Ltd. v. Heritage Park, Inc., 91 F.3d 625, 628 (4th Cir.1996); United States v. Klaphake, 64 F.3d 435, 437 (8th Cir.1995).

If the government wishes to have more than one case agent-witness in the courtroom, it may designate one as its representative under Rule 615(b) and attempt to establish that the second is essential to the presentation of its case and therefore exempt under Rule 615(c). United States v. Phibbs, 999 F.2d 1053, 1072–73 (6th Cir.1993). Compare United States v. Green, 293 F.3d 886, 892 (5th Cir.2002) (exempting three agents, each from different agency, in complex case with lengthy and geographically broad investigation), with United States v. Hickman, 151 F.3d 446, 453–54 (5th Cir.1998) (absent finding that case was complex, trial court erred in exempting two case agents from rule as government's representatives); United States v. Jackson, 60 F.3d 128, 134–36 (2d Cir.1995) (court has discretion to exempt more than one witness under particular subdivision of rule, but should do so only rarely).

    (d)   Rule 615(d) serves as a reminder that Congress has enacted some statutory exemptions to the Rule. 18 U.S.C.A. § 3771 (as well as Federal Rule of Criminal Procedure 60) provides that a crime victim may not be excluded from a trial unless the court determines, by clear and convincing evidence, the victim's testimony would be materially altered if the victim heard other testimony. See, e.g., United States v. Maldonado-Passage, 4 F.4th 1097, 1102–03 (10th Cir.2021) (target of murder-for-hire scheme who suffered emotional and pecuniary harm but was not physically injured qualified as "victim"); In re Mikhel, 453 F.3d 1137, 1139 (9th Cir.2006) (court must find that it is "highly likely" that victim-witness will alter testimony). 18 U.S.C.A. § 3510(a) provides that, in a non-capital case, any victim of the crime for which the defendant is on trial may not be excluded from the trial on the ground that the victim might, during the sentencing hearing, make a statement or present information to the court relating to the sentence. 18 U.S.C.A. § 3510(b) creates an analogous exemption for capital cases. It provides that a victim may not be excluded from the trial because the victim might, during the sentencing hearing, testify as to the effect of the offense on the victim or the victim's family, or as to any other factor for which notice is required under 18 U.S.C.A. § 3593(a).

    (3)   **Rebuttal witnesses permitted.** The court may allow a witness who was present in the courtroom despite an invocation of the Rule to be called as a rebuttal witness. United States v. Hargrove, 929 F.2d 316, 320–21 (7th Cir.1991).

    (4)   **Prohibiting disclosure of and access to trial testimony.** Rule 615(b) was amended in 2023 to expressly authorize courts to enter orders that extend beyond excluding witnesses from the courtroom. It allows courts to prohibit (1) others from disclosing trial testimony to excluded witnesses and (2) witnesses from accessing trial testimony. This includes prohibiting witnesses from monitoring trials that are being streamed or have been posted online. Even before this amendment, many courts had concluded that their authority under Rule 615 extended to such matters. United States v. Ali, 991 F.3d 561, 568 (4th Cir.2021) ("District courts frequently employ their discretionary authority to strengthen their sequestration orders outside of the courtroom.").

    Courts may also allow counsel to cross-examine witnesses about whether they have colluded on their testimony. United States v. Ali, 991 F.3d 561, 569–70 (4th Cir.2021). An order prohibiting a criminal defendant not to consult with counsel overnight is unconstitutional, Geders v. United States, 425 U.S. 80, 96 S.Ct. 1330 (1976), but a ban on such communication during a brief recess is permissible. Perry v. Leeke, 488 U.S. 272, 280–81, 109 S.Ct. 594, 600 (1989).

    (5)   **When rule is applicable.** Courts often exercise their discretion to exclude potential witnesses during opening arguments and proffers of proof where testimony may be offered or summarized. Weinstein's Evidence ¶ 615[02]. Rule 615 also applies to suppression hearings. United States v. Brewer, 947 F.2d 404, 408–10 (9th Cir.1991). Federal Rule of Civil Procedure 30(c), however, expressly provides that Rule 615 is inapplicable to depositions. A protective order may be sought under Federal Rule of Civil Procedure 26(c)(5) to exclude other persons from a deposition.

    (6)   **Sanctions for non-compliance.** The appropriate sanction for a violation of a Rule 615 order lies in the court's discretion. Cruz v. Maverick County, 957 F.3d 563, 572 (5th Cir.2020). The court has the power to exclude the offending witness, strike his testimony, or declare a mistrial, but these should be reserved for the most egregious violations. See United States v. Cropp, 127 F.3d 354, 363 (4th Cir.1997) ("The remedy of exclusion is so severe that it is generally employed only when there has been a showing that a party or a party's counsel caused the violation."); United States v. Green, 305 F.3d 422, 428 (6th Cir.2002) (exclusion appropriate when there are "indications that the witness has remained in court with the 'consent, connivance, procurement or knowledge' of the party seeking his testimony"). Less draconian sanctions available include allowing opposing counsel to interrogate the witness about the nature and scope of the violation, instructing the jury to consider the nature of the violation in assessing the witness's credibility, and holding the witness in contempt. United States v. Smith, 441 F.3d 254, 263 (4th Cir.2006); United States v. McMahon, 104 F.3d 638 (4th Cir.1997).

ARTICLE VII

OPINIONS AND EXPERT TESTIMONY

Rule 701. Opinion Testimony by Lay Witnesses

If a witness is not testifying as an expert, testimony in the form of an opinion is limited to one that is:

(a)   rationally based on the witness's perception;

(b)   helpful to clearly understanding the witness's testimony or to determining a fact in issue; and

(c)   not based on scientific, technical, or other specialized knowledge within the scope of Rule 702.

AUTHORS' COMMENTS

(1)   Scope and purpose of Rule 701. The common law prohibition on lay opinion testimony was based partly on the assumption that facts and opinions are easily distinguishable and partly on the notion that jurors are as well equipped to draw inferences from the facts supplied by a lay witness as is the witness. Rule 701 abandons the common law's nominally rigid approach to lay testimony, opting for a more pragmatic rule. United States v. Stadtmauer, 620 F.3d 238, 262 (3d Cir.2010). It is designed to insure that the jury is presented with testimony in the form most likely to help it resolve the contested issues. While jurors will often benefit from hearing the witness relate concrete details, sometimes they will be aided by hearing a lay witness relate his conclusions. Therefore, Rule 701 allows a lay witness to testify in the form of an opinion or inference when the opinion or inference (1) is rationally based on the witness's perception and (2) would help the fact finder to understand clearly the testimony or determine a fact in issue. The last clause of Rule 701 precludes litigants from offering expert testimony under the guise of lay opinion testimony as a means of evading the discovery and reliability requirements associated with expert testimony. Great Lakes Ins. SE v. Wave Cruiser LLC, 36 F.4th 1346, 1357–58 (11th Cir.2022).

Because of pretrial disclosure requirements for expert witnesses, courts are increasingly called upon to decide whether testimony about what appears to be specialized matters constitutes lay or expert testimony. This arises with particular frequency with respect to law enforcement officials and case agents, witnesses knowledgeable about businesses, and medical personnel. Courts are most likely to conclude that law enforcement officials and case agents qualify as lay witnesses when they are testifying about matters reflecting personal knowledge gained in investigating the case at bar. E.g., United States v. Cristerna-Gonzalez, 962 F.3d 1253, 1259 (10th Cir.2020) ("Although a law-enforcement officer's testimony based on knowledge derived from the investigation of the case at hand is typically regarded as lay testimony, opinion testimony premised on the officer's professional experience as a whole is expert testimony."); United States v. Kilpatrick, 798 F.3d 365, 379–85 (6th Cir.2015) (agents based testimony on years-long involvement in investigation of case; United States v. Macedo-Flores, 788 F.3d 181, 191–92 (5th Cir.2015) (agents testified about meaning of code words based on their involvement in underlying investigation). But cf. United States v. Agramonte-Quezada, 30 F.4th 1, 20–21 (1st Cir.2022) (testimony about drug distribution practices by agent not involved in case at bar was lay testimony). Similarly, courts are most likely to find that witnesses testifying about specialized business matters qualify as lay witnesses when they testify about knowledge gained in the course of their regular involvement in the ordinary affairs of the business in question. E.g., United States v. Afriyie, 929 F.3d 63, 69–70 (2d Cir.2019) (director of private investment firm testified as lay witness about proposed transaction in which he was involved and whether certain information was nonpublic); United States v. Kerley, 784 F.3d 327, 337 (6th Cir.2015) (witness provided lay testimony if it was "derived from personal knowledge gained through participation in the business's day-to-day affairs). With regard to medical personnel, courts focus on whether the witness is testifying about treatment the witness personally gave. E.g., Williams v. Mast Biosurgery USA, Inc., 644 F.3d 1312, 1317 (11th Cir.2011) (treating physician testifies as lay witness when testimony concerns observations based on personal knowledge, but testifies as an expert when "testimony is based on a hypothesis").

Example—Lay and expert testimony. In In re: Taxotere (Docetaxel) Products Liability Litigation, 26 F.4th 256 (5th Cir.2022), defendant offered deposition testimony given by its designated corporate representative, an oncologist who was its former associate vice president of global pharmacovigilance and epidemiology. The testimony related to clinical trials of the drug in question. The court of appeals held that the trial court properly admitted parts of the testimony as lay witness testimony; the clinical trials were conducted while the witness stilled worked for defendant. But the appellate court held that the trial court erred in admitting testimony relating to a reanalysis of clinical trial data that he prepared during the litigation. This constituted expert testimony, and the trial court had admitted it without performing a *Daubert* gatekeeping analysis.

Example—Lay and expert testimony. In United States v. Wilson, 605 F.3d 985, 1025–26 (D.C. Cir.2010), the court affirmed the trial court's exclusion of the testimony of former drug dealers regarding their interpretation of taped phone calls the prosecution had introduced into evidence. Because the former drug dealers did not have personal knowledge of the drug conspiracy in issue, they could not testify as lay witnesses. Lacking firsthand knowledge of the drug conspiracy, "such witnesses may testify only when qualified as experts."

Example—Lay and expert testimony. In United States v. Jones, 739 F.3d 364, 368–70 (7th Cir.2014), the court held that a detective's testimony about the production and operation of dye packs (used by banks as "bait money") constituted expert testimony. But the detective's testimony that he had seen burn marks when a dye pack exploded near a person's skin and about his investigation into the bank robbery in issue constituted admissible lay testimony.

(2) Opinion must be rationally based on witness's perception. The requirement that a witness's opinion must be "rationally based on the witness's perception" comprises two elements. First, it echoes the personal knowledge requirement of Rule 602. United States v. Kaplan, 490 F.3d 110, 118–19 (2d Cir.2007) (lay opinion inadmissible in absence of evidence that it was based on first-hand knowledge); United States v. Garcia, 413 F.3d 201, 211 (2d Cir.2005). Second, it mandates that the opinion must be one that a reasonable person could draw from the underlying facts. United States v. Riddle, 103 F.3d 423, 428–29 (5th Cir.1997); Soden v. Freightliner Corp., 714 F.2d 498, 511 (5th Cir.1983). The requirement thus eliminates opinions based on hearsay, e.g., United States v. Freeman, 498 F.3d 893, 903 (9th Cir.2007); speculation, e.g., United States v. Howell, 17 F.4th 673, 682–85 (6th Cir.2021); and irrational reasoning, e.g., United States v. Cox, 633 F.2d 871 (9th Cir.1980). Implicit in this requirement is that courts may require a lay witness to disclose the basis for the witness's opinion so the court can determine whether the opinion is rationally based on the facts. United States v. Williams, 827 F.3d 1134, 1156–57 (D.C. Cir.2016).

(3) Helpfulness requirement. Lay opinion testimony is also restricted to those instances in which hearing the opinion would help the jury to understand the witness's testimony or determine a fact in issue. Among the factors that affect whether a lay witness's opinion meets this test are:

• The extent to which the testimony goes to the heart of the case. The more central the issue, the more the witness should be required to provide concrete details. Hester v. BIC Corp., 225 F.3d 178, 182 (2d Cir.2000); United States v. Allen, 10 F.3d 405, 414 (7th Cir.1993).

• The amount of factual matter subsumed in the opinion. Compare Government of Virgin Islands v. Knight, 989 F.2d 619, 629–30 (3d Cir.1993) (holding admissible an opinion that defendant fired gun accidentally) with United States v. Noel, 581 F.3d 490, 496–97 (7th Cir.2009) (holding inadmissible testimony that images on defendant's computer met federal definition of child pornography).

• The ability or inability of the witness to convey the information in the form of specific facts. E.g., United States v. Yazzie, 976 F.2d 1252, 1255–56 (9th Cir.1992).

- The extent to which the jury is equally well-positioned to draw the inferences from the underlying data. United States v. Diaz, 951 F.3d 148, 156–57 (3d Cir.2020) (excluding agent's testimony about defendant's role in drug conspiracy); United States v. Freeman, 730 F.3d 590, 595–99 (6th Cir.2013) (excluding agent's interpretation of phone calls and of ordinary English language terms).

- The need for the testimony. Wactor v. Spartan Transportation Corp., 27 F.3d 347, 350–51 (8th Cir.1994).

(4) Illustrative cases. Numerous cases exist in which federal courts have permitted lay witnesses to offer their opinions. Among the range of opinions admitted are:

- An opinion that a truck driver was "in total control" when his truck was struck. Robinson v. Bump, 894 F.2d 758, 762–63 (5th Cir.1990).

- An opinion that a developer never intended to carry out promises made to purchasers. Winant v. Bostic, 5 F.3d 767, 772–73 (4th Cir.1993).

- A landowner's opinion regarding value of her property after a pipeline was built across it. Sabal Train Transmission, LLC v. 3.921 Acres of Land in Lake County, Florida, 947 F.3d 1362, 1368–70 (11th Cir.2020).

- An opinion that the person shown in a videotape or bank surveillance photo was the defendant United States v. Ware, 69 F.4th 830, 849–51 (11th Cir.2023) (discussing cases). But see United States v. Earls, 704 F.3d 466, 472 (7th Cir.2012); United States v. Jadlowe, 628 F.3d 1, 23–24 (1st Cir.2010) (excluding such testimony).

- An opinion concerning another person's state of mind or knowledge. United States v. Goodman, 633 F.3d 963, 966–69 (10th Cir.2011) (testimony about defendant's declining mental health). But cf. United States v. Wantuch, 525 F.3d 505, 512–14 (7th Cir.2008) (although "lay opinion testimony regarding mental states is admissible under Rule 701," court holds inadmissible testimony that defendant knew his actions were illegal).

- An opinion that a business operation was a "scam," or that submitted reports were "fraudulent." United States v. Hoffecker, 530 F.3d 137, 170–71 (3d Cir.2008) (scam); United States v. Eaden, 37 F.4th 1307, 1312–13 (7th Cir.2022) (fraudulent).

- An opinion as to the meaning of "code words" used by fellow conspirators. United States v. Valbrun, 877 F.3d 440, 443–44 (1st Cir.2017). Compare United States v. Hill, 63 F.4th 335, 354–57 (5th Cir.2023) (affirming admissibility officer's lay opinion regarding meaning of code words) with United States v. Freeman, 730 F.3d 590, 592–99 (6th Cir.2013) (officer's extensive interpretations of intercepted conversations not admissible as lay opinion) (citing cases).

- An opinion that the vestibule in which plaintiff slipped was safe. Getter v. Wal-Mart Stores, Inc., 66 F.3d 1119, 1124 (10th Cir.1995).

(5) No expert testimony. Expert testimony is admissible only if meets the reliability requirements set forth in Rule 702. Moreover, both Federal Rule of Civil Procedure 26 and Federal Rule of Criminal Procedure 16 include special disclosure requirements for expert witnesses. By stipulating that lay witness testimony may not be based on scientific, technical or other specialized knowledge within the scope of Rule 702, Rule 701 ensures that litigants cannot circumvent expert testimony rules by presenting expert testimony in lay witness clothing. Advisory Committee's Note to 2000 amendment to Rule 701; United States v. Savage, 970 F.3d 217, 284 (3d Cir.2020). Note that the rules distinguish between lay and expert testimony, not lay and expert witnesses. United States v. White, 492 F.3d 380, 403 (6th Cir.2007). A witness may present both lay and expert testimony in the same case. United States v. Freeman, 498 F.3d 893, 903–04 (9th Cir.2007). Admissibility of the lay opinions will be governed by Rule 701; admissibility of the expert opinions, by Rule 702.

Example. In United States v. Perkins, 470 F.3d 150 (4th Cir.2006), police officers who saw defendant kick his victim were permitted to testify as lay witnesses about the reasonableness of the kicks. Other officers who had not witnessed the kicking should not have been permitted to testify as lay witnesses. They testified in response to hypothetical questions, and should have been qualified as experts before being permitted to testify.

Example. In United States v. Christian, 673 F.3d 702, 709–10 (7th Cir.2012), an FBI agent testified as a lay witness when he demonstrated for the jury the arm movements made by the defendant, but testified as an expert when he gave an opinion, based on his twenty years of experience, about the significance of those arm movements.

Although a single witness may offer both lay and expert testimony, courts have increasing warned of the dangers that dual-role witnesses present. E.g., United States v. Rodriguez, 971 F.3d 1005, 1019 (9th Cir.2020); United States v. Rios, 830 F.3d 403, 414–15 (6th Cir.2016). So when a witness offers both lay and expert testimony, the trial court may need to take appropriate steps to mitigate the danger of jury confusion. United States v. Haines, 803 F.3d 713, 730–33 (5th Cir.2015). These may include prohibiting the witness from switching back and forth between lay and expert testimony, United States v. Jett, 908 F.3d 252, 269–70 (7th Cir.2018), prefacing questions to indicate the capacity in which the witness is testifying, United States v. Holguin, 51 F.4th 841, 862–63 (9th Cir.2022), and giving a jury instruction. United States v. Hall, 20 F.4th 1085, 1103 (6th Cir.2022); United States v. Garcia, 752 F.3d 382, 292 (4th Cir.2014).

(6)   Grounds for objecting. An objection to a lay opinion may certainly be phrased in terms of the governing standard articulated in Rule 701 (e.g., not based on personal knowledge, not helpful). But an objection will often prove more effective if it is supported with an explanation as to why the opinion is not rational or not helpful.

(a)   If the witness seeks to offer an opinion on a subject that calls for expertise not possessed by the witness, the opinion is not one that would be either rational or helpful. See Asplundh Mfg. Div. v. Benton Harbor Engineering, 57 F.3d 1190 (3d Cir.1995) (lay witness did not have sufficient knowledge to give opinion regarding cause of accident and design of hydraulic cylinder). Lay witness testimony, however, is not restricted to matters within the common knowledge of ordinary jurors. United States v. Paiva, 892 F.2d 148, 157 (1st Cir.1989) (lay witness who had experience with cocaine permitted to testify that substance was cocaine).

(b)   Where the witness testifies as to a mixed question of law and fact, the witness's opinion will not be helpful unless the witness understands the underlying legal standard. See United States v. Scop, 846 F.2d 135, 139–42 (2d Cir.1988).

(c)   Opinions stated in conclusory terms and that amount to little more than "choosing up sides" by telling the jury that the defendant "breached his contract" or was "negligent" are not helpful because they do not inform the jury as to the underlying facts. Village of Freeport v. Barrella, 814 F.3d 594, 611 (2d Cir.2016) (condemning opinions that "merely tell the jury what result to reach"); United States v. Garcia, 413 F.3d 201, 214 (2d Cir.2005).

CROSS-REFERENCES

Common Objections (Chapter 3)

24.   Conclusion of law, lay witness

55.   Lay opinion testimony

56.   Lay witness testifying as expert

89.   Speculation, question calls for

Treatises

5 Graham, Handbook of Federal Evidence §§ 701:0–701:1 (9th ed. 2020)

1 McCormick, Evidence § 11 (8th ed. 2020)

29 Wright and Gold, Federal Practice and Procedure §§ 6251–6255 (2d ed. 2016)

Rule 702. Testimony by Expert Witnesses

A witness who is qualified as an expert by knowledge, skill, experience, training, or education may testify in the form of an opinion or otherwise if the proponent demonstrates to the court that it is more likely than not that:

(a)   the expert's scientific, technical, or other specialized knowledge will help the trier of fact to understand the evidence or to determine a fact in issue;

(b) the testimony is based on sufficient facts or data;

(c) the testimony is the product of reliable principles and methods; and

(d) the expert's opinion reflects a reliable application of the principles and methods to the facts of the case.

AUTHORS' COMMENTS

(1) Scope and purpose of Rule 702. Rule 702 governs the admissibility of expert testimony. Because the resolution of many cases requires an understanding of scientific, technical or other types of specialized principles or information, experts traditionally have been used to provide such information to jurors and to apply their expertise to the facts in the case. Before admitting expert testimony, the court must be satisfied that the following conditions are met: (1) the witness qualifies as an expert; (2) the subject matter of the testimony is an appropriate one for expert testimony; (3) the expert testimony will assist the fact finder in deciding the case; and (4) the expert's opinion is sufficiently reliable. Rule 702(b)–(d) articulates three criteria for courts to use in judging the reliability of an expert's opinion.

Rule 702 was amended in 2023 to clarify that the court must apply a preponderance of the evidence standard in making its admissibility determination. A trial court's decision to admit or exclude expert testimony will not be reversed unless the court abused its discretion. Wellogix, Inc. v. Accenture, LLP, 716 F.3d 867, 881 (5th Cir.2013).

(2) Qualifications of an expert. The burden of establishing a witness's qualifications lies with his proponent. This should be done before the witness begins to relate the substance of his testimony. Ordinarily, opposing counsel should be given the opportunity to conduct a voir dire examination to test the qualifications of a tendered expert. Freeman v. Package Machinery Co., 865 F.2d 1331, 1337 (1st Cir.1988).

(a) There are no definite guidelines for determining the knowledge, skill or experience required either in a particular case or of a particular witness. "The test is whether, under the totality of the circumstances, the witness can be said to be qualified as an expert in a particular field through any one or more of the five bases enumerated in Rule 702—knowledge, skill, experience, training, or education." Santos v. Posadas de Puerto Rico Associates, Inc., 452 F.3d 59, 64 (1st Cir.2006).

> **Example—Qualified by experience.** In Correa v. Cruisers, A Division of KCS Int'l, Inc., 298 F.3d 13, 25–26 (1st Cir.2002), the plaintiffs offered a witness to testify about the defectiveness of a marine engine's fuel management system. Although the witness's educational background might not have qualified him as an expert, his experience repairing various marine and fuel-injection engines for more than twenty years provided a sufficient basis for the court to find him qualified.

> **Example—Lack of qualifications.** In Pan American World Airways, Inc. v. Port Authority of N.Y. and N.J., 995 F.2d 5, 10 (2d Cir.1993), plaintiff claimed that defendant negligently maintained the runways at JFK Airport. The trial court refused to qualify plaintiff's proposed witness as an expert, finding that he had never completed local air traffic control training, had little experience in large airports, and was entirely unfamiliar with ground procedures at JFK.

(b) Licensure or certification in the particular discipline is not a per se requirement. Pagés-Ramírez v. Ramírez-González, 605 F.3d 109, 114 (1st Cir.2010).

> **Example.** In United States v. Members of Estate of Boothby, 16 F.3d 19, 22–23 (1st Cir.1994), the trial court properly allowed a Corps of Engineers official to testify that a houseboat constituted a permanently moored structure. Even though the witness was not a nautical architect, she was sufficiently familiar with both the Corps' regulations and the vessel at issue to qualify as an expert.

(c) A witness's qualifications as an expert must be measured with respect to the opinions the witness seeks to give. Lebron v. Secretary of Florida Dept. of Children and Families, 772 F.3d 1352, 1368 (11th Cir.2014) ("Expertise in one field does not qualify a witness to testify about others.").

> **Example.** In Hall v. Flannery, 840 F.3d 922, 927–30 (7th Cir.2016), the court held that a pediatric neurosurgeon was qualified to state his opinion that a child's death was not attributable

to a seizure following a cranioplasty, but not that the death was caused by focal interstitial chronic inflammation of the heart.

Example. In Jones v. Lincoln Electric Co., 188 F.3d 709, 723–24 (7th Cir.1999), the trial court properly allowed a witness with expertise in material science and metallurgy to testify about the chemical composition of welding fumes and how they are generated. But the court of appeals held that the lower court abused its discretion when it allowed the witness to testify about the medical effects of the welding fumes.

(3) Subject matter of expert testimony—Generally. Rule 702 provides that expert testimony is admissible if it concerns "scientific, technical, or other specialized knowledge" that "will help the trier of fact to understand the evidence or to determine a fact in issue." This embraces a wide variety of subjects. Examples include:

- Testimony concerning the rules and regulations relating to IOLTA accounts. United States v. Cohen, 887 F.3d 77, 85 (1st Cir.2018).

- Testimony as to whether the release of fumes was caused by a fire or chemical reaction. Maffei v. Northern Insurance Co. of New York, 12 F.3d 892, 897–98 (9th Cir.1993).

- Testimony about drug dealing and drug use. United States v. Cushing, 10 F.4th 1055, 1079–80 (10th Cir.2021) (methamphetamine slang, culture, and dealing protocol); United States v. Haines, 803 F.3d 713, 727 (5th Cir.2015) (drug code, jargon; citing cases); United States v. York, 572 F.3d 415, 423 (7th Cir.2009). But see United States v. Hawkins, 934 F.3d 1251, 1264–67 (11th Cir.2019) (expert went beyond interpreting coded language and impermissibly testified to meaning of uncoded, ordinary language); United States v. Medina-Copete, 757 F.3d 1092, 1100–05 (10th Cir.2014) (trial court abused discretion in admitting expert testimony about narco-saints).

- Testimony providing background information about radical Islam and jihad. United States v. Benkahla, 530 F.3d 300, 308–09 (4th Cir.2008).

- Testimony explaining the meaning of coded or slang expressions. United States v. Delva, 922 F.3d 1228, 1251 (11th Cir.2019) (citing cases); United States v. Amuso, 21 F.3d 1251, 1263–64 (2d Cir.1994) (terminology of organized crime families). But see United States v. Cruz, 363 F.3d 187, 193–97 (2d Cir.2004) (expert not permitted to testify about meaning of "to watch someone's back").

- Testimony about police practices in a case alleging excessive use of force. Knight Through Kerr v. Miami-Dade County, 856 F.3d 795, 807–11 (11th Cir.2017).

- Testimony about the reliability of eyewitness identifications. See, e.g., United States v. Brownlee, 454 F.3d 131, 140–44 (3d Cir.2006) (court improperly excluded testimony concerning relationship between eyewitness's confidence and accuracy of identification); United States v. Smithers, 212 F.3d 306 (6th Cir.2000) (admissible in certain circumstances). But see United States v. Hall, 165 F.3d 1095, 1103–08 (7th Cir.1999) (affirming exclusion of such testimony and citing cases).

- Testimony about how coercive interrogation techniques can lead to false confessions. Tekoh v. County of Los Angeles, 75 F.4th 1264, 1265–66 (9th Cir.2023).

(4) Subject matter of expert testimony—Beyond common understanding. Rule 702 abandons the common-law requirement that the subject matter of the testimony be one that is beyond the common understanding of the lay juror. United States v. Lamarre, 248 F.3d 642, 648 (7th Cir.2001) ("Trial courts are not compelled to exclude all expert testimony merely because it overlaps with matters within the jury's experience."); United States v. Brawner, 173 F.3d 966, 969 (6th Cir.1999) ("well settled that 'necessity' is not a condition precedent for the admissibility of opinion testimony" under Rule 702); Kopf v. Skyrm, 993 F.2d 374, 377 (4th Cir.1993) (subject matter of expert testimony "need not be arcane or even especially difficult to comprehend"). Nevertheless, courts often conclude that expert testimony on such matters fails to meet the helpfulness requirement of Rule 702. United States v. Kime, 99 F.3d 870, 884 (8th Cir.1996) (expert testimony concerning reliability of eyewitness testimony not helpful); United States v. Montas, 41 F.3d 775, 781–84 (1st Cir.1994) (expert testimony that drug smugglers check bags and travel under pseudonyms not helpful).

(5) Reliability of expert testimony—Generally. Rule 702(b)–(d) codifies the principles articulated in a series of cases beginning with Daubert v. Merrell Dow Pharmaceuticals, Inc., 509 U.S. 579, 113 S.Ct. 2786 (1993). As discussed in more detail in the following paragraphs, these cases hold that trial judges should admit expert testimony only if they first determine that the proffered opinions are reliable. This reliability determination has three components: (1) the expert must base the opinion upon sufficient facts or data; (2) the expert must ground the opinion in reliable principles and methods; and (3) the expert's opinion must reflect a reliable application of the principles and methods to the facts of the case. Although this standard applies to all experts, its application may vary depending upon whether the subject matter of the testimony is rooted in science or some technical or other specialized area of knowledge.

(6) Admissibility of scientific expert testimony—Daubert factors. For many years, federal courts held that the admissibility of novel scientific evidence was governed by the *Frye* test, which required the proponent of such evidence to demonstrate that the scientific theory or technique was generally accepted in the relevant scientific community. Frye v. United States, 293 Fed. 1013 (D.C.Cir.1923). In 1993, the now-famous *Daubert* case held that the *Frye* test was no longer viable. Daubert v. Merrell Dow Pharmaceuticals, Inc., 509 U.S. 579, 113 S.Ct. 2786 (1993). The Supreme Court noted that neither the text nor the history of Federal Rule 702 evinces an intent to retain *Frye*. Moreover, the general acceptance test is at odds with the Rules' "general approach of relaxing the traditional barriers to 'opinion' testimony." Id. at 587, 113 S.Ct. at 2794. But while the Court cast aside the *Frye* test, it insisted that trial judges have the responsibility to act as gatekeepers and to admit a scientific opinion only if it is shown to be reliable. The Court's opinion included a list of factors for trial judges to consider in determining reliability under Rule 702:

- Whether the theory or technique in question has been or can be tested.

- Whether the theory or technique has been subjected to peer review and publication.

- The known or potential rate of error of the particular theory or technique, and whether means exist for controlling its operation.

- The extent to which the theory or technique has been accepted.

The *Daubert* list of factors was non-exclusive, and courts have added other factors to the list, including:

- Whether the expert testimony is based on research the expert has conducted independent of the litigation. Daubert v. Merrell Dow Pharmaceuticals, Inc., 43 F.3d 1311, 1317 (9th Cir.1995).

Example. In Mike's Train House, Inc. v. Lionel, L.L.C., 472 F.3d 398, 408 (6th Cir.2006), the court of appeals held that the trial court abused its discretion in allowing an expert to testify, noting that the expert had created the precise methodology at issue for the purpose of the litigation.

- The existence and maintenance of standards controlling the technique's operation. Anderson v. Raymond Corp., 61 F.4th 505, 509 (7th Cir.2023).

- Whether the expert has adequately accounted for obvious alternative explanations. Michaels v. Avitech, Inc., 202 F.3d 746, 753 (5th Cir.2000).

- Whether the expert has employed in the courtroom "the same level of intellectual rigor that characterizes the practice of an expert in the relevant field." Kumho Tire Co., Ltd. v. Carmichael, 526 U.S. 137, 152, 119 S.Ct. 1167, 1176 (1999); Milward v. Acuity Specialty Products Group, Inc., 639 F.3d 11, 26 (1st Cir.2011).

- Whether there is "too great an analytical gap" between the data and the opinion. General Electric Co. v. Joiner, 522 U.S. 136, 144, 118 S.Ct. 512, 519 (1997).

- The experience of the expert. United States v. Mallory, 902 F.3d 584, 593–94 (6th Cir.2018); F & H Coatings, LLC v. Acosta, 900 F.3d 1214, 1222–24 (10th Cir.2018).

All these factors can be helpful means of assessing whether the three components of reliability now set forth in Rule 702 have been met. See also Advisory Committee Note to 2000 amendments to Rule 702.

Once a court determines that the evidence is reliable, it must then satisfy itself that the evidence will assist the jury. In *Daubert*, the Court equated this inquiry with the question of relevance; that is, the evidence will assist the jury if it is "sufficiently tied to the facts of the case." 509 U.S. at 591, 113 S.Ct. at 2796.

Finally, even if the court determines that the demands of Rule 702 have been satisfied, Rule 403 may still provide grounds for exclusion. The court must therefore keep in mind that expert testimony possesses great potential for misleading the jury.

(7) Scientific evidence—Illustrations. Among the types of scientific evidence accepted or rejected are:

- DNA evidence—accepted. United States v. Gissantaner, 990 F.3d 457 (6th Cir.2021) (DNA sorting); United States v. Beverly, 369 F.3d 516, 530–31 (6th Cir.2004) (mitochondrial DNA); United States v. Beasley, 102 F.3d 1440, 1445–48 (8th Cir.1996) (polymerase chain reaction method); United States v. Davis, 40 F.3d 1069, 1073–75 (10th Cir.1994); United States v. Chischilly, 30 F.3d 1144, 1151–58 (9th Cir.1994).

- Airplane identification with forward-looking infrared device—accepted. United States v. Sanchez, 829 F.2d 757, 759 (9th Cir.1987).

- Testimony that radiation-induced cataracts can be identified through mere observation—rejected. O'Conner v. Commonwealth Edison Co., 13 F.3d 1090, 1106–07 (7th Cir.1994).

- Shoeprint evidence—accepted. United States v. Smith, 697 F.3d 625, 634–35 (7th Cir.2012) (citing cases).

- Determination of causation through differential diagnosis. Messick v. Novartis Pharmaceuticals Corp., 747 F.3d 1193, 1197–99 (9th Cir.2014) (citing cases). See Hendrix ex rel. G.P. v. Evenflo Co., 609 F.3d 1183, 1194–97 (11th Cir.2010) (discussing how differential diagnosis should be performed).

- Testimony about the accuracy of eyewitness identifications. United States v. Langan, 263 F.3d 613, 620–24 (6th Cir.2001) (surveying cases and upholding exclusion).

- Polygraph evidence—limited acceptance. United States v. Piccinonna, 885 F.2d 1529 (11th Cir.1989) (admissible upon stipulation or for impeachment or corroboration). United States v. Henderson, 409 F.3d 1293, 1301–03 (11th Cir.2005) (affirming finding that polygraph was unreliable); United States v. Cordoba, 194 F.3d 1053 (9th Cir.1999) (affirming district court's finding that polygraph was unreliable); United States v. Thomas, 167 F.3d 299, 308–09 (6th Cir.1999) (affirming exclusion of polygraph, but declining to decide whether *Daubert* effects general rule of admissibility); United States v. Posado, 57 F.3d 428 (5th Cir.1995) (rejecting per se rule of inadmissibility). But see United States v. Prince-Oyibo, 320 F.3d 494, 497–501 (4th Cir.2003) (affirming per se rule of inadmissibility).

- Fingerprint matches. United States v. Ware, 69 F.4th 830, 846–48 (11th Cir.2023) ("long accepted"; citing cases).

- Handwriting analysis. E.g., United States v. Foust, 989 F.3d 842, 844–48 (10th Cir.2021); United States v. Prime, 431 F.3d 1147, 1151–54 (9th Cir.2005) (citing cases); Deputy v. Lehman Bros., Inc., 345 F.3d 494, 509 (7th Cir.2003) (citing cases).

- Firearm tool-mark identification. United States v. Hunt, 63 F.4th 1229 (10th Cir.2023) (extensive discussion upholding admissibility).

- Testimony about location based on cell-phone and cell-tower records. United States v. Hill, 818 F.3d 289, 295–99 (7th Cir.2016) (cautioning that testimony must indicate level of precision that can be achieved).

(8) Applicability of Daubert to non-scientific evidence. The trial judge's gatekeeping function applies to expert testimony based on technical and other specialized knowledge as well as scientific testimony. Kumho Tire Co. Ltd. v. Carmichael, 526 U.S. 137, 119 S.Ct. 1167 (1999). Where the testimony's "factual basis, data, principles, methods, or their application are called sufficiently into question . . . the trial judge must determine whether the testimony has 'a reliable basis in the knowledge and experience of [the relevant] discipline.'" 526 U.S. at 149, 119 S.Ct. at 1174 (quoting *Daubert,* 509 U.S. at 592). In evaluating the reliability of nonscientific expert testimony, a court may have to consider factors other than those listed in *Daubert.* 526 U.S. at 150, 119 S.Ct. at 1175. Whether one or more of the *Daubert* factors will be pertinent depends on the nature of the issue, the area of the expertise, and the subject of the testimony. The ultimate objective of the gatekeeping function is the same for all expert testimony: "It is to make certain that an expert, whether basing testimony upon professional studies or personal experience, employs in the courtroom the same level of intellectual rigor that characterizes the practice of an expert in the relevant field." 526 U.S. at 152, 119 S.Ct. at 1176.

Kumho emphasizes that a finding that an expert employed a methodology that is generally accepted in the particular field may not be sufficient to justify admission of the expert's conclusion. The court must further inquire into the reasonableness of using that methodology to reach the particular conclusion in the case. 526 U.S. at 152–53, 119 S.Ct. at 1176–77. See Blue Dane Simmental Corp. v. American Simmental Ass'n, 178 F.3d 1035, 1039–41 (8th Cir.1999) (excluding testimony by economist who used method of analysis typically used within field, but not to reach type of conclusions to which expert sought to testify). On the other hand, in nonscientific fields that are based on specialized knowledge, the expert's experience and training may be the primary factor that the court uses to determine reliability. United States v. Holguin, 51 F.4th 841, 856, 858 (9th Cir.2022); United States v. Martinez-Armestica, 846 F.3d 436, 444–45 (1st Cir.2017). But the court must still make a reliability determination. United States v. Valencia-Lopez, 971 F.3d 891, 899 (9th Cir.2020) (although witness was qualified, court still had "unwavering gatekeeping obligation to determine reliability").

(9) Grounds for finding lack of reliability or helpfulness. There are numerous reasons why an expert's opinion might not be sufficiently reliable or helpful to qualify for admission under Rule 702. The same reasons may contribute to a court's decision to exclude an opinion under Rule 403 because its probative value is substantially outweighed by the danger of unfair prejudice, confusion of issues, etc. The following are among the grounds for excluding such evidence.

(a) *Lack of relevance.* Expert testimony should be excluded if it is not relevant to an issue in the case. In Daubert v. Merrell Dow Pharmaceuticals, Inc., 509 U.S. 579, 591, 113 S.Ct. 2786, 2796 (1993), the Supreme Court stressed that the expert testimony must have a valid connection to the issues presented.

Example—Inadmissible. In McMahon v. Robert Bosch Tool Corp., 5 F.4th 900, 903–04 (8th Cir.2021), the plaintiff claimed that a saw was defectively designed because its removable handle involuntarily detached from the saw's base even though the plaintiff neither slid a lock pin nor depressed the release button. The trial court properly excluded plaintiff's expert witness's defective-design opinion as irrelevant because the expert assumed that the plaintiff had pressed the release button.

Example—Inadmissible. In United States v. Williams, 934 F.3d 1122, 1130–32 (10th Cir.2019), defendant was convicted of lying to the VA about having served in combat overseas. He did this so he could receive VA benefits for combat-related PTSD. The trial court properly excluded as irrelevant defendant's proffered expert testimony that he suffered from PTSD. Whether he actually suffered from PTSD was immaterial; what mattered was that he lied about serving in overseas combat.

Example—Inadmissible. In Superior Production Partnership v. Gordon Auto Body Parts Co., 784 F.3d 311, 324–35 (6th Cir.2015), the trial court properly excluded expert testimony about putative losses from predatory behavior because the expert's analysis was premised on measures that the law rejected.

(b) *Expert testimony not needed.* The court may exclude expert testimony where the witness is no more capable than the jury of drawing a conclusion or where the testimony would intrude upon the judge's role. See generally Jimenez v. City of Chicago, 732 F.3d 710, 721 (7th Cir.2013) ("It is the role of the judge, not an expert witness, to instruct the jury on the applicable principles of law . . . ."); Burkhart v. Washington Metro. Area Transit Auth., 112 F.3d 1207, 1213 (D.C.Cir.1997) ("Each courtroom comes equipped with a 'legal expert,' called a judge, and it is his or her province alone to instruct the jury on the relevant legal standards."). Common examples of expert testimony that has been held inadmissible include:

- Testimony concerning domestic law. United States v. Fallon, 61 F.4th 95, 108–10 (3d Cir.2023) (disallowing testimony of law professor on contract law); Nieves-Villanueva v. Soto-Rivera, 133 F.3d 92, 99–101 (1st Cir.1997) (citing cases). But see United States v. Offill, 666 F.3d 168, 175 (4th Cir.2011) (allowing testimony about securities registration requirements and exemptions).

- Testimony that the weight a plaintiff had to lift to perform his job was unreasonable. Persinger v. Norfolk & Western Ry. Co., 920 F.2d 1185, 1188 (4th Cir.1990).

- Testimony about the hazards of off-loading a vessel in heavy seas. Peters v. Five Star Marine Service, 898 F.2d 448, 449–50 (5th Cir.1990).

- Testimony that another witness is lying or telling the truth. United States v. Hill, 749 F.3d 1250, 1255–63 (10th Cir.2014) (citing cases).

- An opinion about what was happening on a video that the jury could view for itself. Prosper v. Martin, 989 F.3d 1242, 1248–49 (11th Cir.2021).

(c) *Based on unreliable, speculative, or incomplete data.* An expert's opinion may be excluded if based on unreliable, speculative, or incomplete data.

Example—Inadmissible. In Stephens v. Union Pacific R. Co., 935 F.3d 852 (9th Cir.2019), the plaintiff claimed his mesothelioma was caused by secondary exposure to asbestos resulting from his father's carrying home asbestos to which he had been exposed at work. The trial court properly excluded plaintiff's causation experts from testifying because the record barely contained any evidence to support their assumptions that plaintiff's father had been exposed to asbestos and provided no basis for assuming that plaintiff had been secondarily exposed to it.

Example—Inadmissible. In Conroy v. Vilsack, 707 F.3d 1163, 1170 (10th Cir.2013), a gender and age discrimination case, the trial court properly excluded the testimony of plaintiff's expert, who based his opinion on mistaken beliefs about a number of relevant facts. "The proponent of expert testimony is required to show, among other things, that the expert's opinion is '*based on facts* which satisfy Rule 702's reliability requirements.' " (quoting Dodge v. Cotter Corp., 328 F.3d 1212, 1222 (10th Cir.2003)).

Example—Inadmissible. In UGI Sunbury LLC v. A Permanent Easement for 1.7575 Acres, 949 F.3d 825, 833–35 (3d Cir.2020), the trial court abused its discretion in allowing condemnees' expert to testify regarding the diminution in property value that would result from running an underground pipeline across condemnees' property. The expert presented no quantifiable data to explain or clarify his opinion about what he called "stigma damage."

(d) *Based on questionable theories.* If the theories underlying the expert's opinion are themselves questionable, the opinion may not be helpful to the jury.

Example—Inadmissible. In United States v. Montgomery, 635 F.3d 1074, 1088–92 (8th Cir.2011), the district court properly excluded expert testimony that the results of a positron emission tomography (PET) scan was consistent with a diagnosis of pseudocyesis. The expert's opinion that increased hypothalamic activity revealed by the PET scan is related to pseudocyesis was simply a working hypothesis and lacked scientific support.

(e) *Too conjectural.* Experts do not have to be absolutely certain in their conclusions, and courts have rejected a rigid "reasonable medical certainty" threshold test. Stutzman v. CRST, Inc., 997 F.2d 291, 294–95 (7th Cir.1993). Nevertheless, factfinders will not be helped by hearing an opinion that is unduly tentative or hedged.

Example—Inadmissible. In Tamraz v. Lincoln Electric Co., 620 F.3d 665, 669–672 (6th Cir.2010), the speculative nature of an expert's opinion that plaintiff's Parkinson's Disease was caused by his exposure to manganese rendered the opinion inadmissible. The expert's reasoning included speculation that a link exists between manganese and Parkinson's, that plaintiff was genetically predisposed to Parkinson's, and that, even assuming manganese could cause Parkinson's, that it caused plaintiff's Parkinson's.

(f) *Conclusory.* Testimony that is phrased largely in conclusory terms may prove far less helpful than testimony that provides the jury with information which it is capable of using to draw its own conclusions. Thus, a witness's direct opinion about a party's guilt or innocence is ordinarily inadmissible. United States v. Lockett, 919 F.2d 585, 590 (9th Cir.1990). Testimony that strongly suggests an expert's opinion about guilt or innocence, but which is less directly expressed is, however, more likely to be admitted.

Example—Admissible. In United States v. Boney, 977 F.2d 624, 628–31 (D.C.Cir.1992), the court upheld the trial judge's decision to admit the testimony of a police officer in which he responded to a thinly disguised hypothetical question in a way that left little doubt that he was expressing his opinion that the defendants were playing certain roles in a cocaine sale.

(g) *Too great a gap between data and opinion.* Even if the underlying data are solid and the principles or theories relied upon by the expert are proven, the expert's opinion may be excluded if "there is simply too great an analytical gap between the data and the opinion proffered." General Electric Co. v. Joiner, 522 U.S. 136, 118 S.Ct. 512, 519 (1997). The *Joiner* decision thus recognizes that an expert's conclusions and methodology are not always entirely distinct from one another. Id.

Example—Inadmissible. In General Electric Co. v. Joiner, 522 U.S. 136, 118 S.Ct. 512, 519 (1997), the Court held that the animal and epidemiological studies upon which the plaintiff's experts relied were insufficient, either individually or in combination, to support the experts' conclusion that the plaintiff's exposure to PCB's contributed to his cancer.

(h) *Opinion beyond bounds of reliable application of methodology.* Rule 702(d) was amended in 2023 to highlight that an expert's opinions may not exceed the bounds that a reliable application of the expert's basis and methodology would allow. The Advisory Committee warned especially of the danger of forensic experts overstating their conclusions. "Forensic experts should avoid assertions of absolute or one hundred percent certainty—or to a reasonable degree of scientific certainty—if the methodology is subjective and thus potentially subject to error." Advisory Committee's Note to 2023 amendment. Where possible, courts should require experts to provide estimates of known or potential error rates of their methodology. Id. Cf. United States v. Reynolds, 86 F.4th 332, 348–50 (6th Cir.2023) (discussing different types of error rates).

(10) Procedures for determining reliability. Pre-trial hearings, rulings based on the paper record, trial hearings outside the jury's presence, and rulings on post-trial motions are routinely employed by trial courts to determine the reliability of proffered expert testimony. The choice of the particular procedure lies within the trial court's discretion. United States v. Phillipos, 849 F.3d 464, 471 (1st Cir.2017) ("we have made clear that '[t]here is no particular procedure that the trial court is required to follow in executing its gatekeeping function' ") (quoting Smith v. Jenkins, 732 F.3d 51, 64 (1st Cir.2013)); United States v. Esformes, 60 F.4th 621, 635–36 (11th Cir.2023). Whatever procedure is used, trial courts must determine the reliability of the proffered testimony, United States v. Ruvalcaba-Garcia, 923 F.3d 1183, 1189 (9th Cir.2019), and appellate courts occasionally chastise trial courts for failing to ensure the creation of a developed record and to make specific findings on the record. E.g., United States v. Holguin, 51 F.4th 841, 851, 853 (9th Cir.2022); Sardis v. Overhead Door Corp., 10 F.4th 268, 282–84 (10th Cir.2021); Certain Underwriters at Lloyd's, London v. Axon Pressure Products Inc., 951 F.3d 251, 269–70 (5th Cir.2020).

(11) Mixed question of law and fact. Except for opinions as to an accused's mental state or condition, an expert's opinion on a mixed question of law and fact is not rendered inadmissible merely because it goes to an ultimate issue. Rule 704. But such testimony may be inadmissible under Rule 702 if the expert lacks a proper understanding of the underlying legal standard or if the expert has reached beyond his area of expertise to draw his conclusion.

Example—Admissible. In Fiataruolo v. United States, 8 F.3d 930, 941–42 (2d Cir.1993), taxpayers sought to establish that they were not "responsible persons" for a construction contractor's unpaid withholding taxes. In the course of testifying about the payroll procedures used by the family-run construction firm and its violation of established accounting procedures, the taxpayer's expert expressed his opinion that the taxpayer was not a "responsible person" within the meaning of the Internal Revenue Code. Terming this a close question, the court of appeals held that the trial court did not abuse its discretion in allowing the testimony. The witness did not merely provide a conclusory opinion and the trial court instructed the jury that the expert's views were not binding.

Example—Inadequately explored legal criteria. In Andrews v. Metro North Commuter R. Co., 882 F.2d 705, 708–09 (2d Cir.1989), the court of appeals held that the trial judge abused his discretion in allowing an expert to testify that the defendant railroad was negligent in its operation of a train. The expert did not state the legal criteria upon which he based his opinion and thus there was no way to determine whether he applied the correct legal standard in arriving at his conclusion of "negligence."

Example—Beyond expertise. In Berry v. City of Detroit, 25 F.3d 1342, 1349–53 (6th Cir.1994), the court of appeals held the trial court improperly allowed plaintiff's expert to testify that the Police Department's failure properly to discipline officers led to the shooting of plaintiff's son. Although the expert had, among other things, served as a sheriff and conducted seminars in police management techniques, he lacked the expertise to testify about the effects of lax disciplinary efforts on an entire police force.

CROSS-REFERENCES

Common Objections (Chapter 3)

23.   Conclusion of law, expert witness
32.   Expert lacks sufficient basis for opinion
33.   Expert may not relate hearsay basis for opinion
34.   Expert not qualified
36.   Expert opinion is speculative, conjectural
37.   Expert opinion not helpful
56.   Lay witness testifying as expert
86.   Scientific evidence not admissible
89.   Speculation, question calls for
92.   Truthfulness of another's testimony

Checklists and Foundations (Chapter 4)

5A.   Qualifying an Expert
5B.   Expert Testimony—Reliability Factors

Treatises

5 Graham, Handbook of Federal Evidence §§ 702:1–702:6 (9th ed. 2020)
1 McCormick, Evidence §§ 12–18, 202–211 (8th ed. 2020)
29 Wright and Gold, Federal Practice and Procedure §§ 6261–6270 (2d ed. 2016)

Rule 703. Bases of an Expert's Opinion Testimony

An expert may base an opinion on facts or data in the case that the expert has been made aware of or personally observed. If experts in the particular field would reasonably rely on those kinds of facts or data in forming an opinion on the subject, they need not be admissible for the opinion to be admitted. But if the facts or data would otherwise be inadmissible, the proponent of the opinion may disclose them to the jury only if their probative value in helping the jury evaluate the opinion substantially outweighs their prejudicial effect.

AUTHORS' COMMENTS

     (1)   **Scope and purpose of Rule 703.** An expert's opinion may be based on facts or data (1) that the expert has personally observed; (2) of which the expert is made aware of at trial; and (3) of which the expert is made aware of outside of court, but did not personally observe. Even if the facts or data underlying an expert's opinion would not themselves be admissible at trial, the expert's opinion may be admitted so long as other experts in the field would reasonably rely on the same kinds of facts or data in forming such an opinion.

     But even if the expert's opinion is ruled admissible, Rule 703 makes clear that the facts or data underlying that opinion are not automatically admissible. If the underlying facts or data would otherwise be inadmissible, the proponent of the expert's opinion may disclose them to the jury only if the court determines that their probative value in helping the jury evaluate the expert's opinion substantially outweighs their prejudicial effect.

     (2)   **Focus is on litigated facts.** Rule 703 focuses on the types of facts particular to the litigation that serve as the basis for an expert's opinion. The manner in which the expert has acquired his expertise—through formal education, lectures, experience, reading, etc.—falls within the bounds of Rule 702.

178

(3) Opinion based on personal knowledge. An expert may base an opinion on his own personal knowledge of the litigated facts. The treating physician is commonly cited as the paradigm. See Advisory Committee's Note.

(4) Opinion based on facts in evidence. An expert is permitted to state an opinion even when he lacks personal knowledge of the litigated facts. As has traditionally been the rule, the expert may be informed at trial of facts not within his personal knowledge by having counsel pose them to him in the form of a hypothetical question. See, e.g., Ramey v. Shalala, 26 F.3d 58, 59 (8th Cir.1994). Alternatively, the expert may learn the facts by listening to the testimony that establishes the facts. See, e.g., United States v. Crabtree, 979 F.2d 1261, 1270 (7th Cir.1992). Any facts comprising a hypothetical question must be admitted into evidence, at least by the close of the case. Fluckey v. Chicago & Northwestern Transp. Co., 838 F.2d 302, 303 (8th Cir.1988). See the discussion of Rule 705 infra.

(5) Opinion based on facts not in evidence. Rule 703 provides that expert opinions may be based on facts or data (such as hearsay) that would not otherwise be admissible in evidence if they are the kinds of facts or data that experts in the testifying expert's field would reasonably rely on in forming such opinions. The rule goes beyond eliminating the need to introduce otherwise admissible underlying data; expert opinion may be predicated solely on inadmissible evidence such as hearsay.

> **Example.** In United States v. Thornton, 642 F.3d 599, 606–07 (7th Cir.2011), an ATF agent was permitted to testify about where certain ammunition was manufactured. He based his opinion in part on written materials provided by ammunition manufacturers.

> **Example.** In Boim v. Holy Land Foundation for Relief and Development, 549 F.3d 685, 702–05 (7th Cir.2008), an expert in terrorism was permitted to base his opinion that the men who shot the plaintiffs' son were Hamas gunmen in large part on information he obtained from websites of Islamic movements and Islamic terrorist organizations.

> **Example.** In South Central Petroleum, Inc. v. Long Bros. Oil Co., 974 F.2d 1015, 1018–19 (8th Cir.1992), an expert who calculated an offset credit for profits generated by an oil well based his opinion on triple hearsay. He used information obtained from a commercial production service, which obtained it from the state, which obtained it from the operator of the well. Because even the opponent agreed this information is the type of data reasonably relied upon by experts in this field, the court admitted the testimony.

(6) Reasonable reliance requirement. If an expert seeks to base an opinion on facts neither perceived by him personally nor introduced into evidence, the trial judge must determine, pursuant to Rule 104(a), both that the facts or data relied upon by the expert are the kinds of facts or data that experts in the particular field rely upon and that such reliance is reasonable. See, e.g., Sandifer v. Hoyt Archery, Inc., 907 F.3d 802, 808–09 (5th Cir.2018) (trial court did not abuse discretion in finding that biomechanics experts do not reasonably rely on propensity evidence in forming opinions).

(a) *Determining reasonable reliance—sources.* The trial court may consider the expert's own testimony concerning the types of data that are reasonably relied upon by experts in his field. Ward v. Dixie National Life Ins. Co., 595 F.3d 164, 182 (4th Cir.2010); e.g., United States v. Jackson, 58 F.4th 541, 552–53 (1st Cir.2023) (expert testified he always checked particular database and used usual reference materials and that they are reasonably relied on by other experts). In addition, other experts may be called to testify, see, e.g., In re Swine Flu Immunization Prod. Liability Litigation, 508 F.Supp. 897, 904 (D.Colo.1981), aff'd sub nom., Lima v. United States, 708 F.2d 502 (10th Cir.1983), learned treatises may be consulted, see, e.g., United States v. Tranowski, 659 F.2d 750, 755 (7th Cir.1981), and judicial notice may be taken, Ambrosini v. Labarraque, 966 F.2d 1464, 1467 (D.C.Cir.1992), regarding the types of data that are reasonably relied upon by experts in the field.

(b) *Scrutiny of specific facts.* The trial court must scrutinize the specific facts relied upon by the expert to ensure that the expert's reliance is reasonable in the particular case. The more an expert relies on inadmissible facts that the court finds to be untrustworthy, the less likely it is that the reliance is reasonable. No precise formula exists, however, for determining when an expert's reliance becomes unreasonable.

> **Example—Admissible.** In United States v. Locascio, 6 F.3d 924, 937–38 (2d Cir.1993), the prosecution presented expert testimony about the operation, structure, membership, and

terminology of organized crime families, some of which was based on hearsay. The court of appeals upheld the admission of the testimony, noting that law enforcement agents routinely rely upon such hearsay in the course of their duties.

Example—Inadmissible. In Carrizosa v. Chiquita Brands Int'l, Inc., 47 F.4th 1278, 1322–23 (11th Cir.2022), the trial court held inadmissible testimony by one of plaintiffs' experts that paramilitary organizations had murdered their relatives. The opinion was based partially on a statement by plaintiffs' counsel that "over 90% of the [2,000] cases he investigated were committed by the paramilitaries." The appellate court affirmed. "The hearsay statement of counsel, absent independent investigation or verification, is not the type of evidence on which an expert like Mr. Ortega would reasonably rely to form an opinion."

Example—Inadmissible. In Gopalratnam v. Hewlett-Packard Co., 877 F.3d 771, 788–89 (7th Cir.2017), the court of appeals held that the trial court did not abuse its discretion when it excluded the opinion of one expert that relied on another expert's opinions that the trial court had held were insufficiently reliable to be admitted under Rule 702.

(c) *Reasonable reliance requirement limited.* The reasonable reliance standard simply allows an expert to base an opinion on facts or data even if they would not themselves be admissible in evidence; by the terms of Rule 703, this standard does not apply to opinions that are based on admissible facts or data. Claar v. Burlington Northern R. Co., 29 F.3d 499, 501 (9th Cir.1994). Many courts, however, have ignored this limitation and relied on Rule 703 to exclude expert testimony for lack of reasonable reliance on admissible facts or data. E.g., Ealy v. Richardson-Merrell, Inc., 897 F.2d 1159, 1161–63 (D.C.Cir.1990). Of course, an expert's unreasonable reliance on facts or data—even if they would be admissible—is grounds for a court's exercising its gatekeeping responsibility under Rule 702 to exclude the expert's opinion as unreliable. See Authors' Comment 702(9).

(d) *Confrontation clause.* Whether the Confrontation Clause limits an expert's ability to base an opinion on inadmissible, testimonial hearsay is still an open question. Several courts of appeals have indicated that an expert may offer an independent opinion that is based partially on such testimonial hearsay. See, e.g., United States v. Pablo, 696 F.3d 1280, 1288 (10th Cir.2012); United States v. Ayala, 601 F.3d 256, 275 (4th Cir.2010). The Supreme Court's latest Confrontation Clause opinion did little, if anything, to clarify this issue, see Williams v. Illinois, 567 U.S. 50, 132 S.Ct. 2221 (2012) (4–1–4 opinion), and the Court promptly vacated the *Pablo* decision and remanded it for further consideration. Pablo v. United States, 567 U.S. 948, 133 S.Ct. 56 (2012). But all the justices seemed to agree that the Confrontation Clause forbids an expert from serving merely as a conduit for inadmissible, testimonial hearsay, even though they could not agree whether, in the case under consideration, the expert had done this. See Authors' Comment (8) infra.

(7) Admissibility of underlying data. The first two sentences of Rule 703 authorize the admission of an expert's opinion that is based on facts or data that themselves would be inadmissible in evidence. Whether the otherwise inadmissible facts or data should be disclosed to the jury is a different question. See Wi-LAN Inc. v. Sharp Electronics Corp., 992 F.3d 1366, 1374 (Fed.Cir.2021). Rule 703 now provides that the trial judge must balance the probative value of disclosing such facts or data to the jury against the prejudicial effect of disclosure. Otherwise inadmissible facts or data have probative value to the extent that they would assist the jury in evaluating the expert's opinion; their prejudicial effect derives from the danger that the jury will misuse the evidence for substantive purposes. Turner v. Burlington Northern Santa Fe R. Co., 338 F.3d 1058, 1062 (9th Cir.2003). The trial judge may admit such evidence only when the probative value substantially outweighs the danger of unfair prejudice. E.g., United States v. Leeson, 453 F.3d 631, 637–38 (4th Cir.2006). Cf. In re Hanford Nuclear Reservation Litig., 534 F.3d 986, 1012 (9th Cir.2008) ("reports of other experts cannot be admitted even as impeachment evidence unless the testifying expert based his opinion on the hearsay in the examined report or testified directly from the report"). But, as a badly-divided Supreme Court revealed in Williams v. Illinois, 567 U.S. 50, 132 S.Ct. 2221 (2012), it may sometimes be difficult to determine whether the inadmissible facts or data have any legitimate explanatory power independent of their truth.

(8) Expert as hearsay conduit. The trial court must insure that an expert witness is truly testifying as an expert and not merely serving as a conduit through which hearsay is brought before the jury. Factory Mut. Ins. Co. v. Alon USA L.P., 705 F.3d 518, 524 (5th Cir.2013). An expert must do more than merely relate inadmissible hearsay to the jury. The expert's value as a witness must derive from his ability to apply his expertise to the facts and draw inferences from them. United States v. Palacios, 677 F.3d 234, 243 (4th Cir.2012).

Example—Admissible and Inadmissible. In United States v. Cazares, 788 F.3d 956, 975–78 (9th Cir.2015), an expert on a particular street gang was properly permitted to testify generally about the gang members' attitudes towards black people, but should not have been permitted to testify about who gang members and other officers identified as the most violent members of the gang.

Example—Inadmissible. In Pelster v. Ray, 987 F.2d 514, 525–27 (8th Cir.1993), the plaintiffs sought to prove that the defendants fraudulently sold them a car with a rolled-back odometer and called a state revenue investigator to testify that hundreds of cars sold by defendants had rolled-back odometers. The court of appeals held that the testimony should not have been admitted because the witness was merely relating hearsay to the jury and was not presenting conclusions that were the product of expertise applied to the facts.

In criminal cases, the Confrontation Clause also prevents an expert merely from serving as a conduit for the presentation of inadmissible, testimonial hearsay to the jury. Williams v. Illinois, 567 U.S. 50, 80–81, 132 S.Ct. 2221, 2241 (2012) (Alito, J., plurality); 567 U.S. at 123–25, 132 S.Ct. at 2267 (Kagan, J., dissenting). See United States v. Garcia, 793 F.3d 1194, 1212–16 (10th Cir.2015); United States v. Johnson, 587 F.3d 625, 635 (4th Cir.2009) ("Allowing a witness simply to parrot 'out-of-court testimonial statements of cooperating witnesses and confidential informants directly to the jury in the guise of expert opinion' would provide an end run around *Crawford*.") (quoting United States v. Lombardozzi, 491 F.3d 61, 72 (2d Cir.2007)). Cf. Bullcoming v. New Mexico, 564 U.S. 647, 131 S.Ct. 2705 (2011) (Confrontation Clause bars prosecution from offering testimonial forensic laboratory report through in-court testimony of lab analyst who neither performed or observed performance of reported test nor signed testimonial certification).

(9) Opinions based on constitutionally or statutorily inadmissible material. Although Rule 703 provides that experts may base opinions on facts or data that are otherwise inadmissible, they may be barred from doing so if the underlying information is rendered inadmissible by some constitutional prohibition. See Estelle v. Smith, 451 U.S. 454, 101 S.Ct. 1866 (1981) (psychiatrist should not have been permitted to state opinion about defendant's future dangerousness where opinion was based on statements taken from defendant in violation of *Miranda*). Similarly, policy-based statutory prohibitions on the admissibility of certain evidence may not be circumvented by allowing an expert to base an opinion on such materials. Robertson v. Union Pacific R. Co., 954 F.2d 1433, 1435 (8th Cir.1992) (expert may not base opinion contained in reports rendered inadmissible by 23 U.S.C.A. § 409 [now § 407]).

CROSS-REFERENCES

Common Objections (Chapter 3)

26.   Confrontation Clause: Hearsay
32.   Expert lacks sufficient basis for opinion
33.   Expert may not relate hearsay basis for opinion
35.   Expert opinion based solely on hearsay not reasonably relied upon

Treatises

6 Graham, Handbook of Federal Evidence § 703:1 (9th ed. 2020)

1 McCormick, Evidence §§ 14–17 (8th ed. 2020)

29 Wright and Gold, Federal Practice and Procedure §§ 6271–6275 (2d ed. 2016)

Rule 704. Opinion on an Ultimate Issue

(a) In General—Not Automatically Objectionable. An opinion is not objectionable just because it embraces an ultimate issue.

(b) Exception. In a criminal case, an expert witness must not state an opinion about whether the defendant did or did not have a mental state or condition that constitutes an element of the crime charged or of a defense. Those matters are for the trier of fact alone.

AUTHORS' COMMENTS

(1) Scope and purpose of Rule 704. Rule 704(a) provides that otherwise admissible opinion testimony is not objectionable merely because it reaches an ultimate issue to be decided by the fact finder. This removes the court from the business of determining whether or not an opinion goes to the ultimate issue and eliminates objections that simply assert that the testimony "invades the province of the jury" or embraces an "ultimate issue." See McCormick, Evidence § 12 (5th ed. 1999). Despite this, opinion testimony must still be otherwise admissible. United States v. Campbell, 963 F.3d 309, 313–14 (4th Cir.2020). The major effect of Rule 704(a), therefore, is to shift the battleground to whether the opinion is admissible under the standards of Rules 701, 702 and 403. See Advisory Committee's Note.

Rule 704(b), enacted in the wake of John Hinckley's acquittal by reason of insanity in the shooting of President Reagan, qualifies the general rule set forth in Rule 704(a). Applicable only to experts testifying in criminal cases, Rule 704(b) bars them from opining that the defendant either had or did not have a mental state or condition that constitutes an element of the crime charged or a defense to the crime charged.

(2) Opinions on ultimate issues—Factors affecting admissibility. While a trial court's decision to admit or exclude opinion testimony is ordinarily reviewed only on an abuse of discretion standard, Kopf v. Skyrm, 993 F.2d 374, 378 (4th Cir.1993), appellate courts frequently comment that the admissibility of the opinion testimony under review presents a close question. E.g., United States v. Simpson, 7 F.3d 186, 189 (10th Cir.1993). Appellate courts appear to focus on the following factors in conducting their review.

- The extent to which the witness discussed the facts underlying the conclusion and did not simply make conclusory assertions. Fiataruolo v. United States, 8 F.3d 930, 941–42 (2d Cir.1993); Karns v. Emerson Electric Co., 817 F.2d 1452, 1459 (10th Cir.1987).

- The extent to which the witness is able to convey the information in the form of specific facts. E.g., United States v. Yazzie, 976 F.2d 1252, 1255–56 (9th Cir.1992).

- The extent to which the opposing party has attempted to introduce testimony of a similar tenor. United States v. Aggarwal, 17 F.3d 737, 743 (5th Cir.1994).

- The thoroughness of the cross-examination afforded the opposing party by the trial court. United States v. Logan, 641 F.2d 860, 863 (10th Cir.1981).

- The extent to which a legal term used by the witness corresponds to its lay meaning. Compare Burkhart v. Washington Metro. Area Transit Auth., 112 F.3d 1207, 1212–14 (D.C.Cir.1997) (holding inadmissible testimony phrased in terms of legal standards imposed by Americans with Disabilities Act); Torres v. County of Oakland, 758 F.2d 147, 151 (6th Cir.1985) (holding inadmissible testimony that employer discriminated against plaintiff because of her national origin) with United States v. Sheffey, 57 F.3d 1419, 1422–29 (6th Cir.1995) (holding admissible eyewitnesses' testimony that defendant was driving recklessly and with extreme indifference to human life).

- The extent to which the witness used a legal term as a factual rather than a legal conclusion. Compare Woods v. Lecureux, 110 F.3d 1215, 1219–21 (6th Cir.1997) (witness's testimony that defendant was "deliberately indifferent" involved use of legal term and was properly excluded) with Heflin v. Stewart Co., Tenn., 958 F.2d 709, 715 (6th Cir.1992) (witness's use of "deliberate indifference" reflected his view of the seriousness of defendant's failures, not a legal conclusion).

- The extent to which the witness's testimony tracked the relevant legal standard and gave the appearance of instructing the jury on the law. United States v. Duncan, 42 F.3d 97, 102–03 (2d Cir.1994).

- Whether the trial judge cautioned the jury that it was not bound by the expert's opinion. E.g., Karns v. Emerson Electric Co., 817 F.2d 1452, 1459 (10th Cir.1987).

(3) Opinions on ultimate issues—Illustrations. Because the admissibility of opinions relating to ultimate issues often turns on the particulars of the case, generalizations about what types of opinions are permitted are difficult. Nevertheless, the following are examples of opinions that have been admitted.

- Testimony that a product was unreasonably dangerous under the consumer expectation test. Werth v. Makita Electric Works, Ltd., 950 F.2d 643, 649–50 (10th Cir.1991).

- An IRS agent's opinion that funds on hand were not income. United States v. Toushin, 899 F.2d 617, 620 n. 4 (7th Cir.1990).

- An expert's opinion that check kiting had occurred. United States v. Winkle, 477 F.3d 407, 416–17 (6th Cir.2007).

- An expert's opinion that any investment program using the term "prime bank" is a fraud. United States v. Dazey, 403 F.3d 1147, 1171–72 (10th Cir.2005).

The following are examples of opinions that have been held inadmissible.

- An opinion that the plaintiff's conduct was neither justified nor warranted under the circumstances. Hygh v. Jacobs, 961 F.2d 359, 364 (2d Cir.1992).

- An opinion that an employer discriminated against the plaintiff because of her national origin. Torres v. County of Oakland, 758 F.2d 147, 151 (6th Cir.1985).

- Testimony from plaintiff's expert that the defendant police officers had been negligent. Shahid v. City of Detroit, 889 F.2d 1543, 1547–48 (6th Cir.1989).

- An SEC investigator's opinion that the defendant "manipulated" stock and committed "fraud." United States v. Scop, 846 F.2d 135, 140–42 (2d Cir.1988), on reh'g, 856 F.2d 5 (2d Cir.1988).

- An expert's opinion about an accused's guilt. United States v. Alonso, 48 F.3d 1536, 1540 (9th Cir.1995).

(4) Drug cases. Numerous cases discuss the admissibility of opinion testimony by law enforcement agents concerning defendants' roles in drug transactions and whether defendants' possession of the drugs was for personal use or for distribution. The decisions are not always consistent. Compare, e.g., United States v. Dunnican, 961 F.3d 859, 875–77 (6th Cir.2020) (holding admissible testimony that marijuana was "packed for resale") and United States v. Cotton, 22 F.3d 182, 185 (8th Cir.1994) (holding admissible testimony that amount of crack cocaine seized was indicative of distribution) with United States v. Archuleta, 737 F.3d 1287, 1297–98 (10th Cir.2013) (holding inadmissible expert's response that hypothetical person in same situation as defendant would have requisite knowledge) and United States v. Watson, 260 F.3d 301 (3d Cir.2001) (holding inadmissible opinion "it was possess [sic] with intent to distribute"); United States v. Mitchell, 996 F.2d 419, 421–22 (D.C.Cir.1993) (holding inadmissible testimony that intent of person carrying bags of cocaine "was intent to distribute"). Admission in these cases often appears to depend on the directness with which the opinion is phrased. Thus, courts are more willing to admit an expert's opinion when he makes it clear that his opinion is based on his knowledge of general criminal practices and not on any special knowledge of the particular defendant's mental processes. See United States v. Henry, 848 F.3d 1, 11–12 (1st Cir.2017) (noting expert's opinion was based on quantity of drugs and packaging and "did not attempt to offer any special insight" into defendant's "actual mental state"). See also United States v. Sosa, 897 F.3d 615, 619–20 (5th Cir.2018) (expert could testify about typical roles within drug trafficking organization generally, but should not have been permitted to testify about where defendant fit into structure); United States v. Medeles-Cab, 754 F.3d 316, 320–24 (5th Cir.2014) (discussing characteristics of improper drug courier profile evidence); United States v. Toms, 136 F.3d 176, 184–86 (D.C.Cir.1998) (disapproving generally of "mirroring hypotheticals").

(5) Grounds for objecting. Rule 704(a) simply eliminates the "ultimate issue" objection to opinion testimony. The proffered opinion—whether lay or expert—may still be objectionable for any of a number of reasons: because a lay witness is not capable of rendering such an opinion, the opinion goes beyond the realm of an expert witness's expertise, the fact finder would not be helped by hearing the opinion, or the probative value of the opinion is substantially outweighed by the danger that it would be unfairly prejudicial, confuse the issues or mislead the jury.

(a) *Lay witness not qualified to testify.* Some conclusions may be drawn only by witnesses who possess special expertise. E.g., Randolph v. Collectramatic, Inc., 590 F.2d 844, 848 (10th Cir.1979).

(b) *Inadequately explored legal criteria.* An opinion as to a mixed question of law and fact will not be helpful unless it is based on a proper understanding of the underlying legal criteria. United States v. Richter, 796 F.3d 1173, 1194–96 (10th Cir.2015); United States v. Whitted, 11 F.3d 782, 785 (8th Cir.1993).

(c) *Choosing up sides.* Opinions stated solely in conclusory terms that amount to little more than telling the jury what result to reach are not helpful and thus not "otherwise admissible." Hygh v. Jacobs, 961 F.2d 359, 364 (2d Cir.1992).

(d) *Testimony in form of opinion not necessary.* If the jury is equally well positioned to draw a conclusion from the facts, the opinion may not be helpful. E.g., Salas v. Carpenter, 980 F.2d 299, 304–05 (5th Cir.1992). Testimony by which a witness attempts to instruct the jury as to the law is similarly unhelpful. United States v. Jungles, 903 F.2d 468, 477 (7th Cir.1990).

(e) *Opinion beyond witness's expertise.* Conclusions as to mixed questions of law and fact may involve considerations that are outside the scope of the witness's expertise. E.g., Berry v. City of Detroit, 25 F.3d 1342, 1351 (6th Cir.1994); United States v. Scop, 846 F.2d 135, 140–42 (2d Cir.1988) (witness could not base opinion on personal assessment of another witness's credibility), on reh'g, 856 F.2d 5 (2d Cir.1988).

(6) Opinions about accused's mental state. Rule 704(b) provides that expert opinion testimony concerning one particular type of ultimate issue is per se inadmissible. An expert testifying about an accused's mental state or condition may not offer an opinion as to whether the accused possessed a mental state or condition that constitutes an element of (a) the crime charged or (b) a defense to the crime charged. E.g., United States v. Brown, 871 F.3d 532, 539 (7th Cir.2017) (excluding expert opinion that defendant police officer acted reasonably under the circumstances); United States v. Bennett, 161 F.3d 171, 182–85 (3d Cir.1998). Experts, however, remain free to testify to facts from which a jury might infer the accused's mental state. United States v. Soler-Montalvo, 44 F.4th 1, 14 (1st Cir.2022). For example, an expert may testify that the accused does or does not suffer from a mental disease or defect and to describe the characteristics and effects of such a disease or defect. United States v. Samples, 456 F.3d 875, 884 (8th Cir.2006) (expert may testify to symptoms and qualities of accused's mental illness and whether illness generally affects ability to understand nature and quality of one's actions, but may not make subjective comments about whether accused's mental state affected his ability to understand wrongfulness of his actions); United States v. Thigpen, 4 F.3d 1573, 1579–80 (11th Cir.1993) (testimony that schizophrenia does not necessarily deprive person of ability to understand wrongfulness of actions held admissible).

Example. In United States v. Finley, 301 F.3d 1000, 1015–16 (9th Cir.2002), the court held the trial court erred in excluding defendant's psychological expert. His opinion that the defendant had an atypical belief system did not constitute an opinion that the defendant did not knowingly commit fraud. The trial court properly ruled, however, that the expert could not testify about the defendant's specific beliefs concerning the fraudulent nature of the particular financial instruments.

Rule 704(b) applies to expert opinion about any mental state. It is not restricted to testimony concerning insanity. E.g., United States v. Stahlman, 934 F.3d 1199, 1220–22 (11th Cir.2019) (intent to act out sexual fantasy rather than have sex with minor); United States v. Offill, 666 F.3d 168, 176–77 (4th Cir.2011) (intent to evade securities regulation requirement); United States v. Anchrum, 590 F.3d 795, 804–05 (9th Cir.2009) (why hypothetical drug dealer would possess a firearm); United States v. Campos, 217 F.3d 707 (9th Cir.2000) (defendant's knowledge that vehicle contained drugs).

Although originally enacted to limit the scope of testimony from mental health experts when a defendant raises an insanity defense, courts agree that Rule 704(b) applies to experts in all fields. United States v. Smart, 98 F.3d 1379, 1388 (D.C.Cir.1996) ("it is now well-established that Rule 704(b) applies to all cases in which an expert testifies as to a mental state or condition constituting an element of the crime charged or defense thereto"). E.g., United States v. Lara, 23 F.4th 459, 475–76 (5th Cir.2022) (holding that expert's opinion that drug couriers usually know they are transporting drugs constituted inadmissible testimony about drug trafficking defendant's state of mind); United States v. Miner, 774 F.3d 336, 349 (6th Cir.2015) (applying Rule 704(b) to government agent testifying as expert in criminal tax case). Cf. United States v. Jaffal, 79 F.4th 582, 603 (6th Cir.2023) ("Law-enforcement officers are 'routinely allowed to testify that circumstances are consistent with [the] distribution of drugs rather than personal use.'") (quoting United States v. Swafford, 385 F.3d 1026, 1030 (6th Cir.2004)).

In November 2023, the Supreme Court granted certiorari in a case that may define the contours of Rule 704(b)'s ban on expert opinions about a defendant's mental state. United States v. Diaz, 2023 WL 314309 (9th Cir.2023) (rejecting claim that expert's testimony about drug traffickers' use of unknowing couriers was functional equivalent of opinion about defendant's mental state), cert. granted, 144 S.Ct. 392 (2023).

Federal Rule of Criminal Procedure 12.2(b) requires a defendant who intends to introduce expert testimony relating to a mental disease or defect or any other mental condition of the defendant that bears upon his guilt to provide the prosecution notice of his intent to do so.

CROSS-REFERENCES

Common Objections (Chapter 3)

23.   Conclusion of law, expert witness

24.   Conclusion of law, lay witness

58.   Mental state or condition of accused

93.   Ultimate issue

Treatises

6 Graham, Handbook of Federal Evidence §§ 704:1–704:2 (9th ed. 2020)

1 McCormick, Evidence §§ 12, 16 (8th ed. 2020)

29 Wright and Gold, Federal Practice and Procedure §§ 6281–6286 (2d ed. 2016)

Rule 705. Disclosing the Facts or Data Underlying an Expert's Opinion

Unless the court orders otherwise, an expert may state an opinion—and give the reasons for it—without first testifying to the underlying facts or data. But the expert may be required to disclose those facts or data on cross-examination.

AUTHORS' COMMENTS

(1) Scope and purpose of Rule 705. Rule 705 governs the presentation of expert testimony. Designed to eliminate the need to resort to a hypothetical question in many instances, it thus affords counsel greater flexibility in the manner in which she may present expert testimony. Note, however, that Federal Rule of Civil Procedure 26 and Federal Rule of Criminal Procedure 16 both require pre-trial disclosure of the basis and reasons for an expert's opinion.

(2) Prior disclosure generally not required. Rule 705 abandons the traditional requirement that compelled experts to disclose the facts upon which they based their opinions prior to relating their opinions. Instead, Rule 705 provides that experts may state their opinions without first testifying to the underlying facts or data. In theory at least, an expert's direct examination may consist only of the recitation of his qualifications and his conclusions. No explanation need be provided. As a practical matter, however, such a bare-bones offering is unlikely to prove effective.

To the extent that an expert does not disclose on direct examination the facts underlying his opinion, the burden of probing the basis of the expert's opinion shifts to the cross-examiner. University of Rhode Island v. A.W. Chesterton Co., 2 F.3d 1200, 1218 (1st Cir.1993). The cross-examiner is, of course, free to do this. If the cross-examination reveals that the expert lacks an adequate basis for his opinions, the court should strike the testimony. United States v. Sepulveda, 15 F.3d 1161, 1183 (1st Cir.1993).

(3) Court may require prior disclosure. Although an expert is ordinarily allowed to give his opinion without first testifying to its basis, Rule 705 empowers the court to order prior disclosure. The rule, however, provides no guidance as to when the court should require such disclosure. As the clear design of Rule 705 is to allow counsel to present expert testimony as expeditiously as possible and to rely on the adversary to explore any weaknesses in the testimony, courts should intervene infrequently.

One situation in which courts have not been reluctant to require disclosure is in connection with summary judgment motions. Courts have demanded that expert opinions in summary judgment affidavits consist of more than conclusory statements, although a detailed recitation of the data underlying the opinion need not be included. Hayes v. Douglas Dynamics, Inc., 8 F.3d 88, 92 (1st Cir.1993).

(4) Admissibility of underlying facts. Implicit in Rule 705's command that an expert may state an opinion without first disclosing the facts or data underlying the opinion is the notion that it is ordinarily permissible for an expert to disclose the underlying facts and data. Rule 703 also implicitly accepts this notion, but imposes one important limitation on it. When the underlying facts or data are otherwise inadmissible, they may be disclosed to the jury only if the court determines that the probative value of revealing them substantially outweighs the danger of unfair prejudice.

(a)   If the underlying facts or data are themselves admissible, the expert should be allowed to disclose them to the jury and no limiting instruction is necessary.

> **Example.** If a physician testifies about a patient's condition, he may disclose the facts underlying his opinion, including statements made to him by the patient. Even though these statements may be hearsay, they may qualify for admission under Rule 803(4) and are thus admissible as substantive evidence as well as to explain the basis for the physician's opinion.

(b)   If the underlying facts and data would be otherwise inadmissible, they possess probative value only insofar as they may help the jury to evaluate the expert's opinion. Paddack v. Dave Christensen, Inc., 745 F.2d 1254, 1262–63 (9th Cir.1984). Unfortunately, as a badly-divided Supreme Court revealed in Williams v. Illinois, 567 U.S. 50, 132 S.Ct. 2221 (2012), it may sometimes be difficult to determine whether the inadmissible facts or data have any legitimate explanatory power independent of their truth. But if and when they do, revealing such evidence to the jury still creates the risk that the jurors will impermissibly use the inadmissible facts or data as substantive evidence. Therefore, several options are open to the court:

•   The court may allow the expert to disclose the underlying facts and then give a limiting instruction to the jury. Brennan v. Reinhart Institutional Foods, 211 F.3d 449, 451 (8th Cir.2000); Engebretsen v. Fairchild Aircraft Corp., 21 F.3d 721, 729 (6th Cir.1994).

•   The court may restrict the expert to a description of the types of underlying data upon which he relied, but not allow the expert to give any details. United States v. W.R. Grace, 504 F.3d 745, 761 (9th Cir.2007).

> **Example.** In Marsee v. United States Tobacco Co., 866 F.2d 319, 322–24 (10th Cir.1989), a physician testified that plaintiff's oral cancer was caused by snuff. He based his opinion in part on his awareness of other oral cancer cases involving young snuff users. His knowledge of these other cases came from telephone conversations with doctors whose names he had been given by plaintiff's lawyer. Although the trial court permitted him to testify that he was aware of other oral cancer cases involving young snuff users, it refused to allow him to relate details of these cases.

•   The court may prohibit any mention whatsoever of the otherwise inadmissible material. Mike's Train House, Inc. v. Lionel, L.L.C., 472 F.3d 398, 409 (6th Cir.2006).

(c)   Opposing counsel may not use cross-examination as a means of bringing inadmissible hearsay or opinions before the jury. Thus, counsel may not bring before the jury inadmissible hearsay reports or data to impeach the testifying expert if the expert did not rely on the material in question. Polythane Systems, Inc. v. Marina Ventures International, Ltd., 993 F.2d 1201, 1207–08 (5th Cir.1993).

(5)   Hypothetical questions—Generally. Traditionally, the hypothetical question took either of two forms. Where the expert had observed the testimony of other witnesses, counsel could simply ask him to assume the truth of the facts stated by a particular witness or witnesses and base his opinion upon such facts. More often, the expert would be asked to state an opinion based upon a set of facts recited to him by counsel, the truth of which he was to assume. The hypothetical question thus: (1) supplied data to a testifying expert who lacked familiarity with the facts; (2) informed the jury of the data upon which the expert's opinion was grounded; and (3) restricted the basis of the expert's opinion to those facts in evidence.

As Rule 705 provides that an expert may testify without first disclosing the basis of his opinion, counsel is no longer required to resort to the hypothetical question. Rule 705, however, does not prohibit its use. Taylor v. Burlington Northern R. Co., 787 F.2d 1309, 1317 (9th Cir.1986). Indeed, when an expert lacks knowledge of the facts upon which his opinion is to be predicated, a hypothetical question will be the only way to proceed.

(6)   Hypothetical questions—Procedure. When counsel chooses to use a hypothetical question, the traditional rules governing such questions apply. The form of a hypothetical question is left to the trial court's discretion, subject to these strictures. Kuras v. International Harvester Co., 820 F.2d 15, 18 (1st Cir.1987).

(a)   Counsel may include in a hypothetical question only those facts already in evidence or that will be introduced before the close of evidence, or inferences reasonably drawn from those facts. Toucet v. Maritime Overseas Corp., 991 F.2d 5, 10 (1st Cir.1993) ("a hypothetical question should include only those facts supported by the evidence").

Example—Inadmissible. In United States v. Stinson, 647 F.3d 1196, 1213–14 (9th Cir.2011), the prosecution posed a series of hypothetical questions to defendant's expert, several of which were based on matters that were not introduced into evidence. The court of appeals held this constituted prosecutorial misconduct.

(b)   The facts included in the question need not be established to a high degree of certainty. Matter of P & E Boat Rentals, Inc., 872 F.2d 642, 653 (5th Cir.1989). The question must contain a sufficient number of relevant facts to yield a helpful opinion, Iconco v. Jensen Construction Co., 622 F.2d 1291, 1301 (8th Cir.1980), but it need not refer to all of the relevant facts in evidence.

Example—Admissible. In Piotrowski v. Southworth Prods. Corp., 15 F.3d 748, 753 (8th Cir.1994), the plaintiff's treating physician was asked a hypothetical question that failed to mention that the plaintiff had seen a chiropractor once or twice some four years before the accident in question. The court permitted the question, finding that the omission of this fact did not render the hypothetical misleading.

(c)   On cross-examination, opposing counsel may ask the expert to assume that facts included in the original hypothetical are not true or that other facts are true.

CROSS-REFERENCES

Common Objections (Chapter 3)

32.   Expert lacks sufficient basis for opinion
33.   Expert may not relate hearsay basis for opinion
40.   Hypothetical question includes facts not in evidence
41.   Hypothetical question not helpful

Treatises

6 Graham, Handbook of Federal Evidence § 705:1–705:3 (9th ed. 2020)

1 McCormick, Evidence §§ 14–17 (8th ed. 2020)

29 Wright and Gold, Federal Practice and Procedure §§ 6291–6295 (2d ed. 2016)

Rule 706. Court-Appointed Expert Witnesses

(a)   **Appointment Process.** On a party's motion or on its own, the court may order the parties to show cause why expert witnesses should not be appointed and may ask the parties to submit nominations. The court may appoint any expert that the parties agree on and any of its own choosing. But the court may only appoint someone who consents to act.

(b)   **Expert's Role.** The court must inform the expert of the expert's duties. The court may do so in writing and have a copy filed with the clerk or may do so orally at a conference in which the parties have an opportunity to participate. The expert:

    (1)   must advise the parties of any findings the expert makes;

    (2)   may be deposed by any party;

    (3)   may be called to testify by the court or any party; and

    (4)   may be cross-examined by any party, including the party that called the expert.

(c)   **Compensation.** The expert is entitled to a reasonable compensation, as set by the court. The compensation is payable as follows:

(1) in a criminal case or in a civil case involving just compensation under the Fifth Amendment, from any funds that are provided by law; and

(2) in any other civil case, by the parties in the proportion and at the time that the court directs—and the compensation is then charged like other costs.

(d) Disclosing the Appointment to the Jury. The court may authorize disclosure to the jury that the court appointed the expert.

(e) Parties' Choice of Their Own Experts. This rule does not limit a party in calling its own experts.

AUTHORS' COMMENTS

(1) Scope and purpose of Rule 706. Rule 706, which empowers the court to appoint an expert of its own choosing, was promulgated largely in response to concerns over expert shopping and "the venality of some experts." Advisory Committee's Note. See Armstrong v. Brown, 768 F.3d 975, 987 (9th Cir.2014) ("A Rule 706 expert typically acts as an advisor to the court on complex scientific, medical, or technical matters."). Rule 706 envisions a neutral expert who will serve the court's interest and not that of a particular party. Stevenson v. Windmoeller & Hoelscher Corp., 39 F.4th 466, 470 (7th Cir.2022). Previously, Federal Rule of Criminal Procedure 28 (since amended) provided for court-appointed experts in criminal cases. Despite the high hopes of some, courts have used Rule 706 rather sparingly. Rachel v. Troutt, 820 F.3d 390, 397 (10th Cir.2016). But see Claiborne v. Blauser, 934 F.3d 885, 901 n. 7 (9th Cir.2019) (noting that courts have regularly appointed experts to review medical records and testify about prior medical needs and treatment).

The court's obligation to appoint experts to assist indigent criminal defendants is rooted in the Constitution and 18 U.S.C.A. § 3006A(e). See Ake v. Oklahoma, 470 U.S. 68, 105 S.Ct. 1087 (1985).

(2) Procedures. In its discretion the court may appoint an expert *sua sponte* or on the motion of a party. The expert selected may be one agreed to by the parties or one chosen by the court. Rule 706(b) requires the court to keep the parties informed of the expert's duties and the expert to advise the parties of any findings she makes. Rule 706(b) also empowers parties to depose, call, and cross-examine a court-appointed expert. The court may also call a court-appointed expert to testify. See generally Monolithic Power Systems, Inc. v. O2 Micro International Ltd., 558 F.3d 1341 (Fed.Cir.2009) (trial court did not abuse discretion in appointing independent expert); Federal Trade Comm'n v. Enforma Natural Products, 362 F.3d 1204, 1212–15 (9th Cir.2004) (discussing difference between technical advisor to court and expert appointed under Rule 706).

Rule 706(c) provides details about the compensation of the expert. See Ledford v. Sullivan, 105 F.3d 354, 360–61 (7th Cir.1997).

Rule 706(d) authorizes the court to inform the jury that the expert was appointed by the court. The Advisory Committee Note states that this provision "seems to be essential if the use of court appointed experts is to be fully effective."

The appointment by the court of its own witness in no way limits the parties in calling their own experts. Rule 706(e).

CROSS-REFERENCES

Treatises

6 Graham, Handbook of Federal Evidence §§ 706:1–706:2 (9th ed. 2020)

1 McCormick, Evidence § 17 (8th ed. 2020)

29 Wright and Gold, Federal Practice and Procedure §§ 6301–6305 (2d ed. 2016)

ARTICLE VIII

HEARSAY

Rule 801. Definitions That Apply to This Article; Exclusions From Hearsay

(a) Statement. "Statement" means a person's oral assertion, written assertion, or nonverbal conduct, if the person intended it as an assertion.

(b) Declarant. "Declarant" means the person who made the statement.

(c) Hearsay. "Hearsay" means a statement that:

    (1) the declarant does not make while testifying at the current trial or hearing; and

    (2) a party offers in evidence to prove the truth of the matter asserted in the statement.

(d) Statements That Are Not Hearsay. A statement that meets the following conditions is not hearsay:

    (1) *A Declarant-Witness's Prior Statement.* The declarant testifies and is subject to cross-examination about a prior statement, and the statement:

        (A) is inconsistent with the declarant's testimony and was given under penalty of perjury at a trial, hearing, or other proceeding or in a deposition;

        (B) is consistent with the declarant's testimony and is offered:

            (i) to rebut an express or implied charge that the declarant recently fabricated it or acted from a recent improper influence or motive in so testifying; or

            (ii) to rehabilitate the declarant's credibility as a witness when attacked on another ground; or

        (C) identifies a person as someone the declarant perceived earlier.

    (2) *An Opposing Party's Statement.* The statement is offered against an opposing party and:

        (A) was made by the party in an individual or representative capacity;

        (B) is one the party manifested that it adopted or believed to be true;

        (C) was made by a person whom the party authorized to make a statement on the subject;

        (D) was made by the party's agent or employee on a matter within the scope of that relationship and while it existed; or

        (E) was made by the party's coconspirator during and in furtherance of the conspiracy.

    The statement must be considered but does not by itself establish the declarant's authority under (C); the existence or scope of the relationship under (D); or the existence of the conspiracy or participation in it under (E).

AUTHORS' COMMENTS

    (1) Scope and purpose of Rule 801. Paragraphs (a) through (c) of Rule 801 contain the basic definition of hearsay. The definition is similar to that of the common law. Paragraph (d) of Rule 801 lists two categories of out-of-court statements that are deemed to be nonhearsay even though they are offered to prove the matter asserted: certain prior statements by witnesses, and party admissions. The exemptions from the hearsay rule listed in paragraph (d) function just like the exceptions in Rules 803, 804, and 807.

(2) Definition of hearsay; hearsay exemptions for prior statement by witness and admission by party-opponent. The definition of hearsay in Rule 801(a)–(c) and the exemptions from hearsay in Rule 801(d) are discussed in the sections that follow.

CROSS-REFERENCES

Common Objections (Chapter 3)

26.   Confrontation Clause: Hearsay

39.   Hearsay

Treatises

6 Graham, Handbook of Federal Evidence §§ 801:0–801:26 (9th ed. 2020)

1 McCormick, Evidence §§ 34, 36, 47, 144, 160; 2 id. §§ 245–252, 254–265 (8th ed. 2020)

30B Wright & Bellin, Federal Practice and Procedure §§ 6701–6782 (2018)

30 Wright & Blinka, Federal Practice and Procedure §§ 6321–6695 (2d ed. 2020)

Rule 801(a)–(c).   Definition of Hearsay

(a) Statement. "Statement" means a person's oral assertion, written assertion, or nonverbal conduct, if the person intended it as an assertion.

(b) Declarant. "Declarant" means the person who made the statement.

(c) Hearsay. "Hearsay" means a statement that:

    (1) the declarant does not make while testifying at the current trial or hearing; and

    (2) a party offers in evidence to prove the truth of the matter asserted in the statement.

* * *

AUTHORS' COMMENTS

(1) Nonverbal conduct as hearsay. Testimony about a person's out-of-court nonverbal conduct can constitute hearsay, but only if the conduct was intended as an assertion.

Example—Hearsay. Testimony that a person pointed to a particular vehicle when asked to locate the source of drugs was assertive conduct and hearsay under Rule 801(a)(2). United States v. Caro, 569 F.2d 411, 416 n. 9 (5th Cir.1978).

Example—Hearsay. "Here, Dr. Boswell made the video in response to an FBI request, with the purpose of demonstrating the proper performance of nerve-block injections. Accordingly, because of Dr. Boswell's intent, we conclude that his conduct during the course of the video is an assertion of proper medical performance and is, therefore, a statement under Rule 801(a) of the Federal Rules of Evidence." United States v. Martinez, 588 F.3d 301, 311 (6th Cir.2009).

Example—Nonhearsay. "Appellants contend that testimony concerning drug sales * * * made by Ambriz prior to the existence of any conspiracy between him and appellants was inadmissible hearsay. As to the earlier drug sales, we note that Ambriz by his nonverbal conduct in consummating the transactions clearly did not intend an assertion. Accordingly evidence of the prior sales was not hearsay * * *." United States v. Astorga-Torres, 682 F.2d 1331, 1335 (9th Cir.1982).

Example—Nonhearsay. Evidence that U.S. mining inspector ate his lunch in area alleged to have been unsafe, and that other inspectors who observed area issued no citations, nonhearsay as evidence of safety. Boggs v. Blue Diamond Coal Co., unpublished decision cited in United States v. Zenni, 492 F.Supp. 464, 468 n. 18 (E.D.Ky.1980).

Example—Nonhearsay. "[T]he district court did not err in admitting Officer Arambula's testimony that he saw Officer Ligsay inspect the fish hold of the Clara Luz, the vessel that the officers stopped before encountering the Cristiano Ronaldo, and that in his opinion Officer Ligsay did not appear concerned during and after the inspection. While Officer Arambula's testimony permitted the Government to argue that the Clara Luz did not contain anything suspicious and therefore could not have been the source of the cocaine found in the water, Savala Cisneros has not shown that Officer Ligsay's nonverbal conduct constituted a statement. Nonverbal conduct can constitute a statement where the person intended the conduct to communicate a message, but nothing in the record suggests that Officer Ligsay intended through his conduct to communicate any message to Officer Arambula." United States v. Hernandez, 864 F.3d 1292, 1307 (11th Cir.2017).

(2) Matter implied by utterance. The hearsay rule is not violated if an out-of-court utterance is offered to prove a matter implied by, but not asserted in, the utterance.

Example—Nonhearsay. In a prosecution for illegal bookmaking, it was not hearsay for government agents to testify that while searching defendant's premises pursuant to warrant, agents answered the telephone several times, and unknown callers stated directions for placing bets on sporting events. United States v. Zenni, 492 F.Supp. 464 (E.D.Ky.1980).

Example—Nonhearsay. In drug prosecution, it was not hearsay for officer to testify that unidentified caller to defendant's "beeper" asked, "Did you get the stuff?" and "Where is Dog [codefendant's nickname]?" United States v. Lewis, 902 F.2d 1176, 1179 (5th Cir.1990).

Example—Nonhearsay. "The question, 'Is this Kenny?' cannot reasonably be construed to be an intended assertion, express or implied. * * * [I]t might be possible to imply that the declarant believed Mr. Jackson was in possession of the pager and therefore he was the person responding by telephone to the declarant's message. The mere fact, however, that the declarant conveyed a message with her question does not make the question hearsay. * * * Rather, the important question is whether an assertion was intended. We find it hard to believe in this case that the declarant intended to assert that Mr. Jackson was in possession of the pager and that he was responding to her call." United States v. Jackson, 88 F.3d 845, 848 (10th Cir.1996).

Example—Nonhearsay. "The assertion Herlinda made was that Ybarra would not come home as long as the police were there. The statement was offered to prove that Ybarra lived at the house. Whether Ybarra would come home and, if not, why not, was not at issue in the trial. Therefore, the statement was not offered to prove the truth of the matter asserted and, by definition, was not hearsay." United States v. Ybarra, 70 F.3d 362, 366 (5th Cir.1995).

Example—Nonhearsay. "We have doubts, however, that the declaration in question—the handwritten words 'Date of RPT: 12/31/01'—constitutes a 'statement' under the hearsay rule. * * * White stated that the purpose of the HPL Create Sheet is to request information about a claim from the data processing department. In this sense, the information on the HPL Create Sheet is more in the nature of an inquiry than an assertion. Courts have held that questions and inquiries are generally not hearsay because the declarant does not have the requisite assertive intent, even if the question 'convey[s] an implicit message' or provides information about the declarant's assumptions or beliefs." Lexington Ins. Co. v. Western Pennsylvania Hosp., 423 F.3d 318, 329 (3d Cir.2005).

Example—Nonhearsay. "At trial, Alvarez argued that the surreptitiously recorded videotape of her resignation was strong exculpatory evidence. In particular, Perera's statement that, "there's no fraud whatsoever here, doctor," showed that Alvarez was not privy to the fraudulent scheme. The government objected to the tape's admission on the basis that it was hearsay, and the district court sustained the objection and excluded the videotape from evidence. The district court erred when it excluded the videotape. The relevant comment on the tape was not hearsay at all because it was not being offered for the truth of the matter asserted. See Fed. R. Evid. 801(c). Alvarez sought to admit the statement not as evidence that there was no fraud at St. Jude, a point which no defendant contested, but as evidence that she did not know of the fraud." United States v. Mateos, 623 F.3d 1350, 1355 (11th Cir.2010).

Example—Nonhearsay. Witness's testimony that defendant said, "go to the front door" was not hearsay since it was not an assertion of fact. United States. v. Ned, 637 F.3d 562 (5th Cir.2011).

Example—Nonhearsay. "The government argues that this was a question, not a 'statement' or an 'assertion' and therefore was not hearsay. Love, on the other hand, argues that the question implicitly asserted Deloney's identity and confirmed his role in the deal. Because the phrase communicated this information, Love argues, it should have been excluded as hearsay. * * * Unfortunately for Love, the federal courts do not take this approach. We held in United States v. Thomas that questions are not 'statements' and therefore are not hearsay." United States v. Love, 706 F.3d 832, 839–40 (7th Cir.2013).

Example—Hearsay. "We hold that while some questions may constitute non-hearsay, where the declarant intends the question to communicate an implied assertion and the proponent offers it for this intended message, the question falls within the definition of hearsay. * * * It is widely recognized that the grammatical form of a verbal utterance does not govern whether it fits within the definition of hearsay. * * * Because there may be instances where a party attempts to admit hearsay by cloaking statements under the guise of a question, the focus of the inquiry should be on what the declarant intended to say, whether implied or directly asserted. * * * Fernando's intent in asking for Torres's truck on three separate occasions in the span of a week and a half is apparent: Fernando wanted control of Torres's truck on the U.S.-side of the border. In other words, Fernando intended the implied assertion rather than the express one, and Torres offered the questions for this intended implied message to show it was Fernando who was calling the shots and who unknowingly set him up on the drug importation scheme." United States v. Torres, 794 F.3d 1053, 1059–61 (9th Cir.2015).

Example—Hearsay. "Here, although the record is ambiguous, it was not unreasonable for the district court to conclude—for purposes of Rule 801—that the government met its burden in showing that Pulliam's 'what gun' remark was a statement. This remark was coupled with a statement of denial: 'I don't know what you're talking about, and I didn't throw a gun in the bushes.' In this context, it is unlikely that Pulliam was genuinely curious as to which specific gun the officers were questioning him about. As the district court noted, Pulliam's remark seems more like a rhetorical question 'equivalent to saying: I don't know what you're talking about.' And since 'what gun,' in context, reads as a substantive assertion meant to deny knowledge rather than a question meant to elicit a response, the district court did not abuse its discretion in excluding this statement as inadmissible hearsay." United States v. Pulliam, 973 F.3d 775, 783–84 (7th Cir.2020).

(3) Nonhearsay statements. An out-of-court statement is not inadmissible as hearsay if it has relevancy apart from the truth of the matter that it asserts or implies. If the making of the statement is in itself relevant, evidence that the statement was made is not barred by the hearsay rule.

Example—Admissible. A statement offered to show the reason for an investigation. United States v. Woods, 684 F.3d 1045, 1062 (11th Cir.2012) ("[T]his testimony was not introduced to prove the truth of the matter asserted, i.e., that the images found on Woods's computer matched images of known child pornography. * * * Rather, the testimony explained how the government selected which images recovered from Woods's computers to subject to in-depth analysis."); Suggs v. Stanley, 324 F.3d 672, 681–82 (8th Cir.2003) ("The district court also instructed the jury that the statements were to be used only to show why the officer went to Gilbert's house, not to prove that anything stated by the dispatcher or the caller were true."); United States v. Aguwa, 123 F.3d 418, 421 (6th Cir.1997); United States v. Mejia, 909 F.2d 242, 247 (7th Cir.1990) ("Evidence about the tip the DEA received was relevant to show something other than the tip's truth. That evidence was relevant to show why the DEA was watching Mejia's home, a fact that in no way depended upon the tip's truth.").

Example—Inadmissible. "In this case, the 'background' evidence offered by Detective Hamilton was entirely unnecessary to explain the context of the police investigation of Hinson. The reason the police focused their investigation on Hinson was perfectly clear: After arresting Pingry, he told the police that Hinson was his supplier. The government offered ample admissible evidence to show that this conversation took place, and Detective Nicholson's testimony that she had heard that someone named 'Kevin' was Pingry's supplier was, therefore, completely unnecessary to explain the police's subsequent actions. Where the government introduces evidence that bears on the ultimate issue in a case but that is not necessary to explain the background of a police investigation, the only reasonable conclusion we can reach is that the evidence was offered, not as background, but as support for the government's case against the defendant. * * * That purpose is impermissible, and this evidence should not have been admitted." United States v. Hinson, 585 F.3d 1328, 1337 (10th Cir.2009).

Example—Admissible. Informer's side of taped conversation with accused, necessary to place accused's admissions in context and make them intelligible, "were offered only for context and not for the truth of the matter asserted, [and therefore] are not hearsay under Federal Rule of Evidence 801(c)." United States v. Catano, 65 F.3d 219, 224–25 (1st Cir.1995). Accord, United States v. Jaffal, 79 F.4th 582, 598–99 (6th Cir.2023) (statements by defendant's girlfriend in recorded conversations with him and another person); United States v. Fernandez, 914 F.3d 1105, 111–12 (7th Cir.2019); United States v. Smith, 816 F.3d 479, 481 (7th Cir.2016).

Example—Admissible. A statement offered to show declarant's knowledge of facts, not the facts stated. Crowley v. L.L. Bean, Inc. 303 F.3d 387, 408 (1st Cir.2002) (reference by a supervisor to "Crowley's little stalker," when offered to show management's awareness of a co-worker's behavior, and not to show that the co-worker was actually a stalker, was not hearsay); Bennett v. Nucor Corp., 656 F.3d 802, 811 (8th Cir.2011) (district court properly allowed plaintiffs to question company spokesman about statements in a letter and a complaint alleging workplace discrimination after he denied knowledge of the documents' existence).

Example—Admissible. "Law enforcement officials discovered two notes when they searched the Okie Street warehouse. The first, addressed to 'Steve S,' specified different 'PPMs' (parts per million) of a certain additive that were to be used for 'Little guys,' 'Med guys,' and 'Big guys'; reminded the intended recipient to 'spray'; and instructed him to 'get Bob F to wire up and help you set up.' The second note included the phrase 'when SJ's back' and instructed the intended recipient to 'clean tanks,' 'spray' and 'rap [sic] water pipes.' Defendants argue that the trial court should have excluded the notes because they contained inadmissible hearsay. The short answer to this argument is that the defendants are simply wrong. The notes do not contain any hearsay statements. Instead, they are instructions from one participant in the conspiracy to another concerning the care and feeding of marijuana plants. Documents of this sort are obviously relevant regardless of whether the instructions they contain were ever followed." United States v. Balthazard, 360 F.3d 309, 318 (1st Cir.2004).

Example—Admissible. "Joseph's testimony as to the allegation made by the social workers was offered to explain why Joseph suspended Garner and started an investigation, not to prove the truth of the social workers' allegation that Garner received a patient's Social Security check. Joseph's testimony that she considered the findings of the investigation in deciding to terminate Garner was relevant to refute Garner's claim that the failure to terminate white employees who bought items from patients was proof of disparate treatment reflecting race discrimination and retaliation. * * * Evidence demonstrating the employer's state of mind is 'of crucial importance in wrongful discharge cases.' " Garner v. Missouri Dep't of Mental Health, 439 F.3d 958, 960 (8th Cir.2006).

Example—Admissible. "Included in the government's evidence was a photograph depicting the Pontiac Parisienne automobile that was payment for the murder-for-hire and two photographs of Hyles and Cannon posing together. The three photographs were found in Cannon's jail property and have writing on the back associating Hyles and Cannon. On the back of the picture of the Pontiac was written 'Da-Pony G' "Ride." ' The two pictures of Hyles and Cannon had ' "2" of Da Most Wanted' and ' "Bo" Playa's 2-Da-Casket' written on the back, respectively. The government offered the photographs and the writing on the back as evidence of the importance of the Pontiac to Cannon, and to show Hyles's association with Cannon in the conspiracy case. * * * Regarding Hyles's hearsay argument, we agree with the government that the writings on the pictures are not hearsay. * * * The writings were not offered to prove that Hyles was a 'Boss Playa' or one of the 'Most Wanted.' There is no suggestion that the jury was told what these phrases mean. Indeed, it is the fact that there is writing on the back of these pictures and that Hyles and Cannon found the pictures important enough to write on that makes them important; what exactly was written on them does not matter." United States v. Hyles, 479 F.3d 958, 969 (8th Cir.2007).

Example—Admissible. In prosecution for mortgage fraud scheme, "sale records were admissible, not to prove that the purchase prices reflected the true value of the properties, but for the limited purpose of showing that these prices were lower than those listed on the mortgage loan applications. Accordingly, they were not within the scope of the hearsay rule." United States v. Appolon, 695 F.3d 44, 62 (1st Cir.2012).

Example—Admissible. "The government was not trying to figure out whether it was true that the particular patient whose name Diaz wrote had visited the clinic sixteen out of twenty times. The witnesses were simply explaining what the notes were talking about, not whether they were accurate. If it turned out the notes were wrong—say, if a patient had only been to the clinics six times, not sixteen—that wouldn't have contradicted any testimony or government argument. Simply put, the government didn't care whether it was true that a patient went there sixteen times." United States v. Chavez, 951 F.3d 349, 358–59 (6th Cir.2020).

If the statement has no relevancy apart from its truth, however, it is hearsay.

Example—Inadmissible. "In the instant case, however, the government's espoused reason for introducing the testimony—to explain why Detective Pomerleau drove by Meserve's house on the evening of the robbery—is completely irrelevant to the government's case. * * * In light of the government's baldly pretextual basis for the introduction of Craig's out-of-court statement, this court is not prepared to say that the statement is admissible non-hearsay." United States v. Meserve, 271 F.3d 314, 320 (1st Cir.2001).

Example—Inadmissible. "Contrary to the Government's position, the police officers' testimony about the 911 call, in the context of this case, was effectively offered to prove the truth of the statements made, rather than to show background. This renders the statements hearsay under Federal Rule of Evidence 801(c)(2), and thereby inadmissible under Rule 802. It is true that background information that explains how law enforcement came to be involved might not be hearsay because it is offered not for the truth of the matter asserted, but rather to show why the officers acted as they did. In this case, however, the anonymous 911 caller's description was neither relevant nor material because the officers' background or state of mind were never at issue at Nelson's trial." United States v. Nelson, 725 F.3d 615, 620 (6th Cir.2013) (citation omitted).

    (4) Nonhearsay statements—Verbal acts. One common type of nonhearsay statement is usually referred to as a "verbal act" or "operative fact": a statement the making of which has substantive legal significance.

Example. The words that constitute the offer, acceptance, or terms of a contract. Crawford v. Tribeca Lending Corp., 815 F.3d 121, 125–26 (2d Cir.2016); West Coast Truck Lines, Inc. v. Arcata Community Recycling, Inc., 846 F.2d 1239, 1246 n. 5 (9th Cir.1988).

Example. A certificate of insurance issued by the FDIC, as evidence of "the fact of the legal relationship of insurer and insured." United States v. Bellucci, 995 F.2d 157, 161 (9th Cir.1993).

Example. A certificate of consent executed pursuant to a statute by the government of Panama, to prove that Panama had consented to the search of a Panamanian vessel by U.S. officials. United States v. Rojas, 53 F.3d 1212, 1216 (11th Cir.1995).

Example. Words that operate as a conveyance. Hanson v. Johnson, 161 Minn. 229, 201 N.W. 322 (1924) (words constituting a partition of crops between landlord and tenant farmer).

Example. Tape recorded conversations of illegal gambling. United States v. Boyd, 566 F.2d 929, 937 (5th Cir.1978).

Example. Ballots, to show the votes cast. Local 512, Warehouse & Office Workers' Union v. N.L.R.B., 795 F.2d 705, 713 n. 4 (9th Cir.1986).

Example. Threats, in a prosecution for threatening court officers. United States v. Jones, 663 F.2d 567, 571 (5th Cir.1981).

Example. Inquiry for a murder for hire. United States v. Childs, 539 F.3d 552, 559 (6th Cir.2008).

Example. Money orders. United States v. Davis, 596 F.3d 852, 856–57 (D.C.Cir.2010) ("They are legally operative documents with a meaning independent of the truth of the words they display.

* * * As 'verbal acts', their significance 'lies solely in the fact that [they were] made, [so] no issue is raised as to the truth of anything asserted.' ").

Example. Credit union vice president's instruction to auditor to remove a particular loan from the audit report. Michigan First Credit Union v. Cumis Ins. Soc., Inc., 641 F.3d 240, 251 (6th Cir.2011).

Example. "These files were not introduced for the purpose of establishing the truth of the assertions contained therein, but rather, as instrumentalities of the crimes in question. To the extent that the government relied on any representations contained within these documents, the representations' probative value was not for their truth. Indeed, the government sought to admit them for a wholly different purpose—'to prove that the statements were made,' and to later demonstrate 'through other admissible evidence[ ] that [the statements] were false.' Consequently, they are not hearsay." United States v. Appolon, 715 F.3d 362, 372 (1st Cir.2013).

(5) Nonhearsay statements—Verbal parts of acts. A closely related category of nonhearsay utterance is often called "verbal parts of acts." In this category, the utterance establishes the legal character of an act that it accompanies.

Example. The words that accompany the delivery of money or property may establish a gift, a loan, a bribe, a bet, or payment of a debt. McCormick, Evidence § 249 (7th ed. 2013).

Example. Declarations by an occupant of land, offered to show that the possession was adverse. Sanders v. Worthington, 382 S.W.2d 910, 916 (Tex.1964).

(6) Nonhearsay statements—To show effect on state of mind of listener or reader. Another common type of nonhearsay utterance is a statement that is offered to show the effect on one who heard or read the statement.

Example. In a prosecution of a man for murder of his wife, it was error to exclude the defendant's offered testimony that a woman had told him shortly before the homicide that his wife had had sexual relations with two other men. McClure v. State, 575 S.W.2d 564 (Tex.Crim.App.1979).

Example. Words that establish notice or knowledge, where notice or knowledge of a person is relevant. Smedra v. Stanek, 187 F.2d 892 (10th Cir.1951) (testimony "that Dr. Stanek had been told by someone in the operating room that the sponge count did not come out right"); Player v. Thompson, 259 S.C. 600, 193 S.E.2d 531 (1972) (testimony that motor vehicle inspector told defendants prior to accident that car's tires were unsafe).

Example. Statements that tend to establish that a party acted in good or bad faith. Bush v. Dictaphone Corp., 161 F.3d 363, 366–67 (6th Cir.1998) (statements to management by employees supervised by age-discrimination plaintiff that he was abusive or unstable, offered to show reasons other than age for plaintiff's demotion and termination); United States v. Mays, 69 F.3d 116, 120–21 (6th Cir.1995) (prosecution for fraudulently selling orange juice as "pure" with knowledge that it was adulterated with sugar; proper to admit as nonhearsay scientific test reports by customers showing sugar, which were presented to defendants, who continued to sell the product without change); United States v. Rubin, 591 F.2d 278, 283 (5th Cir.1979) (in prosecution of union official for embezzlement by taking unauthorized salary increases, error to exclude his testimony that union presidents told him that the union constitution was to be interpreted flexibly, not strictly); Moore v. Sears, Roebuck & Co., 683 F.2d 1321 (11th Cir.1982) (records by Moore's supervisor as to Moore's conduct not hearsay when not offered to prove the conduct but to show Sears in good faith fired Moore for reason other than age).

Example. "Johnson is correct that the district court erred in excluding George Qua's statement. * * * Johnson testified that he used one of his Buicks 'sparingly' because he 'knew it was going to be worth a lot of money.' And when Johnson's counsel asked him for the basis of his belief, he cited his conversation with Qua. The court excluded this evidence as hearsay. But we agree with Johnson that Qua's statement was offered not to show that the car was actually 'the last big Buick off the assembly line,' or even that it was in fact worth the amount Johnson claimed. Instead, it was offered to establish the basis for Johnson's belief about the value of his car. The court should have admitted this statement with a limiting instruction to the jury regarding its proper scope." United States v. Johnson, 79 F.4th 684, 700–01 (6th Cir.2023).

Example. After Costello, a Government witness, was impeached with contradictory statements he made to an investigator, he testified on redirect that the reason he made the contradictory statements was "that an individual, Bob Daldeegan, had approached him and told him that if he testified against LaBue his job would remain safe." Daldeegan's statement was not hearsay; it was not offered for its truth, but to show why Costello made the contradictory statements. United States v. Marshall, 75 F.3d 1097, 1113 (7th Cir.1996).

Example. "Officer LaFave also testified that the information reported to dispatch included the name of Thomas Davis, a description of the car, the license plate number BEW 7533, and that Davis had been seen with a gun. In addition, Officer LaFave confirmed that the information was broadcast over the police radio, and that 'if someone had a police scanner [and was listening], they would have heard that information.' This testimony, read in context, fairly precisely provides an explanation of what Defendant subsequently did and said that afternoon: midway through his ride in and around the neighborhood, Defendant entered and soon emerged from a house saying that 'somebody called the boys on us.' A short while later, Defendant announced his plan to exchange the Chevy Cobalt for another. A logical inference is that Defendant had access to a police scanner—perhaps in the house he visited—and came to know that local officers thought he had a gun and were actively searching for him in a particular car. The woman's statement [to dispatch] was not offered to prove the truth of its content. It explained (perhaps only incidentally) what the officer did and, more importantly, it established a foundation for the evidence about the visit to the house that would demonstrate Defendant's actions and culpable state of mind. In short, the jury was properly invited to focus on Defendant's reaction to the statement, not the 'truth' of its substance." United States v. Davis, 577 F.3d 660, 667 (6th Cir.2009).

Example. "Bady argues the district court erred in permitting Sergeant Peter to testify a paramedic told Sergeant Peter that Bady had assaulted a firefighter. * * * The district court determined the challenged paramedic's statement was admissible because the officers did not offer it to establish Bady had assaulted a firefighter, but 'to establish the totality of the circumstances relevant to determining whether the force used in seizing Bady was objectively reasonable.' Indeed, Bady acknowledges the truth at issue in this case is 'not whether Bady had actually assaulted a firefighter,' but 'whether the statement was made at all.' Offered for that purpose, the contested statement is not hearsay and the district court did not err in admitting it." Bady v. Murphy-Kjos, 628 F.3d 1000, 1002–03 (8th Cir.2011).

Example. "[T]he defendants were offering the testimony about Bowling's alleged statements not to prove that a stated-income loan does permit what Bowling told them it did, but to explain what they had heard him tell them (and that they believed what he told them) when they made the application. It is not hearsay * * *. The defendants wanted to testify not that Bowling had told them the truth but that his lies, undetected by them, had made them misunderstand the meaning of 'borrower's income' in an application for a stated-income loan." United States v. Phillips, 731 F.3d 649, 653 (7th Cir.2013).

Example. "A witness's statement is not hearsay if the witness is reporting what someone told the witness and what the witness thought she meant, and that statement is offered as an explanation of what the witness was thinking at the time or what motivated him to do something. In this context, the out-of-court statement is not being offered as evidence that its contents are true." United States v. Leonard-Allen, 724 F.3d 780, 785 (7th Cir.2013).

Example. " 'The victim's fearful state of mind is a crucial element in proving extortion. The testimony of victims as to what others said to them, and the testimony of others as to what they said to victims is admitted not for the truth of the information in the statements but for the fact that the victim heard them and that they would have tended to produce fear in his mind.' Because such fear-illustrating statements also often refer to acts of the defendant, courts should, upon request, instruct the jury that such statements may only be used as evidence of fear, not evidence of the defendant's acts. * * * Such 'fear' evidence in extortion cases is similar to, but distinguishable from, evidence admissible under the hearsay exception at Federal Rule of

Evidence 803(3). Rule 803(3) allows witnesses to recount hearsay statements (that is, statements offered to prove the truth of the statements' factual content) when the statement's original declarant is expressing his or her then-existing state of mind. * * * The difference is this: when the out-of-court statement is an expression of fear being offered to prove the existence of the fear expressed in the statement, this is a hearsay statement that may be admissible under Rule 803(3). When, however, the statement is not the victim/declarant's expression of his or her own fear, but a statement made to (or in the presence of) the victim by someone else that would tend to be a fear-inducing statement, such evidence is not hearsay." United States v. Kilpatrick, 798 F.3d 365, 386 (6th Cir.2015) (citations omitted).

Example. "Here, borrower complaints about illegal practices by Moseley's business served to put Moseley on notice of their potential illegality. That he continued to operate his business despite this notice makes the complaints probative of his intent to violate the law." United States v. Moseley, 980 F.3d 9, 27 (2d Cir.2020).

(7) Nonhearsay statements—Machine generated data. Raw data generated by machines are not normally "statements" subject to the hearsay rule or the Confrontation Clause. United States v. Lizarraga-Tirado, 789 F.3d 1107, 1109–10 (9th Cir.2015); United States v. Lamons, 532 F.3d 1251, 1264 (11th Cir.2008).

Example—Admissible. "In the case before us, the 'statements' in question are alleged to be the assertions that Washington's blood sample contained PCP and alcohol. But those statements were never made by the technicians who tested the blood. The most the technicians could have said was that the printed data from their chromatograph machines showed that the blood contained PCP and alcohol. The machine printout is the only source of the statement, and no person viewed a blood sample and concluded that it contained PCP and alcohol. Yet, the very same data that would have permitted the lab technicians to say that the blood contained PCP and alcohol were also seen and interpreted by Dr. Levine. Moreover, those data were the only basis upon which Dr. Levine stated in court that the blood sample contained PCP and alcohol. In short, the inculpating 'statement'—that Washington's blood sample contained PCP and alcohol—was made by the machine on printed sheets, which were given to Dr. Levine. The technicians could neither have affirmed or denied independently that the blood contained PCP and alcohol because all the technicians could do was to refer to the raw data printed out by the machine. Thus, the statements to which Dr. Levine testified in court—the blood sample contained PCP and alcohol—did not come from the out-of-court technicians, and so there was no violation of the Confrontation Clause." United States v. Washington, 498 F.3d 225, 230 (4th Cir.2007).

Example—Inadmissible. "Machine-generated records usually do not qualify as 'statements' for hearsay purposes but can become hearsay when developed with human input. In United States v. Morrissey, we determined that a spreadsheet similar to the reports at issue here was hearsay. 895 F.3d 541, 547, 554 (8th Cir.2018). The spreadsheet indicated which files the testifying officer believed to be child pornography and which files NCMEC had previously identified as child pornography. * * * Like in Morrissey, the computer-generated reports offered against Juhic contained inadmissible hearsay. The 'child-notable' and 'series' notations are out-of-court statements offered for the truth of the matter asserted: that the videos and images were child pornography. While the reports may have been computer-generated, human statements and determinations were used to classify the files as child pornography. It was only after a human determined that a file contained child pornography that the hash value or series information was inserted into the computer program and automatically noted in future reports. The human involvement in this otherwise automated process makes the notations hearsay." United States v. Juhic, 954 F.3d 1084, 1089 (8th Cir.2020).

CROSS-REFERENCES

Common Objections (Chapter 3)

Treatises

6 Graham, Handbook of Federal Evidence §§ 801:1–801:10 (9th ed. 2020)

2 McCormick, Evidence §§ 246, 248–250 (8th ed. 2020)

30B Wright & Bellin, Federal Practice and Procedure §§ 6701–6729 (2018)

Rule 801(d)(1).   A Declarant-Witness's Prior Statement

* * *

(d) Statements That Are Not Hearsay. A statement that meets the following conditions is not hearsay:

    (1) *A Declarant-Witness's Prior Statement.* The declarant testifies and is subject to cross-examination about a prior statement, and the statement:

        (A) is inconsistent with the declarant's testimony and was given under penalty of perjury at a trial, hearing, or other proceeding or in a deposition;

        (B) is consistent with the declarant's testimony and is offered:

            (i) to rebut an express or implied charge that the declarant recently fabricated it or acted from a recent improper influence or motive in so testifying; or

            (ii) to rehabilitate the declarant's credibility as a witness when attacked on another ground; or

        (C) identifies a person as someone the declarant perceived earlier.

* * *

AUTHORS' COMMENTS

    (1) Prior statements by witnesses—In general. At common law, a prior statement by a witness normally was regarded as hearsay, inadmissible to prove its truth, unless it happened to fall within some hearsay exception. Prior statements were generally admissible, under certain conditions, only for the limited purposes of impeachment or rehabilitation. Under Rule 801(d)(1), some, but by no means all, prior statements by a witness are accorded full substantive admissibility.

    (2) Prior inconsistent statements. Rule 801(d)(1)(A) accords substantive admissibility only to certain prior testimonial inconsistent statements. A prior inconsistent statement that does not qualify as substantive evidence under Rule 801(d)(1)(A) is hearsay. Such a statement may be admissible for impeachment, subject to the requirements of Rule 613, but a limiting instruction must be given upon request, "to explain to the jury that the impeachment evidence is only to reflect on the witness' credibility and is not to be used to establish facts." United States v. Miller, 664 F.2d 94, 97–98 (5th Cir.1981).

    "In applying Rule 801(d)(1)(A), 'inconsistency is not limited to diametrically opposed answers but may be found in evasive answers, inability to recall, silence, or changes of position.' " United States v. Matlock, 109 F.3d 1313, 1319 (8th Cir.1997).

    Example—Admissible. "McDowell's mother Donia * * * made statements in her testimony before the grand jury that implicated McDowell, Cooper, Harris, and Presley in drug-trafficking activities. At trial, however, Donia claimed that, while she remembered testifying before the grand jury, she did not remember making the incriminating statements and did not know about the group's alleged illicit activities. * * * She therefore made statements during her testimony at trial that were inconsistent with her admissions before the grand jury. * * * The rule is designed for situations like the one the prosecutors faced in this case." United States v. Cooper, 767 F.3d 721, 729 (7th Cir.2014).

    A party may not call a witness for the primary purpose of impeaching the witness with prior statements that would be otherwise inadmissible. United States v. Hogan, 763 F.2d 697, 702 (5th Cir.1985); United States v. Webster, 734 F.2d 1191, 1192 (7th Cir.1984).

Occasionally courts have admitted prior inconsistent statements not qualifying under Rule 801(d)(1)(A) as substantive evidence using Rule 803(24). United States v. Valdez-Soto, 31 F.3d 1467, 1470–73 (9th Cir.1994).

(3) Prior inconsistent statements—"Other proceeding." The term "other proceeding" in Rule 801(d)(1)(A) includes grand jury. United States v. Distler, 671 F.2d 954, 958–59 (6th Cir.1981). It does not extend to "station house" interrogations by investigating law enforcement officers, even if the statement is written and sworn. United States v. Day, 789 F.2d 1217, 1222–23 (6th Cir.1986).

Example—Admissible. When defendant's coconspirator who had pled guilty testified, he disputed the contents of his "factual basis" in the plea agreement documents. The factual basis was properly used as substantive evidence under Rule 801(d)(1)(A). United States v. McClaren, 13 F.4th 386, 415 (5th Cir.2021).

(4) Prior consistent statements—In general. Normally a witness may not be corroborated by proof of prior statements consistent with the witness's testimony. United States v. Williams, 573 F.2d 284, 289 (5th Cir.1978); United States v. Weil, 561 F.2d 1109, 1111 (4th Cir.1977). Rule 801(d)(1)(B)(i) permits, and accords nonhearsay status to, a prior statement by a witness that is consistent with the witness's testimony and that is offered to rebut an express or implied charge against him of recent fabrication or improper influence or motive.

Example—Admissible. "On cross-examination of Price, Reliford's attorney challenged the witness's recollection of events: 'Mr. Price, your memory gets better with time, doesn't it?' On redirect, the court granted the Government's motion to admit written statements Price had given to police [shortly after the crime]. The prior written statements were consistent with Price's testimony on the stand recounting the sequence of events at the carjacking. * * * It was proper for the court to admit the witness's prior consistent statements after the defense attorney had challenged his recollection." United States v. Reliford, 58 F.3d 247, 249–50 (6th Cir.1995).

Example—Admissible. "Stone's position * * * was that appellants created the claim of the pre-existing oral contract only after incurring the loss of their investment through the collapse of the magazine, and this theme was stressed throughout his cross-examinations and arguments. Ambrosini had no motive to falsify at the time he prepared the excluded documents: such a motive to falsify would arise only when California Business News failed, and all of the contested documents were prepared prior to that time." Phoenix Associates III v. Stone, 60 F.3d 95, 104 (2d Cir.1995).

Example—Admissible. "Conroy attempted to impeach Tail as to her testimony about whether the porch light was on, the number of adults at home, her missing clothes, and an encounter with Conroy at Slow Bear's home. Following cross-examination, the government attempted to rehabilitate Tail with prior consistent statements regarding her desire to end her relationship with Conroy. * * * While the statements admitted to rehabilitate Tail did not specifically relate to the subject matter of the statements impeached by Conroy, it is not an abuse of discretion for a district court to admit prior consistent statements 'relevant to any other portion made the subject of cross-examination,' * * * when doing so is 'necessary to show the seriousness of the claimed inconsistencies,' as a result of 'serious efforts ha[ving] been made to show recent fabrication or improper motive.'" United States v. Conroy, 424 F.3d 833, 839–840 (8th Cir.2005).

Example—Admissible. "In this case, the declarants, Chi and Lian, both testified at trial and were subject to cross examination. Liu challenged the credibility of Lian and Chi by presenting evidence that the women had received financial assistance from the FBI. Liu implied Lian and Chi fabricated their testimony in order to receive financial assistance from the FBI. Agent Barry, the proponent, testified about the content of Lian and Chi's statements before the FBI began providing them with financial assistance. Lian and Chi's statements, as presented by Agent Barry, were largely consistent with their in-court testimony. Accordingly, all four elements are satisfied by Agent Barry's testimony. Rather than reversible error, this is a textbook example of when to apply Federal Rule of Evidence 801(d)(1)(B), and we conclude the district court did not abuse its discretion when it permitted Agent Barry to testify about Lian and Chi's prior consistent statements." United States v. Chang Da Liu, 538 F.3d 1078, 1086 (9th Cir.2008).

Example—Admissible. "Bonin also argues the district court erred by admitting the text messages sent from the theater by witness Patrick Alfich. * * * In the government's rebuttal case, Alfich testified regarding text messages he sent immediately after witnessing Bonin's outbursts. The statements contained in those text messages were admitted as prior consistent statements under Fed. R. Evid. 801(d)(1)(B). * * * Bonin's testimony on direct and cross-examination directly contradicted Alfich and implied that Alfich's testimony about Bonin's false statements, threats, and behavior was fictional." United States v. Bonin, 932 F.3d 523, 542 (7th Cir.2019).

Example—Inadmissible. "[W]e consider the degree of fit between the putative prior consistent statement and the charge of fabrication that it is offered to rebut. * * * Did the government make an express or implied charge that Chiu recently fabricated the claim that Anderson had occasionally possessed Chiu's computer and passwords? * * * The record shows that the government certainly challenged Chiu's credibility broadly, as well as his claim that someone else had downloaded the images to his computer without his knowledge. But the government never bothered to contest the predicate yet separate claim that Anderson could occasionally access the computer and passwords. * * * And the government's distinction between these claims makes sense in light of its theory at trial. In proving that Chiu possessed the material, the government did not rely on his exclusive ability to access his computer. Rather, it pointed to evidence that someone had actually accessed the pornographic files nearly contemporaneously with actual access of Chiu's work files." United States v. Chiu, 36 F.4th 294, 300–01 (1st Cir.2022), cert. denied, 143 S.Ct. 336 (2022).

The rule altered the common law only insofar as it grants substantive status; it does not change the circumstances in which a prior consistent statement is permitted or forbidden. Tome v. United States, 513 U.S. 150, 115 S.Ct. 696 (1995); United States v. Quinto, 582 F.2d 224, 233–34 (2d Cir.1978).

(5) Prior consistent statements—Prior statement must antedate improper influence or motive to fabricate. To be admissible under Rule 801(d)(1)(B)(i), the consistent statement must have been made before the alleged improper influence or the attachment of the alleged motive to fabricate. Tome v. United States, 513 U.S. 150, 115 S.Ct. 696 (1995); United States v. Portillo, 969 F.3d 144, 173–74 (5th Cir.2020), cert. denied, 141 S.Ct. 1275 (2021); United States v. Awon, 135 F.3d 96, 100 (1st Cir.1998) (improper to admit prior consistent statements of prosecution witnesses; "The motive to fabricate alleged by the defense—desire for leniency—was the same when the Neves brothers first spoke with police as at the time of their testimony at trial."). Compare, e.g., United States v. Anderson, 303 F.3d 847, 859 (7th Cir.2002) ("The defense counsel's theory was that the coconspirators communicated with each other after their arrests while they were incarcerated in proximity to each other, and that they decided to frame Anderson to reduce their own sentences. The post-arrest statements by those witnesses implicating Anderson, taken before any opportunity to consult arose, were thus admissible to refute the claim that they decided to falsely implicate him later."); United States v. Prieto, 232 F.3d 816, 819–21 (11th Cir.2000) ("In [*Awon*] the court held that two brothers' statements were equally contaminated by a motive to fabricate when they first spoke with police as when they subsequently testified at trial. In that case, however, both brothers testified that they spoke with investigators only after the potential benefits of cooperation had already been discussed. * * * Here, the trial judge found that Palacios made his statements before any discussion of cooperation. * * * [W]hether a witness had a motive to fabricate when a prior consistent statement was made is a factual question properly decided by the district court and subject to reversal only for a clear abuse of discretion.").

"A prior consistent statement need not rebut all motives to fabricate, but only the specific motive alleged at trial." United States v. Wilson, 355 F.3d 358, 361–62 (5th Cir.2003) ("Even though Osborne may have also had a motive to fabricate when he wrote the letter, * * * the motive to write the letter was different than the motive to fabricate arising from his plea bargains charged at trial."). Accord, United States v. Kootswatewa, 893 F.3d 1127, 1135 (9th Cir.2018).

(6) Prior consistent statements—2014 addition of Rule 801(d)(1)(B)(ii). "The intent of the amendment is to extend substantive effect to consistent statements that rebut other attacks on a witness—such as the charges of inconsistency or faulty memory. * * * It does not allow impermissible bolstering of a witness. * * * The amendment does not make any consistent statement admissible that was not admissible previously—the only difference is that prior consistent statements otherwise admissible for rehabilitation are now admissible substantively as well." Advisory Committee's Note.

Example—Admissible. "During cross examination, Child 3 told defense counsel that he did not recall the events of that night until he was shown photographs. On redirect examination however, Child 3 clarified that he recalled the events prior to being shown any photographs. Subsequently, Kruithoff testified that, prior to Kruithoff showing Child 3 the images, Child 3 informed Kruithoff that he was aware of the fact that nude photographs of him were taken. * * * Previously, a prior consistent statement could only be admitted for the truth of the matter asserted to rebut a charge of recent fabrication. However, in 2014, subparagraph (B) was split into two clauses, including the new clause (ii), which allows prior consistent statements to be admitted for the truth of the matter asserted if offered 'to rehabilitate the declarant's credibility as a witness when attacked on another ground.' 'The intent of the amendment is to extend substantive effect to consistent statements that rebut other attacks on a witness—such as the charges of inconsistency or faulty memory.' (Advisory Committee's Note to 2014 Amendment). Defendant certainly attacked Child 3 on the basis of a faulty memory * * *. Child 3's statement to Kruithoff was a consistent statement that rebutted Defendant's attack on Child 3's purportedly faulty memory, and therefore, the district court's admission of the testimony was proper." United States v. Cox, 871 F.3d 479, 487 (6th Cir.2017) (citations omitted).

Example—Inadmissible. "We do not agree that the Romo brothers' statements were admissible under 801(d)(1)(B)(ii). The government cites several instances where the defendants identified inconsistencies between the brothers' earlier statements and their testimony at trial. * * * In all cases, however, these inconsistencies were identified by the defendants in order to make a broader point: that the brothers subsequently changed their stories in order to get favorable deals from the government. * * * Put differently, the defendants accused the Romo brothers of inconsistency only to support their claim that the brothers fabricated their stories—a motive that fits squarely within 801(d)(1)(B)(i), and not the alternative 801(d)(1)(B)(ii). * * * Here, the plain language of 801(d)(1)(B)(ii) precludes the admission of the prior consistent statements under these circumstances because the defendants did not attack the Romo brothers on 'another ground.' " United States v. Portillo, 969 F.3d 144, 173–74 (5th Cir.2020), cert. denied, 141 S.Ct. 1275 (2021).

Example—Admissible. "In contrast to the Romo brothers' statements, the government identifies at least one portion of Portillo's cross examination of Merla where Portillo questioned Merla's memory of the events surrounding Robert Lara's killing. * * * Portillo's attack on Merla's memory was sufficient to justify the admission of his prior consistent statement under Rule 801(d)(1)(B)(ii)." United States v. Portillo, 969 F.3d 144, 176 (5th Cir.2020), cert. denied, 141 S.Ct. 1275 (2021).

Example—Admissible. "In its cross-examination of Wood, defense counsel highlighted the aspects of Wood's 2012 statements to the State College police that seemed most inconsistent with her trial testimony. By introducing Royer's testimony, which recounted Wood's statements to police in full and largely matched the version of events that Wood had recounted at trial, the government plainly sought to rebut the charge of inconsistency and to rehabilitate Wood's credibility by placing the alleged discrepancies in context. Royer's testimony concerning Wood's 2012 statements may be fairly interpreted as statements that were 'consistent with [Wood's] testimony and [were] offered' 'to rehabilitate [Wood's] credibility as a witness when attacked on a[ ] ground' other than recent fabrication or recent improper influence or motive." United States v. Purcell, 967 F.3d 159, 197 (2d Cir.2020).

(7) Prior identification of a person. Rule 801(d)(1)(C) permits showing that a witness identified a person, such as the accused in a criminal case, on a previous occasion. The previous identification may have been at a lineup, a "show-up" (a one-on-one viewing), from a photograph (such as a "photo lineup") or a sketch, at a previous hearing, or under any other circumstances. United States v. Lopez, 271 F.3d 472, 483–84 (3d Cir.2001) (witness, who recanted at trial, told officer that he had seen defendants near the scene on the night of the crime); United States v. Lewis, 565 F.2d 1248, 1251–52 (2d Cir.1977). There is no requirement that the witness first be impeached. 6 Graham, Handbook of Federal Evidence § 801:13 (8th ed. 2016).

The rule does not limit proof of the prior identification to testimony by the identifying witness; another witness who was present, such as a police officer, may testify to the previous identification. United States v. Brink, 39 F.3d 419, 426 (3d Cir.1994).

The prior identification need not be consistent with the witness's testimony. United States v. Lopez, 271 F.3d 472, 483–84 (3d Cir.2001) (witness denied having told officer that he had seen defendants near the scene on the night of the crime); United States v. Anglin, 169 F.3d 154, 159 (2d Cir.1999) (witness unable to identify defendant in court); United States v. Brink, 39 F.3d 419, 426 (3d Cir.1994) (bank teller identified defendant, whose eyes are light hazel, at trial and testified she was unable to remember robber's eye color; error to deny substantive evidence status to her description of robber as dark eyed to FBI agent the day after the robbery); United States v. O'Malley, 796 F.2d 891, 899 (7th Cir.1986) (witness acknowledged but repudiated prior identification); United States v. Jarrad, 754 F.2d 1451, 1456 (9th Cir.1985) (witness denied making previous identification); United States v. Lewis, 565 F.2d 1248, 1252 (2d Cir.1977) (witness pointed out deputy federal marshal in court rather than defendant).

The requirement that the witness be "subject to cross-examination about the statement" is not violated by the witness having, or purporting to have, no present recollection of the identity of the person. United States v. Owens, 484 U.S. 554, 561–63, 108 S.Ct. 838, 844 (1988).

(8) **Witness must be subject to cross-examination on prior statement.** It is a requirement of all subparts of Rule 801(d)(1) that the witness-declarant be subject to cross-examination concerning the prior statement. United States v. Torrez-Ortega, 184 F.3d 1128, 1131–32 (10th Cir.1999) (error to admit under Rule 801(d)(1)(A) grand jury testimony of witness who claimed self-incrimination and refused to testify despite grant of immunity); United States v. West, 670 F.2d 675, 686–87 (7th Cir.1982) (Rule 801(d)(1)(B)). This requirement is satisfied if the witness is available to be recalled for recross-examination. United States v. Piva, 870 F.2d 753, 758 (1st Cir.1989).

CROSS-REFERENCES

Common Objections (Chapter 3)

39. Hearsay

Treatises

6 Graham, Handbook of Federal Evidence §§ 801:11–801:14 (9th ed. 2020)

1 McCormick, Evidence §§ 34, 36, 47; 2 id. § 251 (8th ed. 2020)

30B Wright & Bellin, Federal Practice and Procedure §§ 6731–6764 (2018)

Rule 801(d)(2).   An Opposing Party's Statement

* * *

(d) **Statements That Are Not Hearsay.** A statement that meets the following conditions is not hearsay:

* * *

(2) *An Opposing Party's Statement.* The statement is offered against an opposing party and:

    (A) was made by the party in an individual or representative capacity;

    (B) is one the party manifested that it adopted or believed to be true;

    (C) was made by a person whom the party authorized to make a statement on the subject;

    (D) was made by the party's agent or employee on a matter within the scope of that relationship and while it existed; or

    (E) was made by the party's coconspirator during and in furtherance of the conspiracy.

The statement must be considered but does not by itself establish the declarant's authority under (C); the existence or scope of the relationship under (D); or the existence of the conspiracy or participation in it under (E).

* * *

AUTHORS' COMMENTS

    (1) Admissions and statements against interest distinguished. The exemption from the hearsay rule for party admissions should not be confused with the hearsay exception for statements against interest, Rule 804(b)(3). Unlike the declaration against interest, a statement by a party qualifies as an admission even if it was not against interest when made. United States v. Turner, 995 F.2d 1357, 1363 (6th Cir.1993); People of Territory of Guam v. Ojeda, 758 F.2d 403, 408 (9th Cir.1985). "[T]he statements need neither be incriminating, inculpatory, against interest, nor otherwise inherently damaging to the declarant's case." United States v. Reed, 227 F.3d 763, 770 (7th Cir.2000).

    (2) Admissions in opinion form. Rule 801(d)(2) places no restrictions on the admissibility of admissions based on any fact-opinion distinction. Russell v. United Parcel Service, Inc., 666 F.2d 1188, 1190 (8th Cir.1981). Rule 701, the opinion rule, applies only to "testimony."

    (3) First-hand knowledge not required. The first-hand knowledge requirement does not apply to party admissions. Lexington Ins. Co. v. Western Pennsylvania Hosp., 423 F.3d 318, 330 n. 7 (3d Cir.2005); United States v. Goins, 11 F.3d 441, 443 (4th Cir.1993); Mahlandt v. Wild Canid Survival & Research Center, Inc., 588 F.2d 626, 630–31 (8th Cir.1978).

    (4) Admissions by accused. In criminal cases, statements by an accused made prior to arrest are admissible against him as admissions. United States v. Matlock, 415 U.S. 164, 172 & n. 8, 94 S.Ct. 988, 994 & n. 8 (1974). It is not required that the accused knew that he was incriminating himself by making the statement. People of Territory of Guam v. Ojeda, 758 F.2d 403, 408 (9th Cir.1985). Statements by an accused made after arrest, to be admissible, must satisfy the requirements of the *Miranda* doctrine. Miranda v. Arizona, 384 U.S. 436, 86 S.Ct. 1602 (1966).

    (5) Adoptive admissions. Rule 801(d)(2)(B) covers so-called adoptive admissions, including admissions by silence or acquiescence.

        Example—Adoptive admission. "By reprinting the newspaper articles and distributing them to person with whom defendants were doing business, defendants unequivocally manifested their adoption of the inflated statements made in the newspaper articles." Wagstaff v. Protective Apparel Corp., 760 F.2d 1074, 1078 (10th Cir.1985).

        Example—Adoptive admission. "[W]here * * * the government has indicated in a sworn affidavit to a judicial officer that it believes particular statements are trustworthy, it may not sustain an objection to the subsequent introduction of those statements on grounds that they are hearsay." United States v. Morgan, 581 F.2d 933, 938 (D.C.Cir.1978). Accord, United States v. Warren, 42 F.3d 647, 655 (D.C.Cir.1994).

        Example—Adoptive admission. "When Monroe told Officer Dunston that he could get another rock of crack from 'my buddy,' Beckham immediately got up from his chair, walked over to a stash of crack that was packaged for distribution, and began to open it. By that action, Beckham indicated his endorsement of Monroe's statement." United States v. Beckham, 968 F.2d 47, 52 (D.C.Cir.1992).

        Example—Adoptive admission. "[D]efendant Lawal heard the questions he was being asked by Agent Hein, responded affirmatively and adopted the contents of Agent Hein's question, 'You knew it was China White heroin?' by replying, 'yes.' In a similar manner, Lawal's answers to Agent Hein's other questions were adoptive admissions." United States v. Jinadu, 98 F.3d 239, 245 (6th Cir.1996).

        Example—Adoptive admission. University president's acceptance of contents of grievance committee's report and his implementation of its recommendations without disclaimer served as adoption of the report. Pilgrim v. Trustees of Tufts College, 118 F.3d 864, 870 (1st Cir.1997).

        Example—Adoptive admission. "According to Tsachres's trial testimony, he never opened the envelope containing the PSG Appraisal. Nevertheless, * * * it is uncontradicted that Tsachres knowingly brought the PSG Appraisal to CPB and handed it to the chairman. At this point, Tsachres manifested an intent to adopt the PSG Appraisal. He went to the bank with the hope of inducing it to provide him with a loan. As part of this inducement, he provided CPB with the PSG Appraisal. Tsachres does not know whether CPB relied upon the PSG Appraisal before finalizing the loan three days later. But by providing the PSG Appraisal in a package of materials upon which he knew the bank might rely when deciding whether to make him the loan, he 'manifested an adoption or belief in the truth' of the PSG Appraisal." Transbay Auto Service, Inc. v. Chevron USA Inc., 807 F.3d 1113, 1121 (9th Cir.2015).

Example—Adoptive admission. "We begin by addressing Recio's challenge to the admission of the rap lyric posted on Facebook. * * * Recio did not use quotation marks, attribute the lyric to the artist, or provide other signals to indicate to his Facebook audience that someone else authored the words in his post. Nor did he include additional explanation, commentary, or criticism that could refute an inference that he adopted the lyric as his own words. * * * [T]he facts here were sufficient for a jury to infer that Recio adopted the rap lyric as his own statement." United States v. Recio, 884 F.3d 230, 234–35 (9th Cir.2018).

Example—Adoptive admission. "Here, Officer Barrios's red marks on Santos's annotated Form N-400 Application are nonhearsay under Rule 801(d)(2)(B) as an adopted statement by an opposing party. * * * Santos expressly adopted Officer Barrios's corrections in red ink on the Form N-400 by, at the end of the interview, signing Part 13 of the application, swearing or affirming under penalty of perjury that the annotated Form N-400 with those corrections was 'true and correct to the best of [his] knowledge and belief.' * * * Under the circumstances, Santos's adoption of Officer Barrios's corrections in red ink is unequivocal." United States v. Santos, 947 F.3d 711, 724 (11th Cir.2020), cert. denied, 141 S.Ct. 1048 (2021).

Example—Not adoptive admission. "Plaintiffs contend that Steve Winwood manifested his adoption of the entire article—including Davis's statement that *Gimme Some Lovin'* used *Ain't That a Lot of Loving*'s bass riff—by reproducing it on his website. But as the Supreme Court has noted, '[m]erely hosting a document on a Web site does not indicate that the hosting entity adopts the document as its own statement or exercises control over its content.' Janus Capital Grp., Inc. v. First Derivative Traders, 564 U.S. 135, 148 n.12, 131 S.Ct. 2296 (2011). * * * Although posting a statement on a webpage might imply one's general agreement with it, Rule 801(d)(2)(B) requires an actual 'manifest[ation]' of one's adoption of a statement or belief in it." Parker v. Winwood, 938 F.3d 833, 837–38 (6th Cir.2019).

Example—Admission by acquiescence or silence. "When an accusatory statement is made in the defendant's presence and hearing, and he understands and has an opportunity to deny it, the statement and his failure to deny are admissible against him." United States v. Moore, 522 F.2d 1068, 1075 (9th Cir.1975).

Example—Admission by acquiescence or silence. "[T]he mere failure to respond to a letter does not indicate an adoption unless it was reasonable under the circumstances for the sender to expect the recipient to respond and to correct erroneous assertions." Southern Stone Co., Inc. v. Singer, 665 F.2d 698, 702 (5th Cir.1982).

Example—Admission by acquiescence or silence. "[T]he court properly admitted Desaigoudar's out-of-court response—next question please—to an accusation in a press conference that the defendants were cooking the books. * * * [U]nder the circumstances, the natural response to such an accusation would be to address or deny it. It therefore [was] an adoptive admission." United States v. Henke, 222 F.3d 633, 642 (9th Cir.2000).

(6) Post-arrest silence. Post-arrest silence of an accused who has received the *Miranda* warnings may not be used against the accused. Doyle v. Ohio, 426 U.S. 610, 96 S.Ct. 2240 (1976). If the *Miranda* warnings have not been given, however, silence of an accused after arrest may be used if otherwise relevant and admissible. Fletcher v. Weir, 455 U.S. 603, 102 S.Ct. 1309 (1982). Prearrest silence not induced by government action may be used. Jenkins v. Anderson, 447 U.S. 231, 100 S.Ct. 2124 (1980).

(7) Authorized admissions; agent or servant admissions; "in-house" statements. Rules 801(d)(2)(C) and (D) include statements by the agent or servant to the principal or employer or to another agent or employee of the principal. Reid Bros. Logging Co. v. Ketchikan Pulp Co., 699 F.2d 1292, 1306–07 & n. 25 (9th Cir.1983); Mahlandt v. Wild Canid Survival & Research Center, Inc., 588 F.2d 626, 629–31 (8th Cir.1978); Kingsley v. Baker/Beech-Nut Corp., 546 F.2d 1136, 1141 (5th Cir.1977).

(8) Agent or servant admissions—Not limited to "speaking agents." Under Rule 801(d)(2)(D), so long as the agent's or servant's statement is made during the existence of the employment relationship and concerns a matter within the scope of the employment, it is admissible against the principal, even though the employee had no authority to speak for the principal. Corley v. Burger King Corp., 56 F.3d 709, 710 (5th Cir.1995); Nekolny v. Painter, 653 F.2d 1164, 1171–72 (7th Cir.1981). But see United States v. Riley, 621 F.3d 312, 338 (3d Cir.2010) ("[T]his rule requires that when making an admission on behalf of the defendant, the declarant be both authorized and acting within the scope of employment.").

The statement must, however, be made "while the relationship" and must concern "a matter within the scope of that relationship."

Example—Inadmissible. Statements made by an employee in his resignation letter were not admissible against the employer under Rule 801(d)(2)(D). Young v. James Green Management, Inc., 327 F.3d 616, 622–23 (7th Cir.2003). Accord, In re DePuy Orthopaedics, Incorporated, Pinnacle Hip Implant Product Liability Litigation, 888 F.3d 753, 786–87 (5th Cir.2018).

Example—Admissible. "The employee's station within the organization is not relevant to the Rule 801(d)(2) analysis. * * * The relevant inquiry is whether the employee's statement was made within the scope of employment. * * * Here, there is no question that Falco and Madden made the challenged statements within the scope of their employment. Both were department officials involved in personnel management, and the statements related to a possible personnel action against McDonough." McDonough v. City of Quincy, 452 F.3d 8, 21 (1st Cir.2006).

Example—Inadmissible. In age discrimination case, declarant Gillis' statements were not admitted under Rule 801(d)(2)(D) because nothing in witness Robbins' testimony supported the conclusion that "Gillis was speaking as an agent of BellSouth at the time he made these statements. * * * It is in reality nothing but the inadmissible opinion of Gillis." Rowell v. BellSouth Corp., 433 F.3d 794, 800 (11th Cir.2005).

Example—Admissible. "[Safety Officer] Kroner's report meets all of the Rule's criteria to be classified as non-hearsay. Undisputably, the report that was offered by Mister against his employer Metra, was prepared in the usual course of business, by Metra's Safety Officer (the agent) investigating Mister's work accident. Rule 801(d)(2)(D) does not require anything else along the lines of internal verification of the report's contents. * * * Accordingly, we believe that the district court erred in this finding and that Kroner's report does fall within the confines of Rule 801(d)(2)(D)." Mister v. Northeast Ill. Commuter R.R. Corp., 571 F.3d 696, 698–99 (7th Cir.2009).

Example—Admissible. "As Director of the Office of Security, it is undisputed that Flannery was empowered to speak on the subject of promotions within the Office and was involved generally in the promotion process. * * * Regardless of whether or not Talavera has shown that Flannery was personally involved in the June 2004 promotion, and regardless of exactly when the statements were made, they are directly relevant to the question of whether impermissible gender discrimination may have played a part in Streufert's promotion decision." Talavera v. Shah, 638 F.3d 303, 310 (D.C.Cir.2011).

Example—Admissible. "[A] statement may concern a matter within the scope of employment—even though the declarant is no longer involved with that particular matter when the statement is made—so long as the declarant was involved with that matter at some prior point in his or her employment. Additionally, a matter may fall within the scope of a declarant's employment even though the declarant did not have final decision-making authority on that matter." Weil v. Citizens Telecon Services Co., LLC, 922 F.3d 993, 999 (9th Cir.2019).

(9) Agent or servant admissions—Preliminary questions of fact. If an issue is presented whether the declarant was in fact an agent or employee of the party against whom the statement is offered, or whether the statement concerned a matter within the scope of the agency or employment, the issue is for the court under Rule 104(a), with proponent having the burden of proof. Merrick v. Farmers Ins. Group, 892 F.2d 1434, 1440 (9th Cir.1990). The second sentence of Rule 801(d)(2), added by amendment in 1997, provides that the contents of the out-of-court statement shall be considered but are not alone sufficient to establish the existence or the scope of the declarant's authority or agency or employment relationship.

(10) Unidentified declarant. It is not necessary that the declarant be identified by name, so long as the evidence is otherwise sufficient to show that the declarant bore the necessary relationship to the party and that the subject matter of the statement concerned the declarant's job. Medical Center at Elizabeth Place, LLC v. Atrium Health System, 817 F.3d 934, 944–45 (6th Cir.2016); Lexington Ins. Co. v. Western Pennsylvania Hosp., 423 F.3d 318, 330 n. 7 (3d Cir.2005); Davis v. Mobil Oil Exploration & Producing Southeast, Inc., 864 F.2d 1171, 1173–74 (5th Cir.1989).

(11) Attorneys; government agents; expert witnesses. An attorney's statement in the course of representing a client may be admissible against the client as an agent admission under Rule 801(d)(2)(D). United States v. GAF Corp., 928 F.2d 1253, 1259 (2d Cir.1991). However, the unique nature of the attorney-client relationship demands that a trial court exercise caution in admitting statements that are the product of this relationship. United States v. Jung, 473 F.3d 837, 841 (7th Cir.2007). See also United States v. James, 712 F.3d 79, 102 (2d Cir.2013) (an accused is allowed to introduce a prosecutor's statement from a prior trial when the prosecution offered an inconsistent assertion of fact at the prior trial and the prosecution can offer no "innocent" explanation for the contradiction; the district court must determine by a preponderance of the evidence that an innocent explanation for the inconsistency does not exist). In criminal cases, it has been held that out-of-court statements by government agents are not admissible against the government under Rule 801(d)(2)(D). United States v. Prevatte, 16 F.3d 767, 779 n. 9 (7th Cir.1994); United States v. Kampiles, 609 F.2d 1233, 1246 (7th Cir.1979); United States v. Durrani, 659 F.Supp. 1183, 1185 (D.Conn.1987), aff'd, 835 F.2d 410 (2d Cir.1987). Contra, United States v. Branham, 97 F.3d 835, 851 (6th Cir.1996). The testimony of an expert witness called by a party to testify on its behalf in one case is not admissible against the party in a subsequent case under Rule 801(d)(2) unless there is a finding that the witness was an agent of the party authorized to speak on its behalf. HTC Corporation v. Telefonaktiebolaget LM Ericsson, 12 F.4th 476, 489–90 (5th Cir.2021); Kirk v. Raymark Industries, Inc., 61 F.3d 147, 163–64 (3d Cir.1995).

(12) Coconspirator admissions—In general. Although more frequently used in criminal cases, coconspirator admissions may arise in civil cases as well. World of Sleep, Inc. v. La-Z-Boy Chair Co., 756 F.2d 1467, 1474 (10th Cir.1985); Filco v. Amana Refrigeration, Inc., 709 F.2d 1257, 1267 (9th Cir.1983). It is not necessary that a conspiracy be charged in the indictment or pleadings. United States v. Maldonado-Rivera, 922 F.2d 934, 962 (2d Cir.1990). If there is a charge of conspiracy, acquittal on the conspiracy charge does not render statements inadmissible under Rule 801(d)(2)(E). United States v. Peralta, 941 F.2d 1003, 1005–07 (9th Cir.1991). The conspiracy that forms the basis for admitting coconspirators' statements need not be the same conspiracy for which the accused is charged. United States v. Lara, 181 F.3d 183, 196 (1st Cir.1999); United States v. Ellis, 156 F.3d 493, 497 (3d Cir.1998).

At least two circuits have held that a lawful joint enterprise can constitute a "conspiracy" for purposes of 801(d)(2)(E). United States v. Nelson, 732 F.3d 504, 515 (5th Cir.2013); United States v. Brockenborrugh, 575 F.3d 726, 735–36 (D.C.Cir.2009).

A statement of one coconspirator is admissible against another member who joined after the statement was made. United States v. Arrellano, 757 F.3d 623, 634 (7th Cir.2014); United States v. Lampley, 68 F.3d 1296, 1301 (11th Cir.1995) (citing cases from other circuits). Conspirators do not have to have contact with, or even know, all of the other conspirators. United States v. Frazier, 213 F.3d 409, 415 (7th Cir.2000). It is not necessary that the identity of the declarant be established. United States v. El-Mezain, 664 F.3d 467, 505 (5th Cir.2011); United States v. Smith, 223 F.3d 554, 570 (7th Cir.2000); United States v. Squillacote, 221 F.3d 542, 563 (4th Cir.2000). The testifying witness need not be a member of the conspiracy. United States v. Dinwiddie, 618 F.3d 821, 836 (8th Cir.2010). Statements by a cooperating coconspirator to known authorities, made after the commencement of cooperation, are not admissible because such statements are not made "in furtherance of the conspiracy." United States v. Villasenor, 664 F.3d 673, 682 (7th Cir.2011); United States v. Singh, 494 F.3d 653, 659 (8th Cir.2007).

If a conspirator effectively withdraws, coconspirator statements made after that date are not admissible against him. United States v. Nagelvoort, 856 F.3d 1117, 1128 (7th Cir.2017). It is the defendant's burden to prove the withdrawal. Id.; United States v. Hall, 212 F.3d 1016, 1023 (7th Cir.2000). Ceasing active participation in the conspiracy, by itself, is not sufficient to prove withdrawal. United States v. Vallone, 752 F.3d 690, 697 (7th Cir.2014). Withdrawal requires an " 'affirmative action * * * to disavow or defeat the purpose' of the conspiracy." Smith v. United States, 568 U.S. 106, 133 S.Ct. 714, 720 (2013) (quoting Hyde v. United States, 225 U.S. 347, 369, 32 S.Ct. 793 (1912)).

Coconspirator statements that are made during and in furtherance of a conspiracy are not considered testimonial and so their use does not implicate the Confrontation Clause. United States v. Hargrove, 508 F.3d 445, 449 (7th Cir.2007). Accord, United States v. Mayfield, 909 F.3d 956, 962–63 (8th Cir.2018).

The corroboration requirement focuses on the existence of the conspiracy and other elements of the rule, not on the contents of the statements sought to be introduced. United States v. Damra, 621 F.3d 474, 493 (6th Cir.2010) ("Damra * * * is wrongly focusing on whether there was corroboration of the *contents* of Fawaz's statements; our case law requires instead corroboration of 'defendant's knowledge of and participation in the conspiracy.' * * * Whether there was confirmation of the contents of any one statement is not dispositive, provided that there was independent evidence offered corroborating the court's preliminary factual determinations that the conspiracy existed, that the defendant was a member of that conspiracy, and that the statements were made in furtherance of the conspiracy.").

(13) Coconspirator admissions—Preliminary questions of fact. The issues of the existence of a conspiracy, its pendency, whether the party against whom it was offered was a member, and whether the statement was made in furtherance of it, are for the court under Rule 104(a). Bourjaily v. United States, 483 U.S. 171, 175–76, 107 S.Ct. 2775, 2778 (1987). The standard of proof to be applied by the court to these preliminary fact issues, even in a criminal case, is preponderance of the evidence. 483 U.S. at 175, 107 S.Ct. at 2778. The content of the coconspirator's statement itself may be considered by the court as evidence on the preliminary issues. 483 U.S. at 176, 107 S.Ct. at 2779. The second sentence of Rule 801(d)(2), added by amendment in 1997, provides that the contents of the out-of-court statement are not alone sufficient to establish the preliminary facts. This issue was not before the Supreme Court in *Bourjaily*, but the Courts of Appeals have uniformly required some independent evidence. "This requirement can be satisfied by the testimony of nonconspirators or by corroboration of facts contained in the statements of the conspirators." United States v. Petty, 132 F.3d 373, 380 (7th Cir.1997).

> **Example—Inadmissible.** "Kadamovas argues Mikhel's letter was inadmissible because 'once a party withdraws from a conspiracy subsequent statements by a coconspirator do not fall within this exemption.' The government responds that the conspiracy had revived by the time of Mikhel's letter. The problem with the government's argument, however, is that there is no proof of the conspiracy reviving other than the contested hearsay. We may consider contested hearsay in determining whether the Rule 801(d)(2)(E) exemption applies, but there must also be 'some evidence, aside from the proffered statements, of the existence of the conspiracy and the defendant's involvement.' Here, Mikhel's letter was the only evidence of an ongoing conspiracy to escape after Kadamovas's withdrawal. The letter was therefore inadmissible hearsay." United States v. Mikhel, 889 F.3d 1003, 1049 (9th Cir.2018) (citations omitted).

The trial court is not required to enter express findings into the record as to the preliminary facts; it suffices that the facts are supported by evidence of record. United States v. Sinclair, 109 F.3d 1527, 1533–35 (10th Cir.1997); United States v. South, 28 F.3d 619, 625 n. 2 (7th Cir.1994).

Where a district court instructed to the jury that it must first determine whether a conspiracy existed before considering the statements of the co-conspirators, there was no reversible error where the appellate court was satisfied that the district court had made its own initial determination of the existence of a conspiracy; "the district court's instruction was not erroneous, for it merely provided the defendant with unnecessary double protection." United States v. Scott, 642 F.3d 791, 798–99 (9th Cir.2011).

CROSS-REFERENCES

Common Objections (Chapter 3)

39. Hearsay

Treatises

6 Graham, Handbook of Federal Evidence §§ 801:15–801:26 (9th ed. 2020)

1 McCormick, Evidence §§ 53, 144, 160; 2 id. §§ 254–265 (8th ed. 2020)

30B Wright & Bellin, Federal Practice and Procedure §§ 6771–6782 (2018)

Rule 802. The Rule Against Hearsay

Hearsay is not admissible unless any of the following provides otherwise:

- a federal statute;

- these rules; or

- other rules prescribed by the Supreme Court.

AUTHORS' COMMENTS

(1) Scope and purpose of Rule 802. Rule 802 is the basic hearsay rule, i.e., hearsay is inadmissible except as elsewhere provided by the rules of evidence, by other court rules, or by statute.

(2) Admissible hearsay. Rule 801(d) exempts certain categories of statements from hearsay. The many hearsay exceptions in the evidence rules are found in Rules 803, 804, and 807. Other court rules and statutes authorizing the admissibility of hearsay are cross-referenced after the evidence rule to which they most closely relate (Rule 801, 802, 803, or 804, and/or a particular part of Rule 801, 803, or 804).

(3) Hearsay and the constitutional right of confrontation—In general. Prior to Crawford v. Washington, 541 U.S. 36, 124 S.Ct. 1354 (2004), Supreme Court caselaw on hearsay and the constitutional right of confrontation requires distinguishing among four categories of hearsay statements: (i) prior statements by witnesses who testify in the present proceeding under oath and are subject to cross-examination concerning the prior statement; (ii) former testimony of presently unavailable witnesses; (iii) other hearsay falling within a "firmly rooted" exception; and (iv) hearsay not falling within a "firmly rooted" exception. In *Crawford*, the Supreme Court adopted a fundamentally new approach to confrontation and hearsay. The new approach does not change the treatment of evidence in the first two categories—prior statements by witnesses and former testimony—but it substantially changes the treatment of hearsay statements by nontestifying declarants offered under hearsay exceptions, whether firmly rooted or not.

(4) Hearsay and the constitutional right of confrontation—Prior statements by witnesses. Substantive admission of a prior statement by a witness who testifies in the present proceeding under oath and subject to cross-examination concerning the prior statement does not offend the constitutional right of confrontation, California v. Green, 399 U.S. 149, 90 S.Ct. 1930 (1970), even if the witness denies making the prior statement, Nelson v. O'Neil, 402 U.S. 622, 91 S.Ct. 1723 (1971), or testifies to a lack of memory of the event, United States v. Owens, 484 U.S. 554, 559–60, 108 S.Ct. 838, 842–43 (1988).

(5) Hearsay and the constitutional right of confrontation—Former testimony—Constitutional requirement of unavailability. In order for former testimony to be constitutionally admissible against an accused, the prosecution must establish that the witness is unavailable despite good faith efforts to produce the witness at trial. Ohio v. Roberts, 448 U.S. 56, 100 S.Ct. 2531 (1980); Mancusi v. Stubbs, 408 U.S. 204, 92 S.Ct. 2308 (1972); Barber v. Page, 390 U.S. 719, 88 S.Ct. 1318 (1968).

Although at one time the Supreme Court suggested that an unavailability requirement might apply more broadly to hearsay, Ohio v. Roberts, supra, 448 U.S. at 65, 100 S.Ct. at 2538, subsequently the Court has indicated that "unavailability analysis is a necessary part of Confrontation Clause inquiry only when the challenged out-of-court statements were made in the course of a prior judicial proceeding." White v. Illinois, 502 U.S. 346, 352, 112 S.Ct. 736, 741 (1992).

(6) Hearsay and the constitutional right of confrontation—Pre-*Crawford*—"Firmly rooted" exception. Prior to *Crawford*, the Supreme Court held that "where proffered hearsay has sufficient guarantees of reliability to come within a firmly rooted exception to the hearsay rule, the Confrontation Clause is satisfied." White v. Illinois, 502 U.S. 346, 352, 112 S.Ct. 736, 741 (1992). Most of the hearsay exemptions and exceptions specifically denominated in Rules 801(d)(2), 803, and 804 undoubtedly qualify as "firmly rooted." The Supreme Court has identified as "firmly rooted" the exceptions for excited utterances and statements made for medical treatment, White v. Illinois, supra, 502 U.S. at 352, 112 S.Ct. at 741, and coconspirator statements, Bourjaily v. United States, 483 U.S. 171, 184, 107 S.Ct. 2775, 2783 (1987). Many other exceptions were identified as "firmly rooted" by courts of appeals. E.g., United States v. Hale, 978 F.2d 1016, 1021 (8th Cir.1992) (Rule 803(10)); United States v. Beckham, 968 F.2d 47, 51 (D.C.Cir.1992) (adoptive admissions under Rule 801(d)(2)(B)); United States v. Saks, 964 F.2d 1514, 1525–26 (5th Cir.1992) (Rule 801(d)(2)(D)); United States v. Ray, 930 F.2d 1368, 1371 (9th Cir.1990) (Rule 803(6)). Declarations against penal interest inculpating the accused and offered by the prosecution under Rule 804(b)(3) did not qualify as within a "firmly rooted" exception. Lilly v. Virginia, 527 U.S. 116, 134, 119 S.Ct. 1887, 1899 (1999) (plurality opinion).

(7) Hearsay and the constitutional right of confrontation—Pre-*Crawford*—Not within a "firmly rooted" exception. Prior to *Crawford*, the Supreme Court held that if the hearsay offered against an accused did not fall within a "firmly rooted" exception—for example, if it was offered under the "residual" exception, Rule 807—then the Confrontation Clause required a showing of "particularized guarantees of trustworthiness." Idaho v. Wright, 497 U.S. 805, 110 S.Ct. 3139 (1990); Ohio v. Roberts, 448 U.S. 56, 66, 100 S.Ct. 2531, 2539 (1980). " '[P]articularized guarantees of trustworthiness' must be shown from the totality of the circumstances, but * * * the relevant circumstances include only those that surround the making of the statement and that render the declarant particularly worthy of belief." Idaho v. Wright, 497 U.S. at 819, 110 S.Ct. at 3148. The evidence "must possess indicia of reliability by virtue of its inherent trustworthiness, not by reference to other evidence at trial"—i.e., not by corroboration. 497 U.S. at 822, 110 S.Ct. at 3150.

(8) Hearsay and the constitutional right of confrontation—*Crawford*—Testimonial vs. nontestimonial hearsay. After carefully reviewing the historical background of the Confrontation Clause, the *Crawford* Court concluded that the reliability approach of Ohio v. Roberts and its progeny was unsound. Instead, the first issue should be whether the hearsay statement is "testimonial" in nature. If so, the constitutional right of confrontation and cross-examination is absolute, and no showing of reliability, whether based on a "firmly rooted" exception or particularized indicia, can substitute. On the other hand, if the hearsay is "nontestimonial" in nature, the Court suggested (though it did not hold) that it may raise no Confrontation Clause issue at all. See 541 U.S. at 51, 124 S.Ct. at 1364 ("This focus also suggests that not all hearsay implicates the Sixth Amendment's core concerns. An off-hand, overheard remark might be unreliable evidence and thus a good candidate for exclusion under hearsay rules, but it bears little resemblance to the civil-law abuses the Confrontation Clause targeted."); 541 U.S. at 68, 124 S.Ct. at 1374 ("Where nontestimonial hearsay is at issue, it is wholly consistent with the Framers' design to afford the States flexibility in their development of hearsay law—as does *Roberts,* and as would an approach that exempted such statements from Confrontation Clause scrutiny altogether."). But see 541 U.S. at 53, 124 S.Ct. at 1365 ("In sum, even if the Sixth Amendment is not solely concerned with testimonial hearsay, that is its primary object, and interrogations by law enforcement officers fall squarely within that class.").

The Court did not attempt to state a single definition of "testimonial." Instead, it recited with approval a group of definitions, leaving the precise categorization of various kinds of hearsay utterances for future case law:

> Various formulations of this core class of "testimonial" statements exist: "*ex parte* in-court testimony or its functional equivalent—that is, material such as affidavits, custodial examinations, prior testimony that the defendant was unable to cross-examine, or similar pretrial statements that declarants would reasonably expect to be used prosecutorially," Brief for Petitioner 23; "extrajudicial statements * * * contained in formalized testimonial materials, such as affidavits, depositions, prior testimony, or confessions," White v. Illinois, 502 U.S. 346, 365, 112 S.Ct. 736 (1992) (Thomas, J., joined by Scalia, J., concurring in part and concurring in judgment); "statements that were made under circumstances which would lead an objective witness reasonably to believe that the statement would be available for use at a later trial," Brief for National Association of Criminal Defense Lawyers et al. as Amici Curiae 3. These formulations all share a common nucleus and then define the Clause's coverage at various levels of abstraction around it. Regardless of the precise articulation, some statements qualify under any definition—for example, ex parte testimony at a preliminary hearing.

> Statements taken by police officers in the course of interrogations are also testimonial under even a narrow standard.

541 U.S. at 51–52, 124 S.Ct. at 1364.

Among the federal cases applying *Crawford,* a number are quite straightforward because the hearsay admitted was plainly testimonial. E.g., United States v. Gilbert, 391 F.3d 882, 883–85 (7th Cir.2004) (nontestifying wife's statements admitted under Rule 807); United States v. Cromer, 389 F.3d 662, 670–79 (6th Cir.2004) (statements of confidential informer); United States v. Rodriguez-Marrero, 390 F.3d 1, 16–17 (1st Cir.2004) (codefendant's confession); United States v. Bruno, 383 F.3d 65, 77–78 (2d Cir.2004) (plea allocutions and grand jury testimony); United States v. Rashid, 383 F.3d 769, 775–76 (8th Cir.2004) (statements of nontestifying codefendant). But see United States v. Vasilakos, 508 F.3d 401, 408 (6th Cir.2007) (reading codefendants' redacted civil-case depositions into evidence at the defendants' trial did not offend the Confrontation Clause where the government substituted names in the deposition statements with the neutral noun "person" or phrase "another person," and "the declarant-codefendants' deposition statements did not ineluctably implicate" the complaining defendants).

In Melendez-Diaz v. Massachusetts, 557 U.S. 305, 129 S.Ct. 2527 (2009), the Court held that forensic laboratory "certificates of analysis" stating that seized substances contained cocaine were inadmissible testimonial statements. Four justices dissented. Accord, Bullcoming v. New Mexico, 564 U.S. 647, 131 S.Ct. 2705 (2011).

Where an accused who did not speak English was questioned through an interpreter, testimony by the questioning officer as to what the interpreter said the accused said was held to violate the Confrontation Clause. United States v. Charles, 722 F.3d 1319, 1322–31 (11th Cir.2013).

"Where an officer's testimony leads 'to the clear and logical inference that out-of-court declarants believed and said that [the defendant] was guilty of the crime charged,' Confrontation Clause protections are triggered. * * * Officer testimony regarding statements made by witnesses is thus inadmissible where it allows a jury to reasonably infer the defendant's guilt. Similarly, a prosecutor's questioning may introduce a testimonial statement by a nontestifying witness, thus implicating the Confrontation Clause. Here, Detective Schultz's testimony introduced Brown's out-of-court testimonial statements by implication. * * * In fact, the prosecutor's questions appeared designed to elicit hearsay testimony without directly introducing Brown's statements. Brown's statements were testimonial because they were made under interrogation, and the primary purpose of that interrogation was to establish 'past events potentially relevant to later criminal prosecution.' " United States v. Kizzee, 877 F.3d 650, 657–58 (5th Cir.2017).

Held nontestimonial: recorded statements by murdered stalking victim to her therapist, United States v. Gonzalez, 905 F.3d 165, 202 (3d Cir.2018) ("Belford's statements to her therapist are not testimonial in nature. As her therapist testified, the purpose of Belford's visits were to receive therapy to treat her anxiety and depression. The purpose of a visit to a therapist is not to create a record for a future criminal case."); statements by sexually abused child to pediatrician, United States v. Peneaux, 432 F.3d 882, 896 (8th Cir.2005) ("Where statements are made to a physician seeking to give medical aid in the form of diagnosis or treatment, they are presumptively nontestimonial."); INS warrant of deportation, United States v. Cantellano, 430 F.3d 1142, 1145–46 (11th Cir.2005); INS Form I-213, United States v. Noria, 945 F.3d 847, 849–58 (5th Cir.2019) ("An 'I-213 is an official record routinely prepared by an [immigration] agent as a summary of information obtained at the time of the initial processing of an individual suspected of being an alien unlawfully present in the United States.' Put more simply, it 'is a record of an immigration inspector's conversation with an alien who will probably be subject to removal.' Typically, an I-213 'includes, inter alia, the individual's name, address, immigration status, the circumstances of the individual's apprehension, and any substantive comments the individual may have made.' "); recorded coconspirator statements, United States v. Stewart, 433 F.3d 273, 291–93 (2d Cir.2006); United States v. Jordan, 509 F.3d 191, 201 (4th Cir.2007) (statements against penal interest made to friend; "To our knowledge, no court has extended *Crawford* to statements made by a declarant to friends or associates.") (accord, United States v. Alvarado, 816 F.3d 242, 250–52 (4th Cir.2016)); United States v. Hendricks, 395 F.3d 173, 180–82 (3d Cir.2005); diary entries of murdered wife, Parle v. Runnels, 387 F.3d 1030, 1037 (9th Cir.2004); unwitting statements of coconspirator to confidential informer, United States v. Saget, 377 F.3d 223, 229–30 (2d Cir.2004); excited utterance in police call by murder victim, Leavitt v. Arave, 383 F.3d 809, 830 n. 22 (9th Cir.2004); statements made for the purposes of obtaining medical treatment during an ongoing emergency, United States v. Santos, 589 F.3d 759, 763 (5th Cir.2009).

In United States v. Foreman, 84 F.4th 615, 619–20 (5th Cir.2023), the Fifth Circuit distinguished *Noria,* supra, and held that a different INS report, Form G-166F, violated the Confrontation Clause. "At bottom, an alien-smuggling investigation report is not 'essentially ministerial' as this court found the I-213 to be in *Noria.* Instead, it is a criminal investigation report—the sort of document the Federal Rules of Evidence, and even the *Noria* decision itself, explicitly note are inadmissible hearsay." Id. at 620.

An excited utterance, even if made to law enforcement (such as a 911 call), may be nontestimonial. A call for help, even if it recounts facts that incriminate another, is not testimonial. But once "the dust has settled," the declarant is secure, and law enforcement or other investigative questioning has begun, the line to testimonial has been crossed, even though the declarant may still be under a state of excitement sufficient for Rule 803(2). "Statements are nontestimonial when made in the course of police interrogation under circumstances objectively indicating that the primary purpose of the interrogation is to enable police assistance to meet an ongoing emergency. They are testimonial when the circumstances objectively indicate that there is no such ongoing emergency, and that the primary purpose of the interrogation is to establish or prove past events potentially relevant to later criminal prosecution." Davis v. Washington, 547 U.S. 813, 126 S.Ct. 2266 (2006).

In Michigan v. Bryant, 562 U.S. 344, 131 S.Ct. 1143 (2011), the Court extended the *Davis* concept of "ongoing emergency" to classify as nontestimonial statements to police by a mortally wounded man describing the shooting that had occurred blocks away about 25 minutes earlier. "[T]here was an ongoing emergency here where an armed shooter, whose motive for and location after the shooting were unknown, had mortally wounded Covington within a few blocks and a few minutes of the location where the police found Covington." 562 U.S. at 373, 131 S.Ct. at 1154. "Because the circumstances of the encounter as well as the statements and actions of Covington and the police objectively indicate that the 'primary purpose of the interrogation' was 'to enable police assistance to meet an ongoing emergency,' Covington's identification and description of the shooter and the location of the shooting were not testimonial hearsay." 562 U.S. at 377–78, 131 S.Ct. at 1166. The Court emphasized that the "primary purpose" issue is the objectively apparent purpose of all of the participants taken together, considering all circumstances—not the actual subjective purpose of any particular person, such as the declarant.

Bryant also reiterated, 562 U.S. 344, 359 & n. 5, 131 S.Ct. 1143, 1155 (2011), that the admissibility of a nontestimonial statement "is the concern of state and federal rules of evidence, not the Confrontation Clause."

In Ohio v. Clark, 576 U.S. 237, 135 S.Ct. 2173 (2015), the Supreme Court upheld admission of hearsay statements by a three-year-old child with visible injuries identifying his abuser in response to questions from a teacher. "Because at least some statements to individuals who are not law enforcement officers could conceivably raise confrontation concerns, we decline to adopt a categorical rule excluding them from the Sixth Amendment's reach. Nevertheless, such statements are much less likely to be testimonial than statements to law enforcement officers." 576 U.S. at 246, 135 S.Ct. at 2181. In addition, "Statements by very young children will rarely, if ever, implicate the Confrontation Clause." 576 U.S. at 247–248, 135 S.Ct. at 2182. For an example of a case where a federal court found a very young child's statement to have been testimonial, see McCarley v. Kelly, 801 F.3d 652, 664–65 (6th Cir.2015).

A number of lower-court federal and state cases following *Clark* concern statements by sexual assault victims during questioning by a sexual assault nurse examiner (SANE). Whether particular statements are excluded as testimonial or admitted as nontestimonial is very context-specific, and redaction line-by-line may be performed. United States v. Norwood, 982 F.3d 1032, 1045–51 (7th Cir.2020).

The Seventh Circuit found *Davis* to support the conclusion that "the mere fact a person creating a business record (or other similar record) knows the record might be used for criminal prosecution does not by itself make that record testimonial" because the decision "necessarily rejects a strict adherence to denominating as testimonial all statements made under circumstances where a reasonable person would know the statements might be used as evidence of a crime." United States v. Ellis, 460 F.3d 920, 926 (7th Cir.2006) ("While the medical professionals in this case might have thought their observations would end up as evidence in a criminal prosecution, the objective circumstances of this case indicate that their observations and statements introduced at trial were made in nothing else but the ordinary course of business.").

Sometimes, however, "business records" may be testimonial. United States v. Cameron, 699 F.3d 621, 653–54 (1st Cir.2012) ("Our holding today does not mean that non-testimonial business records somehow become testimonial simply because the government seeks to use them as evidence against a criminal defendant. However, if business records are testimonial, then a defendant must be given an opportunity to confront the authors of those records. What the government did in this case was seek to introduce, absent confrontation of the authors, out-of-court statements that: (1) did not exist before criminal activity was discovered; (2) stated conclusions (though perhaps obvious ones) about the meaning of underlying data; (3) were created for the express purpose of reporting criminal activity and identifying the perpetrator of that activity; and (4) were reported to a government-funded entity that serves as a conduit for passing information to law enforcement. This, we hold, the government cannot do.").

A defendant may, by engaging in conduct that procures a declarant's unavailability, forfeit his right to confrontation. In Giles v. California, 554 U.S. 353, 128 S.Ct. 2678 (2008), the Supreme Court held such forfeiture occurs only when defendant acted with the purpose of making the declarant unavailable to testify. A defendant's wrongdoing that results in the unavailability of the declarant—but done without the intent to procure that unavailability to testify—does not result in the defendant's forfeiting his Confrontation Clause right.

Although *Crawford* created a new procedural rule, it is not a "watershed rule" of criminal procedure implicating the "fundamental fairness" of the criminal proceeding. Therefore, *Crawford* does not apply retroactively. Whorton v. Bockting, 549 U.S. 406, 127 S.Ct. 1173 (2007).

CROSS-REFERENCES

Common Objections (Chapter 3)

39.   Hearsay

Treatises

6 Graham, Handbook of Federal Evidence §§ 802:1–802:2:2 (9th ed. 2020)

2 McCormick, Evidence §§ 245–246, 252–253 (8th ed. 2020)

30B Wright & Bellin, Federal Practice and Procedure §§ 6791–6795 (2018)

30 Wright & Blinka, Federal Practice and Procedure §§ 6321–6695 (2d ed. 2020)

Rule 803. Exceptions to the Rule Against Hearsay—Regardless of Whether the Declarant Is Available as a Witness

The following are not excluded by the rule against hearsay, regardless of whether the declarant is available as a witness:

(1)   ***Present Sense Impression.*** A statement describing or explaining an event or condition, made while or immediately after the declarant perceived it.

(2)   ***Excited Utterance.*** A statement relating to a startling event or condition, made while the declarant was under the stress of excitement that it caused.

(3)   ***Then-Existing Mental, Emotional, or Physical Condition.*** A statement of the declarant's then-existing state of mind (such as motive, intent, or plan) or emotional, sensory, or physical condition (such as mental feeling, pain, or bodily health), but not including a statement of memory or belief to prove the fact remembered or believed unless it relates to the validity or terms of the declarant's will.

(4)   ***Statement Made for Medical Diagnosis or Treatment.*** A statement that:

(A)   is made for—and is reasonably pertinent to—medical diagnosis or treatment; and

(B)   describes medical history; past or present symptoms or sensations; their inception; or their general cause.

(5)   ***Recorded Recollection.*** A record that:

(A)   is on a matter the witness once knew about but now cannot recall well enough to testify fully and accurately;

(B)   was made or adopted by the witness when the matter was fresh in the witness's memory; and

(C)   accurately reflects the witness's knowledge.

If admitted, the record may be read into evidence but may be received as an exhibit only if offered by an adverse party.

(6)   ***Records of a Regularly Conducted Activity.*** A record of an act, event, condition, opinion, or diagnosis if:

212

(A) the record was made at or near the time by—or from information transmitted by—someone with knowledge;

(B) the record was kept in the course of a regularly conducted activity of a business, organization, occupation, or calling, whether or not for profit;

(C) making the record was a regular practice of that activity;

(D) all these conditions are shown by the testimony of the custodian or another qualified witness, or by a certification that complies with Rule 902(11) or (12) or with a statute permitting certification; and

(E) the opponent does not show that the source of information or the method or circumstances of preparation indicate a lack of trustworthiness.

(7) *Absence of a Record of a Regularly Conducted Activity.* Evidence that a matter is not included in a record described in paragraph (6) if:

(A) the evidence is admitted to prove that the matter did not occur or exist;

(B) a record was regularly kept for a matter of that kind; and

(C) the opponent does not show that the possible source of the information or other circumstances indicate a lack of trustworthiness.

(8) *Public Records.* A record or statement of a public office if:

(A) it sets out:

    (i) the office's activities;

    (ii) a matter observed while under a legal duty to report, but not including, in a criminal case, a matter observed by law-enforcement personnel; or

    (iii) in a civil case or against the government in a criminal case, factual findings from a legally authorized investigation; and

(B) the opponent does not show that the source of information or other circumstances indicate a lack of trustworthiness.

(9) *Public Records of Vital Statistics.* A record of a birth, death, or marriage, if reported to a public office in accordance with a legal duty.

(10) *Absence of a Public Record.* Testimony—or a certification under Rule 902—that a diligent search failed to disclose a public record or statement if the testimony or certification is admitted to prove that:

(A) the record or statement does not exist; or

(B) a matter did not occur or exist, if a public office regularly kept a record or statement for a matter of that kind.

(11) *Records of Religious Organizations Concerning Personal or Family History.* A statement of birth, legitimacy, ancestry, marriage, divorce, death, relationship by blood or marriage, or similar facts of personal or family history, contained in a regularly kept record of a religious organization.

(12) *Certificates of Marriage, Baptism, and Similar Ceremonies.* A statement of fact contained in a certificate:

(A) made by a person who is authorized by a religious organization or by law to perform the act certified;

(B) attesting that the person performed a marriage or similar ceremony or administered a sacrament; and

    (C) purporting to have been issued at the time of the act or within a reasonable time after it.

(13) *Family Records.* A statement of fact about personal or family history contained in a family record, such as a Bible, genealogy, chart, engraving on a ring, inscription on a portrait, or engraving on an urn or burial marker.

(14) *Records of Documents That Affect an Interest in Property.* The record of a document that purports to establish or affect an interest in property if:

    (A) the record is admitted to prove the content of the original recorded document, along with its signing and its delivery by each person who purports to have signed it;

    (B) the record is kept in a public office; and

    (C) a statute authorizes recording documents of that kind in that office.

(15) *Statements in Documents That Affect an Interest in Property.* A statement contained in a document that purports to establish or affect an interest in property if the matter stated was relevant to the document's purpose—unless later dealings with the property are inconsistent with the truth of the statement or the purport of the document.

(16) *Statements in Ancient Documents.* A statement in a document that was prepared before January 1, 1998, and whose authenticity is established.

(17) *Market Reports and Similar Commercial Publications.* Market quotations, lists, directories, or other compilations that are generally relied on by the public or by persons in particular occupations.

(18) *Statements in Learned Treatises, Periodicals, or Pamphlets.* A statement contained in a treatise, periodical, or pamphlet if:

    (A) the statement is called to the attention of an expert witness on cross-examination or relied on by the expert on direct examination; and

    (B) the publication is established as a reliable authority by the expert's admission or testimony, by another expert's testimony, or by judicial notice.

If admitted, the statement may be read into evidence but not received as an exhibit.

(19) *Reputation Concerning Personal or Family History.* A reputation among a person's family by blood, adoption, or marriage—or among a person's associates or in the community—concerning the person's birth, adoption, legitimacy, ancestry, marriage, divorce, death, relationship by blood, adoption, or marriage, or similar facts of personal or family history.

(20) *Reputation Concerning Boundaries or General History.* A reputation in a community—arising before the controversy—concerning boundaries of land in the community or customs that affect the land, or concerning general historical events important to

(21) *Reputation Concerning Character.* A reputation among a person's associates or in the community concerning the person's character.

(22) *Judgment of a Previous Conviction.* Evidence of a final judgment of conviction if:

    (A) the judgment was entered after a trial or guilty plea, but not a nolo contendere plea;

    (B) the conviction was for a crime punishable by death or by imprisonment for more than a year;

    (C) the evidence is admitted to prove any fact essential to the judgment; and

(D) when offered by the prosecutor in a criminal case for a purpose other than impeachment, the judgment was against the defendant.

The pendency of an appeal may be shown but does not affect admissibility.

(23) *Judgments Involving Personal, Family, or General History or a Boundary.* A judgment that is admitted to prove a matter of personal, family, or general history, or boundaries, if the matter:

(A) was essential to the judgment; and

(B) could be proved by evidence of reputation.

(24) **[Other exceptions.]** [Transferred to Rule 807.]

AUTHORS' COMMENTS

(1) Scope and purpose of Rule 803. Rule 803 lists twenty-three exceptions to the hearsay rule that may be invoked without regard to whether the declarant is available to testify.

(2) Hearsay exceptions under Rule 803. The more important exceptions listed in Rule 803 are discussed in the sections that follow. The other exceptions seldom arise and most questions concerning them can be answered by reference to the text of the rule.

CROSS-REFERENCES

Common Objections (Chapter 3)

39. Hearsay

Treatises

7 Graham, Handbook of Federal Evidence §§ 803:0–803:24 (9th ed. 2020)

1 McCormick, Evidence § 191; 2 id. §§ 208, 257, 268–300, 321–324 (8th ed. 2020)

30B Wright & Bellin, Federal Practice and Procedure §§ 6801–6953 (2018)

Rule 803(1).   Present Sense Impression

The following are not excluded by the rule against hearsay, regardless of whether the declarant is available as a witness:

(1) *Present Sense Impression.* A statement describing or explaining an event or condition, made while or immediately after the declarant perceived it.

* * *

AUTHORS' COMMENTS

(1) No requirement that witness be in position to check declarant's statement. Rule 803(1) does not require that the witness who recounts the hearsay utterance have had an opportunity to observe and check what the declarant describes. United States v. Obayagbona, 627 F.Supp. 329, 339 (E.D.N.Y.1985) (Weinstein, C.J.).

(2) Lapse of time between event and statement. The rule requires that the declaration, if not simultaneous with the event, be made "immediately thereafter." "Immediately" permits only a "slight lapse" of time. Advisory Committee's Note to Rule 803(1).

Example—Inadmissible. "Here, too much time had passed between when Mr. Rush spoke with Mr. Manfre and when he spoke with Mr. Strozier to call the transaction a present-sense impression. At the very least, there was an intervening walk or drive between the time of the discussion with Mr. Manfre and the time when Mr. Rush spoke with Mr. Strozier. The present-sense-impression exception to the hearsay rule is rightfully limited to statements made while a declarant perceives an event or immediately thereafter, and we decline to expand it to cover a declarant's relatively recent memories. The opportunity for strategic modification undercuts the reliability that spontaneity insures." United States v. Manfre, 368 F.3d 832, 840 (8th Cir.2004).

Example—Inadmissible. "The record does not reflect how long it took Benitez to travel from the restaurant to Hernandez's paint and body shop, engage in conversation with Cruz and Hernandez, obtain the cocaine sample, and return to the restaurant and engage in further conversation, before turning the cocaine and one of Hernandez's business cards over to Pherson. It is clear, however, that Benitez's statement to Pherson was not made immediately following Benitez's receipt of the cocaine." United States v. Cruz, 765 F.2d 1020, 1024 (11th Cir.1985).

Example—Inadmissible. "[W]e are * * * unaware of any legal authority for the proposition that 50 minutes after the fact may appropriately be considered 'immediately thereafter.' On the contrary, given the clear language of the rule and its underlying rationale, courts consistently require substantial contemporaneity." United States v. Green, 541 F.3d 176, 181 (3d Cir.2008).

Example—Admissible. "Ms. Hawkins' 911 call was placed with sufficient contemporaneity to the underlying events to be admissible under Rule 803(1). The occupants of apartment 204 placed a 911 call at approximately 1:07 a.m. complaining about a disturbance in apartment 304. Ms. Hawkins placed her 911 call at approximately 1:14 a.m. from a nearby SuperAmerica convenience store. Further, Ms. Hawkins stated that 'my husband just pulled a gun out on me.' " United States v. Hawkins, 59 F.3d 723, 730 (8th Cir.1995), vac'd on other grounds, 516 U.S. 1168, 116 S.Ct. 1257 (1996).

(3) "Describing or explaining." The exception in Rule 803(1) covers only statements "describing or explaining an event or condition." This is stricter than Rule 803(2), which extends to statements "relating to a startling event or condition." United States v. Boyce, 742 F.3d 792, 798 (7th Cir.2014).

Example—Inadmissible. The trial court properly excluded defendant's offer of his own statement to officers, "That is my gym bag, but Taylor put it in the trunk." The subject matter of the statement "was not what the declarant was presently perceiving when the statement was made, but rather something which had occurred at a remote previous time, namely whenever the gym bag was placed in the trunk." United States v. Phelps, 572 F.Supp. 262, 265 (E.D.Ky.1983).

(4) Personal knowledge. A hearsay declarant, like a witness, must have personal knowledge of the matter the statement is offered to prove. Advisory Committee's Note to Rule 803. Accordingly, a statement offered as a present sense impression is excluded in the absence of evidence sufficient to support a finding that the declarant personally perceived the matter. United States v. Gonzalez, 764 F.3d 159, 169 (2d Cir.2014); Hynes v. Coughlin, 79 F.3d 285, 294 (2d Cir.1996).

Example—Inadmissible. Trial court properly excluded 911 tape of declarant describing alleged police beating of plaintiff, because of a "basis to suspect that [declarant] did not witness the events he described, but instead had relayed to the 911 operator descriptions by other people who had been observing from the windows of [declarant]'s house." Bemis v. Edwards, 45 F.3d 1369, 1373–74 (9th Cir.1995).

CROSS-REFERENCES

Treatises

7 Graham, Handbook of Federal Evidence § 803:1 (9th ed. 2020)

2 McCormick, Evidence § 271 (8th ed. 2020)

30B Wright & Bellin, Federal Practice and Procedure §§ 6811–6816 (2018)

Rule 803(2). Excited Utterance

The following are not excluded by the rule against hearsay, regardless of whether the declarant is available as a witness:

* * *

(2) *Excited Utterance.* A statement relating to a startling event or condition, made while the declarant was under the stress of excitement that it caused.

* * *

AUTHORS' COMMENTS

(1) Excitement. "[W]hen a hearsay statement is offered under this exception, the trial court must make a preliminary factual determination that the declarant was so excited or distraught at the moment of utterance that he did not reflect (or have an opportunity to reflect) on what he was saying." United States v. McLennan, 563 F.2d 943, 948 (9th Cir.1977).

Example—Inadmissible. "Billie made her statement approximately one hour after the assault. Bennally made her statement even later. Both had spoken to several persons before telling Nez they had been raped. They had time to think about their actions and to invent an excuse about their late arrival at the dorm with alcohol on their breath." United States v. Sherlock, 962 F.2d 1349, 1365 (9th Cir.1989).

Example—Inadmissible. " 'The rationale of the excited utterance exception is that "the stress of nervous excitement or physical shock stills the reflective faculties, thus removing an impediment to truthfulness." ' * * * In this case, D.D. initially fabricated a story about how she tripped when she told her mother how she became bloodied. Minutes later, she returned and told her mother the truth. This court concludes that D.D.'s statements demonstrate a level of reflection that prohibit their admission as an 'excited utterance.' " United States v. DeMarce, 564 F.3d 989, 997 (8th Cir.2009) (citations omitted).

Example—Admissible. "This case is not a close call. A drunk person forcing his way inside and shoving a loaded gun in your face—in front of your young children—is on the higher end of the startling-event spectrum." United States v. Lundy, 83 F.4th 615, 619 (6th Cir.2023).

(2) Proof of startling event and declarant's perception of it. The contents of the statement itself, along with circumstances including the declarant's appearance, behavior, and condition, may be relied upon to establish the occurrence of an exciting event, United States v. Moore, 791 F.2d 566, 570–71 (7th Cir.1986), and the declarant's personal perception of it, McLaughlin v. Vinzant, 522 F.2d 448, 451 (1st Cir.1975).

Example—Admissible. "Mr. Moltzan testified that Mr. Cluff seemed 'excited'; he 'appeared nervous, kind of fidgety,' and unable to 'stop moving.' Mr. Cluff testified that he was in considerable pain, and, in fact, vomited on his way out of the cell. * * * Although Mr. Floyd, a federal marshal, testified that Mr. Cluff was alert and without disorientation or confusion when he requested medical attention, alertness is not tantamount to lack of excitement, or even lack of shock." United States v. Pursley, 577 F.3d 1204, 1221–22 (10th Cir.2009).

(3) "Relating to a startling event." The subject matter requirement of Rule 803(2) is significantly more liberal than that of Rule 803(1). Rule 803(1) is limited to statements "describing or explaining an event or condition"; Rule 803(2) embraces statements "relating to a startling event or condition." United States v. Boyce, 742 F.3d 792, 798 (7th Cir.2014); People of the Territory of Guam v. Cepeda, 69 F.3d 369, 372 (9th Cir.1995).

Example—Admissible. Slip and fall; bystander's statement, "I told them to clean it up about two hours ago—an hour and a half ago," admissible under Rule 803(2). David by Berkeley v. Pueblo Supermarket, 740 F.2d 230, 234–35 (3d Cir.1984).

The startling event that triggers the statement need not be the crime or event out of which the litigation arises.

Example—Admissible. "First, viewing the 'photograph of the individual that she recognized as her husband committing a bank robbery' was a startling event. Second, according to Trombitas' testimony, Mrs. Parks uttered the words 'oh, my God, that looks like Johnny,' as soon as she saw the photograph, and therefore before she could have had an opportunity to 'contrive or misrepresent.' Third, Mrs. Parks identified Crockett in her very first statement upon seeing the photograph, and then with tears in her eyes, reaffirmed that identification, evidence of the fact that she was still under the stress of the moment." United States v. Beverly, 369 F.3d 516, 540 (6th Cir.2004).

Example—Admissible. "Pagan explained that after hearing the sound of Irizarry's truck, Minor Y 'got very nervous. Her eyes got really big. She started moving her fingers, and she started looking everywhere when she said that she heard the sound of the car.' She also began to cry and continued to do so throughout her conversation with Pagan and her sister. Minor Y testified at trial that when she heard the sound of Irizarry's truck, she knew 'he was going to my house to get me.' Pagan went as far as to characterize Minor Y as 'hysterical' during their conversation. While hearing a truck is not in and of itself startling, when that truck is associated with the two recent sexual assaults that Minor Y had allegedly experienced, hearing that sound could have had the potential to 're-excite' Minor Y (and clearly seemed to do so). The prospect of a third consecutive weekend of sexual abuse, when the second had been a dramatic escalation from the first, was undoubtedly frightening for Minor Y." United States v. Irizarry-Sisco, 87 F.4th 38, 45–48 (1st Cir.2023).

(4) Lapse of time. Rule 803(2) requires that the statement be made while the declarant was under the stress caused by the exciting event. If the event is sufficiently startling, the period of stress may persist for some time. "[S]everal factors must be considered, including: (1) The lapse of time between the event and the declarations; (2) the age of the declarant; (3) the physical and mental state of the declarant; (4) the characteristics of the event; (5) the subject matter of the statements." Morgan v. Foretich, 846 F.2d 941, 947 (4th Cir.1988). Accord, United States v. Marrowbone, 211 F.3d 452 (8th Cir.2000).

Example—Admissible. Rape victim's statements to her sister, made several minutes after assault, were properly admitted. Victim's statements to police officer were also admissible, even though they were made an hour after assault and in response to questioning, because officer testified that victim was still visibly upset. United States v. Frost, 684 F.3d 963, 974–75 (10th Cir.2012).

Example—Admissible. "The [district] court seems to have truncated the event, limiting its discussion of Christiansen's statement relative only to the singular event of Christiansen's witnessing of Brunsting's impact with the tree. For example, the court discusses the 'four to five minutes' between the accident and Christiansen's statement to Benson, necessarily implying that the 'startling event' occurred on the chairlift. Limiting the discussion in that manner was an abuse of discretion. It was the whole of the event that is relevant for purposes of the Rule 803(2) analysis: witnessing a near-fatal traumatic accident from the chairlift and immediately rushing to the scene where Brunsting was unconscious, bleeding from the mouth, turning blue and believed to be near death, as others tried to stabilize him until medical assistance arrived. It was a chaotic scene and Christiansen realized the gravity of the accident—that she might indeed be witnessing a man's death. The difference between the two definitions of what constitutes the 'event' for purposes of the Rule 803(2) analysis is pivotal, as there was little or no time lapse between the latter-defined 'event' and the statement at issue because the statement was made contemporaneously with the singular startling event." Brunsting v. Lutsen Mts. Corp., 601 F.3d 813, 818–19 (8th Cir.2010).

Example—Admissible. Statement by shooting victim made up to thirty minutes after attack. United States v. Baptiste, 264 F.3d 578, 590–91 (5th Cir.2001).

Example—Admissible. Statement by fifteen-year-old rape victim to her mother one half hour after assault, properly admitted. United States v. Rivera, 43 F.3d 1291, 1296 (9th Cir.1995).

Example—Admissible. Statements by four-year-old child one or one and one-half hours after suffering serious injuries were properly admitted. Haggins v. Warden, Fort Pillow State Farm, 715 F.2d 1050, 1057–58 (6th Cir.1983).

Example—Admissible. Statement by victim fifteen minutes after assault and after driving twelve miles to grandmother's house at speeds up to 120 miles per hour, properly admitted. United States v. Golden, 671 F.2d 369, 371 (10th Cir.1982).

Example—Inadmissible. Statement by one defendant to his girlfriend several hours after robbery that other defendant had already spent robbery money on drugs and given some away, not admissible as excited utterance. United States v. Moss, 544 F.2d 954, 958 (8th Cir.1976).

Example—Inadmissible. "Several hours passed between the events of the morning of January 24 and 25 and the time Mrs. Wesela spoke to Detective Schmitz. Mrs. Wesela was not under a continuous threat; to the contrary, she was at work and away from Wesela for a full workday.

That she was able to go to work demonstrates that she had regained at least some of her composure and emotional control. Therefore, although Wesela engaged in a pattern of threatening behavior, one cannot say that Mrs. Wesela was under continuous, uninterrupted stress and excitement. By accepting a lesser state of mental angst as enough to satisfy Rule 803(2), the district court applied the wrong legal standard." United States v. Wesela, 223 F.3d 656 (7th Cir.2000).

Example—Inadmissible. "The allegations of sexual abuse were made about three hours after the event occurred. In addition, these statements were made by a teenager, not by a small child. * * * L.D.'s actions also do not show continuous excitement or stress from the time of the event until the time of the statements. * * * Officer Takes the Gun testified that when he arrived at the house, L.D. was standing with a group of people and, when handcuffed, said nothing about the incident with Marrowbone. It was only when L.D. was about to be placed in the patrol car for transport to jail that he raised a ruckus and began making these statements. * * * Based on the lapse of time, age, motive to lie, and known actions of L.D., we are wholly unconvinced these statements were excited utterances." United States v. Marrowbone, 211 F.3d 452 (8th Cir.2000).

(5) Response to questioning. If the requisite stress is shown, a statement may qualify even if it was made in response to questioning. United States v. Irizarry-Sisco, 87 F.4th 38, 47 (1st Cir.2023); United States v. Joy, 192 F.3d 761, 766–67 (7th Cir.1999).

(6) Unidentified bystanders. Statements by unidentified bystanders are not "ipso facto inadmissible" but "are admissible if they otherwise meet the criteria of 803(2)." Miller v. Keating, 754 F.2d 507, 510 (3d Cir.1985).

CROSS-REFERENCES

Treatises

7 Graham, Handbook of Federal Evidence § 803:2 (9th ed. 2020)

2 McCormick, Evidence § 272 (8th ed. 2020)

30B Wright & Bellin, Federal Practice and Procedure §§ 6811, 6817–6822 (2018)

Rule 803(3).   Then-Existing Mental, Emotional, or Physical Condition

The following are not excluded by the rule against hearsay, regardless of whether the declarant is available as a witness:

* * *

(3) *Then-Existing Mental, Emotional, or Physical Condition.* A statement of the declarant's then-existing state of mind (such as motive, intent, or plan) or emotional, sensory, or physical condition (such as mental feeling, pain, or bodily health), but not including a statement of memory or belief to prove the fact remembered or believed unless it relates to the validity or terms of the declarant's will.

* * *

AUTHORS' COMMENTS

(1) Four categories covered by Rule 803(3). Rule 803(3) covers four distinct categories of statements: (i) statements of present bodily condition; (ii) statements of present state of mind or emotion, offered to prove a state of mind or emotion of the declarant that is "in issue" in the case; (iii) statements of present state of mind—usually intent, plan, or design—offered to prove subsequent conduct of the declarant in accordance with the state of mind; and (iv) state-of-mind statements of a testator, offered on certain issues in will cases.

(2) Present bodily condition. Statements indicating a present physical condition of the declarant are admissible under Rule 803(3) whether made to a physician or to a lay person. This exception does not extend to statements of past conditions or external facts. Ochs v. Martinez, 789 S.W.2d 949, 959 (Tex.App.1990); 2 McCormick, Evidence § 273 (7th ed.2013). A statement of a past condition or an external

219

fact may, however, be admissible under Rule 803(4), if it is made for the purpose of medical diagnosis or treatment.

(3) Statement of present state of mind or emotion, offered to prove a state of mind or emotion of the declarant that is "in issue" in the case. In innumerable instances, the rules of substantive law treat the state or condition of mind or emotion of a person as an element of a crime, cause of action, or defense. In any of these cases, statements by the person in question indicating a then existing relevant state or condition of mind or feeling are admissible.

> **Example—Admissible.** In extortion case, victim's fearful state of mind is an essential element; therefore, victim's expressions of fear are admissible. United States v. Collins, 78 F.3d 1021, 1036 (6th Cir.1996); United States v. Adcock, 558 F.2d 397, 404 (8th Cir.1977).

> **Example—Admissible.** " 'The victim's fearful state of mind is a crucial element in proving extortion. The testimony of victims as to what others said to them, and the testimony of others as to what they said to victims is admitted not for the truth of the information in the statements but for the fact that the victim heard them and that they would have tended to produce fear in his mind.' Because such fear-illustrating statements also often refer to acts of the defendant, courts should, upon request, instruct the jury that such statements may only be used as evidence of fear, not evidence of the defendant's acts. * * * Such 'fear' evidence in extortion cases is similar to, but distinguishable from, evidence admissible under the hearsay exception at Federal Rule of Evidence 803(3). Rule 803(3) allows witnesses to recount hearsay statements (that is, statements offered to prove the truth of the statements' factual content) when the statement's original declarant is expressing his or her then-existing state of mind. * * * The difference is this: when the out-of-court statement is an expression of fear being offered to prove the existence of the fear expressed in the statement, this is a hearsay statement that may be admissible under Rule 803(3). When, however, the statement is not the victim/declarant's expression of his or her own fear, but a statement made to (or in the presence of) the victim by someone else that would tend to be a fear-inducing statement, such evidence is not hearsay." United States v. Kilpatrick, 798 F.3d 365, 386 (6th Cir.2015) (citations omitted).

> **Example—Admissible.** Defendant's out-of-court statement offered by him to show lack of criminal intent. "While the government was attempting to show that Bennie had the specific intent to conspire in a drug scheme, Bennie's reply to Buford on the telephone tends to show that his intent was to help 'capture' Hackney." United States v. Peak, 856 F.2d 825, 833 (7th Cir.1988).

> **Example—Admissible.** In trademark infringement and "passing off" case, statements by members of the public indicating their confusion as to source of product were admissible under Rule 803(3). Source Services Corp. v. Source Telecomputing Corp., 635 F.Supp. 600, 612 (N.D.Ill.1986). Accord, Lahoti v. Vericheck, Inc., 636 F.3d 501, 509 (9th Cir.2011); Fun-Damental Too, Ltd. v. Gemmy Industries Corp., 111 F.3d 993, 1003–04 (2d Cir.1997).

> **Example—Admissible.** In suit alleging race discrimination in termination of plaintiff's employment, racist comments by management personnel were admissible under Rule 803(3). Talley v. Bravo Pitino Restaurant, Ltd., 61 F.3d 1241, 1249–50 (6th Cir.1995).

> **Example—Admissible.** In antitrust case, statements by customers of plaintiffs as to why they were purchasing instead from defendants. Callahan v. A.E.V., Inc., 182 F.3d 237, 250–53 (3d Cir.1999).

(4) Must be statement of declarant's, not another's, state of mind. Rule 803(3) applies only to a statement describing a state of mind of the declarant; Rule 803(3) "does not authorize receipt of a statement by one person as proof of another's state of mind." Hong v. Children's Memorial Hospital, 993 F.2d 1257, 1265 (7th Cir.1993).

> **Example—Inadmissible.** "Ms. Meyers asserts that Mr. O'Boyle's remark falls under the state of mind exception to the hearsay rule. See Fed. R. Evid. 803(3). But, this exception would cover Mr. O'Boyle's state of mind, not the superintendent's. See United States v. Joe, 8 F.3d 1488, 1493 n. 4 (10th Cir.1993) ('An out-of-court statement relating a third party's state of mind falls outside the scope of the hearsay exception because such a statement necessarily is one of memory or belief.'). Mr. O'Boyle's state of mind is irrelevant: The rigging was allegedly done by the

superintendent, not Mr. O'Boyle. Thus, the state of mind exception would not support the admissibility of Mr. O'Boyle's alleged remark." Meyers v. Eastern Oklahoma County Technology Center, 776 F.3d 1201, 1207 (10th Cir.2015).

(5)   Statement of present state of mind—usually intent, plan, or design—offered to prove subsequent conduct of the declarant in accordance with the state of mind. In the famous case of Mutual Life Insurance Co. of New York v. Hillmon, 145 U.S. 285, 12 S.Ct. 909 (1892), the United States Supreme Court extended the hearsay exception for state-of-mind statements to a case in which the declarant's mental state was not in issue, but was merely relevant evidence on an external fact dispute, concerning the declarant's conduct at a subsequent time. The so-called *Hillmon* doctrine, allowing state-of-mind statements to show subsequent conduct of the declarant, is carried forward in Rule 803(3). Shelden v. Barre Belt Granite Employer Union Pension Fund, 25 F.3d 74, 79 (2d Cir.1994); United States v. Astorga-Torres, 682 F.2d 1331, 1335–36 (9th Cir.1982).

(6)   Relevancy of declarant's subsequent conduct. Of course, the conduct sought to be proved by the statement must be relevant. T. Harris Young & Assoc., Inc. v. Marquette Electronics, Inc., 931 F.2d 816, 828 (11th Cir.1991); United States v. Scrima, 819 F.2d 996, 1000 (11th Cir.1987) ("Under these facts, Scrima's subjective belief as to his wealth is totally irrelevant. The statement was offered to prove the fact that the defendant actually had the money not that he thought he had it. Consequently, the statement was not admissible under Rule 803(3).").

(7)   Memory or belief statements prohibited. Statements of "memory or belief to prove the fact remembered or believed"—except in will cases—are not admissible on the state-of-mind theory. United States v. Rodriguez-Pando, 841 F.2d 1014, 1019 (10th Cir.1988).

Example—Inadmissible. "What Iglesias said was offered to show not only that he was remorseful, but also that he had stolen the belts. Rule 803(3) expressly prohibits the use of a statement of then-existing state of mind in this way." United States v. Samaniego, 345 F.3d 1280, 1283 (11th Cir.2003).

Example—Inadmissible. "Here Aquarium would like to have had Mr. Murray testify to Lerner's statement of memory, that is, Lerner's recollection of the telephone conversation, in order to prove the fact remembered, i.e., the contents of that conversation. This is among the type of testimony that the final phrase of Rule 803(3) was designed to preclude." Marshall v. Commonwealth Aquarium, 611 F.2d 1, 5 (1st Cir.1979).

Example—Inadmissible. "Ms. Joe's statement to Dr. Smoker, though indicating her state of mind, also included a statement of why she was afraid (i.e., because she thought her husband might kill her). This portion of Ms. Joe's statement is clearly a 'statement of memory or belief' expressly excluded by the Rule 803(3) exception." United States v. Joe, 8 F.3d 1488, 1492–93 (10th Cir.1993).

Example—Inadmissible. "[T]he defendants' criminal intent or lack thereof in January 1983, when the statements were made, was not an issue at their trial; rather, the issue at trial was whether the defendants had been involved in a fuel-stealing scheme two years earlier. The defendants are attempting to introduce statements relevant to their state of mind in 1983 as indicative of their actions before that time. Admission of such evidence is prohibited by Fed. R. Evid. 803(3) * * *." United States v. Jackson, 780 F.2d 1305, 1315 (7th Cir.1986).

Example—Inadmissible. "Turolla's e-mails contain hearsay statements expressing his then existing state of mind (i.e., 'I hate to be in this predicament;' 'I am at my wits end;' 'I am concerned for the future') as well as assertions of why Turolla had these feelings (i.e., descriptions of conversations, interactions, incidents, and problems he was allegedly having with Plaintiff). The statements explaining why Turolla had these feelings are expressly outside the state-of-mind exception." McInnis v. Fairfield Communities, Inc., 458 F.3d 1129, 1143 (10th Cir.2006).

Example—Partly admissible, partly inadmissible. Prosecution for sexual abuse of 11-year-old girl. Over hearsay objections, the mother of the girl was permitted to testify to the girl's account of the crime after the girl awoke her in the middle of the night with a facial laceration. "Limited portions of the mother's testimony are based upon D.D.'s statements concerning her physical state—she was bleeding because Joseph DeMarce hit and tried to rape her. Those statements were properly admitted. This court concludes that the remaining testimony of the mother, however, does not recount statements of D.D.'s present condition, but states D.D.'s memory. The testimony should not have been admitted under Rule 803(3)." United States v. DeMarce, 564 F.3d 989, 996 (8th Cir.2009).

(8) Joint conduct. Although the matter is controversial, most courts admit a statement of A that he or she intends to do an act with B as evidence of both A's and B's subsequent conduct. E.g., United States v. Pheaster, 544 F.2d 353, 374–80 (9th Cir.1976). Some courts require independent evidence corroborating the conduct of B. United States v. Delvecchio, 816 F.2d 859, 862–63 (2d Cir.1987).

(9) Testator statements. The peculiar feature of this category of state-of-mind statements is that it is not restricted by the prohibition against statements of memory or belief that limits all the other categories. This special treatment applies only to a testator's statement that "relates to the execution, revocation, identification, or terms" of the will. It does not extend, for example, to a statement concerning the conduct of others influencing the terms of the will. Atherton v. Gaslin, 194 Ky. 460, 239 S.W. 771 (1922); Barnum v. State, 7 S.W.3d 782, 789–90 & n. 5 (Tex.App.1999).

CROSS-REFERENCES

Treatises

7 Graham, Handbook of Federal Evidence § 803:3 (9th ed. 2020)

2 McCormick, Evidence §§ 273–276 (8th ed. 2020)

30B Wright & Bellin, Federal Practice and Procedure §§ 6831–6836 (2018)

Rule 803(4).   Statement Made for Medical Diagnosis or Treatment

The following are not excluded by the rule against hearsay, regardless of whether the declarant is available as a witness:

* * *

    (4) *Statement Made for Medical Diagnosis or Treatment.* A statement that:

        (A) is made for—and is reasonably pertinent to—medical diagnosis or treatment; and

        (B) describes medical history; past or present symptoms or sensations; their inception; or their general cause.

* * *

AUTHORS' COMMENTS

(1) Not limited to treating physicians. Rule 803(4) is not limited to statements for purposes of medical treatment; it extends to statements to a nontreating physician consulted solely for purposes of expert testimony ("diagnosis *or* treatment"). O'Gee v. Dobbs Houses, Inc., 570 F.2d 1084, 1089 (2d Cir.1978).

(2) Statements as to cause of condition. Rule 803(4) includes a statement by the patient concerning the cause of his condition, so long as it meets the test of "reasonably pertinent to medical diagnosis or treatment." The Advisory Committee's Note explains: "Statements as to fault would not ordinarily qualify under this latter language. Thus a patient's statement that he was struck by an automobile would qualify but not his statement that the car was driven through a red light." The key word in the Advisory Committee's comment is "ordinarily." In many instances, a statement "as to fault" will be pertinent to treatment and will therefore be admissible under the exception.

Example—Admissible. Statement by sexually abused child to doctor identifying father or stepfather as abuser. United States v. Longie, 984 F.2d 955, 959 (8th Cir.1993); United States v. George, 960 F.2d 97, 99 (9th Cir.1992); United States v. Renville, 779 F.2d 430, 435–36 (8th Cir.1985).

Example—Admissible. Statements by child victim of sexual assault to medical personnel; court rejected argument that reliability of statements was undermined because child, on account of age, was not able to understand medical relationship and necessity of telling truth. United States

222

v. Pacheco, 154 F.3d 1236, 1240–41 (10th Cir.1998). Accord, United States v. Edward J., 224 F.3d 1216, 1219–20 (10th Cir.2000); United States v. Norman T., 129 F.3d 1099, 1105–06 (10th Cir.1997) (five-year-old child). Contra, United States v. Sumner, 204 F.3d 1182, 1185 (8th Cir.2000) ("[I]t must be shown that the child understands the 'medical significance of being truthful,' i.e., the role of the medical health professional in trying to help or heal her, which triggers the motivation to be truthful."); Olesen v. Class, 164 F.3d 1096, 1098 (8th Cir.1999).

Example—Admissible. Statements by mother of thirteen-year-old blind, speech-impaired daughter to nurse, describing attempted sexual assault by child's father. Lovejoy v. United States, 92 F.3d 628, 632 (8th Cir.1996).

Example—Admissible. Statement by sexually abused wife to doctor identifying estranged husband as abuser. United States v. Joe, 8 F.3d 1488, 1494–95 (10th Cir.1993).

Example—Admissible. Statement by victim to physician that she was raped. United States v. Cherry, 938 F.2d 748, 756–57 (7th Cir.1991); United States v. Iron Thunder, 714 F.2d 765, 772–73 (8th Cir.1983).

Example—Admissible. Prosecution of defendant for murder of his wife and mother-in-law; mother-in-law's physician testified that he diagnosed and treated her for "situational depression," relying in part upon her statements "that her son-in-law had been physically abusive to her daughter, and that 'she felt he might kill them both.' " State v. Moen, 309 Or. 45, 55–58, 786 P.2d 111, 118–21 (1990).

Example—Admissible. "While the district court was correct that Willingham's statements about a firearm being pointed at her were not relevant to her physical injuries, it is clear from the physicians' notes that Willingham was also seeking treatment for emotional trauma. Willingham's statements to her doctors indicate that her emotional trauma stemmed, in part, from having a firearm pointed at her; therefore, these statements were relevant to her diagnosis and treatment." Willingham v. Crooke, 412 F.3d 553, 562 (4th Cir.2005).

Example—Admissible. "The statements by the medical professionals in this case that the victims' wounds and burns were the result of abuse or torture (as opposed to, for example, a vehicular or workplace accident) were statements of causation. * * * These records do not assign any fault for the abuse or torture, nor do they insinuate impermissibly that the 'abuse' or 'torture' satisfied any particular statutory or legal definition of those terms. The district court did not abuse its discretion in admitting the unredacted medical records into evidence." United States v. Belfast, 611 F.3d 783, 819 (11th Cir.2010).

Example—Inadmissible. Statement to physician that injuries were caused by "excessive force." Roberts v. Hollocher, 664 F.2d 200, 204–05 (8th Cir.1981).

    (3) Statements to nonphysicians. "Under the exception the statement need not have been made to a physician. Statements to hospital attendants, ambulance drivers, or even members of the family might be included." Advisory Committee's Note to Rule 803(4). Statements to nonphysicians are frequently admitted under the rule. E.g., Davignon v. Clemmey, 322 F.3d 1, 8 (1st Cir.2003) (statements by family to family therapist and social worker concerning the emotional distress the children suffered at the hands of defendants); United States v. Newman, 965 F.2d 206, 210 (7th Cir.1992) (clinical psychologist); United States v. Balfany, 965 F.2d 575, 581 (8th Cir.1992) (statements by abused child to psychologist and social worker identifying abuser); Navarro de Cosme v. Hospital Pavia, 922 F.2d 926, 933 (1st Cir.1991) (social worker).

    (4) Statements by doctor to patient. Rule 803(4) does not cover statements by a doctor or other medical personnel to the patient. Bombard v. Fort Wayne Newspapers, Inc., 92 F.3d 560, 564 (7th Cir.1996); Bulthuis v. Rexall Corp., 789 F.2d 1315, 1316 (9th Cir.1985) ("Rule 803(4) applies only to statements made by the patient to the doctor, not the reverse.").

    (5) Statements between doctors. Rule 803(4) does not extend to statements between physicians. Field v. Trigg County Hospital, Inc., 386 F.3d 729, 736 (6th Cir.2004) (statements made by consulting physicians to the treating physician).

CROSS-REFERENCES

Treatises

7 Graham, Handbook of Federal Evidence § 803:4 (9th ed. 2020)

2 McCormick, Evidence §§ 277, 278, 324.3 (8th ed. 2020)

30B Wright & Bellin, Federal Practice and Procedure §§ 6841–6849 (2018)

Rule 803(5).   Recorded Recollection

The following are not excluded by the rule against hearsay, regardless of whether the declarant is available as a witness:

* * *

(5) *Recorded Recollection.* A record that:

     (A) is on a matter the witness once knew about but now cannot recall well enough to testify fully and accurately;

     (B) was made or adopted by the witness when the matter was fresh in the witness's memory; and

     (C) accurately reflects the witness's knowledge.

If admitted, the record may be read into evidence but may be received as an exhibit only if offered by an adverse party.

* * *

AUTHORS' COMMENTS

(1) Memorandum not to go to jury room. The second sentence of Rule 803(5) denies the memorandum entrance to the jury room as an exhibit of the proponent "in order to prevent the trier of fact from being overly impressed by the writing." United States v. Judon, 567 F.2d 1289, 1294 (5th Cir.1978). See also Research Systems Corp. v. IPSOS Publicite, 276 F.3d 914, 923 (7th Cir.2002) (proper for court to exclude memorandum when offered as an exhibit rather than to be read).

(2) "Fresh memory." Rule 803(5)'s requirement that the memorandum or record "was made or adopted by the witness when the matter was fresh in the witness's memory" is far less strict than Rule 803(6)'s requirement of "at or near the time." United States v. Patterson, 678 F.2d 774, 779–80 (9th Cir.1982) (witness's grand jury testimony reporting conversations with defendant admitted under Rule 803(5) though recorded testimony given "at least ten months" after the conversations); United States v. Williams, 571 F.2d 344, 348 (6th Cir.1978) (memorandum of conversations made six months afterward).

(3) Memorandum not made but adopted by witness. Rule 803(5) extends to a memorandum or record "adopted" by a witness, such as where the witness orally recounted a matter to another who reduced the account to a written statement which the witness then verified. United States v. Lewis, 954 F.2d 1386, 1394 (7th Cir.1992).

(4) Form of memorandum. A transcript, made by others, of a taped telephone call between the sponsoring witness and another, qualified under Rule 803(5). United States v. Rommy, 506 F.3d 108, 138–139 (2d Cir.2007).

CROSS-REFERENCES

Checklists and Foundations (Chapter 4)

5.   Foundation for Recorded Recollection

Treatises

7 Graham, Handbook of Federal Evidence § 803:5 (9th ed. 2020)

2 McCormick, Evidence §§ 279–283 (8th ed. 2020)

30B Wright & Bellin, Federal Practice and Procedure §§ 6851–6857 (2018)

Rule 803(6), (7).   Records of a Regularly Conducted Activity

The following are not excluded by the rule against hearsay, regardless of whether the declarant is available as a witness:

* * *

(6) ***Records of a Regularly Conducted Activity.*** A record of an act, event, condition, opinion, or diagnosis if:

(A) the record was made at or near the time by—or from information transmitted by—someone with knowledge;

(B) the record was kept in the course of a regularly conducted activity of a business, organization, occupation, or calling, whether or not for profit;

(C) making the record was a regular practice of that activity;

(D) all these conditions are shown by the testimony of the custodian or another qualified witness, or by a certification that complies with Rule 902(11) or (12) or with a statute permitting certification; and

(E) the opponent does not show that the source of information or the method or circumstances of preparation indicate a lack of trustworthiness.

(7) ***Absence of a Record of a Regularly Conducted Activity.*** Evidence that a matter is not included in a record described in paragraph (6) if:

(A) the evidence is admitted to prove that the matter did not occur or exist;

(B) a record was regularly kept for a matter of that kind; and

(C) the opponent does not show that the possible source of the information or other circumstances indicate a lack of trustworthiness.

* * *

AUTHORS' COMMENTS

(1)   Foundation for business record. The foundation for qualifying a business record under Rule 803(6) consists of four basic elements:

(a)   the record was made and kept in the course of a regularly conducted business activity;

(b)   it was the regular practice of the business activity to make the record; i.e., it is a routine record;

(c)   the record was made at or near the time of the event that it records;

(d)   the record was made by, or from information transmitted by, a person with knowledge; the person with knowledge must have acted in the regular course of business, or as it is sometimes put, must have had a business duty to report.

The foregoing elements must be shown by the testimony of the custodian or "another qualified witness," or by certification under Rule 902(11) or (12). "Another qualified witness" is any person who can credibly testify that the records satisfy the requirements of the exception. United States v. Console, 13 F.3d 641, 657 (3d Cir.1993); Wallace Motor Sales, Inc. v. American Motors Sales Corp., 780 F.2d 1049, 1060–61 (1st Cir.1985).

Whether the supporting witness is the custodian or another person, it is not required that the witness have personal knowledge of the contents of the particular entry or the circumstances in which it was made. It suffices that the witness can testify that the records generally satisfy the conditions of the rule. United States v. Collins, 799 F.3d 554, 584 (6th Cir.2015) ("[T]he meaning of '[another] qualified witness should be given the broadest interpretation.' The foundation for admitting evidence under Rule 803(6) 'may be laid, in whole or in part, by the testimony of a government agent or other person outside the organization whose records are sought to be admitted. The only requirement is that the witness be familiar with the record keeping system.'") (citations omitted); Conoco Inc. v. Department of Energy, 99 F.3d 387, 391–92 (Fed.Cir.1996); F.D.I.C. v. Staudinger, 797 F.2d 908, 910 (10th Cir.1986); United States v. Lieberman, 637 F.2d 95, 100 (2d Cir.1980).

> **Example—Admissible.** "The business records exception to the hearsay rule clearly does not require that the witness have personal knowledge of the entries in the records. The witness need only have knowledge of the procedures under which the records were created. * * * Thus, Richardson's lack of memory with regard to the specific entries in the records does not affect their admissibility under Fed. R. Evid. 803(6)." United States v. Wables, 731 F.2d 440, 449 (7th Cir.1984).

> **Example—Admissible.** The custodian who testifies to the foundation for a business record need not have been the custodian at the time the record was made. United States v. Scallion, 533 F.2d 903, 915 (5th Cir.1976).

> **Example—Admissible.** The foundation witness need not have been employed by the business at the time of the making of the record. United States v. Smith, 609 F.2d 1294, 1301–02 (9th Cir.1979).

> **Example—Inadmissible.** A state police officer was not a "qualified witness" to lay the foundation for a state crime laboratory chemist's report, because he had no personal knowledge about how the reports were prepared or maintained. United States v. Riley, 236 F.3d 982, 984–85 (8th Cir.2001).

> **Example—Inadmissible.** " * * * Weber was not a 'custodian or other qualified witness' because he did not know when or how the documents were prepared. * * * Weber testified that he had seen the documents while attending a meeting at Allied-Signal. However, he failed to testify concerning the record-keeping process related to them, a requirement for admissibility of documents under the business records exception." Fonar Corp. v. General Elec. Co., 107 F.3d 1543 (Fed.Cir.1997).

> **Example—Inadmissible.** "The district court did not err in ruling that Barner was not qualified to lay the foundation. Barner's expertise in statistics and in the computer program used did not give him any knowledge about I-10 East Pharmacy's record keeping practices. He knew about the pharmacy computer system, how to operate the system, and how to extract information from it, but that is not knowledge about the pharmacy's record keeping. * * * Amidst all of his unquestioned expertise, Barner lacked this necessary familiarity." United States v. Brown, 553 F.3d 768, 793 (5th Cir.2008).

Rules 902(11) and (12) were added by amendment in 2000. They permit establishment of all foundation elements by certification of the custodian or other qualified person, thereby obviating foundation testimony at trial.

(2) Computer records. The fact that records are kept by computer does not result in any special foundation requirements beyond those set forth in the rule. United States v. Linn, 880 F.2d 209, 216 (9th Cir.1989); United States v. Vela, 673 F.2d 86, 90 (5th Cir.1982).

(3) "Business." The first element of the basic foundation is easily satisfied because of the breadth of the definition of "business," which includes any "regularly conducted activity." The activity may be that of an individual, so long as it is done, and the records are kept, regularly. Keogh v. Commissioner of Internal Revenue, 713 F.2d 496, 499–500 (9th Cir.1983) (personal diary of wages and tips kept by casino employee admissible under Rule 803(6)).

(4) "Regular practice." The second element, routineness, goes to the heart of the theory of trustworthiness of business records. Reliability does not attach to a statement just because a person engaged in a business activity writes it down; it is essential to any claim of reliability that the statement be of a type that persons engaged in the activity record routinely.

> **Example—Inadmissible.** "None [of the letters] are a record made in the 'regular practice' of the construction business. Instead, his letters have all the earmarks of being motivated and generated to further Timberlake's interest, with litigation actually not far around the corner. The same holds true for the October 13 letter from Abowitz, Timberlake's counsel, to James, counsel

for Fidelity, demanding that Fidelity cover Timberlake's loss." Timberlake Construction Co. v. United States Fidelity & Guaranty Co., 71 F.3d 335, 342 (10th Cir.1995).

Example—Inadmissible. "We find no indication in the record that Comp-U-Med obtained appraisals of this sort as a 'regular practice' of its business. There is thus no foundation for admitting it as Comp-U-Med's business record." Waddell v. C.I.R., 841 F.2d 264, 267 (9th Cir.1988).

Example—Admissible. "LeShore's challenge to the bait money list is that even though the bank regularly kept this record, it was irregularly compiled (in this case, remade): a new list was made only after the theft (or loss) of an existing bait money packet. * * * This argument overstates the spirit of both the rule and the exception. The chief concern with hearsay evidence is that it lacks sufficient indicia of reliability. Even though the bank did not compile its bait money list regularly, it verified the list three times per year. * * * Indeed, all of the factors suggested by the Advisory Committee as central to the justification for the exception are met in this case: systematic checking, regularity and continuity (giving rise to precision), actual reliance by the business, and compilation and verification by someone whose duty it is to do so." United States v. LeShore, 543 F.3d 935, 942 (7th Cir.2008).

(5) "At or near the time." The third requirement is that the record be made "at or near the time" of the recorded event. "Timeliness is essential because 'any trustworthy habit of making regular business records will ordinarily involve the making of the record contemporaneously.'" Abascal v. Fleckenstein, 820 F.3d 561, 565 (2d Cir.2016) (quoting United States v. Strother, 49 F.3d 869, 876 (2d Cir.1995)). The requirement is satisfied if the record was made "a reasonable time thereafter." Seattle-First Nat'l Bank v. Randall, 532 F.2d 1291, 1296 (9th Cir.1976).

Example—Inadmissible. Memorandum prepared November 5, 1976 providing "history and background of the transaction" from December 5, 1975 to June 19, 1976 did not satisfy timeliness requirement of Rule 803(6). United States v. Lemire, 720 F.2d 1327, 1350 (D.C.Cir.1983).

Example—Admissible. "[A]lthough the physical documents were not generated when the parties contracted for the shipment of Lozen's grapes, they were produced from the same electronic information that was generated contemporaneously. For the purposes of Rule 803(6), 'it is immaterial that the business record is maintained in a computer rather than in company books.'" Sea-Land Service, Inc. v. Lozen International, LLC., 285 F.3d 808, 819 (9th Cir.2002).

(6) "By—or from information transmitted by—someone with knowledge"; outsider statements; double hearsay. The employee who makes the record or entry need not have personal knowledge of the facts recorded, but some person who is a member of the organized activity must have personal knowledge. The requisite knowledge may be inferred circumstantially. United States v. Lieberman, 637 F.2d 95, 100 (2d Cir.1980) ("In light of the complexities of modern business, direct proof of actual knowledge of the person making the record or providing the information is not required, and the requisite knowledge may be inferred from the fact that it was someone's business to obtain such information."). There is no requirement that the person whose knowledge was the basis for the entry be identified, so long as it is shown that it was the regular practice of the activity to receive information from a person with knowledge. United States v. Reyes, 157 F.3d 949, 952 (2d Cir.1998).

If a business record incorporates a statement by a person who is not part of the regular organized activity and who thus has no "business duty" to make the report—an "outsider" to the organized activity—and the record is offered to prove the truth of the incorporated statement, the record will be treated as "double hearsay." The statement by the outside declarant will be inadmissible for its truth unless it independently falls within an exception to or exemption from the hearsay rule.

Example—Inadmissible. "Thus, it is well established that although entries in a police or investigating officer's report which result from the officer's own observations and knowledge may be admitted, statements made to the officer by third parties under no business duty to report may not." United States v. Snyder, 787 F.2d 1429, 1434 (10th Cir.1986).

Example—Inadmissible. "Although the adjuster's report might otherwise qualify as a business record within the meaning of Rule 803(6), Belsky's statement does not satisfy the rule's requirements because there was no showing that he had a duty to report the information he was quoted as having given." United States v. Bortnovsky, 879 F.2d 30, 34 (2d Cir.1989).

Example—Inadmissible. Bank records containing customers' statements that their credit cards were stolen. United States v. Ismoila, 100 F.3d 380, 392–93 (5th Cir.1996).

Example—Inadmissible. "[W]e conclude that the district court erred in admitting Exhibit 1-BBB and Exhibits 22, 23, and 24 under Rule 803(6). It is undisputed that the crucial information in the AOL and PACER records—specifically, the information concerning the identity of the user of the 'rablechman' AOL account and the user of PACER account 'RB 1071'—was provided by a third party over the Internet, not by an employee of AOL or PACER." United States v. Blechman, 657 F.3d 1052, 1066 (10th Cir.2011).

Example—Admissible. Police report incorporating statement by party, offered against the party. Rosario v. Amalgamated Ladies' Garment Cutters' Union, Local 10 of I.L.G.W.U., 605 F.2d 1228, 1250–51 (2d Cir.1979).

Example—Admissible. Transcript of statement routinely taken by insurance company from employee of party, offered against the party. Wright v. Farmers Co-Op of Arkansas and Oklahoma, 681 F.2d 549, 553 (8th Cir.1982).

Example—Admissible. Western Union "to-send-money" forms on which sender had written his name, address, etc., where government did not offer the forms to prove the truth of the sender's assertion of identity, but rather on the theory that the names were fictitious names established by other evidence as aliases of defendant. United States v. Cestnik, 36 F.3d 904, 907–09 (10th Cir.1994).

Example—Admissible. "The Hoseltons are correct when they argue that the out-of-court statements in Williams's notes by other declarants do not meet the requirements of Rule 803(6). In the case of Exhibit A-60, however, the statements of the other declarant or declarants are not offered to show the truth of the matters asserted in the statements." Hoselton v. Metz Baking Co., 48 F.3d 1056, 1061 (8th Cir.1995).

Where the source of information is an outsider, the statement may be admitted on a showing of a regular practice of verification by an employee of the business; for example, records of customers' identities may be received if a practice of examination of identification cards is established. United States v. Reyes, 157 F.3d 949, 952 (2d Cir.1998). Compare Rowland v. American General Finance, Inc., 340 F.3d 187, 194–95 (4th Cir.2003) (customer letter complaining about an employee kept in employer's files, inadmissible hearsay); United States v. Santos, 201 F.3d 953, 963 (7th Cir.2000) ("The fact that statements made by strangers to the business become a part of its records, such as the complaints which were placed in the Board of Ethics' files, does not make them business records unless they are verified by the business and thus adopted and become the business's own statements. * * * That did not happen here. The complaints were inadmissible hearsay interleaved with admissible business records").

A document prepared by a third party may qualify as a business record under Rule 803(6) if the business integrated the document into its records and relied upon it, provided that circumstances support the trustworthiness of the document. Residential Funding Co., LLC v. Terrace Mortg. Co., 725 F.3d 910, 921 (8th Cir.2013) ("[A] record created by a third party and used as part of another entity's records meets the business records exception, so long as the entity relied on the accuracy of that record and the remaining requirements of Rule 803(6) are met."); United States v. Adefehinti, 510 F.3d 319, 326 (D.C. Cir.2007) ("[S]everal courts have found that a record of which a firm takes custody is thereby 'made' by the firm within the meaning of the rule (and thus is admissible if all the other requirements are satisfied). We join those courts.") (citing cases); United States v. Grant, 56 M.J. 410, 414–15 (U.S.C.A.A.F. 2002) (Texas medical laboratory report incorporated into records of military hospital in Turkey; "[A] record incorporated by a second entity may be admitted under Mil.R.Evid. 803(6) on the testimony of a 'qualified witness' of the incorporating entity alone if certain criteria are met. First, the incorporating entity must obviously procure and keep the record in the normal course of its business. Second, the entity must show that it relies on the accuracy of the incorporated record in its business. Finally, there must be 'other circumstances indicating the trustworthiness of the document.' " [citations omitted]).

(7) "Lack of trustworthiness" proviso. Courts are likely to invoke the "lack of trustworthiness" proviso with regard to documents prepared in anticipation of litigation, or under circumstances similarly suggesting a motive to misrepresent.

> **Example—Inadmissible.** "The incident report was prepared by a non-witness Hardee's employee and contained not only a description of the condition of the parking lot as dry, not wet or oily, but also a statement attributed to a 'friend' of Mrs. Scheerer that the cause of the accident was Mrs. Scheerer's 'slick shoes.' * * * We hold the incident report was not admissible as a business record under Fed. R. Evid. 803(6) because the source of the information contained therein was never identified at trial. * * * In the absence of any evidence about the source of that information, we cannot test its reliability or trustworthiness. * * * In addition, the incident report was inadmissible as a business record under Fed. R. Evid. 803(6) because it had been prepared in anticipation of litigation." Scheerer v. Hardee's Food Systems, Inc., 92 F.3d 702, 706 (8th Cir.1996).

> **Example—Inadmissible.** "The report is no more trustworthy because Geary prepared it than if Underwriters had done so. Whether Underwriters compiled the report as part of an internal investigation with in-house employees or whether Underwriters hired an outside investigator to prepare the report, the conclusion remains that the primary motive for initially preparing the report was to prepare for litigation. * * * Litigants cannot evade the trustworthiness requirement of Rule 803(6) by simply hiring an outside party to investigate an accident and then arguing that the report is a business record because the investigator regularly prepares such reports as part of his business." Certain Underwriters at Lloyd's, London v. Sinkovich, 232 F.3d 200, 205 (4th Cir.2000).

> **Example—Inadmissible.** "Clearly, the report in this case was not kept in the course of a regularly conducted business activity, but rather was specially prepared at the behest of the FBI and with the knowledge that any information it supplied would be used in an ongoing criminal investigation. * * * In finding this report inadmissible under Rule 803(6), we adhere to the well-established rule that documents made in anticipation of litigation are inadmissible under the business records exception." United States v. Blackburn, 992 F.2d 666, 670 (7th Cir.1993).

> **Example—Inadmissible.** "[W]e find the Ragan memorandum inadmissible because the circumstances of its preparation indicate a lack of trustworthiness. It was drafted not as part of a regular routine by Pan-Islamic to reflect the true state of its marketing efforts, but was drafted for the express purpose of preventing Sonatrach from cancelling the contract. As such, it was written in the most optimistic light Ragan thought the facts would warrant." Pan-Islamic Trade Corp. v. Exxon Corp., 632 F.2d 539, 560 (5th Cir.1980).

A party's accident report may be viewed with skepticism if offered by that party under Rule 803(6); however, such a report can be introduced by the party's opponent under Rule 802(d)(2)(D). Mister v. Northeast Ill. Commuter R.R. Corp., 571 F.3d 696, 698–99 (7th Cir.2009) (injury report prepared by railroad's employee was admissible against it without requiring internal verification of the contents of the report).

A party need not prove that business records are accurate before they are admitted. Generally, objections that records contain inaccuracies, ambiguities, or omissions go to weight rather than admissibility. United States v. Smith, 804 F.3d 724, 729–30 (5th Cir.2015); United States v. Scholl, 166 F.3d 964, 978 (9th Cir.1999).

(8) Reports inadmissible under Rule 803(8)(B) or (C). If a public record or report is inadmissible against an accused in a criminal case under Rule 803(8) because of the limitations in Rule 803(8)(B) or (C), the record or report generally cannot be admitted under Rule 803(6) even though it might otherwise meet all the requirements of Rule 803(6). United States v. Brown, 9 F.3d 907, 911 (11th Cir.1993); United States v. Oates, 560 F.2d 45, 84 (2d Cir.1977).

(9) Absence of entry. Rule 803(7) permits proof of the nonoccurrence or nonexistence of a matter by showing that no record of it is found in regularly kept records that would be expected to have recorded it if it did occur or exist. A presentation under Rule 803(7) requires, first, a foundation sufficient to qualify the record under Rule 803(6). Second, either the record must be introduced, or the custodian or other qualified witness must testify that a diligent search failed to disclose the matter. United States v. Rich, 580 F.2d 929, 938 (9th Cir.1978). The best evidence rule is not violated by testimony that a writing does not contain any reference to a matter. Advisory Committee's Note to Rule 1002.

CROSS-REFERENCES

Checklists and Foundations (Chapter 4)
2.   Foundation for Business Record
Treatises
7 Graham, Handbook of Federal Evidence §§ 803:6, 803:7 (9th ed. 2020)
2 McCormick, Evidence §§ 284–294, 324.1 (8th ed. 2020)
30B Wright & Bellin, Federal Practice and Procedure §§ 6861–6873 (2018)

Rule 803(8)–(10). Public Records

The following are not excluded by the rule against hearsay, regardless of whether the declarant is available as a witness:

* * *

(8) *Public Records.* A record or statement of a public office if:

   (A) it sets out:

      (i) the office's activities;

      (ii) a matter observed while under a legal duty to report, but not including, in a criminal case, a matter observed by law-enforcement personnel; or

      (iii) in a civil case or against the government in a criminal case, factual findings from a legally authorized investigation; and

   (B) the opponent does not show that the source of information or other circumstances indicate a lack of trustworthiness.

(9) *Public Records of Vital Statistics.* A record of a birth, death, or marriage, if reported to a public office in accordance with a legal duty.

(10) *Absence of a Public Record.* Testimony—or a certification under Rule 902—that a diligent search failed to disclose a public record or statement if:

   (A) the testimony or certification is admitted to prove that

      (i) the record or statement does not exist; or

      (ii) a matter did not occur or exist, if a public office regularly kept a record or statement for a matter of that kind; and

   (B) in a criminal case, a prosecutor who intends to offer a certification provides written notice of that intent at least 14 days before trial, and the defendant does not object in writing within 7 days of receiving the notice—unless the court sets a different time for the notice or the objection.

* * *

AUTHORS' COMMENTS

   (1)   Foundation; business records distinguished. The foundation for a public record or report under Rule 803(8) need only establish that the document is authentic and that it contains one of the three types of matters specified in the rule. It is not necessary to show that the public record or report was regular or made at or near the time of the event recorded. Matter of Oil Spill by the Amoco Cadiz, 954 F.2d 1279, 1308 (7th Cir.1992) ("The public-document exception to the hearsay rule does not contain the requirement of the business records exception (Rule 803(6)) that the documents be kept in the course of a regularly

230

conducted activity."); United States v. Versaint, 849 F.2d 827, 832 (3d Cir.1988) ("Fed. R. Evid. 803(8) does not require that a report be made at or near the time of the event it is describing.").

(2) Types of public documents covered. Despite the liberal breadth of the public records exception, it does not embrace every document created by public agencies. To be admissible, the document must fall within one of the three specific categories designated in the rule.

Example—Inadmissible. Draft of proposed letter from area director of Office of Federal Contract Compliance Programs. Figures v. Board of Public Utilities, 967 F.2d 357, 360 (10th Cir.1992).

Example—Inadmissible. Transcript of state court proceeding reflecting state trial judge's opinion that settlement was reasonable. Trustees of University of Pennsylvania v. Lexington Ins. Co., 815 F.2d 890, 905 (3d Cir.1987).

Example—Admissible—"[T]he office's activities." Certificate executed pursuant to statute by government of Panama, consenting to search of Panamanian vessel by U.S. authorities. United States v. Rojas, 53 F.3d 1212, 1216 (11th Cir.1995).

Example—Admissible—"[T]he office's activities." Firearm serial number report kept by Bureau of Alcohol, Tobacco and Firearms. United States v. Johnson, 722 F.2d 407, 410 (8th Cir.1983).

Example—Admissible—"[M]atter observed." Copies of Menominee Tribal Roll, containing certificates of enrollment of defendants, kept by tribal enrollment clerk. United States v. Torres, 733 F.2d 449, 455 n. 5 (7th Cir.1984).

Example—Admissible—"[M]atter observed." Transcript of court reporter, to prove testimony was given. United States v. Arias, 575 F.2d 253, 254 (9th Cir.1978).

Example—Admissible—"Matters observed." Return of service completed by tribal police officer, to show that service had taken place. United States v. Fryberg, 854 F.3d 1126, 1131–32 (9th Cir.2017).

Example—Admissible—"[F]actual findings." Consumer Products Safety Commission reports that examined and tested fireworks failed to comply with safety standards. United States v. Midwest Fireworks Mfg. Co., Inc., 248 F.3d 563, 566–67 (6th Cir.2001).

Example—Admissible—"[F]actual findings." Results of NLRB investigation. Local Union No. 59, Int'l Bhd. of Elec. Workers v. Namco Elec., Inc., 653 F.2d 143, 145 (5th Cir.1981).

Example—Admissible—"[F]actual findings." USDA transaction reports. Haskell v. U.S.D.A., 930 F.2d 816, 819 (10th Cir.1991).

Example—Admissible—"[F]actual findings." Decision of administrative law judge for state department of labor that employee had not made misrepresentation to employer. Henry v. Daytop Village, Inc., 42 F.3d 89, 96 (2d Cir.1994).

Example—Admissible—"[F]actual findings." Police department's report of internal investigation of incident giving rise to excessive force claim. English v. District of Columbia, 651 F.3d 1, 8 (D.C.Cir.2011).

Example—Admissible—"Factual findings." State Department reports that "contain both factual findings and conclusions on Sudan's support for terrorism in general and al Qaeda in particular." Owens v. Republic of Sudan, 864 F.3d 751 (D.C.Cir.2017).

Example—Admissible—"Factual findings." OSHA reports of fatalities and catastrophes. Crawford v. ITW Food Equipment Group, LLC, 977 F.3d 1331, 1347–50 (11th Cir.2020).

(3) Lack of trustworthiness proviso. Reports offered under Rule 803(8) are presumed admissible; the burden is on the party opposing the admission of the report to prove its untrustworthiness. Beech Aircraft Corp. v. Rainey, 488 U.S. 153, 167, 109 S.Ct. 439, 448 (1988).

Example—Admissible. "The appellant has not carried this burden. His argument boils down to a plaint that the district court lacked adequate information about the procedures surrounding the creation of the I-296 form. But this plaint puts the burden in the wrong place. Rule 803(8) is a pathway to admissibility, anchored in the concept that public officials will perform their responsibilities appropriately. The party challenging the admissibility of a public record that is relevant and that conforms to the requirements of Rule 803(8)(A) can challenge its admission only by making an affirmative showing that the record is untrustworthy under Rule 803(8)(B). Under this standard, a paucity of evidence concerning the extent to which creating the form was a routine procedure cannot, by itself, constitute such an affirmative showing. In other words, to show untrustworthiness, the appellant cannot simply identify a lack of proof regarding the circumstances surrounding the creation of the form but, rather, must show that something specific, resulting from those circumstances, adversely affected the trustworthiness of the form." United States v. Fuentes-Lopez, 994 F.3d 66, 70–71 (1st Cir.2021) (citations omitted).

Four factors are frequently cited as bearing on the determination of trustworthiness: "(1) the timeliness of the investigation; (2) the investigator's skill or experience; (3) whether a hearing was held; and (4) possible bias when reports are prepared with a view to possible litigation." Id., 488 U.S. at 168 n. 11, 109 S.Ct. at 449 n. 11; Advisory Committee's Note to Rule 803(8).

Example—Inadmissible. "The inference of doctoring, even in the case of the unamended version of the January 6 minutes, is strong, and the public-records exception to the hearsay rule is inapplicable when the 'circumstances indicate lack of trustworthiness.' * * * The provision is tailor-made for a case in which the records are controlled by the defendants themselves rather than by clerks assumed to be disinterested." United States v. Spano, 421 F.3d 599, 604 (7th Cir.2005).

Example—Inadmissible. EEOC letter of determination is not per se admissible, but may be excluded based upon Rule 403 balancing of probative value versus negative factors. Coleman v. Home Depot, Inc., 306 F.3d 1333 (3d Cir.2002).

Example—Admissible. "As the district court's explication makes plain, the court did not base its ruling on the manner in which the death certificate was completed, the sources of information utilized, the credentials of the person completing it, or how the record was maintained. Instead, the court premised its ruling on the substance of what the death certificate contained. This was error: Rule 803(8) does not authorize a trial court to deem evidence untrustworthy (and thus inadmissible) simply because the court finds the gist of the evidence incredible or unpersuasive." Blake v. Pellegrino, 329 F.3d 43, 48 (1st Cir.2003).

Example—Inadmissible. "Martin's testimony before the MDOE examiner was not trustworthy at this stage in the investigation because she was so involved in the illegal conduct and not yet charged. She had a significant motive to lie about the falsity of food program claims. Since Martin's testimony was unreliable, the examiner's report relying on that testimony is likewise unreliable and therefore inadmissible. The district court did not err in excluding it." United States v. Jackson-Randolph, 282 F.3d 369, 381 (6th Cir.2002).

Example—Inadmissible. "The report is incomplete because its exhibits are not attached. Its author is unidentified and unknown, making it impossible to assess the author's skill or experience. No hearing was held. The document does not appear even to be a final report, as distinct from an internal draft: 'It [the Department of Labor] did not issue the report or send it to either party at any time before this litigation; rather, it became available only because Plaintiff filed a request pursuant to the Freedom of Information Act. * * * Accordingly, we—like the district court—do not consider the disputed portion of the DOL Report as evidence in our analysis of the successorship issue." Sullivan v. Dollar Tree Stores, Inc., 623 F.3d 770, 778 (9th Cir.2010).

Example—Inadmissible. The district court properly excluded an EPA report where "[a] prominent disclaimer on the report states that the 'information provided does not necessarily reflect the views of the [EPA], and no official endorsement should be inferred.' The disclaimer further states that the report is 'not sufficiently detailed nor is it intended to be used directly for environmental assessments or decision making.' " Junk v. Terminix Intern. Co., 628 F.3d 439, 449 (8th Cir.2010).

Example—Admissible. "In short, FEG has adduced no evidence that the OSHA reports lack trustworthiness. All FEG has done is hypothesize that the investigators might have been biased, unskilled, or inexperienced (notwithstanding OSHA's published assurances that its investigators shall be 'appropriately trained or experienced,' and notwithstanding the common sense notion that a public official would act with particular care when investigating a fatality or catastrophe). We are unwilling to conclude that mere anonymity—in the absence of any evidence of lack of trustworthiness—is sufficient for a court to infer that OSHA investigators were biased, unskilled, or inexperienced. * * * FEG has adduced no evidence at all—apart from bald speculation—that any of the OSHA reports lack trustworthiness." Crawford v. ITW Food Equipment Group, LLC, 977 F.3d 1331, 1349 (11th Cir.2020).

(4) "[F]actual findings." The term "factual findings" in Rule 803(8)A(iii) includes opinions or conclusions of a factual nature, such as the cause of an accident. Beech Aircraft Corp. v. Rainey, 488 U.S. 153, 109 S.Ct. 439 (1988). It does not extend, however, to legal conclusions. Hines v. Brandon Steel Decks, Inc., 886 F.2d 299, 302–03 (11th Cir.1989). Accord, Sullivan v. Dollar Tree Stores, Inc., 623 F.3d 770, 777 (9th Cir.2010).

(5) Double hearsay. Public records may present "double hearsay" problems similar to those frequently presented in business records. Most courts treat these situations as with private business records; they will not admit for its truth a statement by an outsider declarant having no official duty to report, unless the statement happens to fit within another hearsay exception or exemption. E.g., Jordan v. Binns, 712 F.3d 1123, 1133 (7th Cir.2013) ("[T]hird-party statements contained in a police report do not become admissible for their truth by virtue of their presence in a public record and instead must have an independent basis for admissibility."); United States v. Mackey, 117 F.3d 24, 28 (1st Cir.1997) (FBI report recording statement by defendant's bookie that defendant had won $60,000 in baseball bets); Miller v. Field, 35 F.3d 1088, 109–92 (6th Cir.1994) (statements by victim, witnesses, and others contained in police reports); United States v. Sallins, 993 F.2d 344, 347 (3d Cir.1993) (statements by caller recorded in police 911 record).

(6) Limitations in criminal cases—In general. Rule 803(8) contains two limitations specific to criminal cases: the "matters observed" type of record or report is inadmissible if it reports or records "matter observed by law-enforcement personnel"; and a "factual findings" type of record or report is not admissible against the accused.

If a public record or report is inadmissible against an accused in a criminal case under Rule 803(8) the record or report generally cannot be admitted under Rule 803(6) even though it might otherwise meet all the requirements of Rule 803(6). United States v. Brown, 9 F.3d 907, 911 (11th Cir.1993); United States v. Oates, 560 F.2d 45, 84 (2d Cir.1977). Cf. United States v. Pena-Gutierrez, 222 F.3d 1080, 1086–87 (9th Cir.2000) (same if offered under Rule 803(5)). Some courts, however, have held that the limitations in Rule 803(8) do not compel the exclusion of a document otherwise admissible under Rule 803(6) if the author testifies. E.g., United States v. Sokolow, 91 F.3d 396, 404–05 (3d Cir.1996).

(7) "[M]atter observed by law-enforcement personnel." The exclusion in Rule 803(8) applies to observations made by police officers and other law enforcement personnel in connection with an investigation. It does not apply to routine, ministerial, objective observations recorded in nonadversarial circumstances.

Example—Admissible. Warrant of deportation. United States v. Loyola-Dominguez, 125 F.3d 1315, 1317–18 (9th Cir.1997); United States v. Agustino-Hernandez, 14 F.3d 42, 43 (11th Cir.1994); United States v. Quezada, 754 F.2d 1190, 1193–94 (5th Cir.1985).

Example—Admissible. I-213 immigration forms, which were labeled a "Record of Deportable/ Inadmissible Alien"; "the admitted forms are a ministerial, objective observation detailing how the aliens were repatriated, and do not implicate the purposes animating the law enforcement exception." United States v. Torralba-Mendia, 784 F.3d 652, 664 (9th Cir.2015). Accord, United States v. Noria, 945 F.3d 847 (5th Cir.2019).

Example—Admissible. Calibration report of a breathalyzer maintenance operator. United States v. Wilmer, 799 F.2d 495, 501 (9th Cir.1986).

Example—Admissible. Computer printout listing identification numbers of vehicles reported stolen. United States v. Enterline, 894 F.2d 287, 290–91 (8th Cir.1990).

Courts have disagreed as to whether the exclusion applies to a forensic chemist's drug analysis. Compare United States v. Baker, 855 F.2d 1353, 1359–60 (8th Cir.1988) (no), with United States v. Oates, 560 F.2d 45, 63–84 (2d Cir.1977) (yes).

The exclusion does not apply to evidence offered by the accused. United States v. Smith, 521 F.2d 957, 965–67 (D.C.Cir.1975).

CROSS-REFERENCES

Checklists and Foundations (Chapter 4)
4.   Foundation for Public Record or Report
Treatises
7 Graham, Handbook of Federal Evidence §§ 803:8–803:10 (9th ed. 2020)
2 McCormick, Evidence §§ 295–297, 300 (8th ed. 2020)
30B Wright & Bellin, Federal Practice and Procedure §§ 6881–6905 (2018)

Rule 803(18). Statements in Learned Treatises, Periodicals, or Pamphlets

The following are not excluded by the rule against hearsay, regardless of whether the declarant is available as a witness:

* * *

(18) *Statements in Learned Treatises, Periodicals, or Pamphlets.* A statement contained in a treatise, periodical, or pamphlet if:

(A) the statement is called to the attention of an expert witness on cross-examination or relied on by the expert on direct examination; and

(B) the publication is established as a reliable authority by the expert's admission or testimony, by another expert's testimony, or by judicial notice.

If admitted, the statement may be read into evidence but not received as an exhibit.

* * *

AUTHORS' COMMENTS

(1)   Foundation. A foundation for a learned treatise normally consists of testimony by a qualified expert that the item is recognized in the relevant discipline as a reliable authority. Schneider v. Revici, 817 F.2d 987, 991 (2d Cir.1987); Dawsey v. Olin Corp., 782 F.2d 1254, 1264 (5th Cir.1986). It is not sufficient that the article appears in a particular periodical. Twin City Fire Ins. Co. v. Country Mutual Ins. Co., 23 F.3d 1175 (7th Cir.1994). Although the rule recognizes the possibility that the authority of the material can be established by judicial notice, this is unlikely to occur in practice. E.g., Hemingway v. Ochsner Clinic, 608 F.2d 1040, 1047 (5th Cir.1979).

(2)   Treatise is substantive evidence, but not received as an exhibit. When statements in a publication are admitted under Rule 803(18) on cross-examination, they become substantive evidence rather than merely impeachment evidence. Tart v. McGann, 697 F.2d 75, 78 (2d Cir.1982). Statements from a properly qualified publication may be read into evidence by an expert on direct examination. United States v. An Article of Drug, 661 F.2d 742, 745 (9th Cir.1981); United States v. Sene X Eleemosynary Corp., Inc., 479 F.Supp. 970, 975 (S.D.Fla.1979). The publication may not, however, be received as an exhibit to be taken into the jury room. Dartez v. Fibreboard Corp., 765 F.2d 456, 465 (5th Cir.1985); Johnson v. William C. Ellis & Sons Iron Works, Inc., 609 F.2d 820, 822–23 (5th Cir.1980).

(3)   May only be presented in conjunction with expert testimony. Rule 803(18) permits learned publications to be used only in conjunction with testimony by an expert witness, either on direct or cross-examination. It is not be proper for an attorney to introduce or read into evidence from a publication, however fully authenticated and established as authoritative, except while examining an expert witness. Dartez v. Fibreboard Corp., 765 F.2d 456, 465 (5th Cir.1985); Zwack v. State, 757 S.W.2d 66, 67–69 (Tex.App.1988); Advisory Committee's Note to Rule 803(18).

(4)   **Not limited to "treatises, periodicals, or pamphlets."** Courts have extended Rule 803(18) to other media, such as videotapes. Costantino v. Herzog, 203 F.3d 164, 170–71 (2d Cir.2000).

CROSS-REFERENCES

Treatises

7 Graham, Handbook of Federal Evidence § 803:18 (9th ed. 2020)

2 McCormick, Evidence § 321 (8th ed. 2020)

30B Wright & Bellin, Federal Practice and Procedure § 6938 (2018)

Rule 804. Exceptions to the Rule Against Hearsay—When the Declarant Is Unavailable as a Witness

(a)   **Criteria for Being Unavailable.** A declarant is considered to be unavailable as a witness if the declarant:

(1)   is exempted from testifying about the subject matter of the declarant's statement because the court rules that a privilege applies;

(2)   refuses to testify about the subject matter despite a court order to do so;

(3)   testifies to not remembering the subject matter;

(4)   cannot be present or testify at the trial or hearing because of death or a then-existing infirmity, physical illness, or mental illness; or

(5)   is absent from the trial or hearing and the statement's proponent has not been able, by process or other reasonable means, to procure:

    (A)   the declarant's attendance, in the case of a hearsay exception under Rule 804(b)(1) or (6); or

    (B)   the declarant's attendance or testimony, in the case of a hearsay exception under Rule 804(b)(2), (3), or (4).

But this subdivision (a) does not apply if the statement's proponent procured or wrongfully caused the declarant's unavailability as a witness in order to prevent the declarant from attending or testifying.

(b)   **The Exceptions.** The following are not excluded by the rule against hearsay if the declarant is unavailable as a witness:

(1)   *Former Testimony.* Testimony that:

    (A)   was given as a witness at a trial, hearing, or lawful deposition, whether given during the current proceeding or a different one; and

    (B)   is now offered against a party who had—or, in a civil case, whose predecessor in interest had—an opportunity and similar motive to develop it by direct, cross-, or redirect examination.

(2)   *Statement Under the Belief of Imminent Death.* In a prosecution for homicide or in a civil case, a statement that the declarant, while believing the declarant's death to be imminent, made about its cause or circumstances.

(3)   *Statement Against Interest.* A statement that:

    (A) a reasonable person in the declarant's position would have made only if the person believed it to be true because, when made, it was so contrary to the declarant's proprietary or pecuniary interest or had so great a tendency to invalidate the declarant's claim against someone else or to expose the declarant to civil or criminal liability; and

    (B) is supported by corroborating circumstances that clearly indicate its trustworthiness, if it is offered in a criminal case as one that tends to expose the declarant to criminal liability.

  (4) *Statement of Personal or Family History.* A statement about:

    (A) the declarant's own birth, adoption, legitimacy, ancestry, marriage, divorce, relationship by blood or marriage, or similar facts of personal or family history, even though the declarant had no way of acquiring personal knowledge about that fact; or

    (B) another person concerning any of these facts, as well as death, if the declarant was related to the person by blood, adoption, or marriage or was so intimately associated with the person's family that the declarant's information is likely to be accurate.

  (5) **[Other exceptions.]** [Transferred to Rule 807.]

  (6) *Statement Offered Against a Party That Wrongfully Caused the Declarant's Unavailability.* A statement offered against a party that wrongfully caused—or acquiesced in wrongfully causing—the declarant's unavailability as a witness, and did so intending that result.

AUTHORS' COMMENTS

  (1) **Scope and purpose of Rule 804.** Like Rule 803, Rule 804 contains exceptions to the hearsay rule. Its five exceptions, however, may be used only if the declarant is unavailable to testify at the trial.

  (2) **Definition of unavailability; hearsay exceptions.** The definition of unavailability and the more important exceptions listed in Rule 804 are discussed in the sections that follow. The other exceptions seldom arise and most questions concerning them can be answered by reference to the text of the rule.

CROSS-REFERENCES

Common Objections (Chapter 3)

36.   Hearsay

Treatises

7 Graham, Handbook of Federal Evidence §§ 804:0–804:5 (9th ed. 2020)

2 McCormick, Evidence §§ 253–254, 301–320, 322, 324 (8th ed. 2020)

30B Weight & Bellin, Federal Practice and Procedure §§ 6961–7036 (2018)

Rule 804(a). Criteria for Being Unavailable

(a) **Criteria for Being Unavailable.** A declarant is considered to be unavailable as a witness if the declarant:

  (1) is exempted from testifying about the subject matter of the declarant's statement because the court rules that a privilege applies;

  (2) refuses to testify about the subject matter despite a court order to do so;

  (3) testifies to not remembering the subject matter;

  (4) cannot be present or testify at the trial or hearing because of death or a then-existing infirmity, physical illness, or mental illness; or

(5) is absent from the trial or hearing and the statement's proponent has not been able, by process or other reasonable means, to procure:

    (A) the declarant's attendance, in the case of a hearsay exception under Rule 804(b)(1) or (6); or

    (B) the declarant's attendance or testimony, in the case of a hearsay exception under Rule 804(b)(2), (3), or (4).

But this subdivision (a) does not apply if the statement's proponent procured or wrongfully caused the declarant's unavailability as a witness in order to prevent the declarant from attending or testifying.

* * *

AUTHORS' COMMENTS

(1) Grounds of unavailability. Rule 804(a) names five separate grounds that suffice to constitute unavailability: (1) a claim of privilege, (2) refusal to testify, (3) lack of memory, (4) death or physical or mental illness or infirmity, and (5) absence from the hearing and inability of the proponent to procure the declarant's attendance or testimony by process or other reasonable means. The listed grounds are illustrative, not exclusive. For example, a child declarant who is incompetent to testify on account of immaturity is unavailable. Gregory v. State of North Carolina, 900 F.2d 705, 707 n. 6 (4th Cir.1990).

(2) Burden of showing unavailability on proponent. The burden of showing unavailability of the declarant is on the proponent of the hearsay evidence. Garcia-Martinez v. City and County of Denver, 392 F.3d 1187, 1192 (10th Cir.2004); United States v. Fuentes-Galindo, 929 F.2d 1507, 1510 (10th Cir.1991).

(3) Claim of privilege. Normally an actual claim of privilege in court is required. United States v. Oropeza, 564 F.2d 316, 325 n. 8 (9th Cir.1977); Advisory Committee's Note to Rule 804(a)(1). Where the privilege that would be invoked is self-incrimination and the circumstances clearly indicate that such a claim would be exercised, however, an actual invocation is often not required. E.g., United States v. Miller, 954 F.3d 551, 561–62 (2d Cir.2020), pet. for cert. filed; United States v. Williams, 927 F.2d 95, 98–99 (2d Cir.1991). Actual invocation may be excused in other circumstances as well. Jennings v. Maynard, 946 F.2d 1502, 1505 (10th Cir.1991). A defendant cannot invoke his Fifth Amendment privilege and then claim that he is thus an unavailable hearsay declarant. United States v. Hughes, 535 F.3d 880, 882 (8th Cir.2008).

(4) Refusal to testify. An actual order of the court directing the witness to testify is required. United States v. Zappola, 646 F.2d 48, 54 (2d Cir.1981).

(5) Lack of memory. See Lamonica v. Safe Hurricane Shutters, Inc., 711 F.3d 1299 (11th Cir.2013) ("Appellants contend that Ibacache was unavailable because he testified that he did not remember his conversation with Leiva. However, Rule 804(a)(3) applies only if the declarant is unable to remember the 'subject matter,' i.e., if 'he has no memory of the events to which his hearsay statements relate.' The fact that the witness does not remember making the statements themselves is irrelevant.") (citation omitted).

(6) Illness or infirmity. "[T]he judge must consider both the duration and the severity of the illness. With regard to duration, it is not essential to a finding of unavailability that the illness be permanent. The duration of the illness need only be in probability long enough so that, with proper regard to the importance of the testimony, the trial cannot be postponed." Burns v. Clusen, 798 F.2d 931, 937 (7th Cir.1986). See also United States v. McGuire, 307 F.3d 1192, 1204 (9th Cir.2002) ("It was not inappropriate for the district court to have credited Sesnon's doctor's written opinion that Sesnon's pregnancy (she was twenty-eight weeks pregnant) made her unable to undergo the stresses of testimony. * * * A pregnancy in its seventh month poses special risks for a mother and her unborn child that may be exacerbated by the stress of trial. These risks in late pregnancy, when attested to by a physician, are an 'infirmity' within the meaning of the Rule.").

Example—Unavailable. "The court did not abuse its discretion in determining that LaMie was unavailable to testify at the January 2007 trial. * * * LaMie's medical problems were severe and chronic. Her doctors did not expect her condition to improve and in fact twice indicated that, as time passed, LaMie had grown even more ill and less able to endure the rigors of interstate travel

237

and live testimony. * * * Two months before trial, LaMie was morbidly obese, suffering from brittle diabetes, peripheral neuropathy, biliary cirrhosis, lipomatosis and other severe and chronic conditions. By all accounts, her mobility was severely limited. Her many problems were not expected to improve in a few months' time. * * * LaMie's ability to travel locally to her lawyer's office for a deposition did not change the analysis of her ability to travel interstate and endure courtroom testimony. * * * In short, the district court's January 8, 2007 assessment of LaMie * * * was timely and sound given the severe, chronic and deteriorating nature of the medical problems from which LaMie suffered." United States v. McGowan, 590 F.3d 446, 454–55 (7th Cir.2009).

(7) Absence from hearing; sufficiency of efforts to obtain attendance or testimony. In criminal cases in which former testimony is offered against an accused, the sufficiency of efforts by the prosecution to produce the witness at trial is judged by a constitutional standard. The test is described as "good faith efforts." Ohio v. Roberts, 448 U.S. 56, 74–77, 100 S.Ct. 2531, 2543–45 (1980); Barber v. Page, 390 U.S. 719, 724–25, 88 S.Ct. 1318, 1321–22 (1968). The question whether the declarant's attendance or testimony could be obtained by reasonable means "cannot be divorced from the significance of the witness to the proceeding at hand, the reliability of the former testimony, and whether there is reason to believe that the opposing party's prior cross exam[ination] was inadequate." United States v. Johnson, 108 F.3d 919, 922 (8th Cir.1997). "Where the government itself bears some responsibility for the difficulty of procuring the witness, such as by deporting the witness, the government will have to make greater exertions to satisfy the standard of good-faith and reasonable efforts than it would have if it had not played any role. * * * In a case such as this one, in which the government knew or should have known of the potential need for the witness's testimony before he was deported, the government's duty to make good-faith, reasonable efforts to ensure the witness's presence arises before the witness leaves the United States." United States v. Burden, 934 F.3d 675, 686–87 (D.C.Cir.2019).

Even in civil cases, it is not sufficient that the declarant is not amenable to process, if the declarant's attendance might have been procured by "other reasonable means." For example, if the declarant resides outside the reach of process but has indicated a willingness to appear at trial voluntarily, the hearsay may be inadmissible.

Example—Inadmissible. "As with his Federal Rule of Civil Procedure 32 argument, Garcia-Martinez has put forth no evidence showing that alternative options for testifying had been exhausted. He made no attempt to obtain a temporary visa to reenter the country for the limited purpose of attending trial or show that an effort to do so would certainly have been denied. Nor did he demonstrate that alternatives to live testimony, such as a testimony via video-conferencing, were unavailable. The only explanation of Garcia-Martinez's absence from trial comes from statements of his attorney to the district court at the evidentiary hearing. Thus, Garcia-Martinez has not demonstrated that 'a good faith effort was made to obtain the declarant's presence at trial using reasonable means.' " Garcia-Martinez v. City and County of Denver, 392 F.3d 1187, 1193 (10th Cir.2004).

If absence alone is relied upon as the ground of unavailability, Rule 804(a)(5) requires that the proponent show an inability to obtain the testimony (such as by deposition) as well as the attendance of the declarant, if the hearsay statement is offered under Rule 804(b)(2), (3), or (4). Campbell by Campbell v. Coleman Co., Inc., 786 F.2d 892, 896 (8th Cir.1986) (error to admit statements under Rule 804(b)(3); declarant not unavailable because his deposition had been taken). The requirement of attempt to depose declarant does not apply to statements offered under Rule 804(b)(1) or (6).

CROSS-REFERENCES

Treatises

7 Graham, Handbook of Federal Evidence § 804:00 (9th ed. 2020)

2 McCormick, Evidence § 253 (8th ed. 2020)

30B Wright & Bellin, Federal Practice and Procedure §§ 6961–6969 (2018)

Rule 804(b)(1).   Former Testimony

* * *

(b) The Exceptions. The following are not excluded by the rule against hearsay if the declarant is unavailable as a witness:

(1) *Former Testimony.* Testimony that:

(A) was given as a witness at a trial, hearing, or lawful deposition, whether given during the current proceeding or a different one; and

(B) is now offered against a party who had—or, in a civil case, whose predecessor in interest had—an opportunity and similar motive to develop it by direct, cross-, or redirect examination.

* * *

AUTHORS' COMMENTS

(1) Depositions. In addition to Rule 804(b)(1), a deposition may be admissible in a civil case under Fed. R. Civ. P. 32(a)(3), or in a criminal case under Fed. R. Crim. P. 15 or 18 U.S.C.A. §§ 3503, 3509(b)(2). As provided in Rule 802, these sources may permit hearsay beyond the ambit of Rule 804(b)(1). Any conflict is resolved in favor of admissibility.

(2) Opportunity to develop the testimony. Only opportunity is required; there need not have been actual examination of the witness by the party or predecessor in interest. United States v. Koon, 34 F.3d 1416, 1427 (9th Cir.1994), aff'd in part, rev'd in part on other grounds, 518 U.S. 81, 116 S.Ct. 2035 (1996); DeLuryea v. Winthrop Laboratories, etc., 697 F.2d 222, 227 (8th Cir.1983); United States v. Zurosky, 614 F.2d 779, 791–93 (1st Cir.1979). Moreover, it need not have been an opportunity for cross-examination; direct examination suffices. Hence, grand jury testimony may be admitted against the government, provided that the similar motive requirement is met in the particular circumstances. United States v. Salerno, 505 U.S. 317, 321–29, 112 S.Ct. 2503, 2507–10 (1992); United States v. DiNapoli, 8 F.3d 909 (2d Cir.1993); United States v. Omar, 104 F.3d 519, 523–24 (1st Cir.1997) (upholding exclusion upon finding lack of opportunity and similar motive in the circumstances); United States v. Miller, 904 F.2d 65, 68 (D.C.Cir.1990).

(3) Similar motive to develop the testimony. Generally, a party or predecessor in interest is regarded as having a similar motive to develop the testimony when the issue to which the testimony related at the former hearing is substantially identical to the issue in the present proceeding. United States v. Koon, 34 F.3d 1416, 1427 (9th Cir.1994), aff'd in part, rev'd in part on other grounds, 518 U.S. 81, 116 S.Ct. 2035 (1996); United States v. DiNapoli, 8 F.3d 909 (2d Cir.1993); United States v. Miller, 904 F.2d 65, 68 (D.C.Cir.1990); United States v. Licavoli, 725 F.2d 1040, 1048 (6th Cir.1984) ("Here the issues in the cases were nearly identical, since in the state cases the defendants were charged with murder and conspiracy to commit murder, and in the RICO prosecution these two acts constituted the predicate acts for the RICO conviction."). Absolute identity of the issue is not required. United States v. McFall, 558 F.3d 951, 963 (9th Cir.2009) (Rule 804(b)(1) "does not require an identical quantum of motivation").

Example—Inadmissible. "The government's motive at the plea hearing, however, was only to establish a factual basis for Lindsey's guilty plea, and to ensure that the plea that [*sic*] was knowing and voluntary. See Fed. R. Crim. P. 11(b). The government had no motive to develop Lindsey's testimony about whether Dunn knowingly possessed the firearm, because Dunn's involvement was immaterial to the validity of Lindsey's guilty plea." United States v. Dunn, 76 F.4th 1062, 1066 (8th Cir.2023).

Example—Inadmissible. "Even if we assumed that the SEC and the DOJ are the same party, the agencies did not have sufficiently similar motives. First, the stakes and burdens of proof were different: The SEC was in the discovery phase in relation to potential civil enforcement actions, whereas the DOJ was investigating for potential criminal involvement after a grand jury indictment. Second, the focuses and motivations of the investigations were different: The SEC was likely developing a factual background regarding wrongdoing at the company generally, whereas the DOJ would have been gathering evidence to convict specific individuals. Third, the lack of cross-examination shows the agencies' different trial strategies: The SEC deposition excerpts show no sign of cross-examination or additional follow-up questions after Simmons denied his involvement and that he had any conversations with Baker. In contrast, for the reasons we have already explained, the agencies were not coordinating their activity to a degree that would have led the SEC lawyer to cross-examine Simmons like a criminal prosecutor would have." United States v. Baker, 923 F.3d 390, 401–02 (5th Cir.2019).

Differences as to tactics or strategy, however reasonable, are disregarded. United States v. Mann, 161 F.3d 840, 861 (5th Cir.1998) (discovery deposition taken in related civil proceeding admitted in criminal case; "Rule 804(b)(1) * * * does not require that the party against whom the prior testimony is offered had a compelling tactical or strategic incentive to subject the testimony to cross-examination, only that an opportunity and similar motive to develop the testimony existed."); United States v. Koon, 34 F.3d 1416, 1427 (9th Cir.1994) ("Appellants did not lack the opportunity to cross-examine Briseno; they lacked only some of the tools which were later developed by the government or by appellants themselves, and which appellants argue would have allowed them to cross-examine Briseno to better effect."), aff'd in part, rev'd in part on other grounds, 518 U.S. 81, 116 S.Ct. 2035 (1996); Hendrix v. Raybestos-Manhattan, Inc., 776 F.2d 1492, 1506 (11th Cir.1985) ("[A]s a general rule, a party's decision to limit cross-examination in a discovery deposition is a strategic choice and does not preclude his adversary's use of the deposition at a subsequent proceeding."); United States v. Zurosky, 614 F.2d 779, 791–93 (1st Cir.1979) (testimony taken on motion to suppress; witness later claimed self-incrimination; "Defense counsel made a tactical decision not to question Smith; this does not mean they were denied an opportunity to do so.").

(4) **"[P]redecessor in interest."** Courts applying Rule 804(b)(1) in civil cases have generally interpreted the phrase "predecessor in interest" not in the narrow, common-law sense of privity, but broadly to encompass any party with a similar interest and motive. Supermarket of Marlinton, Inc. v. Meadow Gold Dairies, Inc., 71 F.3d 119, 128 (4th Cir.1995); New England Mutual Life Ins. Co. v. Anderson, 888 F.2d 646, 651 (10th Cir.1989); Dykes v. Raymark Industries, Inc., 801 F.2d 810, 816 (6th Cir.1986); Lloyd v. American Export Lines, Inc., 580 F.2d 1179, 1185–87 (3d Cir.1978); Rule v. International Ass'n. of Bridge, Structural & Ornamental Ironworkers, Local Union No. 396, 568 F.2d 558, 569 (8th Cir.1977).

CROSS-REFERENCES

Treatises

7 Graham, Handbook of Federal Evidence § 804:1 (9th ed. 2020)

2 McCormick, Evidence §§ 301–308 (8th ed. 2020)

30B Wright & Bellin, Federal Practice and Procedure §§ 6971–6975 (2018)

Rule 804(b)(3). Statement Against Interest

* * *

(b) **The Exceptions.** The following are not excluded by the rule against hearsay if the declarant is unavailable as a witness:

* * *

(3) *Statement Against Interest.* A statement that:

(A) a reasonable person in the declarant's position would have made only if the person believed it to be true because, when made, it was so contrary to the declarant's proprietary or pecuniary interest or had so great a tendency to invalidate the declarant's claim against someone else or to expose the declarant to civil or criminal liability; and

(B) is supported by corroborating circumstances that clearly indicate its trustworthiness, if it is offered in a criminal case as one that tends to expose the declarant to criminal liability.

* * *

AUTHORS' COMMENTS

(1) Opposing-party statements distinguished. An out-of-court statement by a party offered against the party is admissible under Rule 801(d)(2), and is not subject to the requirements of Rule 804(b)(3). The party statement need not have been against interest when made, United States v. Turner, 995 F.2d 1357, 1363 (6th Cir.1993); People of Territory of Guam v. Ojeda, 758 F.2d 403, 408 (9th Cir.1985); insofar as it disserves the party-declarant's interest, it need not do so in any particular way.

(2) Statements against penal interest—In general. In order to be against penal interest, the statement need not be an outright confession of guilt. United States v. Paguio, 114 F.3d 928, 933 (9th Cir.1997); United States v. Barrett, 539 F.2d 244, 251 (1st Cir.1976). All that is required is that the statement tend to subject the declarant to criminal liability to such an extent that a reasonable person would not make the statement unless it were true. United States v. Garcia, 897 F.2d 1413, 1420 (7th Cir.1990); United States v. Lang, 589 F.2d 92, 97 (2d Cir.1978). A statement may qualify though made to a friend, confederate, cellmate, or family member. United States v. Mills, 704 F.2d 1553, 1562 (11th Cir.1983) (one inmate to another); United States v. Mock, 640 F.2d 629, 631 (5th Cir.1981) (to former wife); United States v. Goins, 593 F.2d 88, 91 (8th Cir.1979) (to daughter and to friend); United States v. Barrett, supra, 539 F.2d at 249–51 (to acquaintance during card game). Compare United States v. Hammers, 942 F.3d 1001, 1010–11 (10th Cir.2019) (statement in suicide note not against penal interest "because 'penal interest * * * [is] of no moment to a dead man.'"); United States v. Awer, 770 F.3d 83, 93–94 (1st Cir.2014) ("The district court found Johnson's statements to her attorneys [claiming responsibility for the drugs] could not come in under Rule 804(b)(3) because they would not have exposed her to criminal liability. We agree.").

(3) Statements against penal interest offered to exculpate accused; corroboration requirement. Courts have identified a variety of factors or circumstances that are relevant to the court's determination whether a statement against penal interest offered to exculpate an accused possesses sufficient corroborating circumstances that clearly indicate its trustworthiness.

> **Example.** Factors include (1) the relationship between the declarant and the accused (the absence of a close relationship makes it less likely that the story is fabricated for the benefit of the accused); (2) whether the statement was made voluntarily after Miranda warnings; (3) whether there is evidence that the statement was made in order to curry favor with authorities. United States v. Jackson, 540 F.3d 578, 589 (7th Cir.2008). Accord, American Automotive Accessories, Inc. v. Fishman, 175 F.3d 534, 541 (7th Cir.1999); United States v. Nagib, 56 F.3d 798, 805 (7th Cir.1995).

> **Example.** "Factors to be considered in such an analysis include: '(1) whether there is any apparent motive for the out-of-court declarant to misrepresent the matter, (2) the general character of the speaker, (3) whether other people heard the out-of-court statement, (4) whether the statement was made spontaneously, (5) the timing of the declaration and the relationship between the speaker and the witness.'" United States v. One Star, 979 F.2d 1319, 1322 (8th Cir.1992).

> **Example.** "Factors relevant to trustworthiness include the time of the declaration and the party to whom it was made, the existence of corroborating evidence, the extent to which the declaration is really against the declarant's interest, and the availability of the declarant as a witness." United States v. Ospina, 739 F.2d 448, 452 (9th Cir.1984).

It has also been held that "for a statement to be admissible under the exception, there must be indicia of trustworthiness of the specific, 'essential' assertions, not merely of other facts contained in the statement." United States v. Mackey, 117 F.3d 24, 29 (1st Cir.1997).

(4) Statements against penal interest that inculpate accused, offered by prosecution. Prior to amendment in 2010, Rule 804(b)(3) by terms required corroborating circumstances clearly indicating the trustworthiness of an against-penal-interest statement only if the statement was offered to exculpate the accused. Because of constitutional (Confrontation Clause) concerns, however, courts had, even before the amendment, imposed a similar corroboration/trustworthiness requirement upon statements inculpating the accused. Williamson v. United States, 512 U.S. 594, 605, 114 S.Ct. 2431, 2437 (1994) (not reaching issue); United States v. Costa, 31 F.3d 1073, 1077 (11th Cir.1994); United States v. Harty, 930 F.2d 1257, 1264–65 (7th Cir.1991); United States v. Candoli, 870 F.2d 496, 509 (9th Cir.1989); United States v. Alvarez, 584

F.2d 694, 701 (5th Cir.1978). The requirement has also been applied in a civil case. American Automotive Accessories, Inc. v. Fishman, 175 F.3d 534, 541 (7th Cir.1999).

A statement against interest offered by the prosecution to inculpate another was held not to be firmly rooted exception for Confrontation Clause analysis. Lilly v. Virginia, 527 U.S. 116, 134, 119 S.Ct. 1887, 1899 (1999) (plurality opinion).

(5) "Collateral" statements. In Williamson v. United States, 512 U.S. 594, 114 S.Ct. 2431 (1994), the Supreme Court held that the Rule 804(b)(3) "does not allow admission of non-self-inculpatory statements, even if they are made within a broader narrative that is generally self-inculpatory." 512 U.S. at 600–01, 114 S.Ct. at 2435. Therefore, a statement in a co-perpetrator's confession that incriminates the accused is admissible under the provision only if the particular statement is also sufficiently against the declarant's interest to be reliable. 512 U.S. at 604, 114 S.Ct. at 2437; United States v. Costa, 31 F.3d 1073, 1077–79 (11th Cir.1994).

> **Example—Inadmissible.** "Wheeler's statement that Mendoza had delivered the methamphetamine was not sufficiently against her penal interest to warrant admission under Rule 804(b)(3). Wheeler agreed to cooperate with authorities after she was caught red-handed with $16,000 in drug money. Initially, she denied that Mendoza was involved in the transaction and named someone else as her source. It was only after the agents apprehended Mendoza near the drop site location and confronted her with this fact that she pointed the finger at Mendoza. At that point, she had nothing to lose by implicating him. Moreover, she may reasonably have believed that by implicating Mendoza she would curry favor with the authorities and lessen her own punishment." United States v. Mendoza, 85 F.3d 1347, 1352 (8th Cir.1996).

> **Example—Admissible.** "[A] statement inculpating both the declarant and the defendant may be sufficiently reliable to be admissible in the circumstances that obtain here—i.e., where the statement is made in a noncustodial setting to an ally, rather than to a law enforcement official, and where the circumstances surrounding the portion of the statement that inculpates the defendant provide no reason to suspect that this portion of the statement is any less trustworthy than the portion that inculpates the declarant." United States v. Barone, 114 F.3d 1284, 1295–96 (1st Cir.1997).

> **Example—Admissible.** "Williamson does not mean that the trial judge must always parse the statement and let in only the inculpatory part. It means that the statement must be examined in context, to see whether as a matter of common sense the portion at issue was against interest and would not have been made by a reasonable person unless he believed it to be true. Sometimes that requires exclusion of part of the statement, sometimes not. A reasonable man caught with a trunk full of cocaine, like the unavailable declarant in Williamson, might well imagine that he could advance his own penal interest by fingering someone else. But Paguio Sr.'s statement that 'my son had nothing to do with it' was not an attempt to 'shift blame or curry favor.'" United States v. Paguio, 114 F.3d 928, 933 (9th Cir.1997).

The *Williamson* treatment of collateral statements applies in civil cases as well. Silverstein v. Chase, 260 F.3d 142, 146–47 (2d Cir.2001).

CROSS-REFERENCES

Treatises

7 Graham, Handbook of Federal Evidence § 804:3 (9th ed. 2020)

2 McCormick, Evidence §§ 316–320 (8th ed. 2020)

30B Wright & Bellin, Federal Practice and Procedure §§ 6991–7000 (2018)

Rule 804(b)(6).   Statement Offered Against a Party That Wrongfully Caused the Declarant's Unavailability

* * *

(b) The Exceptions. The following are not excluded by the rule against hearsay if the declarant is unavailable as a witness:

* * *

(6) *Statement Offered Against a Party That Wrongfully Caused the Declarant's Unavailability.* A statement offered against a party that wrongfully caused—or acquiesced in wrongfully causing—the declarant's unavailability as a witness, and did so intending that result.

AUTHORS' COMMENTS

(1) Background and purpose of Rule 804(b)(6). Rule 804(b)(6) was added by amendment in 1997. According to its drafters, it is "a prophylactic rule to deal with abhorrent behavior 'which strikes at the heart of the system of justice itself.' " Advisory Committee's Note to Rule 804(b)(6), citing United States v. Mastrangelo, 693 F.2d 269, 273 (2d Cir.1982).

(2) Criminal act not required; rule applies to all parties. The wrongdoing that invokes Rule 804(b)(6) need not consist of a criminal act. Advisory Committee's Note to Rule 804(b)(6). The rule applies to all parties, including the government. Id.

Direct, personal participation is not required.

Example—Admissible. "Rivera contends that the district court improperly imputed the acts of others to him for purposes of Rule 804(b)(6). He maintains that the Paz murder could not have been committed by him, since he was incarcerated, and Rule 804(b)(6) only allows the court to admit hearsay if the defendant has personally committed the wrongful act which caused the declarant's unavailability. Rivera misreads the Rule. * * * [T]he plain language of the Rule supports the district court's holding that a defendant need only tacitly assent to wrongdoing in order to trigger the Rule's applicability. Active participation or engagement, or, as Rivera would have it, the personal commission of the crime, is not required." United States v. Rivera, 412 F.3d 562, 567 (4th Cir.2005).

(3) Rule applies in prosecution for homicide of declarant. The rule has been applied to admit statements by the victim in a homicide prosecution where the motive for the homicide was to silence a potential witness to other crimes. United States v. Emery, 186 F.3d 921, 926 (8th Cir.1999). In Giles v. California, 554 U.S. 353, 128 S.Ct. 2678 (2008), the Supreme Court noted that every commentator of which it was aware had concluded that this exception applies only when the wrongdoer acted with the purpose of making the witness unavailable to testify.

(4) Burden as to showing of wrongful conduct. In accordance with most, though not all, of previous case law, the usual Rule 104(a) preponderance of the evidence standard applies to the preliminary determination whether a party has engaged in conduct justifying a forfeiture under the rule. United States v. Johnson, 767 F.3d 815, 820–23 (9th Cir.2014); United States v. Rivera, 412 F.3d 562, 566–67 (4th Cir.2005); United States v. Zlatogur, 271 F.3d 1025, 1027–29 (11th Cir.2001); United States v. Dhinsa, 243 F.3d 635, 654 (2d Cir.2001); Advisory Committee's Note to Rule 804(b)(6).

(5) Conspiracy. Where the unavailability of the declarant resulted from the acts of a party's coconspirator, "mere participation in a conspiracy does not suffice—yet participation may suffice when combined with findings that the wrongful act at issue was in furtherance and within the scope of an ongoing conspiracy and reasonably foreseeable as a natural or necessary consequence thereof." United States v. Cherry, 217 F.3d 811, 820 (10th Cir.2000).

CROSS-REFERENCES

Treatises

7 Graham, Handbook of Federal Evidence § 804:5 (9th ed. 2020)

2 McCormick, Evidence § 265 (8th ed. 2020)

30B Wright & Bellin, Federal Practice and Procedure §§ 7031–7036 (2018)

Rule 805. Hearsay Within Hearsay

Hearsay within hearsay is not excluded by the rule against hearsay if each part of the combined statements conforms with an exception to the rule.

AUTHORS' COMMENTS

(1) **Scope and purpose of Rule 805.** Rule 805 declares a principle long recognized at common law: even what is often called "double" or "multiple" hearsay may be admissible if an exception properly applies to each "layer" of hearsay. In other words, exceptions may be "stacked."

> **Example—Admissible.** Notes by witness, read to jury as recorded recollection under Rule 803(5), which recounted statements by coconspirators, Rule 801(d)(2)(E). United States v. Steele, 685 F.2d 793, 809 (3d Cir.1982).

> **Example—Admissible.** Coconspirator statement, Rule 801(d)(2)(E), quoting statement of state of mind, Rule 803(3). United States v. Diez, 515 F.2d 892, 895–96 & n. 2 (5th Cir.1975).

> **Example—Admissible.** Witness testified that declarant, immediately after telephone call to party's business, quoted party's secretary quoting party. Admissible triple hearsay, by virtue of Rules 803(1), 801(d)(2)(D), 801(d)(2)(A), and 805. United States v. Portsmouth Paving Corp., 694 F.2d 312, 321–23 (4th Cir.1982).

CROSS-REFERENCES

Treatises

8 Graham, Handbook of Federal Evidence § 805:1 (9th ed. 2020)

2 McCormick, Evidence § 324.1 (8th ed. 2020)

30B Wright & Bellin, Federal Practice and Procedure §§ 7041–7044 (2018)

Rule 806. Attacking and Supporting the Declarant's Credibility

When a hearsay statement—or a statement described in Rule 801(d)(2)(C), (D), or (E)—has been admitted in evidence, the declarant's credibility may be attacked, and then supported, by any evidence that would be admissible for those purposes if the declarant had testified as a witness. The court may admit evidence of the declarant's inconsistent statement or conduct, regardless of when it occurred or whether the declarant had an opportunity to explain or deny it. If the party against whom the statement was admitted calls the declarant as a witness, the party may examine the declarant on the statement as if on cross-examination.

AUTHORS' COMMENTS

(1) **Scope and purpose of Rule 806.** Rule 806 recognizes that a hearsay declarant whose statement is admitted is like a witness, and therefore the declarant should be, so far as possible, subject to impeachment and rehabilitation like a witness.

(2) **Impeachment or rehabilitation must be such as would be permissible with a witness.** To be admissible under Rule 806, the impeachment or rehabilitation evidence must be such that it would have been admissible to impeach or to rehabilitate the declarant had the declarant testified as a witness at the trial in which the statement was received. United States v. Finley, 934 F.2d 837, 839 (7th Cir.1991); United States v. Moody, 903 F.2d 321, 328–29 (5th Cir.1990).

(3) **Calling of declarant as hostile witness.** The last sentence of Rule 806 in effect permits a party against whom a hearsay statement has been introduced to call the declarant as a hostile witness, so that the calling party may ask leading questions and impeach the declarant-witness as if the declarant-witness had been called by the party who introduced the hearsay statement.

CROSS-REFERENCES

Treatises

8 Graham, Handbook of Federal Evidence § 806:1 (98th ed. 2020)

1 McCormick, Evidence § 37; 2 id. § 324.2 (8th ed. 2020)

30B Wright & Bellin, Federal Practice and Procedure §§ 7051–7053 (2018)

Rule 807. Residual Exception

(a) In General. Under the following conditions, a hearsay statement is not excluded by the rule against hearsay even if the statement is not admissible under a hearsay exception in Rule 803 or 804:

  (1) the statement is supported by sufficient guarantees of trustworthiness—after considering the totality of circumstances under which it was made and evidence, if any, corroborating the statement; and

  (2) it is more probative on the point for which it is offered than any other evidence that the proponent can obtain through reasonable efforts.

(b) Notice. The statement is admissible only if the proponent gives an adverse party reasonable notice of the intent to offer the statement—including its substance and the declarant's name—so that the party has a fair opportunity to meet it. The notice must be provided in writing before the trial or hearing—or in any form during the trial or hearing if the court, for good cause, excuses a lack of earlier notice.

AUTHORS' COMMENTS

(1) Rule 807 combines former Rules 803(24) and 804(b)(5). Rule 807 was created by an amendment in 1997 which combined former Rules 803(24) and 804(b)(5). "This was done to facilitate additions to Rules 803 and 804. No change in meaning is intended." Advisory Committee's Note to Rule 807.

(2) Trial court's discretion. Trial courts are accorded wide discretion in applying the residual exception.

  Example. " 'Rule [807] provides a trial court with some flexibility when it must make a determination as to the admissibility of hearsay evidence, and there is no specific rule governing admissibility.' * * * The relevant benchmark is not how we would have ruled had we been standing in the trial judge's shoes, but rather, 'whether any reasonable person could agree with the district court.' " Doe v. United States, 976 F.2d 1071, 1076–77 (7th Cir.1992).

  Example. "[A]n appellate court should be 'particularly hesitant to overturn a trial court's admissibility ruling under the residual hearsay exception absent a "definite and firm conviction that the court made a clear error of judgment in the conclusion it reached based upon a weighing of the relevant factors." ' " United States v. North, 910 F.2d 843, 909 (D.C.Cir.1990).

(3) Three requirements. For evidence to be admitted under the residual hearsay exception, three requirements must be met:

  (1) The proponent must give the adverse party the notice specified in Rule 807.

  (2) The hearsay statement must be supported by sufficient guarantees of trustworthiness. The court must consider the totality of circumstances under the statement was made and any corroborating evidence.

  (3) The statement must be more probative on the point for which it is offered than any other evidence that the proponent could obtain through reasonable effort.

(4) Notice requirement. Most courts treat the notice requirement flexibly, and hold that lack of pretrial notice does not preclude admissibility so long as the opponent is given a fair opportunity to prepare to contest the use of the evidence. United States v. Panzardi-Lespier, 918 F.2d 313, 317 (1st Cir.1990); United States v. Calkins, 906 F.2d 1240, 1245–46 (8th Cir.1990).

(5) Equivalent circumstantial guarantees of trustworthiness. In Idaho v. Wright, 497 U.S. 805, 110 S.Ct. 3139 (1990), a criminal case involving an application of a state version of Rule 807, the Supreme Court held that if hearsay offered against an accused did not fall within a "firmly rooted" exception—for example, if it is offered under a residual exception like Rule 807—then the Confrontation Clause required a showing of "particularized guarantees of trustworthiness." See also Ohio v. Roberts, 448 U.S. 56, 66, 100 S.Ct. 2531, 2539 (1980). " '[P]articularized guarantees of trustworthiness,' " the Court went on, "must be shown from the totality of the circumstances, but * * * the relevant circumstances include only those that surround the making of the statement and that render the declarant particularly worthy of belief." Idaho v. Wright, 497 U.S. at 819, 110 S.Ct. at 3148. The evidence "must possess indicia of reliability by virtue of its inherent trustworthiness, not by reference to other evidence at trial"—i.e., not by corroboration. 497 U.S. at 822, 110 S.Ct. at 3150.

The restriction against supporting a finding of trustworthiness by reference to corroboration announced in Idaho v. Wright is part of Confrontation Clause doctrine, not an interpretation of Rule 807. Brumley v. Albert E. Brumley & Sons, Inc., 727 F.3d 574, 578 (6th Cir.2013); United States v. Valdez-Soto, 31 F.3d 1467, 1470–71 (9th Cir.1994) (affirming admission of prior inconsistent statement by witness under residual exception where trial court relied in part on corroborating evidence to support finding of trustworthiness). Therefore, the restriction by terms applied only to evidence offered against an accused. With regard to evidence offered against the government or in a civil case, it has (and remains) possible that the Supreme Court would extend the Idaho v. Wright approach as an interpretation of the phrase "circumstantial guarantees of trustworthiness" in Rule 807, but it has not yet done so. As a matter of Confrontation Clause doctrine, the Court's subsequent overruling of the Ohio v. Roberts line of cases in Crawford v. Washington, see Authors' Comments on Rule 802, supra, renders moot the Idaho v. Wright analysis. According to *Crawford*, the correct determination under the Confrontation Clause is never trustworthiness, but whether the statement is "testimonial."

In Williamson v. United States, 512 U.S. 594, 114 S.Ct. 2431 (1994), the Supreme Court held, in the context of Rule 804(b)(3), that the word "statement" means "a single declaration or remark" rather than a "report or narrative." 512 U.S. at 597–99, 114 S.Ct. at 2434–35. The Court of Appeals for the Sixth Circuit has held that this restrictive definition of "statement" is applicable to all the hearsay exceptions, so that when applying the residual exception "a court, when determining the admissibility of a narrative, must examine it sentence by sentence and rule upon the admissibility of each 'single declaration or remark.' " United States v. Canan, 48 F.3d 954, 960 (6th Cir.1995).

Courts have cited many factors as bearing upon circumstantial trustworthiness.

Example. Relevant circumstances include whether the statement was made under oath, whether it concerned matters within the declarant's personal knowledge, whether the declarant recanted the statement, whether there is evidence that the declarant is unreliable, and whether other evidence seriously undermines the content of the statement. United States v. Donlon, 909 F.2d 650, 654 (1st Cir.1990).

Example. "Wright identified several factors that trial courts may consider in evaluating the reliability of a child's hearsay statement, including spontaneity, consistent repetition, the mental state of the child at the time the statement was made, use of terminology unexpected of a child of similar age, and lack of motive to fabricate." Doe v. United States, 976 F.2d 1071, 1075 (7th Cir.1992). Accord, United States v. Wandahsega, 924 F.3d 868, 881–82 (6th Cir.2019).

(6) Material fact. The requirement that the statement be offered as evidence of a material fact is seemingly redundant with Rules 401 and 402. "[W]hat is probably meant is that the exception should not be used for trivial or collateral matters." United States v. Iaconetti, 406 F.Supp. 554, 559 (E.D.N.Y.1976) (Weinstein, J.), aff'd, 540 F.2d 574 (2d Cir.1976). Accord, United States v. Gaitan-Acevedo, 148 F.3d 577, 589 (6th Cir.1998).

(7) Necessity—More probative than other available evidence. Courts sometimes exclude hearsay offered under the residual exception where the declarant or another person with personal knowledge is available to testify concerning the matter, Eisenstadt v. Centel Corp., 113 F.3d 738, 743 (7th Cir.1997); Noble v. Alabama Dept. of Environmental Management, 872 F.2d 361, 366 (11th Cir.1989); United States v. Scrima, 819 F.2d 996, 1001 (11th Cir.1987), or where a more persuasive document might have been obtained, Conoco Inc. v. Department of Energy, 99 F.3d 387, 394 (Fed.Cir.1996) (summaries not complying with Rule 1006 not admissible under residual exception where underlying records and proper summary were obtainable).

(8)   General purposes of rules and interests of justice. The requirement that the general purposes of the rules and the interest of justice be served by admission of the statement is redundant with Rule 102.

CROSS-REFERENCES

Treatises

8 Graham, Handbook of Federal Evidence § 807:1 (9th ed. 2020)

2 McCormick, Evidence § 324 (8th ed. 2020)

30B Wright & Bellin, Federal Practice and Procedure §§ 7061–7068 (2018)

ARTICLE IX

AUTHENTICATION AND IDENTIFICATION

Rule 901. Authenticating or Identifying Evidence

(a)   In General. To satisfy the requirement of authenticating or identifying an item of evidence, the proponent must produce evidence sufficient to support a finding that the item is what the proponent claims it is.

(b)   Examples. The following are examples only—not a complete list—of evidence that satisfies the requirement:

(1)   *Testimony of a Witness with Knowledge.* Testimony that an item is what it is claimed to be.

(2)   *Nonexpert Opinion About Handwriting.* A nonexpert's opinion that handwriting is genuine, based on a familiarity with it that was not acquired for the current litigation.

(3)   *Comparison by an Expert Witness or the Trier of Fact.* A comparison with an authenticated specimen by an expert witness or the trier of fact.

(4)   *Distinctive Characteristics and the Like.* The appearance, contents, substance, internal patterns, or other distinctive characteristics of the item, taken together with all the circumstances.

(5)   *Opinion About a Voice.* An opinion identifying a person's voice—whether heard firsthand or through mechanical or electronic transmission or recording—based on hearing the voice at any time under circumstances that connect it with the alleged speaker.

(6)   *Evidence About a Telephone Conversation.* For a telephone conversation, evidence that a call was made to the number assigned at the time to:

(A)   a particular person, if circumstances, including self-identification, show that the person answering was the one called; or

(B)   a particular business, if the call was made to a business and the call related to business reasonably transacted over the telephone.

(7)   *Evidence About Public Records.* Evidence that:

(A)   a document was recorded or filed in a public office as authorized by law; or

(B)   a purported public record or statement is from the office where items of this kind are kept.

247

(8) *Evidence About Ancient Documents or Data Compilations.* For a document or data compilation, evidence that it:

    (A) is in a condition that creates no suspicion about its authenticity;

    (B) was in a place where, if authentic, it would likely be; and

    (C) is at least 20 years old when offered.

(9) *Evidence About a Process or System.* Evidence describing a process or system and showing that it produces an accurate result.

(10) *Methods Provided by a Statute or Rule.* Any method of authentication or identification allowed by a federal statute or a rule prescribed by the Supreme Court.

AUTHORS' COMMENTS

(1) Scope and purpose of Rule 901. Rule 901 prescribes the general principles of authentication and identification and gives a number of examples of foundations that satisfy the requirements.

(2) General principles of authentication. Rule 901(a) prescribes that authentication or identification of an item requires only evidence sufficient to support a finding—a "prima facie case"—that the item is genuine. A bona fide dispute as to authenticity or identity is not to be decided by the judge, but rather is to go to the jury. Ricketts v. City of Hartford, 74 F.3d 1397, 1409–11 (2d Cir.1996); United States v. McGlory, 968 F.2d 309, 328–29 (3d Cir.1992). In other words, conflicting evidence on genuineness goes to weight, not admissibility, so long as some reasonable person could believe that the item is what it is claimed to be. Ricketts v. City of Hartford, supra, 74 F.3d at 1411; United States v. Johnson, 637 F.2d 1224, 1247 (9th Cir.1980).

    Example—Admissible. "The district court's determination that it 'was not satisfied that the voice on the tape was that of Davis' * * * is inconsistent with these principles. So long as a jury is entitled to reach a contrary conclusion, it must be given the opportunity to do so. * * * [T]he district court erred in excluding the tape on authentication grounds without making a finding that no rational juror could have concluded that Davis made the statement at issue." Ricketts v. City of Hartford, supra, 74 F.3d at 1411.

    Example—Admissible. "We have repeatedly noted that '[t]he burden of proof for authentication is slight.' * * * When we combine White's testimony with the circumstantial evidence of the authenticity of the document, in particular the fact that it was produced by Lexington pursuant to discovery requests, we believe that there is a sufficient foundation for a jury to determine that this document is what it is purported to be: a Lexington HPL Create Sheet. * * * While it is troubling to us that the author of the handwritten notations remains unknown, and that White could not be sure of correct date, there does not appear to be any genuine dispute that the HPL Create Sheet was filled out by a Lexington employee for the purpose for which this sheet is typically used, i.e., to search for data on a claim." Lexington Ins. Co. v. Western Pennsylvania Hosp., 423 F.3d 318, 329 (3d Cir.2005).

    Example—Admissible. "Giraldo argues this evidence was insufficient because neither Vargas nor Pablo Diaz, another official involved in duplicating the tapes, had listened to all of the tapes to ensure a perfect duplication. But that is not the standard for authentication. Despite the fact that no one listened to each tape from beginning to end, the district court heard evidence relating to the integrity of the duplication procedures and the quality of the machinery. Based upon this showing, we conclude that the court did not abuse its discretion by determining that the recordings were authentic as a matter of reasonable probability." United States v. Celis, 608 F.3d 818, 842 (D.C.Cir.2010).

    Example—Admissible. "The district court did not abuse its discretion by admitting the transcripts, or clearly err in accepting as fact Detective Clifton's authenticating testimony. Detective Clifton testified that he participated in the online chats and the transcripts were accurate copies of those conversations. His testimony was sufficient 'competent evidence' to authenticate the transcripts." United States v. Lanzon, 639 F.3d 1293, 1301 (11th Cir.2011).

Example—Admissible. District court properly admitted a jacket where three police officers testified jacket was the jacket defendant was wearing on the night of his arrest even though officers admitted on cross-examination they did not know where the jacket had been prior to its receipt by the lab several months after defendant's arrest or whether it had been tampered with. United States v. Summers, 666 F.3d 192, 201 (4th Cir.2011).

Example—Inadmissible. "The VK profile page was helpful to the government's case only if it belonged to Zhyltsou—if it was his profile page, created by him or someone acting on his behalf— and thus tended to establish that Zhyltsou used the moniker 'Azmadeuz' on Skype and was likely also to have used it for the Gmail address from which the forged birth certificate was sent, just as Timku claimed. * * * It is uncontroverted that information about Zhyltsou appeared on the VK page: his name, photograph, and some details about his life consistent with Timku's testimony about him. But there was no evidence that Zhyltsou himself had created the page or was responsible for its contents." United States v. Vayner, 769 F.3d 125, 131–33 (2d Cir.2014).

Example—Admissible. "The authenticity of Janica's social media account is not at issue in this case—that is, the account's ownership is not relevant. The photographs were introduced as images of Vázquez-Soto on a motorcycle trip, not as part of a social media statement by Janica. Thus, what is at issue is only the authenticity of the photographs, not the Facebook page. * * * Accordingly, the ordinary rules of authentication apply, and the question we must ask in assessing the district court's ruling is whether there was sufficient evidence for a reasonable factfinder to conclude that the photographs were what the government represented they were— photographs of Vázquez-Soto. * * * In determining whether the photographs were authentic, the jurors could examine the photographs and rely on their own observations of Vázquez-Soto in the courtroom. Under these circumstances, a reasonable factfinder could conclude that the photographs depicted Vázquez-Soto." United States v. Vásquez-Soto, 939 F.3d 365, 373–74 (1st Cir.2019).

(3) Illustrations. Rule 901(b) lists nine examples of authentication techniques, plus a tenth provision incorporating by reference any additional methods that might be recognized by statute or court rule. The examples are explicitly stated not to be exclusive. United States v. Simpson, 152 F.3d 1241, 1249–50 (10th Cir.1998); United States v. Jimenez Lopez, 873 F.2d 769, 772 (5th Cir.1989).

(4) Testimony of witness with knowledge; chain of custody. In the case of an object or document that has unique or distinctive characteristics, testimony of a single person who perceived the item at the relevant time normally suffices to identify it in court. Reyes v. United States, 383 F.2d 734 (9th Cir.1967).

Example—Admissible. "Here, Diaz testified that he was fluent in both Spanish and English, was able to read both languages, had listened to the wiretap recordings, and believed the translated transcripts accurately reflected the recorded conversations. Because Diaz had himself been a party to each of the conversations, he was in an excellent position to authenticate the transcripts." United States v. Curbelo, 726 F.3d 1260, 1271 (11th Cir.2013).

Where the object is not distinctive in appearance, a so-called "chain of custody" may be required in order to establish that the item presented at trial is indeed the same one that had a role in the events in issue. A chain of custody consists of testimony of each person who had custody of the item, from the time of its discovery or initial connection with the case to the time of its presentation at trial. United States v. Zink, 612 F.2d 511, 514 (10th Cir.1980).

When real evidence is offered, often its condition as well as its identity is important. When this is so, a proper foundation must include evidence that the item is in substantially the same condition when presented as at the legally material time, e.g., the time of the accident, the time of first discovery, etc. United States v. Barrow, 448 F.3d 37, 42–43 (1st Cir.2006) (broken bottles properly admitted where DEA chemist testified that he received the bottles "in heat-sealed bags inside Customs boxes," and after performing tests for drugs, "he put the bottles in a DEA heat-sealed bag, initialed the bag, and then placed and sealed it in a DEA box," and his testimony "showed that the bottles were broken after he had tested their contents."); United States v. Dickerson, 873 F.2d 1181, 1185 (9th Cir.1988). Like identity, continuity of condition can sometimes be shown by a single witness. If any plausible material change in the object would be palpable, it suffices that the witness who identifies the object also testifies that it appears to be in the same condition as when previously perceived by him. Hammett v. State, 578 S.W.2d 699, 708 (Tex.Crim.App.1979). If, on the other hand, the object is of a nature that admits a risk of material but impalpable change—such as a chemical or bodily fluid specimen—then mere assertion by the identifying witness of the absence of any apparent change in its condition may not suffice. In such a case, continuity of condition must be established by a chain of custody. It is not required, however, that all possibility of tampering or adulteration be eliminated. United States v. Collins, 715 F.3d 1032, 1035–36 (7th Cir.2013) ("We acknowledge that Flores did not testify at trial and that no government agents were present when Flores made the recordings, but merely raising the possibility of tampering is not sufficient to render evidence inadmissible."). In re Exxon Valdez, 270 F.3d 1215, 1249 (9th Cir.2001) (blood test results showing alcohol content properly admitted despite "remarkable mishandlings" of sample, where evidence was sufficient for a reasonable juror to find identity and unchanged condition); United States v. Olson, 846 F.2d 1103, 1116 (7th Cir.1988); Ballou v. Henri Studios, Inc., 656 F.2d 1147, 1154–55 (5th Cir.1981). A defect in the chain of custody normally goes to the weight, not the admissibility, of the evidence. United States v. Jackson, 345 F.3d 59, 65 (2d Cir.2003); United States v. Briley, 319 F.3d 360, 363–64 (8th Cir.2003); United States v. Gorman, 312 F.3d 1159, 1162 (10th Cir.2002) ("One officer testified that all evidence taken from inside the truck was placed on the hood of the truck and the box of ammunition was among those items. He said he took the evidence from the truck hood and transported it to the police station. Another officer testified to receiving, securing and accounting for the evidence, including the box of ammunition. Although these officers could not identify who found the box of ammunition, their testimony was sufficient foundation when placed in context and considered in light of all factual circumstances."); United States v. Matta-Ballesteros, 71 F.3d 754, 768–69 (9th Cir.1995).

(5) Photographs, motion pictures, videotapes, and sound recordings. A photograph may generally be authenticated by testimony that it is a fair and accurate representation of the actual scene or event. It is not necessary that the photographer or any person who saw the making of the photograph testify. United States v. Clayton, 643 F.2d 1071, 1074 (5th Cir.1981). But see Griffin v. Bell, 694 F.3d 817, 827 (7th Cir.2012) (holding that the district court "did not abuse its discretion in requiring Griffin to produce the maker of the video before allowing admission of still photos extracted from it" where there were "many valid reasons to call into question the authenticity of the video and still photographs, and many questions about the video that could be answered only by the student who produced the recording."). A motion picture or videotape may be authenticated on the same foundation as a still photograph. Saturn Mfg., Inc. v. Williams Patent Crusher & Pulverizer Co., 713 F.2d 1347, 1357 (8th Cir.1983). A sound recording may be authenticated by a similar foundation, establishing the accuracy of the recording and identifying the speakers. United States v. Lance, 853 F.2d 1177, 1181 (5th Cir.1988); United States v. Jones, 730 F.2d 593, 597 (10th Cir.1984).

> **Example—Admissible.** "The Federal Rules of Evidence require audio and video recordings to be authenticated. Fed. R. Evid. 901. We have adopted a non-exhaustive list of factors for a court to consider in determining whether a proper foundation has been laid to authenticate recordings. United States v. McMillan, 508 F.2d 101 (8th Cir.1974). We consider whether a party has established that (1) the device was capable of recording, (2) the operator of the recording device was competent, (3) the recording is authentic and correct, (4) the recording has not been changed, (5) the recording has been preserved, (6) any speakers in the recording are identified, and (7) the conversation was voluntary. Id. at 104. To be able to identify a speaker in a recording, a witness only needs to have "heard the voice of the alleged speaker at any time." Id. at 105 (quotation omitted); see also Fed. R. Evid. 901(b)(5). * * * We have repeatedly cautioned that the McMillan factors are not to be applied rigidly. * * * The McMillan factors are 'merely helpful guidelines.' A recording can be admitted 'even if not every factor is explicitly and completely met,' as long as the totality of the circumstances satisfy a court that the recording is reliable" United States v. Kimble, 54 F.4th 538, 547 (8th Cir.2022).

(6) Nonexpert opinion on handwriting. While the extent of the witness's familiarity generally goes to the weight to be given his testimony rather than admissibility, there must be a minimal factual basis from which sufficient familiarity might reasonably have been acquired, in the absence of which the opinion evidence may properly be excluded. United States v. Binzel, 907 F.2d 746, 749 (7th Cir.1990).

Under Rule 901(b)(2), a lay witness is not competent to give an opinion on handwriting if his familiarity with the putative author's hand was acquired for purposes of the litigation. The purpose of this limitation is to reserve such testimony to experts testifying under Rule 901(b)(3).

Example—Admissible. "An investigator who becomes familiar with the defendant's handwriting for the purpose of solving a crime is different from a lay witness who makes a handwriting comparison so he can testify about it at trial. That investigator is in the same position as any other lay witness who, as part of his job or in his day-to-day affairs, has seen examples of the defendant's handwriting * * *. His opinion about the defendant's handwriting is not categorically barred by Rule 901(b)(2)." United States v. Iriele, 977 F.3d 1155, 1167 (11th Cir.2020).

(7) Comparison by trier or expert witness. Rule 901(b)(3), unlike the common law, does not require that an exemplar or specimen be found by the court to be genuine. It suffices if the exemplar or specimen is "authenticated," i.e., supported by evidence sufficient to support a finding that it is genuine. United States v. Mangan, 575 F.2d 32, 42 (2d Cir.1978). Comparison may be made by the trier of fact alone or with the assistance of an expert witness. United States v. Walker, 32 F.4th 377, 393 (4th Cir.2022) ("As for the other screenshot, which is a photograph of a letter purportedly written on December 23, 2019, the jury was capable of concluding on its own that the letter was written by Appellant. '[T]he trier of fact' may authenticate a document by comparing it 'with an authenticated specimen' like the intercepted letter Appellant admits he wrote to Davis. Fed. R. Evid. 901(b)(3). For instance, the jury could compare the handwriting in both letters. See United States v. Dozie, 27 F.3d 95, 98 (4th Cir.1994) (per curiam). The jury could also compare the similar words and phrases used in and the similar content of both letters. Fed. R. Evid. 901(b)(4)."), cert denied, 143 S.Ct. 450 (2022); United States v. Cavallo, 790 F.3d 1202, 1230 (11th Cir.2015); United States v. Spano, 421 F.3d 599, 604–05 (7th Cir.2005) ("No handwriting expert testified about the genuineness of the contested signatures. The checks and other documents were all copies, and in closing argument the prosecutor began to argue that handwriting experts are unable to authenticate signatures on copies. The defense rightly objected on the ground that no expert testimony or other basis had been provided for that implausible argument, and the judge ordered it stricken. It is doubtful that the argument helped the prosecutor; told that even an expert can't verify the genuineness of signatures on copies, a juror asked to do just that might doubt his ability to do so, and vote to acquit. In any event, no rule of evidence makes a jury incompetent to determine the genuineness of a signature by comparing it to a signature known to be genuine."); United States v. Alvarez-Farfan, 338 F.3d 1043, 1045 (9th Cir.2003) ("The district court abused its discretion in preventing the jury from comparing the documents. The law does not require 'a questioned document examiner to vouch for the similarity of handwriting,' but instead, allows the jury to determine for itself whether the same person's handwriting appears on two documents."); United States v. Wylie, 919 F.2d 969, 978 (5th Cir.1990).

(8) Circumstances and contents. Rule 901(b)(4) encompasses authentication by circumstances and contents.

Example—Admissible. "Federal Rule of Evidence 901(b) provides examples of appropriate methods of authentication, including reliance on '[t]he appearance, contents, substance, internal patterns, or other distinctive characteristics of the item.' Fed. R. Evid. 901(b)(4). This list is not exhaustive, however, and it is clear that the Government may authenticate documents with other types of circumstantial evidence, including the circumstances surrounding the documents' discovery"; citing cases "considering that notes were found in trash outside of defendant's residence as evidence of authenticity," "that documents were produced in response to a discovery request as evidence of authenticity," "holding that exhibits found in defendant's warehouse were adequately authenticated simply by their being found there," and "concluding that small number of people who knew the information in the evidence supported finding of authenticity." United States v. Turner, 718 F.3d 226, 232–33 (3d Cir.2013).

Example—Admissible. "The written materials were found in an isolated and remote area where law enforcement agents observed no one other than Harvey. The materials were within Harvey's campsite; indeed, they were next to Harvey's own bed. The writings also make numerous references to Harvey's beloved dog, Drigo. These distinctive characteristics and circumstances are sufficient to support a finding that the materials were written by Harvey." United States v. Harvey, 117 F.3d 1044, 1049 (7th Cir.1997).

Example—Admissible. An e-mail was authenticated when (1) it bore the purported author's e-mail address, (2) the contents reflected detailed knowledge of the purported author's conduct, (3) the author identified himself using the purported author's nickname, and (4) in a telephone conversation shortly after the e-mail, the purported author made the same requests as in the e-mail. United States v. Siddiqui, 235 F.3d 1318, 1322–23 (11th Cir.2000).

Example—Admissible. "To authenticate the text messages, the government needed only to 'produce evidence sufficient to support a finding' that the messages were actually sent and received by Lewisbey. Fed. R. Evid. 901(a). The government clearly did so. The iPhone was confiscated from Lewisbey at the time of his arrest, and in a recorded phone call from the jail, he told his mother that the police took his phone. The Samsung device was recovered from his bedroom at his parents' home, a room that both parents identified as belonging exclusively to him. The 'Properties' section of the iPhone described the phone as 'Big Dave's,' and the contacts directory included information for Lewisbey's mother listed under the heading 'Mom,' and also the name and number of his former attorney. Both phones listed contact information for the Texas Home Depot stores where Lewisbey used to work. And the confidential informant arranged gun sales with Lewisbey on the Samsung phone. That's more than enough to establish that the two phones were indeed Lewisbey's. See Fed. R. Evid. 901(b)(4)." United States v. Lewisbey, 843 F.3d 653, 658 (7th Cir.2016).

Example—Admissible. "Lewisbey's admission that the Facebook posts were his is enough for authentication, but if more were needed, the Facebook page lists Lewisbey's nickname, his date of birth, and his place of residence (Houston) where he lived prior to Illinois. The email addresses associated with the Facebook account correspond to both the email linked with Lewisbey's iPhone and his former email address at the University of Kansas. The Facebook page contains more than 100 photos of Lewisbey—including a profile picture—and many of the Facebook photos match photos also found on Lewisbey's iPhone. The Facebook application on Lewisbey's iPhone was linked to this Facebook account. And messages on the account discuss Lewisbey's trips to gun shows in Fort Wayne and Indianapolis on dates when gun shows actually occurred at these locations." United States v. Lewisbey, 843 F.3d 653, 658 (7th Cir.2016).

Example—Admissible. "We agree with the Third and Seventh Circuits: the Government may authenticate social media evidence with circumstantial evidence linking the defendant to the social media account. The Government did that here. First, the Government linked the same cell phone number—in Kevin Lamm's name—to both accounts. Second, the same images that appeared on Lamm's Facebook account appeared on the Malone account. Third, Lamm had copies of those images on memory cards in his apartment. Fourth, those same memory cards also contained screenshots of private messages only the Malone account could access. Fifth, other online subscriptions found on Lamm's computer used an email address containing the name Mike Malone. Taken together, this evidence provided a rational basis for the district court to pass the question of authentication to the jury." United States v. Lamm, 5 F.4th 942, 948 (8th Cir.2021) (citation and footnote omitted).

Authorship of a letter or identity of a telephone speaker may be established by evidence that the letter or statement exhibited special knowledge peculiar to the purported writer or speaker. United States v. Eisenberg, 807 F.2d 1446, 1452–53 (8th Cir.1986). The traditional "reply letter doctrine" is an instance of this special knowledge method of circumstantial authentication.

Example—Admissible. "Because the evidence showed that the caller was a male, Carpenter was the only male living at the residence to which three of the calls were traced, three more calls were traced to pay phones near Carpenter's residence, and the pay-phone and residential-phone conversations were similar in substance, we conclude the district court did not abuse its discretion in allowing the tape recordings into evidence." United States v. Carpenter, 70 F.3d 520, 521 (8th Cir.1995).

(9) Voice identification; telephone calls. Rule 901(b)(5) permits voice identification based upon familiarity acquired "at any time," including in anticipation of litigation. United States v. Panico, 435 F.3d 47, 48 (1st Cir.2006) (Two state policemen identified defendant's voice; one officer had known defendant from childhood while the other had heard his voice five or six times prior to trial.); United States v. Puentes, 50 F.3d 1567, 1577 (11th Cir.1995) ("Inspector Perez testified that he became familiar with Puentes's voice during the two-month wiretap surveillance. This testimony satisfied the requirements of rule 901(b)(5).").

"Minimal familiarity is sufficient." United States v. Saulter, 60 F.3d 270, 276 (7th Cir.1995). Accord, United States v. Plunk, 153 F.3d 1011, 1023 (9th Cir.1998).

> **Example—Admissible.** "[A] witness's claim to have heard a defendant in open court should not be accepted as per se sufficient to show minimal familiarity for Rule 901(b)(5) purposes. Courts should examine what actually transpired at the court proceeding in question to ensure that the defendant actually spoke enough to give a listener minimal familiarity with his or her voice. There may well be situations in which a defendant said so little that a listener could not claim the minimal familiarity our case law requires; and in such a situation, a court would be justified in finding that the voice identification was not admissible. Here, while Cook spoke relatively little at his pretrial appearance (by his count, 62 words in total) he did go beyond simply responding 'yes' or 'no' to inquiries by the court and spoke a number of sentences." United States v. Jones, 600 F.3d 847, 858 (7th Cir.2010).

> **Example—Admissible.** Trial court properly allowed witness to testify that he had spoken to defendant over telephone, even though witness had no prior familiarity with defendant's voice, where witness was an appraiser of businesses, telephone conversation was an interview to see if he could assess value of an asset defendant was considering for sale, speaker identified himself by defendant's name, and government introduced a letter, signed by defendant, that memorialized the agreement reached in the conversation. United States v. De Simone, 699 F.3d 113, 126–27 (1st Cir.2012).

Rule 901(b)(6) covers identification of the party who received a telephone call. Identification of the calling party is normally established under example (5) or (4); self-identification alone is insufficient. United States v. Garrison, 168 F.3d 1089, 1092–93 (8th Cir.1999); United States v. Khan, 53 F.3d 507, 516 (2d Cir.1995); United States v. Orozco-Santillan, 903 F.2d 1262, 1266 (9th Cir.1990).

(10) Ancient documents. "Federal Rule of Evidence 901(b)(8) governs the admissibility of ancient documents. The Rule states that a document is admissible if it '(A) is in such condition as to create no suspicion concerning its authenticity, (B) was in a place where it, if authentic, would likely be, and (C) has been in existence 20 years or more at the time it is offered.' The question of whether evidence is suspicious, and therefore inadmissible, is within the trial court's discretion. United States v. Kairys, 782 F.2d 1374, 1379 (7th Cir.1986). Although Rule 901(b)(8) requires that the document be free of suspicion, that suspicion goes not to the content of the document, but rather to whether the document is what it purports to be. Id. Therefore, whether the contents of the document correctly identify the defendant goes to its weight and is a matter for the trier of fact." United States v. Demjanjuk, 367 F.3d 623, 630–31 (6th Cir.2004). See also United States v. Mandycz, 447 F.3d 951, 966 (6th Cir.2006) ("Because Mandycz does not argue, much less prove, that the Soviet interrogation records are not what they purport to be—Soviet interrogation records— his contention fails.").

CROSS-REFERENCES

Common Objections (Chapter 3)

13.   Authentication insufficient
16.   Chain of custody not established (real evidence)
42.   Identification insufficient
70.   Photograph, motion picture, videotape, or sound recording not authenticated

Checklists and Foundations (Chapter 4)

10.   Steps in Offering an Exhibit (Documentary, Real, or Illustrative Evidence)

Treatises

8 Graham, Handbook of Federal Evidence §§ 901:1–901:10 (9th ed. 2020)

2 McCormick, Evidence §§ 214, 218–228 (8th ed. 2020)

31 Wright & Gold, Federal Practice and Procedure §§ 7101–7015 (2000)

Rule 902. Evidence That Is Self-Authenticating

The following items of evidence are self-authenticating; they require no extrinsic evidence of authenticity in order to be admitted:

(1) ***Domestic Public Documents That Are Sealed and Signed.*** A document that bears:

    (A) a seal purporting to be that of the United States; any state, district, commonwealth, territory, or insular possession of the United States; the former Panama Canal Zone; the Trust Territory of the Pacific Islands; a political subdivision of any of these entities; or a department, agency, or officer of any entity named above; and

    (B) a signature purporting to be an execution or attestation.

(2) ***Domestic Public Documents That Are Not Sealed but Are Signed and Certified.*** A document that bears no seal if:

    (A) it bears the signature of an officer or employee of an entity named in Rule 902(1)(A); and

    (B) another public officer who has a seal and official duties within that same entity certifies under seal—or its equivalent—that the signer has the official capacity and that the signature is genuine.

(3) ***Foreign Public Documents.*** A document that purports to be signed or attested by a person who is authorized by a foreign country's law to do so. The document must be accompanied by a final certification that certifies the genuineness of the signature and official position of the signer or attester—or of any foreign official whose certificate of genuineness relates to the signature or attestation or is in a chain of certificates of genuineness relating to the signature or attestation. The certification may be made by a secretary of a United States embassy or legation; by a consul general, vice consul, or consular agent of the United States; or by a diplomatic or consular official of the foreign country assigned or accredited to the United States. If all parties have been given a reasonable opportunity to investigate the document's authenticity and accuracy, the court may, for good cause, either:

    (A) order that it be treated as presumptively authentic without final certification; or

    (B) allow it to be evidenced by an attested summary with or without final certification.

(4) ***Certified Copies of Public Records.*** A copy of an official record—or a copy of a document that was recorded or filed in a public office as authorized by law—if the copy is certified as correct by:

    (A) the custodian or another person authorized to make the certification; or

    (B) a certificate that complies with Rule 902(1), (2), or (3), a federal statute, or a rule prescribed by the Supreme Court.

(5) ***Official Publications.*** A book, pamphlet, or other publication purporting to be issued by a public authority.

(6) ***Newspapers and Periodicals.*** Printed material purporting to be a newspaper or periodical.

(7) ***Trade Inscriptions and the Like.*** An inscription, sign, tag, or label purporting to have been affixed in the course of business and indicating origin, ownership, or control.

(8) ***Acknowledged Documents.*** A document accompanied by a certificate of acknowledgment that is lawfully executed by a notary public or another officer who is authorized to take acknowledgments.

(9) ***Commercial Paper and Related Documents.*** Commercial paper, a signature on it, and related documents, to the extent allowed by general commercial law.

(10) ***Presumptions Under a Federal Statute.*** A signature, document, or anything else that a federal statute declares to be presumptively or prima facie genuine or authentic.

(11) *Certified Domestic Records of a Regularly Conducted Activity.* The original or a copy of a domestic record that meets the requirements of Rule 803(6)(A)–(C), as shown by a certification of the custodian or another qualified person that complies with a federal statute or a rule prescribed by the Supreme Court. Before the trial or hearing, the proponent must give an adverse party reasonable written notice of the intent to offer the record—and must make the record and certification available for inspection—so that the party has a fair opportunity to challenge them.

(12) *Certified Foreign Records of a Regularly Conducted Activity.* In a civil case, the original or a copy of a foreign record that meets the requirements of Rule 902(11), modified as follows: the certification, rather than complying with a federal statute or Supreme Court rule, must be signed in a manner that, if falsely made, would subject the maker to a criminal penalty in the country where the certification is signed. The proponent must also meet the notice requirements of Rule 902(11).

(13) *Certified Records Generated by an Electronic Process or System.* A record generated by an electronic process or system that produces an accurate result, as shown by a certification of a qualified person that complies with the certification requirements of Rule 902(11) or (12). The proponent must also meet the notice requirements of Rule 902(11).

(14) *Certified Data Copied from an Electronic Device, Storage Medium, or File.* Data copied from an electronic device, storage medium, or file, if authenticated by a process of digital identification, as shown by a certification of a qualified person that complies with the certification requirements of Rule 902(11) or (12). The proponent also must meet the notice requirements of Rule 902(11).

AUTHORS' COMMENTS

(1)　Scope and purpose of Rule 902. Rule 902 lists several categories of documents which are self-authenticating, i.e., they do not need evidence of authenticity (genuineness) to be admissible.

(2)　Effect of self-authentication. If a document falls into one of the listed categories, the proponent is not required to present any authenticating evidence in order to introduce it. The opponent may still challenge the genuineness of the document, however, and may offer evidence to support such an attack. Reed v. State, 811 S.W.2d 582, 587 (Tex.Crim.App.1991). If the opposing evidence is sufficient to support a finding that the document is not authentic, the issue will go to the trier of fact. Furthermore, Rule 902 only addresses the authentication issue. A document that is self-authenticating may nevertheless be inadmissible for other reasons, such as the best evidence rule, the hearsay rule, or a privilege. United States v. Bellucci, 995 F.2d 157, 160 (9th Cir.1993).

(3)　Certified copies of public records. Examples of documents admissible under Rule 902(4):

• 　Copy of record of United States Postal Service bearing certification under seal of Service. United States v. Moore, 555 F.2d 658, 661 (8th Cir.1977).

• 　Copy of Texas state court judgment certified by custodian of records of Texas Department of Corrections. United States v. Huffhines, 967 F.2d 314, 320 (9th Cir.1992).

• 　Tape recording of arraignment and plea before federal magistrate, certified by deputy clerk. United States v. Lechuga, 975 F.2d 397, 399 (7th Cir.1992).

• 　IRS Certificate of Assessment and Payments accompanied by IRS Certificate of Official Record bearing seal and signature of manager of certification unit of the regional service center. United States v. Bisbee, 245 F.3d 1001, 1006–07 (8th Cir.2001).

• 　Penitentiary packet certified by coordinator of the Offender Records Unit of the Oklahoma Department of Corrections. United States v. Watson, 650 F.3d 1084, 1090 (8th Cir.2011).

• 　Outstanding arrest warrant signed by judge. Moore v. City of Desloge, Mo., 647 F.3d 841, 848 (8th Cir.2011).

A public document not qualifying under paragraphs (1), (2), (3) or (4) may nevertheless be rendered self-authenticating under some other provision of Rule 902, such as Rule 902(8) (Acknowledged Documents). United States v. M'Biye, 655 F.2d 1240, 1243 (D.C.Cir.1981).

(4) Commercial paper and related documents. The effect of Rule 902(9) is to refer to certain provisions of the Uniform Commercial Code that create presumptive authenticity for various commercial instruments, or parts of them, in some circumstances. Three sections of the Code have this effect: § 1–202 (third party documents), § 3–307(a) (signatures on negotiable instruments) and § 3–510 (protests, bank stamps or tickets indicating dishonor, and bank records showing dishonor).

(5) Presumptions under statutes or other rules. Examples of statutory self-authentication provisions that are made applicable under Rule 902(10):

- Signature on SEC registration presumed genuine. 15 U.S.C.A. § 77f(a).

- Individual's name on corporate return is prima facie evidence of authority to sign return. 26 U.S.C.A. § 6062.

(6) Certified business records. Rules 902(11) and (12) were added by amendment in 2000. They permit establishment of all foundation elements for records admissible under Rule 803(6) by certification of the custodian or other qualified person, thereby obviating foundation testimony at trial. They require "reasonable" pretrial written notice. United States v. Daniels, 723 F.3d 562, 580–81 (5th Cir.2013) ("[A]lthough the Government failed to give timely pretrial notice of its intention to use attestations to introduce the business records, the district court crafted two suitable remedies so as to afford the defendants the opportunity to test the adequacy of the foundations established by the declarations. The defendants did not avail themselves of these remedies. Moreover, the defendants had three days to assess the foundation of the business records the Government sought to introduce, a duration not materially unlike the five-day notice that we considered sufficient in [United States v. Olguin, 643 F.3d 384, 391 (5th Cir.2011)]. While it might not be the best practice to admit records upon three days' review in the midst of trial, we cannot say that it constitutes an abuse of discretion.").

Paragraphs (13) and (14) were added in 2017. Paragraph (13) "sets forth a procedure by which parties can authenticate certain electronic evidence other than through the testimony of a foundation witness. * * * A proponent establishing authenticity under this Rule must present a certification containing information that would be sufficient to establish authenticity were that information provided by a witness at trial." Advisory Committee's Note. Paragraph (14) has a similar purpose and effect. As explained by the Advisory Committee.

Today, data copied from electronic devices, storage media, and electronic files are ordinarily authenticated by "hash value." A hash value is a number that is often represented as a sequence of characters and is produced by an algorithm based upon the digital contents of a drive, medium, or file. * * * This amendment allows self-authentication by a certification of a qualified person that she checked the hash value of the proffered item and that it was identical to the original. The rule is flexible enough to allow certifications through processes other than comparison of hash value, including by other reliable means of identification provided by future technology.

CROSS-REFERENCES

Common Objections (Chapter 3)

13. Authentication insufficient
41. Identification insufficient
70. Photograph, motion picture, videotape, or sound recording not authenticated

Checklists and Foundations (Chapter 4)

10. Steps in Offering an Exhibit (Documentary, Real, or Illustrative Evidence)

Treatises

8 Graham, Handbook of Federal Evidence §§ 902:1–902:10 (9th ed. 2020)

2 McCormick, Evidence §§ 218, 228, 300 (8th ed. 2020)

31 Wright & Gold, Federal Practice and Procedure §§ 7131–7148 (2000)

Rule 903. Subscribing Witness's Testimony

A subscribing witness's testimony is necessary to authenticate a writing only if required by the law of the jurisdiction that governs its validity.

AUTHORS' COMMENTS

(1) Scope and purpose of Rule 903. At common law, if an instrument was attested by subscribing witnesses, it could not be authenticated without producing at least one of the attesters or showing them all to be unavailable. Under Rule 903, production of or accounting for attesting witnesses is required only if the law governing the validity of the document so requires. Today very few writings will present such a requirement. The most important are wills in some states.

CROSS-REFERENCES

Treatises

8 Graham, Handbook of Federal Evidence § 903:1 (9th ed. 2020)

2 McCormick, Evidence § 220 (8th ed. 2020)

31 Wright & Gold, Federal Practice and Procedure §§ 7151–7154 (2000)

ARTICLE X

CONTENTS OF WRITINGS, RECORDINGS, AND PHOTOGRAPHS

Rule 1001. Definitions That Apply to This Article

In this article:

(a) A "writing" consists of letters, words, numbers, or their equivalent set down in any form.

(b) A "recording" consists of letters, words, numbers, or their equivalent recorded in any manner.

(c) A "photograph" means a photographic image or its equivalent stored in any form.

(d) An "original" of a writing or recording means the writing or recording itself or any counterpart intended to have the same effect by the person who executed or issued it. For electronically stored information, "original" means any printout—or other output readable by sight—if it accurately reflects the information. An "original" of a photograph includes the negative or a print from it.

(e) A "duplicate" means a counterpart produced by a mechanical, photographic, chemical, electronic, or other equivalent process or technique that accurately reproduces the original.

AUTHORS' COMMENTS

(1) Scope and purpose of Rule 1001. Rule 1001, Definitions, must be read in conjunction with other rules which employ the defined terms and thereby give them legal significance. For example, Rule 1002 states the basic best evidence rule, that ordinarily the "original" (defined in Rule 1001(d)) of a "writing" (defined in Rule 1001(a)) is required in order to prove its content. Rule 1001(e) defines "duplicate"; but the legal significance of the concept is contained in Rule 1003, which tells us that most of the time a "duplicate" is as good as an "original."

(2) Writings. Rule 1001(a) and (b) are merely definitions. The existence of an item related to the case that fits the definition does not by itself mean that production of the item is required. Under Rule 1002, the original writing is demanded, as at common law, only when a party seeks "to prove the content" of it. Many times a writing exists that bears some connection with the case but the best evidence rule does not require its production because no party seeks to prove its content. See the Authors' Comments to Rule 1002, infra.

(3) Inscribed chattels. The best evidence rule's requirement of production of the original is not rigidly applied when the "writing" is a so-called "inscribed chattel" rather than a document. Instead, the trial judge has discretion whether to require the original item, "in light of such factors as the need for precise information as to the exact inscription, the ease or difficulty of production, and the simplicity or complexity of the inscription." McCormick, Evidence § 232 (5th ed. 1999). See United States v. Duffy, 454 F.2d 809, 811–13 (5th Cir.1972) (upholding admission of oral testimony concerning a laundry mark on a shirt).

(4) Artwork, drawings, designs; "other form of data compilation." Artwork, drawings, designs, and the like are included within the coverage of the definition of "writings." Seiler v. Lucasfilm, Ltd., 808 F.2d 1316, 1320 (9th Cir.1986). A witness's description of a Global Positioning System monitor display, showing the location and movements of a boat, violated Rule 1002 because the display was a "writing." United States v. Bennett, 363 F.3d 947, 953 (9th Cir.2004).

(5) Photographs. Although the best evidence rule in this codification extends to photographs, this extension seldom has practical consequences. For one reason, Rule 1001(d) gives "the negative or print from it" equal status as originals. Moreover, under Rule 1002, the requirement of an original arises only when a party seeks "to prove its content." See the Authors' Comments to Rule 1002, infra.

(6) Original. There can be more than one "original." If each party to a contract, lease, sale, or other transaction receives or retains a copy of the instrument that embodies or evidences the transaction, each copy is an original. Greater Kansas City Laborers Pension Fund v. Thummel, 738 F.2d 926, 928 (8th Cir.1984) (agreements executed in quadruplicate by carbon copies, all "originals"). For example, each part of a credit card formpack ("bank copy," "merchant copy," "customer copy") is an original. United States v. Rangel, 585 F.2d 344 (8th Cir.1978).

The phrase "the writing * * * itself" means the writing the content of which is sought to be proved in the case.

> **Example.** "[W]hat is an original for some purposes may be a duplicate for others. Thus a bank's microfilm record of checks cleared is the original as a record. However, a print offered as a copy of a check whose contents are in controversy is a duplicate." Advisory Committee's Note to Federal Rule 1001.

> **Example.** Defendant, a federal employee, had submitted travel expense vouchers accompanied by photocopies of altered charge card receipts. The photocopies were "originals" in this context, since they were the writings actually submitted by defendant for reimbursement. United States v. Rangel, 585 F.2d 344 (8th Cir.1978).

> **Example.** "Ms. Cartier was not trying to prove the contents of the rented master tape. She was trying to show Mr. Jackson had access to her version of 'Dangerous' through her demo tapes. * * * The 'original' for which Ms. Cartier is trying to demonstrate the contents was the demo tape." Cartier v. Jackson, 59 F.3d 1046, 1049 (10th Cir.1995).

(7) Duplicate. A duplicate is a type of copy which is ordinarily admissible to prove the contents of the original, under Rule 1003. Basically, any mechanically created reproduction is a duplicate; a manually created reproduction, because of the risk of human error, is not. In the absence of stipulation, a proper foundation that a writing is a duplicate of another consists of testimony by a person with personal knowledge of the contents of the original that the offered writing is an accurate reproduction of it, produced by some identified process "that accurately reproduces the original."

(8) Transcript of sound recording. A transcript offered in lieu of an available recording would be objectionable on best evidence grounds, being neither the original nor a duplicate of the recording. United States v. Chavez, 976 F.3d 1178, 1199 (10th Cir.2020) (reversible error to admit English translation of foreign-language recording that was not introduced). However, when offered in conjunction with the original or a duplicate recording, a properly authenticated transcript is admissible to assist the trier in understanding the recording. United States v. Wright, 932 F.2d 868, 880 (10th Cir.1991). When a transcript is used in this manner in conjunction with a recording, it is not "substantive evidence"—the recording is— and, at least if the party-opponent so requests, the judge should instruct the jury accordingly. United States v. Doerr, 886 F.2d 944, 966 (7th Cir.1989). Courts have disagreed as to whether the transcript should be taken into the jury room. Compare United States v. Vinson, 606 F.2d 149, 155 (6th Cir.1979) (no), with

United States v. Doerr, 886 F.2d 944, 966 (7th Cir.1989) (proper), and United States v. Rengifo, 789 F.2d 975, 982–83 (1st Cir.1986) (trial court's discretion).

CROSS-REFERENCES

Common Objections (Chapter 3)

14.   Best evidence not being offered

Treatises

8 Graham, Handbook of Federal Evidence §§ 1001:1–1001:3 (9th ed. 2020)

2 McCormick, Evidence §§ 232, 235–236 (8th ed. 2020)

31 Wright & Gold, Federal Practice and Procedure §§ 7161–7167 (2000)

Rule 1002. Requirement of the Original

An original writing, recording, or photograph is required in order to prove its content unless these rules or a federal statute provides otherwise.

AUTHORS' COMMENTS

(1) Scope and purpose of Rule 1002. Rule 1002 states the best evidence rule. The key to its application is in the phrase "to prove its content." The rule only applies, and requires production of the original, when a party seeks to prove the content of the original. The rule does not come into operation every time a writing (or recording or photograph) exists containing a matter that a party seeks to prove. This is so even if a writing may be the "best" evidence of the matter, in the sense of most convincing. As explained below, the rule only operates when either (1) a writing is itself the thing to be proved, or (2) a party seeks to prove a matter by using a writing as evidence of it.

(2) Rule applicable—Writing is itself the thing to be proved. In cases involving written contracts, deeds, wills, libels, or materials claimed to be obscene, the substantive law accords ultimate legal significance to the writing, by operation of the statute of frauds, parol evidence rule, etc. Therefore, in these instances the transaction can only be proven by the writing, and a party seeking to prove it necessarily must prove the content of the writing, and must comply with the best evidence rule.

> **Example.** In prosecution for fraud, best evidence rule applied to proof of contents of letter alleged to be fraudulent. United States v. Taylor, 648 F.2d 565, 570 (9th Cir.1981).

(3) Rule applicable—Party chooses to use writing as evidence of a matter. The best evidence rule also applies in instances in which, although the ultimate fact to be determined is not a written transaction, a party chooses a writing as evidence of it. For example, suppose that in a negligence case P offers to establish D's negligence by D's statement in a letter admitting a negligent act. The rule applies to the letter.

> **Example.** A witness's description of a Global Positioning System monitor display, showing the location and movements of a boat, violated Rule 1002 because the display was a "writing," and the testimony was offered to prove the contents, i.e., the location and movements of the boat. United States v. Bennett, 363 F.3d 947, 953–54 (9th Cir.2004).

(4) Rule inapplicable—Party may prove non-writing event although writing exists that happens to record the event. To be distinguished from the situations described in paragraphs (2) and (3), supra, are the many situations in which the best evidence rule does not require production of a writing that happens to contain matter that a party can prove without the writing.

> **Example.** A person who heard an oral conversation may testify to the content of the conversation even if a tape recording of the conversation exists. United States v. Branham, 97 F.3d 835, 853 (6th Cir.1996); United States v. Fagan, 821 F.2d 1002, 1008–09 n. 1 (5th Cir.1987); United States v. Gonzales-Benitez, 537 F.2d 1051, 1053–54 (9th Cir.1976).

> **Example.** A witness with knowledge could testify to the cost of items, in lieu of producing written records. "No evidentiary rule * * * prohibits a witness from testifying to a fact simply because the

fact can be supported by written documentation." R & R Associates, Inc. v. Visual Scene, Inc., 726 F.2d 36, 38 (1st Cir.1984).

Example. A corporate officer with personal knowledge could testify to the amount of fringe benefits paid to an employee, without producing written company records. D'Angelo v. United States, 456 F.Supp. 127, 131 (D.Del.1978), aff'd, 605 F.2d 1194 (3d Cir.1979). On the other hand, if the witness lacks independent knowledge, but derives his knowledge from the written records, then his testimony in lieu of the records would violate the rule.

Example. Witness who testified that she had opened a California bank account, acquired a California driver's license, and taken California community college courses was not required to produce documentation of her bank account, license, or college transcripts. Rodriguez v. Señor Frog's de la Isla, Inc., 642 F.3d 28, 34 (1st Cir.2011).

(5) Rule inapplicable—Proof of absence of matter in writing. By weight of authority, the rule does not apply to testimony that written records have been examined and found not to contain a certain matter. Advisory Committee's Note to Rule 1002; 2 McCormick, Evidence § 233 (7th ed. 2013).

(6) Rule inapplicable—Existence or date of writing. Considerable authority holds that the rule does not apply to evidence that a writing exists, United States v. Sliker, 751 F.2d 477, 483–84 (2d Cir.1984) (insurance policy), or to evidence of some other fact about it such as its date, United States v. Jones, 958 F.2d 520, 521 (2d Cir.1992) (secondary evidence that tax return was timely filed), as distinguished from evidence of its terms. As Wigmore noted, however, "[t]estimony about a document cannot go very far without referring to its terms." 4 Wigmore, Evidence § 1242 (Chadbourn rev. 1972).

(7) Photographs; X-rays. Best evidence problems seldom arise with photographs, for three reasons: (1) in most instances the party wishes to introduce the photograph; rarely would he instead offer testimony about it; (2) the usual device of using a photograph to illustrate a witness's oral testimony does not constitute proof of its contents, and the rule is inapplicable; (3) Rule 1001(d) defines "original" as to photographs very liberally.

On the other hand, there are situations where the contents of a photograph are sought to be proved. In these instances the rule applies, and oral testimony describing the photograph would be incompetent. United States v. Levine, 546 F.2d 658, 667–68 (5th Cir.1977) (Rule 1002 applied to film in obscenity case).

With respect to X-rays, however, the Advisory Committee's Note to Rule 1002 points out that Rule 703 permits expert testimony based upon matters not in evidence, and Rule 803(6) would permit medical records containing a radiologist's interpretation of an X-ray without the X-ray itself.

(8) Other admissibility objections. "The best evidence rule is *not* an exception to the general rule excluding the admission of hearsay. Instead, [w]hile Rule 1002 limits the admissibility of evidence offered to prove the contents of a writing * * * satisfying Rule 1002 does not mean that the evidence in question is necessarily admissible. The evidence remains subject to other admissibility objections under the Evidence Rules and the Constitution. Specifically, the evidence frequently also raises admissibility issues under the rules regulating hearsay and authentication." McInnis v. Fairfield Communities, Inc., 458 F.3d 1129, 1144 (10th Cir.2006).

CROSS-REFERENCES

Common Objections (Chapter 3)

14. Best evidence not being offered

Treatises

8 Graham, Handbook of Federal Evidence §§ 1002:1–1002:5 (9th ed. 2020)

2 McCormick, Evidence §§ 229–231, 233 (8th ed. 2020)

31 Wright & Gold, Federal Practice and Procedure §§ 7181–7185 (2000)

Rule 1003. Admissibility of Duplicates

A duplicate is admissible to the same extent as the original unless a genuine question is raised about the original's authenticity or the circumstances make it unfair to admit the duplicate.

AUTHORS' COMMENTS

(1) Scope and purpose of Rule 1003. Rule 1003 makes duplicates (defined in Rule 1001(e))—such as photocopies—freely admissible in lieu of the original in most circumstances.

"[A] duplicate of a duplicate is a duplicate for purposes of Federal Rule of Evidence 1003." In re Griffin, 719 F.3d 1126, 1127 (9th Cir.2013).

(2) Genuine question about the original's authenticity. While a party is generally free to substitute a duplicate for an original, if the case presents a jury question whether the original document is a forgery, the jury should receive the original. Therefore, Rule 1003 provides that in this situation the proponent may not use a duplicate if he is in a position to produce the original. United States v. Haddock, 956 F.2d 1534, 1545–46 (10th Cir.1992). If, however, the proponent is excused from production of the original—because, for example, it has been lost or destroyed—then any secondary evidence, including a duplicate, will be permitted, as provided in Rule 1004.

(3) Unfair to admit the duplicate. The second exception to the general admissibility of duplicates is where "the circumstances make it unfair to admit the duplicate."

Example—Inadmissible. "[W]hen only a part of the original is reproduced and the remainder is needed for cross-examination or may disclose matters qualifying the part offered or otherwise useful to the opposing party." Advisory Committee's Note to Federal Rule 1003.

Example—Inadmissible. In a prosecution for theft of a Social Security check from the mail, it was improper to admit an incomplete photocopy of the check as evidence. United States v. Alexander, 326 F.2d 736, 742–43 (4th Cir.1964).

Example—Inadmissible. In a civil fraud action, it was proper to exclude photocopies, prepared for trial, of portions of business records of plaintiff Japanese corporation, where the original records were in Japan, plaintiff offered no excuse for failure to produce them, and defendant had no opportunity to examine the originals to determine whether other, omitted portions might also be relevant. Toho Bussan Kaisha, Ltd. v. American President Lines, Ltd., 265 F.2d 418, 422–24 (2d Cir.1959).

Example—Admissible. "[T]he copies of the expense account reports were not prepared with litigation in mind; they came from the microfiche records that Mellon Bank collects in the ordinary course of its business. And the district court undertook a detailed examination of the omitted portions of the originals before finding that the omissions would not have affected the usefulness of the duplicates." United States v. Sinclair, 74 F.3d 753, 760 (7th Cir.1996).

Example—Inadmissible. Photocopy of date-stamped DOJ decision letter was inadmissible where key information therein was barely legible and original was never produced. Lozano v. Ashcroft, 258 F.3d 1160, 1166 (10th Cir.2001).

CROSS-REFERENCES

Common Objections (Chapter 3)

14. Best evidence not being offered

Treatises

8 Graham, Handbook of Federal Evidence § 1003:1 (9th ed. 2020)

2 McCormick, Evidence § 236 (8th ed. 2020)

31 Wright & Gold, Federal Practice and Procedure §§ 8001–8004 (2000)

Rule 1004. Admissibility of Other Evidence of Content

An original is not required and other evidence of the content of a writing, recording, or photograph is admissible if:

(a) all the originals are lost or destroyed, and not by the proponent acting in bad faith;

(b) an original cannot be obtained by any available judicial process;

(c) the party against whom the original would be offered had control of the original; was at that time put on notice, by pleadings or otherwise, that the original would be a subject of proof at the trial or hearing; and fails to produce it at the trial or hearing; or

(d) the writing, recording, or photograph is not closely related to a controlling issue.

AUTHORS' COMMENTS

(1) Scope and purpose of Rule 1004. Rule 1004 codifies the common law doctrines excusing a party from compliance with the best evidence rule in various circumstances.

(2) No degrees of secondary evidence. If any of the four conditions listed in Rule 1004 is established, the proponent is then free to prove the contents of a writing, recording, or photograph by any secondary evidence he chooses. As explained in the Advisory Committee's Note, "The rule recognizes no 'degrees' of secondary evidence."

> **Example.** In a breach of warranty action against a seller of insulation, it was proper to permit the buyer to testify to the contents of seller's promotional brochure, which was destroyed in the fire, despite the availability of a similar brochure. Neville Const. Co. v. Cook Paint and Varnish Co., 671 F.2d 1107, 1109 (8th Cir.1982).

> **Example.** In a criminal case, a police officer could testify to the contents of a lost note written by defendant, although a typed copy existed. United States v. Standing Soldier, 538 F.2d 196, 202–03 (8th Cir.1976).

> **Example.** "Because the district court in this case could admit any form of secondary testimony once the tape was destroyed and because there was no evidence of bad faith, the agent's oral testimony was properly admitted." United States v. Billingsley, 160 F.3d 502, 505 n. 2 (8th Cir.1998).

(3) Originals lost or destroyed. Proof that the original is lost normally consists of testimony describing a fruitless diligent search. Cartier v. Jackson, 59 F.3d 1046, 1048 (10th Cir.1995); 5 Graham, Handbook of Federal Evidence § 1004.2 (8th ed. 2016); 2 McCormick, Evidence § 237 (7th ed. 2013). Occasionally direct evidence of destruction or loss may be shown. United States v. McGaughey, 977 F.2d 1067, 1071 (7th Cir.1992). Sufficiency of the foundation is regarded as a matter within the trial court's discretion. Cartier v. Jackson, 59 F.3d 1046, 1048 (10th Cir.1995); United States v. Shoels, 685 F.2d 379, 384 (10th Cir.1982); Wright v. Farmers Co-Op of Arkansas and Oklahoma, 681 F.2d 549, 553 (8th Cir.1982).

(4) Bad faith destruction by proponent. Intentional destruction by the proponent by no means forecloses use of exception (1); bad faith must appear.

> **Example—Not bad faith destruction.** Proponent destroyed the original in the regular course of business. United States v. Workinger, 90 F.3d 1409, 1415 (9th Cir.1996); United States v. Conry, 631 F.2d 599, 600 (9th Cir.1980).

> **Example—Not bad faith destruction.** Proponent re-recorded wire to tape by process that erased original which otherwise could not be played back. United States v. Balzano, 687 F.2d 6, 7–8 (1st Cir.1982).

> **Example—Not bad faith destruction.** Negligent destruction. Gryder's Estate v. Commissioner, 705 F.2d 336, 338 (8th Cir.1983).

See also Vodusek v. Bayliner Marine Corp., 71 F.3d 148, 156 (4th Cir.1995) ("Even if a court determines not to exclude secondary evidence, it may still permit the jury to draw unfavorable inferences against the party responsible for the loss or destruction of the original evidence. An adverse inference about a party's consciousness of the weakness of his case, however, cannot be drawn merely from his negligent loss or destruction of evidence; the inference requires a showing that the party knew the evidence was relevant to some issue at trial and that his wilful conduct resulted in its loss or destruction.").

(5) Original not obtainable. A sufficient foundation for secondary evidence under Rule 1004(b) consists of showing (1) the original is in the possession of a third party, and (2) proponent has unsuccessfully sought to obtain the original from the third party by appropriate subpoena duces tecum. United States v. Taylor, 648 F.2d 565, 570 (9th Cir.1981). The rule's reference to "any available judicial process or procedure" "includes subpoena duces tecum as an incident to the taking of a deposition in another jurisdiction." Advisory Committee's Note to Rule 1004(2). Considerable authority suggests, however, that the rule will be construed not to impose "unreasonable" burdens in this regard. United States v. Marcantoni, 590 F.2d 1324, 1329–30 (5th Cir.1979).

A civil trial subpoena duces tecum may be served at any place within the district of the issuing court or within 100 miles of the courthouse. Fed. R. Civ. P. 45(b)(2). A criminal trial subpoena may be served anywhere in the nation. Fed. R. Crim. P. 17(e). Under certain conditions in both civil and criminal cases, a national or resident of the United States who is in a foreign country may be subpoenaed for trial. 28 U.S.C.A. § 1783. A civil deposition subpoena duces tecum may reach any person in the nation. Fed. R. Civ. P. 28(a), 45. Civil Rule 28(b) prescribes mechanisms for depositions in foreign countries. These devices may not function in practice in particular instances, however.

(6) Original in possession of opponent. Under Rule 1004(c), a party may prove the content of a document by secondary evidence upon showing (1) possession or control of the original by the opponent, and (2) opponent's knowledge or notice, at any time sufficiently in advance of the hearing to have brought the original, that the terms or contents of the original would be in issue. Whether these conditions have been established is to be determined by the judge. Rule 1008, infra.

(7) Effect of possession and notice. The notice served under this provision does not compel the party to produce the original; it merely justifies the admission of secondary evidence to prove contents. Thus it is no substitute, if the original is desired, for a subpoena duces tecum, Fed. R. Civ. P. 45, or a discovery request for production, Fed. R. Civ. P. 34. The only sanction for ignoring a Rule 1004(4) notice is overruling of an objection to secondary evidence.

(8) Sufficiency of notice. Sufficiency of the notice should be determined by practical, not technical standards. Oral notice may suffice in proper circumstances. Walters v. State, 102 Tex.Crim. 243, 247, 277 S.W. 653, 656 (1925). Moreover, many cases demonstrate that implied notice may result from the nature of the controversy as stated in the pleadings, where a writing or instrument is central to the litigation.

Example—Implied notice. Suit on insurance policy. McConnell Const. Co. v. Insurance Co. of St. Louis, 428 S.W.2d 659, 661–62 (Tex.1968).

Example—Implied notice. Prosecution for robbery put defendants on notice that serial numbers of stolen "bait bills" would be subject of proof at the trial. United States v. Marcantoni, 590 F.2d 1324, 1329–30 (5th Cir.1979).

(9) Collateral matters. If a witness in the course of testifying refers to a writing which is not a part of the underlying dispute, Rule 1004(d) obviates production of that "collateral" writing, even if strictly speaking the witness has testified to the terms or contents of it. Three factors that preponderate in the determination of collateralness are "the centrality of the writing to the principal issues of the litigation, the complexity of the relevant features of the writing, and the existence of a genuine dispute as to the contents of the writing." 2 McCormick, Evidence § 234 (7th ed. 2013).

Example. Party could examine own witness about contents of a flyer about the case, without producing the flyer, to show how witness learned of the case and came to testify. Jackson v. Crews, 873 F.2d 1105, 1110 (8th Cir.1989).

Example. Plaintiffs could establish their standing as aggrieved owners in a zoning case by their testimony, without producing title instruments. Farr v. Zoning Board of Appeals, 139 Conn. 577, 95 A.2d 792 (1953).

Example. Plaintiff in an action for rent could testify that he purchased the premises from lessor and took assignment of the lease, without producing title documents. Prudential Ins. Co. v. Black, 572 S.W.2d 379, 380–81 (Tex.Civ.App.1978).

CROSS-REFERENCES

Common Objections (Chapter 3)

14.   Best evidence not being offered

Treatises

8 Graham, Handbook of Federal Evidence §§ 1004:1–1004:5 (9th ed. 2020)

2 McCormick, Evidence §§ 234, 237–239, 241 (8th ed. 2020)

31 Wright & Gold, Federal Practice and Procedure §§ 8011–8017 (2000)

Rule 1005. Copies of Public Records to Prove Content

The proponent may use a copy to prove the content of an official record—or of a document that was recorded or filed in a public office as authorized by law—if these conditions are met: the record or document is otherwise admissible; and the copy is certified as correct in accordance with Rule 902(4) or is testified to be correct by a witness who has compared it with the original. If no such copy can be obtained by reasonable diligence, then the proponent may use other evidence to prove the content.

AUTHORS' COMMENTS

(1) Scope and purpose of Rule 1005. Under Rule 1005, production of the original of a public record is never required, because, as explained by the federal Advisory Committee, "[r]emoving them from their usual place of keeping would be attended by serious inconvenience to the public and to the custodian." Instead of the original, proponent must offer a certified or "compared" copy; only if such a copy cannot "be obtained by reasonable diligence" may other evidence of contents be offered.

Rule 1005 addresses only the best evidence aspect of public record evidence. United States v. Ruffin, 575 F.2d 346, 356 (2d Cir.1978). Other rules address the authentication and hearsay aspects. Under Rule 901(b)(7), evidence of custody in a proper place, by itself, is sufficient to authenticate any public record. More importantly, under Rule 902(4), a copy of any public record that is "certified as correct by the custodian or other person authorized to make the certification" is self-authenticating. Several hearsay exceptions apply to various public records. See Rules 803(8)–(10), (14), and (22)–(23), supra.

(2) Copy need not be duplicate. A certified or compared copy may or may not be a duplicate as defined in Rule 1001(e); that is immaterial. If it is a certified or compared copy, it is admissible under Rule 1005 whether or not it is a duplicate. United States v. Torres, 733 F.2d 449, 455 n. 5 (7th Cir.1984). If it is not certified or compared, it is not admissible even if it is a duplicate.

(3) Recorded private documents. Application of Rule 1005 sometimes requires careful attention to the question of which writing is the "original" that the proponent seeks to prove. This may be particularly necessary where the evidence concerns "a document that was recorded and filed in a public office as authorized by law," as opposed to "an official record." Recorded documents often are copies of original private documents, such as deeds or encumbrances on real property. After recordation, the private original is returned to the owner. In this situation, there are really two "originals": the owner's document is the original as the conveyance, but the recorded copy is the original as the public record. If a party seeks to prove the terms of an original conveyance, he may do so by proving the public record in accordance with Rule 1005, but he is not required to do so. He might instead offer the original conveyance, or a duplicate, or show an excuse under Rule 1004 for nonproduction of the original (such as loss or destruction or possession by opponent and notice) and offer any form of secondary evidence. Amoco Production Co. v. United States, 619 F.2d 1383, 1389–90 (10th Cir.1980) (Rule 1005 not applicable to proof of terms of lost original deed). On the other hand, a party may seek to prove not the terms of the conveyance, but the public record, since for some purposes (such as establishing record notice) the latter would be the material issue. In that case only such proof as stated in Rule 1005 would be proper.

CROSS-REFERENCES

Treatises

8 Graham, Handbook of Federal Evidence § 1005:1 (9th ed. 2020)

2 McCormick, Evidence § 240 (8th ed. 2020)

31 Wright & Gold, Federal Practice and Procedure §§ 8031–8034 (2000)

Rule 1006. Summaries to Prove Content

The proponent may use a summary, chart, or calculation to prove the content of voluminous writings, recordings, or photographs that cannot be conveniently examined in court. The proponent must make the originals or duplicates available for examination or copying, or both, by other parties at a reasonable time or place. And the court may order the proponent to produce them in court.

AUTHORS' COMMENTS

(1) Scope and purpose of Rule 1006. Rule 1006 codifies prior common law on the use of summaries as evidence of the contents of documents too voluminous to be conveniently presented in their entirety.

(2) Underlying materials must be admissible. Summary evidence is admissible under Rule 1006 only if the underlying materials are admissible. United States v. Pelullo, 964 F.2d 193, 204 (3d Cir.1992).

(3) Underlying materials need not be introduced or produced in court. The underlying materials need not be introduced in evidence, and the rule provides that whether to require that they be produced in court is a matter of the court's discretion. United States v. Hemphill, 514 F.3d 1350, 1359 (D.C. Cir.2008) ("the point of Rule 1006 is to avoid introducing all the documents"); United States v. Bakker, 925 F.2d 728, 736 (4th Cir.1991); United States v. Strissel, 920 F.2d 1162, 1163 (4th Cir.1990).

(4) Foundation. A proper foundation for a summary must establish the admissibility of the underlying materials and the accuracy of the summary. Needham v. White Laboratories, Inc., 639 F.2d 394, 403 (7th Cir.1981). Although the rule does not specify that the person who prepared a written summary, chart, or other exhibit must testify, "[a]s a practical matter it would be very difficult to authenticate the chart, summary, or calculation, or to establish its accuracy without calling as a witness the person who is responsible for its preparation." 5 Weinstein's Evidence ¶ 1006[06].

(5) Underlying material, not summary itself, must be made available. The rule requires that the underlying material, not the summary itself, be made available to the adverse party before trial. United States v. Mazkouri, 945 F.3d 293 (5th Cir.2019); Coates v. Johnson & Johnson, 756 F.2d 524, 549–50 (7th Cir.1985). But see Air Safety, Inc. v. Roman Catholic Archbishop of Boston, 94 F.3d 1, 7 (1st Cir.1996) ("Common sense dictates that this guaranteed access, designed to give the opponent the ability to check the summary's accuracy and prepare for cross-examination, * * * must include unequivocal notice of the party's intent to invoke Rule 1006. * * * Thus, to satisfy the 'made available' requirement, a party seeking to use a summary under Rule 1006 must identify its exhibit as such, provide a list or description of the documents supporting the exhibit, and state when and where they may be reviewed.").

(6) Voluminousness. "Rule 1006 does not require that it be literally impossible to examine all the underlying records, but only that in-court examination would be an inconvenience." United States v. Possick, 849 F.2d 332, 339 (8th Cir.1988).

Example—Admissible. "In the present case, the district court did not err in admitting the summaries. The government's evidence was incredibly voluminous, and it would have been incomprehensible to the jury without summarization." United States v. Thompson, 518 F.3d 832, 859 (10th Cir.2008).

Example—Admissible. In deciding whether to admit summaries, "district courts are advised to carefully weigh the volume and complexity of the materials. These two factors have an inversely proportionate relationship: as either the volume or complexity increases, relatively less is required of the other factor." United States v. Appolon, 695 F.3d 44, 62 (1st Cir.2012).

(7) Types of summaries. The "summary" permitted by the rule may be either a tangible exhibit or testimony. Nichols v. Upjohn Co., 610 F.2d 293, 293–94 (5th Cir.1980) (oral testimony of physician summarizing contents of 94,000 page F.D.A. new drug application). Abridged recordings, resulting from edited voluminous originals, have been received under this rule. United States v. Segines, 17 F.3d 847, 853–54 (6th Cir.1994) ("composite tape" of selected conversations taped during wiretap). See also United States v. Harms, 442 F.3d 367, 376 (5th Cir.2006) (admission of time-line and accompanying oral testimony).

Rule 1006 does not embrace a "summary," prepared by the lawyers trying the case, of the other evidence and exhibits; "such a summary is a written argument." United States v. Grajales-Montoya, 117

F.3d 356, 361 (8th Cir.1997). Accord, United States v. Buck, 324 F.3d 786 (5th Cir.2003) ("The diagram was plainly a pedagogical aid. It was not introduced, per the proper use of rule 1006, to summarize documents or other evidence too voluminous to present effectively and efficiently to the jury. Rather, the diagram summarized evidence that had already been presented. * * * It was proper for the diagram to be shown to the jury, to assist in its understanding of testimony and documents that had been produced, but the diagram should not have been admitted as an exhibit or taken to the jury room." [footnotes omitted]); United States v. Irvin, 656 F.3d, 1151, 1160 (10th Cir.2011) ("[T]he core prejudicial impact of this inadmissible exhibit" was "the compelling simplicity with which Exhibit 1–2 reduced weeks of complex testimony and inadmissible hearsay into an easily digested summary."). Rule 1006 does not contemplate nor authorize "summary witnesses"—witnesses who are presented primarily to summarize the testimony of other witnesses, and exhibits, in a complex case. United States v. Nguyen, 504 F.3d 561, 572 (5th Cir.2007) ("Although the district court may admit summary witness testimony in limited circumstances, this court has repeatedly warned of its dangers. We have stressed that the purpose of summary evidence 'is not simply to allow the Government to repeat its entire case-in-chief shortly before jury deliberations.' Summary witnesses may 'not be used as a substitute for, or a supplement to, closing argument.' ").

> **Example—Inadmissible.** "Because Exhibit 1000 summarizes both admissible voluminous records and witness testimony, it cannot be neatly classified as either a voluminous-records summary or a pedagogical device. The government contends that Rule 1006 alone allows for the full admission of Exhibit 1000. We reject this argument outright. * * * Witness testimony is not a record that falls within the purview of Rule 1006 * * *. * * * Although our precedent suggests that hybrid devices that summarize both witness testimony and voluminous records may be admissible in unusual cases involving highly 'complex testimony or transactions,' we hold that Exhibit 1000 was inadmissible for two distinct reasons. First, Exhibit 1000 on numerous occasions dramatically and provocatively reframes witness testimony in an argumentative manner, which alone probably renders the summary inadmissible * * *. Further, with respect to the recordings of Heurung's conference calls, which the parties agree constitute voluminous records, Exhibit 1000 regularly labels statements Heurung made during these calls as being 'false and misleading,' 'exaggerations,' or 'material misrepresentations and omissions * * *.' * * * [T]he government's argumentative recasting of Heurung's statements certainly would have rendered the government's summaries of his conference calls inadmissible under this rule. The government cannot sidestep Rule 1006 merely by smuggling an argumentative summary of voluminous records into a hybrid exhibit and seeking admission of the exhibit * * *." United States v. Hawkins, 796 F.3d 843, 866 (8th Cir.2015) (citations omitted).

> **Example—Inadmissible.** "The district court allowed the government to present portions of Lucas's twelve to thirteen hours of civil deposition testimony by having Velasquez paraphrase some of its content. * * * This paraphrasing is effectively a summary of Lucas's deposition testimony, all of which was admitted into evidence by agreement and was available for the jury to review. It was error to permit Velasquez to paraphrase the deposition testimony, which was insufficiently complex. Our decisions finding adequate complexity include, for example, * * * 'seventeen days of technical testimony.' In contrast, the summary here was of portions of a long deposition rather than complex investigations. The government instead could have shown the relevant clips from the deposition; complexity did not bar it from doing so." United States v. Lucas, 849 F.3d 638, 644 (5th Cir.2017) (citations omitted).

(8) Limits on the role of summary witnesses. "[T]here are strict limits on the role of summary witnesses. The trial court must ensure that the witness does not 'usurp the jury's fact-finding function by summarizing or describing not only what is in evidence but also what inferences should be drawn from that evidence.' We have repeatedly warned that summary witnesses 'should not draw controversial inferences or pronounce[ ] judgment[.]' 'Another danger to be guarded against is that the jury will treat summary testimony "as additional evidence or as corroborative of the truth[,]" ' rather than just a compilation of existing evidence into a manageable format." United States v. Abou-Khatwa, 40 F.4th 666, 685 (D.C. Cir.2022) (citations omitted).

> **Example—Inadmissible.** "The first two charts have asterisks next to some of the subscribers' names. Hinson testified that these asterisks signified that Abou-Khatwa had used them as 'dummies'—that is, fake files. Previous testimony had explained that the term 'dummy' meant a

'fake,' and that a 'dummy' could be created for example by 'taking customers from [business] A and customers from B, and putting them in C.' * * * Hinson, though, went beyond summarizing records and instead claimed to be able to identify specific subscribers as dummies. * * * That testimony went too far. In claiming to identify certain individuals as dummies, Hinson was no longer summarizing the voluminous records reviewed but instead was adding her own inference regarding specific modifications of information by Abou-Khatwa as identifiers of the fake subscribers. In other words, she went beyond summarizing and started opining." United States v. Abou-Khatwa, supra, at 687.

(9)   Rule 1006 only governs summaries prepared for use at trial. Rule 1006, with its dual requirements of establishing admissibility of, and providing opponent with an opportunity for inspection of, underlying materials, only applies to a summary that is created for use at trial. A business record made and kept in the regular course of business, properly qualified according to the requirements of Rule 803(6), is not subject to these two Rule 1006 requirements, even though it may in fact be a "summary" of some underlying materials. United States v. Draiman, 784 F.2d 248, 256 n. 6 (7th Cir.1986).

CROSS-REFERENCES

Common Objections (Chapter 3)

91.   Summary not admissible

Checklists and Foundations (Chapter 4)

7.   Foundation for Summary of Voluminous Writings

Treatises

8 Graham, Handbook of Federal Evidence § 1006:1 (9th ed. 2020)

2 McCormick, Evidence § 233 (8th ed. 2020)

31 Wright & Gold, Federal Practice and Procedure §§ 8041–8045 (2000)

Rule 1007. Testimony or Statement of a Party to Prove Content

The proponent may prove the content of a writing, recording, or photograph by the testimony, deposition, or written statement of the party against whom the evidence is offered. The proponent need not account for the original.

AUTHORS' COMMENTS

(1)   Scope and purpose of Rule 1007. Rule 1007 allows proof of the contents of a writing by the opposing party's testimony or deposition or written admission, but not by an oral out-of-court admission. The common-law version of this doctrine allowed extrajudicial oral admissions.

(2)   Illustrations. In a case concerning a written contract, the terms of the contract may be shown by opposing party's deposition or trial testimony, or by a letter in which he describes the terms, but not by testimony of another witness to the party's oral statement describing the terms.

(3)   Oral admission permissible when nonproduction of original excused under Rule 1004. The exclusion of oral admissions ceases when nonproduction of the original has been excused under Rule 1004 and secondary evidence generally has become admissible. To return to the contract case example, after a showing that the original contract has been lost or destroyed (Rule 1004(a)), or that it is in the opposing party's possession and he had notice that its terms would be in issue (Rule 1004(c)), testimony of any witness to the party's oral description of the contract's terms would become admissible.

CROSS-REFERENCES

Treatises

8 Graham, Handbook of Federal Evidence § 1007:1 (9th ed. 2020)

2 McCormick, Evidence § 242 (8th ed. 2020)

31 Wright & Gold, Federal Practice and Procedure §§ 8051–8054 (2000)

Rule 1008. Functions of the Court and Jury

Ordinarily, the court determines whether the proponent has fulfilled the factual conditions for admitting other evidence of the content of a writing, recording, or photograph under Rule 1004 or 1005. But in a jury trial, the jury determines—in accordance with Rule 104(b)—any issue about whether:

(a) an asserted writing, recording, or photograph ever existed;

(b) another one produced at the trial or hearing is the original; or

(c) other evidence of content accurately reflects the content.

AUTHORS' COMMENTS

(1) Scope and purpose of Rule 1008. Rule 1008 governs the allocation, between the judge and the jury, of authority to make fact determinations concerning Article X issues. Its effect is consistent with that of the more general provision on judge-jury allocation in applying the rules of evidence, Rule 104. The purpose of Rule 1008, like Rule 104, is to leave to the jury all "ultimate" or "central" fact issues on which evidence creating a jury issue has been presented, while requiring the judge, as usual, to make preliminary fact determinations that the technical rules of evidence require.

The great majority of fact issues arising in connection with the best evidence doctrines are for the trial judge to resolve. It is only where a fact issue is among the few specified in the second sentence of Rule 1008 that it is for the jury. Even in those instances, the judge is required to exercise the usual control over the submission of jury issues. That is, the judge must determine whether evidence has been presented sufficient to support a finding of the matter.

(2) Issues for jury. Under the second sentence of Rule 1008, three issues are made jury questions because they "go beyond the mere administration of the rule preferring the original and into the merits of the controversy." Advisory Committee's Note to Federal Rule 1008.

> **Illustration—Issue (a).** "For example, plaintiff offers secondary evidence of the contents of an alleged contract, after first introducing evidence of loss of the original, and defendant counters with evidence that no such contract was ever executed." The dispute goes to the jury, because "[i]f the judge decides that the contract was never executed and excludes the secondary evidence, the case is at an end without ever going to the jury on a central issue." Advisory Committee's Note to Federal Rule 1008.

> **Illustration—Issue (b).** Two documents are produced, the plaintiff claiming one to be the original and the defendant the other. The dispute must go to the jury.

> **Illustration—Issue (c).** Plaintiff, having established that a written contract is lost, testifies to its terms ("other evidence of content," i.e., evidence other than the original). Defendant objects that plaintiff's testimony is inaccurate, and offers his own "correct" version. The issue is for the jury, not the judge.

(3) Issues for judge. The more normal case, covered by the first sentence of the rule, in which a preliminary fact issue is for the judge, is illustrated by the federal Advisory Committee as follows: "Thus, the question whether the loss of the originals has been established, or of the fulfillment of other conditions specified in Rule 1004, supra, is for the judge." Many other examples may be given. The following issues of fact must be decided by the judge, not the jury, under the allocation made in Rule 1008: (1) whether an item that is the object of proof is a "writing," "recording," or "photograph," within the definitions in Rule 1001; (2) whether a proffered item is an "original" as defined in Rule 1001(d) (unless one of the circumstances described in Rule 1008(a) or (b) is presented); (3) whether a proffered item is a "duplicate" as defined in Rule 1001(e); (4) whether, when a duplicate is offered, one of the two conditions specified in Rule 1003 ("a genuine question is raised about the original's authenticity or the circumstances make it unfair to admit the duplicate") is present, so that the duplicate must be excluded; (5) whether all originals have been lost or destroyed (Rule 1004(a)); (6) whether originals were lost or destroyed by the proponent in bad faith (Rule 1004(a)), Seiler v. Lucasfilm, Ltd., 808 F.2d 1316, 1320–21 (9th Cir.1986); (7) whether no original is obtainable (Rule 1004(b)); (8) whether an original is under the control of the party against whom other evidence of contents is offered, and whether he was put on notice that the content would be a subject of proof (Rule 1004(c)); (9) whether an item is "not closely related to a controlling issue" (Rule 1004(d)); (10) whether a document is either an official record, or a document that was recorded or filed and authorized to be recorded or filed (Rule 1005); (11) whether a copy offered to prove the terms of a public record is properly certified (Rule 1005); (12) whether no certified or compared copy can be obtained by reasonable diligence (Rule 1005); (13) whether an item is so voluminous as to justify summary presentation under Rule 1006; (14) whether the originals of which a summary is offered were reasonably made available to other parties (Rule 1006).

CROSS-REFERENCES

Treatises

8 Graham, Handbook of Federal Evidence § 1008:1 (9th ed. 2020)

2 McCormick, Evidence § 53 (8th ed. 2020)

31 Wright & Gold, Federal Practice and Procedure §§ 8061–8064 (2000)

ARTICLE XI

MISCELLANEOUS RULES

Rule 1101. Applicability of the Rules

(a) **To Courts and Judges.** These rules apply to proceedings before:

- United States district courts;

- United States bankruptcy and magistrate judges;

- United States courts of appeals;

- the United States Court of Federal Claims; and

- the district courts of Guam, the Virgin Islands, and the Northern Mariana Islands.

(b) **To Cases and Proceedings.** These rules apply in:

- civil cases and proceedings, including bankruptcy, admiralty, and maritime cases;

- criminal cases and proceedings; and

- contempt proceedings, except those in which the court may act summarily.

(c) **Rules on Privilege.** The rules on privilege apply to all stages of a case or proceeding.

(d) **Exceptions.** These rules—except for those on privilege—do not apply to the following:

(1) the court's determination, under Rule 104(a), on a preliminary question of fact governing admissibility;

(2) grand-jury proceedings; and

(3) miscellaneous proceedings such as:

- extradition or rendition;

- issuing an arrest warrant, criminal summons, or search warrant;

- a preliminary examination in a criminal case;

- sentencing;

- granting or revoking probation or supervised release; and

- considering whether to release on bail or otherwise.

(e) Other Statutes and Rules. A federal statute or a rule prescribed by the Supreme Court may provide for admitting or excluding evidence independently from these rules.

AUTHORS' COMMENTS

(1) Scope and purpose of Rule 1101. Rule 1101 prescribes the courts, proceedings, and issues to which the rules of evidence apply. The rules apply in most federal court proceedings, including proceedings before bankruptcy judges and magistrates.

(2) Privileges. Privilege rules apply at all stages of all proceedings. It has been held that the work product doctrine is a privilege for this purpose. In re Grand Jury Investigation, 412 F.Supp. 943, 946–47 (E.D.Pa.1976).

(3) Rules inapplicable or applicable only in part. Paragraph (d) lists situations in which the rules, other than privileges, do not apply. Paragraph (e) recognizes that there are proceedings in which the rules apply only in part, in accordance with other particular statutes and court rules.

CROSS-REFERENCES

Treatises

8 Graham, Handbook of Federal Evidence § 1101:1 (9th ed. 2020)

31 Wright & Gold, Federal Practice and Procedure §§ 8071–8079 (2000)

Rule 1102. Amendments

These rules may be amended as provided in 28 U.S.C. § 2072.

Rule 1103. Title

These rules may be cited as the Federal Rules of Evidence.

CHAPTER 3

COMMON OBJECTIONS AND RESPONSES

Table of Objections and Responses

Objections to Form of Question:

1. Ambiguous Question (Rule 611(a))
2. Argumentative Question (Rule 611(a))
3. Asked and Answered (Rule 611(a))
4. Assumes Facts Not in Evidence (Rule 611(a))
5. Compound Question (Rule 611(a))
6. Confusing (Rule 611(a))
7. Harassing the Witness (Rule 611(a))
8. Leading Question (Direct Examination) (Rule 611(c))
9. Leading Question (Cross-Examination) (Rule 611(c))
10. Narrative Testimony, Calls for (Rule 611(a))
11. Repetitious Question (Rule 611(a))
12. Unintelligible Question (Rule 611(a))

Objections to Admissibility:

13. Authentication Insufficient (Rules 901 and 902)
14. Best Evidence Not Being Offered (Rules 1001 and 1002)
15. Bolstering (Rules 607, 608 and 801(d)(1)(B))
16. Chain of Custody Not Established (Real Evidence) (Rule 901)
17. Character Evidence in Form of Opinion Testimony (Rule 405)
18. Character Evidence Inadmissible (Rule 404(a))
19. Character Evidence, Specific Acts Inadmissible (Rule 405)
20. Character Witness, Improper Cross-Examination as to Specific Acts (Rule 405)
21. Character Witness Not Qualified to Testify in the Form of Reputation or Opinion (Rule 405)
22. Compromise of or Offer to Compromise a Civil Claim (Rule 408)
23. Conclusion of Law, Expert Witness (Rules 702 and 704)
24. Conclusion of Law, Lay Witness (Rules 701 and 704)
25. Confrontation Clause: Face-to-Face Confrontation
26. Confrontation Clause: Hearsay
27. Confusion of the Issues (Rule 403)
28. Cross-Examination, Beyond Scope of Direct (Rule 611(b))
29. Cumulative (Rule 403)
30. Dead Man's Act Renders Witness Incompetent (Rule 601)
31. Exclusion of Witness, Violation of (Rule 615)
32. Expert Lacks Sufficient Basis for Opinion (Rule 702)
33. Expert May Not Relate Hearsay Basis for Opinion (Rule 703)
34. Expert Not Qualified (Rule 702)
35. Expert Opinion Based Solely on Hearsay Not Reasonably Relied Upon (Rule 703)
36. Expert Opinion Is Speculative, Conjectural (Rule 702)
37. Expert Opinion Not Helpful (Rule 702)
38. Habit Evidence Not Admissible (Rule 406)
39. Hearsay (Rules 801 and 802)
40. Hypothetical Question Includes Facts Not in Evidence (Rule 705)

OBJECTIONS TO FORM OF QUESTION

1. Ambiguous Question (Rule 611(a))

Your honor, I object. The question is ambiguous.

Authority:

> A question is ambiguous if it may be interpreted in different ways, or is so vague or unclear that it is likely to confuse either the jury or the witness. E.g., United States v. Clark, 613 F.2d 391, 406–07 (2d Cir.1979).

Response:

- Rephrase the question.

2. Argumentative Question (Rule 611(a))

Your honor, I object. The question is argumentative; counsel is trying to make an argument to the jury.

Authority:

> A question is argumentative if it is merely an effort by counsel to make a jury argument, to summarize, draw inferences from, or comment on the evidence, or to ask the witness to testify as to his own credibility. E.g., Smith v. Estelle, 602 F.2d 694, 700 n. 7 (5th Cir.1979) ("Dr. Grigson, you're kind of the hatchet man down here for the District Attorney's Office, aren't you?"), aff'd, 451 U.S. 454, 101 S.Ct. 1866 (1981).

Response:

- Rephrase the question.

3. Asked and Answered (Rule 611(a))

Your honor, I object. The witness has already answered the question.

Authority:

> A question that has already been asked and answered is not likely to elicit additional evidence of probative value and tends to waste time. E.g., United States v. Collins, 996 F.2d 950, 952 (8th Cir.1993).

Responses (as applicable):

- The witness has not yet answered this question.
- Opposing counsel asked this question. I have not.

4. Assumes Facts Not in Evidence (Rule 611(a))

Your honor, I object. The question assumes facts not in evidence.

Authority:

Questions that assume facts not in evidence are generally impermissible. E.g., United States v. Medel, 592 F.2d 1305, 1314 (5th Cir.1979). The proper way to offer evidence is through witnesses and real evidence; counsel is not permitted to testify.

Responses (as applicable):

- Although the particular fact has not been directly proved, its existence may reasonably be inferred from _____, which has been proved.
- The fact will be proved during the testimony of _____.

5. Compound Question (Rule 611(a))

Your honor, I object. Counsel is asking a compound question.

Authority:

A question that combines two or more distinct inquiries is likely to be confusing to the witness and misleading to the jury. E.g., United States v. Smith, 354 F.3d 390, 396 (5th Cir.2003).

Response:

- Rephrase the question.

6. Confusing (Rule 611(a))

Your honor, I object. The question is confusing.

Authority:

Rule 611(a) directs the court to "exercise reasonable control over the mode * * * of examining witnesses * * * and presenting evidence so as to (1) make those procedures effective for determining the truth."

Response:

- Rephrase the question.

7. Harassing the Witness (Rule 611(a))

Your honor, I object. Counsel is trying to harass [embarrass] the witness.

Authority:

Rule 611(a) directs the court to "exercise reasonable control over the mode * * * of examining witnesses * * * and presenting evidence so as to * * * protect witnesses from harassment or undue embarrassment." E.g., United States v. Singh, 628 F.2d 758, 763–64 (2d Cir.1980) (unnecessarily delving into witnesses' personal lives).

Response:

- Rephrase the question.

8. Leading Question (Direct Examination) (Rule 611(c))

Your honor, I object. Counsel is leading the witness.

Authority:

"A leading question is one that suggests to the witness the answer desired by the examiner." McCormick, Evidence § 6 (5th ed. 1999).

Rule 611(c) provides that leading questions "should not" be allowed on direct examination. They are, however, permissible on direct examination where "necessary to develop" a witness's testimony.

Responses (as applicable):

- The question is not leading. The fact that a question calls for a simple yes or no answer does not necessarily make it an impermissibly leading question.

- Leading questions are permitted concerning preliminary or other undisputed matters. United States v. Londondio, 420 F.3d 777, 789 (8th Cir.2005).

- Leading questions are permitted when a witness, because of age, infirmity, language barriers, or memory loss, is unable to convey information meaningfully in response to non-leading questions. E.g., United States v. Torres, 894 F.3d 305, 316–18 (D.C. Cir.2018) (reluctant minor); United States v. Johnson, 519 F.3d 816, 822 (8th Cir.2008) (child); United States v. Ajmal, 67 F.3d 12, 16 (2d Cir.1995) (language); United States v. Callahan, 801 F.3d 606, 623 (6th Cir.2015) (cognitive impairment); Litherland v. Petrolane Offshore Construction Serv., 546 F.2d 129, 134 (5th Cir.1977) (mental deficiency); United States v. Templeman, 965 F.2d 617, 619 (8th Cir.1992) (memory); United States v. Grassrope, 342 F.3d 866, 867–69 (8th Cir.2003) (sexual assault victim); United States v. Greaux-Gomez, 52 F.4th 426, 437–38 (1st Cir.2022) (teen-aged sexual assault victim "shaking uncontrollably and extremely nervous").

- The witness is an adverse party. Rule 611(c).

- The witness is identified with an adverse party. Rule 611(c); e.g., Rosa-Rivera v. Dorado Health, Inc., 787 F.3d 614, 616–17 (1st Cir.2015) (nurse who assisted physician in alleged medical malpractice); Chonich v. Wayne County Community College, 874 F.2d 359, 368 (6th Cir.1989) (employee of party).

- The witness is hostile. Rule 611(c); e.g., National Railroad Pass. Corp. v. Certain Temporary Easements Above R.R. Right of Way, 357 F.3d 36, 42 (1st Cir.2004).

- Rephrase the question.

9. Leading Question (Cross-Examination) (Rule 611(c))

Your honor, I object. Counsel is leading the witness.

Authority:

"A leading question is one that suggests to the witness the answer desired by the examiner." McCormick, Evidence § 6 (5th ed. 1999).

Although Rule 611(c) provides that leading questions "ordinarily" should be allowed on cross-examination, courts may limit the use of such questions when the cross-examiner is interrogating a friendly witness. E.g., Shultz v. Rice, 809 F.2d 643, 654 (10th Cir.1986) (cross-examination of client called by opponent as adverse witness).

Responses (as applicable):

- This is cross-examination. Leading questions are generally allowed and denial of the right to conduct thorough cross-examination is a violation of the constitution. Davis v. Alaska, 415 U.S. 308, 94 S.Ct. 1105 (1974).

- The question is not leading. The fact that a question calls for a simple yes or no answer does not necessarily make it an impermissibly leading question.

- The witness is not friendly.

- Rephrase the question.

10. Narrative Testimony, Calls for (Rule 611(a))

Your honor, I object. Counsel is asking a question that calls for narrative testimony.

Authority:

Rule 611(a) directs the court to "exercise reasonable control over the mode * * * of examining witnesses * * * and presenting evidence so as to (1) make those procedures effective for determining the truth."

Although narrative testimony is not per se objectionable, the court should require counsel to employ more pointed questions when a narrative question is likely to provoke a response containing hearsay or other inadmissible evidence. See United States v. Pless, 982 F.2d 1118, 1123 (7th Cir.1992).

Response:

- Rephrase the question.

11. Repetitious Question (Rule 611(a))

Your honor, I object. The question is unduly repetitious.

Authority:

Unduly repetitious questions are not likely to elicit additional evidence of probative value and tend to waste time. E.g., United States v. Dowdy, 960 F.2d 78, 80 (8th Cir.1992).

Responses (as applicable):

- The witness has not yet answered this question.

- Opposing counsel asked this question. I have not.

12. Unintelligible Question (Rule 611(a))

Your honor, I object. The question is unintelligible.

Authority:

Rule 611(a) directs the court to "exercise reasonable control over the mode * * * of examining witnesses * * * and presenting evidence so as to (1) make those procedures effective for determining the truth."

Response:

- Rephrase the question.

OBJECTIONS TO ADMISSIBILITY

13. Authentication Insufficient (Rules 901 and 902)

Your honor, I object. The evidence has not been properly authenticated.

Authority:

Rule 901 states, "To satisfy the requirement of authenticating or identifying an item of evidence, the proponent must produce evidence sufficient to support a finding that the item is what the proponent claims it is."

Responses (as applicable):

- The evidence is sufficient to support a finding (prima facie case) that the item is genuine—all that is required by Rule 901(a). The issue of actual genuineness is for the jury. United States v. Lanzon, 639 F.3d 1293, 1301 (11th Cir.2011); Ricketts v. City of Hartford, 74 F.3d 1397, 1409–11 (2d Cir.1996); United States v. McGlory, 968 F.2d 309, 328–29 (3d Cir.1992); United States v. Johnson, 637 F.2d 1224, 1247 (9th Cir.1980).

- The item is sufficiently authenticated by a method listed in Rule 901(b), such as:

  - Testimony of witness with knowledge, Rule 901(b)(1); United States v. Curbelo, 726 F.3d 1260, 1271 (11th Cir.2013);

  - Chain of custody, Rule 901(b)(1); United States v. Collins, 715 F.3d 1032, 1035–36 (7th Cir.2013); United States v. Olson, 846 F.2d 1103, 1116 (7th Cir.1988); United States v. Zink, 612 F.2d 511, 514 (10th Cir.1980); a defect in the chain of custody normally goes to the weight, not the admissibility, of the evidence; United States v. Summers, 666 F.2d 192, 201 (4th Cir.2011); United States v. Matta-Ballesteros, 71 F.3d 754, 768–69 (9th Cir.1995);

  - Lay opinion on handwriting, Rule 901(b)(2); United States v. Binzel, 907 F.2d 746, 749 (7th Cir.1990);

  - Comparison with exemplar, Rule 901(b)(3); United States v. Wylie, 919 F.2d 969, 978 (5th Cir.1990); United States v. Mangan, 575 F.2d 32, 42 (2d Cir.1978);

  - Circumstances and contents, Rule 901(b)(4); United States v. Turner, 718 F.3d 226, 232–33 (3d Cir.2013); United States v. Siddiqui, 235 F.3d 1318, 1322–23 (11th Cir.2000); United States v. Harvey, 117 F.3d 1044, 1049 (7th Cir.1997); United States v. Carpenter, 70 F.3d 520, 521 (8th Cir.1995); Denison v. Swaco Geolograph Co., 941 F.2d 1416, 1423 (10th Cir.1991);

  - Voice identification, Rule 901(b)(5); United States v. Jones, 600 F.3d 847, 858 (7th Cir.2010); United States v. Puentes, 50 F.3d 1567, 1577 (11th Cir.1995);

  - Telephone conversation, Rule 901(b)(6); United States v. De Simone, 699 F.3d 113, 126–27 (1st Cir.2012); United States v. Hines, 717 F.2d 1481, 1491 (4th Cir.1983); United States v. Portsmouth Paving Corp., 694 F.2d 312, 321–22 (4th Cir.1982);

  - Public record or report, Rule 901(b)(7); United States v. Wilson, 535 F.2d 521, 523 (9th Cir.1976);

  - Ancient document, Rule 901(b)(8); Threadgill v. Armstrong World Indus., Inc., 928 F.2d 1366, 1375–76 (3d Cir.1991);

- Process or system, Rule 901(b)(9); United States v. Taylor, 530 F.2d 639, 641–42 (5th Cir.1976).

- The item is sufficiently authenticated by appearance and circumstances; the methods listed in Rule 901(b) are not exclusive. United States v. Simpson, 152 F.3d 1241, 1249–50 (10th Cir.1998); United States v. Jimenez Lopez, 873 F.2d 769, 772 (5th Cir.1989).

- The item is self-authenticating under Rule 902, such as:

  - Public document under seal, Rule 902(1), (2), or (3); United States v. Beason, 690 F.2d 439, 444–45 (5th Cir.1982);

  - Certified copy of public record, Rule 902(4); United States v. Watson, 650 F.3d 1084, 1090 (8th Cir.2011); Moore v. City of Desloge, Mo., 647 F.3d 841, 848 (8th Cir.2011); United States v. Bisbee, 245 F.3d 1001, 1006–07 (8th Cir.2001), on remand, 2001 WL 1136811 (S.D.Iowa 2001); United States v. Huffhines, 967 F.2d 314, 320 (9th Cir.1992);

  - Acknowledged (notarized) document, Rule 902(8); United States v. M'Biye, 655 F.2d 1240, 1243 (D.C.Cir.1981);

  - Certified record of regularly conducted activity, Rule 902(11) or (12).

14. Best Evidence Not Being Offered (Rules 1001 and 1002)

Your honor, I object. The evidence is not the best evidence, as required by Rule 1002.

Authority:

Rule 1002 states, "An original writing, recording, or photograph is required in order to prove its content unless these rules or a federal statute provides otherwise."

Responses (as applicable):

- The evidence qualifies as an "original" as defined in Rule 1001(d).

- The evidence qualifies as a "duplicate" as defined in Rule 1001(e), which is admissible under Rule 1003.

- The best evidence rule is inapplicable because the proponent is not seeking "to prove [the] content" of a writing, recording, or photograph, but rather is seeking to prove a non-writing event that happens to be recorded in a writing. Rule 1002. E.g., a person who heard an oral conversation may testify to the content of the conversation even if a tape recording of the conversation exists. United States v. Branham, 97 F.3d 835, 853 (6th Cir.1996); United States v. Fagan, 821 F.2d 1002, 1008–09 n. 1 (5th Cir.1987); United States v. Gonzales-Benitez, 537 F.2d 1051, 1053–54 (9th Cir.1976). Witness who testified that she had opened a California bank account, acquired a California driver's license, and taken California community college courses was not required to produce documentation of her bank account, license, or college transcripts. Rodriguez v. Señor Frog's de la Isla, Inc., 642 F.3d 28, 34 (1st Cir.2011).

- Secondary evidence is admissible under Rule 1004 because the original is lost, destroyed, not obtainable, or in possession of the opponent, or the writing is collateral.

15. Bolstering (Rules 607, 608 and 801(d)(1)(B))

Your honor, I object. Counsel is bolstering the witness by offering evidence of the witness's [character for truthfulness] [prior consistent statement].

Authority:

It is often said that it is improper to "bolster" a witness's credibility before it has been attacked. United States v. Rosario-Diaz, 202 F.3d 54, 65 (1st Cir.2000); United States v. LeFevour, 798 F.2d 977, 983 (7th Cir.1986). Rules 608(a) and 801(d)(1)(B) are particular applications of this rule. Rule 608(a)(2) excludes evidence of a witness's trustworthy character until an attack is made on the witness's veracity. Rule 801(d)(1)(B) defines as non-hearsay only those prior consistent statements that are offered "to rebut an express or implied charge that the declarant recently fabricated" his testimony or "acted from a recent improper influence or motive in so testifying."

But the rules contain no other provision about "bolstering." Thus, the admissibility of other types of evidence offered solely to enhance the credibility of a witness who has not been impeached must be measured against the standards of Rules 401–403.

Responses (as applicable):

- The witness's credibility has been attacked and the evidence is admissible to rehabilitate.

- The prior consistent statement was made before any motive to fabricate arose and is admissible both as substantive evidence and for rehabilitative purposes. Rule 801(d)(1)(B); Tome v. United States, 513 U.S. 150, 115 S.Ct. 696 (1995).

- The prosecution may elicit details of a cooperation agreement entered into with a witness, especially details regarding the consequences of perjurious testimony by the witness. See United States v. Thornton, 197 F.3d 241, 252–53 (7th Cir.1999); United States v. Romer, 148 F.3d 359, 369 (4th Cir.1998); United States v. Spriggs, 996 F.2d 320, 323–24 (D.C.Cir.1993). But see United States v. Wallace, 848 F.2d 1464, 1474 (9th Cir.1988); United States v. Cruz, 805 F.2d 1464, 1479–80 (11th Cir.1986); United States v. Borello, 766 F.2d 46, 56–58 (2d Cir.1985) (inadmissible).

- [For evidence other than character or prior consistent statements.] The evidence is probative and its probative value is not substantially outweighed by the danger of unfair prejudice or the other factors listed in Rule 403. United States v. Scott, 267 F.3d 729, 735 (7th Cir.2001).

16. Chain of Custody Not Established (Real Evidence) (Rule 901)

Your honor, I object. Counsel has not proven a proper chain of custody.

Authority:

Where an object is not distinctive or unique in appearance, or where the object is of a nature that admits a risk of material but impalpable change—such as a chemical or bodily fluid specimen—then the object's identity and continuity of condition must be established by a chain of custody. A chain of custody consists of testimony of each person who had custody of the item, from the time of its discovery or initial connection with the case to the time of its presentation at trial. United States v. Zink, 612 F.2d 511, 514 (10th Cir.1980).

Responses (as applicable):

- The object has unique or distinctive characteristics and any material change in condition would be palpable, so testimony of single witness identifying the object and stating that it is in unchanged condition suffices; a chain of custody is unnecessary. Rule 901(b)(1); Reyes v. United States, 383 F.2d 734 (9th Cir.1967); Hammett v. State, 578 S.W.2d 699, 708 (Tex.Crim.App.1979).

- It is not required that all possibility of tampering or adulteration be eliminated; minor gaps in the chain go to weight, not admissibility. United States v. Collins, 715 F.3d 1032, 1035–36 (7th Cir.2013); United States v. Summers, 666 F.3d 192, 201 (4th Cir.2011); United States v. Matta-Ballesteros, 71 F.3d 754, 768–69 (9th Cir.1995); United States v. Olson, 846 F.2d 1103, 1116 (7th Cir.1988); Ballou v. Henri Studios, Inc., 656 F.2d 1147, 1154–55 (5th Cir.1981).

17. Character Evidence in Form of Opinion Testimony (Rule 405)

Your honor, I object. Character evidence, where admissible, must be shown by reputation, not opinion, testimony.

Authority:

This is no longer a valid objection. At common law, reputation testimony was normally the only permissible method of proof of character. But Rule 405(a) now authorizes the use of opinion testimony as well.

Response:

- Rule 405(a) authorizes the use of opinion testimony.

18. Character Evidence Inadmissible (Rule 404(a))

Your honor, I object. The question calls for evidence of character, which is inadmissible under Rule 404.

Authority:

Rule 404(a) bars the admission of evidence of a person's character or character trait if it is offered to show that the person acted in accordance with that character or character trait on a particular occasion.

Responses (as applicable):

- Character evidence is admissible when a person's character or character trait is in issue; i.e., when it is an essential element of a claim, charge, or defense. United States v. Franco, 484 F.3d 347, 352 (6th Cir.2007) (entrapment—bad character); United States v. Thomas, 134 F.3d 975 (9th Cir.1998) (entrapment—good character); Parrish v. Luckie, 963 F.2d 201, 205 (8th Cir.1992) (civil rights action against a police officer and his police chief; previous acts of violence by defendant police officer admissible to prove the police chief's knowledge of the officer's violent tendencies); Schafer v. Time, Inc., 142 F.3d 1361, 1370–73 (11th Cir.1998) (plaintiff's character in defamation action).

- A criminal defendant may offer evidence of his good character, and the prosecution may rebut. Rule 404(a)(2)(A); United States v. Diaz, 961 F.2d 1417, 1419–20 (9th Cir.1992).

- Evidence of the victim's character is admissible to prove the victim was the initial aggressor. Rule 404(a)(2)(B); United States v. Smith, 230 F.3d 300, 307–08 (7th Cir.2000) (allowing reputation testimony, but excluding specific act evidence); United States v. Yazzie, 188 F.3d 1178, 1189–90 (10th Cir.1999).

- To rebut evidence presented by the defendant of the victim's violent character, the prosecution may offer evidence of the defendant's violent character, Rule 404(a)(2)(B)(ii), as well as the victim's peaceable character. Rule 404(a)(2)(B)(i). In a homicide case, the prosecution may offer evidence of the victim's peaceable character in response to any kind of evidence that the victim was the aggressor. Rule 404(a)(2)(C).

- Evidence of specific acts of sexual assault or child molestation are admissible under Rules 413 (sexual assault), 414 (child molestation) and 415 (either, in civil cases).

- The evidence of the victim's character, acts, or threats, known to the defendant prior to the events in issue, is not being offered as circumstantial evidence to prove the victim's behavior on the occasion in question. It is being offered to support the claimed reasonableness of the defendant's belief as to the immediate necessity to use force in self-defense. United States v. Saenz, 179 F.3d 686, 688–89 (9th Cir.1999); Senra v. Cunningham, 9 F.3d 168, 171–72 (1st Cir.1993).

- The evidence goes to the character of a witness for purposes of impeachment or rehabilitation under Rules 607, 608, and 609. Rule 404(a)(3).

19. Character Evidence, Specific Acts Inadmissible (Rule 405)

Your honor, I object. Evidence of specific acts is inadmissible to prove a person's character.

Authority:

Character normally may be proved only by reputation and/or opinion testimony, not by specific acts. Rule 405(a); United States v. Bautista, 145 F.3d 1140, 1152 (10th Cir.1998).

Rule 405(b) authorizes evidence of specific instances of conduct to prove character only where a trait of a person's character is an ultimate issue in the case under the governing substantive law ("an essential element of a charge, claim, or defense"), a rare situation.

Rule 405(a) permits inquiry as to particular instances of conduct on cross-examination of a character (opinion or reputation) witness, but if the witness answers in the negative, neither the act nor the witness's knowledge of it may be shown by extrinsic evidence; the cross-examiner must abide the witness's answer. United States v. Ling, 581 F.2d 1118, 1121 (4th Cir.1978); United States v. Benedetto, 571 F.2d 1246, 1250 (2d Cir.1978).

Responses (as applicable):

- A trait of the person's character is "in issue" in this case—it is an essential element of a charge, claim, or defense. For example, where the plaintiff contends that the defendant was negligent in entrusting a dangerous instrumentality to a particular servant, the trait of incompetence of the servant to handle the instrumentality safely is an element of the claim. In re Aircrash in Bali, Indonesia, 684 F.2d 1301, 1314–15 (9th Cir.1982); Crawford v. Yellow Cab Co., 572 F.Supp. 1205, 1210 (N.D.Ill.1983).

- The specific act is being offered to prove something other than the person's character; for example, to prove motive, intent, knowledge, or absence of mistake or accident. Rule 404(b).

- Inquiry into relevant specific instances of conduct is permitted on cross-examination of a character or reputation witness. Rule 405(a).

- Evidence of specific acts of sexual assault or child molestation are admissible under Rules 413 (sexual assault), 414 (child molestation) and 415 (either, in civil cases).

20. Character Witness, Improper Cross-Examination as to Specific Acts (Rule 405)

Your honor, I object. Cross-examination of the witness concerning this alleged act is improper because [counsel has not demonstrated a good-faith factual basis] [the alleged

act is not relevant to the character trait to which the witness testified] [it assumes guilt of the crime for which the defendant is now on trial].

Authority:

Rule 405(a) permits inquiry on cross-examination of a character opinion or reputation witness as to relevant particular instances of conduct. However, there are "two important limitations upon judicial discretion in admitting inquiries concerning such prior misconduct: first, a requirement that the prosecution have some good-faith factual basis for the incidents inquired about, and second, a requirement that the incidents inquired about are relevant to the character traits involved at trial." United States v. Wells, 525 F.2d 974, 976 (5th Cir.1976). It is not sufficient as to the first requirement that the prosecutor have a good faith belief that the incidents occurred; there must also be a good faith belief that the events are of a type that are likely to become a matter of general knowledge or reputation in the community. United States v. Monteleone, 77 F.3d 1086, 1090 (8th Cir.1996).

Moreover, it is improper to ask the character witness if his or her opinion would change if the witness assumed the act or acts for which the accused is on trial. United States v. Mason, 993 F.2d 406, 409 (4th Cir.1993) (citing many other cases).

Responses (as applicable):

- Counsel has a good-faith factual basis for the alleged act. United States v. Alvarez, 860 F.2d 801, 828 (7th Cir.1988) (affidavit from F.B.I. agent that defendant told agent she committed act was adequate basis for questions); United States v. Bright, 588 F.2d 504, 512 (5th Cir.1979) (prosecution made required showing of good faith by offer of letter of reprimand).

- The alleged act is relevant to the character traits to which the witness testified. United States v. West, 58 F.3d 133, 141 (5th Cir.1995) (in prosecution for conspiracy to evade federal gasoline taxes, witnesses who testified to defendant's good character for veracity and honesty could be asked whether they had heard about pending state court indictment of defendant for evasion of state gasoline taxes); United States v. Grady, 665 F.2d 831, 834 n. 3 (8th Cir.1981) (witness who testified defendant had good reputation for truth and honesty was properly cross-examined concerning his prior convictions for filing false unemployment claim and making false statement to the police).

- The question does not hypothetically assume guilt of the crime for which the defendant is now on trial. "Asking a character witness whether he has heard of some of the defendant's alleged misbehavior is arguably appropriate, because if the witness has not heard of the behavior, then he may be perceived by the jury as not attuned to the community and the defendant's reputation, and his effectiveness as a character witness is undermined." United States v. Smith-Bowman, 76 F.3d 634, 636 (5th Cir.1996).

21. Character Witness Not Qualified to Testify in the Form of Reputation or Opinion (Rule 405)

Your honor, I object. The witness has not been shown to be qualified to testify to [the person's reputation] [an opinion as to the person's character].

Authority:

A reputation witness must be qualified by showing that the witness has a sufficient acquaintance with the person, the community in which he has lived or worked, and the circles in which he has moved to speak with authority of the terms in which he is generally regarded. United States v. Watson, 669 F.2d 1374, 1381 (11th Cir.1982). Similarly, a witness must have sufficient familiarity to be qualified to express an opinion as to a person's character. United States v. Koessel, 706 F.2d 271, 275 (8th Cir.1983) (witness who had met person only once not qualified).

Responses (as applicable):

- The witness is sufficiently familiar with the person's reputation in the workplace. United States v. Oliver, 492 F.2d 943, 946 (8th Cir.1974).

- Rule 405(a) embraces expert as well as lay opinion as to a person's traits. United States v. Roberts, 887 F.2d 534, 536 (5th Cir.1989); United States v. Hill, 655 F.2d 512, 516–17 (3d Cir.1981); United States v. Staggs, 553 F.2d 1073, 1075 (7th Cir.1977).

22. Compromise of or Offer to Compromise a Civil Claim (Rule 408)

Your honor, I object. Rule 408 excludes evidence of settlements and settlement negotiations.

Authority:

Rule 408 bars the admission of evidence that a party settled or offered to settle a civil claim, and of statements made in the course of settlement negotiations.

Responses (as applicable):

- Rule 408 protects only offers to compromise and compromises of disputed claims. An agreement that was made before a dispute arose is not covered by Rule 408. Cassino v. Reichhold Chem., Inc., 817 F.2d 1338 (9th Cir.1987).

- Rule 408 does not protect ordinary business negotiations. Deere & Co. v. International Harvester Co., 710 F.2d 1551, 1557 (Fed.Cir.1983).

- Statements are protected by Rule 408 only if they were made in an effort to compromise a claim. Lightfoot v. Union Carbide Corp., 110 F.3d 898, 909 (2d Cir.1997).

- In a criminal case, Rule 408(a)(2) authorizes the admission of conduct or a statement made during compromise negotiations that related to a claim by a public office in the exercise of its regulatory, investigative, or enforcement authority.

- Rule 408 excludes compromise evidence only when it is offered to prove the validity of the claim, the invalidity of the claim, or the amount of damages. The evidence here is being offered to prove something else:

  - The bias, prejudice or interest of a witness. Croskey v. BMW of North America, Inc., 532 F.3d 511, 519 (6th Cir.2008).

  - To explain or excuse undue delay. Freidus v. First Nat'l Bank, 928 F.2d 793, 795 (8th Cir.1991).

  - To prove the motive or intent of a party. Bankcard America, Inc. v. Universal Bancard Systems, Inc., 203 F.3d 477, 483–84 (7th Cir.2000); Johnson v. Hugo's Skateway, 949 F.2d 1338, 1345–46 (4th Cir.1991);

  - To enforce the terms of the settlement. Catullo v. Metzner, 834 F.2d 1075, 1079 (1st Cir.1987);

  - To prove knowledge. United States v. Austin, 54 F.3d 394, 399–400 (7th Cir.1995).

  - To prove an effort to obstruct justice. United States v. Technic Services, Inc., 314 F.3d 1031, 1045 (9th Cir.2002).

- Where the statement made in the settlement negotiation constitutes the wrongful conduct that is the basis of the claim. Starter Corp. v. Converse, Inc., 170 F.3d 286, 292–94 (2d Cir.1999); Uforma/Shelby Business Forms, Inc. v. N.L.R.B., 111 F.3d 1284, 1293–94 (6th Cir.1997).

23. Conclusion of Law, Expert Witness (Rules 702 and 704)

Your honor, I object. The witness is being asked to state a conclusion of law.

Authority:

Although Rule 704 does not bar most opinions that go to an ultimate issue or express a conclusion of law, an opinion must still be admissible under Rule 702. Therefore:

- The opinion must be within the scope of the witness's expertise. Cook v. American Steamship Co., 53 F.3d 733, 738–40 (6th Cir.1995).
- The expert must be knowledgeable about the relevant legal standard. Andrews v. Metro North Commuter R. Co., 882 F.2d 705, 708–09 (2d Cir.1989).
- The opinion must be on an appropriate subject for expert testimony. Nieves-Villanueva v. Soto-Rivera, 133 F.3d 92, 99–101 (1st Cir.1997); Askanase v. Fatjo, 130 F.3d 657, 672–73 (5th Cir.1997) (testimony about domestic law improper).
- The opinion must assist the factfinder. United States v. Lockett, 919 F.2d 585, 590 (9th Cir.1990) (opinions about guilt or innocence inadmissible).

Responses (as applicable):

- The above requirements are met.
- An expert may testify as to a conclusion of law if the expert is familiar with the appropriate legal standard. Fiataruolo v. United States, 8 F.3d 930, 941–42 (2d Cir.1993).
- An opinion may be given where the legal standard utilizes the plain meaning of commonly-used words. United States v. Hearst, 563 F.2d 1331 (9th Cir.1977).

24. Conclusion of Law, Lay Witness (Rules 701 and 704)

Your honor, I object. The witness is being asked to state a conclusion of law.

Authority:

Although Rule 704 does not bar a lay opinion that goes to an ultimate issue or expresses a conclusion of law, the opinion must still be admissible under Rule 701, which requires that a lay opinion must be (a) rationally based on the witness's perception and (b) helpful to the factfinder. Therefore:

- The witness must be basing his opinion on personal knowledge. United States v. Rivera, 22 F.3d 430, 434 (2d Cir.1994).
- The witness must be knowledgeable about the relevant legal standard. United States v. Richter, 796 F.3d 1173, 1194–96 (10th Cir.2015).
- The opinion must be one that does not require special expertise. See Randolph v. Collectramatic, Inc., 590 F.2d 844, 848 (10th Cir.1979).
- The opinion must assist the factfinder. Kostelecky v. NL Acme Tool/NL Industries, Inc., 837 F.2d 828, 830 (8th Cir.1988) ("evidence that merely tells the jury what result to reach is not sufficiently helpful to the trier of fact to be admissible").

Responses (as applicable):

- The above requirements are met: the witness is basing his opinion on personal knowledge, is familiar with the appropriate legal standard, the opinion does not require special expertise, and it will be helpful to the fact finder.

- An opinion may be given where the legal standard utilizes the plain meaning of commonly-used words. Torres v. County of Oakland, 758 F.2d 147, 151 (6th Cir.1985).

25. Confrontation Clause: Face-to-Face Confrontation

Your honor, I object. I have a right to confront the witness face-to-face in the courtroom. The witness should not be permitted to testify via [closed-circuit television] [a videotaped deposition].

Authority:

Maryland v. Craig, 497 U.S. 836, 110 S.Ct. 3157 (1990), held that the Confrontation Clause allows a child witness in a child abuse case to testify via closed-circuit television only when the prosecution makes an adequate showing of necessity. In *Craig*, the state successfully demonstrated that resort to closed-circuit television testimony was necessary to protect child witness from the trauma of having to testify in the presence of the defendant. 18 U.S.C.A. § 3509(b) now provides a statutory basis for the use of testimony via closed-circuit television or videotaped depositions in proceedings involving an alleged offense of physical abuse, sexual abuse, or exploitation against a child.

Response:

- The form of the testimony is authorized by 18 U.S.C.A. § 3509(b).

26. Confrontation Clause: Hearsay

Your honor, I object. The evidence is hearsay and violates the Confrontation Clause.

Authority:

In Crawford v. Washington, 541 U.S. 36, 124 S.Ct. 1354 (2004), the Supreme Court adopted a fundamentally new approach to the Confrontation Clause and hearsay. The new approach did not change the treatment of prior statements by witnesses and former testimony, but it substantially changed the treatment of hearsay statements by nontestifying declarants offered under hearsay exceptions, whether firmly rooted or not. Under *Crawford*, the first issue is whether the hearsay statement is "testimonial" in nature. If so, the constitutional right of confrontation and cross-examination is absolute, and no showing of reliability, whether based on a "firmly rooted" exception or particularized indicia, can substitute. On the other hand, if the hearsay is "nontestimonial" in nature, the Confrontation Clause does not apply. Michigan v. Bryant, 562 U.S. 344, 359 & n. 5, 131 S.Ct. 1143, 1155 (2011) (the admissibility of a nontestimonial statement "is the concern of state and federal rules of evidence, not the Confrontation Clause").

There is no single definition of "testimonial," but the concept includes "ex parte in-court testimony or its functional equivalent—that is, material such as affidavits, custodial examinations, prior testimony that the defendant was unable to cross-examine, or similar pretrial statements that declarants would reasonably expect to be used prosecutorially," and "statements that were made under circumstances which would lead an objective witness reasonably to believe that the statement would be available for use at a later trial." *Crawford*, 541 U.S. at 51–52, 124 S.Ct. at 1364.

In order for former testimony to be constitutionally admissible against an accused, the prosecution must establish that the witness is unavailable despite good faith efforts to produce the witness at trial. Ohio v. Roberts, 448 U.S. 56, 100 S.Ct. 2531 (1980).

Affidavits certifying laboratory results "were testimonial statements, and the analysts were 'witnesses' for purposes of the Sixth Amendment. Absent a showing that the analysts were unavailable to testify at trial and that petitioner had a prior opportunity to cross-examine them, petitioner was entitled to 'be confronted with' the analysts at trial." Melendez-Diaz v. Massachusetts, 557 U.S. 305, 311, 129 S.Ct. 2527, 2532 (2009).

Responses (as applicable):

- Substantive admission of a prior statement by a witness who testifies in the present proceeding under oath and subject to cross-examination concerning the prior statement does not offend the constitutional right of confrontation. California v. Green, 399 U.S. 149, 90 S.Ct. 1930 (1970).

- The statement is former testimony of a witness who is now unavailable and who was under oath and subject to cross-examination by the accused, who had a similar motive to develop the testimony when it was given.

- The statement is not "testimonial" in nature. E.g.:

    - An excited utterance, even if made to law enforcement (such as a 911 call), may be nontestimonial. A call for help, even if it recounts facts that incriminate another, is not testimonial. (But once "the dust has settled," the declarant is secure, and law enforcement or other investigative questioning has begun, the line to testimonial has been crossed, even though the declarant may still be under a state of excitement sufficient for Rule 803(2)). Davis v. Washington, 547 U.S. 813, 126 S.Ct. 2266 (2006).

    - The primary purpose of the interrogation was to enable police to meet an ongoing emergency. Michigan v. Bryant, 562 U.S. 344, 377–78 131 S.Ct. 1143, 1166 (2011).

    - Coconspirator statements are generally nontestimonial. United States v. Stewart, 433 F.3d 273, 291–93 (2d Cir.2006).

- Forfeiture by wrongdoing. A defendant does not forfeit by wrongdoing his Confrontation Clause rights solely on a showing that he procured the declarant's unavailability. Confrontation Clause forfeiture by wrongdoing requires that the defendant procure the declarant's unavailability with the intent of making him unavailable as a witness. Giles v. California, 554 U.S. 353, 128 S.Ct. 2678 (2008).

27. Confusion of the Issues (Rule 403)

Your honor, I object. The evidence will cause confusion of the issues.

Authority:

Rule 403 provides that relevant evidence may be excluded if its probative value is substantially outweighed by the danger of confusing the issues. BE & K Construction Co. v. United Brotherhood of Carpenters & Joiners, 90 F.3d 1318, 1331 (8th Cir.1996) ("The videotape improperly focused attention on what took place in International Falls on September 9, 1989 instead of what was actually said at the October 24, 1991 meeting in McGehee, Arkansas."); Grenada Steel Indus., Inc. v. Alabama Oxygen Co., 695 F.2d 883, 888 (5th Cir.1983) (evidence about subsequent design changes in product confused issue of safety of design at time of sale); United States v. Tidwell, 559 F.2d 262, 266 (5th Cir.1977) (evidence that bank recovered its investment confused issue of intent to defraud).

Response:

- The probative value of the evidence outweighs the danger of confusion. The rule 403 "balance should be struck in favor of admission." United States v. Dennis, 625 F.2d 782, 797 (8th Cir.1980). Rule 403 is "an extraordinary remedy to be used sparingly." United States v. Meester, 762 F.2d 867, 875 (11th Cir.1985).

28. Cross-Examination, Beyond Scope of Direct (Rule 611(b))

Your honor, I object. The question asked goes beyond the scope of the matters raised on direct exam.

Authority:

Rule 611(b) provides that cross-examination "should be" limited to subjects raised on direct examination and credibility issues.

Responses:

- The subject matter of direct examination includes all "inferences and implications" arising from the direct testimony. United States v. Moore, 917 F.2d 215, 222 (6th Cir.1990).

- Cross-examination "need only be reasonably related" to direct examination. United States v. Bozovich, 782 F.3d 814, 816 (7th Cir.2015) ("reasonably related" standard should be "liberally interpreted").

- Rule 611(b) authorizes the court to permit cross-examination on matters beyond the scope of direct examination, with the questioning proceeding "as if on direct examination." E.g., United States v. Carter, 910 F.2d 1524, 1530 (7th Cir.1990).

29. Cumulative (Rule 403)

Your honor, I object. The evidence is cumulative and inadmissible under Rule 403.

Authority:

Rule 403 provides that relevant evidence may be excluded if its probative value is substantially outweighed by considerations of "needlessly presenting cumulative evidence." International Minerals & Resources, S.A. v. Pappas, 96 F.3d 586, 596 (2d Cir.1996); United States v. Bejar-Matrecios, 618 F.2d 81, 84 (9th Cir.1980).

Responses:

- The concept of "cumulative" evidence should not be employed to interfere with a party's right to present a persuasive case. For example, evidence that is corroborative of a defendant's testimony should not be excluded as "cumulative." Towner v. State, 685 P.2d 45, 49–50 (Wyo.1984).

- The rule 403 "balance should be struck in favor of admission." United States v. Dennis, 625 F.2d 782, 797 (8th Cir.1980). Rule 403 is "an extraordinary remedy to be used sparingly." United States v. Meester, 762 F.2d 867, 875 (11th Cir.1985).

30. Dead Man's Act Renders Witness Incompetent (Rule 601)

Your honor, I object. The witness is not competent to testify to statements made by the deceased.

Authority:

In civil actions in which state law supplies the rule of decision with respect to an element of a claim or defense, a witness's competency must be determined in accordance with state law. Thus, in a diversity case, a state Dead Man's Act may be applicable. E.g., Lovejoy Electronics, Inc. v. O'Berto, 873 F.2d 1001, 1005 (7th Cir.1989).

Responses (as applicable):

- The witness's testimony goes to an issue as to which federal law governs.
- The requirements of the state's Dead Man's Act are not met.

31. Exclusion of Witness, Violation of (Rule 615)

Your honor, I object. The witness is testifying in violation of The Rule.

Authority:

Rule 615, often referred to as "The Rule," provides for the exclusion of witnesses from the courtroom so that they will be unable to hear the testimony of other witnesses.

Responses (as applicable):

- The witness is exempt from the operation of Rule 615 because he is:
    - A party, Rule 615(a);
    - One officer or employee who has been designated as the representative of a party that is not a natural person, Rule 615(b), United States v. Edwards, 34 F.4th 570, 585 (7th Cir.2022) (case agent).
    - A person whose presence is essential to the presentation of the party's cause, e.g., an expert, Rule 615(c); United States v. Seschillie, 310 F.3d 1208, 1214 (9th Cir.2002) But cf. United States v. Olofson, 563 F.3d 652, 660 (7th Cir.2009) (noting that "Rule 703 is not an automatic exemption for expert witnesses from Rule 615 sequestration").
- A person whose presence is authorized by statute, Rule 615(d); 18 U.S.C. §§ 3510, 3593, 3771.
- Even though the witness was not excluded from the courtroom, the court has the discretion to allow the witness to testify. United States v. Cropp, 127 F.3d 354, 363 (4th Cir.1997).

32. Expert Lacks Sufficient Basis for Opinion (Rule 702)

Your honor, I object. The witness lacks a sufficient basis for his opinion.

Authority:

An expert's opinion is not admissible unless the court finds that it is "based upon sufficient facts or data." Rule 702(1).

Responses (as applicable):

- The expert's opinion is based on the kind of facts or data that experts in her field reasonably rely up on in drawing such inferences. South Central Petroleum, Inc. v. Long Bros. Oil Co., 974 F.2d 1015, 1018–19 (8th Cir.1992).

- An expert is not required to hold an opinion to a "reasonable degree of certainty." Stutzman v. CRST, Inc., 997 F.2d 291, 294–95 (7th Cir.1993).

- Ordinarily, an expert may state an opinion without first disclosing the facts or data underlying the opinion. Rule 705.

33. Expert May Not Relate Hearsay Basis for Opinion (Rule 703)

Your Honor, I object. An expert may not disclose to the jury otherwise inadmissible hearsay even if she based her opinion upon it. Whatever probative value disclosure may have in helping the jury evaluate the expert's opinion does not substantially outweigh the danger that the jury will used the hearsay for its truth.

Authority:

It is true that Rule 703 permits an expert to base an opinion on otherwise inadmissible hearsay or other facts or data so long as the hearsay or the other facts or data are the type of information experts in the particular field reasonably rely on in forming such an opinion. But Rule 703 stipulates that the expert may disclose such facts or data only if the court determines that their probative value in assisting the jury to evaluate the expert's opinion substantially outweighs their prejudicial effect. Turner v. Burlington Northern Santa Fe R. Co., 338 F.3d 1058, 1062 (9th Cir.2003).

Responses (as applicable):

- The underlying facts or data fall within an exception to the hearsay rule and therefore are not "otherwise inadmissible."

- The jury cannot properly evaluate this expert's opinion unless it is permitted to hear what the expert based her opinion on. Brennan v. Reinhart Institutional Foods, 211 F.3d 449, 451 (8th Cir.2000).

34. Expert Not Qualified (Rule 702)

Your honor, I object. The witness is not qualified to testify as an expert. [The witness is not qualified to give an opinion on this particular topic.]

Authority:

A witness must be qualified as an expert before testifying to expert opinions. The burden of establishing a witness's qualifications lies with his proponent. See Pan American World Airways, Inc. v. Port Authority of N.Y. and N.J., 995 F.2d 5, 10 (2d Cir.1993).

Even if a witness is qualified as an expert, the expert testimony must be limited to the scope of his expertise. E.g., Lebron v. Secretary of Florida Dept. of Children and Families, 772 F.3d 1352, 1368 (11th Cir.2014).

Responses (as applicable):

- Rule 702 provides that the requisite expertise may be acquired through knowledge, skill, experience, training or education. Academic certification or licensure is not required to qualify a witness as an expert. Pagés-Ramírez v. Ramírez-González, 605 F.3d 109, 114 (1st Cir.2010).

- Work experience is sufficient to qualify a witness as an expert. F & H Coatings, LLC v. Acosta, 900 F.3d 1214, 1222–24 (10th Cir.2018).

35. Expert Opinion Based Solely on Hearsay Not Reasonably Relied Upon (Rule 703)

Your honor, I object. This expert's opinion is based solely on hearsay of a kind not reasonably relied upon by experts in the witness's field.

Authority:

Rule 703 allows an expert to base an opinion on inadmissible hearsay or other facts or data, but only if the hearsay or other facts or data are the kind of information experts in the particular field reasonably rely on in forming such an opinion.

Moreover, a witness must be truly testifying as an expert and not just as a conduit for hearsay. United States v. Garcia, 793 F.3d 1194, 1212–16 (10th Cir.2015).

Responses (as applicable):

- The witness (or another expert) has testified that the facts upon which he is basing his opinion are the kind of facts reasonably relied upon by experts in the field. Ward v. Dixie National Life Ins. Co., 595 F.3d 164, 182 (4th Cir.2010); Sphere Drake Insurance PLC v. Trisko, 226 F.3d 951, 955 (8th Cir.2000).

- The court may take judicial notice that the facts underlying the opinion are the kind reasonably relied upon by experts in the field. Ambrosini v. Labarraque, 966 F.2d 1464, 1467 (D.C.Cir.1992).

- Reasonable reliance has been demonstrated through learned treatises. United States v. Tranowski, 659 F.2d 750, 755 (7th Cir.1981).

36. Expert Opinion Is Speculative, Conjectural (Rule 702)

Your honor, I object. The witness's opinion is speculative [conjectural] [lacks a reasonable degree of certainty].

Authority:

An expert's opinion is not admissible unless the court finds that it is "based on sufficient facts or data." Rule 702(1).

Responses (as applicable):

- The expert is basing her opinion on the kind of facts or data that experts in her field reasonably rely upon in drawing such inferences. Advent Systems Ltd. v. Unisys Corp., 925 F.2d 670, 682 (3d Cir.1991).

- An expert is not required to hold an opinion to a "reasonable degree of certainty." Stutzman v. CRST, Inc., 997 F.2d 291, 294–95 (7th Cir.1993).

37. Expert Opinion Not Helpful (Rule 702)

Your honor, I object. This expert's opinion will not assist the fact finder either in understanding the evidence or determining a fact in issue because [insert appropriate reason listed below].

Authority:

Rule 702 provides that expert testimony is admissible only when it "will help the trier of fact to understand the evidence or to determine a fact in issue."

The following are among the reasons for concluding that expert testimony will not be helpful.

- It is not relevant to an issue in the case. E.g., Superior Production Partnership v. Gordon Auto Body Parts Co., 784 F.3d 311, 324–35 (6th Cir.2015).

- The witness is no more capable than the jury of drawing conclusions from the facts. Persinger v. Norfolk & Western Ry. Co., 920 F.2d 1185, 1188 (4th Cir.1990).

- The testimony would intrude upon the judge's role. United States v. Fallon, 50 F.4th 336, 351 (3d Cir.2022); Jimenez v. City of Chicago, 732 F.3d 710, 721 (7th Cir.2013); Burkhart v. Washington Metro. Area Transit Auth., 112 F.3d 1207, 1213 (D.C.Cir.1997) (domestic law).

- It is based on speculation or incomplete data. Amorgianos v. National R.R. Passenger Corp., 303 F.3d 256, 268 (2d Cir.2002).

- It is based on questionable theories. Mercado v. Ahmed, 974 F.2d 863, 869–70 (7th Cir.1992).

- There is simply too great an analytical gap between the data and the opinion proffered. General Electric Co. v. Joiner, 522 U.S. 136, 118 S.Ct. 512, 519 (1997).

- The expert lacks sufficient certainty about the opinion. Pinkham v. Burgess, 933 F.2d 1066, 1071 (1st Cir.1991).

Responses (as applicable):

- Expert testimony may be helpful even if it concerns a subject that is not beyond the understanding of the average juror. United States v. Lamarre, 248 F.3d 642, 648 (7th Cir.2001) ("Trial courts are not compelled to exclude all expert testimony merely because it overlaps with matters within the jury's experience."); Kopf v. Skyrm, 993 F.2d 374, 377 (4th Cir.1993) (subject matter of expert testimony "need not be arcane or even especially difficult to comprehend").

- Experts may testify about domestic law in cases such as legal malpractice or securities actions. United States v. Bilzerian, 926 F.2d 1285, 1294–95 (2d Cir.1991).

- The expert is basing her opinion on the types of facts or data that experts in her field reasonably rely upon in drawing such inferences. Advent Systems Ltd. v. Unisys Corp., 925 F.2d 670, 682 (3d Cir.1991).

- An expert is not required to hold an opinion to a "reasonable degree of certainty." Stutzman v. CRST, Inc., 997 F.2d 291, 294–95 (7th Cir.1993).

38. Habit Evidence Not Admissible (Rule 406)

Your honor, I object. Counsel has not established that the conduct qualifies as admissible habit evidence under Rule 406.

Authority:

Rule 406 provides that evidence of a person's habit [an organization's routine practice] is admissible to prove that the person [organization] acted in conformity with that habit [routine practice] on a particular occasion. But the conduct must (1) be particular enough to be considered a "regular response to a repeated specific situation," and have occurred with sufficient (2) frequency and (3) regularity that it can be considered uniform or "semi-automatic" behavior. McCormick, Evidence § 195 (6th ed. 2006); United States v. Angwin, 271 F.3d 786, 799 (9th Cir.2001); Simplex v. Diversified Energy Sys., 847 F.2d 1290, 1293 (7th Cir.1988).

Responses:

- The conduct here is sufficiently particularized, frequent and regular to constitute a habit. E.g., Crawford v. Tribeca Lending Corp., 815 F.3d 121, 124–25 (2d Cir.2016) (attorney's loan signing procedure); Babcock v. General Motors Corp., 299 F.3d 60, 66 (1st Cir.2002) (deceased driver's habit of wearing a seat belt); Meyer v. United States, 638 F.2d 155, 156–58 (10th Cir.1980) (dentist's regular practice of informing patients of potential risks associated with molar extractions).

- The evidence is not being offered as character evidence. The court may give a limiting instruction clarifying this for the jury.

- Evidence of the routine practice of a business poses little danger that it will be misused as character evidence since it refers to a business rather than a person.

39. Hearsay (Rules 801 and 802)

Your honor, I object. Hearsay (or, The question calls for hearsay; or, The document is hearsay).

Authority:

Rule 802 provides that hearsay is not admissible unless it falls within an exception established by a rule or statute.

Responses (as applicable):

- The statement is not hearsay because it is not offered to prove the truth of the matter asserted. Rule 801(a)–(c). E.g., the statement is a verbal act (such as words that constitute the terms of a contract), or a verbal part of an act (such as a statement accompanying delivery of property to show it was a gift), or the statement is relevant to show an effect on the state of mind of the listener (such as words of warning or notice).

- The statement is not hearsay because it is not offered for its truth but only to show the basis of an expert witness's opinion. Rules 703, 705.

- The statement is exempted from hearsay by Rule 801(d), such as:
  - Prior inconsistent testimony by witness, Rule 801(d)(1)(A);
  - Prior consistent statement by witness to rebut charge of recent fabrication or improper influence, Rule 801(d)(1)(B);
  - Prior statement by witness identifying a person, Rule 801(d)(1)(C);
  - Admission by party-opponent, or by agent, employee, or coconspirator of party-opponent, Rule 801(d)(2).

- The statement falls within an exception to the hearsay rule, such as:
  - Present sense impression, Rule 803(1);
  - Excited utterance, Rule 803(2);
  - State of mind of declarant, Rule 803(3);
  - Medical diagnosis or treatment, Rule 803(4);
  - Recorded recollection, Rule 803(5);
  - Business record, Rule 803(6);
  - Public record, Rule 803(8);

- Learned treatise, Rule 803(18);
- Former testimony, Rule 804(b)(1);
- Dying declaration, Rule 804(b)(2);
- Statement against interest, Rule 804(b)(3);
- Personal or family history, Rule 804(b)(4);
- Residual exception, Rules 803(24), 804(b)(5).

40. Hypothetical Question Includes Facts Not in Evidence (Rule 705)

Your honor, I object. Counsel is posing a hypothetical question that contains facts not adduced in evidence.

Authority:

A hypothetical question may consist of facts already in evidence, facts that will be introduced before the close of evidence, and inferences reasonably drawn from those facts. Toucet v. Maritime Overseas Corp., 991 F.2d 5, 10 (1st Cir.1993).

Responses (as applicable):

- The facts included in the question need not be established to a high degree of certainty. Matter of P & E Boat Rentals, Inc., 872 F.2d 642, 653 (5th Cir.1989).
- The question need not refer to all of the relevant facts in evidence.
- An expert may base an opinion on facts not personally known to the expert, even if the facts have not been admitted in evidence, so long as they are the kind of facts reasonably relied on by experts in the particular field in forming opinions on the subject. Rule 703.

41. Hypothetical Question Not Helpful (Rule 705)

Your honor, I object. The hypothetical question posed by counsel omits so many relevant facts that it cannot yield a helpful opinion.

Authority:

Unless a hypothetical question contains a sufficient number of relevant facts, any opinion rendered in response to it will be misleading, unhelpful to the resolution of the case, and inadmissible. Iconco v. Jensen Construction Co., 622 F.2d 1291, 1301 (8th Cir.1980).

Responses (as applicable):

- A hypothetical question need not refer to all of the relevant facts in evidence. Piotrowski v. Southworth Prods. Corp., 15 F.3d 748, 753 (8th Cir.1994).
- Opposing counsel is free on cross-examination to pose to this witness a hypothetical question which includes additional facts.

42. Identification Insufficient (Rules 901 and 902)

Your honor, I object. The evidence has not been properly identified.

Authority:

> Rule 901 states, "To satisfy the requirement of authenticating or identifying an item of evidence, the proponent must produce evidence sufficient to support a finding that the item is what the proponent claims it is."

Responses (as applicable):

- The evidence is sufficient to support a finding (prima facie case) that the item is genuine—all that is required by Rule 901(a). The issue of actual genuineness is for the jury. United States v. Lanzon, 639 F.3d 1293, 1301 (11th Cir.2011); Ricketts v. City of Hartford, 74 F.3d 1397, 1409–11 (2d Cir.1996); United States v. McGlory, 968 F.2d 309, 328–29 (3d Cir.1992); United States v. Johnson, 637 F.2d 1224, 1247 (9th Cir.1980).

- The item is sufficiently identified by a method listed in Rule 901(b), such as:

  - Testimony of a witness with knowledge, Rule 901(b)(1); United States v. Curbelo, 726 F.3d 1260, 1271 (11th Cir.2013);

  - Chain of custody, Rule 901(b)(1); United States v. Collins, 715 F.3d 1032, 1035–36 (7th Cir.2013); United States v. Olson, 846 F.2d 1103, 1116 (7th Cir.1988); United States v. Zink, 612 F.2d 511, 514 (10th Cir.1980); a defect in the chain of custody normally goes to the weight, not the admissibility, of the evidence; United States v. Summers, 666 F.3d 192, 201 (4th Cir.2011); United States v. Matta-Ballesteros, 71 F.3d 754, 768–69 (9th Cir.1995);

  - Lay opinion on handwriting, Rule 901(b)(2); United States v. Binzel, 907 F.2d 746, 749 (7th Cir.1990);

  - Comparison with exemplar, Rule 901(b)(3); United States v. Wylie, 919 F.2d 969, 978 (5th Cir.1990); United States v. Mangan, 575 F.2d 32, 42 (2d Cir.1978);

  - Circumstances and contents, Rule 901(b)(4); United States v. Turner, 718 F.3d 226, 232–33 (3d Cir.2013); United States v. Siddiqui, 235 F.3d 1318, 1322–23 (11th Cir.2000); United States v. Harvey, 117 F.3d 1044, 1049 (7th Cir.1997); United States v. Carpenter, 70 F.3d 520, 521 (8th Cir.1995); Denison v. Swaco Geolograph Co., 941 F.2d 1416, 1423 (10th Cir.1991);

  - Voice identification, Rule 901(b)(5); United States v. Jones, 600 F.3d 847, 858 (7th Cir.2010); United States v. Puentes, 50 F.3d 1567, 1577 (11th Cir.1995);

  - Telephone conversation, Rule 901(b)(6); United States v. De Simone, 699 F.3d 113, 126–27 (1st Cir.2012); United States v. Hines, 717 F.2d 1481, 1491 (4th Cir.1983); United States v. Portsmouth Paving Corp., 694 F.2d 312, 321–22 (4th Cir.1982);

  - Public record or report, Rule 901(b)(7); United States v. Wilson, 535 F.2d 521, 523 (9th Cir.1976);

  - Ancient document, Rule 901(b)(8); Threadgill v. Armstrong World Indus., Inc., 928 F.2d 1366, 1375–76 (3d Cir.1991);

  - Process or system, Rule 901(b)(9); United States v. Taylor, 530 F.2d 639, 641–42 (5th Cir.1976).

- The item is sufficiently identified by appearance and circumstances; the methods listed in Rule 901(b) are not exclusive. United States v. Simpson, 152 F.3d 1241, 1249–50 (10th Cir.1998); United States v. Jimenez Lopez, 873 F.2d 769, 772 (5th Cir.1989).

- The item is self-authenticating under Rule 902, such as:

  - Public document under seal, Rule 902(1), (2), or (3); United States v. Beason, 690 F.2d 439, 444–45 (5th Cir.1982);

  - Certified copy of public record, Rule 902(4); United States v. Watson, 650 F.3d 1084, 1090 (8th Cir.2011); Moore v. City of Desloge, Mo., 647 F.3d 841, 848 (8th Cir.2011); United States v. Bisbee, 245 F.3d 1001, 1006–07 (8th Cir.2001); United States v. Huffhines, 967 F.2d 314, 320 (9th Cir.1992);

  - Acknowledged (notarized) document, Rule 902(8); United States v. M'Biye, 655 F.2d 1240, 1243 (D.C.Cir.1981);

  - Certified record of regularly conducted activity, Rule 902(11) or (12).

43. Impeachment, Bias (Rules 607 and 611)

Your honor, I object. Counsel is offering extrinsic evidence to prove bias without first having questioned the witness about it.

Authority:

Although the rules do not contain an express provision requiring that a witness first be asked about any facts or statements that indicate the witness is biased, some courts have indicated that the impeaching party must afford the impeached witness the opportunity to admit or deny any such facts or statements. See, e.g., United States v. Betts, 16 F.3d 748, 764 (7th Cir.1994). Moreover, it is within the trial court's power to control the mode and order in which evidence is presented. Rule 611.

Responses (as applicable):

- The witness is available to be recalled and thus will have the opportunity to admit or deny the bias.

- The rules do not require that a witness be asked about bias before extrinsic evidence of the bias is offered.

44. Impeachment, Extrinsic Evidence of Prior Conduct Inadmissible (Rule 608)

Your honor, I object. Rule 608 does not allow extrinsic evidence of specific instances of a witness's conduct.

Authority:

Rule 608(b) provides that counsel may cross-examine a witness about specific instances of the witness's conduct for the purpose of attacking the witness's truthful character, but that extrinsic proof of such conduct (other than convictions admissible under Rule 609) is inadmissible. United States v. McGee, 408 F.3d 966, 979–82 (7th Cir.2005).

Responses (as applicable):

- Rule 608(b) applies only when the specific act is offered to prove the witness's character for truthfulness. Specific acts may, however, be offered for other purposes, such as:

  - To prove the witness's bias. E.g., United States v. Abel, 469 U.S. 45, 105 S.Ct. 465 (1984).

- To rebut factual assertions made by the witness on direct examination. E.g., United States v. Antonakeas, 255 F.3d 714, 724–25 (9th Cir.2001).

- To cure a witness's misleading statements as to the extent of his troubles with the law. E.g., United States v. Callaway, 938 F.2d 907, 910–12 (8th Cir.1991).

45. Impeachment of Own Witness (Rule 607)

Your honor, I object. Counsel is impeaching her own witness.

Authority:

Not a valid objection. Rule 607 overturns the common-law rule that prevented a party from impeaching a witness called by that party in the absence of surprise and injury. Rule 607 states, "Any party, including the party that called the witness, may attack the witness's credibility." A party, however, may not call a witness to the stand solely for the purpose of placing otherwise inadmissible evidence before the jury. United States v. Peterman, 841 F.2d 1474, 1479–80 (10th Cir.1988).

See also Objection # 46 if counsel seeks to impeach her own witness with a prior inconsistent statement.

Responses:

- Rule 607 allows a party to impeach its own witness.

- The witness was not called for the sole purpose of placing otherwise inadmissible evidence before the jury. E.g., United States v. Burt, 495 F.3d 733, 736–38 (7th Cir.2007) (witness presented testimony both favorable and unfavorable to prosecution); United States v. West, 22 F.3d 586, 593 (5th Cir.1994) (impeachment by conviction).

46. Impeachment of Own Witness With Prior Inconsistent Statement (Rules 403 and 607)

Your honor, I object. Counsel is trying to impeach her own witness with a prior inconsistent statement. The probative value of the statement for impeachment purposes is substantially outweighed by the danger of unfair prejudice and misleading the jury.

Authority:

Since a witness's own out-of-court statements are hearsay if offered for their truth, a party may not call a witness to the stand primarily for the purpose of impeaching the witness with the otherwise inadmissible hearsay. The probative value of the evidence for impeachment purposes is substantially outweighed by the danger that the jury will use the prior statement as substantive evidence. United States v. Logan, 121 F.3d 1172, 1174–77 (8th Cir.1997); United States v. Ince, 21 F.3d 576, 579–82 (4th Cir.1994).

Responses (as applicable):

- The witness's out-of-court statement is admissible for its truth because it is defined as non-hearsay under Rule 801(d)(1) or falls within an exception to the hearsay rule under Rule 803 or 804. Therefore, it may properly be considered by the jury for its truth.

- The witness was not called primarily for the purpose of impeaching him with his prior statement. United States v. Burt, 495 F.3d 733, 736–38 (7th Cir.2007) (witness presented testimony both favorable and unfavorable to prosecution); United States v. Webster, 734 F.2d 1191, 1193 (7th Cir.1984).

- The probative value of the impeachment is not substantially outweighed by the danger of unfair prejudice. United States v. Buffalo, 358 F.3d 519, 525–28 (8th Cir.2004).

47. Impeachment on Collateral Matter (Rules 403 and 607)

Your honor, I object. Counsel is seeking to introduce evidence on a collateral matter and the probative value of such evidence is substantially outweighed by the danger of unfair prejudice, confusion of the issues, and misleading the jury, as well as by considerations of undue delay.

Authority:

Courts exclude extrinsic evidence when offered to prove a collateral matter. The most common instance in which this arises is when a party seeks to impeach a witness by introducing extrinsic evidence that contradicts an answer given by the witness. The standard for whether a matter is collateral, and thus not susceptible to proof by extrinsic evidence is, "Could the fact, * * * have been shown in evidence for any purpose independently of the contradiction?" 3A Wigmore, Evidence § 1003, at 961 (Chadbourn rev. 1970).

The rules of evidence do not directly address this issue. The admissibility of such evidence, therefore, must be resolved under the balancing test of Rule 403. Morgan v. Covington Township, 648 F.3d 172, 179–80 (3d Cir.2011).

The term is also sometimes used with reference to specific prohibitions on extrinsic evidence imposed by particular rules. For example, although reputation or character witnesses may be cross-examined with "have you heard" or "did you know" questions, Rule 405 provides that extrinsic evidence may not be offered to prove that the incidents alluded to in such questions actually occurred.

Responses (as applicable):

- The extrinsic evidence is not being offered solely to impeach the witness. It is independently relevant to a substantive issue in the case.

- Extrinsic evidence of a contradiction is admissible when a witness is unlikely to have been mistaken about the "collateral" fact were his story true. United States v. Lopez, 979 F.2d 1024, 1034 (5th Cir.1992).

- Bias is not a collateral matter; extrinsic evidence, therefore, is admissible. United States v. Abel, 469 U.S. 45, 52, 105 S.Ct. 465, 469 (1984).

- The capacity of a witness to perceive, remember, or relate an event is not a collateral matter; extrinsic evidence, therefore, is admissible. E.g., United States v. Gonzalez-Maldonado, 115 F.3d 9, 15–17 (1st Cir.1997).

- Extrinsic evidence of a witness's prior inconsistent statement is admissible so long as the witness is afforded the opportunity to explain or deny the statement and opposing counsel is afforded the opportunity to question the witness about it. United States v. Hudson, 970 F.2d 948, 955 (1st Cir.1992).

- Evidence of the specific acts of a witness are not rendered inadmissible by Rule 608(b) when offered to prove something other than a witness's untrustworthy character. E.g., Foster v. General Motors Corp., 20 F.3d 838, 839 (8th Cir.1994) (evidence relevant to a material issue in the case).

48. Impeachment, Prior Conviction Inadmissible (Rule 609)

Your honor, I object. Counsel is improperly trying to impeach the witness with a criminal conviction.

Authority:

Rule 609 allows a witness to be impeached with evidence of a criminal conviction, but only if the conviction was for a crime involving dishonesty or false statement, regardless of the punishment, Rule 609(a)(2), or for a felony, Rule 609(a)(1). A crime does not qualify under Rule 609(a)(2) unless the fact finder was required to find (or the defendant to admit) an act of dishonesty or false statement.

Balancing test for criminal defendant being impeached with a conviction for a felony that did not involve dishonesty or false statement:

- probative value of the conviction as credibility evidence must outweigh its prejudicial effect to the accused.

Balancing test for witnesses other than the accused being impeached with a conviction for a felony that did not involve dishonesty or false statement:

- admissible subject to Rule 403.

Responses (as applicable):

- Rule 609 is not applicable because the conviction is being used to show bias, not untrustworthy character.

- Rule 609 is not applicable because the conviction is being used to rebut a factual assertion made by the witness. E.g., United States v. Norton, 26 F.3d 240 (1st Cir.1994).

- The impeachment is proper because the prior conviction required proof or an admission of an act of dishonesty or false statement by the witness. United States v. Harper, 527 F.3d 396, 408 (5th Cir.2008).

- Although the crime did not involve dishonesty or false statement, it was a felony and

  - [Witness is the accused]: its probative value outweighs its prejudicial effect.

  - [Witness is anyone other than accused]: its probative value is not substantially outweighed by the danger of unfair prejudice.

- The probative value of the conviction is high because it was recent and credibility is an important issue in the case. American Modern Home Ins. Co. v. Thomas, 993 F.3d 1068, 1071 (8th Cir.2021).

49. Incompetent; Witness Is Incompetent (Rules 601 and 403)

Your honor, I object. The witness is incompetent and his testimony should be excluded under Rule 601. Alternatively, the witness lacks sufficient capacity to testify in a meaningful way and his testimony should be excluded under Rule 403.

Authority:

Rule 601 provides that all persons are competent to testify except as otherwise provided in the rules. But some courts maintain that they nevertheless have the power to determine competency. United States v. Barnes, 803 F.3d 209, 219 (5th Cir.2015). Moreover, in civil actions in which state law supplies the rule of decision with respect to an element of a claim or defense, Rule 601 provides that a witness's competency must be determined in accordance with state law.

Moreover, even where federal law governs, under Rule 403 the trial judge may rule that because of the witness's incapacity, the probative value of the person's testimony would be substantially outweighed by the countervailing considerations listed in that rule. United States v. Ramirez, 871 F.2d 582, 584 (6th Cir.1989).

Responses (as applicable):

- Rule 601 unequivocally abolishes all objections to a witness's competency not expressly included in the rules of evidence. Any testimonial deficiencies go to the weight of the witness's testimony, not its admissibility.

- Courts allow witnesses to testify if a minimal threshold level of relevancy is met. E.g., United States v. Villalta, 662 F.2d 1205 (5th Cir.1981).

- A witness's drug or alcohol use does not automatically establish the witness's incompetency. United States v. Ramirez, 871 F.2d 582, 584 (6th Cir.1989) (drug addiction at time of event); United States v. Van Meerbeke, 548 F.2d 415 (2d Cir.1976) (drug use at trial).

- An adjudication that a person is insane or incompetent to stand trial does not automatically establish the witness's incompetency. Andrews v. Neer, 253 F.3d 1052, 1062–63 (8th Cir.2001).

- The witness is competent to testify under governing state law.

50. Insurance (Rule 411)

Your honor, I object. Rule 411 prohibits evidence of liability insurance.

Authority:

Rule 411 excludes evidence that a person was or was not insured when offered to prove that the person was at fault.

Evidence that a party lacks insurance is also inadmissible if it constitutes an improper "plea of poverty." McCormick, Evidence § 201 (6th ed. 2006).

Responses (as applicable):

- Rule 411 does not exclude the evidence because it is being offered to establish a trade custom of limiting liability. Posttape Associates v. Eastman Kodak Co., 537 F.2d 751 (3d Cir.1976).

- Rule 411 does not exclude the evidence because it is being offered to show bias. Conde v. Starlight I, Inc., 103 F.3d 210, 213–14 (1st Cir.1997).

- Rule 411 does not apply because the evidence is being offered to contradict a factual assertion made by the policy owner. Wheeling Pittsburgh Steel Corp. v. Beelman River Terminals, Inc., 254 F.3d 706, 717–18 (8th Cir.2001).

- Rule 411 does not apply because the evidence is being offered to prove the liability of a third party.

- Jurors may be questioned on voir dire about their connections to insurance companies. See Socony Mobil Oil Co. v. Taylor, 388 F.2d 586, 589 (5th Cir.1967).

51. Irrelevant (Immaterial, Not Probative) (Rules 401 and 402)

Your honor, I object. The evidence is irrelevant and inadmissible under Rules 401 and 402.

Authority:

Rule 401 defines "relevant evidence." To be relevant, evidence must possess logical probative value toward some fact that is legally of consequence to the case. Rule 402 provides that evidence which is not relevant is inadmissible.

Responses (as applicable):

- Rule 401 requires only minimal probative value. "Evidence is relevant if 'it has any tendency to make a fact [of consequence] more or less probable than it would be without the evidence.' Fed. R. Evid. 401 (emphasis added). The word 'any' signals that evidence is relevant even if it only slightly or marginally alters the likelihood of a consequential fact." United States v. Leonard-Allen, 739 F.3d 948, 956 (7th Cir.2013). "[T]he test of relevance is very liberal and does not entail a determination of the sufficiency of the evidence." Douglass v. Eaton Corp., 956 F.2d 1339, 1345 (6th Cir.1992).

- The fact of consequence to which the evidence is directed need not be disputed. Advisory Committee's Note to Rule 401. "Background evidence," such as photographs, views of real estate, murder weapons, and basic biographical information concerning a witness, is relevant according to the standard of Rule 401. Id.; Faigin v. Kelly, 184 F.3d 67, 81 (1st Cir.1999); United States v. Blackwell, 853 F.2d 86, 88 (2d Cir.1988); Government of Virgin Islands v. Grant, 775 F.2d 508, 513 (3d Cir.1985); Conway v. Chemical Leaman Tank Lines, Inc., 525 F.2d 927, 930 (5th Cir.1976).

- The relevance of the evidence will become apparent when it is "connected up" as authorized by Rule 104(b).

52. Judge as Witness (Rule 605)

Your honor, I respectfully object as Rule 605 bars a judge from testifying as a witness.

Authority:

Rule 605 provides, "The presiding judge may not testify as a witness at the trial. A party need not object to preserve the issue."

Moreover, remarks or questions from the bench that convey factual information not in evidence constitute impermissible judicial testimony under Rule 605. See United States v. Pritchett, 699 F.2d 317, 318–20 (6th Cir.1983).

Response:

- A judge may testify as a fact witness in a case over which the judge is not presiding. United States v. Frankenthal, 582 F.2d 1102, 1107–08 (7th Cir.1978).

53. Juror as Witness at Trial (Rule 606(a))

Your honor, I object. Under Rule 606 a juror is incompetent to testify as a witness.

Authority:

Rule 606(a) states, "A juror may not testify as a witness before the other jurors at the trial."

The rule gives counsel the right to make this objection out of the presence of the jury.

Response:

- Rule 606(a) does not prevent a juror from being questioned on voir dire or by the court during trial concerning attempted tampering or other such matters. Cf. United States v. Kills Enemy, 3 F.3d 1201, 1204 (8th Cir.1993) (questioning wisdom of permitting former venireman to testify).

54. Juror as Witness to Impeach Verdict (Rule 606(b))

Your honor, I object. A juror is not competent to testify about matters that occurred during jury deliberations.

Authority:

Rule 606(b) prohibits a juror from testifying about (a) any statement that was made or incident that occurred during the jury's deliberations; (b) the effect of anything on that juror's or another juror's vote; or (c) any juror's mental processes concerning the verdict or indictment. It also prohibits a juror's affidavit or evidence of a juror's statement about any of these matters.

Responses (as applicable):

- A juror may testify as to whether extraneous prejudicial information was improperly brought to the jury's attention or whether any outside influence was improperly brought to bear upon a juror. E.g., Oliver v. Quarterman, 541 F.3d 329, 336–40 (5th Cir.2008) (juror consulted Bible); Ewing v. Horton, 914 F.3d 1027, 1029–30 (6th Cir.2019) (juror consulted defendant's Facebook profile and did Google search for case-related information); United States v. Bagnariol, 665 F.2d 877, 883–85 (9th Cir.1981) (jury consulted business publications); Krause v. Rhodes, 570 F.2d 563, 566–70 (6th Cir.1977) (juror subjected to threats).

- A juror may testify about whether a mistake was made in entering the verdict on the verdict form.

- A juror may testify about overt racial bias in the deliberation of a criminal case, Peña-Rodriguez v. Colorado, 580 U.S. 206, 137 S.Ct. 855 (2017), or civil case, Harden v. Hillman, 993 F.2d 465, 478–85 (6th Cir.2021).

- Rule 606(b) does not preclude the testimony of a non-juror who possesses personal knowledge of juror misconduct. United States v. Taliaferro, 558 F.2d 724, 725–26 (4th Cir.1977).

55. Lay Opinion Testimony (Rule 701)

Your honor, I object. The witness is being asked to state an opinion that [is not rationally based on his own perception] [would not be helpful to the jury].

Authority:

Although Rule 701 abandons the common-law rule that barred lay witnesses from testifying in the form of an opinion, the rule still restricts lay opinions to those that (1) are rationally based on the witness's perception and (2) would help the fact finder to understand clearly the testimony or determine a fact in issue. United States v. Hall, 93 F.3d 1337 (7th Cir.1996).

Grounds for excluding lay opinion testimony thus include:

- The witness lacks personal knowledge of the underlying facts. United States v. Garcia, 413 F.3d 201, 211 (2d Cir.2005).

- The witness's conclusion is irrational or speculative. Stagman v. Ryan, 176 F.3d 986, 995–96 (7th Cir.1999); Keller v. United States, 38 F.3d 16, 31 (1st Cir.1994).

- The jury is equally well-positioned to draw the inferences from the underlying data. United States v. Freeman, 730 F.3d 590, 595–99 (6th Cir.2013); United States v. Meises, 645 F.3d 5, 16–17 (1st Cir.2011).

- The witness seeks to offer an opinion on a subject that calls for expertise. Randolph v. Collectramatic, Inc., 590 F.2d 844, 848 (10th Cir.1979).

- The witness seeks to testify as to a mixed question of law and fact and does not understand the underlying legal standard. United States v. Scop, 846 F.2d 135, 139–42 (2d Cir.1988).

Responses (as applicable):

- Rule 701 was designed to allow lay witnesses to testify in the manner most likely to elicit helpful testimony. The trial court has wide latitude in admitting lay opinion testimony. Trademark Research Corp. v. Maxwell Online, Inc., 995 F.2d 326, 339 (2d Cir.1993).

- Demonstrate that the witness has the knowledge necessary to form the opinion.

- Rephrase the question.

56. Lay Witness Testifying as Expert (Rule 701)

Your Honor, I object. A lay witness is not permitted to offer an opinion based on scientific, technical or other specialized knowledge.

Authority:

Rule 701 expressly prohibits a lay witness from testifying to an opinion that is based on "scientific, technical or other specialized knowledge within the scope of Rule 702."

Responses (as applicable):

- The witness is testifying to the type of opinion that lay witnesses are typically allowed to relate. Asplundh Manufacturing. Division v. Benton Harbor Engineering, 57 F.3d 1190, 1196 (3d Cir.1995).

- The witness's testimony is based on personal knowledge gained in investigating the case at bar. United States v. Kilpatrick, 798 F.3d 365, 379–85 (6th Cir.2015); United States v. Macedo-Flores, 788 F.3d 181, 191–92 (5th Cir.2015).

- The witness is testifying about knowledge gained in the course of his regular involvement in the ordinary affairs of the business in question. United States v. Kerley, 784 F.3d 327, 337 (6th Cir.2015); Ryan Development Co. v. Indiana Lumbermens Mut. Ins. Co., 711 F.3d 1165, 1169 (10th Cir.2013).

- The witness is testifying about medical treatment the witness personally gave. E.g., Williams v. Mast Biosurgery USA, Inc., 644 F.3d 1312, 1317 (11th Cir.2011).

57. Medical, Hospital, or Similar Expenses, Payment of (Rule 409)

Your honor, I object. Rule 409 excludes evidence of payment of or offers to pay medical, hospital and similar expenses.

Authority:

Rule 409 bars the admission of evidence of offers to pay or payments of medical, hospital, or similar expenses when offered as proof of the payor's (or offeror's) liability for the injury.

Responses (as applicable):

- The evidence is admissible if offered to prove an issue other than liability. Savoie v. Otto Candies, Inc., 692 F.2d 363, 370 n. 7 (5th Cir.1982) (to prove payment recipient's status as seaman).

- A statement of liability made in connection with such an offer is not rendered inadmissible by Rule 409. See Advisory Committee's Note.

58. Mental State or Condition of Accused (Rule 704(b))

Your honor, I object. The witness is not permitted to state his opinion that the defendant was insane [possessed or lacked the required mental state].

Authority:

Rule 704(b) provides that an expert testifying as to an accused's mental state or condition may not offer an opinion as to whether the accused possessed a mental state or condition that constitutes an element of (a) the crime charged or (b) a defense to the crime charged.

Responses (as applicable):

- A witness may testify that the accused suffers or does not suffer from a mental disease or defect and may describe the characteristics and effects of such a disease or defect. United States v. Samples, 456 F.3d 875, 884 (8th Cir.2006).

- The witness is testifying as a lay witness and Rule 704(b) applies only to experts.

59. Misleading the Jury (Rule 403)

Your honor, the evidence will mislead the jury.

Authority:

Rule 403 provides that relevant evidence may be excluded if its probative value is substantially outweighed by the danger of misleading the jury.

Cases invoking the danger of misleading the jury often refer to the possibility that the jury might attach undue weight to the evidence. Faigin v. Kelly, 184 F.3d 67, 80 (1st Cir.1999) (findings in a sanctions order from a previous trial; "A lay jury is quite likely to give special weight to judicial findings merely because they are judicial findings."); Williams v. Nashville Network, 132 F.3d 1123, 1129 (6th Cir.1997) (probable cause determination by EEOC); United States v. Call, 129 F.3d 1402, 1406 (10th Cir.1997) (polygraph results); Bright v. Firestone Tire & Rubber Co., 756 F.2d 19, 23 (6th Cir.1984) (government report on safety of tire excluded under Rule 403 because the "jury may have been influenced by the official character of the report to afford it greater weight than it was worth").

Demonstrative evidence may be excluded as misleading if it distorts or misrepresents underlying evidence. Cartier v. Jackson, 59 F.3d 1046, 1049 (10th Cir.1995) (in copyright infringement action against singer-composer Michael Jackson, trial court properly excluded plaintiff's demonstrative tapes designed to compare plaintiff's song "Dangerous" with defendant's song of the same title; the tapes altered the tempo, changed the key, repeated musical phrases not repeated in the originals, and spliced together portions not adjacent in the originals; "the changes made to the songs in these recordings were so significant that the tapes no longer represented the songs in question.").

Response:

- The probative value of the evidence outweighs the danger of misleading the jury. The Rule 403 "balance should be struck in favor of admission." United States v. Dennis, 625 F.2d 782, 797 (8th Cir.1980). Rule 403 is "an extraordinary remedy to be used sparingly." United States v. Meester, 762 F.2d 867, 875 (11th Cir.1985).

60. Nonresponsive Answer (Rule 611)

Your honor, I object and move to strike. The witness's answer was nonresponsive and is inadmissible because _____.

Authority:

This objection goes to the form of the answer, rather than the question. Many courts allow only questioning counsel to object and move to strike the answer on this ground. E.g., United States v. Shillingstad, 632 F.3d 1031, 1036 (8th Cir.2011). Opposing counsel may object only if the answer is objectionable on some other ground. Although counsel must object in as timely a manner as possible, the nonresponsiveness of the answer may excuse counsel's failure to object more quickly.

Responses (as applicable):

- Counsel has offered no reason why the evidence is inadmissible. Although the answer was not responsive to the question, the evidence is relevant and otherwise admissible.

- Even when an answer is nonresponsive, counsel must object in as timely a fashion as possible.

61. Other Accidents (Rules 401–403)

Your honor, I object. Evidence of other accidents is irrelevant and inadmissible under Rules 401 and 402 [OR: is inadmissible under Rule 403 because the probative value of such evidence is substantially outweighed by the dangers of unfair prejudice, confusing of the issues and misleading the jury].

Authority:

Evidence of other accidents is inadmissible absent a showing that the other accidents occurred under conditions and circumstances substantially similar to the accident in question. Katzenmeier v. Blackpowder Products, Inc., 628 F.3d 948, 951 (8th Cir.2010); Lovett ex rel. Lovett v. Union Pacific R. Co., 201 F.3d 1074, 1080–81 (8th Cir.2000); Kinser v. Gehl Co., 184 F.3d 1259, 1273 (10th Cir.1999); Nachtsheim v. Beech Aircraft Corp., 847 F.2d 1261, 1268–69 (7th Cir.1988) (citing many other cases).

Similarity of conditions is especially important when the other accidents are offered to show the existence of a dangerous condition or causation. Kinser v. Gehl Co., supra, at 1273;

Even when substantial similarity of circumstances is shown, the evidence is subject to exclusion in the trial court's discretion on account of dangers of unfair prejudice, confusion of issues, and undue expenditure of time in the trial of collateral issues. Nachtsheim v. Beech Aircraft Corp., supra, at 1268–69.

A prior accident may be used to establish notice only if it occurred sufficiently prior to the date of the subject incident that the defendant could have taken steps to remedy the situation. Kinser v. Gehl Co., supra, at 1274.

The admissibility of evidence of absence of accidents is also subject to a foundation showing similarity of conditions, and the trial court's exercise of discretion under Rule 403. Pandit v. American Honda Motor Co., Inc., 82 F.3d 376, 381 (10th Cir.1996); Espeaignnette v. Gene Tierney Co., 43 F.3d 1, 10 (1st Cir.1994); Klonowski v. International Armament Corp., 17 F.3d 992, 996 (7th Cir.1994).

Responses (as applicable):

- The other accidents occurred under substantially similar circumstances and conditions. Therefore, the occurrence of other accidents is relevant to show the existence of a dangerous condition or defect, causation, or notice to the defendant of danger. Kinser v. Gehl Co., 184 F.3d 1259, 1273 (10th Cir.1999); Nachtsheim v. Beech Aircraft Corp., 847 F.2d 1261, 1268–69 (7th Cir.1988) (citing many other cases).

- The other accident is relevant to show notice; therefore, the requirement of similarity is less strict. Kinser v. Gehl Co., supra, at 1273; (citing many other cases); Benedi v. McNeil-P.P.C., Inc., 66 F.3d 1378, 1386 (4th Cir.1995).

- Accidents that would otherwise be inadmissible on account of dissimilarity may become admissible to impeach a witness's broad assertions concerning safety. Cooper v. Firestone Tire & Rubber Co., 945 F.2d 1103, 1105 (9th Cir.1991). But see Drabik v. Stanley-Bostitch, Inc., 997 F.2d 496 (8th Cir.1993).

- The lack of other accidents under similar circumstances and conditions is relevant to show the absence of dangerous condition or defect, lack of causal relation, and lack of notice. Pandit v. American Honda Motor Co., Inc., 82 F.3d 376, 380–81 (10th Cir.1996); Espeaignnette v. Gene Tierney Co., 43 F.3d 1, 9–10 (1st Cir.1994).

62. Other Claims by Plaintiff (Rules 401–403)

Your honor, I object. Evidence of claims made by the plaintiff other than those at issue here is irrelevant and inadmissible under Rules 401 and 402 [OR: is inadmissible under Rule 403 because its probative value is substantially outweighed by the danger of unfair prejudice, confusing the issues or misleading the jury].

Authority:

Evidence of other claims by the plaintiff, offered to show that the present claim lacks merit, is usually excluded on the ground that its probative value is outweighed by the dangers of unfair prejudice, confusing the issues, or misleading the jury. Rule 403; Bunion v. Allstate Ins. Co., 502 F.Supp. 340 (E.D.Pa.1980).

Responses (as applicable):

- Evidence that a plaintiff has brought similar claims that were fraudulent is usually admitted on the ground that it is strongly relevant to the falsity of the present claim. Bunion v. Allstate Ins. Co., 502 F.Supp. 340 (E.D.Pa.1980).

- Evidence of another claim may become relevant on cross-examination of the plaintiff for purposes of impeaching statements made on direct examination. Id.

63. Other Contracts or Transactions Involving a Party (Rules 401–403)

Your honor, I object. Evidence of a party's contracts or transactions other than those at issue here is irrelevant and inadmissible under Rules 401 and 402 [OR: is inadmissible under Rule 403 because its probative value is substantially outweighed by the danger of unfair prejudice, confusing the issues or misleading the jury].

Authority:

Evidence of a party's contracts or transactions other than those at issue in the case is often excluded as irrelevant or because its probative value is substantially outweighed by the dangers of unfair prejudice, confusing the issues, or misleading the jury. E.g., Minnesota Farm Bureau Marketing Corp. v. North Dakota Agricultural Marketing Ass'n, Inc., 563 F.2d 906, 911 (8th Cir.1977).

Response:

- A party's business transactions with third parties in similar circumstances may be relevant to prove the probable terms or meaning of terms of a disputed agreement. Cibro Petroleum Products, Inc. v. Sohio Alaska Petroleum Co., 602 F.Supp. 1520, 1551 (N.D.N.Y.1985), aff'd, 798 F.2d 1421 (Em.App.1986).

64. Other Crimes Evidence; Insufficient Notice of Intent to Offer (Rules 404(b), 413, 414 and 415)

Your honor, I object. I did not receive sufficient notice of the prosecution's intention to offer evidence of the defendant's other crimes as required by Rule 404(b).

Authority:

Rule 404(b)(3) requires the prosecution to give an accused reasonable notice of any other-crimes evidence the prosecutor intends to offer at trial. The notice ordinarily must be in writing and provided before trial.

Rules 413–415 require that the party planning to introduce evidence of other acts of sexual assault or child molestation must disclose such evidence at least 15 days prior to trial.

Responses (as applicable):

- The trial court may, for good cause, allow the prosecutor to provide the required notice in any form during trial.

- The notice requirement does not apply to offenses that are inextricably intertwined with the charged offense ("intrinsic" offenses). Advisory Committee's Note.

65. Other Crimes Evidence Not Adequately Proven (Rules 104(b), 404(b), 413, 414 and 415)

Your honor, I object. Even if the other crimes evidence is offered for a purpose other than proof of propensity, it has not been adequately proven.

Authority:

Although other crimes evidence is not rendered inadmissible by Rule 404 if offered for some purpose other than to prove propensity, the proponent of such evidence still must offer adequate competent evidence to establish that the misconduct occurred and that the accused was the person who committed the misconduct. United States v. Fortenberry, 860 F.2d 628, 632–33 (5th Cir.1988).

Evidence that the defendant committed other sexual assaults or acts of child molestation, offered under Rules 413–415, must also be established with adequate competent proof.

Response:

- Pursuant to Rule 104(b), other crimes evidence is admissible if the trial judge is satisfied that the jury could find by a preponderance of the evidence that the defendant is responsible for, or connected to, the other act from which the evidentiary inference is to be drawn. Huddleston v. United States, 485 U.S. 681, 108 S.Ct. 1496 (1988); United States v. Riddle, 103 F.3d 423, 433 (5th Cir.1997).

66. Other Crimes Evidence Not Admissible to Prove Character (Rules 404(b), 413, 414 and 415)

Your honor, I object. Inquiry into a person's other crimes, wrongs, or acts is barred by Rule 404(b). The issue in this trial is whether the person did what it is claimed she did, not whether she did something wrong at another time.

Authority:

Rule 404(b)(1) embodies the traditional rule that excludes evidence of a person's prior misconduct. The rule is founded on the fear that the jury will conclude from such evidence that the accused is a bad person deserving of punishment and will then render its verdict accordingly. United States v. Linares, 367 F.3d 941, 945–46 (D.C. Cir.2004).

Responses (as applicable):

- Other crimes evidence is admissible if it is "logically relevant * * * to any issue other than the defendant's propensity to commit the crime" and if it survives the balancing test set forth in Rule 403. United States v. Sampson, 980 F.2d 883, 886 (3d Cir.1992).

  Rule 404(b)(2) provides a list of permissible purposes for which such evidence may be admitted, but the list is non-exclusive. Permissible purposes include:

  - To prove the person's intent. United States v. Watson, 766 F.3d 1219, 1237 (10th Cir.2014) (in drug cases); United States v. Misher, 99 F.3d 664 (5th Cir.1996); Turley v. State Farm Mutual Automobile Ins. Co., 944 F.2d 669, 672–75 (10th Cir.1991).

  - To prove a motive for the defendant's commission of the crime charged. United States v. Earls, 704 F.3d 466, 470–72 (7th Cir.2012).

  - To prove identity where the other crime and the offense at issue share one or more distinctive characteristics. This is the *modus operandi* theory. United States v. Simpson, 479 F.3d 492, 498 (7th Cir.2007); United States v. Sanchez, 988 F.2d 1384, 1393 (5th Cir.1993).

  - To prove a person had a special talent or capacity also involved in the charged offense. United States v. Cruz-Garcia, 344 F.3d 951 (9th Cir.2003).

  - To demonstrate a common plan or scheme. United States v. DeCicco, 370 F.3d 206 (1st Cir.2004).

  - To prove knowledge. United States v. Cassell, 292 F.3d 788, 793 (D.C.Cir.2002); United States v. Blitz, 151 F.3d 1002, 1007–08 (9th Cir.1998).

  - To prove absence of mistake. King v. Ahrens, 16 F.3d 265, 269 (8th Cir.1994).

- To support or rebut a claim of entrapment. United States v. Thomas, 134 F.3d 975 (9th Cir.1998) (support); United States v. Emerson, 501 F.3d 804, 812–13 (7th Cir.2007) (rebut).

- Evidence of specific acts of sexual assault or child molestation are admissible under Rule 413 (sexual assault), United States v. Guidry, 456 F.3d 493, 501 (5th Cir.2006); Rule 414 (child molestation), United States v. Hruby, 19 F.4th 963, 965 (6th Cir.2021); and Rule 415 (either, in civil cases), Martinez v. Cui, 608 F.3d 54, 60 (1st Cir.2010).

- Prior specific instances of conduct will be admissible where character is itself an issue; i.e., an essential element of a charge, claim or defense (almost exclusively a civil matter). Parrish v. Luckie, 963 F.2d 201, 205 (8th Cir.1992) (civil rights action against a police officer and his police chief; previous acts of violence by defendant police officer admissible to prove the police chief's knowledge of the officer's violent tendencies). See Rule 405(b).

- "Other crimes" evidence is admissible if the other crime is inextricably intertwined with the charged offense. United States v. Loftis, 843 F.3d 1173, 177–78 (9th Cir.2016); United States v. Kupfer, 797 F.3d 1233, 1238 (10th Cir.2015). But see United States v. Conner, 583 F.3d 1011, 1019 (7th Cir.2009) (criticizing doctrine as often "unhelpfully vague"); United States v. Bowie, 232 F.3d 923, 927–29 (D.C. Cir.2000) (surveying case law and criticizing broad interpretation of "intrinsic offense").

- Although such evidence is often referred to as "other crimes evidence," it is clear from the wording of Rule 404(b) that the other event need not have been criminal, much less have resulted in a prosecution or conviction. United States v. Scott, 677 F.3d 72, 78 (2d Cir.2012).

- There is no requirement that the other act have occurred prior to the one which is the subject of the trial, although that will ordinarily be the case. United States v. Curley, 639 F.3d 50, 51 (2d Cir.2011).

67. Other Crimes Evidence Offered for an Undisputed Point (Rules 403, 404(b), 413, 414 and 415)

Your honor, I object. Even if the other crimes evidence is offered for a purpose other than proof of propensity or is offered under Rules 413–415, it is not offered for a fact in dispute. Therefore it is inadmissible under Rules 403 and 404(b).

Authority:

Even if the evidence is directed at proving an element of the crime charged, the probative value of the evidence is substantially outweighed by the danger of unfair prejudice when the element to which it is directed is not actually the subject of dispute. Old Chief v. United States, 519 U.S. 172, 117 S.Ct. 644 (1997) (defendant's stipulation to fact of prior felony conviction sufficient to prevent prosecution from offering evidence as to name and nature of conviction).

Response:

- Old Chief v. United States, 519 U.S. 172, 117 S.Ct. 644 (1997), renders other crimes evidence inadmissible only when the defendant is being prosecuted for being a felon in possession of a firearm and stipulates to a prior felony. When the prosecution is offering other crimes evidence to prove intent, knowledge, identity, the absence of mistake or accident, etc., the prosecution is entitled to prove how and why the crime was committed in the manner it sees fit. *United States v. Tan*, 254 F.3d 1204, 1213 (10th Cir.2001) (citing and quoting other cases); *United States v. Hill*, 249 F.3d 707, 712 (8th Cir.2001) ("*Old Chief* eliminates the possibility that a defendant can escape the introduction of past crimes under Rule 404(b) by stipulating to the element of the crime at issue").

68. Personal Knowledge Lacking (Rule 602)

Your honor, I object. No showing has been made that the witness has personal knowledge about this matter.

Authority:

Rule 602 provides, "A witness may testify to a matter only if evidence is introduced sufficient to support a finding that the witness has personal knowledge of the matter."

Responses (as applicable):

- A witness's assertion of personal knowledge is sufficient to establish personal knowledge. Personal knowledge may also be inferred from the circumstances. E.g., *United States v. Doe*, 960 F.2d 221, 223 (1st Cir.1992).

- An expert may testify regardless of a lack of personal knowledge. Rule 602.

- A witness may testify to an inference that is fairly drawn from the witness's personal knowledge. *United States v. Flores-Rivera*, 787 F.3d 1, 28 (1st Cir.2015).

- Testimony prefaced by "I believe," "I'm not sure but," etc. is admissible despite the witness's lack of certainty about the matter. E.g., *M.B.A.F.B. Fed. Credit Union v. Cumis Ins. Soc., Inc.*, 681 F.2d 930, 932 (4th Cir.1982).

- Rephrase the question, establishing witness's personal knowledge.

69. Photograph Inflammatory and Unfairly Prejudicial (Rule 403)

Your honor, I object. The photographs are highly inflammatory and unnecessary to prove facts at issue. They are unfairly prejudicial and thus excluded by Rule 403.

Authority:

Rule 403 provides that although relevant, evidence may be excluded if its probative value is substantially outweighed by the danger of unfair prejudice.

Responses:

- Even though gruesome, photographs that depict relevant facts are generally admitted. E.g., *United States v. McRae*, 593 F.2d 700, 707 (5th Cir.1979) (photographs of deceased and death scene).

- The probative value of the evidence outweighs the danger of prejudice. The rule 403 "balance should be struck in favor of admission." *United States v. Dennis*, 625 F.2d 782, 797 (8th Cir.1980). Rule 403 is "an extraordinary remedy to be used sparingly." *United States v. Meester*, 762 F.2d 867, 875 (11th Cir.1985).

70. Photograph, Motion Picture, Videotape, or Sound Recording Not Authenticated (Rule 901)

Your honor, I object. The photograph [motion picture, videotape, or sound recording] has not been properly authenticated.

Authority:

Rule 901 states, "To satisfy the requirement of authenticating or identifying an item of evidence, the proponent must produce evidence sufficient to support a finding that the item is what the proponent claims it is."

Responses (as applicable):

- A photograph may generally be authenticated by testimony that it is a fair and accurate representation of the actual scene or event. It is not necessary that the photographer or any person who saw the making of the photograph testify. United States v. Clayton, 643 F.2d 1071, 1074 (5th Cir.1981).

- A motion picture or videotape may be authenticated on the same foundation as a still photograph. Saturn Mfg., Inc. v. Williams Patent Crusher & Pulverizer Co., 713 F.2d 1347, 1357 (8th Cir.1983).

- A sound recording may be authenticated by a similar foundation, establishing the accuracy of the recording and identifying the speakers. United States v. Lance, 853 F.2d 1177, 1181 (5th Cir.1988); United States v. Jones, 730 F.2d 593, 597 (10th Cir.1984).

71. Pleas and Plea Bargaining (Rule 410)

Your honor, I object. Rule 410 excludes evidence of plea bargains and plea negotiations.

Authority:

Rule 410 excludes evidence that an accused entered a plea of guilty that was later withdrawn or a plea of *nolo contendere* and of statements made in connection with plea proceedings regarding such pleas.

Rule 410 also excludes evidence of any statement made during plea negotiations unless the negotiations resulted in an unwithdrawn guilty plea.

Responses (as applicable):

- Rule 410 does not exclude statements made to law enforcement officers. United States v. Mangine, 302 F.3d 819, 822 (8th Cir.2002) (statements to sheriff's lieutenant).

- Rule 410 is inapplicable because the accused's statements were made without the intent to negotiate a plea. United States v. Edelmann, 458 F.3d 791, 804–06 (8th Cir.2006); United States v. Hare, 49 F.3d 447, 449–51 (8th Cir.1995).

- Rule 410 does not exclude plea evidence when it is offered against someone other than the party who made the plea. United States v. Dortch, 5 F.3d 1056, 1067 (7th Cir.1993).

- Rule 410 allows the accused who made the plea to be impeached with it if he is not a party to the present action. United States v. Dortch, 5 F.3d 1056, 1067 (7th Cir.1993).

- In accordance with the rule of optional completeness, Rule 410 permits the introduction of statements made in a plea proceeding or plea negotiations. United States v. Doran, 564 F.2d 1176, 1177 (5th Cir.1977).

- Evidence of a defendant's statement is admissible in a criminal proceeding for perjury or false statement if the statement was made by the defendant under oath, on the record and in the presence of counsel.

- The defendant knowingly and voluntarily waived his right to have such statements excluded under Rule 410. United States v. Mezzanatto, 513 U.S. 196, 115 S.Ct. 797 (1995). See United States v. Elbeblawy, 899 F.3d 925, 934 (11th Cir.2018) (extent of the waiver depends on the language of the proffer or plea agreement).

72. Prejudicial Effect Outweighs Probative Value (Rule 403)

Your honor, I object. The probative value of this [testimony] [exhibit], if any, is substantially outweighed by the danger of unfair prejudice.

Authority:

Rule 403 provides that although relevant, evidence may be excluded if its probative value is substantially outweighed by the danger of unfair prejudice.

Responses (as applicable):

- The probative value of the evidence outweighs the danger of prejudice.

- The rule 403 "balance should be struck in favor of admission." United States v. Dennis, 625 F.2d 782, 797 (8th Cir.1980). Rule 403 is "an extraordinary remedy to be used sparingly." United States v. Meester, 762 F.2d 867, 875 (11th Cir.1985).

- Rule 403 "does not offer protection against evidence that is merely prejudicial, in the sense of being detrimental to a party's case. Rather, the rule only protects against evidence that is *unfairly* prejudicial." Carter v. Hewitt, 617 F.2d 961, 972 (3d Cir.1980). Accord, United States v. Skillman, 922 F.2d 1370, 1374 (9th Cir.1990).

- "Rule 403 does not provide a shield for defendants who engage in outrageous acts, permitting only the crimes of Caspar Milquetoasts to be described fully to a jury. It does not generally require the government to sanitize its case, to deflate its witnesses' testimony, or to tell its story in a monotone." United States v. Gartmon, 146 F.3d 1015, 1021 (D.C.Cir.1998).

- "Weighing probative value against unfair prejudice under F.R.Evid. 403 means probative value with respect to a material fact if the evidence is believed, not the degree the court finds it believable." Bowden v. McKenna, 600 F.2d 282, 284–85 (1st Cir.1979). Accord, Ballou v. Henri Studios, Inc., 656 F.2d 1147, 1154 (5th Cir.1981).

73. Prior Consistent Statement Not Admissible to Rehabilitate (Rule 613)

Your honor, I object. Counsel may not rehabilitate a witness by offering evidence of her prior consistent statement.

Authority:

A witness who has been impeached with a prior inconsistent statement may rehabilitate herself by effectively explaining away the inconsistency or denying that the statement was made. Ordinarily, however, a witness may not be rehabilitated simply by showing that she made a prior consistent statement. Although prior consistent statements are no longer limited to those offered to rebut an "express or implied charge" that the witness "recently fabricated" her testimony or "acted from a recent improper influence or motive in so testifying," Rule 801(d)(1)(B)(i), the prior consistent statement must still tend to rehabilitate the witness's credibility in a way that is not dependent on the truth of the prior statement.

A prior consistent statement offered to rebut "an express or implied charge" of recent fabrication or that the witness "acted from recent improper influence or motive" must have been made before the alleged improper influence or motive to fabricate arose. Tome v. United States, 513 U.S. 150, 115 S.Ct. 696 (1995).

Responses (as applicable):

- Counsel has implicitly accused the witness of making up her story. This prior statement was made before her alleged motive to fabricate arose.

- The witness's prior statement is not being offered to rehabilitate her. It is independently admissible under [insert applicable hearsay exception].

74. Prior Inconsistent Statement; Extrinsic Evidence Inadmissible (Rule 613(b))

Your honor, I object. Counsel is offering extrinsic evidence to prove that a witness made a prior inconsistent statement without affording the witness an opportunity to explain or deny the statement.

Authority:

Although an impeaching party may offer extrinsic proof of a witness's prior inconsistent statement without first questioning the witness about it, Rule 613(b) still requires that (a) the witness must be afforded the opportunity to explain or deny the statement and (b) opposing counsel must be afforded the opportunity to question the witness about it.

Moreover, extrinsic evidence of a prior inconsistent statement is inadmissible if the inconsistency relates to a collateral matter. United States v. Torres-Correa, 23 F.4th 129, 135–36 (1st Cir.2022).

Responses (as applicable):

- The witness is available to be recalled. United States v. Young, 86 F.3d 944, 949 (9th Cir.1996).

- The court may, in the interests of justice, admit the extrinsic proof even if the witness is not available to be recalled. See Wammock v. Celotex Corp., 793 F.2d 1518, 1523–23 (11th Cir.1986).

- The statement bears on a substantive issue in the case; it is not collateral.

75. Prior Inconsistent Statement; Must Disclose Contents of Writing (Rule 613)

Your honor, I object. Counsel is attempting to impeach the witness with her prior written statement without first disclosing its contents to me.

Authority:

Although Rule 613(a) does not require a cross-examiner to show the witness her written inconsistent statement before examining her about it, it still provides that on request the statement must be shown or its contents disclosed to opposing counsel. United States v. Lawson, 683 F.2d 688, 694 (2d Cir.1982).

Response (as applicable):

- Counsel already has a copy of the written statement.

- Disclose the contents.

76. Privilege, Comment on or Adverse Inference From Invocation (Proposed Rule 513)

Your honor, I object. The invocation of a constitutionally or statutorily recognized privilege cannot ever be burdened by a comment or adverse inference.

Authority:

It is ordinarily improper for counsel or the court to comment upon a claim of privilege. Similarly, no adverse inference may be drawn from a claim of privilege. Griffin v. California, 380 U.S. 609, 85 S.Ct. 1229 (1965).

To the extent practicable, proceedings should be conducted to allow privilege claims to be made out of the jury's presence. United States v. Victor, 973 F.2d 975, 978 (1st Cir.1992) (witness's invocation of privilege against self-incrimination).

Responses (as applicable):

- The invocation of a privilege in a civil case is a proper subject for comment, and an adverse inference may be drawn therefrom. Baxter v. Palmigiano, 425 U.S. 308, 318, 96 S.Ct. 1551, 1558 (1976) (party's invocation); In re High Fructose Corn Syrup Antitrust Litigation, 295 F.3d 651, 663–64 (7th Cir.2002) (non-party's invocation).

77. Privileged (Rules 501–502; Proposed Rules 502–513)

Your honor, I object. The question is calling for privileged information.

Authority:

Rule 501 provides that, except as otherwise provided by the Constitution, federal statutes, or other rules prescribed by the Supreme Court, privileges are to be determined by the principles of the common law as interpreted by the federal courts in light of reason and experience. Rule 502 governs certain waiver questions regarding the attorney-client privilege and work-product protection.

In civil cases, state privilege law applies with respect to an element of a claim or defense as to which state substantive law governs.

The requirements for the traditional common-law privileges are discussed in the Authors' Comments to Proposed Rules 502–513. In addition, the most widely asserted statutory privileges are cross-referenced following the Authors' Comments to Rule 501 and are reproduced in Chapter 3.

Responses (as applicable):

- The privilege asserted is not one created by constitution, statute, or court rule, or recognized by common law. Rule 501.

- Privileges are to be strictly construed. Trammel v. United States, 445 U.S. 40, 100 S.Ct. 906 (1980).

- The requirements of the asserted privilege have not been met. See Authors' Comments to Proposed Rules 502–510.

- The privilege is inapplicable because of the existence of an exception to the privilege. See Authors' Comments to Proposed Rules 502–510.

- The privilege has been waived through the voluntary disclosure of the communication to others. See Authors' Comments to Proposed Rule 511.

- The privilege is not being asserted by the holder or another person entitled to assert it on behalf of the holder. See Authors' Comments to Proposed Rules 502–511.

78. Privileged Attorney-Client Communication (Rule 502; Proposed Rule 503)

Your honor, I object. The question concerns matters privileged under the attorney-client privilege.

Authority:

The attorney-client privilege covers confidential communications between an attorney and client, allowing the client both to refuse to disclose and to prevent others from disclosing such communications. United States v. United Shoe Machinery Corp., 89 F.Supp. 357, 358–59 (D.Mass.1950).

Responses (as applicable):

- The communication at issue was not between a client (or client's representative) and his lawyer (or lawyer's representative). Matter of Fischel, 557 F.2d 209, 211 (9th Cir.1977).

- The communication was not made confidentially. United States v. Lopez, 777 F.2d 543, 552 (10th Cir.1985) (communication made in presence of third party); United States v. Oloyede, 982 F.2d 133, 141 (4th Cir.1992) (communication intended to be disclosed).

- The communication was not made for the purpose of facilitating the rendition of professional legal services. United States v. Williams, 698 F.3d 374, 379–80 (7th Cir.2012) (lawyer may testify that imprisoned client asked lawyer to forward sealed letter to client's cousin asking cousin to fabricate alibi); United States v. Alexander, 287 F.3d 811, 816–17 (9th Cir.2002) (client's threats to commit violent acts against lawyer and others not privileged); Antoine v. Atlas Turner, Inc., 66 F.3d 105, 109–10 (6th Cir.1995) (whether attorney forwarded default judgments to client is not privileged).

- The attorney was acting in a nonlegal capacity. United States v. Spencer, 700 F.3d 317, 320–21 (8th Cir.2012) (privilege not applicable to communications made for preparation of tax return; preparer, who was lawyer, provided no legal advice and was practicing as a CPA); In re Grand Jury Subpoena (Mr. S.), 662 F.3d 65, 72 (1st Cir.2011) (documents created by attorney to facilitate consummation of real estate transaction not privileged); In re Lindsey, 158 F.3d 1263, 1270 (D.C.Cir.1998) (political, strategic or policy advice not privileged).

- The privilege protects only communications and does not protect the underlying facts contained in an attorney-client communication. Upjohn Co. v. United States, 449 U.S. 383, 395–96, 101 S.Ct. 677, 685–86 (1981).

- The privilege does not protect the identity of a client, In re Grand Jury Subpoena, 204 F.3d 516, 520 (4th Cir.2000); fee arrangements, Montgomery County v. Microvote Corp., 175 F.3d 296, 304 (3d Cir.1999); or the general purpose of the work performed; United States v. Legal Services for New York City, 249 F.3d 1077, 1081–82 (D.C.Cir.2001).

- The communication falls within one of the exceptions to the attorney-client privilege found in Proposed Rule 503(d). No privilege exists:

  - If the lawyer's services were knowingly sought or obtained to further a criminal or fraudulent endeavor. United States v. Zolin, 491 U.S. 554, 109 S.Ct. 2619 (1989).

  - As to communications relevant to a dispute between two or more clients who jointly consulted an attorney on a matter of common interest if the communications were made by any of the clients to the lawyer retained or consulted in common. F.D.I.C. v. Ogden Corp., 202 F.3d 454, 461–64 (1st Cir.2000).

  - For other exceptions, see the Authors' Comments to Proposed Rule 503.

79. Privileged; Clergy-Communicant Privilege (Proposed Rule 506)

Your honor, I object. The question calls for a privileged communication made to a member of the clergy.

Authority:

Federal courts (and Proposed Rule 506) recognize a privilege for confidential communications made to a clergyman in his capacity as a spiritual adviser. See In re Grand Jury Investigation, 918 F.2d 374 (3d Cir.1990).

Responses (as applicable):

- The communication was not made to the clergyman in his capacity as a spiritual advisor. Cox v. Miller, 296 F.3d 89, 111 (2d Cir.2002); United States v. Dube, 820 F.2d 886, 889–90 (7th Cir.1987).

- The communication was not made confidentially. In re Grand Jury Investigation, 918 F.2d 374, 385–88 (3d Cir.1990).

80. Privileged Marital Communication (Proposed Rule 505)

Your honor, I object. The proposed testimony of the witness concerns a privileged communication made to her by her husband during their marriage.

Authority:

The marital communication privilege protects against the disclosure of confidential communications made between spouses during their marriage. United States v. White, 974 F.2d 1135, 1138 (9th Cir.1992).

Responses (as applicable):

- The privilege covers only communications, i.e., information conveyed verbally or by acts intended as a substitute for verbal communication. Therefore, observations by a person of his or her spouse's conduct are not protected. United States v. Estes, 793 F.2d 465, 466–67 (2d Cir.1986) (husband's actions in counting, hiding and laundering money not confidential communications).

- The communication is not confidential because it was made in the presence of another person as to whom no other communication privilege attaches, United States v. Taylor, 92 F.3d 1313, 1331–32 (2d Cir.1996), or where the spouses had no expectation of confidentiality. United States v. Madoch, 149 F.3d 596, 602 (7th Cir.1998).

- There is an exception to the privilege as to communications concerning present or future crimes in which both spouses are participants. United States v. Vo, 413 F.3d 1010, 1017 (9th Cir.2005); United States v. Westmoreland, 312 F.3d 302, 308–09 (7th Cir.2002); United States v. Bey, 188 F.3d 1, 4–6 (1st Cir.1999); United States v. Ramirez, 145 F.3d 345, 355–56 (5th Cir.1998).

- There is an exception to the privilege when the communication relates to a crime against the spouse or the child of a spouse. United States v. White Owl, 39 F.4th 527 (8th Cir.2022); United States v. Underwood, 859 F.3d 386, 390–92 (6th Cir.2017).

- The communication was made when the parties' marriage was no longer viable. United States v. Singleton, 260 F.3d 1295, 1300 (11th Cir.2001) ("the privilege is not available when the parties are permanently separated").

81. Privileged; Marital Testimonial Privilege (Proposed Rule 505)

Your honor, I object. The witness is the accused's spouse and therefore cannot be compelled to testify against him.

Authority:

In criminal cases, the testimonial privilege gives an accused's spouse the right to refuse to testify against the accused. Trammel v. United States, 445 U.S. 40, 100 S.Ct. 906 (1980).

Responses (as applicable):

- The witness is testifying voluntarily. The privilege not to testify against a spouse is held by the witness spouse, not the defendant spouse. Trammel v. United States, 445 U.S. 40, 100 S.Ct. 906 (1980).

- The marital testimonial privilege applies only if the witness and the defendant have a viable marriage at the time of testimony. No such viable marriage exists where:

  - The witness and the defendant were never legally married. United States v. Hamilton, 19 F.3d 350, 354 (7th Cir.1994) (defendant's "wife" had not been legally divorced from first husband).

  - The witness and the defendant are separated. United States v. Roberson, 859 F.2d 1376, 1381 (9th Cir.1988).

- The witness spouse may be compelled to testify concerning matters that occurred before the marriage. United States v. Clark, 712 F.2d 299, 302 (7th Cir.1983).

- The witness spouse may be compelled to testify when the testimony relates to the abuse of the spouse or a minor child within the household. United States v. Castillo, 140 F.3d 874, 884–85 (10th Cir.1998) (child); Wyatt v. United States, 362 U.S. 525, 80 S.Ct. 901 (1960) (Mann Act violation). But see United States v. Jarvison, 409 F.3d 1221, 1231–32 (10th Cir.2005) (declining to recognize exception).

- The witness spouse may be compelled to testify when the spouses were joint participants in the crime. United States v. Clark, 712 F.2d 299, 301 (7th Cir.1983). But see United States v. Pineda-Mateo, 905 F.3d 13 (1st Cir.2018) (rejecting exception); In re Grand Jury Subpoena United States, 755 F.2d 1022 (2d Cir.1985) (same), judgment vac'd on other grounds, 475 U.S. 133, 106 S.Ct. 1253 (1986); Appeal of Malfitano, 633

F.2d 276, 278–80 (3d Cir.1980) (same); United States v. Ramos-Osequera, 120 F.3d 1028, 1042 (9th Cir.1997) (same).

- The testimonial privilege does not apply in civil cases. Civil cases recognize a spousal privilege only for confidential communications made during marriage.

- Although the proposed testimony concerns a communication, the witness and the defendant were not married at the time the communication was made.

82. Privileged Physician-Patient Communication (Proposed Rule 504)

Your honor, I object. The question calls for information that is privileged under the physician-patient privilege.

Authority:

Many states recognize a privilege for confidential communications between a patient and physician. Therefore, the federal courts should acknowledge that the principles of the common law, as interpreted in the light of reason and experience, recognize the existence of such a privilege. Jaffee v. Redmond, 518 U.S. 1, 116 S.Ct. 1923 (1996) (looking to state law developments for guidance as to interpretation of psychotherapist-patient privilege); Trammel v. United States, 445 U.S. 40, 100 S.Ct. 906 (1980) (same as to marital privilege). In addition, some federal statutes provide for the confidentiality of certain treatment records.

Responses (as applicable):

- The federal courts unanimously reject a physician-patient privilege. Gilbreath v. Guadalupe Hospital Foundation, 5 F.3d 785, 791 (5th Cir.1993).

- The privilege protects communications only when the patient is seeking or receiving diagnosis or treatment. See United States v. Romo, 413 F.3d 1044, 1046–49 (9th Cir.2005).

- The Supreme Court distinguished ordinary medical care from psychotherapy in Jaffee v. Redmond, 518 U.S. 1, 116 S.Ct. 1923 (1996).

83. Privileged Psychotherapist-Patient Communication (Proposed Rule 504)

Your honor, I object. The proposed testimony concerns a privileged psychotherapist-patient communication.

Authority:

A privilege exists for communications between a patient and a psychiatrist, psychologist, or licensed social worker if made for the purpose of giving or receiving psychotherapy. Jaffee v. Redmond, 518 U.S. 1, 116 S.Ct. 1923 (1996). In addition, several federal statutes provide for confidentiality of certain treatment records.

Responses (as applicable):

- The privilege protects communications only when the patient is seeking or receiving diagnosis or treatment. See United States v. Bolander, 722 F.3d 199, 223 (4th Cir.2013) (communications for obtaining mental condition evaluation rather than diagnosis or treatment not privileged); United States v. Ghane, 673 F.3d 771, 781–84 (8th Cir.2012) (statements during ER intake not privileged).

- The communication falls within an exception to the privilege. E.g., In re Grand Jury Proceedings (Gregory P. Violette), 183 F.3d 71 (1st Cir.1999) (crime-fraud exception); Dixon v. City of Lawton, Oklahoma, 898 F.2d 1443, 1450–51 (10th Cir.1990) (patient-litigant exception); United States v. Glass, 133 F.3d 1356 (10th Cir.1998) (dangerous-patient exception). But see United States v. Ghane, 673 F.3d 771, 784–86 (8th Cir.2012) (rejecting dangerous-patient exception); United States v. Chase, 340 F.3d 978 (9th Cir.2003) (same); United States v. Hayes, 227 F.3d 578 (6th Cir.2000).

84. Privileged Required Report (Proposed Rule 502)

Your honor, I object. Counsel is attempting to introduce a document that is part of a privileged required report.

Authority:

Many statutes that require reports to be made to governmental agencies also provide that the maker of such a report may prevent its disclosure and/or that the public officer or agency to whom the report was made may refuse to disclose it. See the list of statutes cross-referenced following the Authors' Comments to Proposed Rule 502.

Response:

- Not all required reports are privileged. Although this document is a required report, the statute requiring that such reports be made does not give the maker of the report a privilege to prevent its disclosure.

85. Religious Belief or Opinion (Rule 610)

Your honor, I object. Counsel is making an impermissible inquiry into the witness's religious beliefs.

Authority:

Rule 610 bars evidence of a witness's religious beliefs or opinions when offered to attack or support the witness's credibility.

Responses (as applicable):

- The question is not designed to show the witness's untruthful character. It is aimed at demonstrating the witness's bias. Firemen's Fund Ins. Co. v. Thien, 63 F.3d 754, 760–61 (8th Cir.1995); United States v. Teicher, 987 F.2d 112, 118 (2d Cir.1993).
- The witness's religious beliefs are relevant to the merits of the action. United States v. Beasley, 72 F.3d 1518, 1527 (11th Cir.1996); Mauldin v. Upjohn Co., 697 F.2d 644, 649 (5th Cir.1983).

86. Scientific Evidence Not Admissible (Rule 702)

Your honor, I object. My opponent is offering expert testimony based on scientific [tests] [theories] that are not scientifically reliable and that will not assist the fact finder.

Authority:

Daubert v. Merrell Dow Pharmaceuticals, Inc., 509 U.S. 579, 113 S.Ct. 2786 (1993), holds that Rule 702, and not the *Frye* general acceptance test, provides the standard for judging the admissibility of scientific evidence. Rule 702 mandates that scientific evidence is admissible only when it is scientifically reliable and will assist the fact finder. Id.

Moreover, as *Daubert* points out, scientific evidence may be excluded pursuant to Rule 403 because of its tendency to confuse the jury.

Responses (as applicable):

- The testimony is admissible applying the factors set forth in *Daubert* and its progeny:
  - The underlying theory [technique] has or can be tested.
  - The theory [technique] has been subjected to peer review and publication.
  - The theory's [technique's] known or potential rate of error is low and controllable.
  - The theory [technique] has been widely, if not generally, accepted. Daubert v. Merrell Dow Pharmaceuticals, Inc., 509 U.S. 579, 113 S.Ct. 2786 (1993).
  - Whether the expert testimony is based on research the expert has conducted independent of the litigation. Daubert v. Merrell Dow Pharmaceuticals, Inc., 43 F.3d 1311, 1317 (9th Cir.1995).
- The validity of the test or theory has already been accepted and the court may take judicial notice of such. Daubert v. Merrell Dow Pharmaceuticals, Inc., 509 U.S. 579, 113 S.Ct. 2786 (1993).

87. Sexual Conduct or Predisposition of Alleged Victim of Sexual Misconduct; Civil Case (Rule 412)

Your honor, I object. Evidence of other sexual behavior or the sexual predisposition of an alleged victim of sexual misconduct is not admissible.

Authority:

Rule 412(a) excludes in a civil proceeding involving alleged sexual misconduct any evidence (1) that an alleged victim engaged in other sexual behavior or (2) of an alleged victim's sexual predisposition. However, Rule 412(b)(2) provides that such evidence may be admissible if its probative value substantially outweighs the danger of harm to any victim and of unfair prejudice to any party.

Moreover, Rule 412(c) requires that such evidence is admissible only where 14-days' notice has been given and an in camera hearing has been held.

Responses (as applicable):

- The probative value of the evidence substantially outweighs the danger of unfair prejudice to any party and of harm to the alleged victim. Rule 412(b)(2). See Stampf v. Long Island R. Co., 761 F.3d 192, 203 (2d Cir.2014).
- The alleged victim has placed his (her) reputation in controversy. Rule 412(b)(2).
- Prior false accusations by the alleged victim are not considered instances of previous sexual conduct. United States v. Bartlett, 856 F.2d 1071, 1087–89 (8th Cir.1988).
- The sexual behavior was intrinsic to the alleged sexual misconduct in issue and so is not "other" sexual behavior. Advisory Committee's Note.

88. Sexual Conduct or Predisposition of Alleged Victim of Sexual Misconduct; Criminal Case (Rule 412)

Your honor, I object. Evidence of other sexual behavior or the sexual predisposition of an alleged victim of sexual misconduct is not admissible.

Authority:

Rule 412(a) excludes in a criminal proceeding involving alleged sexual misconduct any evidence that (1) an alleged victim of sexual misconduct engaged in other sexual behavior or (2) of an alleged victim's sexual predisposition. Only three narrow exceptions apply, as set forth in Rule 412(b)(1).

Moreover, Rule 412(c) requires that such evidence is admissible only where 14-days' notice has been given and an in camera hearing has been held.

Responses (as applicable):

- Specific instance evidence is admissible if offered to prove that someone other than the accused was the source of semen, injury, or other physical evidence. Rule 412(b)(1)(A); United States v. Begay, 937 F.2d 515, 519–23 (10th Cir.1991).

- Evidence of the alleged victim's sexual conduct with the accused may be offered to prove consent. Rule 412(b)(1)(B); United States v. Saunders, 943 F.2d 388, 390–91 (4th Cir.1991).

- Exclusion of the evidence would violate the accused's constitutional rights. Rule 412(b)(1)(C); Olden v. Kentucky, 488 U.S. 227, 109 S.Ct. 480 (1988).

- Prior false accusations by the alleged victim are not considered instances of sexual conduct. United States v. Bartlett, 856 F.2d 1071, 1087–89 (8th Cir.1988).

- The sexual behavior was intrinsic to the alleged sexual misconduct in issue and so is not "other" sexual behavior. Advisory Committee's Note to Rule 412.

89. Speculation, Question Calls for (Rules 602, 701 and 702)

Your honor, I object. The question calls for the witness to speculate as to what happened.

Authority:

Questions inviting the witness to speculate or guess as to what occurred or caused an event may either run afoul of the personal knowledge requirement (Rules 602 and 701) or constitute an impermissible attempt to elicit an opinion beyond the scope of the witness's expertise (Rule 702). E.g., United States v. Stewart, 104 F.3d 1377, 1383–84 (D.C.Cir.1997); Beissel v. Pittsburgh & Lake Erie R. Co., 801 F.2d 143, 151 (3d Cir.1986).

Responses (as applicable):

- Rephrase the question, establishing the witness's personal knowledge.

- Testimony prefaced by "I believe," "I'm not sure but," etc. is admissible despite the witness's lack of certainty about the matter. E.g., M.B.A.F.B. Fed. Credit Union v. Cumis Ins. Soc., 681 F.2d 930, 932 (4th Cir.1982).

- Experts do not have to be absolutely certain in their conclusions, and courts have rejected a rigid "reasonable medical certainty" threshold test. Stutzman v. CRST, Inc., 997 F.2d 291, 294–95 (7th Cir.1993).

90. Subsequent Remedial Measure (Rule 407)

Your honor, I object. Counsel is offering evidence of a subsequent remedial measure in violation of Rule 407.

Authority:

Rule 407 excludes evidence of a party's subsequent remedial measures as proof of the party's negligence or culpable conduct, the existence of a defect, or the need for a warning or instruction. A subsequent remedial measure is any action that would have made the occurrence of the particular accident or event less likely had it been taken prior to the accident or event. This includes repairs, design changes, policy changes, erection of warning signs, etc.

Responses (as applicable):

- The evidence is admissible because the remedial measure was taken before the accident or event in question occurred. Traylor v. Husqvarna Motor, 988 F.2d 729, 733 (7th Cir.1993).

- The evidence is admissible because the remedial measure was taken by a third party. Millennium Partners, L.P. v. Colmar Storage, LLC, 494 F.3d 1293, 1302–03 (11th Cir.2007).

- The evidence is admissible because the action taken was not a remedial measure. E.g., Brazos River Authority v. GE Ionics, Inc., 469 F.3d 416, 430–31 (5th Cir.2006) (post-accident analysis).

- The evidence is admissible because it is being offered to show something other than negligence, culpable conduct, the existence of a defect, or the need for a warning or instruction. It is being offered to prove [select appropriate use, e.g., ownership, control, prior condition, or feasibility]. Clausen v. Sea-3, Inc., 21 F.3d 1181, 1189–92 (1st Cir.1994) (control); Abernathy v. Eastern Illinois R. Co., 940 F.3d 982, 992–94 (7th Cir.2019) (feasibility).

- The evidence is admissible because it is being offered for impeachment purposes. Muzyka v. Remington Arms Co., Inc., 774 F.2d 1309 (5th Cir.1985).

91. Summary Not Admissible (Rule 1006)

Your honor, I object. The summary does not meet the requirements of Rule 1006, because [the summarized originals have not all been shown to be admissible] [the summary has not been shown to be accurate] [the writings, recordings, or photographs are not so voluminous that they cannot conveniently be examined in court] [the originals, or duplicates, were not made available to us at a reasonable time and place].

Authority:

Rule 1006 provides that the contents of voluminous writings, recordings, or photographs which cannot conveniently be examined in court may be presented in the form of a chart, summary, or calculation, provided that the originals, or duplicates, are made available for examination or copying, or both, by other parties at reasonable time and place.

The underlying materials must be admissible. United States v. Pelullo, 964 F.2d 193, 204 (3d Cir.1992).

A proper foundation must establish the admissibility of the underlying materials and the accuracy of the summary. Needham v. White Laboratories, Inc., 639 F.2d 394, 403 (7th Cir.1981).

Responses (as applicable):

- The underlying materials need not be introduced in evidence, and the rule provides that whether to require that they be produced in court is a matter of the court's discretion. *United States v. Hemphill,* 514 F.3d 1350, 1359 (D.C. Cir.2008); *United States v. Bakker,* 925 F.2d 728, 736 (4th Cir.1991); *United States v. Strissel,* 920 F.2d 1162, 1163 (4th Cir.1990).

- The rule requires that the underlying material, not the summary itself, be made available to the adverse party before trial. *Coates v. Johnson & Johnson,* 756 F.2d 524, 549–50 (7th Cir.1985). But see *Air Safety, Inc. v. Roman Catholic Archbishop of Boston,* 94 F.3d 1, 7 (1st Cir.1996).

- "Rule 1006 does not require that it be literally impossible to examine all the underlying records, but only that in-court examination would be an inconvenience." *United States v. Possick,* 849 F.2d 332, 339 (8th Cir.1988). In deciding whether to admit summaries, "district courts are advised to carefully weigh the volume and complexity of the materials. These two factors have an inversely proportionate relationship: as either the volume or complexity increases, relatively less is required of the other factor." *United States v. Appolon,* 695 F.3d 44, 62 (1st Cir.2012).

- The "summary" permitted by the rule may be either a tangible exhibit or testimony. *Nichols v. Upjohn Co.,* 610 F.2d 293, 293–94 (5th Cir.1980) (oral testimony of physician summarizing contents of 94,000 page F.D.A. new drug application). Abridged recordings, resulting from edited voluminous originals, have been received under this rule. *United States v. Segines,* 17 F.3d 847, 853–54 (6th Cir.1994) ("composite tape" of selected conversations taped during wiretap).

- Rule 1006, with its dual requirements of establishing admissibility of, and providing opponent with an opportunity for inspection of, underlying materials, only applies to a summary that is created for use at trial. A business record made and kept in the regular course of business, properly qualified according to the requirements of Rule 803(6), is not subject to these two Rule 1006 requirements, even though it may in fact be a "summary" of some underlying materials. *United States v. Draiman,* 784 F.2d 248, 256 n. 6 (7th Cir.1986).

92. Truthfulness of Another's Testimony (Rules 608, 701 and 702)

Your honor, I object. The witness is being asked to testify that she believes another witness is testifying truthfully [untruthfully].

Authority:

Although Rule 608 permits a witness to testify as to her opinion concerning another witness's character for truthfulness [untruthfulness], it does not permit a witness to express her opinion that another witness is testifying truthfully [untruthfully]. *United States v. Harris,* 471 F.3d 507, 511 (3d Cir.2006).

Neither does Rule 701 (lay opinions) or Rule 702 (expert opinions) allow a witness to give an opinion that another witness is testifying truthfully [untruthfully] or belongs to a class of persons who testify truthfully [untruthfully]. *United States v. Whitted,* 11 F.3d 782, 785–86 (8th Cir.1993).

Responses (as applicable):

- The witness is not testifying that another witness is telling the truth [lying], but is merely providing specialized information that may help the jury assess the strength of a party's case (e.g., that certain behaviors are commonly associated with child sexual abuse). *United States v. Charley,* 189 F.3d 1251, 1266–68 (10th Cir.1999); *United States v. Johns,* 15 F.3d 740, 743 (8th Cir.1994).

- The witness is not giving an opinion about the truth [falsity] of another witness's testimony, but is merely providing specialized information that may explain why the other witness acted in a certain way (e.g., battered woman's syndrome). United States v. Whitetail, 956 F.2d 857, 859 (8th Cir.1992).

93. Ultimate Issue (Rule 704)

Your honor, I object. The witness is testifying as to an ultimate issue.

Authority:

Although Rule 704(a) provides that otherwise admissible opinion testimony is not objectionable merely because it reaches an ultimate issue, Rule 704(b) allows such an objection when an expert is testifying as to an accused's mental state or condition and seeks to offer an opinion as to whether the accused possessed a mental state or condition that constitutes an element of (a) the crime charged or (b) a defense to the crime charged. United States v. Bennett, 161 F.3d 171, 182–85 (3d Cir.1998).

When a witness, other than an expert covered by Rule 704(b), seeks to testify as to an ultimate issue, objection should be made to such testimony on the grounds that it is not "otherwise admissible" under Rules 701–703. United States v. Barile, 286 F.3d 749, 759–60 (4th Cir.2002).

Responses (as applicable):

- A witness may testify that the accused suffers or does not suffer from a mental disease or defect and may describe the characteristics and effects of such a disease or defect. United States v. Dixon, 185 F.3d 393, 397–402 (5th Cir.1999), appeal after remand 273 F.3d 636 (5th Cir.2001); United States v. Thigpen, 4 F.3d 1573, 1579–80 (11th Cir.1993).

- Rule 704(b) does not apply to experts who are not mental health professionals. See United States v. Gastiaburo, 16 F.3d 582, 588 (4th Cir.1994); United States v. Richard, 969 F.2d 849, 855 n.6 (10th Cir.1992). But see United States v. Mancillas, 183 F.3d 682, 704–06 (7th Cir.1999); United States v. Smart, 98 F.3d 1379, 1388 (D.C.Cir.1996) (most circuits reject this argument); United States v. Valle, 72 F.3d 210, 215–16 (1st Cir.1995).

- The witness is testifying as a lay witness and Rule 704(b) applies only to experts.

- [For testimony not covered by Rule 704(b)]: The opinion is otherwise admissible because the witness discussed the facts underlying the conclusion and did not simply make conclusory assertions. Fiataruolo v. United States, 8 F.3d 930, 941–42 (2d Cir.1993).

- [For testimony not covered by Rule 704(b)]: The opinion is otherwise admissible because the witness is unable to convey the information in the form of specific facts. E.g., United States v. Yazzie, 976 F.2d 1252, 1255–56 (9th Cir.1992).

- [For testimony not covered by Rule 704(b)]: The opinion is otherwise admissible because the witness used the legal term as a factual rather than a legal conclusion. E.g., Heflin v. Stewart Co., Tenn., 958 F.2d 709, 715 (6th Cir.1992), on reconsideration, 968 F.2d 1 (6th Cir.1992).

- [For testimony not covered by Rule 704(b)]: The trial judge may caution the jury that it is not bound by the witness's opinion. E.g., Karns v. Emerson Electric Co., 817 F.2d 1452, 1459 (10th Cir.1987).

CHAPTER 4

CHECKLISTS AND FOUNDATIONS

Table of Checklists and Foundations

CHECKLISTS AND FOUNDATIONS (CL & F)

1. OFFERING AN EXHIBIT (DOCUMENTARY, REAL, OR ILLUSTRATIVE EVIDENCE) (RULES 401, 402, 901 AND 902)

Checklist

1.   Hand exhibit to reporter or clerk.

2.   Ask reporter or clerk to mark it for identification.

3.   Hand exhibit to opposing counsel for inspection.

4.   Hand exhibit to witness.

5.   Ask witness questions to establish

   a.   Relevance (Rules 401, 402).

   b.   Authentication or identification (Rules 901, 902).

   c.   Hearsay exemption or exception, if necessary (Rules 801, 803, 804).

   d.   Best evidence rule compliance or exemption, if necessary (Rules 1001–1007).

6.   Offer exhibit to court as evidence. If illustrative and not substantive evidence, offer "for illustrative purposes only."

7.   Respond to opposing counsel's objections, if any.

8.   Obtain ruling of court on offer.

9.   If admitted, return exhibit to witness for further testimony, if desired, such as reading or describing exhibit.

10.   If desired, ask court's permission to pass exhibit or copies to jury for their examination.

Example: Document

Action for rent due under a written lease of residential premises. The witness is the plaintiff lessor. The witness has testified that she advertised the premises for lease, that the defendant responded to the advertisement, inspected the premises with her, stated to her that he wished to lease the premises in accordance with the advertised terms, and joined her in her office for the purpose of executing the written lease agreement.

Q: What happened next?

A: Mr. Tenant and I filled out a form lease and signed it.

Q: [Handing document to reporter or clerk] I ask that this be marked Plaintiff's Exhibit number 1 for identification. [Reporter or clerk marks document.] [Hand document or copy to opposing counsel.]

Q: Your Honor, may I approach the witness?

A [Judge]: You may.

Q: [Handing document to witness] Ms. Lessor, I hand you a document marked Plaintiff's Exhibit number 1 for identification. Would you examine it, please? [pause] Have you examined it?

A: Yes.

Q: Do you recognize the document?

A: Yes, I do.

Q: What is it?

A: It is the form lease that Mr. Tenant and I signed on June 1, 2019.

Q: How do you recognize it?

A: Well, it has the address and the apartment number filled in in my handwriting, the dates of the lease, the rent—also in my handwriting—and our signatures and the date we signed it, at the end.

Q: Is this the original document or a copy?

A: It is the original.

Q: Does your signature appear on it?

A: Yes it does. It is at the end, in the space marked "Lessor."

Q: Do you recall signing this document on June 1, 2019?

A: Yes, I do.

Q: Does the defendant's signature also appear on the lease?

A: Yes, in the space marked "Lessee" at the end.

Q: Did you personally observe the defendant sign this particular document?

A: Yes.

Q: Your Honor, I offer in evidence the document marked Plaintiff's Exhibit number 1 for identification as Plaintiff's Exhibit number 1.

A [Judge]: It will be received.

Example: Real Evidence

Product liability action against Manufacturer and Retailer of a Widget, alleging that the Widget was defective in manufacture and as a result of the defect it failed during use and injured Plaintiff, the purchaser. The witness, Plaintiff, has testified that she purchased a Widget from Retailer on June 1.

Q: [Handing item to reporter or clerk] I ask that this be marked Plaintiff's Exhibit number 1 for identification. [Reporter or clerk marks item.] [Hand item to opposing counsel.]

Q: Your Honor, may I approach the witness?

A [Judge]: You may.

Q: [Handing item to witness] Ms. Plaintiff, I hand you an object marked Plaintiff's Exhibit number 1 for identification. Would you examine it, please? [pause] Have you examined it?

A: Yes.

Q: Do you recognize this object?

A: Yes, I do.

Q: What is it?

A: It is the Widget that I purchased from Retailer on June 1, 2018.

Q: How do you recognize it?

A: Well, it has the serial number 6389, which I remember, and I recognize the cracked squidgeon, which cracked in the accident on June 2.

Q: Did you have an opportunity to observe the condition of the Widget immediately after the accident on June 2?

A: Yes.

Q: Do you recall today how the Widget appeared at that time?

A: Yes, I do.

Q: Examining the Widget now, how has its condition changed since that time?

A: Not at all. It appears to be in exactly the same condition as after the accident on June 2.

Q: Your Honor, I offer in evidence the Widget marked Plaintiff's Exhibit number 1 for identification.

A [Judge]: It will be received.

Q: I request permission to hand Plaintiff's Exhibit number 1 to the jurors for their inspection.

A: Granted.

2. CHARACTER EVIDENCE (RULES 404 AND 405)

Comments

Although evidence of a person's character evidence is generally not admissible to prove that the person acted in accordance with his character on a particular occasion, there are some important exceptions to this. Most important is the exception that allows an accused to offer evidence of his good character to prove that he did not commit the crime with which he is charged. The accused may establish his good character only through reputation and opinion witnesses.

Example: Reputation

Defendant is on trial for murder. He calls Williams as his first witness.

Q: Do you know Defendant?

A: Yes.

Q: Have long have you known him?

A: Almost seventeen years.

Q: How did you first come to meet him?

A: We were in the Army together, in basic training.

Q: Have you maintained contact with Defendant since then?

A: Oh, yes. After basic training, I didn't see him for a while, but a few years later I ran into him in a restaurant and discovered we were living in the same neighborhood.

Q: Have you seen Defendant often since then?

A: I'd say a couple of times a month on average.

Q: Do you know other people who know Defendant?

A: Yeah. We know lots of people in common.

Q: Are you familiar with Defendant's reputation in the community in which you live for being a gentle and peaceable man?

A: Yes I am.

Q: What is his reputation for gentleness and peaceableness?

A: It is very good.

Example: Opinion

Defendant is on trial for murder. He calls Williams as his first witness.

Q: Do you know Defendant?

A: Yes.

Q: Have long have you known him?

A: Almost seventeen years.

Q: How did you first come to meet him?

A: We were in the Army together, in basic training.

Q: Have you maintained contact with Defendant since then?

A: Oh, yes. After basic training, I didn't see him for a while, but a few years later I ran into him in a restaurant and discovered we were living in the same neighborhood.

Q: Have you seen Defendant often since then?

A: I'd say a couple of times a month on average.

Q: Do you have an opinion as to whether Defendant is a gentle and peaceable man?

A: Yes I do.

Q: What is your opinion?

A: He is a very gentle, peaceable man.

Example: Cross-Examination of Reputation Witness

Defendant is on trial. Williams has testified for the defense that Defendant's reputation in the community for gentleness and peaceableness is very good. The prosecution cross-examines Williams.

Q: You said on direct examination that you have known Williams for seventeen years?

A: Yes.

Q: And that you are familiar with his reputation in the community for peaceableness?

A: Yes.

Q: Have you heard that on December 16, 2013 Defendant assaulted a woman named Michelle Trafert?

[Defense counsel]: Objection. You can't use specific acts to prove a person's character.

[Prosecutor]: I'm simply trying to test just how familiar this witness is with Defendant's reputation, Your Honor.

[Judge]: Objection overruled. [To the witness] You may answer.

A: Yes.

Q: And have you heard that on March 7, 2017 Defendant was involved in a brawl at the Down and Out Bar and stabbed two people?

A: No, I never heard that.

[NOTE: The prosecutor must have a good-faith belief that these incidents occurred. But even if the witness answers, "No, I never heard that," the prosecutor will not be allowed to offer extrinsic evidence to prove that the incidents occurred.]

Example: Cross-Examination of Opinion Witness

Defendant is on trial. Williams has testified for the defense that, in his opinion, Williams is a very gentle, peaceable man. The prosecution cross-examines Williams.

Q: You said on direct examination that you have known Williams for seventeen years?

A: Yes.

Q: And you said that your opinion is that he is—and I quote—a "very gentle, peaceable man"?

A: Yes.

Q: Did you know that on December 16, 2013, Defendant assaulted a woman named Michelle Trafert?

[Defense counsel]: Objection. You can't use specific acts to prove a person's character.

[Prosecutor]: I'm simply trying to test just how well this witness knows the defendant, Your Honor.

[Judge]: Objection overruled. The witness may answer.

A: Yes.

Q: And did you know that on March 7, 2017 Defendant was involved in a brawl at the Down and Out Bar and stabbed two people?

A: No, I didn't know that.

[NOTE: The prosecutor must have a good-faith belief that these incidents occurred. But even if the witness answers, "No, I didn't know that," the prosecutor will not be allowed to offer extrinsic evidence to prove that the incidents occurred.]

3. IMPEACHMENT (RULES 607–613)

A. The Five Methods of Impeachment

Checklist

1. Bias, prejudice, interest. See Authors' Comments to Rule 607.

2. Prior inconsistent statements. Rule 613.

3. Contradiction of witness's testimony. See Authors' Comments to Rule 607.

4.   Capacity of witness to perceive, remember, relate. See Authors' Comments to Rule 607.

5.   Character of witness for truthfulness.

- Reputation or opinion testimony. Rule 608(a).
- Specific acts not resulting in conviction. Rule 608(b).
- Convictions. Rule 609.

B. Bias, Prejudice, Interest

Comments

The rules do not set forth any particular foundation requirement. Typically, however, this type of impeachment is initiated during cross-examination of the witness. Extrinsic proof may also be allowed, especially if the witness denies the bias. Some courts require that the witness be afforded the opportunity to admit or deny the facts or statements that manifest the bias.

Example: Bias—Cross-Examination

Giles testified against the accused. She is now being cross-examined.

Q: This is not the first time you have worked as a police informant is it?

A: No.

Q: You don't do it for free, do you?

A: No.

Q: How much do you get paid?

A: Fifty bucks a case.

Q: And isn't it true that you get paid only if there's a conviction?

A: Yes.

Q: So if Defendant isn't convicted here, you won't get paid a cent will you?

A: No.

Example: Bias—Extrinsic Evidence

Assume Giles denies that she gets paid only if the prosecution succeeds in winning a conviction. During the defense's case-in-chief, defense counsel calls Officer Sanchez.

Q: Officer Sanchez, are you the person in your department who is in charge of informants?

A: Yes.

Q: Does your department use paid informants?

A: Yes.

Q: Does your department pay informants in cases in which a conviction is not obtained?

A: No.

Q: If Defendant is acquitted in this case, will informant Giles be paid?

A: No, she will not.

C. Prior Inconsistent Statements

Comments

The federal rules, unlike the common law, do not require that counsel lay a foundation before asking a witness about her prior inconsistent statement. Nevertheless, most lawyers will still:

1. Get the witness to commit to her direct examination testimony.

2. Lay the foundation, pinpointing

    a.   the time the prior statement was made;

    b.   the place the prior statement was made; and

    c.   the person to whom the prior statement was made.

3. Ask about the statement.

Example: Prior Inconsistent Statement—Oral

The wife of a drowning victim brings a product liability action against the manufacturer of the life preservers used on the victim's boat. A witness for the plaintiff is being cross-examined.

Q: Now, you testified on direct examination that Joe Stern put his life preserver on when you all first went out in the boat the afternoon of his death?

A: Yes.

Q: And that he took it off because several of the buckles were broken and the vest was flapping in the breeze?

A: Yes.

Q: Do you remember being interviewed by a Coast Guard investigator at your home the day after Joe Stern drowned?

A: Yes.

Q: That investigator's name was Bennett, was it not?

A: Yes.

Q: Did Ms. Bennett explain to you that the purpose of the interview was to enable the Coast Guard to determine the precise cause of Joe Stern's death?

A: That's what Ms. Bennett told me.

Q: Because the Coast Guard collected such information so that it could make appropriate recommendations for safer boating?

A: She said that also.

Q: Now, didn't you tell Ms. Bennett during that interview that Joe Stern did not put on his life preserver that day because he said it would interfere with his tan?

A: Yes, I did.

[Plaintiff's counsel]: I object. Hearsay.

[Defense counsel]: We are offering the witness's statement to the Coast Guard investigator as a prior inconsistent statement for impeachment purposes only, not for its truth.

[Judge]: Objection overruled.

[Plaintiff's counsel]: I request that the court so instruct the jury.

[Judge]: Request granted. [Judge instructs jurors that they are to consider the evidence only insofar as it bears on the witness's credibility and may not use it as substantive evidence.]

Example: Prior Inconsistent Statement—Written

The wife of a drowning victim brings a product liability action against the manufacturer of the life preservers used on the victim's boat. A witness for the plaintiff is being cross-examined.

Q: Now, you testified on direct examination that Joe Stern put his life preserver on when you all first went out in the boat the afternoon of his death?

A: Yes.

Q: And that he took it off because several of the buckles were broken and the vest was flapping in the breeze?

A: Yes.

Q: [Handing document to clerk or reporter.] I ask that this document be marked Defendant's Exhibit number 8 for identification. [Reporter or clerk marks document.] [Hand document or copy to opposing counsel.]

Q: May I approach the witness?

A [Judge]: Yes.

Q: [Handing document to witness.] I hand you what has been marked Defendant's Exhibit number 8 for identification. Do you recognize it?

A: Yes.

Q: Could you please tell the jury what it is?

A: It's a description of the incident that I wrote for the Coast Guard.

Q: It's in your handwriting, isn't it?

A: Yes.

Q: Isn't it true that you wrote this less than twenty-four hours after Joe Stern drowned.

A: Yes.

Q: And isn't it true you wrote this because an investigator for the Coast Guard, a Ms. Bennett, asked you to write down as accurately as possible everything you observed relating to Joe Stern's drowning?

A: Yes.

Q: Isn't it true that on the sixth line of this exhibit you wrote, and I quote, "Joe Stern didn't put on his life preserver. He said that he hated life preservers because they got in the way of getting a good tan."

A: Yes.

Q: And you wrote that less than a day after Joe Stern drowned, didn't you?

A: Yes.

Q: Your honor, I offer Defendant's Exhibit 8 into evidence.

[Plaintiff's counsel]: I object. The witness has admitted making the previous statement. No purpose would be served by admitting the entire document into evidence other than exposing the jury to a lot of inadmissible hearsay.

[Judge]: Objection sustained.

D. Contradiction

Comments

A party may attempt to elicit from a witness testimony that contradicts part or all of the witness's own testimony. But extrinsic evidence may be used to contradict the witness only as to matters that are not deemed to be collateral.

Example

Witness Ed Wilson testified for the prosecution that he saw a man with a large scar on his cheek running out of a liquor store carrying a gun and a large gray sack. He also testified that the driver of a red car had to slam on his brakes to avoid hitting the man with the gray sack. The defendant, who has a large scar on his cheek, has been charged with holding up the liquor store. The defense calls Maria Sanchez to the stand.

Q: Ms. Sanchez, could you please tell the jury where you were at 5:45 on the afternoon of June 12.

A: Yes. I was on the southeast corner of Whitlock and Jordan, waiting for a friend to pick me up.

Q: Did you notice anything unusual at that time?

A: Yes. I heard a gunshot come from across the street and looked up a saw a man running out of the liquor store on the corner.

Q: Was that man carrying anything?

A: Yes. He had a gun and a gray bag or sack of some kind.

Q: Were you able to get a good look at the man?

A: Yes. The street isn't very wide there, so I wasn't very far from him at all.

Q: Were you able to see his face clearly?

A: Yes. I got a real good look at his face.

Q: Did he have any scars or other distinguishing characteristics?

[Prosecution]: Objection. Defendant is offering extrinsic evidence on a collateral matter.

[Judge]: Objection overruled.

A: He definitely didn't have any large scars on his face.

Q: Did you notice anyone who had a scar on his face?

A: Yes. Shortly after the man with the gun and the sack ran out, I saw another man run out of the store, yelling, "Someone call the police." That man had a large scar on his cheek.

Q: Did anything else unusual happen when the man with the gray sack ran out of the store?

A: Yes. When he ran out to cross the street a car had to stop really suddenly to avoid hitting him.

Q: Do you know what color car that was?

[Prosecution]: Objection. Defendant is offering extrinsic evidence on a collateral matter.

[Judge]: Objection sustained.

E. Capacity

Comments

A witness may be attacked by showing that any illness, infirmity, condition, or circumstance may have adversely affected the witness's ability accurately to perceive, recall or relate the event in question. No foundation requirement is prescribed by the rules.

Example

Q: Am I correct that your testimony on direct examination was that you saw the driver of the blue car take his eyes off the road just before the collision?

A: Yes.

Q: The accident took place about 11:00 P.M., didn't it?

A: Yes.

Q: On a country road?

A: Yes.

Q: With no lights?

A: Yes.

Q: And the night was overcast, wasn't it?

A: Yes.

Q: So there was no moonlight?

A: That's right.

Q: And I believe you testified that you were about seventy-five feet away from the blue car?

A: Yes.

Q: Isn't it true that you suffer from night blindness?

A: Yes.

Q: In fact, you have so much difficulty seeing at night that you're not able to drive in the dark, are you?

A: No, I can't.

F. Character

Comments

A witness may be impeached by demonstrating the witness's untruthful nature. This may be done through reputation or opinion testimony, by questioning the witness about specific acts of the witness's own conduct that bear on truthfulness, or by establishing that the witness has been convicted of certain types of crimes.

Example: Character—Reputation

Ellen Hairston testified for the plaintiffs. The defendant is conducting a direct examination of Randy West.

Q: Do you know Ellen Hairston?

A: Yes.

Q: Have long have you known her?

A: About twelve years.

Q: How did you meet her?

A: She lives on the next block. Our kids go to the same school. We've done car pools together, school trips, that sort of thing.

Q: Are you familiar with her reputation for honesty in the community in which you live?

A: Yes I am.

Q: What is her reputation for honesty?

A: It is very bad.

Example: Character—Opinion

Ellen Hairston testified for the plaintiffs. The defendant is conducting a direct examination of Randy West.

Q: Do you know Ellen Hairston?

A: Yes.

Q: Have long have you known her?

A: About twelve years.

Q: How did you meet her?

A: She lives on the next block. Our kids go to the same school. We've done car pools together, school trips, that sort of thing.

Q: How well would you say you know Ms. Hairston?

A: Pretty well. I've spent a fair amount of time with her over the past twelve years.

Q: Do you have an opinion as to whether she is an honest person?

A: Yes, I do.

Q: What is your opinion?

A: She is very dishonest.

Example: Character—Specific Instances

Dewey Ramsey is being cross-examined by the defense in a medical malpractice action.

Q: You applied for a $150,000 loan from the First City Bank on January 7, 2019, didn't you?

A: Yes.

Q: Isn't it true that one of the questions on the loan application form asked you to state what your income for 2018 was?

A: Yes.

Q: And you answered that question didn't you?

A: Yes.

Q: Isn't it a fact that at the end of the application, it states, "I affirm that I have read each question on this application carefully and that I have answered each question fully and truthfully."

A: Yes.

Q: And that is right above the signature line—the place where the applicant must sign, is it not?

A: Yes, it is.

Q: And you signed that application form, didn't you?

A: Yes.

Q: Right after the place where it says "I affirm that I have answered each question fully and truthfully."

A: Yes.

Q: Isn't it true that you stated on that application that your 2018 income was $75,000?

A: Yes.

Q: In fact, that wasn't your 2018 income was it?

A: No.

Q: Isn't it true that your 2018 income was less than $30,000?

A: Yes.

Q: So you lied when you filled out that application, didn't you?

A: Well, I wouldn't say I lied.

Q: When you signed the application you affirmed that you read each question carefully, didn't you?

A: Yes.

Q: And you also affirmed that you answered each question truthfully?

A: Yes.

Q: There wasn't any clause in that affirmation that said "every question except the one about my 2018 income," was there?

A: No.

Q: It said "every question," didn't it?

A: Yes.

Q: And you wrote down on that application form that your 2018 income was $75,000?

A: Yes.

Q: That wasn't true, was it?

A: No.

Q: And you knew it wasn't true, didn't you?

A: Yes.

Q: So you lied when you answered that question, didn't you?

A: Yes.

[NOTE: The cross-examiner must have a good-faith belief that the witness engaged in this dishonest conduct. But even if the witness denies it, the cross-examiner will not be allowed to offer extrinsic evidence to prove that the witness engaged in the conduct.]

Example: Character—Convictions

James Maloney, a witness for the prosecution, is being cross-examined.

Q: Isn't it true that on July 17, 2015 you were convicted of perjury, a felony, in Montgomery, Alabama, and were sentenced to six months confinement in prison?

A: Yes.

Q: Isn't it true that on January 24, 2017 you were convicted of lying to an FBI agent, a misdemeanor, in Columbus, Georgia?

A: No.

[NOTE: If the witness denies having been convicted of the crime, the cross-examiner will be allowed to offer extrinsic evidence to prove the conviction.]

G. Impeachment by Convictions—Factors for Balancing Probative Value Against Prejudice

Checklist

1. Impeachment value of prior conviction. The more the crime seems related to veracity, the greater its probative value.

2. Recency of conviction. If the conviction is recent, its probative value is higher.

3. Age at time of conviction. Crimes committed during youth may have less bearing on the witness's present character.

4. Witness's subsequent criminal history. If the witness has subsequent convictions, the probative value is higher.

5. Similarity between conviction and offense under prosecution. If the accused is the witness and the prior conviction is similar to the crime being prosecuted, the prejudicial impact is higher.

6. Importance of credibility issue. If the case is basically a swearing match, the probative value is higher.

7. Danger accused would be deterred from testifying. If the threat of impeachment would deter the accused from testifying, court should consider this as weighing against admissibility.

8. Other evidence of witness's credibility. If other evidence establishes the witness's lack of credibility, the probative value of the conviction is lower.

4. PRESENT RECOLLECTION REFRESHED (RULE 612)

Checklist

1. The witness is unable to recall something.

2. Counsel is unable to jog the witness's memory through questioning. Leading questions are permitted.

3. Counsel should show the writing to the witness and allow the witness to read it silently.

4. If the witness testifies that he now recalls the matter independent of the writing, he may testify to that independent recollection. Recollection has been refreshed.

5. If the witness cannot recall the matter after having reviewed the writing, counsel may lay the foundation for admitting the contents of the writing under the past recollection recorded exception to the hearsay rule, Rule 803(5).

Example

The witness, a burglary victim, is having difficulty recalling what items were missing from her house following the burglary. The prosecutor refreshes her recollection with a police report that is based on information provided to the officer by the witness and her husband. Note that the witness did not create this document and does not have to identify it and that the document is not offered into evidence.

Q: What did you do when you came home that night and found that your house had been broken into?

A: Well, after I called the police I started looking around to see what was missing.

Q: Did you discover anything missing?

A: Yes.

Q: About how many items were missing?

A: Oh, I don't know exactly. Lots.

Q: Could you tell the jury some of the things that were present in your house when you left for the evening but were gone when you returned?

A: The television, my laptop, all my good jewelry—several necklaces, a tiara my mother had given me—, about $50 in cash that I had in my desk.

Q: Anything else?

A: I know there were some other things, but I can't recall them just now.

Q: Were you missing any silverware?

A: Oh, yes. All my silver was gone. I had four place settings of sterling silver. And a silver pitcher that I received as a wedding gift was also missing.

Q: Can you think of anything else that you noticed was missing?

A: No. Again, I know I haven't mentioned everything, but it happened a while ago and I'm having a hard time remembering everything.

Q: Were any other gifts missing?

A: I can't recall anything else right now.

Q: [Handing document to clerk or reporter.] I ask that this document be marked State's Exhibit number 14 for identification. [Reporter or clerk marks document.] [Hand document or copy to opposing counsel.]

Q: May I approach the witness?

A [Judge]: Yes.

Q: [Handing document to witness.] I hand you what has been marked State's Exhibit number 14 for identification. Please read it to yourself. [Pause] Have you read it?

A: Yes.

Q: Please put it down. [Witness does so.] Do you now recall, independent of the document you have just read, what other items were missing from your house?

A: Yes, I do.

Q: Without looking at State Exhibit number 14 for identification, could you please tell the jury what those other items were?

A: Yes. A watch that I had just purchased for my husband's birthday was missing and so was a pair of antique brass candlesticks.

Q: Thank you.

5. EXPERT TESTIMONY (RULE 702)

A. Qualifying an Expert

Comments

Before an expert witness may offer her opinion, the proponent of the expert must demonstrate that she is qualified as an expert. The requisite expertise may be acquired through knowledge, skill, experience, training or education.

Example

The prosecution is attempting to qualify the witness as an expert on drug use and dealing so that she can testify that the amount of crack cocaine seized from the defendant was indicative of distribution rather than personal use.

Q: Detective Gillick, could you please tell us how long you have been a member of the Mollenberg Police Department?

A: Yes. I joined the Department twenty-two years ago.

Q: Have you served continuously since that time?

A: Yes.

Q: Are you assigned to a particular division of the MPD?

A: Yes. I am with the Narcotics Division.

Q: What is your position in the Narcotics Division?

A: I am in charge of the division.

Q: For how long have you run the division?

A: For about ten years.

Q: How long in total have you been associated with the Narcotics Division?

A: Thirteen years.

Q: Before that, what division were you assigned to?

A: I started out in vice, was there for two years, then moved over to homicide, and was there until I transferred into Narcotics.

Q: Have you received any special training in the recognition of drugs and the methods of drug distribution?

A: Yes. Each year for the past five years I have attended a week-long conference for narcotics officers that is run by the Justice Department in Washington, D.C.

Q: What types of things do you cover in these conferences?

A: Pretty much what you would expect. What the newest drugs are, how to recognize them, test for them, how they affect the users. We have lectures on new methods for distribution, how to detect distribution schemes. We're brought up to date on the latest technologies being used by the FBI and when and how we can utilize them. We also have classes on the new legal developments.

Q: Thank you. You mentioned that you are in charge of the Narcotics Division. Is yours a desk job?

A: No. Our police force is not large enough for that. I'm still out on the streets on a regular basis.

Q: Can you tell us approximately how many drug arrests you have participated in over the course of your time in the Narcotics Division?

A: I would guess that it's got to be over a thousand.

Q: Are you aware of the normal usage levels of various drugs?

A: Sure. I could certainly tell you how much a typical user of cocaine, crack cocaine, heroin, marijuana, angel dust, and a lot of other drugs would be using a day.

Q: How have you come to know this?

A: Through a combination of things I guess. My training, my experience, my observations over the years. It's come up in the classes I've attended, I've seen lots of drug use on the streets, made a lot of busts, dealt with drug dealers. After all these years in the job, it's hard to say exactly where I learned any one thing.

Q: Thank you. Are there ways in which people who are selling drugs typically sell and package them?

A: Most definitely.

Q: Are you knowledgeable about these packaging and selling methods?

A: Yes.

Q: How do you know all this?

A: As I said, this is information I have obtained through my experience over the last thirteen years in the division, as well as through the formal training I have received over the years.

B. Reliability Factors

Checklist

1.   Is the expert's opinion:

- based upon sufficient facts or data? Rule 702(b).

- the product of reliable principles and methods Rule 702(c).

2.   Did the witness apply the principles and methods reliably to the facts of the case? Rule 702(d).

Consider, as applicable:

(a)   Whether the theory or technique in question has been or can be tested.

(b)   Whether the theory or technique has been subjected to peer review and publication.

(c)   The known or potential rate of error of the particular theory or technique, and whether means exist for controlling its operation.

(d)   The extent to which the theory or technique has been accepted.

(e)   Whether the expert testimony is based on research the expert has conducted independent of the litigation.

(f)   Whether the expert has adequately accounted for obvious alternative explanations.

(g)   Whether the expert has employed the same care in reaching the litigation-related opinions as the expert employs in performing his or her regular professional work.

(h)   Whether there is "too great an analytical gap" between the data and the opinion.

(i)   The experience of the expert.

3.   Is opinion "sufficiently tied to the facts of the case?"

6. HEARSAY EXCEPTIONS (RULE 803)

A. Foundation for Recorded Recollection (Rule 803(5))

Checklist

1. The record is on a matter the witness once knew about.

2. The witness now cannot recall the matter well enough to testify fully and accurately.

3. The record accurately reflects the witness's knowledge.

Example

Slip-and-fall action against grocery store. The witness is an investigator for grocery's liability insurer, called by the defense. The witness has testified that he telephoned plaintiff after the accident and arranged an interview, which occurred at the plaintiff's office on June 1, 2019.

Q: Did Mr. Plaintiff at that time make any statements to you concerning the accident?

A: Yes.

Q: What exactly did Mr. Plaintiff say?

A: I don't recall the exact statements; this was over a year ago.

Q: [Handing document to reporter or clerk] I ask that this be marked Defendant's Exhibit number 8 for identification. [Reporter or clerk marks document.] [Hand document or copy to opposing counsel.]

Q: Your Honor, may I approach the witness?

A [Judge]: You may.

Q: [Handing document to witness] Mr. Investigator, I hand you a document marked Defendant's Exhibit number 8 for identification. Would you examine it, please? [pause] Have you examined it?

A: Yes.

Q: Do you recognize this document?

A: Yes, I do.

Q: What is it?

A: It's the notes I made on June 1, 2019 during my interview with Mr. Plaintiff.

Q: How do you recognize it?

A: I recognize my handwriting, and the type of note paper I use, and the caption at the top identifying the date and subject.

Q: Would you please read over the notes silently? [pause] Have you read them?

A: Yes.

Q: Please put the notes down for a moment. Now that you have looked at your notes, do you have a present recollection, apart from the notes, of the exact statements that Mr. Plaintiff made to you on June 1, 2019?

A: No. Like I said, it was over a year ago.

Q: How long after your conversation with Mr. Plaintiff did you make these notes?

A: I made them during the interview. As the statements were made, I wrote them down.

Q: Word for word?

A: As closely as I could, I wrote down what he said.

Q: Did you write the statements down accurately?

A: Yes.

Q: Please read the statements made by Mr. Plaintiff as written in your notes.

A: [reads statements].

B. Foundation for Business Record (Rule 803(6))

Checklist

1. The record was made and kept in the course of a regularly conducted business activity.

2. It was the regular practice of the business activity to make the record.

3. The record was made at or near the time of the event that it records.

4. The record was made by, or from information transmitted by, a person with knowledge acting in the regular course of business.

Comments

The foregoing elements must be shown by the testimony, or certification that complies with Rule 902(11), Rule 902(12), or a statute permitting certification, of the custodian or "another qualified witness." "Another qualified witness" is any person who can credibly testify that the records satisfy the requirements of the exception.

It is not required that the witness have personal knowledge of the contents of the particular entry or the circumstances in which it was made. It suffices that the witness can testify that the records generally satisfy the conditions of the rule.

The fact that records are kept by computer does not result in any special foundation requirements beyond those set forth in the rule.

Example

Action for the price of goods sold and delivered. Plaintiff is a lumber company; defendant is a homebuilder. The witness called by plaintiff is Ms. Jane Doe.

Q: Where do you work, Ms. Doe?

A: Duece Lumber Company.

Q: What is your job there?

A: I am the credit manager.

Q: How long have you held that position?

A: About ten years.

Q: So you were employed as credit manager at Duece Lumber Company throughout the year 2019?

A: Yes.

Q: In your job, do you have any duties with regard to billing and customer accounts?

A: I maintain all the billing records for the company.

Q: How are these records prepared and maintained?

A: A salesperson receives a customer's order, either in the store or over the telephone. The salesperson types the order into a computer terminal, then prints out an invoice. The invoice comes out in a five-part formpack. One copy will be for the customer, one for the warehouse, two for my office, and one for inventory control. If the customer is in the store and wants to carry out the goods, they sign the invoice pack at the register and take it to the warehouse to pick up the order. If the goods are to be delivered, the formpack goes to the warehouse and will be carried out with the goods and signed upon delivery by the purchaser.

In either case two parts of the invoice formpack will end up in my office, either from the warehouse or the delivery driver. If it is a credit transaction, I will have a file on the account. Each account is on a monthly billing cycle. When the monthly cycle ends for an account, I prepare a statement in duplicate that summarizes their invoices for that month. That is done on my computer. One copy of the statement and one copy of each invoice goes out to them for payment. One copy of the statement and one copy of the invoices stays in the account file. When payment is received on an account, I stamp or mark the file copy of the statement.

Q: Is the procedure you just described followed with regard to every transaction?

A: Yes.

Q: [Handing document to reporter or clerk] I ask that this be marked Plaintiff's Exhibit number 1 for identification. [Reporter or clerk marks document.] [Hand document or copy to opposing counsel.]

Q: Your Honor, may I approach the witness?

A [Judge]: You may.

Q: [Handing document to witness] Ms. Doe, I hand you a document marked Plaintiff's Exhibit number 1 for identification. Would you examine it, please? [pause] Have you examined it?

A: Yes.

Q: Do you recognize the document?

A: Yes, I do.

Q: What is it?

A: It is my account file for Deadbeat Builders, Inc.

Q: How do you recognize it?

A: It contains our invoice forms and statement forms, all filled out with Deadbeat listed as purchaser.

Q: Are the documents in this file original records of your company, or are they copies?

A: Originals.

Q: Were these records in your custody?

A: Yes. They have been kept in my office from the time they were created until I brought them here this morning.

Q: In the case of the statements, did you personally make the statements?

A: Yes.

Q: Based upon what information?

A: Based upon the invoices sent to my office from the warehouse or the deliverers, as I described.

Q: How long after receipt of the invoices did you prepare the statements?

A: At the end of each billing cycle. Not more than a month.

Q: And was it among your duties to prepare the statements based upon the invoices?

A: Yes.

Q: And who prepared the invoices?

A: Salespersons, as indicated on each one.

Q: And the information on the invoices, would the salesperson have personal knowledge as to that— that is, would the salesperson personally know the goods ordered by the purchaser?

A: Yes.

Q: How long after receipt of the order would the invoice be prepared?

A: Immediately.

Q: Was it among the duties of the salespersons to prepare the invoices as you have described?

A: Yes.

Q: Was it among the duties of the warehouse employees and deliverers to forward copies of the invoices to your office after making a delivery of goods?

A: Yes.

Q: Your Honor, I offer in evidence the document marked Plaintiff's Exhibit number 1 for identification as Plaintiff's Exhibit number 1.

A [Judge]: It will be received.

C. Foundation for Public Record or Report (Rule 803(8))

Checklist

1. The document is a certified copy of a record or report of a public office.

2. The document sets forth either (i) the office's activities, or (ii) a matter observed while under a legal duty to report, or (iii) factual findings from a legally authorized investigation.

Comments

The foundation for a public record or report under Rule 803(8) need only establish that the document is authentic and that it contains one of the three types of matters specified in the rule. It is not necessary to show that the public record or report was regular or made at or near the time of the event recorded.

Example

Wrongful death action. Plaintiffs' decedent was accidentally killed in the collapse of scaffolding at a construction site. There are several defendants. Plaintiff has called as a witness a deputy county medical examiner (coroner), who conducted an autopsy on the body of the decedent. The witness has been qualified as a medical expert in the field of pathology and has testified that she conducted the autopsy on June 1, 2019 at the county morgue.

Q: Dr. Sawbones, did you prepare a report on your autopsy of Mr. Decedent?

A: Yes.

Q: Was the preparation of the report a part of your duties as a deputy county medical examiner?

A: Yes. We are required by law to prepare such a report in all cases where an autopsy is required, such as here, where death appears to have occurred by trauma.

Q: [Handing document to reporter or clerk] I ask that this be marked Plaintiff's Exhibit number 4 for identification. [Reporter or clerk marks document.] [Hand document or copy to opposing counsel.]

Q: Your Honor, may I approach the witness?

A [Judge]: You may.

Q: [Handing document to witness] Mr. Sawbones, I hand you a document marked Plaintiff's Exhibit number 4 for identification. Would you examine it, please? [pause] Have you examined it?

A: Yes.

Q: Do you recognize the document?

A: Yes, I do.

Q: What is it?

A: It is a copy of my official report on the autopsy of Mr. Decedent.

Q: Does the copy you hold bear any certification or seal?

A: Yes. It bears the certification and seal of the office of the Washington County Medical Examiner.

Q: Your Honor, I offer in evidence the document marked Plaintiff's Exhibit number 4 for identification as Plaintiff's Exhibit number 4.

A [Judge]: It will be received.

D. Foundation for Residual Hearsay Exception (Rule 807)

Checklist

1. The proponent must give the adverse party the notice specified in Rule 807.

2. The hearsay statement must be supported by sufficient guarantees of trustworthiness. The court must consider the totality of circumstances under which the statement was made and any corroborating evidence.

3. The statement must be more probative on the point for which it is offered than any other evidence that the proponent could obtain through reasonable effort.

7. FOUNDATION FOR SUMMARY OF VOLUMINOUS WRITINGS (RULE 1006)

Checklist

1. The original writings, recordings, or photographs are voluminous.

2. The originals cannot be conveniently examined in court.

3. The originals or duplicates have been made available for examination or copying, or both, by other parties at a reasonable time and place.

4. The originals would be admissible in evidence.

5. The summary, chart, or calculation offered in lieu of the voluminous originals is fair and accurate.

Example

Prosecution of televangelist for fraud and conspiracy. Among other facts, the government wants to prove that the defendant made numerous solicitations for funds for a real estate development during his ostensibly religious broadcast. The witness is an FBI agent, Gumshoe.

Q: Mr. Gumshoe, what did you do next in the course of your investigation?

A: I obtained a video file of the entire 200 hours of the defendant's television program, "Praise the Lord," that were broadcast between February 2016 and April 2019.

Q: How did you obtain the video file?

A: I asked PTL Television Network, the producer of the show, to provide the file to me, and they did.

Q: Did you view the file?

A: Yes, I did.

Q: The entire 200 hours?

A: Yes.

Q: What did you do then?

A: Using video-editing software, I prepared a one-hour composite video of selections from the original 200 hours and downloaded it onto a thumb drive.

Q: Did you prepare anything besides the composite video?

A: I also prepared a written log, which lists the source of each selection in the composite by date of the original broadcast.

Q: Are the original 200 hours of video marked in that way, as to date of the broadcast?

A: Yes.

Q: Does your composite video fairly and accurately duplicate and summarize the contents of the original 200 hours of video?

A: Yes.

Q: [Handing thumb drive and document to reporter or clerk] I ask that this thumb drive be marked Government's Exhibit number 98 for identification and that this document be marked Government's Exhibit number 99 for identification. [Reporter or clerk marks thumb drive and document.] [Hand thumb drive and document or copy to opposing counsel.]

Q: Your Honor, may I approach the witness?

A [Judge]:   You may.

Q: [Handing thumb drive and document to witness] Mr. Gumshoe, I hand you a thumb drive and a document marked Government's Exhibits numbers 98 and 99 for identification. Would you examine them, please? [pause] Have you examined them?

A: Yes.

Q: Do you recognize them?

A: Yes, I do.

Q: What are they?

A: Number 98 is the thumb drive containing my composite video and number 99 is my log of the composite video.

Q: Your Honor, I ask that the record reflect that the government made the original 200-hour video file available to counsel for the defendant approximately six months prior to the beginning of this trial.

Q [Judge]:   Is that true, counsel?

A [Defendant's counsel]:   Yes, your honor.

Q [Prosecutor]:   Your Honor, I offer in evidence the composite video and document marked Government's Exhibits numbers 98 and 99 for identification as Government's Exhibits 98 and 99.

A [Judge]:   They will be received.

Q: I ask the court's permission to hand copies of Government's Exhibit number 99 to the jurors and to display Government's Exhibit number 98.

A: Granted.

TABLE OF CASES

References are to Rules.

INDEX

References are to Rules.

Abbreviations Used in Index

Rule 609/AC(4) = Federal Rule of Evidence 609 and paragraph (4) of the accompanying Authors' Commentary (Chapter 2)

CL 5 = Checklist or Foundation 5 (Chapter 4)

Substantially same condition, Rule 401/AC(12), Rule 901/AC(4), CL 10
Telephone conversations, Rule 901/AC(9)
Voice identification, Rule 901/AC(9)
Wills, Rule 903
Witness with knowledge, Rule 901/AC(4)

BACKGROUND INFORMATION, Rule 401/AC(6); Rule 608/AC(9)

BAIL
Applicability of rules, Rule 1101

BAPTISMAL CERTIFICATES, Rule 803(12)

BEST EVIDENCE RULE
Generally, Rule 1002
Admissibility of other evidence of contents, Rule 1004
Admission of party, Rule 1007
Certified copy of public record, Rule 1005
Chattels, inscribed, Rule 1001/AC(3)
Collateral matters, Rule 1004/AC(9)
Compared copy, public records, Rule 1005
Counterparts, Rule 1001/AC(6)
Destroyed original, Rule 1004/AC(3), (4)
Duplicates,
    Admissibility, Rule 1003
    Definition, Rule 1001/AC(7)
Inscribed chattels, Rule 1001/AC(3)
Judge and jury, Rule 1008
Lost or destroyed original, Rule 1004/AC(3), (4)
Notice to produce, Rule 1004/AC(6)–(8)
Original,
    Definition, Rule 1001/AC(6)
    Requirement of, Rule 1002
Original in possession of opponent, Rule 1004/AC(6)–(8)
Original lost or destroyed, Rule 1004/AC(3), (4)
Original not obtainable, Rule 1004/AC(5)
Photographs, Rule 1001/AC(5), Rule 1002/AC(7)
Possession of opponent, Rule 1004/AC(6)–(8)
Preliminary questions of fact, Rule 1008
Public records, Rule 1005
Reasonable reliance by expert, Rule 703
Recordings, Rule 1001
Secondary evidence, Rule 1004/AC(2)
Summaries, Rule 1006, CL 7
Testimony of party, Rule 1007
Writing, definition of, Rule 1001/AC(2)–(4)

BIAS, Rule 607/AC(3)–(5)

BODILY CONDITION
Statement of, Rule 803(3)/AC(2)

BODILY DEMONSTRATIONS, Rule 401/AC(13)

BOLSTERING WITNESS, Rule 607/AC(10); Rule 608/AC(6)

BOUNDARIES
Judgment as to, Rule 803(23)
Reputation concerning, Rule 803(20)

BRAND NAMES
Authentication, Rule 902

BUSINESS RECORDS, Rule 803(6), (7); Rule 805; Rule 902(11), (12)/AC(6); CL 6B

BUSINESS ROUTINE, Rule 406/AC(6)–(8)

CERTIFICATE OF REHABILITATION, Rule 609/AC(8)

CERTIFIED BUSINESS RECORDS, Rule 902(11), (12)/AC(6)

CERTIFIED COPIES OF PUBLIC RECORDS
Best Evidence Rule, Rule 1005
Self-authentication, Rule 902/AC(3)

CHAIN OF CUSTODY, Rule 901/AC(4)

CHARACTER EVIDENCE
    See also Character for Truthfulness; Reputation
Generally, Rules 404, 405, 413–415
Accused, Rule 404(a)/AC(1)–(6), (9), (11); Rules 404(b), 405, 413, 414, CL 2
Character "in issue," Rule 404(a)/AC(4), (5); Rule 405/AC(2), (3)
Civil cases, Rules 404, 405, 415
Criminal cases, Rules 404, 405, 413, 414
Cross-examination of character witnesses, Rule 404(a)/AC(6), Rule 405/AC(6)–(11), Rule 608/AC(8), CL 2
Decedent, Rule 404(a)/AC(3), (8)–(10)
Element of charge, claim, or defense, Rule 404(a)/AC(4); Rule 405/AC(2), (3)
Expert opinion testimony, Rule 405/AC(5)
Good character instruction, Rule 404(a)/AC(7)
Method of proof, Rule 404(a)/AC(3)–(11); Rule 405; Rule 413/AC(3); Rule 414/AC(3); Rule 415/AC(3); Rule 608/AC(2)–(5), CL 2, 3F
Opinion testimony, Rule 404(a)/AC(3)–(11), Rule 405, Rule 608/AC(3), CL 2, 3F
Other crimes, wrongs, or acts, Rules 404(b), 413, 414, 415
Party, Rule 404(a)/AC(1)–(6), (11); Rule 404(b), Rules 405, 413, 414, 415
Qualifications of character witness, Rule 405/AC(4), (5); Rule 608/AC(2), (3)
Reputation, hearsay exception, Rule 803(21)
Reputation testimony, Rule 404(a)/AC(3)–(11), Rule 405, Rule 608/AC(2), CL 2, 3F
Specific instances of conduct, Rule 404(a)/AC(3)–(11), Rules 404(b), 405, 413, 414, 415, Rule 608/AC(4)–(5)
Victim, Rule 404(a)/AC(8)–(11), Rule 405, Rule 412/AC(2)–(3)
Witness, Rule 404(a)/AC(12); Rules 608–609

CHARACTER FOR TRUTHFULNESS
Generally, Rule 608, Rule 609, CL 3F
Convictions, Rule 609, CL 3F, 3G
Cross-examination, Rule 608/AC(8), Rule 609
Form of questions, Rule 608/AC(2)–(4), (8)
Opinion testimony, Rule 608/AC(3), (7), CL 3F
Rehabilitation, Rule 608/AC(7)
Reputation, hearsay exception, Rule 803(21)
Reputation testimony, Rule 608/AC(2), (7), CL 3F
Specific acts of fact witness, Rule 608/AC(4)–(5), (8), (10), CL 3F

CHARACTER IN ISSUE, Rule 404(a)/AC(4), (5); Rule 405/AC(2), (3)

CHARACTER OF ACCUSED, Rule 404(a)/AC(1)–(6), (11); Rule 404(b); Rules 405, 413, 414

CHARACTER OF ALLEGED VICTIM, Rule 404(a)/AC(8)–(11), Rule 405
See also Sexual Conduct of Alleged Victim

Federal Rules of Evidence Summary

Hearsay exceptions that apply only if declarant is unavailable (Rule 804):

1. **Former testimony** if party against whom now offered (or in civil case a party with similar interest) had opportunity and similar motive to develop testimony.
2. **Dying declaration** if declarant believed death imminent and statement concerns cause of death (only in homicide and civil cases).
3. **Statement against interest** (pecuniary, proprietary or penal).
4. Statement of **personal or family history.**
5. **Forfeiture by wrongdoing:** a statement offered against a party who has wrongfully caused the declarant's unavailability.

Declarant is unavailable if dead or too ill to testify, outside subpoena power, disobeys subpoena, cannot remember, refuses to testify or is exempt due to privilege (Rule 804(a)). Witness may be available, however, if deposition can be taken.

Hearsay within hearsay may be admitted if exception applies as each level (Rule 805).

If hearsay is admitted, **credibility of declarant may be attacked** and then supported (Rule 806).

Residual exception: a statement not specifically covered in Rule 803 or 804 but having equivalent circumstantial guarantees of trustworthiness, if pretrial notice is given by proponent (Rule 807).

• *Authentication*

Requires **evidence sufficient to support a finding** (prima facie case) that offered evidence is what proponent claims (Rule 901).

Self-authenticating documents need no further proof to authenticate (Rule 902). These include:

1. Domestic public documents that are sealed.
2. Certified domestic public documents not sealed.
3. Foreign public documents signed and certified by consular or diplomatic official.
4. Certified copies of public records.
5. Official publications.
6. Newspapers and periodicals.
7. Trade inscriptions (tags, labels).
8. Documents with certificates of acknowledgment.
9. Commercial paper.
10. Matters declared presumptively authentic by statute.
11. Certified domestic business records.
12. Certified foreign business records.
13. Certified records generated by electronic process or system.
14. Certified data copied from electronic device, storage medium, or file.

Subscribing witness not required to testify (unless state law requires) (Rule 903).

• *Contents of Documents; Requirements of Original*

Original and **duplicate** defined (Rule 1001).

Original generally required to prove contents of writing (Rule 1002).

Duplicates admissible as originals unless (1) genuine question exists as to authenticity of original or (2) it world be unfair to receive duplicate (Rule 1003).

If original **lost or destroyed** (unless in bad faith), **not available**, in **possession of opponent**, or **collateral**, then original not required (Rule 1004).

Public records may be proven by certified copy if obtainable, otherwise by other methods (Rule 1005).

Summaries may be received of voluminous documents; original must be made available (Rule 1006).

Content of writing may be proven by **testimony or written admission** of a party (Rule 1007).

Court decides most preliminary facts, but jury determines (1) whether original ever existed, (2) which of two exhibits is an original, and (3) whether secondary evidence of the contents reflects the contents (Rule 1008).

• *Applicability of Rules*

Rules apply generally to all court proceedings except: as provided by statute; preliminary questions of facts; grand jury; miscellaneous proceedings including extradition, sentencing, and probation, warrant, and bail proceedings. **Privileges** apply at all stages of **all proceedings** (Rule 1101).

Federal Rules of Evidence Summary

- ## General Provisions

  Rules **apply in all court proceedings** except as provided in Rule 1101 (Rule 101).

  Rules construed to achieve **fairness** and **avoid expense** or **delay** (Rule 102).

  Timely and specific **objection** or **motion to strike** required to preserve error in admission of evidence; **offer of proof** required to preserve error in exclusion (Rule 103).

  Judge determines most **preliminary questions** of admissibility and in doing so is not bound by rules of evidence except privileges (Rule 104).

  Judge upon request shall instruct jury as to **limited admissibility** of evidence (Rule 105).

  When a **writing or part of a writing** is offered, judge may require immediate admission of **other part or other writing** if fairness requires (Rule 106).

- ## Judicial Notice

  Notice may be taken of **indisputable fact generally known** in jurisdiction or **established from accurate, unquestionable sources** whether or not requested (Rule 201).

  Judge **must** take notice of fact if supplied with necessary information (Rule 201(c)).

  Party opposing notice should have **opportunity to be heard** upon request (Rule 201(e)).

  In **civil cases**, judicial notice is **conclusive**; in **criminal cases**, judicial notice results in **permissive instruction** (Rule 201(f)).

- ## Presumption in Civil Cases

  In **federal law** civil cases, presumptions **shift burdens of producing evidence only**; no shift in burden of persuasion, unless otherwise provided by statute or court Rule (Rule 301).

  In cases governed by **state law**, effect of presumption is governed by state law.

- ## Relevancy

  Evidence is **relevant** if it tends to make a consequential fact more or less likely (Rule 401).

  Relevant evidence is admissible unless excluded by other rule, statute or constitution: **irrelevant evidence is not admissible** (Rule 402).

  Even relevant evidence is excluded if probative value **substantially outweighed by danger of prejudice, confusion of issues, misleading, or repetition** (Rule 403).

  Character is not admissible to prove an act consistent with character except own character put in issue by accused, or character of victim in limited circumstances, or character for truthfulness of a witness as provided in impeachment rules (Rule 404(a)).

  Other crimes/bad acts are not admissible to show character but may be admissible for other purposes (e.g., to show motive, intent, plan, or identity) (Rule 404(b)).

  Character may be proven by **reputation or opinion; specific acts** admissible only on cross-examination or when character is essential element (directly in issue) (Rule 405).

  Habit or routine practice is admissible to prove conduct in conformity (Rule 406).

  Subsequent remedial measures are inadmissible to prove negligence, culpable conduct, product defect, or need for a warning, but may be admissible for another purpose such as to show ownership, feasibility, or impeachment (Rule 407).

  Compromise, offer of compromise or statement in settlement discussions of disputed claim is not admissible on validity of claim but may be admissible for another purpose such as to show bias of a witness (Rule 408).

  Payment of **medical expenses** is not admissible to prove liability (Rule 409).

  Withdrawn plea of guilty, nolo plea, or statement in plea discussions with prosecutor not normally admissible (Rule 410).

  Liability insurance not admissible to show fault but may be allowed for another purpose such as to show ownership or bias of a witness (Rule 411).

  Prior sexual conduct or sexual character of sex offense or sexual misconduct victim generally not admissible (Rule 412).

  Defendant's prior commission of sexual assault may be shown in prosecution for sexual assault (Rule 413).

Federal Rules of Evidence Summary

Defendant's prior commission of child molestation may be shown in prosecution for child molestation (Rule 414).

Civil party's prior commission of sexual assault or child molestation may be shown in civil action for sexual assault or child molestation (Rule 415).

• *Privileges*

In **federal law** cases, privileges are determined by common law except as provided by Constitution, statute, or court rule; in cases governed by **state law**, privileges are determined by state law (Rule 501).

Rule 502 governs certain **waiver** questions regarding the **attorney-client privilege** and **work product** protection.

• *Witnesses*

All persons are **competent** to testify in **federal law** cases except as other rules provide; in cases governed by **state law**, witness competency is determined by state law (Rule 601).

Personal knowledge is required of all witnesses except experts (Rule 602).

An **oath** or affirmation is required of all witnesses (Rule 603).

Interpreters must qualify as experts and testify under oath (Rule 604).

The **presiding judge** may not testify (Rule 605).

Jurors may not testify at trial; to **impeach verdict** jurors may testify only as to extraneous prejudicial information, outside influence, or clerical mistake in entering verdict (Rule 606).

Any party may impeach a witness's credibility, even party calling witness (Rule 607).

A witness's character for truthfulness can be challenged by **cross-examination about specific acts** probative of untruthfulness or through **opinion or reputation witnesses** (Rule 608).

Conviction of a crime is admissible if (1) felony and prohibitive value outweighs prejudice, or involved false statement and (2) if less than ten years conviction or release (Rule 609).

Religious beliefs are inadmissible to impeach or enhance credibility (Rule 610).

Court controls examination; **cross is limited** to scope of direct; **leading** normally prohibited on direct, except when party calls hostile witness, adverse party, or witness identified with adverse party (Rule 611).

Writing used to refresh witness's recollection on stand must be produced; adverse party may introduce relevant parts (Rule 612).

Prior statements may be used without disclosing to witness; extrinsic proof of prior statements not admissible unless witness given chance to explain (Rule 613).

Court may call witnesses (Rule 614).

Court shall exclude (**sequester**) witnesses upon request, except party, representative of non-natural party, or person whose presence is shown to be essential or authorized by statute (Rule 615).

• *Opinions and Experts*

Lay opinion admissible if based on first-hand knowledge and helpful to trier of fact (Rule 701).

Expert opinion admissible if **reliable and helpful** to trier of fact and witness **qualified** (Rule 702).

Expert opinion may be **based on admissible evidence or facts reasonably relied on** by experts in field (Rule 703).

Opinion may be offered on **ultimate issue**, if otherwise proper (Rule 704).

Expert may state opinion without first giving **underlying facts** unless court requires; underlying facts may be required on cross examination (Rule 705).

Court may appoint experts and direct their compensation (Rule 706).

Federal Rules of Evidence Summary

- ## *Hearsay*

Hearsay is a statement, other than one made by the declarant while testifying at the trial or hearing, offered in evidence to prove the truth of the matter asserted (Rule 801).

Statements include **acts** only if **intended as assertions** by declarant (Rule 801).

Certain **prior statements by a witness** are not hearsay: a prior **inconsistent** statement made under oath as a prior proceeding: a prior **consistent** statement that rebuts a charge of fabrication or improper influence or motive; or a prior **identification of a person** (Rule 801(d)(1)).

Party admissions are not hearsay, including **party's own statement, adopted** statement of another, **authorized** statement by agent, agent or **employee's** statement concerning matter in scope of employment, or **coconspirator** statement (Rule 801(d)(2)).

Hearsay is inadmissible unless an exception exists (by rule or statute) (Rule 802).

Hearsay exceptions that apply whether the declarant is available or not (Rule 803):

1. **Present sense impression** describing an event made while observing the event or immediately thereafter.
2. **Excited utterance** relating to a startling event and made under the stress of the event.
3. **Present mental, emotional, or physical condition**, including intent or plan, but not memory or belief except in will cases.
4. **Statements for medical diagnosis or treatment** including history, and cause of conditions if medically pertinent.
5. **Recorded recollection**: document made with fresh memory of matter witness now cannot completely remember; if admitted, document is read but not received as exhibit unless at behest of adverse party.
6. **Business records** regularly made and kept and based upon personal knowledge of some member of the entity. Custodian or other qualified witness must provide foundation.
7. **Absence of entry** in business records to show nonoccurrence or nonexistence of a matter.
8. **Public records or reports** showing activities of agency, or matters observed pursuant to duty (except by police or other law enforcement personnel in criminal cases), or factual findings resulting from investigation pursuant to legal authority (except against criminal defendant).
9. **Records of vital statistics** such as births, marriages, or deaths.
10. **Absence of public record or entry** to show nonoccurrence of nonexistence of a matter.
11. **Records of religious organizations** to show birth, death, marriage, etc.
12. **Marriage and baptismal certificates.**
13. **Family records** such as Bibles, genealogies, or tombstones.
14. **Recorded document affecting property interests** as proof of content, execution and delivery of original.
15. **Statements in recorded document affecting property interests** if germane.
16. Statements in **ancient documents** (20 years or older and authenticated).
17. **Market reports, commercial publications** of types relied upon by public or professionals.
18. **Learned treatises** if relied on during direct or called to an expert's attention on cross, shown by testimony or judicial notice to be reliable authority; may be read into evidence but not received as exhibits.
19. **Reputation concerning personal or family history** to show birth, marriage, death, relationship, etc.
20. **Reputation concerning boundaries or historical matters** established before dispute arose.
21. **Reputation concerning character.**
22. **Judgment of conviction** of felony to prove a fact essential to the judgment.
23. **Judgment involving personal, family, or general history, or boundaries.**